Prophetic
VIRTUES & MIRACLES

Al-Minhāj al-Sawī (Part I)

Prophetic
VIRTUES & MIRACLES

Al-Minhāj al-Sawī (Part-I)

SHAYKH-UL-ISLAM
DR MUHAMMAD TAHIR-UL-QADRI

First published January 2012
Reprinted July 2012
Reprinted February 2013

Published by Minhaj-ul-Quran Publications
292–296 Romford Road
Forest Gate
London, E7 9HD
United Kingdom

www.minhaj.org | www.minhajuk.org
www.minhajpublications.com

Research Assistants
Shaykh Abdul Aziz Dabbagh, Muhammad Hanif, M Farooq Rana

ISBN: 978-1-908229-01-4

Printed by Mega Printing, Turkey

بِسۡمِ ٱللَّهِ ٱلرَّحۡمَٰنِ ٱلرَّحِيمِ

In the name of Allah, Most Compassionate, Ever-Merciful

Saying of God ﷻ

﴿وَمَآ ءَاتَىٰكُمُ ٱلرَّسُولُ فَخُذُوهُ وَمَا نَهَىٰكُمۡ عَنۡهُ فَٱنتَهُواْ﴾

And whatever the Messenger (ﷺ) gives you, take that and whatever he forbids you, abstain (from that).

[Qurʾān 59:7]

Saying of the Prophet ﷺ

عَنْ أَبِي هُرَيْرَةَ رضي الله عنه أَنَّ رَسُولَ اللهِ ﷺ قَالَ: «مَنْ أَطَاعَنِي فَقَدْ أَطَاعَ اللهَ ﷻ، وَمَنْ عَصَانِي فَقَدْ عَصَى اللهَ ﷻ».

According to Abū Hurayra رضي الله عنه: "Allah's Messenger ﷺ said: 'If someone obeys me, he has obeyed Allah ﷻ, and if someone disobeys me, he has disobeyed Allah ﷻ.'"

[al-Bukhārī and Muslim]

Shaykh-ul-Islam Dr Muhammad Tahir-ul-Qadri

Shaykh-ul-Islam Dr Muhammad Tahir-ul-Qadri is a scholar and intellectual leader of extraordinary proportions. He is a living model of profound classical knowledge, intellectual enlightenment, practical wisdom, pure spirituality, love, harmony and humanism. He is well known for his ardent endeavours to strengthen bonds amongst people by bringing them together through tolerance, dialogue, integration and education. He successfully bridges the past with his image of the future and finds convincing solutions for contemporary problems. Dr Qadri has been teaching Hadith, Qurʾānic exegesis, jurisprudence, theology, Sufism, Prophetic biography, Islamic philosophy and many other rational and traditional sciences to thousands of people, including scholars, students, intellectuals and academics in the east and the west.

Dr Qadri was born in 1951 in the city of Jhang, Pakistan, hailing from a family of Islamic scholars and teachers. His formal religious education was initiated in Medina at the age of 12 in Madrasa al-ʿUlūm al-Sharʿiyya, a traditional school situated in the blessed house of the Companion of the Prophet Muhammad ﷺ, Abū Ayyūb al-Anṣārī ؓ. He completed the traditional studies of classical and Arabic sciences under the tutelage of his father and other eminent scholars of his time. He continued to travel around the Islamic world in pursuit of sacred knowledge, and studied under many famous scholars of Mecca, Medina, Syria, Baghdad, Lebanon, the Maghreb, India and Pakistan, and received around five hundred authorities and chains of transmission from them in Hadith and classical Islamic and spiritual sciences.

Amongst them is an unprecedented, unique, highly blessed and honoured chain of authority which connects him, through four teachers, to ʿAbd al-Razzāq, the son of Sayyidunā Shaykh ʿAbd al-Qādir al-Jīlānī al-Ḥasanī al-Ḥusaynī (of Baghdad), al-Shaykh al-Akbar Muḥyī al-Dīn b. al-ʿArabī [(the author of *al-Futūḥāt al-Makkiyya*) (Damascus)] and Imam Ibn Ḥajar al-ʿAsqalānī, the great Hadith authority of Egypt. Through another chain he is linked to Imam Yūsuf b. Ismāʿīl al-Nabhānī directly via only one teacher. His chains of transmission are published in two of his *thabats* (detailed list): *al-Jawāhir al-Bāhira fī al-Asānīd al-Ṭāhira* and *al-Subul al-Wahabiyya fī al-Asānīd al-Dhahabiyya.*

In the academic sphere, Dr Qadri received a First Class Honours Degree from the University of the Punjab in 1970. After earning his MA in Islamic studies with distinction in 1972 and achieving his LLB in 1974, Dr Qadri began to practise law in the district courts of Jhang. He moved to Lahore in 1978 and joined the University of the Punjab as a lecturer in law and completed his doctorate in Islamic Law. He was later appointed as a professor of Islamic Law and was head of the department of Islamic legislation.

Dr Qadri was also a jurist advisor to the Federal Shariat Court and Appellate Shariah Bench of the Supreme Court of Pakistan and advisor on the development of Islamic Curricula to the Federal Ministry of Education. Within a short span of time, Dr Qadri has emerged as one of the Pakistan's leading Islamic jurists and scholars and one of the world's most renowned and leading authorities on Islam. A prolific author, researcher and orator, Dr Qadri has written around one thousand books, out of which four hundred and thirty have been published, and has delivered over six thousand lectures (in Urdu, English and Arabic) on a wide range of subjects.

Shaykh-ul-Islam Dr Muhammad Tahir-ul-Qadri issued a historic fatwa on the vital matter of suicide bombings and terrorism carried out in the name of Islam. It is regarded as a significant and historic step, the first time that such an explicit and unequivocal decree against the perpetrators of terror has been broadcast so widely. The original fatwa was written in Urdu, and amounts to 600 pages of research and references from the Qurʾān, Hadith, opinions of the Companions ﵃, and the widely accepted classical texts of Islamic scholarship. This historic work has been published in English, while translation into Arabic, Norwegian and other major languages is also in process. Islamic Research Academy of Egypt wrote a detailed description of the fatwa and verified its contents as well.

Dr Qadri is also the founder and head of Minhaj-ul-Quran International (MQI), an organisation with branches and centres in more than ninety countries around the globe; he is the chairman of the Board of Governors of Minhaj University Lahore, which is chartered by the Government of Pakistan; he is the founder of Minhaj Education Society, which has established more than 600 schools and colleges in Pakistan; and he is the chairman of Minhaj Welfare Foundation, an organization involved in humanitarian and social welfare activities globally.

It is difficult to encompass his work and achievements in their entirety. A globally renowned jurist and expert of Islamic legal affairs and most eminent Islamic scholar, the authority on Islam, Shaykh-ul-Islam Dr Muhammad Tahir-ul-Qadri is engaged in spreading the divine guidance and promoting his mission for peace all over the world. Known as the ambassador of peace, love and justice, he is pursuing the emancipation of humankind through Islam and its spiritual teachings and divine practices.

Transliteration Key

ا/آ/ى	ā	ظ	ẓ
ب	b	ع	ʿ
ت	t	غ	gh
ث	th	ف	f
ج	j	ق	q
ح	ḥ	ك	k
خ	kh	ل	l
د	d	م	m
ذ	dh	ن	n
ر	r	ه	h
ز	z	و	w/ū
س	s	ي	y/ī
ش	sh	ة	a
ص	ṣ	ء	ʾ
ض	ḍ	أ	a
ط	ṭ	إ	i

Formulaic Arabic Expressions

(*Ṣalla-llāhu ʿalayhi wa ālihī wa sallam*) an invocation of Allah's blessings and peace upon the Prophet Muhammad and his family: "Allah's blessings and peace be upon him and his family"

(*ʿAlayhis-salām*) an invocation of Allah's blessings and peace upon a Prophet or an angel: "May peace be upon him"

(*ʿAlayhimus-salām*) an invocation of Allah's blessings and peace upon three or more Prophets: "May peace be upon them"

(*Raḍiya-llāhu ʿanhu*) an invocation of Allah's pleasure with a male Companion of the Prophet: "May Allah be pleased with him"

(*Raḍiya-llāhu ʿanhā*) an invocation of Allah's pleasure with a female Companion of the Prophet: "May Allah be pleased with her"

(*Raḍiya-llāhu ʿanhumā*) an invocation of Allah's pleasure with two Companions of the Prophet: "May Allah be pleased with both of them"

(*Raḍiya-llāhu ʿanhum*) an invocation of Allah's pleasure with more than two Companions of the Prophet: "May Allah be pleased with them"

Contents

Commendations

Former Shaykh al-Azhar Professor Dr Muhammad Sayyid Ṭanṭāwī (Egypt)

In the Name of Allah, Most Compassionate, Ever-Merciful

All praises are for Allah alone Who is the Master, the Protector and the Lord Most High. He created (everything in the universe) and then (fulfilling all the requisites) equipoised it to its exact proportion. He determined law (phenomena for every creation) and guided it to its way (of sustaining and functioning according to its specific respective system). Salutations and greetings be invoked on our most beloved chieftain, the venerable and chosen Muhammad, who does not speak out of his (own) desire and whose speech is nothing but the Revelation which is sent down to him. Allah send down His mercy, blessings and peace on him, his family and Companions and all those who follow his Sunna and seek direction from the guidance he has brought for the entire mankind.

Honourable Dr Muhammad Tahir-ul-Qadri sent me his book *al-Minhāj al-Sawī* (Part I) for comments. I have read the book thoroughly. It is a collection of Prophetic traditions divided into different chapters. Each chapter contains traditions relevant to the subject. The translation of all the traditions and references of their sources and origins at footnotes are also one of the salient features of this anthology.

The esteemed author—may Allah reward him his rightful due—has indeed worked most diligently to bring it forth in a highly exhilarating and magnificent format to contribute his part in the revival and promotion of the Sunna of the Holy Messenger ﷺ. In simple and easy mode, it is a great presentation as well as a valuable gift from his side for the erudite luminaries of the *Umma*, research scholars and the most sincere and devoted lovers.

While writing these lines, I pray that may Allah reward Dr Muhammad Tahir-ul-Qadri most benevolently for his bountiful effort to produce such a beneficial work, and may He grant us profit through this book, besides adding it to the Scale of his pious deeds in the ultimate reckoning. Surely Allah is Watchful and Most Capable of doing it.

The Grand Mufti of Egypt
Al-Shaykh Dr ʿAlī Jumuʿa

In the Name of Allah, Most Compassionate, Ever-Merciful

All praises be to Allah, the Sustainer of all the worlds and salutations and greetings be invoked on the most venerable of the Messengers of Allah our Master, the Chosen Muhammad ﷺ, his family and Companions ﷺ. The strenuous struggle ventured by the scholars of the *Umma* in collecting the Prophetic traditions is no secret. The traditions of the Messenger of Allah ﷺ are one of the two kinds of revelation as described in an *al-Musnad*: "Beware! I have been blessed with the Qurʾān and its similitude (i.e., the traditions)." In this connection, a wide variety of books were written and published by the Muslim scholars and traditionists based on narrations and cognizance in order to arrange and compile the traditions and transfer the knowledge of hadith to the coming generations. This exercise made the method of collecting the hadith more and more effective, varied and refined. Some of them imposed the condition on collection of traditions that they must be "sound"; they collected them according to the chapters of jurisprudence such as *Ṣaḥīḥ al-Bukhārī*. The others relaxed this condition of "soundness" like the compilers of *Sunan al-Arbaʿa—al-Nasāʾī, Abū Dāwūd, al-Tirmidhī, Ibn Mājāh*. Among them, there were still others who compiled their narrations compatible with the *masānīd* collected by the Companions ﷺ such as Imam Aḥmad b. Ḥanbal, who did it in his *al-Musnad*, and other books wrote in the same style.

This age of narrating traditions ended with the demise of Ḥāfiẓ Abū Bakr al-Bayhaqī in 458 AH. Then other kinds of anthologies of Prophetic traditions came to the fore. In this period, some scholars sorted out only those hadiths that were based on injunctions and commands; others compiled those based on polite manners, ascetic practices, and heart-softening devotions; and there were still others who obtained the contiguously narrated reports with authentic chains of transmission.

Conforming to the methodology and skills employed by the pioneers and the pious predecessors, the worthy Dr Muhammad Tahir-ul-Qadri also stretched up his sinews to dedicate his services to the promotion and promulgation of the holy Prophetic traditions. He not only sorted out the colossal reservoirs of Prophetic traditions and compiled an excellent collection of hadiths, but also arranged it chapter-wise under different headings like doctrines, beliefs, acts of worship, etiquette and polite manners, heart-softening devotions and virtues and hymns. In addition to that, he also translated it into English for the benefit of English-knowing readers.

It is indeed a commendable and appreciable work. We supplicate in the Divine Presence of Allah Most High that may He reward the author of this book bountifully and grant true benefit to its readers and keen learners. Surely, He is Watchful and its Ordainer; and all praises are for Allah alone, Who is the Lord of all the worlds.

Former Vice-Chancellor al-Azhar Professor Dr Aḥmad ʿUmar Hāshim (Egypt)

In the Name of Allah, Most Compassionate, Ever-Merciful

All praises are for Almighty Allah alone, Who is the Lord of all the worlds, and salutations and greetings on the most revered of the Messengers of Allah our Master, the Chosen Muhammad ﷺ, his family and Companions ؓ.

I have gone through the book *al-Minhāj al-Sawī* (Part I), compiled by Dr Muhammad Tahir-ul-Qadri. It is indeed a great book because it is an excellent collection of the fine traditions of Allah's Messenger ﷺ, and also because this collection comprises traditions on beliefs, practices of worship and exhortations on morality and good manners. It is a commendable effort on the part of the author in that he has made his contribution to the promotion of the most valuable legacy for mankind—the legacy of the holy traditions of the Master of the Basin and of the Praiseworthy Station, the Head of the creation and our Chieftain and Intercessor, the Venerable Chosen Muhammad ﷺ.

There is no doubt in it that the promulgation and preaching of the Prophetic traditions is a source of real triumph in this world and in the Hereafter, betterment in the beliefs and devotion and an excellent service to morality and Shariah.

It is one of those significant books that comprise the roots of Islam—the traditions of Allah's Messenger (the second great source after the Holy Qur'ān) and are in this way a great service to the cause of Islam. Allah may reward Professor Dr Muhammad Tahir-ul-Qadri plenteously on his diligence and hard work put in to produce this book. And his endeavour in the promotion of Prophetic Sunna may be accorded blessing of acceptance in the holy presence of the Messenger of Allah ﷺ. I supplicate Allah to grant me, you and all the Muslims of the world His Kind Forgiveness and bless every reader of this book with benefit and send His mercy, blessings and peace on our Beloved Messenger, his Family and Companions ﷺ.

The Grand Hanafite Mufti of Syria

Al-Shaykh Asʿad Muhammad Saʿīd al-Ṣāgharjī

In the Name of Allah, Most Compassionate, Ever-Merciful

In the Honour of Shaykh-ul-Islam Dr Muhammad Tahir-ul-Qadri (may he live long)

All praises are for Allah alone, Who holds the most exalted and transcendent station. Holy is He, free of all imperfections and deficiencies. He it is Who extended the breasts of Saints for His remembrance, gratitude and perfect devotion. All glory and superiority is meant for Him alone. He it is Who has pledged to safeguard His *Dīn* till the Day of Resurrection, saying: "Surely We have sent down this admonition (the Holy Qurʾān) and We alone are its Protector." And extolled is only He Who has bestowed upon us the affinity with His venerable Messenger and made us members of the best *Umma* (Community). He made this *Umma* elegant with the pragmatic scholars and graced it with the most sincerely devoted Saints in order that His evidence might eternally persevere. It is for this that His venerable Messenger ﷺ said: "My *Umma* (Community) is like rain (drops); it is inconceivable whether its first portion is beneficial or the last one."

Then Allah send the most perfect salutations, blessings and mercy on our Chieftain and Protector, the Venerable and Chosen Muhammad ﷺ, who is the sun emitting the light of the divine gnosis, the radiance of the illumining Truths, the first vicegerent of the Essence of God and most superior of all the creation in excellent morality and conduct. He not only showed the brightest road to mankind, but also left after him two things which if humanity holds fast, it cannot go astray. These two things are: the Holy Book of Allah and the Prophet's Family who are most holy.

To promote and promulgate his call to the Truth, Allah persistently raised such dignified authorities who were the illumining lamps for all the seekers of guidance. May Allah the Exalted prolong our life filled with their love, instilled with love for the venerable Prophet and imbued with the love for his holy family! *Āmīn.*

Surely the knowledge of the Prophetic traditions is most superior to all other branches of knowledge owing to its compatibility with the Qur'ānic disciplines; and rightly so because it is this knowledge that elaborates the Qur'ān's conciseness and interprets Qur'ānic injunctions. This is an established fact that, to promote this knowledge, Allah Most High created such people in every age that would earn laurels with regard to organizing and systematizing it. They include Imam al-Bukhārī and other eminent authorities. All these authorities devised a straight path to collect, compile and arrange the Prophetic traditions for their followers and descendants. And this way, they became most deserving for this supplication of the Beloved Messenger of Allah ﷺ: "May Allah keep him evergreen who heard my instruction, retained and integrated it well and then communicated it to others unchanged as he heard it. So, many of those whom that instruction is conveyed are more intelligent than the ones who hear it directly."

I found opportunity to go through the valuable book *al-Minhāj al-Sawī* (Part I) compiled by Shaykh-ul-Islam Dr Muhammad Tahir-ul-Qadri who is a thinker and intellectual of his age, an outstanding and unrivalled personality of his time and the one who leads into the mysteries of ecstasy and intuitive sayings. He is a pragmatic scholar blessed with the gnosis of Allah, bringing splendour and grandeur to the Qādiriyya order of spiritual discipline. A prolific author, he has included in this anthology such Prophetic traditions as provide guidance and direction to every Muslim in correcting his behaviour, architecting his personality and reforming his society in addition to establishing a link of servanthood, devotion and obedience with his Lord.

This book comprises different chapters and sections that are predicated on subjects like the exalted station of the Prophet ﷺ, his noble virtues, his living status, the gnosis of his esteemed station, intercession, virtues of his kindred, Caliphs and Companions ﷺ, his miracles and the nobility of his *Umma*.

All these chapters have been crowned with the eulogy of the Beloved Messenger of Allah ﷺ in compliance with the Divine Command: *wa tuʿazzirūh-u wa tuwaqqirūh-u*—venerate him the maximum charged with most sincere and persevering reverence. This way, the book is a delightful gift for the lovers of Allah's Messenger ﷺ and those who invoke salutations and greetings on the Holy Prophet ﷺ; such is this comprehensive collection of hadiths. I have not been able to find any like of this book apart from *Riyāḍ al-Ṣāliḥīn* by the eminent authority Abū Zakariyyā al-Nawawī.

This book is a compendium of the venerable Messenger's decrees, instructions, actions and spiritual states. Similarly, the name of the book given to it by the worthy author (Allah protect him and give him long life) also encompasses all the traditions it contains. I supplicate Allah by means of His exalted Messenger to make this book a lighthouse for those who seek guidance. He certainly listens and grants supplications.

اَلْبَابُ الْأَوَّلُ

عَظَمَةُ الرِّسَالَةِ وَشَرَفُ الْمُصْطَفَى ﷺ

CHAPTER 1

THE ESTEEMED MAJESTY OF THE MESSENGERSHIP AND THE HONOURED STATION OF THE CHOSEN PROPHET ﷺ

اَلْفَصْلُ الْأَوَّلُ

فَصْلٌ فِي شَرَفِ النُّبُوَّةِ الْمُحَمَّدِيَّةِ ﷺ

SECTION 1

THE EXALTED STATION OF MUHAMMAD'S PROPHETHOOD

١ / ١. عَنْ جُبَيْرِ بْنِ مُطْعِمٍ ﵁ قَالَ: قَالَ رَسُولُ اللهِ ﷺ: لِي خَمْسَةُ أَسْمَاءَ: أَنَا مُحَمَّدٌ وَأَحْمَدُ، وَأَنَا الْمَاحِي الَّذِي يَمْحُو اللهُ بِيَ الْكُفْرَ وَأَنَا الْحَاشِرُ الَّذِي يُحْشَرُ النَّاسُ عَلَى قَدَمِي وَأَنَا الْعَاقِبُ.

مُتَّفَقٌ عَلَيْهِ.

1/1. According to Jubayr b. Muṭʿim ﵁:

"Allah's Messenger ﷺ said: 'I have five names: I am Muhammad and Aḥmad, I am *al-Māḥī* [the Eraser] with whom Allah erases unbelief, I am *al-Ḥāshir* [the Collector] at whose foot the people

---

[1] Set forth by •al-Bukhārī in *al-Ṣaḥīḥ*: Bk.: *al-Manāqib* [Virtues], Ch.: What has come to us about the names of Allah's Messenger ﷺ, 3/1299 §3339, & Bk.: *al-Tafsīr* [Interpretation], Ch.: Interpretation of *Sūrat al-Saff*, 4/1858 §4614. •Muslim in *al-Ṣaḥīḥ*: Bk.: *al-Faḍāʾil* [Excellent Merits], Ch.: Concerning his names ﷺ, 4/828 §2354. •al-Tirmidhī in *al-Sunan*: Bk.: *al-Adab* [Proper Conduct] according to Allah's Messenger ﷺ, Ch.: What has come to us about the names of the Prophet ﷺ, 5/135 §2840. According to al-Tirmidhī: "This is a fine authentic tradition." •Mālik in *al-Muwaṭṭaʾ*: Bk.: The Names of the Prophet ﷺ, Ch.: The names of the Prophet ﷺ, 2/1004. •al-Dārimī in *al-Sunan*, 2/409 §2775. •Ibn Ḥibbān in *al-Ṣaḥīḥ*, 14/219 §6313. •Aḥmad b. Ḥanbal in *al-Musnad*, 4/80, 84. •al-Ṭabarānī in *al-Muʿjam al-Awsaṭ*, 4/44 §3570, & in *al-Muʿjam al-Kabīr*, 2/120 §1520–1529. •Abū Yaʿlā in *al-Musnad*, 13/388 §7395. •al-Bayhaqī in *Shuʿab al-Īmān*, 2/140 §1397.

will be collected (on the Day of Resurrection), and I am *al-ʿĀqib* [the Last in Succession (of the Prophets)].'"

Agreed upon by al-Bukhārī and Muslim.

٢/ ٢. عَنْ أَبِـي هُرَيْرَةَ ﵁ أَنَّ رَسُوْلَ اللهِ ﷺ قَالَ: إِنَّ مَثَلِي وَمَثَلَ الْأَنْبِيَاءِ مِنْ قَبْلِي، كَمَثَلِ رَجُلٍ بَنَى بَيْتًا فَأَحْسَنَهُ وَأَجْمَلَهُ إِلاَّ مَوْضِعَ لَبِنَةٍ مِنْ زَاوِيَةٍ، فَجَعَلَ النَّاسُ يَطُوْفُوْنَ بِهِ وَيَعْجَبُوْنَ لَهُ وَيَقُوْلُوْنَ: هَلاَّ وُضِعَتْ هَذِهِ اللَّبِنَةُ. قَالَ: فَأَنَا اللَّبِنَةُ وَأَنَا خَاتَمُ النَّبِيِّيْنَ.

مُتَّفَقٌ عَلَيْهِ.

2/2. According to Abū Hurayra ﵁:

"Allah's Messenger ﷺ said: 'My likeness, and the likeness of the Prophets before me, is the likeness of a man who built a house, then adorned it and beautified it, but left the place of an adobe brick in a corner, so the people started encircling it and marvelling at it, saying: 'Why has this adobe brick not been installed?' He said: 'Because I am the adobe brick and I am the Seal of the Prophets (i.e., with me the chain of Prophets has come to an end)!'"

Agreed upon by al-Bukhārī and Muslim.

٣/ ٣. عَنْ أَبِـي مُوْسَى الْأَشْعَرِيِّ ﵁ قَالَ: كَانَ رَسُوْلُ اللهِ ﷺ يُسَمِّي لَنَا نَفْسَهُ أَسْمَاءً. فَقَالَ: أَنَا مُحَمَّدٌ، وَأَحْمَدُ، وَالْمُقَفِّي، وَالْحَاشِرُ، وَنَبِيُّ التَّوْبَةِ، وَنَبِيُّ الرَّحْمَةِ.

رَوَاهُ مُسْلِمٌ وَأَحْمَدُ.

3/3. According to Abū Mūsā al-Ashʿarī ﵁:

---

[2] Set forth by •al-Bukhārī in *al-Ṣaḥīḥ*: Bk.: *al-Manāqib* [Virtues], Ch.: The Seal of the Prophets [*Khātam al-Anbiyā*ʾ] ﷺ, 3/1300 §3341–3342. •Muslim in *al-Ṣaḥīḥ*: Bk.: *al-Faḍāʾil* [Excellent Merits], Ch.: Concerning his being the Seal of the Prophets ﷺ, 4/1791 §2286. •al-Nasāʾī in *al-Sunan al-Kubrā*, 6/436 §11422. •Ibn Ḥibbān in *al-Ṣaḥīḥ*, 14/315 §6405. •Aḥmad b. Ḥanbal in *al-Musnad*, 2/398 §9156.

[3] Set forth by •Muslim in *al-Ṣaḥīḥ*: Bk.: *al-Faḍāʾil* [The Excellent Merits], Ch.: Concerning his names ﷺ, 4/1828 §2355. •al-Ḥākim in *al-Mustadrak*,

"Allah's Messenger ﷺ used to name himself to them in various names for our sake, for he said: 'I am Muhammad and Aḥmad, and *al-Muqaffī* [the Last] and *al-Ḥāshir* [the Collector with whose compliance the people will be collected on the Day of Resurrection], and *Nabī al-Tawba* [the Prophet of Repentance] and *Nabī al-Raḥma* [the Prophet of Mercy].'"

Reported by Muslim and Aḥmad.

٤/ ٤. عَنْ وَاثِلَةَ بْنِ الْأَسْقَعِ رضي الله عنه يَقُوْلُ: سَمِعْتُ رَسُوْلَ اللهِ ﷺ يَقُوْلُ: إِنَّ اللهَ اصْطَفَى كِنَانَةَ مِنْ وَلَدِ إِسْمَاعِيْلَ، وَاصْطَفَى قُرَيْشًا مِنْ كِنَانَةَ، وَاصْطَفَى مِنْ قُرَيْشٍ بَنِي هَاشِمٍ، وَاصْطَفَانِي مِنْ بَنِي هَاشِمٍ.

رَوَاهُ مُسْلِمٌ وَالتِّرْمِذِيُّ، وَقَالَ التِّرْمِذِيُّ: هَذَا حَدِيْثٌ حَسَنٌ.

4/4. According to Wāthila b. al-Asqaʿ رضي الله عنه:

"I heard Allah's Messenger ﷺ say: 'Allah has chosen the tribe of Kināna from the offspring of Ishmael. He has chosen Quraysh from Kināna. He has chosen the Banū Hāshim from Quraysh, and He has chosen me from the Banū Hāshim.'"

Reported by Muslim and al-Timidhī. According to al-Timidhī: "This is a fine tradition."

2/659 §4185–4186. •Ibn Abī Shayba in *al-Muṣannaf*, 6/311 §31692–31693. •Aḥmad b. Ḥanbal in *al-Musnad*, 4/395, 404, 407. •al-Ṭabarānī in *al-Muʿjam al-Awsaṭ*, 4/327 §4338, 4417. •Ibn al-Jaʿd in *al-Musnad*, 1/479 §3322.

4 Set forth by •Muslim in *al-Ṣaḥīḥ*: Bk.: *al-Faḍāʾil* [The Excellent Merits], Ch.: The excellence of the lineage of the Prophet ﷺ, 4/1782 §2276. •al-Tirmidhī in *al-Sunan*: Bk.: *al-Manāqib* [Virtues] according to Allah's Messenger ﷺ, Ch.: What has come to us concerning the excellent merit of the Prophet ﷺ, 5/583 §3605. •Ibn Ḥibbān in *al-Ṣaḥīḥ*, 14/135 §6242. •Aḥmad b. Ḥanbal in *al-Musnad*, 4/107. •al-Bayhaqī in *al-Sunan al-Kubrā*, 6/365 §12852, 3542, & in *Shuʿab al-Īmān*, 2/139 §1391. •Ibn Abī Shayba in *al-Muṣannaf*, 6/317 §31731. •al-Ṭabarānī in *al-Muʿjam al-Kabīr*, 22/66 §161. •Abū Yaʿlā in *al-Musnad*, 13/469 §7485. •al-Lālakāʾī in *Iʿtiqād Ahl al-Sunna*, 4/751 §1400.

٥/٥. عَنْ أَبِي سَعِيْدٍ ﵁ قَالَ: بَيْنَا النَّبِيُّ ﷺ يَقْسِمُ، جَاءَ عَبْدُ اللهِ بْنُ ذِي الْخُوَيْصِرَةِ التَّمِيْمِيُّ فَقَالَ: اعْدِلْ، يَا رَسُوْلَ اللهِ. قَالَ: وَيْحَكَ، وَمَنْ يَعْدِلُ إِذَا لَمْ أَعْدِلْ؟ قَالَ عُمَرُ بْنُ الْخَطَّابِ: ائْذَنْ لِي فَأَضْرِبَ عُنُقَهُ. قَالَ: دَعْهُ، فَإِنَّ لَهُ أَصْحَابًا يَحْقِرُ أَحَدُكُمْ صَلَاتَهُ مَعَ صَلَاتِهِ وَصِيَامَهُ مَعَ صِيَامِهِ. يَمْرُقُوْنَ مِنَ الدِّيْنَ كَمَا يَمْرُقُ السَّهْمُ مِنَ الرَّمِيَّةِ. يُنْظَرُ فِي قُذَذِهِ فَلَا يُوْجَدُ فِيْهِ شَيءٌ، ثُمَّ يُنْظَرُ فِي نَصْلِهِ فَلَا يُوْجَدُ فِيْهِ شَيءٌ، ثُمَّ يُنْظَرُ فِي رِصَافِهِ فَلَا يُوْجَدُ فِيْهِ شَيءٌ، ثُمَّ يُنْظَرُ فِي نَضِيِّهِ فَلَا يُوْجَدُ فِيْهِ شَيءٌ. قَدْ سَبَقَ الْفَرْثَ وَالدَّمَ.

مُتَّفَقٌ عَلَيْهِ.

وَفِي رِوَايَةِ أَحْمَدَ: قَالَ عُمَرُ بْنُ الْخَطَّابِ ﵁: يَا رَسُوْلَ اللهِ، دَعْنِي أَقْتُلْ هَذَا الْمُنَافِقَ الْخَبِيثَ.

5/5. According to Abū Saʿīd ﵁:

---

[5] Set forth by •al-Bukhārī in *al-Ṣaḥīḥ*: Bk.: Calling on the apostates and the intransigents to repent, Ch.: Someone who refrains from fighting the Khawārij because of sympathy, and so that the people will not shun him, 6/2540 §6534, 6532, & Bk.: *al-Manāqib* [Virtues], Ch.: The signs of Prophethood in Islam, 3/1321 §3414, & Bk.: *Faḍāʾil al-Qurʾān* [The Excellent Merits of the Qurʾān], Ch.: Weeping during the recitation of the Qurʾān, 4/1928 §4771, & Bk.: *al-Adab* [Proper Conduct], Ch.: What has come to us about the man's saying: "Woe to you!" 5/2281 §5811. •Muslim in *al-Ṣaḥīḥ*: Bk.: *al-Zakāt* [The Alms-due], Ch.: Concerning the Khawārij and their characteristics, 2/744 §1064. •al-Nasāʾī likewise, on the authority of Abū Barza ﵁, in *al-Sunan,* Bk.: The Prohibition of Bloodshed, Ch.: Someone who unsheathes his sword, then, thrusts it into the people, 7/119 §4103, & in *al-Sunan al-Kubrā*, 6/355 §11220. •Ibn Mājah in *al-Sunan*: Introduction: Ch. Concerning the Khawārij, 1/61 §172. •Ibn al-Jārūd in *al-Muntaqā*, 1/272 §1083. •Ibn Ḥibbān in *al-Ṣaḥīḥ*, 15/140 §6741. •al-Ḥākim, on the authority of Abū Barza ﵁, in *al-Mustadrak*, 2/160 §2647. He said: "This is an authentic tradition." •Aḥmad b. Ḥanbal in *al-Musnad*, 3/56 §11554, 14861. •al-Bayhaqī in *al-Sunan al-Kubrā*, 8/171. •Ibn Abī Shayba in *al-Muṣannaf*, 7/562 §37932. •ʿAbd al-Razzāq in *al-Muṣannaf*, 10/146. •al-Bazzār likewise,

"While the Prophet ﷺ was distributing war gains, ʿAbd Allāh b. Dhū al-Khuwayṣira al-Tamīmī came and said: 'Distribute fairly, O Messenger of Allah!' (On his sarcasm) Allah's Messenger said: 'Woe to you! Who acts fairly, if I do not act fairly?' ʿUmar b. al-Khaṭṭāb said: 'Allow me to strike his neck!' He said: 'Leave him alone, for he has companions! One of you would disdain his own performance of the ritual prayer together with his performance of the ritual prayer, and his own observance of the fast together with his observance of the fast. They zoom off the Religion as the arrow speeds through the game animal. The hunter examines the head of his arrow, but there is nothing on it. Then he examines its cord, but there is nothing on it. Then he examines its shaft, but there is nothing on it. Then he examines its feather, but there is nothing on it. It has flown through the dung and blood (of the game animal without taking any stain on it. These wicked people too, in like manner, go out of the Religion without having any sign of a link with the Religion.)'"

Agreed upon by al-Bukhārī and Muslim.

And in the tradition narrated by Aḥmad: ʿUmar b. al-Khaṭṭāb رضي الله عنه said: "O Messenger of Allah! Let me kill this wicked hypocrite!"

٦/٦. عَنْ أَبِي هُرَيْرَةَ رضي الله عنه عَنِ النَّبِيِّ ﷺ قَالَ: مَا مِنْ مُؤْمِنٍ إِلاَّ وَأَنَا أَوْلَى النَّاسِ بِهِ فِي الدُّنْيَا وَالآخِرَةِ. اقْرَؤُوْا إِنْ شِئْتُمْ: ﴿ٱلنَّبِيُّ أَوْلَىٰ بِٱلْمُؤْمِنِينَ مِنْ أَنفُسِهِمْ﴾ (الأحزاب، ٣٣: ٦). فَأَيُّمَا مُؤْمِنٍ تَرَكَ مَالاً فَلْيَرِثْهُ عَصَبَتُهُ مَنْ كَانُوْا، فَإِنْ تَرَكَ دَيْنًا أَوْ ضِيَاعًا فَلْيَأْتِنِي وَأَنَا مَوْلاَهُ.

رَوَاهُ الْبُخَارِيُّ وَالدَّارِمِيُّ.

6/6. According to Abū Hurayra رضي الله عنه:

---

on the authority of Abū Barza رضي الله عنه, in *al-Musnad*, 9/305 §3846. •al-Ṭabarānī in *al-Muʿjam al-Awsaṭ*, 9/35 §9060. •Abū Yaʿlā in *al-Musnad*, 2/298 §1022. •al-Bukhārī, on the authority of Jābir رضي الله عنه, in *al-Adab al-Mufrad*, 1/270 §774.

[6] Set forth by •al-Bukhārī in *al-Ṣaḥīḥ*: *al-Tafsīr / al-Aḥzāb* [Interpretation / *Sūrat al-Aḥzāb*], Ch.: "The Prophet is closer to the believers than their own

"The Prophet ﷺ said: 'There is no believer to whom I am not the closest of the people in this world and the Hereafter. Recite if you wish: "This (Esteemed) Prophet is nearer to and has a greater claim on the believers than their own souls *[al-Nabiyyu awlā bi al-muʾminīna min anfusi-him].*" (Q.33:6). Whenever a believer leaves some wealth, let it be inherited by his relatives, whoever they may be, and if he leaves a debt or children, let them come to me, for I am their custodian! (And it is the system of the government after me that will fulfil these responsibilities.)'"

Reported by al-Bukhārī and al-Dārimī.

٧/٧. عَنِ الْـمُطَّلِبِ بْنِ أَبِي وَدَاعَةَ ؓ قَالَ: جَاءَ الْعَبَّاسُ ؓ إِلَى رَسُوْلِ اللهِ ﷺ فَكَأَنَّهُ سَمِعَ شَيْئًا، فَقَامَ النَّبِيُّ ﷺ عَلَى الْـمِنْبَرِ فَقَالَ: مَنْ أَنَا؟ قَالُوْا: أَنْتَ رَسُوْلُ اللهِ، عَلَيْكَ السَّلَامُ. قَالَ: أَنَا مُحَمَّدُ بْنُ عَبْدِ اللهِ بْنِ عَبْدِ الْـمُطَّلِبِ. إِنَّ اللهَ خَلَقَ الْخَلْقَ فَجَعَلَنِي فِي خَيْرِهِمْ فِرْقَةً، ثُمَّ جَعَلَهُمْ فِرْقَتَيْنِ فَجَعَلَنِي فِي خَيْرِهِمْ فِرْقَةً، ثُمَّ جَعَلَهُمْ قَبَائِلَ فَجَعَلَنِي فِي خَيْرِهِمْ قَبِيْلَةً، ثُمَّ جَعَلَهُمْ بُيُوْتًا فَجَعَلَنِي فِي خَيْرِهِمْ بَيْتًا وَخَيْرِهِمْ نَسَبًا.

رَوَاهُ التِّرْمِذِيُّ وَأَحْمَدُ، وَقَالَ التِّرْمِذِيُّ: هَذَا حَدِيْثٌ حَسَنٌ.

7/7. According to al-Muṭṭalib b. Abī Wadāʿa ؓ:

"Al-ʿAbbās came to Allah's Messenger ﷺ, for he seemed to have heard something (indecent from unbelievers and was in a rage),

---

selves [*al-Nabiyyu awlā bi al-muʾminīna min anfusi-him*]." (Q.33:6), 4/1795 §4503. •al-Dārimī in *al-Sunan*, 2/341 §2594. •al-Bayhaqī in *al-Sunan al-Kubrā*, 6/238 §12148.

[7] Set forth by •al-Tirmidhī in *al-Sunan*: Bk.: *al-Daʿawāt* [Supplications] according to Allah's Messenger ﷺ, Ch.: (99), 5/543 §3532, & Bk.: *al-Manāqib* [Virtues] according to Allah's Messenger ﷺ, Ch.: The excellent merit of the Prophet ﷺ, 5/584 §3607–3608. •Aḥmad b. Ḥanbal in *al-Musnad*, 1/210 §1788. •al-Bayhaqī in *Dalāʾil al-Nubuwwa*, 1/149. •al-Daylamī in *al-Firdaws bi-Maʾthūr al-Khiṭāb*, 1/41 §95. •al-Ḥusaynī in *al-Bayān wa al-Taʿrīf*, 1/178 §466. •al-Hindī in *Kanz al-ʿUmmāl*, 11/415 §319500.

so the Prophet ﷺ stood on the pulpit and said: 'Who am I?' They said: 'You are Allah's Messenger. Peace be upon you!' He said: 'I am Muhammad, the son of ʿAbd Allāh b. ʿAbd al-Muṭṭalib. Allah created the creatures, so He put me among the best of them (the human beings). Then He divided them into two segments (the Arabs and the non-Arabs) and He put me among the best of them (the Arabs). Then He made them tribes and He put me among the best of them (the tribe of the Quraysh). Then He made them households and He put me among the best of them as a household (Banū Hāshim), and the best of them as a lineage. (So I am the most exalted of the entire creation, my lineage, my tribe, my household and personal glory.)'"

Reported by al-Tirmidhī and Aḥmad. Al-Tirmidhī said: "This is a fine tradition."

٨/٨. عَنْ أَبِي هُرَيْرَةَ رضي الله عنه قَالَ: قَالُوْا: يَا رَسُوْلَ اللهِ، مَتَى وَجَبَتْ لَكَ النُّبُوَّةُ؟ قَالَ: وَآدَمُ بَيْنَ الرُّوْحِ وَالْجَسَدِ.

رَوَاهُ التِّرْمِذِيُّ وَالْحَاكِمُ، وَقَالَ التِّرْمِذِيُّ: هَذَا حَدِيْثٌ حَسَنٌ صَحِيْحٌ. وَقَالَ الْهَيْثَمِيُّ: رَوَاهُ أَحْمَدُ وَالطَّبَرَانِيُّ وَرِجَالُهُ رِجَالُ الصَّحِيْحِ.

وفي رواية: عَنْ مَيْسَرَةَ الْفَجْرِ رضي الله عنه قَالَ: قُلْتُ لِرَسُوْلِ اللهِ ﷺ: مَتَى كُنْتَ نَبِيًّا؟ قَالَ: وَآدَمُ بَيْنَ الرُّوْحِ وَالْجَسَدِ.

رَوَاهُ الْحَاكِمُ وَالطَّبَرَانِيُّ وَالْبُخَارِيُّ فِي الْكَبِيْرِ. وَقَالَ الْحَاكِمُ: هَذَا حَدِيْثٌ صَحِيْحُ الإِسْنَادِ.

وفي رواية: عَنِ ابْنِ عَبَّاسٍ رضي الله عنهما قَالَ: قِيْلَ: يَا رَسُوْلَ اللهِ، مَتَى كُتِبْتَ نَبِيًّا؟ قَالَ: وَآدَمُ بَيْنَ الرُّوْحِ وَالْجَسَدِ.

رَوَاهُ أَحْمَدُ وَالطَّبَرَانِيُّ وَاللَّفْظُ لَهُ وَابْنُ أَبِي عَاصِمٍ. إِسْنَادُهُ صَحِيْحٌ وَرِجَالُهُ كُلُّهُمْ ثِقَاتٌ رِجَالُ الصَّحِيْحِ. وَقَالَ الذَّهَبِيُّ: هَذَا حَدِيْثٌ صَالِحُ السَّنَدِ.

وفي رواية عنه: قَالَ: قُلْتُ: يَا رَسُوْلَ اللهِ، مَتَى أُخِذَ مِيْثَاقُكَ؟ قَالَ: وَآدَمُ بَيْنَ الرُّوْحِ وَالْجَسَدِ. رَوَاهُ الطَّبَرَانِيُّ.

وفي رواية: عَنْ عَبْدِ اللهِ بْنِ شَقِيْقٍ عَنْ رَجُلٍ، قَالَ: قُلْتُ: يَا رَسُوْلَ اللهِ، مَتَى جُعِلْتَ نَبِيًّا؟ قَالَ: وَآدَمُ بَيْنَ الرُّوْحِ وَالْجَسَدِ. رَوَاهُ أَحْمَدُ وَرِجَالُهُ رِجَالُ الصَّحِيْحِ.

وفي رواية: عَنْ عُمَرَ ﷺ قَالَ: يَا رَسُوْلَ اللهِ، مَتَى جُعِلْتَ نَبِيًّا؟ قَالَ: وَآدَمُ مُنْجَدِلٌ فِي الطِّيْنِ. رَوَاهُ أَبُوْنُعَيْمٍ كَمَا ذَكَرَ السُّيُوْطِيُّ وَابْنُ كَثِيْرٍ.

وفي رواية: عَنْ عَامِرٍ ﷺ قَالَ: قَالَ رَجُلٌ لِلنَّبِيِّ ﷺ: مَتَى اسْتُنْبِئْتَ؟ فَقَالَ: وَآدَمُ بَيْنَ الرُّوْحِ وَالْجَسَدِ حِيْنَ أُخِذَ مِنِّي الْـمِيْثَاقُ. رَوَاهُ ابْنُ سَعْدٍ.

8/8. According to Abū Hurayra ﷺ:

"The Companions said: 'O Messenger of Allah, when was Prophethood made incumbent upon you?' He said: 'When Adam was between the spirit and the body (i.e., the spirit and the body had not yet been blended. I was a Prophet at that time as well)!'"

---

[8] Set forth by •al-Tirmidhī in *al-Sunan*: Bk.: *al-Manāqib* [Virtues] according to Allah's Messenger ﷺ, Ch.: The excellent merit of the Prophet ﷺ, 5/585 §3609. •al-Ḥākim in *al-Mustadrak*, 2/665–666 §4609–4610. He said: "This is a tradition with an authentic chain of transmission." •Aḥmad b. Ḥanbal in *al-Musnad*, 4/66; 5/59, 379 §23620. •al-Ṭabarānī in *al-Muʿjam al-Awsaṭ*, 4/272 §4175, & in *al-Muʿjam al-Kabīr*, 12/92 §12571, 12646; 20/353 §833. •Ibn Abī Shayba in *al-Muṣannaf*, 7/369 §36553. •al-Haythamī in *Majmaʿ al-Zawāʾid*, 8/223. •Abū Nuʿaym in *Ḥilya al-Awliyāʾ*, 9/53. •Ibn Saʿd in *al-Ṭabaqāt al-Kubrā*, 7/60. •al-Maqdisī in *al-Aḥādīth al-Mukhtāra*, 9/142 §123. •al-Daylamī in *al-Firdaws bi-Maʾthūr al-Khiṭāb*, 3/284 §4845. •al-Shaybānī in *al-Āḥād wa al-Mathānī*, 5/347 §2918. •al-Khilāl in *al-Sunna*, 1/188 §200. He said: "Its chain of transmission is authentic." •Ibn Abī ʿĀṣim in *al-Sunna*, 1/179 §411. He said: "Its chain of transmission is authentic." •ʿAbd Allāh b. Aḥmad in *al-Sunan*, 2/398 §864. He said: "Its chain of transmission is authentic." •Abū al-Maḥāsin in *Muʿtaṣar al-Mukhtaṣar*, 1/10, •al-bānī in *Silsilat al-Aḥādīth al-Ṣaḥīḥa li al-Albānī*, 4/471 §1856. According to al-Haythamī: "It has been reported by al-Bazzār and al-Ṭabarānī."

Reported by al-Tirmidhī, al-Ḥākim. Al-Tirmidhī said: "This is a fine authentic tradition." And al-Haythamī said: "It is reported by Aḥmad and al-Ṭabarānī and its narrators are reliable."

In one report: According to Maysara al-Fajr: "I said to Allah's Messenger ﷺ: 'When did you become a Prophet?' He said: '(I was a Prophet even) when the creation of Adam was in the phase of the spirit and the body!'"

Reported by al-Ḥākim, al-Ṭabarānī and al-Bukhārī in *al-Kabīr*. According to al-Ḥākim: "This is a tradition with an authentic chain of transmission."

In another report: Ibn ʿAbbās ؓ said: "Someone said: 'O Messenger of Allah, when did you become a Prophet?' He said: '(I was a Prophet even) when the creation of Adam was in the phase of the spirit and the body!'"

Reported by Aḥmad and al-Ṭabarānī (the wording is his) and reported by Ibn Abī ʿĀṣim; its chain of transmission is authentic and its resources are sound and reliable. According to al-Dhahabī: "Its chain of transmission is authentic."

In still another report Ibn Abbās ؓ has been reported as saying: "I said: 'O Messenger of Allah! When was the covenant (of apostolate) taken from you?' He said: '(I was the Prophet even) when Adam's creation was between spirit and body.'"

Reported by al-Ṭabarānī.

According to ʿAbd Allāh b. Shaqīq, one of the Companions said: "O Messenger of Allah! When were you made the Prophet?" He said: "(I was a Prophet even) when the creation of Adam was in the transitional phase of spirit and body."

Reported by Aḥmad and its resources are reliable.

In another report ʿUmar b. al-Khaṭṭāb has been reported as saying: "I submitted: 'O Allah's Messenger, when were you made a Prophet?' He said: '(I was a Prophet even) when the body of Adam was kneaded in clay.'"

Reported by Abū Nuʿaym as mentioned by al-Suyūṭī and Ibn

Kathīr.

According to one report on the authority of ʿĀmir, a man submitted in the presence of the Prophet: 'O Allah's Messenger: When was the exalted station of Prophethood conferred upon you?" He said: "When the covenant of Prophethood was taken from me, Adam was between the spirit and the body."

Reporled by Ibn Saʿd.

٩/ ٩. عَنْ عَائِشَةَ ﵂ عَنْ رَسُوْلِ اللهِ ﷺ عَنْ جِبْرِيْلَ ﵇ قَالَ: قَلَبْتُ مَشَارِقَ الْأَرْضِ وَمَغَارِبَهَا فَلَمْ أَجِدْ رَجُلاً أَفْضَلَ مِنْ مُحَمَّدٍ ﷺ، وَلَمْ أَرَ بَيْتًا أَفْضَلَ مِنْ بَيْتِ بَنِي هَاشِمٍ.

رَوَاهُ الطَّبَرَانِيُّ وَاللاَّلَكَائِيُّ.

9/9. According to ʿĀʾisha ﵂:

"Allah's Messenger ﷺ said that Gabriel ﵇ said: 'I have searched and scrutinized the eastern regions of the earth and its western regions, and I have not discovered any man more excellent than Muhammad ﷺ, nor have I seen any home more excellent than the household of the Banū Hāshim.'"

Reported by al-Ṭabarānī and al-Lālakāʾī.

١٠/ ١٠. عَنْ عَلِيٍّ ﵁ أَنَّ النَّبِيَّ ﷺ قَالَ: خَرَجْتُ مِنْ نِكَاحٍ وَلَـمْ أَخْرُجْ مِنْ سِفَاحٍ، مِنْ لَدُنْ آدَمَ إِلَى أَنْ وَلَدَنِي أَبِـي وَأُمِّي.

رَوَاهُ الطَّبَرَانِيُّ وَالْبَيْهَقِيُّ وَابْنُ أَبِـي شَيْبَةَ.

10/10. According to ʿAlī ﵁:

---

[9] Set forth by •al-Ṭabarānī in *al-Muʿjam al-Awsaṭ*, 6/237 §6285. •al-Haythamī in *Majmaʿ al-Zawāʾid*, 8/217. •Al-Lālakāʾī in *Iʿtiqād Ahl al-Sunna*, 4/752 §1402.

[10] Set forth by •al-Ṭabarānī in *al-Muʿjam al-Awsaṭ*, 5/80 §4728. •Ibn Abī Shayba in *al-Muṣannaf*, 6/303 §31641. •al-Bayhaqī, on the authority of Ibn ʿAbbās ﵁, in *al-Sunan al-Kubrā*, 7/190. •al-Daylamī in *al-Firdaws bi-Maʾthūr al-Khiṭāb*, 2/190 §2949. •al-Haythamī in *Majmaʿ al-Zawāʾid*,

"The Prophet ﷺ said: 'I have emanated from a marriage and I have not emanated from a fornication; from the time of Adam until my father (ʿAbd Allāh) and my mother (Āminā) gave birth to me (the sanctity of my lineage has remained intact).'"

Reported by al-Ṭabarānī, al-Bayhaqī and Ibn Abī Shayba.

١١/١١. عَنْ جَابِرِ بْنِ عَبْدِ اللهِ رضي الله عنهما قَالَ: قُلْتُ: يَا رَسُوْلَ اللهِ، بِأَبِي أَنْتَ وَأُمِّي، أَخْبِرْنِي عَنْ أَوَّلِ شَيءٍ خَلَقَهُ اللهُ تَعَالَى قَبْلَ الْأَشْيَاءِ. قَالَ: يَا جَابِرُ، إِنَّ اللهَ تَعَالَى قَدْ خَلَقَ قَبْلَ الْأَشْيَاءِ نُوْرَ نَبِيِّكَ مِنْ نُورِهِ، فَجَعَلَ ذَلِكَ النُّوْرَ يَدُوْرُ بِالْقُدْرَةِ حَيْثُ شَاءَ اللهُ تَعَالَى، وَلَمْ يَكُنْ فِي ذَلِكَ الْوَقْتِ لَوْحٌ وَلَا قَلَمٌ، وَلَا جَنَّةٌ وَلَا نَارٌ، وَلَا مَلَكٌ وَلَا سَمَاءٌ، وَلَا أَرْضٌ وَلَا شَمْسٌ وَلَا قَمَرٌ، وَلَا جِنِّيٌّ، وَلَا إِنْسِيٌّ. فَلَمَّا أَرَادَ اللهُ تَعَالَى أَنْ يَخْلُقَ الْخَلْقَ قَسَمَ ذَلِكَ النُّورَ أَرْبَعَةَ أَجْزَاءٍ: فَخَلَقَ مِنَ الْجُزْءِ الْأَوَّلِ الْقَلَمَ، وَمِنَ الثَّانِي اللَّوْحَ وَمِنَ الثَّالِثِ الْعَرْشَ، ثُمَّ قَسَمَ الْجُزْءَ الرَّابِعَ أَرْبَعَةَ أَجْزَاءٍ. فَخَلَقَ مِنَ الْأَوَّلِ حَمَلَةَ الْعَرْشِ، وَمِنَ الثَّانِي الْكُرْسِيَّ وَمِنَ الثَّالِثِ بَاقِيَ الْمَلَائِكَةِ. ثُمَّ قَسَمَ الْجُزْءَ الرَّابِعَ أَرْبَعَةَ أَجْزَاءٍ، فَخَلَقَ مِنَ الْأَوَّلِ السَّمَوَاتِ، وَمِنَ الثَّانِي الْأَرْضِيْنَ وَمِنَ الثَّالِثِ الْجَنَّةَ وَالنَّارَ.

رَوَاهُ عَبْدُ الرَّزَّاقِ.

11/11. Jābir b. ʿAbd Allāh is reported having said:

"I said: 'O Messenger of Allah! My mother and father be sacrificed for you, tell me what Allah created first of all.' He said: 'Jābir, certainly Allah created the light of your Prophet from His

8/214. •al-Ḥusaynī in *al-Bayān wa al-Taʿrīf*, 1/294 §784. •al-Hindī in *Kanz al-ʿUmmāl*, 11/402 §31870.

11 Set forth by •ʿAbd al-Razzāq in *al-Muṣannaf*, 1/63 §63. •al-Qasṭallānī in *al-Muwāhib al-Ladunniyyia*, 1/71, and he said: ʿAbd al-Razzāq has set forth on his authority •al-Zurqānī in *Sharḥ al-Muwāhib al-Ladunniyyia*, 1/89–91. •al-ʿAjlūnī in *Kashf al-Khafāʾ*, 1/311 §827.

own light before any other creation. This light travelled where Allah willed and desired. The Tablet, the Pen, Paradise and Hell, the angels, the heaven and the earth, the sun and the moon and the Jinn and Man—nothing had yet been created. When Allah willed to bring into existence the creation, He divided that light into four parts. He made the Pen out of the first part, the Tablet of the second and the Throne of the third. He then further divided the fourth part into another four parts and created the angels that carry the Throne of the first part and the Chair of the second and rest of the angels of the third. He then divided the fourth part into another four parts and created heaven of the first part, earth of the second and Paradise and Hell of the third.

Reported by ʿAbd al-Razzāq.

اَلْفَصْلُ الثَّانِي

فَصْلٌ فِي مَنَاقِبِ النَّبِيِّ ﷺ

Section 2
The Noble Virtues of the Prophet ﷺ

١٢ / ١٢. عَنْ أَبِي هُرَيْرَةَ رضي الله عنه أَنَّ رَسُوْلَ اللهِ ﷺ قَالَ: بُعِثْتُ بِجَوَامِعِ الْكَلِمِ، وَنُصِرْتُ بِالرُّعْبِ. وَبَيْنَا أَنَا نَائِمٌ رَأَيْتُنِي أُتِيْتُ بِمَفَاتِيْحِ خَزَائِنِ الْأَرْضِ فَوُضِعَتْ فِي يَدِي.

مُتَّفَقٌ عَلَيْهِ.

12/12. According to Abū Hurayra رضي الله عنه:

"Allah's Messenger ﷺ said: 'I have been sent with the all-encompassing (i.e., all-inclusive) words, and I have been assisted with awesomeness (i.e., over-dominant and impressive posture). While I was asleep, I saw that the keys of the treasures of the earth were brought for me and placed in my hand!'"

Agreed upon by al-Bukhārī and Muslim.

١٣ / ١٣. عَنِ ابْنِ عَبَّاسٍ رضي الله عنهما قَالَ: جَلَسَ نَاسٌ مِنْ أَصْحَابِ رَسُوْلِ اللهِ ﷺ

---

12 Set forth by •al-Bukhārī in *al-Ṣaḥīḥ*: Bk.: *al-Iʿtiṣām bi al-Kitāb wa al-Sunna* [Adherence to the Book and the Sunna], Ch.: The saying of the Prophet ﷺ: "I have been sent with the totalities of the words," 6/2654 §6845, & Bk.: *al-Jihād* [The Sacred Struggle], Ch.: The saying of the Prophet ﷺ: "I was helped by dreadfulness for the enemy who would still be a month's journey away," 3/1087 §2815, & Bk.: *al-Taʿbīr* [Interpretation], Ch.: The keys in the hand, 6/2573 §6611. •Muslim in *al-Ṣaḥīḥ*: Bk.: *al-Masājid wa Mawāḍiʿ al-Ṣalāt* [Mosques and Places of Ritual Prayer], 1/371 §523. •al-Nasāʾī in *al-Sunan*: Bk.: *al-Jihād* [The Sacred Struggle], Ch.: The necessity of the Sacred Struggle, 6/3–4 §3087–3089. •al-Nasāʾī in *al-Sunan al-Kubrā*, 3/3 §4295. •Aḥmad b. Ḥanbal in *al-Musnad*, 2/264, 455 §7575, 9867. •Ibn Ḥibbān in *al-Ṣaḥīḥ*, 14/277 §6363.

يَنْتَظِرُوْنَهُ. قَالَ: فَخَرَجَ حَتَّى إِذَا دَنَا مِنْهُمْ سَمِعَهُمْ يَتَذَاكَرُوْنَ فَسَمِعَ حَدِيْثَهُمْ، فَقَالَ بَعْضُهُمْ: عَجَبًا إِنَّ اللهَ ﷻ اتَّخَذَ مِنْ خَلْقِهِ خَلِيْلاً، اِتَّخَذَ إِبْرَاهِيْمَ خَلِيْلاً! وَقَالَ آخَرُ: مَاذَا بِأَعْجَبَ مِنْ كَلَامِ مُوْسَى: كَلَّمَهُ تَكْلِيْمًا. وَقَالَ آخَرُ: فَعِيْسَى كَلِمَةُ اللهِ وَرُوْحُهُ. وَقَالَ آخَرُ: آدَمُ اصْطَفَاهُ اللهُ. فَخَرَجَ عَلَيْهِمْ فَسَلَّمَ وَقَالَ: قَدْ سَمِعْتُ كَلَامَكُمْ وَعَجَبَكُمْ أَنَّ إِبْرَاهِيْمَ خَلِيْلُ اللهِ وَهُوَ كَذَلِكَ وَمُوْسَى نَجِيُّ اللهِ وَهُوَ كَذَلِكَ، وَعِيْسَى رُوْحُ اللهِ وَكَلِمَتُهُ وَهُوَ كَذَلِكَ، وَآدَمُ اصْطَفَاهُ اللهُ وَهُوَ كَذَلِكَ. أَلَا وَأَنَا حَبِيْبُ اللهِ وَلَا فَخْرَ، وَأَنَا حَامِلُ لِوَاءِ الْحَمْدِ يَوْمَ الْقِيَامَةِ وَلَا فَخْرَ وَأَنَا أَوَّلُ شَافِعٍ وَأَوَّلُ مُشَفَّعٍ يَوْمَ الْقِيَامَةِ وَلَا فَخْرَ وَأَنَا أَوَّلُ مَنْ يُحَرِّكُ حِلَقَ الْجَنَّةِ فَيَفْتَحُ اللهُ لِي فَيُدْخِلُنِيْهَا وَمَعِيَ فُقَرَاءُ الْمُؤْمِنِيْنَ وَلَا فَخْرَ، وَأَنَا أَكْرَمُ الْأَوَّلِيْنَ وَالْآخِرِيْنَ وَلَا فَخْرَ.

رَوَاهُ التِّرْمِذِيُّ وَالدَّارِمِيُّ.

13/13. According to Ibn ʿAbbās ﷄ:

"Some Companions of Allah's Messenger ﷺ were sitting and waiting for him. In the meanwhile he came. When he drew near to them, he heard them making some conversation. One of them said: 'How amazing it is that Allah chose a bosom friend from among His creatures! He chose Abraham as a bosom friend!' Another said: 'What is more amazing than the discourse of Moses?! He spoke to him directly!' Another said: 'Jesus is the Word of Allah and His Spirit!' Another said: 'Adam was chosen by Allah!' Allah's Messenger ﷺ then approached them, greeted them with the salutation of peace and said: 'I heard your discourse and your amazement that Abraham is Allah's Bosom Friend *[Khalīl Allāh]*, for that is how he is, and that Moses is Allah's Confidant *[Najiyy Allāh]*, for that is how he is, and that Jesus is Allah's Spirit and

[13] Set forth by •al-Tirmidhī in *al-Sunan*: Bk.: *al-Manāqib* [Virtues] according to Allah's Messenger ﷺ, Ch.: The excellent merit of the Prophet ﷺ, 5/587 §3616. •al-Dārimī in *al-Sunan*: Ch.: (8), The excellent merit bestowed upon the Prophet ﷺ, 1/39 §47.

His Word *[Rūḥ Allāh wa Kalimatu-h]*, for that is how he is, and that Adam was chosen by Allah, for that is how he is (the exalted one)! Listen! I am indeed the Beloved of Allah *[Ḥabīb Allāh]*, and that is no boast! I am the bearer of the banner of praise on the Day of Resurrection, and that is no boast, and I am the first intercessor and the first whose intercession is accepted on the Day of Resurrection, and that is no boast! I am the first one to knock the chain of Paradise, for Allah will open the gate for me, then He will cause me to enter it, accompanied by the ascetic and the destitute and the devout believers, and that is no boast! I am the noblest of the first and the last (in the sight of Allah), and that is no boast!'"

Reported by al-Tirmidhī and al-Dārimī.

١٤/ ١٤. عَنْ أَنَسٍ ﷺ قَالَ: قَالَ رَسُوْلُ اللهِ ﷺ: أَنَا أَوَّلُهُمْ خُرُوْجًا وَأَنَا قَائِدُهُمْ إِذَا وَفَدُوْا، وَأَنَا خَطِيْبُهُمْ إِذَا أَنْصَتُوْا، وَأَنَا مُشَفِّعُهُمْ إِذَا حُبِسُوْا، وَأَنَا مُبَشِّرُهُمْ إِذَا أَيِسُوْا. اَلْكَرَامَةُ وَالْمَفَاتِيْحُ يَوْمَئِذٍ بِيَدِيَّ وَأَنَا أَكْرَمُ وَلَدِ آدَمَ عَلَى رَبِّي. يَطُوْفُ عَلَيَّ أَلْفُ خَادِمٍ كَأَنَّهُمْ بَيْضٌ مَكْنُوْنٌ، أَوْ لُؤْلُؤٌ مَنْثُوْرٌ.

رَوَاهُ التِّرْمِذِيُّ وَالدَّارِمِيُّ وَاللَّفْظُ لَهُ.

14/14. According to Anas ﷺ:

"Allah's Messenger ﷺ said: 'I am the first of them to come forth (from the grave). I will be their leader when they will go in congregation. I will be their spokesman when they will be quiet. I will be their intercessor when they will be checked, and I will be their bringer of glad tidings when they are in despair. Nobility

---

[14] Set forth by •al-Tirmidhī in *al-Sunan*: Bk.: *al-Manāqib* [Virtues] according to Allah's Messenger ﷺ, Ch.: The excellent merit of the Prophet ﷺ, 5/585 §3610. •al-Dārimī in *al-Sunan*, (8) Ch.: The excellent merit bestowed upon the Prophet ﷺ, 1/39 §48. •al-Daylamī in *al-Firdaws bi-Ma'thūr al-Khiṭāb*, 1/47 §117. •al-Khilāl in *al-Sunna*, 1/208 §235. •al-Qazwīnī in *al-Tadwīn fī Akhbār Qazwīn*, 1/235. •Ibn al-Jawzī in *Ṣafwat al-Ṣafwa*, 1/182. •al-Munāwī in *Fayḍ al-Qadīr*, 3/40.

and the keys of Paradise will be in my hands on that Day, for I am the noblest of the children of Adam in the sight of my Lord. A thousand servants will circle round me (that Day), as if they are concealed eggs or scattered pearls!'"

> Reported by al-Tirmidhī and al-Dārimī, and this is his wording.

١٥/١٥. عَنْ أُبَيِّ بْنِ كَعْبٍ رضي الله عنه عَنِ النَّبِيِّ ﷺ قَالَ: إِذَا كَانَ يَوْمَ الْقِيَامَةِ كُنْتُ إِمَامَ النَّبِيِّيْنَ، وَخَطِيْبَهُمْ، وَصَاحِبَ شَفَاعَتِهِمْ غَيْرَ فَخْرٍ.

رَوَاهُ التِّرْمِذِيُّ وَابْنُ مَاجَه وَالْحَاكِمُ. وَقَالَ التِّرْمِذِيُّ: هَذَا حَدِيْثٌ حَسَنٌ صَحِيْحٌ، وَقَالَ الْحَاكِمُ: هَذَا حَدِيْثٌ صَحِيْحُ الْإِسْنَادِ.

15/15. According to Ubayy b. Kaʿb (may Allah be pleased with him):

"The Prophet ﷺ said: 'When it is the Day of Resurrection, I shall be the leader of the Prophets, their spokesman and the master of their intercession, without any boast!'"

> Reported by al-Tirmidhī, Ibn Mājah and al-Ḥākim. According to al-Tirmidhī, this is a fine authentic tradition, and according to al-Ḥākim, this is a tradition with an authentic chain of transmission.

١٦/١٦. عَنْ عَمْرِو بْنِ قَيْسٍ رضي الله عنه أَنَّ رَسُوْلَ اللهِ ﷺ قَالَ: نَحْنُ الْآخِرُوْنَ، وَنَحْنُ السَّابِقُوْنَ يَوْمَ الْقِيَامَةِ، وَإِنِّي قَائِلٌ قَوْلًا غَيْرَ فَخْرٍ: إِبْرَاهِيْمُ خَلِيْلُ اللهِ، وَمُوْسَى صَفِيُّ اللهِ، وَأَنَا حَبِيْبُ اللهِ، وَمَعِي لِوَاءُ الْحَمْدِ يَوْمَ الْقِيَامَةِ. وَإِنَّ اللهَ تعالى وَعَدَنِي فِي أُمَّتِي،

---

[15] Set forth by •al-Tirmidhī in *al-Sunan*: Bk.: *al-Manāqib* [Virtues] according to Allah's Messenger ﷺ, Ch.: The excellent merit of the Prophet ﷺ, 5/586 §3613. •Ibn Mājah in *al-Sunan*: Bk.: *al-Zuhd* [Abstinence], Ch.: Concerning intermediation, 2/1443 §4314. •Aḥmad b. Ḥanbal in *al-Musnad*, 5/137–138 §21283, 21290. •al-Ḥākim in *al-Mustadrak*, 1/143 §240, 6969. •ʿAbd b. Ḥumayd in *al-Musnad*, 1/90 §171. •al-Maqdisī in *al-Aḥādīth al-Mukhtāra*, 3/385 §1179. •al-Mizzī in *Tahdhīb al-Kamāl*, 3/118.

وَأَجَارَهُمْ مِنْ ثَلَاثٍ: لَا يَعُمُّهُمْ بِسَنَةٍ، وَلَا يَسْتَأْصِلُهُمْ عَدُوٌّ، وَلَا يَجْمَعُهُمْ عَلَى
ضَلَالَةٍ.

رَوَاهُ الدَّارِمِيُّ.

16/16. According to ʿAmr b. Qays :

"Allah's Messenger said: 'We are the last, and we are the excelling on the Day of Resurrection, and I am making a statement that is no boast: Abraham is Allah's Bosom Friend [*Khalīl Allāh*], Moses is Allah's Sincere Friend [*Ṣafiyy Allāh*], I am Allah's Beloved Friend [*Ḥabīb Allāh*], and with me is the banner of praise on the Day of Resurrection. Allah has promised me for the sake of my Community, and He has granted them protection from three things: (1) He will not encompass them within a drought, (2) an enemy will not annihilate them, and (3) He will not unite them on an error.'"

Reported by al-Dārimī.

١٧/١٧. عَنْ جَابِرٍ أَنَّ النَّبِيَّ قَالَ: أَنَا قَائِدُ الْمُرْسَلِينَ وَلَا فَخْرَ، وَأَنَا خَاتَمُ
النَّبِيِّينَ وَلَا فَخْرَ، وَأَنَا أَوَّلُ شَافِعٍ وَمُشَفَّعٍ وَلَا فَخْرَ.

رَوَاهُ الدَّارِمِيُّ وَالطَّبَرَانِيُّ.

17/17. According to Jābir :

"The Prophet said: 'I am the leader of the Messengers, and that is no boast! I am the Seal of the Prophets, and that is no boast!

---

16 Set forth by •al-Dārimī in *al-Sunan*: (8) Ch.: The excellent merit bestowed upon the Prophet , 1/42 §54. •al-Mubārakfūrī in *Tuḥfat al-Aḥwadhī*, 6/323.

17 Set forth by •al-Dārimī in *al-Sunan*: (8) Ch.: The excellent merit bestowed upon the Prophet , 1/40 §49. •al-Ṭabarānī in *al-Muʿjam al-Awsaṭ*, 1/61 §170. •al-Bayhaqī in *Kitāb al-Iʿtiqād*, 1/192. •al-Haythamī in *Majmaʿ al-Zawāʾid*, 8/254. •al-Dhahabī in *Siyar Aʿlām al-Nubalāʾ*, 10/223. •al-Munāwī in *Fayḍ al-Qadīr*, 3/43.

I am the first to intercede and the first one whose intercession will be accepted, and that is no boast!'"

Reported by al-Dārimī and al-Ṭabarānī.

١٨/١٨. عَنْ أَبِي مُوْسَى الْأَشْعَرِيِّ ﵁ قَالَ: خَرَجَ أَبُوْ طَالِبٍ إِلَى الشَّامِ، وَخَرَجَ مَعَهُ النَّبِيُّ ﷺ فِي أَشْيَاخٍ مِنْ قُرَيْشٍ. فَلَمَّا أَشْرَفُوْا عَلَى الرَّاهِبِ هَبَطُوْا، فَحَلُّوْا رِحَالَهُمْ. فَخَرَجَ إِلَيْهِمُ الرَّاهِبُ. وَكَانُوْا قَبْلَ ذَلِكَ يَمُرُّوْنَ بِهِ فَلاَ يَخْرُجُ إِلَيْهِمْ وَلاَ يَلْتَفِتُ. قَالَ: فَهُمْ يَحُلُّوْنَ رِحَالَهُمْ، فَجَعَلَ يَتَخَلَّلُهُمُ الرَّاهِبُ، حَتَّى جَاءَ فَأَخَذَ بِيَدِ رَسُوْلِ اللهِ ﷺ، فَقَالَ: هَذَا سَيِّدُ الْعَالَمِيْنَ؛ هَذَا رَسُوْلُ رَبِّ الْعَالَمِيْنَ. يَبْعَثُهُ اللهُ رَحْمَةً لِّلْعَالَمِيْنَ. فَقَالَ لَهُ أَشْيَاخٌ مِنْ قُرَيْشٍ: مَا عِلْمُكَ؟ فَقَالَ: إِنَّكُمْ حِيْنَ أَشْرَفْتُمْ مِنَ الْعَقَبَةِ لَمْ يَبْقَ شَجَرٌ وَلاَ حَجَرٌ إِلاَّ خَرَّ سَاجِدًا، وَلاَ يَسْجُدَانِ إِلاَّ لِنَبِيٍّ. وَإِنِّي أَعْرِفُهُ بِخَاتَمِ النُّبُوَّةِ أَسْفَلَ مِنْ غُضْرُوْفِ كَتِفِهِ مِثْلَ التُّفَاحَةِ. ثُمَّ رَجَعَ فَصَنَعَ لَهُمْ طَعَامًا. فَلَمَّا أَتَاهُمْ بِهِ، وَكَانَ هُوَ فِي رِعْيَةِ الْإِبِلِ، قَالَ: أَرْسِلُوْا إِلَيْهِ. فَأَقْبَلَ وَعَلَيْهِ غَمَامَةٌ تُظِلُّهُ. فَلَمَّا دَنَا مِنَ الْقَوْمِ وَجَدَهُمْ قَدْ سَبَقُوْهُ إِلَى فَيْءِ الشَّجَرَةِ. فَلَمَّا جَلَسَ مَالَ فَيْءُ الشَّجَرَةِ عَلَيْهِ، فَقَالَ: انْظُرُوْا إِلَى فَيْءِ الشَّجَرَةِ؛ مَالَ عَلَيْهِ ... قَالَ: أَنْشُدُكُمْ بِاللهِ: أَيُّكُمْ وَلِيُّهُ؟ قَالُوْا: أَبُوْ طَالِبٍ. فَلَمْ يَزَلْ يُنَاشِدُهُ حَتَّى رَدَّهُ أَبُوْ طَالِبٍ.

رَوَاهُ التِّرْمِذِيُّ وَابْنُ أَبِي شَيْبَةَ.

18/18. According to Abū Mūsā al-Ashʿarī ﵁:

"Abū Ṭālib set out towards Syria, and the Prophet ﷺ was also accompanying him among the (affluent) shaykhs of Quraysh. Then, when they drew near to the monk, they alighted, and unfastened

[18] Set forth by •al-Tirmidhī in *al-Sunan*: Bk.: *al-Manāqib* [Virtues] according to Allah's Messenger ﷺ, Ch.: The Prophethood of the Prophet ﷺ, 5/590 §3620. •Ibn Abī Shayba in *al-Muṣannaf*, 6/317 §31733, 36541. •Ibn Ḥibbān in *al-Thiqāt*, 1/42. •al-Iṣbahānī in *Dalāʾil al-Nubuwwa*, 1/45 §19. •al-Ṭabarī in *Taʾrīkh al-Umam wa al-Mulūk*, 1/519.

their camel saddles. The monk came out to meet them. They (the affluent Quraysh) used to pass by him before that too but he would not come out towards them and he would not pay any attention. [However, on this particular occasion] the monk started mingling with them while they were yet unfastening their camel saddles. He came to the Messenger of Allah ﷺ, took hold of his hand and said: 'This is the Chieftain of the worlds! This is the Messenger of the Lord of the worlds! Allah will send him as a mercy for all the worlds!' The shaykhs of Quraysh then said to him: 'How do you know all this?' He said: 'When you drew near to al-ʿAqaba valley, no tree and no stone failed to bow in prostration, and they do not prostrate themselves except for a Prophet. I recognize him by the Seal of Prophethood beneath the scapulum of his shoulder, like the apple.' He then went back and prepared a meal for them. When he brought it to them, while he was in the herd of camels, he said: 'Send for him!' When he came, a cloud provided him shade. When he drew near to the people, he found that they had gone ahead of him to the shadow of the tree. Then, when he [the Prophet ﷺ] sat down, the shadow of the tree bent over him, so he said: 'Look at the shadow of the tree! It has bent over him!' ... He said: 'I adjure you by Allah, which of you is His guardian?' They said: 'Abū Ṭālib!' Then he did not cease adjuring him to send him back till Abū Ṭālib sent him back."

Reported by al-Tirmidhī and Ibn Abī Shayba.

١٩/١٩. عَنْ عَلِيِّ بْنِ أَبِي طَالِبٍ ﵁ قَالَ: كُنْتُ مَعَ النَّبِيِّ ﷺ بِمَكَّةَ، فَخَرَجْنَا فِي بَعْضِ نَوَاحِيْهَا، فَمَا اسْتَقْبَلَهُ جَبَلٌ وَلَا شَجَرٌ إِلَّا وَهُوَ يَقُوْلُ: اَلسَّلَامُ عَلَيْكَ، يَا رَسُوْلَ اللهِ.

رَوَاهُ التِّرْمِذِيُّ وَالدَّارِمِيُّ وَالْحَاكِمُ. وَقَالَ التِّرْمِذِيُّ: هَذَا حَدِيْثٌ حَسَنٌ، وَقَالَ الْحَاكِمُ: هَذَا حَدِيْثٌ صَحِيْحُ الإِسْنَادِ.

19/19. According to ʿAlī b. Abī Ṭālib ﵁:

---

[19] Set forth by •al-Tirmidhī in *al-Sunan*: Bk.: *al-Manāqib* [Virtues]

"I was with the Prophet ﷺ in Mecca, so we set out in one of its directions, and no mountain and no tree on his way came to pass without saying: 'Peace be upon you, O Messenger of Allah!'"

> Reported by al-Tirmidhī, al-Dārimī and al-Ḥākim. According to al-Tirmidhī, this is a fine tradition, and al-Ḥākim said: "This is a tradition with an authentic chain of transmission."

٢٠/ ٢٠. عَنْ أَنَسٍ ؓ أَنَّ النَّبِيَّ ﷺ أُتِيَ بِالْبُرَاقِ لَيْلَةَ أُسْرِيَ بِهِ مُلْجَمًا مُسْرَجًا، فَاسْتَصْعَبَ عَلَيْهِ، فَقَالَ لَهُ جِبْرِيْلُ: أَبِمُحَمَّدٍ تَفْعَلُ هَذَا؟ قَالَ: فَمَا رَكِبَكَ أَحَدٌ أَكْرَمُ عَلَى اللهِ مِنْهُ. قَالَ: فَارْفَضَّ عَرَقًا.

رَوَاهُ التِّرْمِذِيُّ وَأَبُوْ يَعْلَى وَابْنُ حِبَّانَ وَأَحْمَدُ، وَقَالَ التِّرْمِذِيُّ: هَذَا حَدِيْثٌ حَسَنٌ.

20/20. According to Anas ؓ:

"Burāq was brought to the Prophet ﷺ on the night of his Heavenly Ascension, bridled and saddled. (Overjoyed) it danced making it hard to mount it, so Gabriel said to it: 'Is it for Muhammad that you are doing this? You have not been ridden by anyone nobler in the sight of Allah than he!' Hearing this, the Burāq immersed in shame."

---

according to Allah's Messenger ﷺ, Ch.: (6), 5/593 §3626. •al-Dārimī in *al-Sunan*: Ch.: (4), What Allah conferred upon His Prophet, including the belief in him of the trees, the beasts and the jinn, 1/31 §21. •al-Maqdisī in *al-Aḥādīth al-Mukhtāra*, 2/134 §502. •al-Ḥākim in *al-Mustadrak*, 2/677 §4238. •al-Mundhirī in *al-Targhīb wa al-Tarhīb*, 2/150 §1880. •al-Mizzī in *Tahdhīb al-Kamāl*, 14/175 §3103. •al-Jurjānī in *Taʾrīkh Jurjān*, 1/329 §600.

[20] Set forth by •al-Tirmidhī in *al-Sunan*: Bk.: *Tafsīr al-Qurʾān* [Interpretation of the Qurʾān] according to Allah's Messenger ﷺ, Ch.: From *Sūra Banī Isrāʾīl*, 5/301 §3131. •Abū Yaʿlā in *al-Musnad*, 5/459 §3184. •Ibn Ḥibbān in *al-Ṣaḥīḥ*, 1/234 §46. •Aḥmad b. Ḥanbal in *al-Musnad*, 3/164 §12694. •ʿAbd b. Ḥumayd in *al-Musnad*, 1/357 §1185. •al-Maqdisī in *al-Aḥādīth al-Mukhtāra*, 7/23 §2404. •al-Khaṭīb Baghdādī in *Taʾrīkh Baghdād*, 3/435 §1574. •al-ʿAsqalānī in *Fatḥ al-Bārī*, 7/206.

Reported by al-Tirmidhī, Abū Yaʿlā, Ibn Ḥibbān, and Aḥmad. Al-Tirmidhī said: "This is a fine tradition."

٢١/ ٢١. عَنْ أَبِي سَعِيْدٍ ﵁ قَالَ: قَالَ رَسُوْلُ اللهِ ﷺ: أَنَا سَيِّدُ وَلَدِ آدَمَ يَوْمَ الْقِيَامَةِ وَلاَ فَخْرَ، وَبِيَدِي لِوَاءُ الْحَمْدِ وَلاَ فَخْرَ. وَمَا مِنْ نَبِيٍّ يَوْمَئِذٍ آدَمَ فَمَنْ سِوَاهُ إِلاَّ تَحْتَ لِوَائِي؛ وَأَنَا أَوَّلُ مَنْ تَنْشَقُّ عَنْهُ الْأَرْضُ وَلاَ فَخْرَ. قَالَ: فَيَفْزَعُ النَّاسُ ثَلاَثَ فَزَعَاتٍ فَيَأْتُوْنَ آدَمَ ... فذكر الحديث إلى أن قَالَ: فَيَأْتُونَنِي فَأَنْطَلِقُ مَعَهُمْ. قَالَ ابْنُ جُدْعَانَ: قَالَ أَنَسٌ ﵁: فَكَأَنِّي أَنْظُرُ إِلَى رَسُوْلِ اللهِ ﷺ قَالَ: فَآخُذُ بِحَلْقَةِ بَابِ الْجَنَّةِ فَأُقَعْقِعُهَا فَيُقَالُ: مَنْ هَذَا؟ فَيُقَالُ: مُحَمَّدٌ. فَيَفْتَحُوْنَ لِي وَيُرَحِّبُوْنَ بِي فَيَقُولُونَ: مَرْحَبًا. فَأَخِرُّ سَاجِدًا فَيُلْهِمُنِيَ اللهُ مِنَ الثَّنَاءِ وَالْحَمْدِ. فَيُقَالُ لِي: ارْفَعْ رَأْسَكَ وَسَلْ تُعْطَ وَاشْفَعْ تُشَفَّعْ وَقُلْ يُسْمَعْ لِقَوْلِكَ وَهُوَ الْمَقَامُ الْمَحْمُودُ الَّذِي قَالَ اللهُ: ﴿**عَسَىٰ أَن يَبْعَثَكَ رَبُّكَ مَقَامًا مَّحْمُودًا**﴾. (الإسراء، ١٧: ٧٩).

رَوَاهُ التِّرْمِذِيُّ، وَقَالَ: هَذَا حَدِيْثٌ حَسَنٌ صَحِيْحٌ.

وروى ابن ماجه عنه قَالَ: قَالَ رَسُوْلُ اللهِ ﷺ: أَنَا سَيِّدُ وَلَدِ آدَمَ وَلاَ فَخْرَ، وَأَنَا أَوَّلُ مَنْ تَنْشَقُّ الْأَرْضُ عَنْهُ يَوْمَ الْقِيَامَةِ وَلاَ فَخْرَ، وَأَنَا أَوَّلُ شَافِعٍ، وَأَوَّلُ مُشَفَّعٍ وَلاَ فَخْرَ وَلِوَاءُ الْحَمْدِ بِيَدِي يَوْمَ الْقِيَامَةِ وَلاَ فَخْرَ.

21/21. According to Abū Saʿīd al-Khudrī ﵁:

"The Messenger of Allah ﷺ said: 'I will be the leader of the children of Adam on the Day of Resurrection and that is no boast! The banner of praise will be in my hand and that is no boast!

---

[21] Set forth by •al-Tirmidhī in *al-Sunan*: Bk.: *Tafsīr al-Qur'ān* [Interpretation of the Qur'ān] according to Allah's Messenger ﷺ, Ch.: From *Sūra Banī Isrā'īl*, 5/308 §3148. •Ibn Mājah in *al-Sunan*: Bk.: *al-Zuhd* [Abstinence], Ch.: *Dhikr al-Shafāʿa* [Concerning the Intercession], 2/1440 §4308. •al-Mundhirī in *al-Targhīb wa al-Tarhīb*, 4/238 §5509. •al-Lālakā'ī in *Iʿtiqād ahl al-Sunna* [the Doctrine of the people of Sunna], 4/788 §1455.

Adam and all other Prophets will be under my banner (and that is no boast)! I will be the first for whom the earth will split (and that is no boast)!' He said: 'The people will be frightened thrice. They will then approach Adam (and implore intercession from him).' He (Abū Saʿīd) then narrated the hadith in full and said: 'People will then come to me and I will accompany them (for intercession). According to Ibn Judʿān, Anas ﵁ said: 'I visualize I am still beholding Allah's Messenger ﷺ. He said: 'I will take the chain of the Door of Paradise and knock it. They will ask: 'Who is it?' It will be said (to them): 'Muhammad (the Chosen One).' So they will open the door on me and say welcome. I will then fall down in prostration before the Holy Presence of Allah, and He will reveal to me a portion of His praise and hymn. I will be asked: 'Raise your head; you will be granted whatever you supplicate. Intercede; your intercession will be accepted; and say; you will be heard.' (He said:) 'That is the Praiseworthy Station which Allah has promised: *Certainly, your Lord will place you at* "*the Praiseworthy Station*".'" (Q.17:79)

> Reported by al-Tirmidhī and according to him: "This is a fine authentic tradition."

And according to Ibn Mājah, Abū Saʿīd Khudrī reports that Allah's Messenger ﷺ said: "I will be the Chieftain of the Children of Adam and that is no boast. On the Day of Resurrection I will be the first for whom the earth will split and that is no boast! I will be the first to intercede and my intercession will be accepted first of all and that is no boast! And the banner of Allah's praise will be in my hand on the Day of Resurrection and that is also no boast!"

٢٢/ ٢٢. عَنْ نُبَيْهِ بْنِ وَهْبٍ ﵁ أَنَّ كَعْبًا دَخَلَ عَلَى عَائِشَةَ ﵂، فَذَكَرُوْا رَسُوْلَ اللهِ ﷺ فَقَالَ كَعْبٌ: مَا مِنْ يَوْمٍ يَطْلُعُ إِلاَّ نَزَلَ سَبْعُوْنَ أَلْفًا مِنَ الْـمَلاَئِكَةِ حَتَّى يَحُفُّوْا بِقَبْرِ النَّبِيِّ ﷺ يَضْرِبُوْنَ بِأَجْنِحَتِهِمْ، وَيُصَلُّوْنَ عَلَى رَسُوْلِ اللهِ ﷺ، حَتَّى إِذَا أَمْسَوْا عَرَجُوْا

وَهَبَطَ مِثْلُهُمْ فَصَنَعُوْا مِثْلَ ذَلِكَ، حَتَّى إِذَا انْشَقَّتْ عَنْهُ الْأَرْضُ خَرَجَ فِي سَبْعِيْنَ أَلْفًا مِنَ الْـمَلَائِكَةِ يَزِفُّوْنَهُ.

رَوَاهُ الدَّارِمِيُّ وَالْبَيْهَقِيُّ.

22/22. According to Nubayh b. Wahb ﷺ:

"Kaʿb came to ʿĀʾisha ﷺ, and remembered Allah's Messenger ﷺ. Kaʿb said: 'No day dawns without seventy thousand angels descending, until they surround the tomb of the Prophet ﷺ, flapping their wings (for dusting). They invoke blessing upon Allah's Messenger ﷺ until, when they enter the evening, they rise up and the likes of them come down and do the same as that until, when the earth splits on the Day of Resurrection, he will emerge from his grave in the midst of the constellation of seventy thousand angels who will escort him!'"

Reported by al-Dārimī and al-Bayhaqī.

٢٣/٢٣. عَنْ أَبِي أُمَامَةَ ﷺ عَنِ النَّبِيِّ ﷺ قَالَ: إِنَّ اللهَ فَضَّلَنِي عَلَى الْأَنْبِيَاءِ، أَوْ قَالَ: أُمَّتِي عَلَى الْأُمَمِ، وَأَحَلَّ لِيَ الْغَنَائِمَ.

رَوَاهُ التِّرْمِذِيُّ وَالطَّبَرَانِيُّ وَالْبَيْهَقِيُّ. وَقَالَ أَبُوْ عِيْسَى: حَدِيْثُ أَبِي أُمَامَةَ حَدِيْثٌ حَسَنٌ صَحِيْحٌ.

23/23. According to Abū Umāma ﷺ:

---

[22] Set forth by •al-Dārimī in *al-Sunan* (5): Ch.: The honour bestowed by Allah ﷻ upon His Prophet after his demise, 1/57 §94. •al-Bayhaqī in *Shuʿab al-Īmān*, 3/492 §4170. •Ibn Ḥayyān al-Iṣbahānī in *al-ʿAẓama*, 3/1018 §537. •Abū Nuʿaym in *Ḥilya al-Awliyāʾ*, 5/390. •Ibn Kathīr in *Tafsīr al-Qurʾān al-ʿAẓīm*, 3/518, concerning Allah's saying: "He is the One who blesses you, as do His angels… [*Huwa ʾlladhī yuṣallī ʿalay-kum wa malāʾikatu-hu…*]." (Q.33:43).

[23] Set forth by •al-Tirmidhī in *al-Sunan*: Bk.: *al-Siyar ʿan Rasūl Allāh*, Ch: What has come to us about the spoils of war, 4/123 §1553. •al-Ṭabarānī in *al-Muʿjam al-Kabīr*, 8/257 §8001. •al-Rūyānī in *al-Musnad*, 2/308 §1260.

"The Prophet ﷺ said: 'Allah has bestowed upon me merit of excellence greater than all the Prophets (and Messengers),' or he said: 'He granted superiority to my *Umma* over all other *Ummas*, and made the spoils of war lawful for me.'"

Reported by al-Tirmidhī, al-Ṭabarānī and al-Bayhaqī. According to Abū ʿĪsā: "Abū Umāma's report is fine and authentic."

٢٤/ ٢٤. عَنْ أَنَسِ بْنِ مَالِكٍ رضي الله عنه قَالَ: مَرَّ رَسُوْلُ اللهِ ﷺ عَلَى قَوْمٍ قَدْ صَادُوْا ظَبْيَةً فَشَدُّوْهَا إِلَى عَمُوْدِ الْفُسْطَاطِ. فَقَالَتْ: يَا رَسُوْلَ اللهِ، إِنِّي وَضَعْتُ وَلِي خِشْفَانِ. فَاسْتَأْذِنْ لِي أَنْ أُرْضِعَهُمَا ثُمَّ أَعُوْدُ إِلَيْهِمْ. فَقَالَ: أَيْنَ صَاحِبُ هَذِهِ؟ فَقَالَ الْقَوْمُ: نَحْنُ، يَا رَسُوْلَ اللهِ. فَقَالَ: رَسُوْلُ اللهِ ﷺ: خَلُّوْا عَنْهَا حَتَّى تَأْتِيَ خِشْفَيْهَا تُرْضِعُهُمَا وَتَأْتِيَ إِلَيْكُمْ. قَالُوْا: وَمَنْ لَنَا بِذَلِكَ، يَا رَسُوْلَ اللهِ؟ قَالَ: أَنَا. فَأَطْلَقُوْهَا فَذَهَبَتْ فَأَرْضَعَتْ ثُمَّ رَجَعَتْ إِلَيْهِمْ فَأَوْثَقُوْهَا. فَمَرَّ بِهِمُ النَّبِيُّ ﷺ فَقَالَ: أَيْنَ أَصْحَابُ هَذِهِ؟ قَالُوْا: هُوَ ذَا نَحْنُ، يَا رَسُوْلَ اللهِ. قَالَ: تَبِيْعُوْنَهَا؟ قَالُوْا: يَا رَسُوْلَ اللهِ، هِيَ لَكَ. فَخَلُّوْا عَنْهَا فَأَطْلَقُوْهَا فَذَهَبَتْ.

رَوَاهُ الطَّبَرَانِيُّ وَأَبُوْ نُعَيْمٍ.

24/24. According to Anas b. Mālik رضي الله عنه:

"Once the Messenger of Allah ﷺ passed by a group of people. After hunting a she-deer, they had tied it to a bamboo pole. The deer prayed: 'O Messenger of Allah, I have two offsprings whom I have given birth recently. I beseech you to get me permission (from the hunters to go), feed my children and come back.' He asked: 'Who is its owner?' They said: 'O Messenger of Allah! We are its

---

•Bayhaqī in al-*Sunan al-Kubrā*, 1/222 §999 and in al-*Sunan al-Ṣughrā*, 1/180 §245. •al-Haythamī in *Majmaʿ al-Zawāʾid*, 10/16.

[24] Set forth by •al-Ṭabarānī in *al-Muʿjam al-Awsaṭ*, 6/358 §5547. •Abū Nuʿaym in *Dalāʾil al-Nubuwwa*, 376 §274. •Ibn Kathīr in *Shamāʾil al-Rasūl* §347.

owners.' The Messenger of Allah ﷺ said: 'Release this mother deer so that it gets back to you after feeding its offsprings.' They said: 'O Allah's Messenger! Who will guarantee its return?' He said: 'I guarantee.' They then freed the deer. It went to its offsprings, fed them and returned. They tied it. When the Prophet ﷺ passed by them again, he asked: 'Where are its masters?' They said: 'O Messenger of Allah, we are its masters.' He said: 'Will you sell it to me?' They said: 'It belongs to you, O Messenger of Allah!' So they set it free and it went off."

Reported by al-Tabarānī and Abū Nuʿaym.

٢٥/ ٢٥. عَنِ ابْنِ عَبَّاسٍ رضي الله عنهما قَالَ: أَوْحَى اللهُ إِلَى عِيْسَى عليه السلام: يَا عِيْسَى، آمِنْ بِمُحَمَّدٍ وَأْمُرْ مَنْ أَدْرَكَهُ مِنْ أُمَّتِكَ أَنْ يُؤْمِنُوْا بِهِ، فَلَوْ لاَ مُحَمَّدٌ مَا خَلَقْتُ آدَمَ، وَلَوْلاَ مُحَمَّدٌ مَا خَلَقْتُ الْجَنَّةَ وَلاَ النَّارَ. وَلَقَدْ خَلَقْتُ الْعَرْشَ عَلَى الْمَاءِ فَاضْطَرَبَ فَكَتَبْتُ عَلَيْهِ لاَ إِلَهَ إِلاَّ اللهُ مُحَمَّدٌ رَسُوْلُ اللهِ فَسَكَنَ.

رَوَاهُ الْحَاكِمُ، وَقَالَ: هَذَا حَدِيْثٌ صَحِيْحُ الإِسْنَادِ وَوَافَقَهُ الذَّهَبِيُّ.

25/25. According to ʿAbd Allāh b. ʿAbbās رضي الله عنهما:

"Allah revealed to ʿĪsā عليه السلام: 'O ʿĪsā! Believe in (the Messengership of) Muhammad, and command your people also that whoever finds his days must put faith in him. (Beware!) Had Muhammad not been there, I would not have created Adam. Had Muhammad not been there, I would not have created Paradise and Hell. When I built the Throne over water, it tremoured, so I wrote on it: 'There is no God but Allah; Muhammad is Allah's Messenger,' it then came to rest."

Reported by al-Ḥākim who said: "This is a tradition with authentic chain of transmission." Al-Dhahabī also confirmed it.

---

[25] Set forth by •al-Ḥākim in *al-Mustadrak*, 6167ı§4227. •al-Khilāl in *al-Sunna* 1/261 §316. •al-Dhahbī in *Mīzān al-Iʿtidāl*, 5/299 §6336. •al-ʿAsqalānī in *Lisān al-Mīzān*, 4/354 §1040. •Ibn Hayyān in *Ṭabaqāt al-Muḥaddithīn bi Asbahān*, 3/287.

اَلْفَصْلُ الثَّالِثُ

فَصْلٌ فِي أَنَّ الْأَنْبِيَاءَ عليهم السلام أَحْيَاءٌ فِي قُبُوْرِهِمْ بِأَجْسَادِهِمْ

SECTION 3

THE PROPHETS ﷺ ARE PHYSICALLY ALIVE IN THEIR GRAVES

٢٦/٢٦. عَنْ أَوْسِ بْنِ أَوْسٍ رضي الله عنه قَالَ: قَالَ رَسُوْلُ اللهِ ﷺ: إِنَّ مِنْ أَفْضَلِ أَيَّامِكُمْ يَوْمَ الْجُمُعَةِ. فِيْهِ خُلِقَ آدَمُ وَفِيْهِ قُبِضَ وَفِيْهِ النَّفْخَةُ وَفِيْهِ الصَّعْقَةُ. فَأَكْثِرُوْا عَلَيَّ مِنَ الصَّلَاةِ فِيْهِ، فَإِنَّ صَلَاتَكُمْ مَعْرُوْضَةٌ عَلَيَّ. قَالَ: قَالُوْا: يَا رَسُوْلَ اللهِ، كَيْفَ تُعْرَضُ صَلَاتُنَا عَلَيْكَ وَقَدْ أَرِمْتَ؟ يَقُوْلُوْنَ: بَلِيْتَ. قَالَ ﷺ: إِنَّ اللهَ حَرَّمَ عَلَى الْأَرْضِ أَجْسَادَ الْأَنْبِيَاءِ.

رَوَاهُ أَبُوْ دَاوُدَ وَالنَّسَائِيُّ وَابْنُ مَاجَه.

26/26. According to Aws b. Aws رضي الله عنه:

"Allah's Messenger ﷺ said: 'The finest of your days is the Day of Congregation (Friday), on which Adam was created and on which he died, on which the blast of the trumpet will sound [at the Resurrection] and on which the thunderbolt will strike. You must

---

[26] Set forth by •Abū Dāwūd in *al-Sunan*, Bk.: *al-Ṣalāt* [The Ritual Prayer], Ch.: The excellence of Friday, the Day of Congregational Prayer, and the night of Friday, 1/275 §1047, & Bk.: *al-Ṣalāt* [The Ritual Prayer], Ch.: Seeking forgiveness, 2/88 §1531. •al-Nasā'ī in *al-Sunan*, Bk.: *al-Jumu'a* [Friday, the Day of Congregational Prayer], Ch.: The frequency of the invocation of blessing upon the Prophet ﷺ on the Day of Congregational Prayer, 3/91 §1374. •Ibn Mājah in *al-Sunan*, Bk.: *Iqāmat al-Ṣalāt* [Performance of the Ritual Prayer], Ch.: The excellence of the Day of Congregational Prayer, 1/345 §1085.

therefore invoke blessing upon me frequently on that day, for the blessing you invoke is presented to me!' They said: 'O Messenger of Allah, how will the blessing we invoke be presented to you after your departure from life while your holy physical being will have metamorphosed into soil?' He ﷺ replied: 'Indeed, Allah has declared the bodies of the Prophets forbidden to the earth!'"

Reported by Abū Dāwūd, al-Nasā'ī and Ibn Mājah.

٢٧/٢٧. عَنْ أَبِي هُرَيْرَةَ رضي الله عنه أَنَّ رَسُوْلَ اللهِ ﷺ قَالَ: مَا مِنْ أَحَدٍ يُسَلِّمُ عَلَيَّ إِلاَّ رَدَّ اللهُ عَلَيَّ رُوْحِي حَتَّى أَرُدَّ عَلَيْهِ السَّلَامَ.

رَوَاهُ أَبُوْ دَاوُدَ وَأَحْمَدُ.

27/27. According to Abū Hurayra رضي الله عنه:

"Allah's Messenger ﷺ said: 'If one of you greets me with the salutation of peace, I reciprocate greetings, for Allah has restored my spirit to me (and He turns my attention towards it)!'"

Reported by Abū Dāwūd and Aḥmad.

٢٨/٢٨. عَنْ أَبِي الدَّرْدَاءِ رضي الله عنه قَالَ: قَالَ رَسُوْلُ اللهِ ﷺ: أَكْثِرُوْا الصَّلَاةَ عَلَيَّ يَوْمَ الْجُمُعَةِ فَإِنَّهُ مَشْهُوْدٌ تَشْهَدُهُ الْـمَلَائِكَةُ وَإِنَّ أَحَدًا لَنْ يُصَلِّيَ عَلَيَّ إِلاَّ عُرِضَتْ عَلَيَّ صَلَاتُهُ حَتَّى يَفْرُغَ مِنْهَا. قَالَ: قُلْتُ: وَبَعْدَ الْـمَوْتِ؟ قَالَ: وَبَعْدَ الْـمَوْتِ! إِنَّ اللهَ حَرَّمَ عَلَى الْأَرْضِ أَنْ تَأْكُلَ أَجْسَادَ الْأَنْبِيَاءِ فَنَبِيُّ اللهِ حَيٌّ يُرْزَقُ.

رَوَاهُ ابْنُ مَاجَه بِإِسْنَادٍ صَحِيْحٍ.

28/28. According to Abū al-Dardā' رضي الله عنه:

---

[27] Set forth by •Abū Dāwūd in *al-Sunan*, Bk.: *al-Manāsik* [The Pilgrim Ceremonies], Ch.: Visitation of the tombs, 2/218 §2041. •Aḥmad b. Ḥanbal in *al-Musnad*, 2/527 §10827. •al-Bayhaqī in *al-Sunan al-Kubrā*, 15/245 §10050, & in *Shuʿab al-Īmān*, 2/217 §1581, 4161. •Ibn Rāhawayh in *al-Musnad*, 1/453 §526.

[28] Set forth by •Ibn Mājah in *al-Sunan*, Bk.: *al-Janā'iz* [The Funeral

"Allah's Messenger ﷺ said: 'You must invoke blessing upon me frequently on the Day of Congregation (Friday), for it is the witnessed day (the day on which the angels are in attendance and they are present before me in large number). And not one of you will invoke blessing upon me without the blessing he invokes being presented to me, until he concludes it.' I said: 'Even after departing this life?' He said: 'Even after departing this life! Allah has declared it unlawful for the earth to consume the bodies of the Prophets, for Allah's Prophet is a living being who is provided with the means of subsistence.'"

Reported by Ibn Mājah with an authentic chain of transmission.

٢٩/٢٩. عَنِ ابْنِ عُمَرَ رضي الله عنهما قَالَ: قَالَ رَسُوْلُ اللهِ ﷺ: مَنْ زَارَ قَبْرِي بَعْدَ مَوْتِي، كَانَ كَمَنْ زَارَنِي فِي حَيَاتِي.

رَوَاهُ الدَّارَقُطْنِيُّ وَالطَّبَرَانِيُّ وَاللَّفْظُ لَهُ.

29/29. According to Ibn ʿUmar رضي الله عنهما:

"Allah's Messenger ﷺ said: 'If someone visits my tomb after my death, it is as if he has visited me in my lifetime!'"

Reported by al-Dāraquṭnī and al-Ṭabarānī (and the wording is his).

٣٠/٣٠. عَنْ أَبِي هُرَيْرَةَ رضي الله عنه قَالَ: قَالَ رَسُوْلُ اللهِ ﷺ: لَقَدْ رَأَيْتُنِي فِي الْحِجْرِ، وَقُرَيْشٌ تَسْأَلُنِي عَنْ مَسْرَايَ، فَسَأَلَتْنِي عَنْ أَشْيَاءَ مِنْ بَيْتِ الْمَقْدِسِ لَمْ أُثْبِتْهَا، فَكَرِبْتُ كُرْبَةً مَا كَرِبْتُ مِثْلَهُ قَطُّ. قَالَ: فَرَفَعَهُ اللهُ لِي أَنْظُرُ إِلَيْهِ. مَا يَسْأَلُوْنِي عَنْ شَيْءٍ

Ceremonies], Ch.: Concerning the death and burial of the Prophet ﷺ, 1/524 §1637. •al-Mundhirī in *al-Targhīb wa al-Tarhīb*, 2/328 §2582.

29 Set forth by •al-Ṭabarānī in *al-Muʿjam al-Kabīr*, 12/406 §13496. •al-Dāraquṭnī, on the authority of Ḥāṭib رضي الله عنه, in *al-Sunan*, 2/278 §193. •al-Bayhaqī in *Shuʿab al-Īmān*, 3/489 §4154. •al-Haythamī in *Majmaʿ al-Zawāʾid*, 4/2.

إِلاَّ أَنْبَأْتُهُمْ بِهِ. وَقَدْ رَأَيْتُنِي فِي جَمَاعَةٍ مِنَ الْأَنْبِيَاءِ، فَإِذَا مُوسَى ؑ قَائِمٌ يُصَلِّي. فَإِذَا رَجُلٌ ضَرْبٌ جَعْدٌ كَأَنَّهُ مِنْ رِجَالِ شَنُوْءَةَ. وَإِذَا عِيسَى ابْنُ مَرْيَمَ ؑ قَائِمٌ يُصَلِّي؛ أَقْرَبُ النَّاسِ بِهِ شَبَهًا عُرْوَةُ بْنُ مَسْعُودٍ الثَّقَفِيُّ. وَإِذَا إِبْرَاهِيمُ ؑ قَائِمٌ يُصَلِّي، أَشْبَهُ النَّاسِ بِهِ صَاحِبُكُمْ (يَعْنِي نَفْسَهُ). فَحَانَتِ الصَّلَاةُ فَأَمَمْتُهُمْ فَلَمَّا فَرَغْتُ مِنَ الصَّلَاةِ، قَالَ قَائِلٌ: يَا مُحَمَّدُ، هَذَا مَالِكٌ صَاحِبُ النَّارِ فَسَلِّمْ عَلَيْهِ. فَالْتَفَتُّ إِلَيْهِ فَبَدَأَنِي بِالسَّلَامِ.

رَوَاهُ مُسْلِمٌ وَالنَّسَائِيُّ.

30/30. According to Abū Hurayra ؓ:

"Allah's Messenger ﷺ said: 'I saw myself in the Sanctuary, and Quraysh were asking me questions about the Ascension Journey to Heaven. They asked me things about Jerusalem that I did not retain (in memory). So I suffered a distress the like of which I had never suffered. Allah then lifted Bayt al-Maqdis so that I might see it. Whatever they asked about anything, I would (look at it and) and provide them information. I had seen myself in a company of the Prophets, and lo and behold, there was Moses ؑ, busy reciting *ṣalāt*; he had curly hair like the people of Shanūʾa tribe. And lo and behold, (I saw that) there was Mary's son Jesus ؑ, busy reciting *ṣalāt*, the closest of the people in resemblance to him being ʿUrwa b. Masʿūd al-Thaqafī, and lo and behold, there was Abraham ؑ, busy reciting *ṣalāt*, the closest of the people in resemblance to him being your companion (meaning himself)! Then the time of the ritual prayer arrived, so I acted as their prayer-leader, and when I had concluded the ritual prayer, a speaker said: "O Muhammad, this is [the angel] Mālik, the keeper of the Fire of Hell, so greet him with the salutation of peace!" I therefore turned towards him, and he greeted me first with the salutation of peace!'"

---

30 Set forth by •Muslim in *al-Ṣaḥīḥ*: Bk.: *al-Īmān* [Faith], Ch.: Concerning Christ the son of Mary, and the Antichrist, 1/156 §172. •al-Nasāʾī in *al-Sunan al-Kubrā*, 6/455 §11480. •Abū ʿAwāna in *al-Musnad*, 1/116 §350. •Abū Nuʿaym in *Musnad al-Mustakhraj*, 1/239 §433. •al-ʿAsqalānī in *Fatḥ al-Bārī*, 6/487.

Reported by Muslim and al-Nasāʾī.

٣١/٣١. عَنْ أَنَسِ بْنِ مَالِكٍ ﵁ أَنَّ رَسُولَ اللهِ ﷺ قَالَ: أَتَيْتُ (وَفِي رِوَايَةِ هَدَّابٍ:)

مَرَرْتُ عَلَى مُوسَى لَيْلَةَ أُسْرِيَ بِي عِنْدَ الْكَثِيبِ الْأَحْمَرِ وَهُوَ قَائِمٌ يُصَلِّي فِي قَبْرِهِ.

رَوَاهُ مُسْلِمٌ وَالنَّسَائِيُّ وَأَحْمَدُ.

31/31. According to Anas b. Mālik ﵁:

"Allah's Messenger ﷺ said: 'I came to Moses ﷺ, on the night when I was transported on the Heavenly Ascension (in Haddāb's report:) 'I passed by the red sandbank, and (saw that) Moses was busy reciting ṣalāt in his tomb!'"

Reported by Muslim, al-Nasāʾī and Aḥmad.

٣٢/٣٢. عَنْ سَعِيدِ بْنِ عَبْدِ الْعَزِيزِ ﵁ قَالَ: لَمَّا كَانَ أَيَّامُ الْحَرَّةِ لَمْ يُؤَذَّنْ فِي

مَسْجِدِ النَّبِيِّ ﷺ ثَلَاثًا وَلَمْ يُقَمْ وَلَمْ يَبْرَحْ سَعِيدُ بْنُ الْمُسَيَّبِ مِنَ الْمَسْجِدِ، وَكَانَ

لَا يَعْرِفُ وَقْتَ الصَّلَاةِ إِلَّا بِهَمْهَمَةٍ يَسْمَعُهَا مِنْ قَبْرِ النَّبِيِّ ﷺ فَذَكَرَ مَعْنَاهُ.

رَوَاهُ الدَّارِمِيُّ وَانْفَرَدَ بِهِ.

32/32. According to Saʿīd b. ʿAbd al-ʿAzīz ﵁:

---

[31] Set forth by •Muslim in al-Ṣaḥīḥ: Bk.: al-Faḍāʾil [Excellent Merits], Ch.: The excellent merits of Moses ﷺ, 4/1845 §2375. •al-Nasāʾī in al-Sunan, Bk.: Qiyām al-Layl wa Taṭawwuʿ al-Nahār [Night Vigil and Daytime Voluntary Worship], Ch.: Concerning the ritual prayer of Allah's Prophet Moses ﷺ, 3/215 §1631–1632, & in al-Sunan al-Kubrā, 1/419 §1328. •Ibn Ḥibbān in al-Ṣaḥīḥ, 1/242 §50. •al-Ṭabarānī in al-Muʿjam al-Awsaṭ, 8/13 §7806. •Ibn Abī Shayba in al-Muṣannaf, 7/335 §36575. •Abū Yaʿlā in al-Musnad, 6/71 §3325. •ʿAbd b. Ḥumayd in al-Musnad, 1/362 §1205. •al-Daylamī in al-Firdaws bi-Maʾthūr al-Khiṭāb, 4/170 §6529. •al-Haythamī in Majmaʿ al-Zawāʾid, 8/205. •al-ʿAsqalānī in Fatḥ al-Bārī, 6/444.

[32] Set forth by •al-Dārimī in al-Sunan, Ch.: (15), The honour bestowed by Allah ﷻ upon His Prophet ﷺ after his death, 1/56 §93. •al-Khaṭīb al-Tabrīzī in Mishkāt al-Maṣābīḥ, 2/400 §5951. •al-Suyūṭī in Sharḥ Sunan Ibn Mājah,

"During the days of Ḥarrah (when Yazīd commanded invasion of Medina), the call to the ritual prayer was not given in the mosque of the Prophet ﷺ for three days, nor was the imminent beginning of the prayer announced. Saʿīd b. al-Musayyib, an eminent successor (who had taken refuge in the Prophet's mosque), did not leave the mosque (for three days) and did not know the time of the ritual prayer except by means of a mumbling sound that he used to hear from the tomb of the Prophet ﷺ, for he remembered its meaning."

Reported by al-Dārimī uniquely.

٣٣/ ٣٣. عَنْ أَنَسِ بْنِ مَالِكٍ رضي الله عنه قَالَ: قَالَ رَسُوْلُ اللهِ ﷺ: الْأَنْبِيَاءُ أَحْيَاءٌ فِي قُبُوْرِهِمْ يُصَلُّوْنَ. رَوَاهُ أَبُوْ يَعْلَى وَرِجَالُهُ ثِقَاتٌ وَابْنُ عَدِيٍّ وَالْبَيْهَقِيُّ. وَقَالَ ابْنُ عَدِيٍّ: وَأَرْجُوْ أَنَّهُ لَا بَأْسَ بِهِ.

وَالْعَسْقَلَانِيُّ فِي الْفَتْحِ، وَقَالَ: قَدْ جَمَعَ الْبَيْهَقِيُّ كِتَابًا لَطِيْفًا فِي حَيَاةِ الْأَنْبِيَاءِ فِي قُبُورِهِمْ. أَوْرَدَ فِيْهِ حَدِيْثَ أَنَسٍ رضي الله عنه: اَلْأَنْبِيَاءُ أَحْيَاءٌ فِي قُبُورِهِمْ يُصَلُّون. أَخْرَجَهُ مِنْ طَرِيْقِ يَحْيَ بْنِ أَبِي كَثِيرٍ وَهُوَ مِنْ رِجَالِ الصَّحِيْحِ عَنِ الْمُسْتَلِمِ بْنِ سَعِيْدٍ، وَقَدْ وَثَّقَهُ أَحْمَدُ وَابْنُ حِبَّانَ عَنِ الْحَجَّاجِ الْأَسْوَدِ وَهُوَ ابْنُ أَبِي زِيَادٍ الْبَصْرِيُّ. وَقَدْ وَثَّقَهُ أَحْمَدُ وَابْنُ مُعِيْنٍ عَنْ ثَابِتٍ عَنْهُ وَأَخْرَجَهُ أَيْضًا أَبُوْ يَعْلَى فِي مُسْنَدِهِ مِنْ هَذَا الْوَجْهِ وَأَخْرَجَهُ الْبَزَّارُ وَصَحَّحَهُ الْبَيْهَقِيُّ.

33/33. According to Anas b. Mālik رضي الله عنه:

1/291 §4029.

33 Set forth by •Abū Yaʿlā in *al-Musnad*, 6/147 §3425. •Ibn ʿAdī in *al-Kāmil*, 2/327 §460. He said: All these traditions are reported by one narrator alone and I hope they are sound and reliable. •al-Daylamī in *al-Firdaws*, 1/119, §403. •al-ʿAsqalānī in *Fatḥ al-Bārī*, 6/487, and in *Lisān al-Mīzān* 2/175, 246 §787, 1033. He said: al-Bayhaqī reported it and Ibn ʿAdī said: I hope there is no defect in it. •al-Dhahabī in *Mīzān al-iʿtidāl*, 2/200 §270. He said: al-Bayhaqī reported it and *al-Haythamī in Majmaʿ al-Zawāʾid*, 8/211. He said: Abū Yaʿlā and al-Bazzār reported it and resources of Abū Yaʿlā are sound and authentic. •al-Sayyūtī in *Sharḥ ʿalā Sunan al-Nasāʾī*, 4/110. •ʿAẓīm Abādī in *ʿAwn a-Mʿabūd*, 6/19. He said: "I have written a volume on life of Prophets

Allah's Messenger ﷺ said: "The Prophets are alive in their graves and perform the ritual prayers."

> Reported by Abū Yaʿlā with an authentic chain of transmission. Also reported by Ibn ʿAdī and al-Bayhaqī; Ibn ʿAdī says: "In my view, there is no week link in its chain of transmission."

According to al-ʿAsqalānī in *Fatḥ al-Bārī*: "Al-Bayhaqī has written a beautiful book on the tradition that the Prophets are alive in their graves and perform the ritual prayers. He has quoted this tradition reported by Anas b. Mālik ؓ on the authority of Yaḥyā b. Abī Kathīr, who is one of the reporters of the sound tradition. He has reported it from Mustalim b. Saʿīd, and Aḥmad b. Ḥanbal has declared him an authority; and Ibn Ḥibbān has reported it from Ḥajjāj Aswad who is Ibn Abī Ziyād al-Baṣrī, also declared by Aḥmad b. Ḥanbal as authority. Ibn Muʿīn has reported it from Thābit and Abū Yaʿlā has reported it in his *Musnad* on the same authority. Al-Bazzār has reported it and al-Bayhaqī has declared it sound."

---

for the men of learning. •al-Munāwī in *Fayḍ al-Qadīr* 3/184. •al-Shawkānī in *Nayl al-Awṭār*, 5/178. He said: Bayhaqī has declared it sound and has written a volume on it. •al-Zurqānī in *Sharḥ ʿalā Muwaṭṭa Imām Mālik*, 4/357. He said: al-Bayhaqī has compiled a fine book on life of the Prophets and has reported with sound chain of transmission up to Anas ؓ.

اَلْفَصْلُ الرَّابِعُ

فَصْلٌ فِي سَعَةِ عِلْمِ النَّبِيِّ ﷺ وَكَمَالِ مَعْرِفَتِه

Section 4

The Deep Knowledge of the Prophet ﷺ and the Gnosis of His Esteemed Station

٣٤/ ٣٤. عَنْ أَنَسِ بْنِ مَالِكٍ رضي الله عنه أَنَّ النَّبِيَّ ﷺ خَرَجَ حِيْنَ زَاغَتِ الشَّمْسُ، فَصَلَّى الظُّهْرَ. فَلَمَّا سَلَّمَ قَامَ عَلَى الْمِنْبَرِ، فَذَكَرَ السَّاعَةَ، وَذَكَرَ أَنَّ بَيْنَ يَدَيْهَا أُمُوْرًا عِظَامًا، ثُمَّ قَالَ: مَنْ أَحَبَّ أَنْ يَسْأَلَ عَنْ شَيْءٍ فَلْيَسْأَلْ عَنْهُ. فَوَاللهِ، لاَ تَسْأَلُوْنِي عَنْ شَيْءٍ إِلاَّ أَخْبَرْتُكُمْ بِهِ مَا دُمْتُ فِي مَقَامِي هَذَا. قَالَ أَنَسٌ: فَأَكْثَرَ النَّاسُ الْبُكَاءَ وَأَكْثَرَ رَسُوْلُ اللهِ ﷺ أَنْ يَقُوْلَ: سَلُوْنِي. فَقَالَ أَنَسٌ: فَقَامَ إِلَيْهِ رَجُلٌ فَقَالَ: أَيْنَ مَدْخَلِي، يَا رَسُوْلَ اللهِ؟ قَالَ: النَّارُ. فَقَامَ عَبْدُ اللهِ بْنُ حُذَافَةَ فَقَالَ: مَنْ أَبِي، يَا رَسُوْلَ اللهِ؟ قَالَ: أَبُوْكَ حُذَافَةُ. قَالَ: ثُمَّ أَكْثَرَ أَنْ يَقُوْلَ: سَلُوْنِي، سَلُونِي. فَبَرَكَ عُمَرُ عَلَى رُكْبَتَيْهِ فَقَالَ: رَضِيْنَا بِاللهِ رَبًّا، وَبِالإِسْلَامِ دِيْنًا، وَبِمُحَمَّدٍ ﷺ رَسُوْلاً. قَالَ: فَسَكَتَ رَسُوْلُ اللهِ ﷺ حِيْنَ قَالَ عُمَرُ ذَلِكَ، ثُمَّ قَالَ رَسُوْلُ اللهِ ﷺ: وَالَّذِي نَفْسِي بِيَدِهِ، لَقَدْ عُرِضَتْ عَلَيَّ الْجَنَّةُ وَالنَّارُ آنِفًا فِي عُرْضِ هَذَا الْحَائِطِ، وَأَنَا أُصَلِّي، فَلَمْ أَرَ كَالْيَوْمِ فِي الْخَيْرِ وَالشَّرِّ.

مُتَّفَقٌ عَلَيْهِ.

34/34. According to Anas b. Mālik رضي الله عنه:

[34] : Set forth by •al-Bukhārī in *al-Ṣaḥīḥ*: Bk.: *al-Iʿtiṣām bi al-Kitāb wa al-Sunna* [Adherence to the Book and the Sunna], Ch.: The abhorrence of frequent questioning and preoccupation with matters of no concern, 6/2660 §6864, & Bk.: *Mawāqīt al-Ṣalāt* [Set Times of the Ritual Prayer], Ch.:

"The Prophet ﷺ came out when the sun had declined, and offered the midday ritual prayer. Then, having pronounced the salutation of peace, he ascended the pulpit. He spoke about the Final Hour, and mentioned that there are major events and calamities to occur before that; then he said: 'If someone wishes to ask about something, let him ask about it! By Allah, as long as I am standing here, I will answer whatever you ask.' On this the people started weeping profusely, and, out of his majesty, Allah's Messenger ﷺ kept saying: 'Ask me (whatever you want)!' A man therefore approached him and said: 'Where is my abode, O Messenger of Allah?' He said: 'The Fire of Hell!' Then ʿAbd Allāh b. Ḥudhāfa said: 'Who is my father, O Messenger of Allah?' He said: 'Your father is Ḥudhāfa!' Then he said again and again: 'Ask me, ask me!' ʿUmar therefore knelt down on his knee and said: 'We are content with Allah as a Lord, with Islam as a Religion, and with Muhammad ﷺ as a Messenger (and we are to ask nothing)!' Allah's Messenger ﷺ then became silent when ʿUmar said that. Then Allah's Messenger ﷺ said: 'By the One in whose Hand is my soul, the Garden of Paradise and the Fire of Hell have been displayed to me just now in front of this wall, while I was performing the ritual prayer, but I have not viewed good and evil (so vividly) as today!'"

Agreed upon by al-Bukhārī and Muslim.

٣٥ /٣٥. عَنْ عُمَرَ رضي الله عنه يَقُوْلُ: قَامَ فِيْنَا النَّبِيُّ ﷺ مَقَامًا، فَأَخْبَرَنَا عَنْ بَدْءِ الْخَلْقِ حَتَّى دَخَلَ أَهْلُ الْجَنَّةِ مَنَازِلَهُمْ وَأَهْلُ النَّارِ مَنَازِلَهُمْ. حَفِظَ ذَلِكَ مَنْ حَفِظَهُ وَنَسِيَهُ مَنْ نَسِيَهُ.

رَوَاهُ الْبُخَارِيُّ.

The time of noon prayer after mid-day, 1/200 §2001, 2278, & Bk.: *al-ʿIlm* [Knowledge], Ch.: The merit of kneeling down in the presence of the Imam or the narrator, 1/47 §93, & in *al-Adab al-Mufrad*, 1/404 §1184. •Muslim in *al-Ṣaḥīḥ*: Bk.: *al-Faḍāʾil* [Excellent Merits], Ch.: Reverence for the Prophet ﷺ, and refraining from frequent questioning about matters for which there is no urgent need, 4/1832 §2359. •Ibn Ḥibbān in *al-Ṣaḥīḥ*, 1/309 §106. •al-Ṭabarānī in *al-Muʿjam al-Awsaṭ*, 9/72 §9155. •Aḥmad b. Ḥanbal in *al-Musnad*, 3/162 §12681.

35/35. According to ʿUmar ؓ:

"The Prophet ﷺ stood among us at a place and informed us about everything from the origin of creation until the people of the Garden of Paradise have entered their abodes, and the people of the Fire of Hell have entered their abodes. Whoever has remembered it has remembered it, and whoever has forgotten it has forgotten it."

Reported by al-Bukhārī.

٣٦/٣٦. عَنْ حُذَيْفَةَ ؓ قَالَ: قَامَ فِيْنَا رَسُوْلُ اللهِ ﷺ مَقَامًا. مَا تَرَكَ شَيْئًا يَكُوْنُ فِي مَقَامِهِ ذَلِكَ إِلَى قِيَامِ السَّاعَةِ إِلاَّ حَدَّثَ بِهِ. حَفِظَهُ مَنْ حَفِظَهُ وَنَسِيَهُ مَنْ نَسِيَهُ.

مُتَّفَقٌ عَلَيْهِ وَهَذَا لَفْظُ مُسْلِمٍ.

36/36. According to Ḥudhayfa ؓ:

"Allah's Messenger ﷺ stood among us at a place (and addressed us). He did not leave off anything to describe from his stay among us that day till the advent of the Final Hour. Whoever has

[35] Set forth by •al-Bukhārī in *al-Ṣaḥīḥ*: Bk.: *Badʾ al-Khalq* [The Beginning of Creation], Ch.: What has come to us about Allah's saying: "He is the One who produces creation, then reproduces it, and it is easier for Him *[wa Huwa ʾlladhī yabdaʾu al-khalqa thumma yuʿīdu-hu wa huwa ahwanu ʿalayh]*." (Q.30:27), 3/1166 §3020.

[36] Set forth by •al-Bukhārī in *al-Ṣaḥīḥ*: Bk.: *al-Qadar* [The Decree of Destiny], Ch.: "And the commandment of Allah is a decree determined *[wa kāna amru ʾllāhi qadaran maqdūrā]*." (Q.33:38), 6/2435 §6230. •Muslim in *al-Ṣaḥīḥ*: Bk.: *al-Fitan wa Ashrāṭ al-Sāʿa* [The Troubles and the Portents of the Final Hour], Ch.: The news of the Prophet ﷺ about what will be until the Final Hour, 4/2217 §2891. •al-Tirmidhī likewise, on the authority of Abū Saʿīd al-Khudrī ؓ, in *al-Sunan*, Bk.: *al-Fitan* [The Troubles] according to Allah's Messenger ﷺ, Ch.: What has come to inform us that the Prophet ﷺ told his Companions about what is to be until the Day of Resurrection, 4/483 §2191. •Abū Dāwūd in *al-Sunan*, Bk.: *al-Fitan wa al-Malāḥim* [The Troubles and the Bloody Battles], Ch.: Concerning the troubles and their portents, 4/94 §420. •al-Bazzār in *al-Musnad*, 7/231 §8499. He said: "This is an authentic tradition." •Aḥmad b. Ḥanbal in *al-Musnad*, 5/385 §23322. •al-Ṭabarānī likewise, on the authority of Abū Saʿīd al-Khudrī ؓ, in *Musnad al-Shāmiyyīn*, 2/247 §1278.

remembered it has remembered it, and whoever has forgotten it has forgotten it."

Agreed upon by al-Bukhārī and Muslim, and this is the wording of Muslim.

٣٧ /٣٧. عَنْ عَمْرِو بْنِ أَخْطَبَ ﵁ قَالَ: صَلَّى بِنَا رَسُوْلُ اللهِ ﷺ الْفَجْرَ. وَصَعِدَ الْـمِنْبَرَ فَخَطَبَنَا حَتَّى حَضَرَتِ الظُّهْرُ، فَنَزَلَ فَصَلَّى ثُمَّ صَعِدَ الْـمِنْبَرَ. فَخَطَبَنَا حَتَّى حَضَرَتِ الْعَصْرُ، ثُمَّ نَزَلَ فَصَلَّى ثُمَّ صَعِدَ الْـمِنْبَرَ. فَخَطَبَنَا حَتَّى غَرَبَتِ الشَّمْسُ، فَأَخْبَرَنَا بِمَا كَانَ وَبِمَا هُوَ كَائِنٌ. قَالَ: فَأَعْلَمُنَا أَحْفَظُنَا.

رَوَاهُ مُسْلِمٌ وَالتِّرْمِذِيُّ.

37/37. According to ʿAmr b. Akhṭab ﵁:

"Allah's Messenger ﷺ led us in the early morning ritual prayer. He ascended the pulpit and addressed us until the time of the midday ritual prayer arrived, so he descended and performed the ritual prayer. Then he ascended the pulpit until the time of the afternoon ritual prayer arrived, so he descended and performed the ritual prayer. Then he ascended the pulpit and addressed us until the sun had set. He thus informed us of whatever had taken place till then and of whatever will take place till the Day of Resurrection. The most knowledgeable of us is therefore the one of us who retains in memory the most."

Reported by Muslim and Tirmidhī.

---

[37] Set forth by •Muslim in *al-Ṣaḥīḥ*: Bk.: *al-Fitan wa Ashrāṭ al-Sāʿa* [The Troubles and the Portents of the Final Hour], Ch.: The news of the Prophet ﷺ about what will be until the Final Hour, 4/2217 §2892. •al-Tirmidhī in *al-Sunan*: Bk.: *al-Fitan* [The Troubles] according to Allah's Messenger ﷺ, Ch.: What has come to inform us that the Prophet ﷺ told his Companions about what is to be until the Day of Resurrection, 4/483 §2191. •Ibn Ḥibbān in *al-Ṣaḥīḥ*, 15/9 §6638. •al-Ḥākim in *al-Mustadrak*, 4/533 §8498. •Abū Yaʿlā in *al-Musnad*, 12/237 §2844. •al-Ṭabarānī in *al-Muʿjam al-Kabīr*, 17/28 §46. •al-Shaybānī in *al-Āḥād wa al-Mathānī*, 4/199 §2183.

٣٨/ ٣٨. عَنْ حُذَيْفَةَ ﵁ أَنَّهُ قَالَ: أَخْبَرَنِي رَسُوْلُ اللهِ ﷺ بِمَا هُوَ كَائِنٌ إِلَى أَنْ تَقُوْمَ السَّاعَةُ. فَمَا مِنْهُ شَيْءٌ إِلاَّ قَدْ سَأَلْتُهُ إِلاَّ أَنِّي لَمْ أَسْأَلْهُ مَا يُخْرِجُ أَهْلَ الْمَدِيْنَةِ مِنَ الْمَدِيْنَةِ.

رَوَاهُ مُسْلِمٌ وَأَحْمَدُ.

38/38. According to Ḥudhayfa ﵁:

"Allah's Messenger ﷺ informed me of what will come into existence until the Final Hour arrives, and there was nothing of it about which I had not asked him, except that I did not ask him what will evict the people of Medina from Medina."

Reported by Muslim and Aḥmad.

٣٩/ ٣٩. عَنِ ابْنِ عَبَّاسٍ ﵄ عَنِ النَّبِيِّ ﷺ قَالَ: أَتَانِي رَبِّي فِي أَحْسَنِ صُوْرَةٍ، فَقَالَ: يَا مُحَمَّدُ، قُلْتُ: لَبَّيْكَ وَسَعْدَيْكَ. قَالَ: فِيْمَ يَخْتَصِمُ الْمَلأُ الأَعْلَى؟ قُلْتُ: رَبِّي، لاَ أَدْرِي، فَوَضَعَ يَدَهُ بَيْنَ كَتِفَيَّ، حَتَّى وَجَدْتُ بَرْدَهَا بَيْنَ ثَدْيَيَّ، فَعَلِمْتُ مَا بَيْنَ الْمَشْرِقِ وَالْمَغْرِبِ.

رَوَاهُ التِّرْمِذِيُّ وَأَبُوْ يَعْلَى. وَقَالَ أَبُوْ عِيْسَى: هَذَا حَدِيْثٌ حَسَنٌ.

وفي رواية عنه: قَالَ: فَعَلِمْتُ مَا فِي السَّمَوَاتِ وَمَا فِي الأَرْضِ وَتَلاَ: ﴿وَكَذَٰلِكَ نُرِىٓ إِبْرَٰهِيمَ مَلَكُوتَ ٱلسَّمَٰوَٰتِ وَٱلْأَرْضِ وَلِيَكُونَ مِنَ ٱلْمُوقِنِينَ﴾ (الأنعام، ٦: ٧٥).

رَوَاهُ التِّرْمِذِيُّ وَأَحْمَدُ وَالدَّارِمِيُّ وَاللَّفْظُ لَهُ.

---

[38] Set forth by •Muslim in *al-Ṣaḥīḥ*: Bk.: *al-Fitan wa Ashrāṭ al-Sāʿa* [The Troubles and the Portents of the Final Hour], Ch.: The news of the Prophet ﷺ about what will be until the Final Hour, 4/2217 §2892. •al-Ḥākim in *al-Mustadrak*, 4/472 §8311. •al-Bazzār in *al-Musnad*, 7/222 §2795. •al-Ṭayālisī *in al-Musnad*, 1/58 §433. •Ibn Manda in *Kitāb al-Īmān*, 2/912 §996. He said: "Its chain of transmission is authentic." •al-Muqriʾ in *al-Sunan al-Wārida fī al-Fitan*, 4/889 §458.

وفي رواية: عَنْ مُعَاذِ بْنِ جَبَلٍ ﷺ قَالَ: فَتَجَلَّى لِي كُلُّ شَيْءٍ وَعَرَفْتُ.

رَوَاهُ التِّرْمِذِيُّ وَأَحْمَدُ وَالطَّبَرَانِيُّ، وَقَالَ أَبُوْ عِيْسَى: هَذَا حَدِيْثٌ حَسَنٌ صَحِيْحٌ.

وفي رواية: عَنْ أَبِي أُمَامَةَ ﷺ قَالَ: فَعَلِمْتُ فِي مَقَامِي ذَلِكَ مَا سَأَلَنِي عَنْهُ مِنْ أَمْرِ الدُّنْيَا وَالآخِرَةِ.

رَوَاهُ الطَّبَرَانِيُّ وَالرُّوْيَانِيُّ.

وفي رواية: فَعَلِمْتُ مِنْ كُلِّ شَيْءٍ وَبَصَرْتُهُ.

رَوَاهُ الطَّبَرَانِيُّ.

وفي رواية: عَنْ جَابِرِ بْنِ سَمُرَةَ ﷺ قَالَ: فَمَا سَأَلَنِي عَنْ شَيْءٍ إِلاَّ عَلِمْتُهُ.

رَوَاهُ ابْنُ أَبِي شَيْبَةَ وَابْنُ أَبِي عَاصِمٍ. إِسْنَادُهُ حَسَنٌ وَرِجَالُهُ ثِقَاتٌ.

39/39. According to Ibn ʿAbbās ﷺ:

"The Prophet ﷺ said: 'My Lord came to me (during the Ascension Night) in an exceptionally beautiful (and splendid) form (matching His Glory), and He said: "O Muhammad!" I submitted:

---

[39] Set forth by •al-Tirmidhī in *al-Sunan*: Bk.: *Tafsīr al-Qurʾān* [Interpretation of the Qurʾān] according to Allah's Messenger ﷺ, Ch.: From *Sūra Ṣād*, 5/366–368 §3233–3235. •al-Dārimī in *al-Sunan*: Bk.: *al-Ruʾyā* [Visions], Ch.: Seeing the Lord in one's sleep, 2/170 §2149. •Aḥmad b. Ḥanbal in *al-Musnad*, 1/368 §3484, & in *al-Musnad*, 4/66, and in *al-Musnad*, 5/243 §22162–23258. •al-Ṭabarānī in *al-Muʿjam al-Kabīr*, 8/290 §8117; 20/109, 141 §216, 290. •al-Rūyānī in *al-Musnad*, 1/429 §656; 2/299 §1241. •Abū Yaʿlā in *al-Musnad*, 4/475 §2608. •al-Shaybānī in *al-Āḥād wa al-Mathānī*, 5/49 §2585. •ʿAbd b. Ḥumayd in *al-Musnad*, 1/228 §682. •Ibn Abī ʿĀṣim in *al-Sunna*, 1/203 §465. Ibn Abī ʿĀṣim said: "Its chain of transmission is excellent and its sources are reliable." •ʿAbd Allāh b. Aḥmad in *al-Sunna*, 2/489 §1121. •al-Ḥakīm al-Tirmidhī in *Nawādir al-Uṣūl*, 3/120. •al-Mundhirī in *al-Targhīb wa al-Tarhīb*, 1/159 §591. •Ibn ʿAbd al-Barr in *al-Tamhīd*, 24/323. •al-Haythamī in *Majmaʿ al-Zawāʾid*, 7/176–178.

"My Lord! At Your service, recurrently at Your obedient service!" He said: "What does the Sublime Assembly (of angels) argue about?" I submitted: "My Lord, I do not know!" Then Allah placed His Mighty Hand between my shoulders, until I felt its coolness between my breasts, so I came to know what is between the east and the west."'"

Reported by al-Tirmidhī and Abū Yaʿlā. And Abū ʿĪsā said: "This is an excellent tradition."

In one version, he said: "So I came to know what is in the heavens and in the earth," and he recited this Verse: "And thus We showed Abraham the kingdoms of the heavens and the earth (i.e., miracles of creation), so that he might be one of those endowed with the eye of certitude *[wa ka-dhālika nurī Ibrāhīma malakūta al-samāwāti wa al-arḍi wa li-yakūna min al-mūqinīn]*." (Q.6:75).

Reported by al-Tirmidhī, Aḥmad and al-Dārimī (the wording is his).

In one version: According to Muʿādh b. Jabal ؓ, the Prophet ﷺ said: "So (the truth of) everything was manifested to me and I knew (all entirely)."

Reported by al-Tirmidhī, Aḥmad and al-Ṭabarānī and Abū ʿĪsā said: "This is a fine authentic tradition."

In one version: According to Abū Umāma ؓ, the Prophet ﷺ said: "So I learnt, at the same station, whatever He asked me about this world and the Hereafter."

Reported by al-Ṭabarānī and al-Rūyānī.

In one version: "So I acquired the knowledge of the truth of everything (of this world and the Hereafter), and I observed it as well."

Reported by al-Ṭabarānī.

In one version: According to Jābir b. Samura ؓ, the Prophet ﷺ said: "Whenever I was asked about anything, I knew it. (So it never happened after it that He asked me about something and I did not know it.)"

Reported by Ibn Abī Shayba and Ibn Abī ʿĀṣim. Its chain of transmission is excellent and its sources are reliable.

٤٠/ ٤٠. عَنْ أَنَسٍ ؓ فِي رواية طويلة أَنَّ رَسُوْلَ اللهِ ﷺ شَاوَرَ حِيْنَ بَلَغَنَا إِقْبَالُ أَبِي سُفْيَانَ، وَقَامَ سَعْدُ بْنُ عُبَادَةَ ؓ فَقَالَ: وَالَّذِي نَفْسِي بِيَدِهِ، لَوْ أَمَرْتَنَا أَنْ نُخِيْضَهَا الْبَحْرَ لَأَخَضْنَاهَا. وَلَوْ أَمَرْتَنَا أَنْ نَضْرِبَ أَكْبَادَهَا إِلَى بَرْكِ الْغِمَادِ لَفَعَلْنَا. قَالَ: فَنَدَبَ رَسُوْلُ اللهِ ﷺ النَّاسَ، فَانْطَلَقُوْا حَتَّى نَزَلُوْا بَدْرًا، فَقَالَ رَسُوْلُ اللهِ ﷺ: هَذَا مَصْرَعُ فُلَانٍ. قَالَ: وَيَضَعُ يَدَهُ عَلَى الْأَرْضِ، هَاهُنَا وَهَاهُنَا. قَالَ: فَمَا مَاتَ أَحَدُهُمْ عَنْ مَوْضِعِ يَدِ رَسُوْلِ اللهِ ﷺ.

رَوَاهُ مُسْلِمٌ وَأَبُوْ دَاوُدَ.

40/40. According to Anas ؓ, in the course of a detailed report:

"Allah's Messenger ﷺ took counsel, when we received the news of the approach of [the caravan of] Abū Sufyān, and Saʿd b. ʿUbāda ؓ stood up and said: 'By the One in whose Hand my soul is, if you command us to plunge our horses into the sea, we would plunge them, and if you command us to strike their chests against the hills of Bark of al-Ghimād, we would do so!' Allah's Messenger ﷺ then

---

[40] Set forth by •Muslim in *al-Ṣaḥīḥ*: Bk.: *al-Jihād wa al-Siyar* [The Sacred Struggle and the military expeditions], Ch.: The Battle of Badr, 3/1403 §1779, & similarly in Bk.: The Garden of Paradise and the Quality of its Felicity and its Inhabitants, Ch.: Demonstration of the seat of the deceased in the Garden of Paradise or the Fire of Hell, and confirmation of the torment of the grave and taking refuge therefrom, 4/2202 §2873. •Abū Dāwūd in *al-Sunan*: Bk.: *al-Jihād* [The Sacred Struggle], Ch.: The prisoner of war is disarmed, beaten and bound, 3/58 §2071. •al-Nasāʾī in *al-Sunan*: Bk.: *al-Janāʾiz* [Funeral Ceremonies], Ch.: The spirits of the believers, 4/108 §2074, & in *al-Sunan al-Kubrā*, 1/665 §2201. •Ibn Ḥibbān in *al-Ṣaḥīḥ*, 11/24 §4722. •Aḥmad b. Ḥanbal in *al-Musnad*, 3/219 §13320. •al-Bazzār in *al-Musnad*, 1/340 §222. •Ibn Abī Shayba in *al-Muṣannaf*, 7/362 §36708. •al-Ṭabarānī in *al-Muʿjam al-Awsaṭ*, 8/219 §8453, & in *al-Muʿjam al-Ṣaghīr*, 2/233 §1085. •Abū Yaʿlā in *al-Musnad*, 6/69 §3322. •Ibn al-Jawzī in *Ṣafwat al-Ṣafwa*, 1/102. •al-Khaṭīb al-Tabrīzī in *Mishkāt al-Maṣābīḥ*, 2/381 §5871.

commissioned the people, so they dashed off until they reached Badr, whereupon Allah's Messenger ﷺ declared: 'This is So-and-so's place of slaughter,' placing his hand on the ground, here and there, so not one of the infidels died away from the place where Allah's Messenger ﷺ laid his hand!"

Reported by Muslim and Abū Dāwūd.

٤١/ ٤١. عَنْ أَنَسٍ ؓ أَنَّ النَّبِيَّ ﷺ نَعَى زَيْدًا وَجَعْفَرًا وَابْنَ رَوَاحَةَ ؓ لِلنَّاسِ قَبْلَ أَنْ يَأْتِيَهُمْ خَبَرُهُمْ، فَقَالَ: أَخَذَ الرَّايَةَ زَيْدٌ فَأُصِيْبَ، ثُمَّ أَخَذَ جَعْفَرٌ فَأُصِيْبَ، ثُمَّ أَخَذَ ابْنُ رَوَاحَةَ فَأُصِيْبَ – وَعَيْنَاهُ تَذْرِفَانِ – حَتَّى أَخَذَ الرَّايَةَ سَيْفٌ مِنْ سُيُوْفِ اللهِ، حَتَّى فَتَحَ اللهُ عَلَيْهِمْ.

رَوَاهُ الْبُخَارِيُّ وَالنَّسَائِيُّ وَأَحْمَدُ.

41/41. According to Anas ؓ:

"The Prophet ﷺ announced the deaths of Zayd, Jaʿfar and Ibn Rawāḥa ؓ to the people before their news came to them, saying: 'Now Zayd held the banner, but he is martyred; now Jaʿfar held it, but he is martyred, then Ibn Rawāḥa held it, but he is martyred,'—his eyes welled while telling all this—(then said:) 'Then one of the

---

[41] Set forth by •al-Bukhārī in *al-Ṣaḥīḥ*: Bk.: *al-Maghāzī* [Military Expeditions], Ch.: The Battle of Muʾta from the land of Syria, 4/1554 §4014, & Bk.: *al-Janāʾiz* [Funeral Ceremonies], Ch.: The man should announce the death to the family of the deceased in person, 1/420 §1189, & Bk.: *al-Jihād* [The Sacred Struggle], Ch.: The desire for martyrdom, 3/1030 §2645, & Ch.: Someone who behaves imperiously in war without official authority, if he is afraid of the enemy, 3/1115 §2898, & Bk.: *al-Manāqib* [Virtues], Ch.: The signs of Prophethood in Islam, 3/1328 §3431, & Bk.: *Faḍāʾil al-Ṣaḥāba* [The Excellent Merits of the Companions], Ch.: The virtues of Khālid b. al-Walīd ؓ, 3/1372 §3547. •al-Nasāʾī likewise in *al-Sunan al-Kubrā*, 5/180 §8604. •Aḥmad b. Ḥanbal in *al-Musnad*, 1/204 §1750. •al-Ḥākim in *al-Mustadrak*, 3/337 §5295. He said: "This is a tradition with an authentic chain of transmission." •al-Ṭabarānī in *al-Muʿjam al-Kabīr*, 2/105, §1459–1461. •al-Khaṭīb al-Tabrīzī in *Mishkāt al-Maṣābīḥ*, 2/384 §5887.

swords of Allah (Khālid b. al-Walīd) held the banner, until Allah granted victory over them!'"

Reported by al-Bukhārī, al-Nasāʾī and Aḥmad.

٤٢ / ٤٢. عَنْ أَنَسِ بْنِ مَالِكٍ ﷺ قَالَ: إِنَّ رَجُلاً كَانَ يَكْتُبُ لِرَسُوْلِ اللهِ ﷺ فَارْتَدَّ عَنِ الإِسْلَامِ، وَلَحِقَ بِالْـمُشْرِكِيْنَ، وَقَالَ: أَنَا أَعْلَمُكُمْ. إِنْ كُنْتُ لَأَكْتُبُ مَا شِئْتُ. فَمَاتَ ذَلِكَ الرَّجُلُ فَقَالَ النَّبِيُّ ﷺ: إِنَّ الأَرْضَ لَـمْ تَقْبَلْهُ. وَقَالَ أَنَسٌ: فَأَخْبَرَنِي أَبُوْ طَلْحَةَ أَنَّهُ أَتَى الأَرْضَ الَّتِي مَاتَ فِيْهَا فَوَجَدَهُ مَنْبُوْذًا، فَقَالَ: مَا شَأْنُ هَذَا؟ فَقَالُوْا: دَفَنَّاهُ مِرَارًا فَلَمْ تَقْبَلْهُ الأَرْضُ.

رَوَاهُ مُسْلِمٌ وَأَحْمَدُ وَاللَّفْظُ لَهُ وَالْبَيْهَقِيُّ.

42/42. According to Anas b. Mālik ﷺ:

"A man used to work as a scribe for Allah's Messenger ﷺ, but he apostatized from Islam and joined the polytheists, and he said: 'I am more knowledgeable than you. I wrote whatever I wished!' That man then died, so the Prophet ﷺ said: 'The earth has not accepted him!'"

Anas also said: "Abū Ṭalḥa informed me that he came to the land in which he died, and he found him discarded (by the grave), so he said: 'What is the matter with this person?' They said: 'We buried him several times, but the earth did not accept him!'"

Reported by Muslim, Aḥmad (the wording is his) and al-Bayhaqī.

---

[42] Set forth similarly by •Muslim in *al-Ṣaḥīḥ*: Bk.: The Characteristics of the Hypocrites and the rules related to them, Ch.: 4/2145 §2781. •Aḥmad b. Ḥanbal in *al-Musnad*, 3/120 §12236, 13348. •al-Bayhaqī in al-Sunan *al-Ṣughrā*, 1/568 §1054. •ʿAbd b. Ḥumayd in *al-Musnad*, 1/381 §1278. •al-Khaṭīb al-Tabrīzī in *Mishkāt al-Maṣābīḥ*, 2/387 §5798. •Abū al-Maḥāsin in *Muʿtaṣar al-Mukhtaṣar*, 2/188.

الْفَصْلُ الْخَامِسُ

فَصْلٌ فِي أَنَّ الْأُمَّةَ تُسْئَلُ عَنْ مَكَانَةِ النَّبِيِّ ﷺ فِي الْقُبُوْرِ

Section 5

The *Umma* will be Questioned in the Grave about the Esteemed Station of the Prophet ﷺ

٤٣/ ٤٣. عَنْ أَنَسِ بْنِ مَالِكٍ ﵁ قَالَ: قَالَ رَسُوْلُ اللهِ ﷺ: إِنَّ الْعَبْدَ إِذَا وُضِعَ فِي قَبْرِهِ، وَتَوَلَّى عَنْهُ أَصْحَابُهُ وَإِنَّهُ لَيَسْمَعُ قَرْعَ نِعَالِهِمْ. أَتَاهُ مَلَكَانِ فَيُقْعِدَانِهِ، فَيَقُوْلَانِ: مَا كُنْتَ تَقُوْلُ فِي هَذَا الرَّجُلِ، لِمُحَمَّدٍ ﷺ؟ فَأَمَّا الْمُؤْمِنُ فَيَقُوْلُ: أَشْهَدُ أَنَّهُ عَبْدُ اللهِ وَرَسُوْلُهُ. فَيُقَالُ لَهُ: انْظُرْ إِلَى مَقْعَدِكَ مِنَ النَّارِ. قَدْ أَبْدَلَكَ اللهُ بِهِ مَقْعَدًا مِنَ الْجَنَّةِ. فَيَرَاهُمَا جَمِيْعًا. قَالَ: وَأَمَّا الْمُنَافِقُ وَالْكَافِرُ فَيُقَالُ لَهُ: مَاكُنْتَ تَقُوْلُ فِي هَذَا الرَّجُلِ؟ فَيَقُوْلُ: لَا أَدْرِي، كُنْتُ أَقُوْلُ مَا يَقُوْلُ النَّاسُ، فَيُقَالُ: لَا دَرَيْتَ وَلَا تَلَيْتَ، وَيُضْرَبُ بِمَطَارِقَ مِنْ حَدِيْدٍ ضَرْبَةً، فَيَصِيْحُ صَيْحَةً يَسْمَعُهَا مَنْ يَلِيْهِ غَيْرَ الثَّقَلَيْنِ.

مُتَّفَقٌ عَلَيْهِ وَهَذَا لَفْظُ الْبُخَارِيِّ.

43/43. According to Anas b. Mālik ﵁:

---

43 Set forth by •al-Bukhārī in *al-Ṣaḥīḥ*: Bk.: *al-Janāʾiz* [Funeral Ceremonies], Ch.: What has come to us about the torment of the tomb, 1/462 §1308, & Bk.: *al-Janāʾiz* [Funeral Ceremonies], Ch.: The deceased hears the tread of the shoes, 1/448 §1673. •Muslim in *al-Ṣaḥīḥ*: Bk.: The Garden of Paradise and the Qualities of its Felicity and its Inhabitants, Ch.: What is spent in this world by the people of the Garden of Paradise and the people of the Fire of Hell, 4/2200 §2870. •Abū Dāwūd in *al-Sunan*, Bk.: The Sunna, Ch.: Enquiring about the tomb and the torment of the tomb, 4/238 §4752. •al-Nasāʾī in *al-Sunan*,Bk.: *al-Janāʾiz* [Funeral Ceremonies], Ch.: Enquiring about the tomb,

"Allah's Messenger ﷺ said: 'When the servant is placed in his grave, and his companions turn away from him (after the burial), he hears the thumping of their shoes. Then two angels come to him and make him sit down. They ask: "What were you accustomed to saying about this (exalted) personage (Holy Prophet) Muhammad ﷺ?" As for the believer, he says: "I bear witness that he is Allah's (perfect) servant and His (true) Messenger." So he will be told: "(In case you could not recognize him then) look at your seat amid the Fire of Hell! But (owing to recognition of his station) Allah has exchanged it for you with a seat amid the Garden of Paradise!" So he will see both of them (in their entirety). As for the hypocrite or the unbeliever, he will be asked: "What were you accustomed to saying about this personage (the Holy Prophet Muhammad ﷺ)?" He will say: "I do not know! I used to say whatever the people said!" He will therefore be told: "You did not know and you did not try to know," and he will be smitten with hammers of iron, so he will scream (in the torment of pain) that is heard by those near him, apart from the human beings and the jinn.'"

Agreed upon by al-Bukhārī and Muslim, and this is the wording of al-Bukhārī.

٤٤/ ٤٤. عَنْ أَسْمَاءَ بِنْتِ أَبِي بَكْرٍ رضي الله عنهما أَنَّهَا قَالَتْ فِي رِوَايَةٍ طَوِيْلَةٍ: فَلَمَّا انْصَرَفَ رَسُوْلُ اللهِ ﷺ حَمِدَ اللهَ وَأَثْنَى عَلَيْهِ ثُمَّ قَالَ: مَا مِنْ شَيءٍ كُنْتُ لَمْ أَرَهُ إِلاَّ قَدْ رَأَيْتُهُ فِي مَقَامِي هَذَا، حَتَّى الْجَنَّةَ وَالنَّارَ، وَلَقَدْ أُوْحِيَ إِلَيَّ أَنَّكُمْ تُفْتَنُوْنَ فِي الْقُبُوْرِ مِثْلَ أَوْ قَرِيْبَ مِنْ فِتْنَةِ الدَّجَّالِ - لاَ أَدْرِي أَيَّ ذَلِكَ قَالَتْ أَسْمَاءُ - يُؤْتَى أَحَدُكُمْ فَيُقَالُ: مَا عِلْمُكَ بِهَذَا الرَّجُلِ؟ فَأَمَّا الْمُؤْمِنُ أَوِ الْمُوْقِنُ فَيَقُوْلُ: هُوَ مُحَمَّدٌ رَسُوْلُ اللهِ، جَاءَنَا بِالْبَيِّنَاتِ وَالْهُدَى، فَأَجَبْنَا وَآمَنَّا وَاتَّبَعْنَا فَيُقَالُ: نَمْ صَالِحًا فَقَدْ عَلِمْنَا إِنْ كُنْتَ لَمُؤْمِنًا وَأَمَّا الْمُنَافِقُ أَوِ الْمُرْتَابُ - لاَ أَدْرِي أَيَّ ذَلِكَ قَالَتْ أَسْمَاءُ - فَيَقُوْلُ: لاَ أَدْرِي. سَمِعْتُ

4/97 §2051. •Aḥmad b. Ḥanbal in *al-Musnad*, 3/126 §12293.

النَّاسَ يَقُوْلُوْنَ شَيْئًا فَقُلْتُهُ.

مُتَّفَقٌ عَلَيْهِ وَهَذَا لَفْظُ الْبُخَارِيِّ.

44/44. According to an extensive narration of Asmāʾ, the daughter of Abū Bakr ﵄:

"When Allah's Messenger ﷺ concluded (the eclipse ritual prayer), he praised Allah and extolled Him, then said: 'There is nothing which I have not seen in this station of mine, even the Garden of Paradise and the Fire of Hell. And it has been revealed to me that you will be put to test in the graves with a trial like or close to that of the Antichrist *[al-Dajjāl]* (I do not know which of the two things Asmāʾ said). An angel will come to every one of you and ask: "What is your knowledge of this personage (the Holy Prophet Muhammad ﷺ)?" As for the believer, or the one having certitude, he will say: "He is Muhammad, the Messenger of Allah. He has come to us with the clear proofs and right guidance, so we have responded, believed and followed." He will therefore be told: "Sleep at ease, for we have acknowledged that you are indeed a believer!" As for the hypocrite or the one having doubt (I do not know which of the two things Asmāʾ said), he will say: "I do not know! I heard the people saying something, so I would say the same."'"

Agreed upon by al-Bukhārī and Muslim, and this is the wording of al-Bukhārī.

---

44 Set forth by •al-Bukhārī in *al-Ṣaḥīḥ*: Bk.: *al-Wūḍūʾ* [The Minor Ritual Ablution], Ch.: Someone who does not perform the minor ritual ablution except because of a heavy fainting fit, 1/79 §182, & Bk.: *al-Jumuʿa* [Friday, the Day of Congregational Prayer], Ch.: The ritual prayer performed by the women together with the men during the solar eclipse, 1/358 §1005, & Ch.: Emulating the customs of Allah's Messenger ﷺ, 6/2657 §6857. •Muslim in *al-Ṣaḥīḥ*: Bk.: *al-Kusūf* [The Solar Eclipse], Ch.: What was shown to the Prophet ﷺ in the prayer of the solar eclipse, with regard to the Garden of Paradise and the Fire of Hell, 2/624 §905. •Mālik in *al-Muwaṭṭāʾ*, 1/189 §447. •Aḥmad b. Ḥanbal in *al-Musnad*, 6/345 §26970.

٤٥/ ٤٥. عَنْ أَبِي هُرَيْرَةَ ﷺ قَالَ: قَالَ رَسُوْلُ اللهِ ﷺ: إِذَا قُبِرَ الْمَيِّتُ، أَوْ قَالَ أَحَدُكُمْ، أَتَاهُ مَلَكَانِ أَسْوَدَانِ أَزْرَقَانِ. يُقَالُ لِأَحَدِهِمَا الْمُنْكَرُ وَالآخَرُ النَّكِيْرُ. فَيَقُوْلاَنِ: مَا كُنْتَ تَقُوْلُ فِي هَذَا الرَّجُلِ؟ فَيَقُوْلُ مَا كَانَ يَقُوْلُ: هُوَ عَبْدُ اللهِ وَرَسُوْلُهُ. أَشْهَدُ أَنْ لاَ إِلَهَ إِلاَّ اللهُ وَأَنَّ مُحَمَّدًا عَبْدُهُ وَرَسُوْلُهُ. فَيَقُوْلاَنِ: قَدْ كُنَّا نَعْلَمُ أَنَّكَ تَقُوْلُ هَذَا. ثُمَّ يُفْسَحُ لَهُ فِي قَبْرِهِ سَبْعُوْنَ ذِرَاعًا فِي سَبْعِيْنَ، ثُمَّ يُنَوَّرُ لَهُ فِيْهِ، ثُمَّ يُقَالُ لَهُ: نَمْ. فَيَقُوْلُ: أَرْجِعُ إِلَى أَهْلِي فَأُخْبِرُهُمْ؟ فَيَقُوْلاَنِ: نَمْ كَنَوْمَةِ الْعَرُوْسِ الَّذِي لاَ يُوْقِظُهُ إِلاَّ أَحَبُّ أَهْلِهِ إِلَيْهِ، حَتَّى يَبْعَثَهُ اللهُ مِنْ مَضْجَعِهِ ذَلِكَ. وَإِنْ كَانَ مُنَافِقًا قَالَ: سَمِعْتُ النَّاسَ يَقُوْلُوْنَ فَقُلْتُ مِثْلَهُ. لاَ أَدْرِي. فَيَقُوْلاَنِ: قَدْ كُنَّا نَعْلَمُ أَنَّكَ تَقُوْلُ ذَلِكَ. فَيُقَالُ لِلْأَرْضِ: الْتَئِمِي عَلَيْهِ فَتَلْتَئِمُ عَلَيْهِ فَتَخْتَلِفُ فِيْهَا أَضْلاَعُهُ فَلاَ يَزَالُ فِيْهَا مُعَذَّبًا حَتَّى يَبْعَثَهُ اللهُ مِنْ مَضْجَعِهِ ذَلِكَ.

رَوَاهُ التِّرْمِذِيُّ وَحَسَّنَهُ وَابْنُ حِبَّانَ.

45/45. According to Abū Hurayra ﷺ:

"Allah's Messenger ﷺ said: 'When the deceased (or he may have said: one of you) is buried, two blue-eyed angels having dark complexion will come to him, one of them called Munkar and the other Nakīr, and they will ask him (the buried): "What were you accustomed to saying about this most esteemed man?" He will say what he used to say, namely: "He is Allah's servant and His Messenger. I bear witness that there is no God but Allah, and that Muhammad is His (perfect) servant and His (true) Messenger!" They will therefore say: "We already knew that you would say that!" Then his grave is expanded seventy square cubits each side

[45] Set forth by •al-Tirmidhī in *al-Sunan*: Bk.: *al-Janā'iz* [Funeral Ceremonies], Ch.: What has come to us about the torment of the tomb, 3/383 §1071. •Ibn Ḥibbān in *al-Ṣaḥīḥ*, 7/386 §3117. •Ibn Abī Shayba in *al-Muṣannaf*, 3/56 §12062. •Ibn Abī ʿĀṣim in *al-Sunna*, 2/416 §864. •al-Mundhirī in *al-Targhīb wa al-Tarhīb*, 4/199 §5399. •al-Mubārakfūrī in *Tuḥfat al-Aḥwadhī*, 4/156. •al-Munāwī in *Fayḍ al-Qadīr*, 2/331.

and is filled with light. He is then told: "Sleep (at ease)," so he will say: "Shall I return to my family and inform them?" They say: "Sleep like the bridegroom, who is not awakened except by the dearest to him in his family, until Allah resurrects him from that bed of his (on the Day of Rising)!" But if he is a hypocrite, he will say (in reply to the question): "I heard the people speaking, so I said the same as they did. I do not know (whether it was right or wrong)!" The angels will therefore say: "We already knew that you would say that!" The earth will then be told: "Coalesce over him," so it will coalesce over him (i.e., press him) until his ribs will be interlocked. He will thus be constantly tormented in it, until Allah resurrects him from that bed of his (on the Day of Rising).'"

Reported by al-Tirmidhī and Ibn Ḥibbān and al-Tirmidhī declared it fine.

٤٦/ ٤٦. عَنْ عَائِشَةَ وَأَبِـي هُرَيْرَةَ رضي الله عنهما عَنِ النَّبِيِّ ﷺ قَالَ: وَأَمَّا فِتْنَةُ الْقَبْرِ فَبِي تُفْتَنُوْنَ وَعَنِّي تُسْأَلُوْنَ. فَإِذَا كَانَ الرَّجُلُ الصَّالِحُ أُجْلِسَ فِي قَبْرِهِ غَيْرَ فَزِعٍ وَلَا مَشْعُوْفٍ ثُمَّ يُقَالُ لَهُ: فِيْمَ كُنْتَ؟ فَيَقُوْلُ: فِي الإِسْلَامِ. فَيُقَالُ: مَا هَذَا الرَّجُلُ الَّذِي كَانَ فِيْكُمْ؟ فَيَقُوْلُ: مُحَمَّدٌ رَسُوْلُ اللهِ. جَاءَنَا بِالْبَيِّنَاتِ مِنْ عِنْدِ اللهِ سبحانه وتعالى فَصَدَّقْنَاهُ. فَيُقَالُ لَهُ: هَلْ رَأَيْتَ اللهَ؟ فَيَقُوْلُ: مَا يَنْبَغِي لِأَحَدٍ أَنْ يَرَى اللهَ. فَيُفْرَجُ لَهُ فُرْجَةٌ قِبَلَ النَّارِ فَيَنْظُرُ إِلَيْهَا يَحْطِمُ بَعْضُهَا بَعْضًا. فَيُقَالُ لَهُ: أُنْظُرْ إِلَى مَا وَقَاكَ اللهُ سبحانه وتعالى. ثُمَّ يُفْرَجُ لَهُ فُرْجَةٌ إِلَى الْجَنَّةِ فَيَنْظُرُ إِلَى زَهْرَتِهَا وَمَا فِيْهَا فَيُقَالُ لَهُ: هَذَا مَقْعَدُكَ. وَيُقَالُ لَهُ: عَلَى الْيَقِيْنِ كُنْتَ وَعَلَيْهِ مُتَّ وَعَلَيْهِ تُبْعَثُ إِنْ شَاءَ اللهُ تَعَالَى.

رَوَاهُ ابْنُ مَاجَه وَأَحْمَدُ وَإِسْنَادُهُ صَحِيْحٌ.

46/46. According to ʿĀʾisha and Abū Hurayra (may Allah be pleased with them):

---

46 Set forth by •Ibn Mājah in *al-Sunan*: Bk.: *al-Zuhd* [Abstinence], Ch.: Concerning the tomb and the decay, 2/1426 §4268. •Aḥmad b. Ḥanbal in *al-Musnad*, 6/139 §25133. •Ibn Manda in *al-Īmān*, 2/967 §1067. •ʿAbd Allāh b. Aḥmad in *al-Sunna*, 1/308 §602. •al-ʿAsqalānī in *Fatḥ al-Bārī*, 3/240.

"The Prophet ﷺ said: 'As for the trial in the grave, you will be tried and questioned about me. So the righteous man will be seated in his grave, neither afraid nor insane, then he will be asked: "What Religion (*Dīn*) you believed in?" He will say: "In Islam," so he will be asked: "What is this personage who was among you?" He will say: "Muhammad is the Messenger of Allah ﷺ. He came to us with the clear proofs from the presence of Allah ﷻ, so we believed in him!" He will then be asked: "Have you seen Allah?" He will say: "It is not possible for anyone to see Allah." So a crevice will be opened for him in the direction of the Fire of Hell, and he will behold it, one part of it crushing another. He will then be told: "Observe what Allah ﷻ has protected you from!" Then a crevice will be opened for him in the direction of the Garden of Paradise, so he will behold its beauty and what it contains, and he will be told: "This is your seat (in Paradise)!" He will also be told: "You spent your life with certitude and with that you died, and with that you will be raised, if Allah Most High so wills!"'"

Reported by Ibn Mājah and Aḥmad, with an authentic chain of transmission.

٤٧ / ٤٧. عَنْ أَبِي سَعِيْدٍ الْخُدْرِيِّ رضي الله عنه قَالَ: شَهِدْتُ مَعَ رَسُوْلِ اللهِ ﷺ جِنَازَةً. فَقَالَ رَسُوْلُ اللهِ ﷺ: أَيُّهَا النَّاسُ، إِنَّ هَذِهِ الْأَمَّةَ تُبْتَلَى فِي قُبُوْرِهَا، فَإِذَا الإِنْسَانُ دُفِنَ فَتَفَرَّقَ عَنْهُ أَصْحَابُهُ، جَاءَهُ مَلَكٌ فِي يَدِهِ مِطْرَاقٌ فَأَقْعَدَهُ. قَالَ: مَا تَقُوْلُ فِي هَذَا الرَّجُلِ؟ فَإِنْ كَانَ مُؤْمِنًا قَالَ: أَشْهَدُ أَنْ لَا إِلَهَ إِلَّا اللهُ وَأَنَّ مُحَمَّدًا عَبْدُهُ وَرَسُوْلُهُ. فَيَقُوْلُ: صَدَقْتَ. ثُمَّ يُفْتَحُ لَهُ بَابٌ إِلَى النَّارِ فَيَقُوْلُ: هَذَا كَانَ مَنْزِلُكَ لَوْ كَفَرْتَ بِرَبِّكَ، فَأَمَّا إِذَا آمَنْتَ فَهَذَا مَنْزِلُكَ. فَيُفْتَحُ لَهُ بَابٌ إِلَى الْجَنَّةِ، فَيُرِيْدُ أَنْ يَنْهَضَ إِلَيْهِ فَيَقُوْلُ لَهُ: اسْكُنْ. وَيُفْسَحُ لَهُ فِي قَبْرِهِ.

رَوَاهُ أَحْمَدُ وَابْنُ أَبِي عَاصِمٍ.

47/47. According to Abū Saʿīd al-Khudrī ﷺ:

"I attended a funeral together with Allah's Messenger ﷺ, so Allah's Messenger ﷺ said: 'O people, this *Umma* (Community) of mine will be put to trial in their graves, so when the person is buried and his companions go away from him, an angel will come to him with a hammer and make him sit down, saying: "What do you say about this man?" If he is a believer, he will say: "I bear witness that there is no God but Allah, and that Muhammad is His (most exalted) servant and His Messenger." So the angel will say: "You have told the truth!" A gate to the Fire of Hell will then be opened for him, so he will say: "This would have been your abode if you had disbelieved in your Lord, but since you have believed, this (Paradise) will be your abode!" A gate to the Garden of Paradise will then be opened for him, and he (overjoyed) will wish to rise up towards it, so the angel will say to him: "Stop," and expansion will be made for him in his grave."'"

Reported by Aḥmad and Ibn Abī ʿĀṣim.

٤٨/٤٨. عَنْ أَسْمَاءَ بِنْتِ أَبِـي بَكْرٍ رضي الله عنهما فِي رواية طويلة قَالَتْ: قَالَ رَسُوْلُ اللهِ ﷺ: أَيُّهَا النَّاسُ، إِنَّهُ لَمْ يَبْقَ شَيْءٌ لَمْ أَكُنْ رَأَيْتُهُ إِلاَّ وَقَدْ رَأَيْتُهُ فِي مَقَامِي هَذَا وَقَدْ أُرِيْتُكُمْ تُفْتَنُوْنَ فِي قُبُوْرِكُمْ. يُسْأَلُ أَحَدُكُمْ: مَا كُنْتَ تَقُوْلُ؟ وَمَا كُنْتَ تَعْبُدُ؟ فَإِنْ قَالَ: لاَ أَدْرِي، رَأَيْتُ النَّاسَ يَقُوْلُوْنَ شَيْئًا فَقُلْتُهُ وَيَصْنَعُوْنَ شَيْئًا فَصَنَعْتُهُ، قِيْلَ لَهُ: أَجَلْ، عَلَى الشَّكِّ عِشْتَ وَعَلَيْهِ مُتَّ. هَذَا مَقْعَدُكَ مِنَ النَّارِ. وَإِنْ قَالَ: أَشْهَدُ أَنْ لاَ إِلَهَ إِلاَّ اللهُ وَأَنَّ مُحَمَّدًا رَسُوْلُ اللهِ، قِيْلَ لَهُ: عَلَى الْيَقِيْنِ عِشْتَ وَعَلَيْهِ مُتَّ. هَذَا مَقْعَدُكَ مِنَ الْجَنَّةِ.

رَوَاهُ أَحْمَدُ وَإِسْنَادُهُ حَسَنٌ.

[47] 22: Set forth by •Aḥmad b. Ḥanbal in *al-Musnad*, 3/3 §11013, 14864. •Ibn Abī ʿĀṣim in *al-Sunna*, 2/417 §565. •ʿAbd Allāh b. Aḥmad in *al-Sunna*, 2/612 §1456.

48/48. According to Asmāʾ, the daughter of Abū Bakr ﵄, in the course of a detailed report:

"Allah's Messenger ﷺ said: 'O people, there is nothing left that I have not seen, but that I am seeing it in this station of mine! I have seen you being tried in your graves. Every one of you will be asked: "What were you accustomed to saying about this most exalted man (referring to Allah's Messenger ﷺ)? What were you accustomed to worshipping?" If he says: "I do not know! I heard the people saying something, so I said it, and doing something, so I did it," he will be told: "Yes, indeed! You have lived in the state of doubt and in it you have died. This is your seat amid the Fire of Hell!" If he says: "I bear witness that there is no God but Allah, and that Muhammad is the Messenger of Allah," he will be told: "In the state of certainty you have lived, and in it you have died. This is your seat amid the Garden of Paradise!"'"

Reported by Aḥmad with an excellent chain of transmission.

٤٩/ ٤٩. عَنْ أَنَسِ بْنِ مَالِكٍ ﵁ في رواية طويلة قَالَ: إِنَّ رَسُوْلَ اللهِ ﷺ قَالَ: إِنَّ الْـمُؤْمِنَ إِذَا وُضِعَ فِي قَبْرِهِ أَتَاهُ مَلَكٌ، فَيَقُوْلُ لَهُ: مَا كُنْتَ تَعْبُدُ؟ فَإِنَّ اللهَ هَدَاهُ قَالَ: كُنْتُ أَعْبُدُ اللهَ. فَيُقَالُ لَهُ: مَا كُنْتَ تَقُوْلُ فِي هَذَا الرَّجُلِ؟ فَيَقُوْلُ: هُوَ عَبْدُ اللهِ وَرَسُوْلُهُ. فَمَا يُسْأَلُ عَنْ شَيْءٍ غَيْرِهَا... فَيَقُوْلُ: دَعُوْنِي حَتَّى أَذْهَبَ فَأُبَشِّرَ أَهْلِي. فَيُقَالُ لَهُ: اسْكُنْ.

رَوَاهُ أَبُوْ دَاوُدَ وَأَحْمَدُ.

49/49. According to Anas b. Mālik ﵁, in the course of a detailed report:

---

48 Set forth by •Aḥmad b. Ḥanbal in *al-Musnad*, 6/354, and its chain of transmission is excellent.

49 Set forth by •Abū Dāwūd in *al-Sunan*: Bk.: The Sunna, Ch.: Enquiry about the tomb and the torment of the tomb, 4/238 §4751. •Aḥmad b. Ḥanbal in *al-Musnad*, 3/233 §13472. •al-Mundhirī in *al-Targhīb wa al-Tarhīb*, 4/194 §5394. •al-ʿAsqalānī in *Fatḥ al-Bārī*, 3/237.

"Allah's Messenger ﷺ said: 'When the believer is laid in his grave, an angel will come to him and ask him: "What were you accustomed to worshipping?" Since Allah has guided him aright, he will say: "I used to worship Allah!" He will then be asked: "What were you accustomed to saying about this personage (the Holy Prophet Muhammad ﷺ)?" He will say: "He is Allah's servant and His Messenger," so he will not be asked about anything else." ... Then he will say: "Leave me alone, until I go and give the good tidings to my family," so he will be told: "Stay (here with joy and comfort)!"'"

Reported by Abū Dāwūd and Aḥmad.

٥٠/ ٥٠. عَنِ الْبَرَاءِ بْنِ عَازِبٍ رضي الله عنه قَالَ: خَرَجْنَا مَعَ رَسُوْلِ اللهِ ﷺ فِي جِنَازَةِ رَجُلٍ مِنْ الْأَنْصَارِ فَانْتَهَيْنَا إِلَى الْقَبْرِ وَلَـمَّا يُلْحَدْ، فَجَلَسَ رَسُوْلُ اللهِ ﷺ وَجَلَسْنَا حَوْلَهُ كَأَنَّمَا عَلَى رُءُوْسِنَا الطَّيْرُ. وَفِي يَدِهِ عُوْدٌ يَنْكُتُ بِهِ فِي الْأَرْضِ فَرَفَعَ رَأْسَهُ فَقَالَ: اسْتَعِيْذُوْا بِاللهِ مِنْ عَذَابِ الْقَبْرِ مَرَّتَيْنِ أَوْ ثَلَاثًا وَقَالَ: وَإِنَّهُ لَيَسْمَعُ خَفْقَ نِعَالِهِمْ إِذَا وَلَّوْا مُدْبِرِيْنَ حِيْنَ يُقَالُ لَهُ: يَا هَذَا مَنْ رَبُّكَ؟ وَمَا دِيْنُكَ؟ وَمَنْ نَبِيُّكَ؟

وفي رواية له قَالَ: وَيَأْتِيهِ مَلَكَانِ فَيُجْلِسَانِهِ فَيَقُوْلَانِ لَهُ: مَنْ رَبُّكَ؟ فَيَقُوْلُ: رَبِّيَ اللهُ، فَيَقُوْلَانِ لَهُ: مَا دِيْنُكَ؟ فَيَقُوْلُ: دِيْنِيَ الإِسْلَامُ، فَيَقُوْلَانِ لَهُ: مَا هَذَا الرَّجُلُ الَّذِي بُعِثَ فِيْكُمْ؟ قَالَ: فَيَقُوْلُ: هُوَ رَسُوْلُ اللهِ ﷺ فَيَقُوْلَانِ: وَمَا يُدْرِيْكَ؟ فَيَقُوْلُ: قَرَأْتُ كِتَابَ اللهِ فَآمَنْتُ بِهِ وَصَدَّقْتُ.

وفي رواية له: فَذَلِكَ قَوْلُ اللهِ سبحانه وتعالى: ﴿يُثَبِّتُ ٱللَّهُ ٱلَّذِينَ ءَامَنُواْ بِٱلْقَوْلِ ٱلثَّابِتِ فِى ٱلْحَيَوٰةِ ٱلدُّنْيَا وَفِى ٱلْأَخِرَةِ﴾، (إبراهيم، ١٤: ٢٧). قَالَ: فَيُنَادِي مُنَادٍ مِنَ السَّمَاءِ أَنْ قَدْ صَدَقَ عَبْدِي فَأَفْرِشُوْهُ مِنَ الْجَنَّةِ وَافْتَحُوْا لَهُ بَابًا إِلَى الْجَنَّةِ وَأَلْبِسُوْهُ مِنَ الْجَنَّةِ. قَالَ: فَيَأْتِيْهِ مِنْ رَوْحِهَا وَطِيْبِهَا. قَالَ: وَيُفْتَحُ لَهُ فِيْهَا مَدَّ بَصَرِهِ.

رَوَاهُ أَبُوْ دَاوُدَ وَأَحْمَدُ.

50/50. According to al-Barā' b. 'Āzib ﷺ:

"We went out with Allah's Messenger ﷺ in the funeral procession of a man from among the Anṣār, so we eventually reached the grave. It had not yet been dug. Allah's Messenger ﷺ sat down, and we also sat down around him (silent and still) as if the birds were sitting on our heads. There was a stick in his hand, with which he was scratching up the ground, so he raised his head and said, two or three times: 'Seek refuge with Allah from the torment of the graves!' He also said: 'He will surely hear the tread of their shoes, when they (his companions of the world) turn their backs to go away. Then he is asked: "O man, who is your Lord, what is your Religion, and who is your Prophet?'""

In one report of his: "He said: 'Two angels will come to him and make him sit down, then they will say to him: "Who is your Lord?" He will say: "My Lord is Allah!" Then they will say to him: "What is your Religion?" He will say: "My Religion is Islam!" Then they will say to him: "What is this man who was sent to you?" He will say: "He is (our Master Muhammad) Allah's Messenger ﷺ!" They will then ask: "What lets you know?" He will say: "I have read the Book of Allah, so I have believed in him and affirm him as true!"'"

In another report of his: "[He said]: 'Such is the saying of Allah ﷻ: "Allah keeps the believers firm-footed in the life of this world as well as in the Hereafter with (the blessing) of this Firm Word *[yuthabbitu 'llāhu 'lladhīna āmanū bi al-qawl al-thābiti fī al-ḥayāti al-dunyā wa fī al-ākhira].*" (Q.14:27). So a herald will therefore proclaim from heaven: "My servant has told the truth, so spread carpets for him from the Garden of Paradise, open for him a gate to the Garden of Paradise, and clothe him in the attire of Garden of Paradise!" Some of its air and its perfume will thus come to him, and his grave will be expanded for him as far as his eye can see!'"

Reported by Abū Dāwūd and Aḥmad.

---

[50] Set forth by •Abū Dāwūd in *al-Sunan*: Bk.: The Sunna, Ch.: Enquiry about the tomb and the torment of the tomb, 4/238 §4751. •Aḥmad b. Ḥanbal in *al-Musnad*, 3/233.

اَلْفَصْلُ السَّادِسُ

فَصْلٌ فِي الشَّفَاعَةِ يَوْمَ الْقِيَامَةِ

Section 6

Intercession on the Day of Resurrection

٥١/٥١. عَنْ آدَمَ بْنِ عَلِيٍّ ﷺ قَالَ: سَمِعْتُ ابْنَ عُمَرَ ﷺ يَقُوْلُ: إِنَّ النَّاسَ يَصِيْرُوْنَ يَوْمَ الْقِيَامَةِ جُثًا. كُلُّ أُمَّةٍ تَتْبَعُ نَبِيَّهَا. يَقُوْلُوْنَ: يَا فُلَانُ، اشْفَعْ، يَا فُلَانُ، اشْفَعْ، حَتَّى تَنْتَهِيَ الشَّفَاعَةُ إِلَى النَّبِيِّ ﷺ. فَذَلِكَ يَوْمَ يَبْعَثُهُ اللهُ الْمَقَامَ الْمَحْمُوْدَ.

رَوَاهُ الْبُخَارِيُّ وَالنَّسَائِيُّ.

51/51. According to Ādam b. ʿAlī ﷺ:

"I heard Ibn ʿUmar ﷺ say: 'The people will become, on the Day of Resurrection, congregated into communities, each following its Prophet and saying: "O So-and-so, intercede, O So-and-so, intercede," until the intercession finally reaches the (final) Prophet ﷺ. So that day Allah will raise him to the Praiseworthy Station *[al-Maqām al-Maḥmūd]*.'"

Reported by al-Bukhārī and al-Nasāʾī.

٥٢/٥٢. عَنْ عَبْدِ اللهِ بْنِ عُمَرَ ﷺ قَالَ: قَالَ النَّبِيُّ ﷺ: إِنَّ الشَّمْسَ تَدْنُوْ يَوْمَ

---

[51] Set forth by •al-Bukhārī in *al-Ṣaḥīḥ*: Bk.: *Tafsīr al-Qurʾān* [Interpretation of the Qurʾān], Ch.: His saying: "Perhaps your Lord will send you to a definite station," 4/1748 §4441. •al-Nasāʾī in *al-Sunan al-Kubrā*, 6/381 §295. •Ibn Manda in *Kitāb al-Īmān*, 2/871 §927.

الْقِيَامَةِ حَتَّى يَبْلُغَ الْعَرَقُ نِصْفَ الْأُذُنِ. فَبَيْنَاهُمْ كَذٰلِكَ اسْتَغَاثُوْا بِآدَمَ، ثُمَّ بِمُوْسَى، ثُمَّ بِمُحَمَّدٍ ﷺ.

رَوَاهُ الْبُخَارِيُّ.

52/52. According to ʿAbd Allāh b. ʿUmar ﷺ:

"The Prophet ﷺ said: 'The sun will draw near on the Day of Resurrection, until the sweat (due to its heat) reaches the middle of the ear. In this state people will appeal for help to Adam, then to Moses, then (after their regrets) to Muhammad ﷺ!"

Reported by al-Bukhārī.

٥٣ / ٥٣. عَنْ أَنَسِ بْنِ مَالِكٍ ﷺ قَالَ: قَالَ رَسُوْلُ اللهِ ﷺ: شَفَاعَتِي لِأَهْلِ الْكَبَائِرِ مِنْ أُمَّتِي.

رَوَاهُ التِّرْمِذِيُّ وَأَبُوْ دَاوُدَ، وَقَالَ التِّرْمِذِيُّ: هَذَا حَدِيْثٌ حَسَنٌ صَحِيْحٌ.

53/53. According to Anas b. Mālik ﷺ:

---

52 Set forth by •al-Bukhārī in *al-Ṣaḥīḥ*: Bk.: *al-Zakāt* [The Alms-due], Ch.: Someone who begs too much of the people, 2/536 §1405. •al-Ṭabarānī in *al-Muʿjam al-Awsaṭ*, 8/30 §8725. •al-Bayhaqī in *Shuʿab al-Īmān*, 3/269 §3509. •Ibn Manda in *Kitāb al-Īmān*, 2/854 §884. •al-Daylamī in *al-Firdaws bi-Maʾthūr al-Khiṭāb*, 2/377 §3677. •al-Haythamī in *Majmaʿ al-Zawāʾid*, 10/371, and he confirmed it.

53 Set forth by •al-Tirmidhī in *al-Sunan*, Bk.: *Ṣifat al-Qiyāma wa al-Raqāʾiq wa al-Waraʿ* [The spectacle of the Day of Resurrection, the Softening of Hearts, and Piety] according to Allah's Messenger ﷺ, Ch.: What has come to us concerning mediation [*shafāʿa*], 4/625 §2435. •Abū Dāwūd in *al-Sunan*: Bk.: The Sunna, Ch.: Concerning mediation, 4/236 §4739. •Ibn Mājah, on the authority of Jābir ﷺ, in *al-Sunan*: Bk.: *al-Zuhd* [Abstinence], Ch.: Concerning mediation, 2/1441 §4310. •al-Ḥākim in *al-Mustadrak*, 1/139 §228. He said: "This tradition is authentic in accordance with the stipulation of al-Bukhārī and Muslim." •Abū Yaʿlā in *al-Musnad*, 6/40 §3284. •al-Ṭabarānī in *al-Muʿjam al-Ṣaghīr*, 1/272 §448. •al-Ṭayālisī in *al-Musnad*, 1/233 §1669.

"Allah's Messenger ﷺ said: 'My intercession is for those members of my Community who perpetrated major sins!'"

Reported by al-Tirmidhī and Abū Dāwūd. According to al-Tirmidhī: "This is a fine authentic tradition."

٥٤/ ٥٤. عَنْ أَبِي مُوْسَى الْأَشْعَرِيِّ رضي الله عنه قَالَ: قَالَ رَسُوْلُ اللهِ ﷺ: خُيِّرْتُ بَيْنَ الشَّفَاعَةِ وَبَيْنَ أَنْ يُّدْخَلَ نِصْفُ أُمَّتِي الْجَنَّةَ. فَاخْتَرْتُ الشَّفَاعَةَ لِأَنَّهَا أَعَمُّ وَأَكْفَى. أَتَرَوْنَهَا لِلْمُتَّقِيْنَ؟ لاَ، وَلَكِنَّهَا لِلْمُذْنِبِيْنَ الْخَطَّائِيْنَ الْـمُتَلَوِّثِيْنَ.

رَوَاهُ ابْنُ مَاجَه وَأَحْمَدُ.

54/54. According to Abū Mūsā al-Ashʿarī رضي الله عنه:

"Allah's Messenger ﷺ said: 'I was given the choice between intercession and only half of my Community being admitted into the Garden of Paradise (without reckoning), so I have chosen intercession because that will suffice (the entire *Umma*). You may deem it provided only for the truly devout? No, but that (intercession) is for the sinners, the erring and the evildoers.'"

Reported by Ibn Mājah and Aḥmad.

٥٥/ ٥٥. عَنْ عَوْفِ بْنِ مَالِكٍ الْأَشْجَعِيِّ رضي الله عنه قَالَ: قَالَ رَسُوْلُ اللهِ ﷺ: أَتَدْرُوْنَ مَا خَيَّرَنِي رَبِّيَ اللَّيْلَةَ؟ قُلْنَا: اللهُ وَرَسُوْلُهُ أَعْلَمُ. قَالَ: فَإِنَّهُ خَيَّرَنِي بَيْنَ أَنْ يُدْخَلَ نِصْفُ أُمَّتِي الْجَنَّةَ وَبَيْنَ الشَّفَاعَةِ، فَاخْتَرْتُ الشَّفَاعَةَ. قُلْنَا: يَا رَسُوْلَ اللهِ، ادْعُ اللهَ أَنْ يَجْعَلَنَا مِنْ أَهْلِهَا. قَالَ: هِيَ لِكُلِّ مُسْلِمٍ.

رَوَاهُ ابْنُ مَاجَه وَالْحَاكِمُ وَالطَّبَرَانِيُّ، وَقَالَ الْحَاكِمُ: هَذَا حَدِيْثٌ صَحِيْحٌ عَلَى شَرْطِ مُسْلِمٍ.

---

[54] Set forth by •Ibn Mājah in *al-Sunan*: Bk.: *al-Zuhd* [Abstinence], Ch.: Concerning mediation, 2/1441 §4311. •Aḥmad b. Ḥanbal, on the authority of Ibn ʿUmar رضي الله عنه, in *al-Musnad*, 2/75 §5452. •al-Bayhaqī in *al-Iʿtiqād*, 1/202. •al-Haythamī in *Majmaʿ al-Zawāʾid*, 1/387.

55/55. According to ʿAwf b. Mālik al-Ashjaʿī ﷺ:

"Allah's Messenger ﷺ said: 'Do you know what choice my Lord has given me tonight?' We said: 'Allah and His Messenger know best!' He said: 'He has given me the choice between only half of my Community being admitted (without reckoning) into the Garden of Paradise and intercession, so I have chosen intercession.' We said: 'O Messenger of Allah, supplicate Allah to include us among those who deserve intercession!' He said: 'It is meant for every Muslim!'"

Reported by Ibn Mājah and al-Ḥākim and al-Ṭabarānī. According to al-Ḥākim: "This is an authentic tradition in conformity with the stipulation of Muslim."

٥٦/٥٦. عَنِ ابْنِ عُمَرَ رضي الله عنهما قَالَ: قَالَ رَسُوْلُ اللهِ ﷺ: مَنْ زَارَ قَبْرِي وَجَبَتْ لَهُ شَفَاعَتِي.

رَوَاهُ الدَّارَقُطْنِيُّ وَالْبَيْهَقِيُّ.

56/56. According to ʿAbd Allāh b. ʿUmar ﷺ:

"Allah's Messenger ﷺ said: 'If someone visits my tomb, my intercession will necessarily be available to him!'"

Reported by al-Dāraquṭnī and al-Bayhaqī.

٥٧/٥٧. عَنْ أَبِي حَازِمٍ عَنْ سَهْلِ بْنِ سَعْدٍ رضي الله عنه أَنَّ رَسُوْلَ اللهِ ﷺ قَالَ: لَيَدْخُلَنَّ الْجَنَّةَ مِنْ أُمَّتِي سَبْعُوْنَ أَلْفًا، أَوْ سَبْعُ مِائَةِ أَلْفٍ (لَا يَدْرِي أَبُوْ حَازِمٍ أَيُّهُمَا قَالَ)

---

[55] Set forth by •Ibn Mājah in *al-Sunan*: Bk.: *al-Zuhd* [Abstinence], Ch.: Concerning mediation, 2/1444 §4317. •al-Ḥākim in *al-Mustadrak*, 1/135 §221. •al-Ṭabarānī in *al-Muʿjam al-Kabīr*, 18/68 §126, & in *Musnad al-Shāmiyyīn*, 1/326 §575. •Ibn Manda in *al-Īmān*, 20/873 §932.

[56] Set forth by •al-Dāraquṭnī, in *al-Sunan*, 2/278 §195. •al-Bayhaqī in *Shuʿab al-Īmān*, 3/490 §4159. •al-Haythamī in *Majmaʿ al-Zawāʾid*, 4/2. He said: " It has been reported by al-Bazzār." •al-Hakīm al-Tirmizī in *Nawādir al-Usūl*, 2/67.

مُتَمَاسِكُونَ آخِذٌ بَعْضُهُمْ بَعْضًا. لَا يَدْخُلُ أَوَّلُهُمْ حَتَّى يَدْخُلَ آخِرُهُمْ. وُجُوْهُهُمْ عَلَى صُورَةِ الْقَمَرِ لَيْلَةَ الْبَدْرِ.

مُتَّفَقٌ عَلَيْهِ.

57/57. According to Abū Ḥāzim, on the authority of Sahl b. Saʿd رضي الله عنه:

"Allah's Messenger ﷺ said: 'Seventy thousand members of my *Umma* (Community) will surely enter the Garden of Paradise, or seven hundred thousand (Abū Ḥāzim does not remember which of the two numbers he said), holding tight to one another. The first of them will not enter until the last of them enters (he will watch the entry of his hundreds and thousands of people); their faces will be in the form of the moon on the night of the full moon!'"

Agreed upon by al-Bukhārī and Muslim.

٥٨/٥٨. عَنْ أَبِي سَعِيْدٍ الْخُدْرِيِّ رضي الله عنه قَالَ: قَالَ رَسُوْلُ اللهِ ﷺ: مَا مُجَادَلَةُ أَحَدِكُمْ فِي الْحَقِّ يَكُوْنُ لَهُ فِي الدُّنْيَا بِأَشَدَّ مُجَادَلَةً مِنَ الْمُؤْمِنِيْنَ لِرَبِّهِمْ فِي إِخْوَانِهِمُ الَّذِيْنَ أُدْخِلُوْا النَّارَ. قَالَ: يَقُوْلُوْنَ: رَبَّنَا، إِخْوَانُنَا كَانُوْا يُصَلُّوْنَ مَعَنَا وَيَصُوْمُوْنَ مَعَنَا وَيَحُجُّوْنَ مَعَنَا فَأَدْخَلْتَهُمُ النَّارَ. قَالَ: فَيَقُوْلُ: اذْهَبُوْا فَأَخْرِجُوْا مَنْ عَرَفْتُمْ مِنْهُمْ. قَالَ: فَيَأْتُوْنَهُمْ فَيَعْرِفُوْنَهُمْ بِصُوَرِهِمْ. فَمِنْهُمْ مَنْ أَخَذَتْهُ النَّارُ إِلَى أَنْصَافِ سَاقَيْهِ وَمِنْهُمْ مَنْ أَخَذَتْهُ إِلَى كَعْبَيْهِ، فَيُخْرِجُوْنَهُمْ، فَيَقُوْلُوْنَ: رَبَّنَا، قَدْ أَخْرَجْنَا مَنْ أَمَرْتَنَا. قَالَ: وَيَقُوْلُ: أَخْرِجُوْا مَنْ كَانَ فِي قَلْبِهِ وَزْنُ دِيْنَارٍ مِنَ الْإِيْمَانِ ثُمَّ قَالَ: مَنْ كَانَ فِي قَلْبِهِ وَزْنُ نِصْفِ دِيْنَارٍ حَتَّى

---

57 Set forth by •al-Bukhārī in *al-Ṣaḥīḥ*: Bk.: *al-Riqāq* [The Softening of Hearts], Ch.: The quality of the Garden of Paradise and the Fire of Hell, 5/2399 §6187, & in Bk.: *al-Riqāq* [The Softening of Hearts], Ch.: Seventy thousand will enter the Garden of Paradise without reckoning, 5/2396 §6177. •Muslim in *al-Ṣaḥīḥ*: Bk.: *al-Īmān* [Faith], Ch.: Evidence of the entry of parties of the Muslims into the Garden of Paradise without reckoning and without punishment, 1/198 §219.

يَقُوْلَ: مَنْ كَانَ فِي قَلْبِهِ وَزْنُ ذَرَّةٍ. قَالَ أَبُوْسَعِيْدٍ: فَمَنْ لَمْ يُصَدِّقْ فَلْيَقْرَأْ هَذِهِ الآيَةَ: ﴿إِنَّ ٱللَّهَ لَا يَغْفِرُ أَن يُشْرَكَ بِهِۦ وَيَغْفِرُ مَا دُونَ ذَٰلِكَ لِمَن يَشَآءُ﴾ إِلَى ﴿عَظِيمًا﴾. (النساء، ٤: ٤٨).

رَوَاهُ الْبُخَارِيُّ وَالنَّسَائِيُّ وَاللَّفْظُ لَهُ وَابْنُ مَاجَه.

58/58. According to Abū Saʿīd al-Khudrī ﵁:

"Allah's Messenger ﷺ said: 'No argument made by one of you, for the sake of the truth, is more serious for him in this world than the argument presented by the believers to their Lord for the sake of their brethren who have been caused to enter the Fire of Hell. They will say: "Our Lord! Our brethren used to perform the ritual prayer together with us, they used to fast together with us, and they used to perform the Pilgrimage together with us, yet You have caused them to enter the Fire of Hell!" He will say: "Go and bring forth those of them whom you have recognized!" They will therefore come to them and identify them by their faces. There will be some of them whom the Fire of Hell has seized up to the middle of their lower legs, and some of them whom it has seized up to their ankles, so they will bring them forth and say: "Our Lord, we have brought forth those whom You commanded us to take out!" He will say: "Bring forth anyone whose heart contains the weight of a gold coin of faith!" Then He will say: "... anyone whose heart contains the weight of half a gold coin of faith," until He says: "... anyone whose heart contains the weight of an atom!"'"

Abū Saʿīd said: "If someone has not been convinced, let him read this Qurʾānic Verse: 'Indeed, Allah does not forgive that anything be associated with Him; all else He forgives to whom He

---

[58] Set forth by •al-Bukhārī in *al-Ṣaḥīḥ*: Bk.: *al-Tawḥīd* [The Affirmation of Oneness], Ch.: Allah's saying ﷻ: "That day will faces be resplendent, looking towards their Lord *[wujūhun yawmaʾidhin nāḍira: ilā Rabbi-hā nāẓira]*." (Q.75:22–23), 6/2707 §7001. •al-Nasāʾī in *al-Sunan*: Bk.: *al-Īmān wa al-Sharāʾiʿ* [Faith and the Rules of the Sacred Law], Ch.: The increase of faith, 8/112 §5010. •Ibn Mājah in *al-Sunan*, Introduction: Ch.: Concerning faith, 1/23 §60. •al-Ḥākim in *al-Mustadrak*, and he said: "This is a tradition with an authentic chain of transmission." 4/626 §8736. •Aḥmad b. Ḥanbal in *al-Musnad*, 3/94 §117. •Ibn Rāshid in *al-Jāmiʿ*, 11/410.

wills. Whoever associates anything with Allah has surely forged a mighty sin *[inna ʾllāha lā yaghfiru an yushraka bi-hi wa yaghfiru mā dūna dhālika li-man yashāʾ: wa man yushrik bi-ʾllāhi fa-qadi ʾftarā ithman ʿaẓīmā].*' (Q.4:48)."

Reported by al-Bukhārī and al-Nasāʾī (the wording is his) and Ibn Mājah.

٥٩/٥٩. عَنْ أَنَسِ بْنِ مَالِكٍ ﷺ قَالَ: قَالَ رَسُوْلُ اللهِ ﷺ: يَصُفُّ النَّاسُ يَوْمَ الْقِيَامَةِ صُفُوْفًا (وَقَالَ ابْنُ نُمَيْرٍ: أَهْلُ الْجَنَّةِ) فَيَمُرُّ الرَّجُلُ مِنْ أَهْلِ النَّارِ عَلَى الرَّجُلِ، فَيَقُوْلُ: يَا فُلَانُ، أَمَا تَذْكُرُ يَوْمَ اسْتَسْقَيْتَ فَسَقَيْتُكَ شَرْبَةً؟ قَالَ: فَيَشْفَعُ لَهُ. وَيَمُرُّ الرَّجُلُ فَيَقُوْلُ: أَمَا تَذْكُرُ يَوْمَ نَاوَلْتُكَ طَهُوْرًا؟ فَيَشْفَعُ لَهُ. وَيَقُوْلُ: يَا فُلَانُ، أَمَا تَذْكُرُ يَوْمَ بَعَثْتَنِي فِي حَاجَةِ كَذَا وَكَذَا؟ فَذَهَبْتُ لَكَ. فَيَشْفَعُ لَهُ.

رَوَاهُ ابْنُ مَاجَه وَأَبُوْ يَعْلَى.

59/59. According to Anas b. Mālik ﷺ:

"Allah's Messenger ﷺ said: 'People will draw in rows on the Day of Resurrection (the people of Paradise, according to Ibn Numayr). One of the dwellers of Hell will pass by one of the residents of Paradise and say: O So-and so! Do you remember one day you asked for water and I served you with water? So the one from Paradise will intercede for the one from Hell. Then another one will pass by someone and say: Do you remember once I provided you water for purification? So he will intercede for him. (Likewise) someone will say: O So-and so! Do you remember once you sent me to do some work for you and I went for your sake? So he will intercede for him.'"

Reported by Ibn Mājah and Abū Yaʿlā.

---

[59] Set forth by •Ibn Mājah in *al-Sunan*: Bk.: *al-Adab* [Proper Conduct], Ch: *Faḍl Ṣadaqa al-Māʾa* [The Excellent Merit of donating water], 2/1215 §3685. Abū Yaʿlā *in Musnad*, 7/78 §3006. •al-Ṭabarānī in *al-Muʿjam al-Awsaṭ*, 6/317 §6511. •al-Mundhirī in *al-Targhīb wa al-Tarhīb*, 2/39 §1415. •al-Haythamī in *Majmaʿ al-Zawāʾid*, 19/382. •al-Qurtubī in *Jāmiʿ al-Aḥkām al-Qurʾān*, 3/275.

اَلْفَصْلُ السَّابِعُ

فَصْلٌ فِي أَجْرِ حُبِّ النَّبِيِّ ﷺ وَالصُّحْبَةِ الصَّالِحَةِ

Section 7

The Reward for Love of the Prophet ﷺ and the Company of the Righteous People

٦٠/ ٦٠. عَنْ أَنَسٍ ﷺ أَنَّ رَجُلاً سَأَلَ النَّبِيَّ ﷺ عَنِ السَّاعَةِ، فَقَالَ: مَتَى السَّاعَةُ؟ قَالَ: وَمَاذَا أَعْدَدْتَ لَهَا؟ قَالَ: لاَ شَيْءَ (وفي رواية أحمد: قَالَ: مَا أَعْدَدْتُ لَهَا مِنْ كَثِيرِ عَمَلٍ لاَ صَلاَةٍ وَلاَ صِيَامٍ) إِلاَّ أَنِّي أُحِبُّ اللهَ وَرَسُوْلَهُ ﷺ. فَقَالَ: أَنْتَ مَعَ مَنْ أَحْبَبْتَ. قَالَ أَنَسٌ: فَمَا فَرِحْنَا بِشَيْءٍ فَرَحَنَا بِقَوْلِ النَّبِيِّ ﷺ: أَنْتَ مَعَ مَنْ أَحْبَبْتَ. قَالَ أَنَسٌ: فَأَنَا أُحِبُّ النَّبِيَّ ﷺ وَأَبَا بَكْرٍ وَعُمَرَ وَأَرْجُوْ أَنْ أَكُوْنَ مَعَهُمْ بِحُبِّي إِيَّاهُمْ وَإِنْ لَمْ أَعْمَلْ بِمِثْلِ أَعْمَالِهِمْ.

مُتَّفَقٌ عَلَيْهِ.

60/60. According to Anas ﷺ:

[60] Set forth by •al-Bukhārī in *al-Ṣaḥīḥ*: Bk.: *al-Manāqib* [Virtues], Ch.: The virtues of ʿUmar b. al-Khaṭṭāb Abū Ḥafṣ al-Qurashī al-ʿAdawī, 3/1349 §3485, & Bk.: *al-Adab* [Proper Conduct], Ch.: What has come to us about the man's saying: "Woe to you!" 5/2285 §5815. •Muslim in *al-Ṣaḥīḥ*: Bk.: *al-Birr wa al-Ṣila wa al-Ādāb* [Piety, Affinity and Good Manners], Ch.: The man is together with the one he loves, 4/2032 §2639. •al-Tirmidhī in *al-Sunan*: Bk.: *al-Zuhd* [Abstinence] according to Allah's Messenger ﷺ, Ch.: What has come to inform us that the man is together with the one he loves, 4/595 §2385. Abū ʿĪsā said: "This is an authentic tradition." •Abū Dāwūd in *al-Sunan*: Bk.: *al-Adab* [Proper Conduct], Ch.: The man's informing the man of his love for him, 4/333 §5127. •al-Bukhārī in *al-Adab al-Mufrad*, 1/129

"A man asked the Prophet ﷺ about the Final Hour, saying: 'When is the Final Hour?' He said: 'What have you prepared for it?' The man said: 'Nothing, (and in Aḥmad's version: I have not prepared much good work for it, neither ritual prayer nor fasting,) except that I love Allah and His Messenger ﷺ.' So he said: '(On the Day of Resurrection) you are together with those you love!'" Anas said: "We (the Companions) have never felt so glad as on this decree of Allah's Messenger that you will be together with those you love. I therefore love the Prophet ﷺ and Abū Bakr and ʿUmar, and I hope that I shall also be together with them because of my loving them, even if I do not perform the like of their good works."

Agreed upon by al-Bukhārī and Muslim.

٦١/ ٦١. عَنْ أَنَسِ بْنِ مَالِكٍ رضي الله عنه أَنَّ أَعْرَابِيًّا قَالَ لِرَسُوْلِ اللهِ ﷺ: مَتَى السَّاعَةُ، يَا رَسُوْلَ اللهِ؟ قَالَ لَهُ رَسُوْلُ اللهِ ﷺ: مَا أَعْدَدْتَ لَهَا؟ قَالَ: حُبَّ اللهِ وَرَسُوْلِهِ. قَالَ: أَنْتَ مَعَ مَنْ أَحْبَبْتَ.

مُتَّفَقٌ عَلَيْهِ وَهَذَا لَفْظُ مُسْلِمٍ.

61/61. According to Anas b. Mālik رضي الله عنه:

"A Bedouin said to the Messenger of Allah ﷺ: 'When is the Final Hour, O Messenger of Allah?' Allah's Messenger ﷺ asked him: 'What have you prepared for it?' He said: 'The love of Allah and His Messenger. (That is the sole asset of my life.)" He said: 'You are together with those you love!'"

---

§352. •Aḥmad b. Ḥanbal in *al-Musnad*, 3/104, 168, 178 §12032, 12738, 12846. •Ibn Ḥibbān in *al-Ṣaḥīḥ*, 10/308 §105. •Abū Yaʿlā in *al-Musnad*, 5/372 §3023. •al-Ṭabarānī in *al-Muʿjam al-Awsaṭ*, 8/254 §8556.

[61] Set forth by •al-Bukhārī in *al-Ṣaḥīḥ*: Bk.: *al-Adab* [Proper Conduct], Ch.: The sign of love for the sake of Allah, 3/1349 §3485. •Muslim in *al-Ṣaḥīḥ*: Bk.: *al-Birr wa al-Ṣila wa al-Ādāb* [Piety, Affinity and Good Manners], Ch.: The man is together with the one he loves, 4/2032 §2639. •al-Tirmidhī in *al-Sunan*: *al-Zuhd* [Abstinence] according to Allah's Messenger ﷺ, Ch.: What has come to inform us that the man is together with the one he loves, 4/595 §2385.

Agreed upon by al-Bukhārī and Muslim, and this is the wording of Muslim.

٦٢/ ٦٢. عَنْ أَنَسِ بْنِ مَالِكٍ ﷺ قَالَ: بَيْنَمَا أَنَا وَالنَّبِيُّ ﷺ خَارِجَانِ مِنَ الْمَسْجِدِ فَلَقِيَنَا رَجُلٌ عِنْدَ سُدَّةِ الْمَسْجِدِ، فَقَالَ: يَا رَسُوْلَ اللهِ، مَتَى السَّاعَةُ؟ قَالَ النَّبِيُّ ﷺ: مَا أَعْدَدْتَ لَهَا؟ فَكَأَنَّ الرَّجُلَ اسْتَكَانَ ثُمَّ قَالَ: يَا رَسُوْلَ اللهِ، مَا أَعْدَدْتُ لَهَا كَبِيْرَ صِيَامٍ وَلاَ صَلاَةٍ وَلاَ صَدَقَةٍ وَلَكِنِّي أُحِبُّ اللهَ وَرَسُوْلَهُ. قَالَ: أَنْتَ مَعَ مَنْ أَحْبَبْتَ.

مُتَّفَقٌ عَلَيْهِ.

62/62. According to Anas b. Mālik ﷺ:

"While I and the Prophet ﷺ were leaving the mosque, a man encountered us at the gate of the mosque, so he said: 'O Messenger of Allah, when is the Final Hour?' The Prophet ﷺ said: 'What have you prepared for it?' The man remained quiet for a while; then he said: 'O Messenger of Allah, I have not prepared much fasting for it, nor ritual prayer, nor charitable donation, but I love Allah and His Messenger!" He said: 'You are together with those you love!'"

Agreed upon by al-Bukhārī and Muslim.

---

[62] Set forth by •al-Bukhārī in *al-Ṣaḥīḥ*: Bk.: *al-Aḥkām* [The Rules of Law], Ch.: Judgement and formal legal opinion in the spiritual path, 6/2615 §6734, & Bk.: *al-Adab* [Proper Conduct], Ch.: What has come to us about the man's saying: "Woe to you!" 5/2282 §5815, & Bk.: *al-Adab* [Proper Conduct], Ch.: The sign of the love of Allah ﷻ according to His saying: "Say: 'If you love Allah, follow me; Allah will love you *[qul in kuntum tuḥibbūna ʾllāha fa-ʾttabiʿūnī yuḥbib-kumu ʾllāhu]*.'" (Q.3:31), 5/2285 §5816–5819, & Bk.: The excellent merits of the Companions of the Prophet ﷺ, Ch.: The virtues of ʿUmar b. al-Khaṭṭāb, 3/1349 §3485. •Muslim in *al-Ṣaḥīḥ*: Bk.: *al-Birr wa al-Ṣila wa al-Ādāb* [Piety, Affinity and Good Manners], Ch.: The man is together with the one he loves, 4/2032–2033 §2639. •al-Tirmidhī likewise in *al-Sunan*: Bk.: *al-Zuhd* [Abstinence] according to Allah's Messenger ﷺ, Ch.: What has come to inform us that the man is together with the one he loves, 4/595 §2385, and he declared it authentic. •Ibn Khuzayma in *al-Ṣaḥīḥ*, 3/149 §1796. •Ibn Ḥibbān in *al-Ṣaḥīḥ*, 1/182 §8. •al-Ṭabarānī in *al-Muʿjam al-Awsaṭ*, 7/267 §7465.

٦٣/ ٦٣. عَنْ أَبِي ذَرٍّ ﷺ أَنَّهُ قَالَ: يَا رَسُوْلَ اللهِ، اَلرَّجُلُ يُحِبُّ الْقَوْمَ وَلَا يَسْتَطِيْعُ أَنْ يَعْمَلَ كَعَمَلِهِمْ. قَالَ: أَنْتَ، يَا أَبَا ذَرٍّ، مَعَ مَنْ أَحْبَبْتَ. قَالَ: فَإِنِّي أُحِبُّ اللهَ وَرَسُوْلَهُ. قَالَ: فَإِنَّكَ مَعَ مَنْ أَحْبَبْتَ. قَالَ: فَأَعَادَهَا أَبُوْ ذَرٍّ فَأَعَادَهَا رَسُوْلُ اللهِ ﷺ.

رَوَاهُ أَبُوْ دَاوُدَ وَأَحْمَدُ وَالْبَزَّارُ بِإِسْنَادٍ جَيِّدٍ.

63/63. Abū Dharr ﷺ is reported as having said:

"O Messenger of Allah, a man loves the people, but he does not behave as they behave!" He said: "O Abū Dharr, you are together with those you love!" Abū Dharr said: "I love Allah and His Messenger!" He said: "O Abū Dharr, you are together with those you love!" Then Abū Dharr submitted again; so Allah's Messenger ﷺ also repeated it."

Reported by Abū Dāwūd, Aḥmad and al-Bazzār with a perfect chain of transmission.

٦٤/ ٦٤. عَنْ عَبْدِ اللهِ بْنِ مُغَفَّلٍ ﷺ قَالَ: قَالَ رَجُلٌ لِلنَّبِيِّ ﷺ: يَا رَسُوْلَ اللهِ، وَاللهِ، إِنِّي لَأُحِبُّكَ. فَقَالَ: انْظُرْ مَاذَا تَقُوْلُ. قَالَ: وَاللهِ، إِنِّي لَأُحِبُّكَ. فَقَالَ: انْظُرْ مَاذَا تَقُوْلُ. قَالَ: وَاللهِ، إِنِّي لَأُحِبُّكَ، ثَلَاثَ مَرَّاتٍ. فَقَالَ: إِنْ كُنْتَ تُحِبُّنِي فَأَعِدَّ لِلْفَقْرِ تِجْفَافًا، فَإِنَّ الْفَقْرَ أَسْرَعُ إِلَى مَنْ يُحِبُّنِي مِنَ السَّيْلِ إِلَى مُنْتَهَاهُ.

رَوَاهُ التِّرْمِذِيُّ وَابْنُ حِبَّانَ، قَالَ أَبُوْ عِيْسَى: هٰذَا حَدِيْثٌ حَسَنٌ.

64/64. According to ʿAbd Allāh b. Mughaffal ﷺ:

---

[63] Set forth by •Abū Dāwūd in *al-Sunan*, Bk.: *al-Adab* [Proper Conduct], Ch.: The man's informing the man of his love for him, 4/333 §5126. •al-Bazzār in *al-Musnad*, 9/373 §395. •Ibn Ḥibbān in *al-Ṣaḥīḥ*, 2/315 §556. •al-Dārimī in *al-Sunan*, 2/414 §2787. •Aḥmad b. Ḥanbal in *al-Musnad*, 5/156 §61416, 21501. •al-Bukhārī in *al-Adab al-Mufrad*, 1/128 §351. •al-Mundhirī in *al-Targhīb wa al-Tarhīb*, 4/15 §4598.

[64] Set forth by •al-Tirmidhī in *al-Sunan*, Bk.: *al-Zuhd* [Abstinence] according to Allah's Messenger ﷺ, Ch.: What has come to us about the excellent merit

"A man said to the Prophet ﷺ: 'O Messenger of Allah! By Allah, indeed, I love you.' So he said: 'Consider what you are saying!' He again said: 'By Allah, indeed, I love you, and Allah's Messenger said: '(Once more) consider what you are saying!' He said three times: 'By Allah, I love you indeed,' so the Apostle said: 'If you do love me, you must prepare armour for poverty, because poverty comes more quickly to someone who loves me than the flood to its climax!'"

Reported by al-Tirmidhī and Ibn Ḥibbān. Abū ʿĪsā said: "This is a fine tradition."

٦٥/ ٦٥. عَنْ أَنَسِ بْنِ مَالِكٍ رضي الله عنه عَنِ النَّبِيِّ ﷺ أَنَّهُ قَالَ: لَا يُؤْمِنُ أَحَدُكُمْ حَتَّى يَكُوْنَ اللهُ وَرَسُوْلُهُ أَحَبَّ إِلَيْهِ مِمَّا سِوَاهُمَا، وَحَتَّى يُقْذَفَ فِي النَّارِ أَحَبَّ إِلَيْهِ مِنْ أَنْ يَعُوْدَ فِي الْكُفْرِ، (وفي رواية: أَنْ يَرْجِعَ يَهُودِيًّا أَوْ نَصْرَانِيًّا) بَعْدَ أَنْ نَجَّاهُ اللهُ مِنْهُ، وَلَا يُؤْمِنُ أَحَدُكُمْ حَتَّى أَكُوْنَ أَحَبَّ إِلَيْهِ مِنْ وَلَدِهِ وَوَالِدِهِ وَالنَّاسِ أَجْمَعِيْنَ.

رَوَاهُ أَحْمَدُ وَابْنُ حِبَّانَ.

65/65. According to Anas b. Mālik رضي الله عنه:

"The Prophet ﷺ said: 'None of you will truly believe until Allah and His Messenger are dearer to him than everything apart from them, and until being cast into the Fire of Hell is dearer to him than reverting to unbelief (and in one version: than returning to being a Jew or a Christian), after Allah has rescued him from it, and none of you will truly believe until I am dearer to him than his offspring and his father, and than the people altogether!'"

---

of poverty, 4/576 §2350. •Ibn Ḥibbān in *al-Ṣaḥīḥ*, 7/185 §2922. •al-Bayhaqī in *Shuʿab al-Īmān*, 2/173 §1471. •al-Rūyānī *in al-Musnad*, 2/88 §872. •al-Haythamī in *Mawārid al-Ẓamʾān*, 1/620 §2505. •al-Ḥusaynī in *al-Bayān wa al-Taʿrīf*, 1/292 §777. •al-Mizzī in *Tahdhīb al-Kamāl*, 12/398.

[65] Set forth by •Aḥmad b. Ḥanbal in *al-Musnad*, 3/207 §13174; 3/278 §13991–13992; 3/230 §13431. •Ibn Ḥibbān in *al-Ṣaḥīḥ*, 1/473 §237. •ʿAbd b. Ḥumayd in *al-Musnad*, 1/394 §1328. •Ibn Manda in *al-Īmān*, 1/433 §283. •Ibn Rajab in *Jāmiʿ al-ʿUlūm wa al-Ḥikam*, 1/33.

Reported by Aḥmad and Ibn Ḥibbān.

٦٦/ ٦٦. عَنْ عَائِشَةَ ﵂ قَالَتْ: جَاءَ رَجُلٌ إِلَى رَسُوْلِ اللهِ ﷺ فَقَالَ: يَا رَسُوْلَ اللهِ، إِنَّكَ لَأَحَبُّ إِلَيَّ مِنْ نَفْسِي وَإِنَّكَ لَأَحَبُّ إِلَيَّ مِنْ أَهْلِي وَأَحَبُّ إِلَيَّ مِنْ وَلَدِي! وَإِنِّي لَأَكُوْنُ فِي الْبَيْتِ، فَأَذْكُرُكَ فَمَا أَصْبِرُ حَتَّى آتِيَكَ فَأَنْظُرُ إِلَيْكَ. وَإِذَا ذَكَرْتُ مَوْتِي وَمَوْتَكَ عَرَفْتُ أَنَّكَ إِذَا دَخَلْتَ الْجَنَّةَ رُفِعْتَ مَعَ النَّبِيِّيْنَ، وَأَنِّي إِذَا دَخَلْتُ الْجَنَّةَ حَسِبْتُ أَنْ لَا أَرَاكَ. فَلَمْ يَرُدَّ إِلَيْهِ رَسُوْلُ اللهِ ﷺ شَيْئًا حَتَّى نَزَلَ جِبْرِيْلُ بِهَذِهِ الْآيَةِ: ﴿وَمَن يُطِعِ ٱللَّهَ وَٱلرَّسُولَ فَأُوْلَٰٓئِكَ مَعَ ٱلَّذِينَ أَنْعَمَ ٱللَّهُ عَلَيْهِم...﴾. (النساء، ٤:٦٩). فَدَعَا بِهِ فَقَرَأَهَا عَلَيْهِ.

رَوَاهُ الطَّبَرَانِيُّ وَأَبُوْنُعَيْمٍ.

66/66. According to ʿĀʾisha ﵂:

"A man came to Allah's Messenger ﷺ and said: 'O Messenger of Allah, you are indeed dearer to me than myself, and you are indeed dearer to me than my family and dearer to me than my offspring! When I am home I keep remembering you and I shall not have patience until I come to you and behold you! If I think of your death and my own death, I am aware that you will make your effulgent appearance in the Garden of Paradise elevated to the highest station amongst the Prophets. But I am afraid when I enter the Garden of Paradise, I may be deprived of beholding your countenance.' Allah's Messenger ﷺ did not give him any response, until Gabriel ﵇ descended with this Qurʾānic Verse: 'And whoever obeys Allah and His Messenger, they are the people who shall be in the company of those (spiritual dignitaries on the Last Day) whom Allah has blessed with His (special) favour... *[wa man yuṭiʿi ʾllāha wa al-Rasūla fa-ulāʾika maʿa alladhīna anʿama Allāhu ʿalay-him...].*' (Q.4:69). Then he summoned him and recited it to him."

---

66 Set forth by •al-Ṭabarānī in *al-Muʿjam al-Awsaṭ*, 1/152 §477, & in *al-Muʿjam al-Ṣaghīr*, 1/53 §52. •Abū Nuʿaym in *Ḥilya al-Awliyāʾ*, 4/240, 8/125. •al-Haythamī in *Majmaʿ al-Zawāʾid*, 7/7. •Ibn Kathīr in *Tafsīr al-Qurʾān al-ʿAẓīm*, 1/524. •al-Suyūṭī in *al-Durr al-Manthūr*, 2/182.

Reported by al-Ṭabarānī and Abū Nuʿaym.

٦٧/ ٦٧. عَنْ عَبْدِ الرَّحْمَنِ بْنِ سَعْدٍ ﷺ قَالَ: خَدِرَتْ رِجْلُ ابْنِ عُمَرَ ﷺ فَقَالَ لَهُ رَجُلٌ: اذْكُرْ أَحَبَّ النَّاسِ إِلَيْكَ. فَقَالَ: (يَا) مُحَمَّدَاهُ.

رَوَاهُ الْبُخَارِيُّ فِي الأَدَبِ.

67/67. According to ʿAbd al-Raḥmān b. Saʿd ﷺ:

"The foot of Ibn ʿUmar ﷺ became numb, so a man said to him: 'Remember the dearest of the people to you!' He called out (loudly): '(O) Muhammad, aaah!'"

Reported by al-Bukhārī in *al-Adab*.

٦٨/ ٦٨. عَنْ أَبِي هُرَيْرَةَ ﷺ عَنِ النَّبِيِّ ﷺ، قَالَ: إِذَا أَحَبَّ اللهُ الْعَبْدَ، نَادَى جِبْرِيْلَ: إِنَّ اللهَ يُحِبُّ فُلَانًا فَأَحْبِبْهُ. فَيُحِبُّهُ جِبْرِيْلُ، فَيُنَادِي جِبْرِيْلُ فِي أَهْلِ السَّمَاءِ: إِنَّ اللهَ يُحِبُّ فُلَانًا فَأَحِبُّوْهُ. فَيُحِبُّهُ أَهْلُ السَّمَاءِ، ثُمَّ يُوضَعُ لَهُ الْقَبُوْلُ فِي الأَرْضِ.

مُتَّفَقٌ عَلَيْهِ.

68/68. According to Abū Hurayra ﷺ:

---

[67] Set forth by •al-Bukhārī in *al-Adab al-Mufrad*, 1/335 §964. •Ibn al-Jaʿd in *al-Musnad*, 1/369 §2539. •Ibn Saʿd in *al-Ṭabaqāt*, 4/154. •Ibn al-Sunnī in *ʿAmal al-Yawm wa al-Layla*, §168, 170, 172. •al-Qāḍī ʿIyāḍ in *al-Shifā*, 1/498 §1218. •Yaḥyā b. Muʿīn in *al-Tārīkh*, 4/24 §2953. •al-Munāwī in *Fayḍ al-Qadīr*, 1/399. •al-Mizzī in *Tahdhīb al-Kamāl*, 17/142.

[68] Set forth by •al-Bukhārī in *al-Ṣaḥīḥ*: Bk.: *Badʾ al-Khalq* [The Beginning of Creation], Ch.: Concerning the angels, 3/1175 §3037, & Bk.: *al-Adab* [Proper Conduct], Ch.: Compassionate love from Allah ﷻ, 5/2246 §5693, & Bk.: *al-Tawḥīd* [The Affirmation of Oneness], Ch.: The Lord's conversation with Gabriel, and Allah's summoning the angels, 6/2721 §7047. •Muslim in *al-Ṣaḥīḥ*: Bk.: *al-Birr wa al-Ṣila wa al-Ādāb* [Piety, Affinity and Good Manners], Ch.: If Allah loves a servant, He endears him to His servants, 4/2030 §2637. •Mālik in *al-Muwaṭṭāʾ*, Bk.: *al-Shiʿr* [Poetry], Ch.: What has come to us about those who love one another for the sake of Allah, 2/953 §1710. •Ibn Ḥibbān in *al-Ṣaḥīḥ*, 2/86 §365. •al-Ṭabarānī in *al-Muʿjam al-*

"The Prophet ﷺ said: 'If Allah loves the servant, He calls Gabriel (and ordains): "Allah loves So-and-so, so you must love him!" Gabriel will love him, so Gabriel will proclaim to the people of heaven: "Allah loves So-and-so, so you must love him!" The people of heaven will therefore love him, and acceptance is then imbued in (the hearts of) the people on earth.'"

Agreed upon by al-Bukhārī and Muslim.

٦٩/٦٩. عَنْ أَبِي مُوْسَى رضي الله عنه عَنِ النَّبِيِّ ﷺ قَالَ: مَثَلُ الْجَلِيْسِ الصَّالِحِ وَالسُّوْءِ كَحَامِلِ الْمِسْكِ وَنَافِخِ الْكِيْرِ. فَحَامِلُ الْمِسْكِ إِمَّا أَنْ يُحْذِيَكَ، وَإِمَّا أَنْ تَبْتَاعَ مِنْهُ، وَإِمَّا أَنْ تَجِدَ مِنْهُ رِيْحًا طَيِّبَةً. وَنَافِخُ الْكِيْرِ إِمَّا أَنْ يُحْرِقَ ثِيَابَكَ، وَإِمَّا أَنْ تَجِدَ رِيْحًا خَبِيْثَةً.

مُتَّفَقٌ عَلَيْهِ.

69/69. According to Abū Mūsā رضي الله عنه:

"The Prophet ﷺ said: 'The contrast between the righteous companion and the evil one is like the contrast between the bearer of musk and the blower of bellows. As for the bearer of musk, either he gives you a share, or you purchase from him, or you obtain from him a fragrant aroma. As for the blower of bellows, either he burns your clothes, or you obtain a nauseating odour.'"

Agreed upon by al-Bukhārī and Muslim.

Awsaṭ, 3/160 §2800. •Aḥmad b. Ḥanbal in *al-Musnad*, 2/413 §9341, 10685. •al-Bayhaqī in Kitāb *al-Zuhd al-Kabīr*, 2/301 §805. •Ibn ʿUmar al-Azdī in *Musnad al-Rabīʿ*, 1/45 §67. •Ibn Rāhawayh in *al-Musnad*, 1/366 §375. •Abū al-Maḥāsin in *Muʿtaṣar al-Mukhtaṣar*, 2/228.

[69] Set forth by •al-Bukhārī in *al-Ṣaḥīḥ*: Bk.: *al-Dhabāʾiḥ wa al-Ṣayd* [Slaughter Animals and Hunting Game], Ch.: Musk, 5/2104 §5214, & Bk.: *al-Buyūʿ* [Sales], Ch.: The perfumer and the sale of musk, 2/741§1995. •Muslim in *al-Ṣaḥīḥ*: Bk.: *al-Birr wa al-Ṣila wa al-Ādāb* [Piety, Affinity and Good Manners], Ch.: Commendation of keeping company with the righteous and avoidance of the wicked, 4/2026 §7270, 7307. •al-Bayhaqī in *Shuʿab al-Īmān*, 7/54 §9435. •al-Qaḍāʿī in *Musnad al-Shihāb*, 2/288 §1380. •al-Rūyānī in *al-Musnad*, 1/318 §974. •al-Mundhirī in *al-Targhīb wa al-Tarhīb*, 4/24 §4638.

٧٠/ ٧٠. عَنْ أَبِـي هُرَيْرَةَ ﷺ قَالَ: قُلْنَا: يَا رَسُوْلَ اللهِ، مَا لَنَا إِذَا كُنَّا عِنْدَكَ رَقَّتْ قُلُوْبُنَا، وَزَهِدْنَا فِي الدُّنْيَا، وَكُنَّا مِنْ أَهْلِ الآخِرَةِ. فَإِذَا خَرَجْنَا مِنْ عِنْدِكَ فَآنَسْنَا أَهَالِيْنَا، وَشَمَمْنَا أَوْلَادَنَا أَنْكَرْنَا أَنْفُسَنَا. فَقَالَ رَسُوْلُ اللهِ ﷺ: لَوْ أَنَّكُمْ تَكُوْنُوْنَ إِذَا خَرَجْتُمْ مِنْ عِنْدِي كُنْتُمْ عَلَى حَالِكُمْ ذَلِكَ لَزَارَتْكُمُ الْـمَلَائِكَةُ فِي بُيُوْتِكُمْ، وَلَوْ لَـمْ تُذْنِبُوْا لَجَاءَ اللهُ بِخَلْقٍ جَدِيْدٍ كَي يُذْنِبُوْا فَيَغْفِرَ لَهُمْ.

رَوَاهُ التِّرْمِذِيُّ وَابْنُ حِبَّانَ.

70/70. According to Abū Hurayra ﷺ:

"We said: 'O Messenger of Allah, what is the matter with us? If we are in your presence, our hearts are softened, we abstain from this world, and we are among the people of the Hereafter. If we leave your presence, and then consort with our relatives and savour our children, our hearts undergo a change.' Allah's Messenger ﷺ said: 'If you were still in that state of yours when you left my presence, the angels would surely visit you in your homes, and if you did not sin, Allah would surely bring forth new people, so that they would sin and He would forgive them!'"

Reported by al-Tirmidhī and Ibn Ḥibbān.

٧١/ ٧١. عَنْ أَبِـي مُوْسَى ﷺ قَالَ: قَالَ رَسُوْلُ اللهِ ﷺ: مَثَلُ الْجَلِيْسِ الصَّالِحِ مَثَلُ الْعَطَّارِ؛ إِنْ لَـمْ يُصِبْكَ مِنْهُ، أَصَابَكَ رِيْحُهُ. وَمَثَلُ الْجَلِيْسِ السُّوْءِ مَثَلُ الْقَيْنِ؛ إِنْ لَـمْ يُحرِقْكَ بِشَرَرِهِ، عَلَقَ بِكَ مِنْ رِيْحِهِ.

رَوَاهُ ابْنُ حِبَّانَ وَالْبَزَّارُ وَأَحْمَدُ، وَقَالَ الْحَاكِمُ: هَذَا حَدِيْثٌ صَحِيْحُ الإِسْنَادِ.

---

[70] Set forth by •al-Tirmidhī in *al-Sunan*: Bk.: *Ṣifat al-Janna* [The Quality of the Garden of Paradise] according to Allah's Messenger ﷺ, Ch.: What has come to us about the Garden of Paradise and its felicity, 4/672 §2526. •Ibn Ḥibbān in *al-Ṣaḥīḥ*, 16/396 §3787. •al-Ṭayālisī in *al-Musnad*, 1/337 §2583. •al-Bayhaqī in *Shuʿab al-Īmān*, 5/409 §7101. •ʿAbd b. Ḥumayd in *al-Musnad*, 1/415 §1420. •Ibn al-Mubārak in *al-Zuhd*, 1/380 §1075.

71/71. According to Abū Mūsā ﵁:

"Allah's Messenger ﷺ said: 'The likeness of the righteous companion is the likeness of the perfume vendor; even if it does not touch you directly, its fragrant aroma reaches you. The likeness of the evil companion is the likeness of the blacksmith; even if the sparks (of his furnace) do not burn you, the offensive odour of his furnace does affect you.'"

Reported by Ibn Ḥibbān, al-Bazzār and Aḥmad. According to al-Ḥākim: "This is a tradition with an authentic chain of transmission."

٧٢/ ٧٢. عَنْ أَبِي سَعِيْدٍ ﵁ أَنَّهُ سَمِعَ رَسُوْلَ اللهِ ﷺ يَقُوْلُ: لَا تُصَاحِبْ إِلَّا مُؤْمِنًا، وَلَا يَأْكُلْ طَعَامَكَ إِلَّا تَقِيٌّ.

رَوَاهُ التِّرْمِذِيُّ وَأَبُوْ دَاوُدَ، وَقَالَ أَبُوْ عِيْسَى: هَذَا حَدِيْثٌ حَسَنٌ.

72/72. According to Abū Saʿīd ﵁, he heard Allah's Messenger ﷺ say:

---

[71] Set forth by •Ibn Ḥibbān in *al-Ṣaḥīḥ*, 2/341 §579. •al-Bazzār in *al-Musnad*, 8/44 §3027, 3190. •Aḥmad b. Ḥanbal in *al-Musnad*, 4/404 §19624. •al-Ḥākim in *al-Mustadrak*, 4/312 §7749. •Abū Yaʿlā in *al-Musnad*, 7/274 §4295. •al-Maqdisī in *al-Aḥādīth al-Mukhtāra*, 6/199 §2215–2216. He said: "Its chain of transmission is authentic." •al-Qaḍāʿī in *Musnad al-Shihāb*, 2/287 §1377. •Ibn Khallād in *Amthāl al-Ḥadīth*, 1/113 §77–78. •Ibn Abī ʿĀṣim in *Kitāb al-Zuhd*, 1/274. •al-Haythamī in *Majmaʿ al-Zawāʾid*, 8/61. He said: "Its chain of transmission is excellent."

[72] Set forth by •al-Tirmidhī in *al-Sunan*: Bk.: *al-Zuhd* [Abstinence] according to Allah's Messenger ﷺ, Ch.: What has come to us about the companionship of the believer, 4/600 §2395. •Abū Dāwūd in *al-Sunan*: Bk.: *al-Adab* [Proper Conduct], Ch.: Someone who is commanded to keep company, 4/259 §4832. •Ibn Ḥibbān in *al-Ṣaḥīḥ*, 2/314 §554–560. •al-Dārimī in *al-Sunan*, 2/140 §2057. •al-Ḥākim in *al-Mustadrak*, 4/143 §7169. He said: "This tradition has an authentic chain of transmission." •al-Ṭabarānī in *al-Muʿjam al-Awsaṭ*, 3/277 §3136. •Abū Yaʿlā in *al-Musnad*, 2/484 §1315. •al-Bayhaqī in *Shuʿab al-Īmān*, 7/42 §9383. •Ibn al-Mubārak in *al-Zuhd*, 1/124 §364. •al-Daylamī in *al-Firdaws bi-Maʾthūr al-Khiṭāb*, 5/351 §8403. •al-Mundhirī in *al-Targhīb wa al-Tarhīb*, 4/15 §4599.

"Do not make friends except with a (true) believer, and let no one eat your food except a pious devotee!"

Reported by al-Tirmidhī and Abū Dāwūd. Abū ʿĪsā said: "This is a fine tradition."

اَلْفَصْلُ الثَّامِنُ

فَصْلٌ فِي التَّبَرُّكِ بِالنَّبِيِّ ﷺ وَآثَارِهِ

Section 8

The Acquisition of Blessing from the Prophet ﷺ and his Relics

٧٣/ ٧٣. عَنِ السَّائِبِ ابْنِ يَزِيْدَ ﵁ يَقُوْلُ: ذَهَبَتْ بِي خَالَتِي إِلَى النَّبِيِّ ﷺ فَقَالَتْ: يَا رَسُوْلَ اللهِ، إِنَّ ابْنَ أُخْتِي وَجِعٌ. فَمَسَحَ رَأْسِي وَدَعَا لِي بِالْبَرَكَةِ. ثُمَّ تَوَضَّأَ، فَشَرِبْتُ مِنْ وَضُوئِهِ. ثُمَّ قُمْتُ خَلْفَ ظَهْرِهِ، فَنَظَرْتُ إِلَى خَاتَمِ النُّبُوَّةِ بَيْنَ كَتِفَيْهِ، مِثْلَ زِرِّ الْحَجَلَةِ.

مُتَّفَقٌ عَلَيْهِ.

73/73. According to al-Sā᾿ib b. Yazīd ﵁:

"My maternal aunt took me to the Prophet ﷺ, and she said: 'O Messenger of Allah, my sister's son is in pain,' so he caressed my head with his hand and supplicated for blessing on my behalf.

---

73 Set forth by •al-Bukhārī in *al-Ṣaḥīḥ*, Bk.: *al-Wuḍū᾿* [The Minor Ritual Ablution], Ch.: Making use of the remnants of people's minor ritual ablution, 1/81 §187, & Bk.: *al-Manāqib* [Virtues], Ch.: The patronymic appellation [*kunya*] of the Prophet ﷺ, 3/1301, 3347 & Ch.: The Seal of Prophethood [*Khātam al-Nubuwwa*], 3/1301 §3348, & Bk.: *al-Marḍā* [The Ailing], Ch.: Someone who escorts the sick youngster in order to supplicate for him, 5/2146 §5346, & Bk.: *al-Daʿawāt* [Supplications], Ch.: The supplication of blessing for the youngsters, and rubbing their heads, 5/2337 §5991. •Muslim in *al-Ṣaḥīḥ*: Bk.: *Faḍā᾿il* [The Excellent Merits], Ch.: The establishment of the Seal of Prophethood [*Khātam al-Nubuwwa*], its quality and its place on his body ﷺ, 4/1823 §2345. •al-Nasā᾿ī in *al-Sunan al-Kubrā*, 4/361 §7518. •al-Ṭabarānī in *al-Muʿjam al-Kabīr*, 7/157 §6682. •al-Shaybānī in *al-Āḥād wa al-Mathānī*, 4/379 §2420, 3430.

Then he performed the minor ritual ablution, so I drank from the water he used for his ablution. Then I stood behind his back, so I beheld the Seal of Prophethood between his shoulders, like the egg of a pigeon (or a similar bird)."

Agreed upon by al-Bukhārī and Muslim.

٧٤/ ٧٤. عَنْ أَبِي جُحَيْفَةَ ﵁ يَقُوْلُ: خَرَجَ عَلَيْنَا رَسُوْلُ اللهِ ﷺ بِالْهَاجِرَةِ، فَأُتِيَ بِوَضُوْءٍ فَتَوَضَّأَ، فَجَعَلَ النَّاسُ يَأْخُذُوْنَ مِنْ فَضْلِ وَضُوئِهِ فَيَتَمَسَّحُوْنَ بِهِ. فَصَلَّى النَّبِيُّ ﷺ الظُّهْرَ رَكْعَتَيْنِ، وَالْعَصْرَ رَكْعَتَيْنِ، وَبَيْنَ يَدَيْهِ عَنَزَةٌ. وَقَالَ أَبُوْ مُوْسَى: دَعَا النَّبِيُّ ﷺ بِقَدَحٍ فِيْهِ مَاءٌ، فَغَسَلَ يَدَيْهِ وَوَجْهَهُ فِيْهِ وَمَجَّ فِيْهِ، ثُمَّ قَالَ لَهُمَا: اشْرَبَا مِنْهُ، وَأَفْرِغَا عَلَى وُجُوْهِكُمَا وَنُحُوْرِكُمَا.

وفي رواية عنه: قَالَ: رَأَيْتُ رَسُوْلَ اللهِ ﷺ فِي قُبَّةٍ حَمْرَاءَ مِنْ أَدَمٍ، وَرَأَيْتُ بِلَالًا أَخَذَ وَضُوْءَ رَسُوْلِ اللهِ ﷺ، وَرَأَيْتُ النَّاسَ يَبْتَدِرُوْنَ ذَاكَ الْوَضُوْءَ، فَمَنْ أَصَابَ مِنْهُ شَيْئًا تَمَسَّحَ بِهِ، وَمَنْ لَمْ يُصِبْ مِنْهُ شَيْئًا أَخَذَ مِنْ بَلَلِ يَدِ صَاحِبِهِ، ثُمَّ رَأَيْتُ بِلَالًا أَخَذَ عَنَزَةً فَرَكَزَهَا، وَخَرَجَ النَّبِيُّ ﷺ فِي حُلَّةٍ حَمْرَاءَ مُشَمِّرًا. صَلَّى إِلَى الْعَنَزَةِ بِالنَّاسِ رَكْعَتَيْنِ، وَرَأَيْتُ النَّاسَ وَالدَّوَابَّ يَمُرُّوْنَ مِنْ بَيْنَ يَدَيِ الْعَنَزَةِ.

رَوَاهُ الْبُخَارِيُّ وَمُسْلِمٌ مُخْتَصَرًا.

74/74. According to Abū Juḥayfa ﵁:

---

74 Set forth by •al-Bukhārī in *al-Ṣaḥīḥ*: Bk.: *al-Wuḍū'* [The Minor Ritual Ablution], Ch.: Making use of the remnants of people's minor ritual ablution, 1/80 §185, & Bk.: *al-Ṣalāt fi' al-Thiyāb* [The Ritual Prayer in Garments], Ch.: The ritual prayer in red attire, 1/147 §369, Ch.: The tunic of the Imam is the tunic of those behind him, 1/187 §473, & Ch.: The ritual prayer towards the *ʿanaza* [short spear with an iron tip at its lower end], 1/188 §477, & Ch.: The tunic in Mecca and elsewhere, 1/188 §479, & Bk.: *al-Adhān* [The Call to Prayer], Ch.: The call to prayer for the travellers, if they are a congregations, and the announcement that the prayer is about to begin, and likewise at ʿArafa and a gathering, 1/227 §607, & Bk.: *al-Manāqib* [Virtues], Ch.:

"Allah's Messenger ﷺ came out to us in the midday heat, so water was brought and he performed the minor ritual ablution. The people then started taking from the surplus of the water used for his ablution, and wiping themselves with it. The Prophet ﷺ performed the midday ritual prayer consisting of two cycles, and the afternoon ritual prayer consisting of two cycles, while there was a spear in front of him. Abū Mūsā said: 'The Prophet ﷺ called for a bowl containing water, then he washed his hands and his face in it and spat his mouthwash into it. Then he said to them (Abū Mūsa al-Ashʿarī and Abū ʿĀmir al-Ashʿarī): 'Drink from it, and pour it over your faces and your chests!'"

In one report, he said: "I saw Allah's Messenger ﷺ in a red leather tent, and I saw Bilāl take the water used by Allah's Messenger ﷺ for his minor ritual ablution. I also saw the people rushing to that water, so anyone who obtained something from it wiped himself with it, and if someone failed to obtain something from it, he took from the moisture of his companion's hand. Then I saw Bilāl seize a spear and fix it in the ground, and the Prophet ﷺ emerged in a tucked-up red garment. Facing towards the spear, he led the people in two cycles of ritual prayer, and I saw the people and the riding animals passing in front of the spear."

Reported by al-Bukhārī and Muslim in brief.

٧٥/ ٧٥. عَنْ مَحْمُوْدِ بْنِ الرَّبِيْعِ رضي الله عنه قَالَ: وَهُوَ الَّذِي مَجَّ رَسُوْلُ اللهِ ﷺ فِي وَجْهِهِ

The quality of the Prophet ﷺ, 3/1304 §3373, & Bk.: *al-Maghāzī* [Military Expeditions], Ch.: The campaign of *al-Ṭāʾif*, 4/1573 §4073, & Bk.: *al-Libās* [Clothing], Ch.: Tucking up the garments, 5/2182 §5449, & Bk.: *al-Wuḍūʾ* [The Minor Ritual Ablution], Ch.: The major ritual ablution [*ghusl*] and the minor ritual ablution [*wuḍūʾ*] in the dyeing vat, the large drinking vessel, timber and stones, 1/83 §193. •Muslim in *al-Ṣaḥīḥ*: Bk.: *Faḍāʾil al-Ṣaḥāba* [The Excellent Merits of the Companions], Ch.: The excellent merits of Abū Mūsa and Abū ʿĀmir, the Ashʿarīs, رضي الله عنهما, 4/1943 §2497. •Abū Yaʿlā in *al-Musnad*, 13/301 §301.

وَهُوَ غُلَامٌ مِنْ بِئْرِهِمْ. وَقَالَ عُرْوَةُ عَنِ الْمِسْوَرِ وَغَيْرِهِ يُصَدِّقُ كُلُّ وَاحِدٍ مِّنْهُمَا صَاحِبَهُ: وَإِذَا تَوَضَّأَ النَّبِيُّ ﷺ كَادُوْا يَقْتَتِلُوْنَ عَلَى وَضُوئِهِ.

رَوَاهُ الْبُخَارِيُّ وَأَحْمَدُ وَابْنُ حِبَّانَ.

75/75. According to Maḥmūd b. al-Rabīʿ ؓ, he is the one in whose face when he was a child Allah's Messenger ﷺ spat his mouthwash taking water from their well, and also according to ʿUrwa, on the authority of al-Miswar and others and each of them validates his companion:

"When the Prophet ﷺ performed the minor ritual ablution, the Companions ؓ would almost fight with one another over the water he used for the purpose!"

Reported by al-Bukhārī, Aḥmad and Ibn Ḥibbān.

٧٦/ ٧٦. عَنِ الْمِسْوَرِ بْنِ مَخْرَمَةَ وَمَرْوَانَ ؓ قَالَا: إِنَّ عُرْوَةَ جَعَلَ يَرْمُقُ أَصْحَابَ النَّبِيِّ ﷺ بِعَيْنَيْهِ. قَالَ: فَوَاللهِ، مَا تَنَخَّمَ رَسُوْلُ اللهِ ﷺ نُخَامَةً إِلَّا وَقَعَتْ فِي كَفِّ رَجُلٍ مِنْهُمْ فَدَلَكَ بِهَا وَجْهَهُ وَجِلْدَهُ. وَإِذَا أَمَرَهُمُ ابْتَدَرُوْا أَمْرَهُ. وَإِذَا تَوَضَّأَ كَادُوْا يَقْتَتِلُوْنَ عَلَى وَضُوئِهِ. وَإِذَا تَكَلَّمَ خَفَضُوْا أَصْوَاتَهُمْ عِنْدَهُ وَمَا يُحِدُّوْنَ إِلَيْهِ النَّظَرَ تَعْظِيْمًا لَهُ. فَرَجَعَ عُرْوَةُ إِلَى أَصْحَابِهِ فَقَالَ: أَيْ قَوْمِ، وَاللهِ، لَقَدْ وَفَدْتُ عَلَى الْمُلُوْكِ، وَوَفَدْتُ عَلَى قَيْصَرَ وَكِسْرَى وَالنَّجَاشِيِّ، وَاللهِ، إِنْ رَأَيْتُ مَلِكًا قَطُّ يُعَظِّمُهُ أَصْحَابُهُ مَا يُعَظِّمُ

---

75 Set forth by •al-Bukhārī in *al-Ṣaḥīḥ*: Bk.: *al-Wuḍū*ʾ [The Minor Ritual Ablution], Ch.: Making use of the remnants of people's minor ritual ablution, 1/81 §186, & Bk.: *al-ʿIlm* [Knowledge], Ch.: When is the hearing of the infant correct? 1/41 §77, & Bk.: *al-Daʿawāt* [The Supplications], Ch.: The supplication of blessing for the youngsters, and rubbing their heads, 53/2338 §5993. •Ibn Ḥibbān in *al-Ṣaḥīḥ*, 11/221 §4872. •ʿAbd al-Razzāq in *al-Muṣannaf*, 5/336 §9720. •Aḥmad b. Ḥanbal in *al-Musnad*, 4/329. •al-Ṭabarānī in *al-Muʿjam al-Kabīr*, 20/12 §13. •al-Bayhaqī in *al-Sunan al-Kubrā*, 9/220, & in *Shuʿab al-Īmān*, 5/333 §6829. •al-ʿAsqalānī in *Fatḥ al-Bārī*, 11/151 §5993.

أَصْحَابُ مُحَمَّدٍ ﷺ مُحَمَّدًا. وَاللهِ، إِنْ تَنَخَّمَ نُخَامَةً إِلاَّ وَقَعَتْ فِي كَفِّ رَجُلٍ مِنْهُمْ فَدَلَكَ بِهَا وَجْهَهُ وَجِلْدَهُ. وَإِذَا أَمَرَهُمُ ابْتَدَرُوا أَمْرَهُ. وَإِذَا تَوَضَّأَ كَادُوا يَقْتَتِلُوْنَ عَلَى وَضُوئِهِ. وَإِذَا تَكَلَّمَ خَفَضُوا أَصْوَاتَهُمْ عِنْدَهُ وَمَا يُحِدُّوْنَ إِلَيْهِ النَّظَرَ تَعْظِيْمًا لَهُ.

رَوَاهُ الْبُخَارِيُّ وَأَحْمَدُ.

76/76. According to al-Miswar b. Makhrama and Marwān ☺:

"'Urwa (when he came to the Messenger of Allah as an advocate of the unbelievers) kept observing the Companions of the Prophet (and saw how they would practise extreme veneration of the Holy Messenger of Allah ﷺ). He said: 'By Allah, whenever Allah's Messenger ﷺ cleared his throat of some secretion or saliva, one of his Companions would take it on the palm of his hand so he would rub it on his face and his skin. If he gave them a command, they would make haste to obey his command. If he performed the minor ablution, they would almost fight with one another over the water he has used for the purpose. If he spoke, they would lower their voices in his presence, and would not raise their looks to see him in deep love, submissiveness and reverence for him (permeating their hearts).' 'Urwa therefore returned to his companions and said: 'O my people, by Allah, I have visited the kings! I have visited Caesar, Chosroes and Najāshī, and by Allah, I have never seen a king revered by his companions to the extent that the Companions of Muhammad ﷺ revere Muhammad! By Allah, whenever Allah's Messenger ﷺ cleared his throat of some sputum or saliva, one of his Companions would take it on the palm of his hand so he would rub it on his face and his skin. If he gave them a command, they would make haste to obey his command. If he performed the minor ablution, they would almost fight with one

---

[76] Set forth by •al-Bukhārī in *al-Ṣaḥīḥ*: Bk.: *al-Shurūṭ* [The Stipulations], Ch.: The stipulations applied to the Sacred Struggle, reconciliation with the warriors, and ransom, 2/974 §2581. •Aḥmad b. Ḥanbal in *al-Musnad*, 4/329. •al-Ṭabarānī in *al-Muʿjam al-Kabīr*, 20/9 §13. •Ibn Ḥibbān in *al-Ṣaḥīḥ*, 11/216 §4872. •al-Bayhaqī in *al-Sunan al-Kubrā*, 9/220.

another over the water he has used for the purpose. If he spoke, they would lower their voices in his presence, and would not raise their looks to see him in deep love, submissiveness and reverence for him (permeating their hearts).'"

Reported by al-Bukhārī and Aḥmad.

٧٧/ ٧٧. عَنْ أَنَسِ بْنِ مَالِكٍ ﵁ قَالَ: لَمَّا رَمَى رَسُوْلُ اللهِ ﷺ الْجَمْرَةَ وَنَحَرَ نُسُكَهُ وَحَلَقَ، نَاوَلَ الْحَالِقُ شِقَّهُ الْأَيْمَنَ فَحَلَقَهُ، ثُمَّ دَعَا أَبَا طَلْحَةَ الْأَنْصَارِيَّ فَأَعْطَاهُ إِيَّاهُ، ثُمَّ نَاوَلَهُ الشِّقَّ الْأَيْسَرَ، فَقَالَ: احْلِقْ. فَحَلَقَهُ، فَأَعْطَاهُ أَبَا طَلْحَةَ، فَقَالَ: اقْسِمْهُ بَيْنَ النَّاسِ.

رَوَاهُ مُسْلِمٌ وَالتِّرْمِذِيُّ، وَقَالَ التِّرْمِذِيُّ: هَذَا حَدِيْثٌ حَسَنٌ صَحِيْحٌ.

77/77. According to Anas b. Mālik ﵁:

"When Allah's Messenger ﷺ threw the pebbles at Jamra, and slaughtered his sacrificial animal, he turned the right side of his holy head before the barber and he shaved the holy hair off. Then Allah's Messenger summoned Abū Ṭalḥā al-Anṣārī and gifted all the shaved hair to him. Then he asked the barber for the left half and said: 'Shave,' so he shaved it. Then he gave it to Abū Ṭalḥā and said: 'Distribute it among the people!'"

Reported by Muslim and al-Tirmidhī. And al-Tirmidhī said: "This is a fine authentic tradition."

---

77 Set forth by •Muslim in *al-Ṣaḥīḥ*: Bk.: *al-Ḥajj* [The Pilgrimage], Ch.: Explanation of the customary practice of the Day of Sacrifice [*Yawm al-Naḥr*], which is that the Pilgrim throws, then slaughters, then shaves, 2/948 §1305. •al-Tirmidhī in *al-Sunan*: Bk.: *al-Ḥajj* [The Pilgrimage] according to Allah's Messenger ﷺ, Ch.: What has come to us about which side of the head is shaved first, 3/255 §912. •Abū Dāwūd in *al-Sunan*: Bk.: *al-Manāsik* [The Pilgrim Ceremonies], Ch.: Shaving and shortening the hair, 2/203 §1981. •al-Nasā'ī in *al-Sunan al-Kubrā*, 2/449 §4114. •Aḥmad b. Ḥanbal in *al-Musnad*, 3/111 §12113. •Ibn Ḥibbān in *al-Ṣaḥīḥ*, 9/191 §1743. •Ibn Khuzayma in *al-Ṣaḥīḥ*, 4/299 §2928. •al-Ḥākim in *al-Mustadrak*, 1/647 §1743. He said: "This is an authentic tradition."

٧٨/ ٧٨. عَنْ أَنَسِ بْنِ مَالِكٍ ﷺ قَالَ: لَقَدْ رَأَيْتُ رَسُوْلَ اللهِ ﷺ، وَالْحَلاَّقُ يَحْلِقُهُ وَأَطَافَ بِهِ أَصْحَابُهُ، فَمَا يُرِيْدُوْنَ أَنْ تَقَعَ شَعْرَةٌ إِلاَّ فِي يَدِ رَجُلٍ.

رَوَاهُ مُسْلِمٌ وَأَحْمَدُ.

78/78. According to Anas b. Mālik ﷺ:

"I once saw Allah's Messenger ﷺ while the barber was shaving him, and his Companions were encircling him, (each one of them) making utmost effort not to let even a single hair drop but into the hands of one of them!"

Reported by Muslim and Aḥmad.

٧٩/ ٧٩. عَنِ ابْنِ سِيْرِيْنَ قَالَ: قُلْتُ لِعُبَيْدَةَ: عِنْدَنَا مِنْ شَعَرِ النَّبِيِّ ﷺ، أَصَبْنَاهُ مِنْ قِبَلِ أَنَسٍ ﷺ، أَوْ مِنْ قِبَلِ أَهْلِ أَنَسٍ ﷺ، فَقَالَ: لَأَنْ تَكُوْنَ عِنْدِي شَعَرَةٌ مِنْهُ أَحَبَّ إِلَيَّ مِنَ الدُّنْيَا وَمَا فِيْهَا.

رَوَاهُ الْبُخَارِيُّ.

79/79. According to Ibn Sīrīn:

"I said to ʿUbayda: 'We have some hairs of the Prophet ﷺ, which we obtained from the possession of Anas ﷺ, or from the possession of the family of Anas,' so he said: 'To have one hair of his in my possession would surely be dearer to me than this world and what it contains!'"

Reported by al-Bukhārī.

---

78 Set forth by •Muslim in *al-Ṣaḥīḥ*: Bk.: *al-Faḍāʾil* [Excellent Merits], Ch.: The nearness of the Prophet ﷺ to the people, and their enjoyment of its blessing, 4/1812 §2325. •Aḥmad b. Ḥanbal in *al-Musnad*, 3/133, 137 §12423. •ʿAbd b. Ḥumayd in *al-Musnad*, 1/380 §1273.

79 Set forth by •al-Bukhārī in *al-Ṣaḥīḥ*: Bk.: *al-Wuḍūʾ* [The Minor Ritual Ablution], Ch.: The water with which the person washes some hair, for it was an unseen gift, 7/67 §13188. •al-Bayhaqī in *al-Sunan al-Kubrā*, 7/67 §13188.

٨٠/ ٨٠. عَنْ عَبْدِ اللهِ ﷺ مَوْلَى أَسْمَاءَ بِنْتِ أَبِي بَكْرٍ ﷺ فِي رِوَايَةٍ طَوِيلَةٍ قَالَ: أَخْبَرَتْنِي أَسْمَاءُ بِنْتُ أَبِي بَكْرٍ ﷺ عَنْ جُبَّةِ النَّبِيِّ ﷺ فَقَالَتْ: هَذِهِ جُبَّةُ رَسُوْلِ اللهِ ﷺ. فَأَخْرَجَتْ إِلَيَّ جُبَّةَ طَيَالِسَةٍ كِسْرَوَانِيَّةٍ؛ لَهَا لِبْنَةُ دِيْبَاجٍ فَرْجَيْهَا مَكْفُوْفَيْنِ بِالدِّيْبَاجِ. فَقَالَتْ: هَذِهِ كَانَتْ عِنْدَ عَائِشَةَ حَتَّى قُبِضَتْ، فَلَمَّا قُبِضَتْ قَبَضْتُهَا وَكَانَ النَّبِيُّ ﷺ يَلْبَسُهَا، فَنَحْنُ نَغْسِلُهَا لِلْمَرْضَى؛ يُسْتَشْفَى بِهَا.

رَوَاهُ مُسْلِمٌ وَأَبُوْ دَاوُدَ.

80/80. According to ʿAbd Allāh ﷺ, the freedman of Asmāʾ, the daughter of Abū Bakr ﷺ, in the course of a detailed report:

"Asmāʾ, the daughter of Abū Bakr ﷺ, informed me about the cloak of the Prophet ﷺ. She said: 'This is the cloak of Allah's Messenger ﷺ,' and she showed me a cloak in the form of a royal Persian shawl, a thick streaked Caesarian one (ascribed to Caesar) with a breast of brocaded silk and both of its apertures hemmed with brocaded silk. Then she said: 'This was in the possession of ʿĀʾisha ﷺ until she departed this life, so I took it when she passed away. This is the cloak the Prophet ﷺ used to wear. So we wash it for the sick to be restored to health (by drinking the water obtained from its wash)!'"

Reported by Muslim and Abū Dāwūd.

٨١/ ٨١. عَنْ أَنَسِ بْنِ مَالِكٍ ﷺ قَالَ: كَانَ النَّبِيُّ ﷺ يَدْخُلُ بَيْتَ أُمِّ سُلَيْمٍ ﷺ فَيَنَامُ عَلَى فِرَاشِهَا وَلَيْسَتْ فِيْهِ. قَالَ: فَجَاءَ ذَاتَ يَوْمٍ فَنَامَ عَلَى فِرَاشِهَا. فَأُتِيَتْ فَقِيْلَ

---

80 Set forth by •Muslim in *al-Ṣaḥīḥ*: Bk.: *al-Libās wa al-Zīna* [Clothing and Adornment], Ch.: Prohibition of the use of the container of gold and silver for the men, 3/1641§2069. •Abū Dāwūd in *al-Sunan*: Bk.: *al-Libās* [Clothing], Ch.: The licence applied to the badge and the silk thread, 4/49 §4054. •al-Bayhaqī in *al-Sunan al-Kubrā*, 2/423 §4010, & in *Shuʿab al-Īmān*, 5/141 §6108. •Abū ʿAwāna in *al-Musnad*, 1/230 §511. •Ibn Rāhawayh in *al-Musnad*, 1/133 §30.

لَهَا: هَذَا النَّبِيُّ ﷺ نَامَ فِي بَيْتِكِ، عَلَى فِرَاشِكِ. قَالَ: فَجَاءَتْ وَقَدْ عَرِقَ وَاسْتَنْقَعَ عَرَقُهُ عَلَى قِطْعَةِ أَدِيمٍ عَلَى الْفِرَاشِ. فَفَتَحَتْ عَتِيدَتَهَا فَجَعَلَتْ تُنَشِّفُ ذَلِكَ الْعَرَقَ فَتَعْصِرُهُ فِي قَوَارِيرِهَا. فَفَزِعَ النَّبِيُّ ﷺ فَقَالَ: مَا تَصْنَعِينَ، يَا أُمَّ سُلَيْمٍ؟ فَقَالَتْ: يَا رَسُوْلَ اللهِ، نَرْجُو بَرَكَتَهُ لِصِبْيَانِنَا. قَالَ: أَصَبْتِ.

رَوَاهُ مُسْلِمٌ وَأَحْمَدُ.

81/81. According to Anas b. Mālik ﵁:

"The Prophet ﷺ used to enter the home of Umm Sulaym ﵂, and he used to sleep on her bed when she would not be home. He came one day and slept on her bed. Then she came home, so she was told: 'This is the Prophet ﷺ! He is taking a nap in your house, on your bed!' When she arrived, he had perspired, and his sweat had accumulated on a patch of leather on the bed. She therefore opened her toolbox and started wiping up that sweat, squeezing it into her long-necked bottles. The Prophet ﷺ was alarmed, so he exclaimed: 'What are you doing, O Umm Sulaym?' She said: 'O Messenger of Allah, we will acquire blessing for our children (and will use it as perfume)!' He said: 'You have done the right thing!'"

Reported by Muslim and Aḥmad.

[81] 56: Set forth by •Muslim in *al-Ṣaḥīḥ*: Bk.: *al-Faḍā'il* [Excellent Merits], Ch.: The perfume of the Prophet's sweat ﷺ, and enjoying its blessing, 4/1815 §2331. •Aḥmad b. Ḥanbal in *al-Musnad,* 3/221 §1334, 1339.

اَلْفَصْلُ التَّاسِعُ

فَصْلٌ فِي التَّوَسُّلِ بِالنَّبِيِّ ﷺ وَالصَّالِحِيْنَ

Section 9

Intermediation through the Prophet ﷺ and the Righteous

٨٢/ ٨٢. عَنْ أَنَسٍ رضي الله عنه أَنَّ عُمَرَ بْنَ الْخَطَّابِ رضي الله عنه كَانَ إِذَا قُحِطُوْا اسْتَسْقَى بِالْعَبَّاسِ بْنِ عَبْدِ الْمُطَّلِبِ رضي الله عنه فَقَالَ: اَللّٰهُمَّ، إِنَّا كُنَّا نَتَوَسَّلُ إِلَيْكَ بِنَبِيِّنَا فَتَسْقِيْنَا. وَإِنَّا نَتَوَسَّلُ إِلَيْكَ بِعَمِّ نَبِيِّنَا فَاسْقِنَا. قَالَ: فَيُسْقَوْنَ.

رَوَاهُ الْبُخَارِيُّ وَابْنُ خُزَيْمَةَ وَابْنُ حِبَّانَ.

82/82. According to Anas رضي الله عنه:

"When they were afflicted by drought, ʿUmar b. al-Khaṭṭāb رضي الله عنه would seek intermediation of al-ʿAbbās b. ʿAbd al-Muṭṭalib رضي الله عنه for downpour; so he would say: 'O Allah, we used to seek Your help by means of our Prophet, so You would bring forth rain! We are now seeking Your help by means of the paternal uncle of our Prophet, so give us rain!' The rain would then fall."

Reported by al-Bukhārī, Ibn Khuzayma and Ibn Ḥibbān.

---

[82] Set forth by •al-Bukhārī in *al-Ṣaḥīḥ*: Bk.: *al-Istisqā'* [The Prayer for Rain], Ch.: The people's asking the Imam to pray for rain when they are afflicted with drought, 1/342 §964, & Bk.: *Faḍā'il al-Ṣaḥāba* [The Excellent Merits of the Companions], Ch.: Concerning al-ʿAbbās b. ʿAbd al-Muṭṭalib رضي الله عنه, 3/1360 §3507. •Ibn Ḥibbān in *al-Ṣaḥīḥ*, 7/110 §2861. •al-Ṭabarānī in *al-Muʿjam al-Awsaṭ*, 3/49 §2437. •al-Bayhaqī in *al-Sunan al-Kubrā*, 3/352 §6220. •al-Shaybānī in *al-Āḥād wa al-Mathānī*, 1/270 §351. •Hibat Allāh in *Karāmāt al-Awliyā'*, 1/135 §87. •Ibn ʿAbd al-Barr in *al-Istīʿāb*, 2/814. •Ibn Jarīr al-Ṭabarī *in Tārīkh al-Umam wa al-Mulūk*, 4/433.

٨٣/٨٣. عَنْ عَبْدِ اللهِ ابْنِ دِينَارٍ ﷺ قَالَ: سَمِعْتُ ابْنَ عُمَرَ ﷺ يَتَمَثَّلُ بِشِعْرِ أَبِي طَالِبٍ:

وَأَبْيَضَ يُسْتَسْقَى الْغَمَامُ بِوَجْهِهِ

ثِمَالُ الْيَتَامَى عِصْمَةٌ لِلْأَرَامِلِ

وَقَالَ عُمَرُ بْنُ حَمْزَةَ: حَدَّثَنَا سَالِمٌ عَنْ أَبِيهِ: رُبَّمَا ذَكَرْتُ قَوْلَ الشَّاعِرِ، وَأَنَا أَنْظُرُ إِلَى وَجْهِ النَّبِيِّ ﷺ يَسْتَسْقِي، فَمَا يَنْزِلُ حَتَّى يَجِيشَ كُلُّ مِيزَابٍ.

وَأَبْيَضَ يُسْتَسْقَى الْغَمَامُ بِوَجْهِهِ

ثِمَالُ الْيَتَامَى عِصْمَةٌ لِلْأَرَامِلِ

وَهُوَ قَوْلُ أَبِي طَالِبٍ.

رَوَاهُ الْبُخَارِيُّ وَابْنُ مَاجَه وَأَحْمَدُ.

83/83. According to ʿAbd Allāh b. Dīnār 🙵:

"I heard Ibn ʿUmar 🙵 quote the poem of Abū Ṭālib:

Clearly the clouds are asked for rain by means of his effulgent face. The protector of the orphans is a refuge for the widows."

ʿUmar b. Ḥamza said: "Sālim told us that his father said: 'I have often recalled the saying of the poet, while beholding the divinely

83 Set forth by •al-Bukhārī in al-Ṣaḥīḥ: Bk.: al-Istisqāʾ [The Prayer for Rain], Ch.: The people's asking the Imam to pray for rain when they are afflicted with drought, 1/342 §963. •Ibn Mājah in al-Sunan: Bk.: Performance of the Ritual Prayer and the Sunna therein, Ch.: What has come to us about the supplication in the Ritual Prayer for Rain, 1/405 §1272. •Aḥmad b. Ḥanbal in al-Musnad, 2/93 §5673, 26. •al-Bayhaqī in al-Sunan al-Kubrā, 3/352 §6218–6219. •al-Khaṭīb in Tārīkh Baghdād, 14/386 §7700. •al-ʿAsqalānī in Taʿlīq al-Taʿlīq, 2/389 §1009. •Ibn Kathīr in al-Bidāya wa al-Nihāya, 4/2 §471. •al-Mizzī in Tuḥfat al-Ashrāf, 5/359 §6775.

illumined face of the Esteemed Messenger of Allah ﷺ praying for rain. So he would not even descend (from the pulpit) until the rain would flow in every channel:

> Clearly the clouds are asked for rain by means of his effulgent face. The protector of the orphans is a refuge for the widows.

—and that is the saying of Abū Ṭālib.'"

Reported by al-Bukhārī, Ibn Mājah and Aḥmad.

٨٤/ ٨٤. عَنْ عُثْمَانَ بْنِ حُنَيْفٍ رضي الله عنه أَنَّ رَجُلاً ضَرِيرَ الْبَصَرِ أَتَى النَّبِيَّ ﷺ فَقَالَ: ادْعُ اللهَ لِي أَنْ يُعَافِيَنِي. فَقَالَ: إِنْ شِئْتَ أَخَّرْتُ لَكَ وَهُوَ خَيْرٌ وَإِنْ شِئْتَ دَعَوْتُ. فَقَالَ: ادْعُهُ. فَأَمَرَهُ أَنْ يَتَوَضَّأَ فَيُحْسِنَ وُضُوءَهُ وَيُصَلِّيَ رَكْعَتَيْنِ وَيَدْعُوَ بِهَذَا الدُّعَاءِ: اَللَّهُمَّ، إِنِّي أَسْأَلُكَ وَأَتَوَجَّهُ إِلَيْكَ بِمُحَمَّدٍ نَبِيِّ الرَّحْمَةِ. يَا مُحَمَّدُ، إِنِّي قَدْ تَوَجَّهْتُ بِكَ إِلَى رَبِّي فِي حَاجَتِي هَذِهِ لِتُقْضَى. اَللَّهُمَّ، فَشَفِّعْهُ فِيَّ.

رَوَاهُ التِّرْمِذِيُّ وَالنَّسَائِيُّ وَابْنُ مَاجَه وَاللَّفْظُ لَهُ. وَقَالَ أَبُوْ عِيسَى: هَذَا حَدِيْثٌ حَسَنٌ صَحِيْحٌ، وَقَالَ أَبُوْ إِسْحَاقَ: هَذَا حَدِيْثٌ صَحِيحٌ، وَقَالَ الْحَاكِمُ: هَذَا حَدِيْثٌ صَحِيْحٌ عَلَى شَرْطِ الشَّيْخَيْنِ، وَقَالَ الْهَيْثَمِيُّ: حَدِيْثٌ صَحِيْحٌ، وَقَالَ الْأَلْبَانِيُّ: صَحِيْحٌ.

84/84. According to ʿUthmān b. Ḥunayf رضي الله عنه:

---

[84] Set forth by •al-Tirmidhī in *al-Sunan*: Bk.: *al-Daʿawāt* [Supplications] according to Allah's Messenger ﷺ, Ch.: (119), 5/569 §3578. •al-Nasāʾī in *al-Sunan al-Kubrā*, 6/168 §10494–10495. •Ibn Mājah in *al-Sunan*, Bk.: Performance of the Ritual Prayer and the Sunna therein, Ch.: What has come to us about the Prayer of Need [*Ṣalāt al-Ḥāja*], 1/441 §1385. •Ibn Khuzayma in *al-Ṣaḥīḥ*, 2/225 §1219. •al-Ḥākim in *al-Mustadrak*, 1/458, 700, 707 §1180, 1909, 1929. •Aḥmad b. Ḥanbal in *al-Musnad*, 4/138 §17240–17242. •al-Ṭabarānī in *al-Muʿjam al-Ṣaghīr*, 1/306 §508, & in *al-Muʿjam al-Kabīr*, 9/30 §8311. •al-Bukhārī in *al-Tārīkh al-Kabīr*, 6/209 §2192. •ʿAbd b. Ḥumayd in *al-Musnad*, 1/147 §379. •al-Nasāʾī in *ʿAmal al-Yawm wa al-Layla*, 1/417 §658–660. •al-Mundhirī in *al-Targhīb wa al-Tarhīb*, 1/272 §1018. •al-

"A blind man came to the Prophet ﷺ and said: 'Supplicate Allah on my behalf, so that He may cure me (restore my eyesight)!' He replied: 'If you wish, I shall delay for you, for that is good, and if you wish, I shall supplicate.' The man said: 'Supplicate Him,' so he commanded him to perform the minor ritual ablution and perform it well, to perform two cycles of ritual prayer, and to supplicate with this supplication: 'O Allah, I submit my request to You, and I supplicate You by means of Muhammad, the Prophet of Mercy! O Muhammad, I have prayed by means of you to my Lord, so that this need of mine may be fulfilled! O Allah, so approve the intercession of Your Beloved Messenger on my behalf!'"

> Reported by al-Tirmidhī, al-Nasāʾī and Ibn Mājah (the wording is his). Abū ʿĪsā said: "This is a fine authentic tradition," Abū Isḥāq said: "This is an authentic tradition," al-Ḥākim said: "This is an authentic tradition in conformity with the stipulation of al-Bukhārī and Muslim," al-Haythamī said: "An authentic tradition," and al-Albānī said: "Authentic."

٨٥/ ٨٥. عَنْ أَبِي الْجَوْزَاءِ أَوْسِ بْنِ عَبْدِ اللهِ رضي الله عنه قَالَ: قُحِطَ أَهْلُ الْمَدِيْنَةِ قَحْطًا شَدِيْدًا فَشَكَوْا إِلَى عَائِشَةَ رضي الله عنها فَقَالَتْ: انْظُرُوْا قَبْرَ النَّبِيِّ ﷺ فَاجْعَلُوا مِنْهُ كُوًى إِلَى السَّمَاءِ حَتَّى لاَ يَكُوْنَ بَيْنَهُ وَبَيْنَ السَّمَاءِ سَقْفٌ. قَالَ: فَفَعَلُوْا. فَمُطِرْنَا مَطَرًا حَتَّى نَبَتَ الْعُشْبُ وَسَمِنَتِ الإِبِلُ حَتَّى تَفَتَّقَتْ مِنَ الشَّحْمِ فَسُمِّيَ عَامَ الْفَتْقِ.

رَوَاهُ الدَّارِمِيُّ.

85/85. According to Abū al-Jawzāʾ Aws b. ʿAbd Allāh رضي الله عنه:

Haythamī in *Majmaʿ al-Zawāʾid*, 2/279.

85 Set forth by •al-Dārimī in *al-Sunan*: Ch. (15): The honour bestowed by Allah عَزَّ وَجَلَّ upon His Prophet ﷺ after his death, 1/56 §92. •al-Khaṭīb al-Tabrīzī in *Mishkāt al-Maṣābīḥ*, 2/400 §5950. •Ibn al-Jawzī in *al-Wafāʾ bi-Aḥwāl al-Muṣṭafā (Ṣall Allāhu ʿalay-hi was sallam)*, 2/801. •Taqiyy al-Dīn al-Sabukī in *Shifāʾ al-Saqām*, 1/128. •al-Qasṭallānī in *al-Mawāhib al-Laduniyya*, 4/276. •al-Zurqānī in *Sharḥ ʿalā al- Muwaṭṭāʾ*, 11/150.

"The people of Medina were afflicted by a severe drought, so they complained to the Mother of the Believers ʿĀʾisha ؓ (of their miserable plight) and she said: 'Visit the holy tomb of the Prophet ﷺ and make an aperture in it towards the sky, so that there will be no roof or barrier between it and the sky!' They acted accordingly. So we were showered with rain until the grass grew and the camels became so fat and swollen in the flanks that (it seemed) they would burst. It was for this reason that the year became known as the year of bursting (of bellies or the year of superabundance)."

Reported by al-Dārimī.

٨٦/ ٨٦. عَنْ مَالِكِ الدَّارِ ؓ قَالَ: أَصَابَ النَّاسَ قَحْطٌ فِيْ زَمَنِ عُمَرَ ؓ، فَجَاءَ رَجُلٌ إِلَى قَبْرِ النَّبِيِّ ﷺ فَقَالَ: يَا رَسُوْلَ اللهِ، اسْتَسْقِ لِأُمَّتِكَ فَإِنَّهُمْ قَدْ هَلَكُوْا. فَأَتَى الرَّجُلَ فِي الْمَنَامِ فَقِيْلَ لَهُ: ائْتِ عُمَرَ فَأَقْرِئْهُ السَّلَامَ، وَأَخْبِرْهُ أَنَّكُمْ مَسْقِيُّوْنَ وَقُلْ لَهُ: عَلَيْكَ الْكِيْسُ! عَلَيْكَ الْكِيْسُ! فَأَتَى عُمَرَ فَأَخْبَرَهُ فَبَكَى عُمَرُ ثُمَّ قَالَ: يَا رَبِّ، لَا آلُوْ إِلَّا مَا عَجَزْتُ عَنْهُ.

رَوَاهُ ابْنُ أَبِي شَيْبَةَ بِإِسْنَادٍ صَحِيْحٍ وَالْبَيْهَقِيُّ فِي الدَّلَائِلِ.

86/86. According to Mālik al-Dār ؓ:

"A drought afflicted the people in the time of ʿUmar ؓ, so a man came to the shrine of the Prophet ﷺ and said: 'O Messenger of Allah, pray for rain for your *Umma* (Community), for they have perished (owing to famine)!' He therefore came to the man in a dream, and he was told: 'Go to ʿUmar and extend to him the salutation of peace and tell him: You will be supplied with

[86] Set forth by •Ibn Abī Shayba in *al-Muṣannaf*, 6/356 §32002. •Ibn Taymiyya in *Iqtiḍāʾ al-Ṣirāṭ al-Mustaqīm*, 1/373. •al-Bayhaqī in *Dalāʾil al-Nubuwwa*, 7/47. •Ibn ʿAbd al-Barr in *al-Istīʿāb*, 3/1149. •al-Subkī in *Shifāʾ al-Saqām*, 1/130. •al-Hindī in *Kanz al-ʿUmmāl*, 8/431 §23535. •Ibn Kathīr in *al-Bidāya wa al-Nihāya*, 5/167. He said: "Its chain of transmission is authentic." •al-ʿAsqalānī in *al-Iṣāba*, 3/484. He said: "It has been reported by Ibn Abī Shayba with an authentic chain of transmission."

water; and also say to him: (The foes of faith are about to kill you so) be sagacious, be sagacious!' He therefore came to ʿUmar and informed him, so ʿUmar wept and said: 'O my Lord, I do not fail to perform except that of which I am incapable!'"

Reported by Ibn Abī Shayba with an authentic chain of transmission; and reported by al-Bayhaqī in *al-Dalāʾil*.

٨٧/ ٨٧. عَنِ ابْنِ عُمَرَ رضي الله عنهما أَنَّهُ قَالَ: اسْتَقَى عُمَرُ بْنُ الْخَطَّابِ رضي الله عنه عَامَ الرَّمَادَةِ بِالْعَبَّاسِ بْنِ عَبْدِ الْمُطَّلِبِ رضي الله عنهما فَقَالَ: اَللَّهُمَّ، هَذَا عَمُّ نَبِيِّكَ الْعَبَّاسُ. نَتَوَجَّهُ إِلَيْكَ بِهِ فَاسْقِنَا. فَمَا بَرِحُوْا حَتَّى سَقَاهُمُ اللهُ. قَالَ: فَخَطَبَ عُمَرُ النَّاسَ فَقَالَ: أَيُّهَا النَّاسُ، إِنَّ رَسُوْلَ اللهِ صلى الله عليه وآله وسلم كَانَ يَرَى لِلْعَبَّاسِ مَا يَرَى الْوَلَدُ لِوَالِدِهِ. يُعَظِّمُهُ وَيُفَخِّمُهُ وَيَبَرُّ قَسَمَهُ. فَاقْتَدُوْا، أَيُّهَا النَّاسُ، بِرَسُوْلِ اللهِ فِي عَمِّهِ الْعَبَّاسِ وَاتَّخِذُوْهُ وَسِيْلَةً إِلَى اللهِ سبحانه وتعالى فِيْمَا نَزَلَ بِكُمْ.

رَوَاهُ الْحَاكِمُ.

87/87. According to Ibn ʿUmar ﷺ:

"ʿUmar b. al-Khaṭṭāb ﷺ prayed for rain in the year of the drought by means of al-ʿAbbās b. ʿAbd al-Muṭṭalib ﷺ. So he said: 'O Allah, this is al-ʿAbbās, the paternal uncle of Your Esteemed Messenger! We pray to You (for Your Kindness and Compassion) by means of him, so quench our thirst!' They were still in prayer when Allah sent upon them torrents of water and quenched their thirst. Then ʿUmar delivered a sermon to the people in which he said: 'O people, Allah's Messenger ﷺ used to see fit for al-ʿAbbās what the son sees fit for his father, extolling him, revering him and respecting his oath. You must therefore follow the example,

---

[87] Set forth by •al-Ḥākim in *al-Mustadrak*, 3/377 §5438. •Ibn ʿAbd al-Barr in *al-Istīʿāb*, 3/98. •al-Suyūṭī in *al-Jāmiʿ al-Ṣaghīr*, 1/305 §559. •al-Dhahabī in *Siyar Aʿlām al-Nubalāʾ*, 2/92. •al-ʿAsqalānī in *Fatḥ al-Bārī*, 2/497. •al-Qasṭallānī in *al-Mawāhib al-Laduniyya*, 4/277. •al-Subkī in *Shifāʾ al-Saqām*, 1/128. •al-Mubārakfūrī in *Tuḥfat al-Aḥwadhī*, 9/348. •al-Munāwī in *Fayḍ al-Qadīr*, 5/215.

O people, of Allah's Messenger in relation to his paternal uncle al-ʿAbbās, and treat him as a means of access to Allah ﷻ in what has befallen you (so that He sends down to you rain and mercy)!'"

Reported by al-Ḥākim.

٨٨/ ٨٨. عَنْ مُصْعَبِ ابْنِ سَعْدٍ ؓ قَالَ: رَأَى سَعْدٌ ؓ أَنَّ لَهُ فَضْلاً عَلَى مَنْ دُوْنَهُ، فَقَالَ النَّبِيُّ ﷺ: هَلْ تُنْصَرُوْنَ وَتُرْزَقُوْنَ إِلاَّ بِضُعَفَائِكُمْ.

رَوَاهُ الْبُخَارِيُّ وَالتِّرْمِذِيُّ.

وفي رواية: عَنْ أَبِي الدَّرْدَاءِ ؓ قَالَ: سَمِعْتُ النَّبِيَّ ﷺ يَقُوْلُ: ابْغُوْنِي فِي ضُعَفَائِكُمْ، فَإِنَّمَا تُرْزَقُوْنَ وَتُنْصَرُوْنَ بِضُعَفَائِكُمْ.

رَوَاهُ التِّرْمِذِيُّ وَأَبُوْ دَاوُدَ وَالنَّسَائِيُّ. وَقَالَ أَبُوْ عِيْسَى: هَذَا حَدِيْثٌ حَسَنٌ صَحِيْحٌ.

88/88. According to Muṣʿab b. Saʿd ؓ:

"Once it occurred to Saʿd ؓ that he was superior to those below him and those financially weaker. So the Prophet ﷺ said: '(Never forget that) you are granted support and sustenance only by means of your weaklings and destitute.'"

---

[88] Set forth by •al-Bukhārī in *al-Ṣaḥīḥ*: Bk.: *al-Jihād* [The Sacred Struggle], Ch.: Someone who seeks the assistance of the weak and the righteous in warfare, 3/1061 §2739. •al-Tirmidhī in *al-Sunan*: Bk.: *al-Jihād* [The Sacred Struggle], according to Allah's Messenger Ch.: What has come to us about seeking the assistance of the destitute Muslims, 4/206 §1702. •Abū Dāwūd in *al-Sunan*: Bk.: *al-Jihād* [The Sacred Struggle], Ch.: Seeking the assistance of the wretched horses and the weaklings, 3/32 §2594. •al-Nasāʾī in *al-Sunan*, Bk.: *al-Jihād* [The Sacred Struggle], Ch.: Seeking the assistance of the weakling, 6/45 §3179, & in *al-Sunan al-Kubrā*, 3/30 §4388. •Aḥmad b. Ḥanbal in *al-Musnad*, 5/198 §21779. •Ibn Ḥibbān in *al-Ṣaḥīḥ*, 11/85 §4767. •al-Ḥākim in *al-Mustadrak*, 2/116, 157 §2509, 2641. He said: "This is a tradition with an authentic chain of transmission." •al-Bayhaqī in *al-Sunan al-Kubrā*, 3/345 §6181; 6/331 §12684. •al-Mundhirī in *al-Targhīb wa al-Tarhīb*, 4/71 §4842–4843.

Reported by al-Bukhārī and al-Tirmidhī.

And in one report: According to Abū al-Dardā’ ﵁:

“I heard the Prophet ﷺ say: ‘Seek me among your destitute, for you are given sustenance due to the destitute and you are provided with support also due to your destitute.’”

Reported by al-Tirmidhī, Abū Dāwūd and al-Nasā’ī. And Abū ‘Īsā said: “This is a fine authentic tradition.”

٨٩/ ٨٩. عَنْ عُمَرَ بْنِ الْخَطَّابِ ﵁، قَالَ: قَالَ رَسُوْلُ اللهِ ﷺ: لَـمَّا أَذْنَبَ آدَمُ ﵇ الذَّنْبَ الَّذِي أَذْنَبَهُ رَفَعَ رَأْسَهُ إِلَى الْعَرْشِ فَقَالَ: أَسْأَلُكَ بِحَقِّ مُحَمَّدٍ ﷺ إِلاَّ غَفَرْتَ لِي. فَأَوْحَى اللهُ إِلَيْهِ: وَمَا مُحَمَّدٌ؟ وَمَنْ مُحَمَّدٌ؟ فَقَالَ: تَبَارَكَ اسْمُكَ؛ لَـمَّا خَلَقْتَنِي رَفَعْتُ رَأْسِي إِلَى عَرْشِكَ فَرَأَيْتُ فِيْهِ مَكْتُوْبًا: لَا إِلَهَ إِلاَّ اللهُ مُحَمَّدٌ رَسُوْلُ اللهِ، فَعَلِمْتُ أَنَّهُ لَيْسَ أَحَدٌ أَعْظَمَ عِنْدَكَ قَدْرًا مِمَّنْ جَعَلْتَ اسْمَهُ مَعَ اسْمِكَ، فَأَوْحَى اللهُ ﵎ إِلَيْهِ: يَا آدَمُ، إِنَّهُ آخِرُ النَّبِيِّيْنَ مِنْ ذُرِّيَّتِكَ، وَإِنَّ أُمَّتَهُ آخِرُ الأُمَمِ مِنْ ذُرِّيَّتِكَ. وَلَوْلَاهُ، يَا آدَمُ، مَا خَلَقْتُكَ.

رَوَاهُ الطَّبَرَانِيُّ.

89/89. According to ‘Umar b. al-Khaṭṭāb ﵁:

“The Messenger of Allah ﷺ said: ‘When Adam blundered, he raised his head towards the sky and submitted: (O Allah!) If You have not forgiven me, I seek (forgiveness) from You by means of (Your Beloved) Muhammad ﷺ. Allah sent down the revelation: ‘Who is Muhammad?’ He said: ‘(O Lord!) Your Name is Glorious; when You created me, I raised my head towards Your Throne and found written there: “There is no God but Allah; Muhammad is the Messenger of Allah.” So I made out that it is some exalted being whose name You have linked with Your Name. Allah ﵎

89 Set forth by •al-Ṭabarānī in *al-Mu‘jam al-Kabīr*, 2/182 §992 and in *al-Mu‘jam al-Awsat*, 6/313 §6502. •al-Haythamī in *Majma‘ al-Zawā’id*, 8/253. •al-Suyūṭī in *al-Jāmi‘ al-Aḥādīth*, 11/94.

then sent down the revelation: "O Adam! He (Muhammad) is the Final Prophet in your lineage, and his *Umma* will also be the last *Umma* of your race. Had he not been there, I would never have created you, O Adam!'"

Reported by al-Ṭabarānī.

٩٠/ ٩٠. عَنْ عَبْدِ اللهِ بْنِ مَسْعُوْدٍ ؓ قَالَ: قَالَ رَسُوْلُ اللهِ ﷺ: إِذَا انْفَلَتَتْ دَابَّةُ أَحَدِكُمْ بِأَرْضٍ فَلَاةٍ فَلْيُنَادِ: يَا عِبَادَ اللهِ، احْبِسُوْا عَلَيَّ، يَا عِبَادَ اللهِ، احْبِسُوْا عَلَيَّ، فَإِنَّ لِلّٰهِ فِي الْأَرْضِ حَاضِرًا سَيَحْبِسُهُ عَلَيْكُمْ.

رَوَاهُ الطَّبَرَانِيُّ وَأَبُوْ يَعْلَى.

وفي رواية: عَنْ عَتَبَةَ بْنِ غَزْوَانَ ؓ عَنْ نَبِيِّ اللهِ ﷺ قَالَ: إِذَا أَضَلَّ أَحَدُكُمْ شَيْأً أَوْ أَرَادَ أَحَدُكُمْ عَوْنًا وَهُوَ بِأَرْضٍ لَيْسَ بِهَا أَنِيْسٌ، فَلْيَقُلْ: يَا عِبَادَ اللهِ، أَغِيْثُوْنِي! يَا عِبَادَ اللهِ، أَغِيْثُوْنِي! فَإِنَّ لِلّٰهِ عِبَادًا لَا نَرَاهُمْ وَقَدْ جُرِّبَ ذٰلِكَ.

رَوَاهُ الطَّبَرَانِيُّ.

90/90. According to ʿAbd Allāh b. Masʿūd ؓ:

"Allah's Messenger ﷺ said: 'If the riding animal of one of you escapes in a desert land, let him cry: "O servants of Allah, detain it for me! O servants of Allah, detain it for me," for there are many (such) servants of Allah on the earth (as) will detain (your riding animal) for you.'"

Reported by al-Ṭabarānī and Abū Yaʿlā.

In one report: According to ʿAtaba b. Ghazwān ؓ:

"The Prophet ﷺ said: 'If some belonging of a person is lost or he intends to seek help while he is in a town where he does not find

---

90 Set forth by •al-Ṭabarānī in *al-Muʿjam al-Kabīr*, 10/217 §10518; 17/117 §290. •Abū Yaʿlā in *al-Musnad*, 9/177 §5269. •al-Daylamī in *al-Firdaws bi-Maʾthūr al-Khiṭāb*, 1/330 §1311. •al-Haythamī in *Majmaʿ al-Zawāʾid*, 10/132.

any help, then he should call out: “O servants of Allah, help me! O servants of Allah, help me,” for certainly Allah has servants whom we do not see (but they have been appointed to help the people), and that has been put to the test.’”

Reported by al-Ṭabarānī.

اَلْفَصْلُ الْعَاشِرُ

فَصْلٌ فِي عَدَمِ نَظِيْرِ النَّبِيِّ ﷺ فِي الْكَوْنِ

Section 10

The Absence of any Equal to the Prophet ﷺ in the Universe

٩١/٩١. عَنِ ابْنِ عُمَرَ رضي الله عنهما قَالَ: نَهَى رَسُوْلُ اللهِ ﷺ عَنِ الْوِصَالِ. قَالُوْا: إِنَّكَ تُوَاصِلُ. قَالَ: إِنِّي لَسْتُ مِثْلَكُمْ؛ إِنِّي أُطْعَمُ وَأُسْقَى.

مُتَّفَقٌ عَلَيْهِ وَهَذَا لَفْظُ الْبُخَارِيِّ.

91/91. According to Ibn ʿUmar رضي الله عنهما:

"Allah's Messenger ﷺ forbade uninterrupted fasting (without taking any meals). The Companions submitted: 'You fast without interruption!' He said: 'I am not like you. I am fed and my thirst is quenched (by my Lord)!'"

Agreed upon by al-Bukhārī and Muslim, and this is the wording of al-Bukhārī.

٩٢/٩٢. عَنْ أَبِي هُرَيْرَةَ رضي الله عنه قَالَ: نَهَى رَسُوْلُ اللهِ ﷺ عَنِ الْوِصَالِ فِي الصَّوْمِ

[91] Set forth by •al-Bukhārī in *al-Ṣaḥīḥ*: Bk.: *al-Ṣawm* [Fasting], Ch.: Sexual intercourse, and someone who says: "There is no fasting during the night, 2/693 §1861. •Muslim in *al-Ṣaḥīḥ*: Bk.: *al-Ṣiyām* [Fasting], Ch.: The prohibition of uninterrupted fasting, 2/774 §1102. •Abū Dāwūd in *al-Sunan*: Bk.: *al-Ṣawm* [Fasting], Ch.: Sexual intercourse, 2/306 §2360. •Mālik in *al-Muwaṭṭā'*, 1/300 §667. •al-Nasā'ī in *al-Sunan al-Kubrā*, 2/241 §3263. •Ibn Ḥibbān in *al-Ṣaḥīḥ*, 8/341 §3575. •al-Bayhaqī in *al-Sunan al-Kubrā*, 4/282 §8157. •Ibn Abī Shayba in *al-Muṣannaf*, 2/330 §9587. •ʿAbd al-Razzāq in *al-Muṣannaf*, 4/268 §7755. •Aḥmad b. Ḥanbal in *al-Musnad*, 2/102 §5795.

فَقَالَ لَهُ رَجُلٌ مِنَ الْـمُسْلِمِيْنَ: إِنَّكَ تُوَاصِلُ، يَا رَسُوْلَ اللهِ. قَالَ: وَأَيُّكُمْ مِثْلِي؟ إِنِّي أَبِيْتُ يُطْعِمُنِي رَبِّي وَيَسْقِيْنِ.

مُتَّفَقٌ عَلَيْهِ وَهَذَا لَفْظُ الْبُخَارِيِّ.

92/92. According to Abū Hurayra ﷺ:

"Allah's Messenger ﷺ forbade uninterrupted fasting, so a man from among the Muslims said to him: 'You fast without interruption, O Messenger of Allah!' He said: 'Which of you is like me? I spend the night in such a state that my Lord feeds me and quenches my thirst as well!'"

Agreed upon by al-Bukhārī and Muslim, and this is the wording of al-Bukhārī.

٩٣/ ٩٣. عَنْ عائِشَةَ ﷺ قَالَتْ: نَهَى رَسُوْلُ اللهِ ﷺ عَنِ الْوِصَالِ رَحْمَةً لَهُمْ، فَقَالُوْا: إِنَّكَ تُوَاصِلُ! قَالَ: إِنِّي لَسْتُ كَهَيْئَتِكُمْ؛ إِنِّي يُطْعِمُنِي رَبِّي وَيَسْقِيْنِ.

مُتَّفَقٌ عَلَيْهِ.

93/93. According to ʿĀʾisha ﷺ:

---

[92] Set forth by •al-Bukhārī in *al-Ṣaḥīḥ*: Bk.: al-Ḥudūd [The Penalties], Ch.: The law related to exemplary punishment and proper conduct, 2/2512 §6459, & Bk.: al-Tamannī [Longing], Ch.: What "if only...." Is permissible, 6/2646 §6815. •Muslim in *al-Ṣaḥīḥ*: Bk.: *al-Ṣiyām* [Fasting], Ch.: The prohibition of uninterrupted fasting, 2/774 §1103. •Ibn Ḥibbān in *al-Ṣaḥīḥ*, 8/341 §3575. •al-Dārimī in *al-Sunan*, 2/15 §1706. •an- Nasāʾī in *al-Sunan al-Kubrā*, 4/242 §3264. •al-Ṭabarānī in *al-Muʿjam al-Awsaṭ*, 2/68 §1274.

[93] Set forth by •al-Bukhārī in *al-Ṣaḥīḥ*: Bk.: *al-Ṣawm* [Fasting], Ch.: Sexual intercourse, and someone who says: "There is no fasting during the night, 2/693 §1863, & Bk.: *al-Tamannī* [Longing], Ch.: What "if only..." is permissible, 6/2645 §6815. •Muslim in *al-Ṣaḥīḥ*: Bk.: *al-Ṣawm* [Fasting], Ch.: The prohibition of uninterrupted fasting, 2/776 §1105. •Aḥmad b. Ḥanbal in *al-Musnad*, 4/282 §8161. •al-Bayhaqī in *al-Sunan al-Kubrā*, 2/153 §6413. •Ibn Rāhawayh in *al-Musnad*, 2/168 §669. •Abū al-Maḥāsin in *Muʿtaṣar al-Mukhtaṣar*, 1/150. •Ibn Rajab in *Jāmiʿ al-ʿUlūm wa al-Ḥikam*, 1/437.

"Allah's Messenger ﷺ forbade uninterrupted fasting, as a mercy for them, so they said: 'You fast without interruption!' He said: 'I am not like your constitution. My Lord feeds me and quenches my thirst as well!'"

Agreed upon by al-Bukhārī and Muslim.

٩٤/ ٩٤. عَنْ أَنَسٍ رضي الله عنه قَالَ: وَاصَلَ النَّبِيُّ ﷺ آخِرَ الشَّهْرِ، وَوَاصَلَ أُنَاسٌ مِنَ النَّاسِ. فَبَلَغَ النَّبِيَّ ﷺ فَقَالَ: لَوْ مُدَّ بِيَ الشَّهْرُ، لَوَاصَلْتُ وِصَالاً يَدَعُ الْمُتَعَمِّقُوْنَ تَعَمُّقَهُمْ. إِنِّي لَسْتُ مِثْلَكُمْ. إِنِّي أَظَلُّ يُطْعِمُنِي رَبِّي وَيَسْقِيْنِ.

مُتَّفَقٌ عَلَيْهِ.

94/94. According to Anas رضي الله عنه:

"Allah's Messenger ﷺ fasted without interruption at the end of the month, and some of the people also fasted without interruption. This came to the attention of the Prophet ﷺ, so he said: 'If the month of Ramaḍān were prolonged for me, I would keep such an uninterrupted fast that those who exceed the bounds to catch up with me would abandon their excess. I am in no way like you. I always have my Lord feeding me and quenching my thirst!'"

Agreed upon by al-Bukhārī and Muslim.

٩٥/ ٩٥. عَنْ أَنَسٍ رضي الله عنه عَنْ رَسُوْلِ اللهِ ﷺ قَالَ: أَتِمُّوا الرُّكُوْعَ وَالسُّجُوْدَ فَوَاللهِ، إِنِّي لَأَرَاكُمْ مِنْ بَعْدِ ظَهْرِي إِذَا مَا رَكَعْتُمْ وَإِذَا مَا سَجَدْتُمْ. وفي حديث سعيد: إِذَا رَكَعْتُمْ

---

94 Set forth by •al-Bukhārī in *al-Ṣaḥīḥ*: Bk.: *al-Tamannī* [Longing], Ch.: What "if only..." is permissible and Allah's saying: "He said: 'If only I had strength to resist you!' [*qāla law anna lī bi-kum quwwatan*]." (Q.11:80), 6/2645 §6814. •Muslim in *al-Ṣaḥīḥ*: Bk.: *al-Ṣiyām* [Fasting], Ch.: The prohibition of uninterrupted fasting, 2/776 §1104. •Ibn Ḥibbān in *al-Ṣaḥīḥ*, 14/325 §6414. •al-Bayhaqī in *al-Sunan al-Kubrā*, 4/282 §8160. •Ibn Abī Shayba in *al-Muṣannaf*, 2/330 §9585. •Aḥmad b. Ḥanbal in *al-Musnad*, 3/124 §12270, 13035, 13092, 13681. •Abū Yaʿlā in *al-Musnad*, 6/36 §3282, 3501. •ʿAbd b. Ḥumayd in *al-Musnad*, 1/400 §1353.

وَإِذَا سَجَدْتُمْ.

مُتَّفَقٌ عَلَيْهِ.

95/95. According to Anas ﷺ:

"Allah's Messenger ﷺ said: 'You must complete the acts of bowing and prostration excellently (in the ritual prayer), for, by Allah, I see you from behind my back when you bow down and when you prostrate yourselves!'" (In Saʿīd's version: "'... if you bow down and prostrate yourselves!'")

Agreed upon by al-Bukhārī and Muslim.

٩٦/٩٦. عَنْ أَبِي هُرَيْرَةَ ﷺ أَنَّ رَسُوْلَ اللهِ ﷺ قَالَ: هَلْ تَرَوْنَ قِبْلَتِي هَاهُنَا؟ فَوَاللهِ، مَا يَخْفَى عَلَيَّ خُشُوْعُكُمْ وَلاَ رُكُوْعُكُمْ. إِنِّي لَأَرَاكُمْ مِنْ وَرَاءِ ظَهْرِي.

مُتَّفَقٌ عَلَيْهِ.

96/96. According to Abū Hurayra ﷺ:

"Allah's Messenger ﷺ said: 'Do you see my direction *(Qibla)* here? By Allah, your submission, humbleness and humility (in your

---

[95] Set forth by •al-Bukhārī in *al-Ṣaḥīḥ*: Bk.: *al-Aymān wa al-Nudhūr* [Oaths and Vows], Ch.: The manner of the Prophet's oath ﷺ, 6/2449 §6268. •Muslim in *al-Ṣaḥīḥ*: Bk.: *al-Ṣalāt* [The Ritual Prayer], Ch.: The command to beautify the ritual prayer, and its completion and humility in it, 1/320 §425. •al-Nasāʾī in *al-Sunan*: Bk.: *al-Taṭbīq* [Not placing hands between knees and thighs while praying], Ch.: The command to complete the prostration, 2/216 §1117, & in *al-Sunan al-Kubrā*, 1/235 §704. •Aḥmad b. Ḥanbal in *al-Musnad*, 3/115 §12169. •Abū Yaʿlā in *al-Musnad*, 5/341 §2971. •ʿAbd b. Ḥumayd *in al-Musnad*, 1/354 §1170.

[96] Set forth by •al-Bukhārī in *al-Ṣaḥīḥ*: Bk.: *al-Ṣalāt* [The Ritual Prayer], Ch.: The Imam's sermon to the people about the completion of the ritual prayer, and mention of the direction of prayer, 1/161 §408, & Bk.: *al-Adhān* [The Call to Prayer], Ch.: Humility in the ritual prayer, 1/259 §708. •Muslim in *al-Ṣaḥīḥ*: Bk.: *al-Ṣalāt* [The Ritual Prayer], Ch.: The command to beautify the ritual prayer, and its completion and humility in it, 1/259 §424. •Aḥmad b. Ḥanbal in *al-Musnad*, 2/303, 365, §8011, 8756, 8864.

hearts) and your (discernable) bowing are not concealed from me! I can indeed see you from behind my back (the same way as I see you in front of me)!'"

Agreed upon by al-Bukhārī and Muslim.

٩٧/٩٧. عَنْ أَبِي هُرَيْرَةَ ؓ قَالَ: صَلَّى بِنَا رَسُوْلُ اللهِ ﷺ يَوْمًا ثُمَّ انْصَرَفَ، فَقَالَ: يَا فُلاَنُ، أَلاَ تُحْسِنُ صَلاَتَكَ؟ أَلاَ يَنْظُرُ الْمُصَلِّي إِذَا صَلَّى كَيْفَ يُصَلِّي؟ فَإِنَّمَا يُصَلِّي لِنَفْسِهِ. إِنِّي، وَاللهِ، لَأُبْصِرُ مِنْ وَرَائِي كَمَا أُبْصِرُ مِنْ بَيْنِ يَدَيَّ.

رَوَاهُ مُسْلِمٌ وَالنَّسَائِيُّ.

97/97. According to Abū Hurayra ؓ:

"Allah's Messenger ﷺ led us in the ritual prayer one day, then he turned around and said: 'O So-and-so! Why do you not perform your ritual prayer rightly? When the worshipper performs the ritual prayer, does he not consider how he is performing the ritual prayer, for he is only praying for himself? By Allah, I surely see from behind me just as I see from in front of me!'"

Reported by Muslim and al-Nasā'ī.

٩٨/٩٨. عَنْ أَبِي هُرَيْرَةَ ؓ قَالَ: صَلَّى بِنَا رَسُوْلُ اللهِ ﷺ الظُّهْرَ وَفِي مُؤَخَّرِ الصُّفُوْفِ رَجُلٌ. فَأَسَاءَ الصَّلاَةَ، فَلَمَّا سَلَّمَ نَادَاهُ رَسُوْلُ اللهِ ﷺ: يَا فُلاَنُ، أَلاَ تَتَّقِي

---

97 Set forth by •Muslim in *al-Ṣaḥīḥ*: Bk.: *al-Ṣalāt* [The Ritual Prayer], Ch.: The command to beautify the ritual prayer, and its completion and humility in it, 1/319 §423. •al-Nasā'ī in *al-Sunan*: Bk.: *al-Imāma* [Prayer-Leadership], Ch.: The bowing posture outside of the row, 2/118 §872, & in *al-Sunan al-Kubrā*, 1/303 §944. •Abū ʿAwāna in *al-Musnad*, 2/105. •al-Bayhaqī in *al-Sunan al-Kubrā*, 2/290 §3398, & in *al-Sunan al-Ṣughrā*, 1/495 §878, & in *Shuʿab al-Īmān*, 3/134 §3113. •al-Mundhirī in *al-Targhīb wa al-Tarhīb*, 1/202 §768.

الله؟ أَلاَ تَرَى كَيْفَ تُصَلِّي؟ إِنَّكُمْ تَرَوْنَ أَنَّهُ يَخْفَى عَلَيَّ شَيْءٌ مِمَّا تَصْنَعُوْنَ؟ وَاللهِ، إِنِّي لَأَرَى مِنْ خَلْفِي كَمَا أَرَى مِنْ بَيْنِ يَدَيَّ.

رَوَاهُ أَحْمَدُ وَابْنُ خُزَيْمَةَ.

98/98. According to Abū Hurayra :

"Allah's Messenger led us in the midday ritual prayer (one day), and there was a man in the rear part of the rows. He performed the ritual prayer badly, so when he pronounced the salutation of peace, Allah's Messenger called out to him: 'O So-and-so! Do you not fear Allah? Do you not see how you perform the ritual prayer? Do you assume that anything you do is concealed from me? By Allah, I see from behind me just as I see from in front of me!'"

Reported by Aḥmad and Ibn Khuzayma.

٩٩/٩٩. عَنْ أَبِي هُرَيْرَةَ ﭭ قَالَ: قَالَ رَسُوْلُ اللهِ ﷺ: أَنَا أَوَّلُ مَنْ تَنْشَقُّ عَنْهُ الْأَرْضُ فَأُكْسَى حُلَّةً مِنْ حُلَلِ الْجَنَّةِ، ثُمَّ أَقُوْمُ عَنْ يَمِيْنِ الْعَرْشِ. لَيْسَ أَحَدٌ مِنَ الْخَلَائِقِ يَقُوْمُ ذَلِكَ الْمَقَامَ غَيْرِي.

رَوَاهُ التِّرْمِذِيُّ وَقَالَ: هَذَا حَدِيْثٌ حَسَنٌ.

99/99. According to Abū Hurayra :

"Allah's Messenger said: 'I am the first from whom the earth (i.e., the grave) will split open, so I shall be attired with one of the garments of the Garden of Paradise. Then I shall arise on the right side of the Heavenly Throne (at the Most Praiseworthy Station),

---

98 Set forth by •Aḥmad b. Ḥanbal in *al-Musnad*, 2/449 §9795. •Ibn Khuzayma in *al-Ṣaḥīḥ*, 1/332 §664. •al-ʿAsqalānī in *Fatḥ al-Bārī*, 2/226.

99 Set forth by •al-Tirmidhī in *al-Sunan*: Bk.: *al-Manāqib* [Virtues] according to Allah's Messenger , Ch.: The excellent merit of the Prophet , 5/585 §3611. •al-Mubārakfūrī in *Tuḥfat al-Aḥwadhī*, 7/92. •al-Munāwī in *Fayḍ al-Qadīr*, 3/41.

and not one of the creatures will occupy that station apart from me!'"

> Reported by al-Tirmidhī, and he said: "This is a fine tradition."

الْفَصْلُ الْحَادِي عَشَرَ

فَصْلٌ فِي تَعْظِيمِ النَّبِيِّ ﷺ

Section 11

Reverence and Veneration of the Prophet ﷺ

١٠٠/ ١٠٠. عَنْ أَبِي قَتَادَةَ ﷺ قَالَ: قَالَ رَسُوْلُ اللهِ ﷺ: إِذَا أُقِيْمَتِ الصَّلَاةُ، فَلَا تَقُوْمُوْا حَتَّى تَرَوْنِي.

مُتَّفَقٌ عَلَيْهِ.

100/100. According to Abū Qatāda ﷺ:

---

[100] Set forth by •al-Bukhārī in *al-Ṣaḥīḥ*: Bk.: *al-Adhān* [The Call to Prayer], Ch.: When the people should stand up, if they see the Imam at the time of the announcement that the ritual prayer is about to begin, 1/228 §611, & Ch.: One should not run to the ritual prayer in great haste, and one should stand in a state of tranquillity and dignity, 1/828 §612, & Bk.: *al-Jumuʿa* [The Friday Congregational Prayer], Ch.: Walking to the congregational prayer, 1/308 §867. •Muslim in *al-Ṣaḥīḥ*: Bk.: *al-Masājid* [The Mosques], Ch.: When the people should stand up for the ritual prayer, 1/422 §604–606. •al-Tirmidhī in *al-Sunan:* Chs: *al-Jumuʿa* [The Friday Congregational Prayer] according to Allah's Messenger, Ch.: What has come to us about speech after the Imam's descent from the pulpit, 2/394 §517, & Chs.: The two Festivals [*al-ʿĪdayn*], Ch.: Abhorrence of the people's waiting for the Imam while they are standing, at the beginning of the ritual prayer, 2/487 §592. •Abū Dāwūd in *al-Sunan*: Bk.: *al-Ṣalāt* [The Ritual Prayer], Ch.: When the ritual prayer is about to be performed, but the Imam has not arrived, they should wait for him sitting down, 1/148 §539. •al-Nasāʾī in *al-Sunan*: Bk.: *al-Adhān* [The Call to Prayer], The second call of the muezzin on the emergence of the Imam, 2/31 §687. •al-Dārimī in *al-Sunan*, 1/323 §1262. •Ibn Ḥibbān in *al-Ṣaḥīḥ*, 5/51 §1755. •Ibn Khuzayma in *al-Ṣaḥīḥ*, 3/14 §1526. •ʿAbd al-Razzāq in *al-Muṣannaf*, 1/504 §1932. •Aḥmad b. Ḥanbal in *al-Musnad*, 5/304 §22640,

"Allah's Messenger ﷺ said: 'When the ritual prayer is announced, you must not stand up until you see me (i.e., stand in my reverence)!'"

Agreed upon by al-Bukhārī and Muslim.

١٠١/١٠١. عَنْ أَنَسِ بْنِ مَالِكٍ الْأَنْصَارِيِّ رضي الله عنه وَكَانَ تَبِعَ النَّبِيَّ ﷺ وَخَدَمَهُ وَصَحِبَهُ، أَنَّ أَبَا بَكْرٍ كَانَ يُصَلِّي لَهُمْ فِي وَجَعِ النَّبِيِّ ﷺ الَّذِي تُوُفِّيَ فِيهِ، حَتَّى إِذَا كَانَ يَوْمُ الْاِثْنَيْنِ وَهُمْ صُفُوْفٌ فِي الصَّلَاةِ، فَكَشَفَ النَّبِيُّ ﷺ سِتْرَ الْحُجْرَةِ، يَنْظُرُ إِلَيْنَا وَهُوَ قَائِمٌ، كَأَنَّ وَجْهَهُ وَرَقَةُ مُصْحَفٍ، ثُمَّ تَبَسَّمَ يَضْحَكُ فَهَمَمْنَا أَنْ نَفْتَتِنَ مِنَ الْفَرَحِ بِرُؤْيَةِ النَّبِيِّ ﷺ، فَنَكَصَ أَبُوْ بَكْرٍ عَلَى عَقِبَيْهِ لِيَصِلَ الصَّفَّ، وَظَنَّ أَنَّ النَّبِيَّ ﷺ خَارِجٌ إِلَى الصَّلَاةِ، فَأَشَارَ إِلَيْنَا النَّبِيُّ ﷺ أَنْ أَتِمُّوْا صَلَاتَكُمْ وَأَرْخَى السِّتْرَ، فَتُوُفِّيَ مِنْ يَوْمِهِ.

مُتَّفَقٌ عَلَيْهِ.

101/101. According to Anas b. Mālik al-Anṣārī رضي الله عنه, who had followed the Prophet ﷺ, served him and was blessed with his companionship as a special servant:

22649, 22666, 22675, 22702. •Abū Yaʿlā in *al-Musnad*, 1/181 §207. •al-Bayhaqī in *al-Sunan al-Kubrā*, 2/20 §2119.

[101] Set forth by •al-Bukhārī in *al-Ṣaḥīḥ*: Bk.: *al-Adhān* [The Call to Prayer], Ch.: The masters of knowledge and excellent merit are most worthy of prayer-leadership, 1/240 §648, & Bk.: *al-Adhān* [The Call to Prayer], Ch.: Is attention paid to a matter which come up? 1/262 §721, & Bk.: *al-Tahajjud* [Night-time Ritual Prayer], Ch.: Someone who brings back the laggard in his ritual prayer, 1/403 §1147, & Bk.: *al-Maghāzī* [Military Expeditions], Ch.: The illness of the Prophet ﷺ and his death, 4/1616 §4183. •Muslim in *al-Ṣaḥīḥ*: Bk.: *al-Ṣalāt* [The Ritual Prayer], Ch.: Appointing someone to lead the people in the ritual prayer as a substitute for the Imam, if his absence is due to illness, travel and other such excuses, 1/316 §419. •al-Nasāʾī likewise in *al-Sunan*: Bk.: *al-Janāʾiz* [Funeral Ceremonies], Ch.: Death on Monday, 4/7 §1831. •Ibn Mājah likewise in *al-Sunan*: Bk.: *al-Janāʾiz* [Funeral Ceremonies], Ch.: What has come to us concerning the illness of Allah's Messenger ﷺ, 1/517 §1624. •Aḥmad b. Ḥanbal in *al-Musnad*, 3/163, 196–197, 211. •Ibn Ḥibbān in *al-Ṣaḥīḥ*, 14/587 §587. •Ibn Khuzayma in *al-Ṣaḥīḥ*, 2/372 §1488.

"Abū Bakr ؓ used to lead them in the ritual prayer during the departing ailment of the Prophet ﷺ. So, it was Monday and the Companions, aligned in rows, were offering the ritual prayer when the Beloved Prophet ﷺ raised the curtain of his sacred chamber and standing there blessed us with his compassionate gaze (we were missing so restlessly and waiting for so impatiently). The effulgent face of our Beloved Prophet seemed like the (illumined) pages of the Holy Qur'ān. (When he glanced at the ritual prayer in progress) he (felt pleased and) smiled. We had nearly ended our ritual prayer due to the extreme joy of having a (blissful and heartening) glimpse (and beholding) of the (pleased and gleaming) holy countenance of our Beloved Prophet.

"Abū Bakr ؓ (felt as if the Holy Messenger of Allah was coming for the ritual prayer, so) he initiated to drag himself on his soles to join the row (behind the leader). But (our Beloved) Prophet ﷺ gave us the gesture to complete our ritual prayer. Then he pulled down the curtain, and he departed us the same day."

Agreed upon by al-Bukhārī and Muslim.

١٠٢/١٠٢. عَنْ سَهْلِ بْنِ سَعْدٍ السَّاعِدِيِّ ؓ أَنَّ رَسُوْلَ اللهِ ﷺ ذَهَبَ إِلَى بَنِي عَمْرِو بْنِ عَوْفٍ لِيُصْلِحَ بَيْنَهُمْ. فَحَانَتِ الصَّلَاةُ، فَجَاءَ الْمُؤَذِّنُ إِلَى أَبِي بَكْرٍ، فَقَالَ: أَتُصَلِّي لِلنَّاسِ فَأُقِيْمَ؟ قَالَ: نَعَمْ. فَصَلَّى أَبُوْ بَكْرٍ، فَجَاءَ رَسُوْلُ اللهِ ﷺ وَالنَّاسُ فِي الصَّلَاةِ فَتَخَلَّصَ حَتَّى وَقَفَ فِي الصَّفِّ. فَصَفَّقَ النَّاسُ، وَكَانَ أَبُوبَكْرٍ لَا يَلْتَفِتُ فِي صَلَاتِهِ؛ فَلَمَّا أَكْثَرَ النَّاسُ التَّصْفِيقَ، الْتَفَتَ، فَرَأَى رَسُوْلَ اللهِ ﷺ، فَأَشَارَ إِلَيْهِ رَسُوْلُ اللهِ ﷺ أَنِ امْكُثْ مَكَانَكَ. فَرَفَعَ أَبُوْ بَكْرٍ ؓ يَدَيْهِ، فَحَمِدَ اللهَ عَلَى مَا أَمَرَهُ بِهِ رَسُوْلُ اللهِ ﷺ مِنْ ذَلِكَ. ثُمَّ اسْتَأْخَرَ أَبُوْ بَكْرٍ حَتَّى اسْتَوَى فِي الصَّفِّ، وَتَقَدَّمَ رَسُوْلُ اللهِ ﷺ. فَلَمَّا انْصَرَفَ، قَالَ: يَا أَبَا بَكْرٍ، مَا مَنَعَكَ أَنْ تَثْبُتَ إِذْ أَمَرْتُكَ؟ فَقَالَ أَبُو بَكْرٍ: مَا كَانَ لِابْنِ أَبِي قُحَافَةَ أَنْ يُصَلِّيَ بَيْنَ يَدَي رَسُوْلِ اللهِ ﷺ. فَقَالَ رَسُوْلُ اللهِ ﷺ: مَا لِي رَأَيْتُكُمْ أَكْثَرْتُمُ التَّصْفِيقَ. مَنْ رَابَهُ شَيْءٌ فِي صَلَاتِهِ فَلْيُسَبِّحْ، فَإِنَّهُ إِذَا سَبَّحَ الْتُفِتَ إِلَيْهِ،

وَإِنَّمَا التَّصْفِيقُ لِلنِّسَاءِ.

مُتَّفَقٌ عَلَيْهِ.

102/102. According to Sahl b. Saʿd al-Sāʿidī ﵁:

"Allah's Messenger ﷺ went to the tribe of ʿAmr b. ʿAwf, to bring about peace among them (on some dispute). In the meanwhile the time for the ritual prayer approached, so the muezzin came to Abū Bakr ﵁ and said: 'Will you lead the people in the ritual prayer, so that I may announce its commencement?' He said: 'Yes,' so Abū Bakr ﵁ started leading the ritual prayer. During the proceedings of the prayer, Allah's Messenger ﷺ also came and passed sharp through the ranks until he reached to stand in the (first) row. The people patted their hands (like clapping to seek the attention of Abū Bakr), but (absorbed in prayer) he would never pay attention to anything else during the ritual prayer. When the sound of patting the hands rose, Abū Bakr got it and perceived (that) the Beloved Messenger of Allah ﷺ (had come, so he decided to step back from his position). But Allah's Messenger ﷺ indicated him to continue

[102] Set forth by •al-Bukhārī in *al-Ṣaḥīḥ*: Bk.: *al-Adhān* [The Call to Prayer], Ch.: If someone enters to lead the people in prayer, then the first Imam arrives, whether or not the first is late, his leading the prayer is permissible according to ʿĀʾisha, on the authority of the Prophet ﷺ, 1/242 §652, & Chs.: Activity in the ritual prayer, Ch.: What is permissible for the men in the ritual prayer, such as glorification and praise, 1/402 §1143, & Ch.: Clapping for the women, 1/403 §1146, & Ch.: The hands in the ritual prayer, 1/407 §1160, & Chs.: *al-Sahw* [Inadvertent Negligence], Ch.: Signalling in the ritual prayer, 1/414 §1177, 2544, 2547, 6767. •Muslim in *al-Ṣalāt*: Ch.: The congregation's putting someone forward to lead them in the ritual prayer, when the Imam is late, 1/316 §421. •Abū Dāwūd in *al-Sunna*: Bk.: *al-Ṣalāt* [The Ritual Prayer], Ch.: Clapping in the ritual prayer, 1/247 §940. •al-Nasāʾī in *al-Sunan*: Bk.: *Ādāb al-Quḍāh* [Proper Procedures of the Judges], Ch.: The governor's approach to his subjects in order to reconcile them, 8/243 §5413, & Bk.: *al-Imāma* [Prayer-leadership], Ch.: If the man from among the subjects comes to the fore, then the governor arrives, is he too late? 2/77 §784. •Mālik in *al-Muwaṭṭāʾ*: Bk.: *Qaṣr al-Ṣalāt fī al-Safar* [Curtailment of the Ritual Prayer while on a Journey], Ch.: Turning around and clapping when the need arises in the ritual prayer, 1/163 §61.

in his position. On this Abū Bakr raised his hands and thanked Almighty Allah, for Allah's Messenger ﷺ had commanded him for the leadership (of the ritual prayer). Then he stepped back into the first row. So Allah's Messenger ﷺ stepped forward (and took the leadership of the ritual prayer). After completing the ritual prayer, he said: 'O Abū Bakr! What prevented you from continuing as leader after I had commanded you?' Abū Bakr submitted: '(O Messenger of Allah!) How dare son of Abū Qaḥāfa lead the ritual prayer in front of Allah's Messenger ﷺ!' After this Allah's Messenger ﷺ said, turning towards the Companions: 'Why should I have seen you clapping hands? If something unexpected happens during the prayer proceedings, one should (loudly) say: "Glory be to Allah (*Subḥān Allāh*)." So if someone pronounces (*Subḥān Allāh*), he should be given attention. As for clapping, that is exclusive to ladies.'"

Agreed upon by al-Bukhārī and Muslim.

١٠٣/١٠٣. عَنِ الْمِسْوَرِ بْنِ مَخْرَمَةَ وَمَرْوَانَ ﵄ قَالَا: إِنَّ عُرْوَةَ جَعَلَ يَرْمُقُ أَصْحَابَ النَّبِيِّ ﷺ بِعَيْنَيْهِ. قَالَ: فَوَاللهِ، مَا تَنَخَّمَ رَسُوْلُ اللهِ ﷺ نُخَامَةً إِلَّا وَقَعَتْ فِي كَفِّ رَجُلٍ مِنْهُمْ فَدَلَكَ بِهَا وَجْهَهُ وَجِلْدَهُ. وَإِذَا أَمَرَهُمُ ابْتَدَرُوْا أَمْرَهُ. وَإِذَا تَوَضَّأَ كَادُوْا يَقْتَتِلُوْنَ عَلَى وَضُوئِهِ. وَإِذَا تَكَلَّمَ خَفَضُوْا أَصْوَاتَهُمْ عِنْدَهُ وَمَا يُحِدُّوْنَ إِلَيْهِ النَّظَرَ تَعْظِيْمًا لَهُ. فَرَجَعَ عُرْوَةُ إِلَى أَصْحَابِهِ فَقَالَ: أَيْ قَوْمِ، وَاللهِ، لَقَدْ وَفَدْتُ عَلَى الْمُلُوْكِ، وَفَدْتُ عَلَى قَيْصَرَ وَكِسْرَى وَالنَّجَاشِيِّ، وَاللهِ، إِنْ رَأَيْتُ مَلِكًا قَطُّ يُعَظِّمُهُ أَصْحَابُهُ مَا يُعَظِّمُ أَصْحَابُ مُحَمَّدٍ ﷺ مُحَمَّدًا. وَاللهِ، إِنْ تَنَخَّمَ نُخَامَةً إِلَّا وَقَعَتْ فِي كَفِّ رَجُلٍ مِنْهُمْ فَدَلَكَ بِهَا وَجْهَهُ وَجِلْدَهُ. وَإِذَا أَمَرَهُمُ ابْتَدَرُوْا أَمْرَهُ. وَإِذَا تَوَضَّأَ كَادُوْا يَقْتَتِلُوْنَ عَلَى وَضُوئِهِ. وَإِذَا تَكَلَّمَ خَفَضُوْا أَصْوَاتَهُمْ عِنْدَهُ وَمَا يُحِدُّوْنَ إِلَيْهِ النَّظَرَ تَعْظِيْمًا لَهُ.

رَوَاهُ الْبُخَارِيُّ وَأَحْمَدُ.

103/103. According to al-Miswar b. Makhrama and Marwān رضي الله عنهما:

"ʿUrwa (when he came to the Messenger of Allah as an advocate of the unbelievers) kept observing the Companions of the Prophet (and saw how they would practise extreme veneration of the Holy Messenger of Allah ﷺ). He said: 'By Allah, whenever Allah's Messenger ﷺ cleared his throat of some secretion or saliva, one of his Companions would take it on the palm of his hand so he would rub it on his face and his skin. If he gave them a command, they would make haste to obey his command. If he performed the minor ablution, they would almost fight with one another over the water he has used for the purpose. If he spoke, they would lower their voices in his presence, and would not raise their looks to see him in deep love, submissiveness and reverence for him (permeating their hearts).' ʿUrwa therefore returned to his companions and said: 'O my people, by Allah, I have visited the kings! I have visited Caesar, Chosroes and Najāshī, and by Allah, I have never seen a king revered by his companions to the extent that the Companions of Muhammad ﷺ revere Muhammad! By Allah, whenever Allah's Messenger ﷺ cleared his throat of some sputum or saliva, one of his Companions would take it on the palm of his hand so he would rub it on his face and his skin. If he gave them a command, they would make haste to obey his command. If he performed the minor ablution, they would almost fight with one another over the water he has used for the purpose. If he spoke, they would lower their voices in his presence, and would not raise their looks to see him in deep love, submissiveness and reverence for him (permeating their hearts).'"

Reported by al-Bukhārī and Aḥmad.

١٠٤/ ١٠٤. عَنْ أَنَسِ بْنِ مَالِكٍ رضي الله عنه أَنَّ النَّبِيَّ ﷺ افْتَقَدَ ثَابِتَ بْنَ قَيْسٍ رضي الله عنه فَقَالَ

---

103 Set forth by •al-Bukhārī in *al-Ṣaḥīḥ*: Bk.: *al-Shurūṭ* [The Stipulations], Ch.: The stipulations applied to the Sacred Struggle, reconciliation with the warriors, and ransom, 2/974 §2581. •Aḥmad b. Ḥanbal in *al-Musnad*, 4/329. •al-Ṭabarānī in *al-Muʿjam al-Kabīr*, 20/9 §13. •Ibn Ḥibbān in *al-Ṣaḥīḥ*, 11/216 §4872. •al-Bayhaqī in *al-Sunan al-Kubrā*, 9/220.

رَجُلٌ: يَا رَسُوْلَ اللهِ، أَنَا أَعْلَمُ لَكَ عِلْمَهُ. فَأَتَاهُ فَوَجَدَهُ جَالِسًا فِي بَيْتِهِ مُنَكِّسًا رَأْسَهُ فَقَالَ: مَا شَأْنُكَ؟ فَقَالَ: شَرٌّ! كَانَ يَرْفَعُ صَوْتَهُ فَوْقَ صَوْتِ النَّبِيِّ ﷺ، فَقَدْ حَبِطَ عَمَلُهُ وَهُوَ مِنْ أَهْلِ النَّارِ. فَأَتَى الرَّجُلُ فَأَخْبَرَهُ أَنَّهُ قَالَ كَذَا وَكَذَا فَقَالَ مُوْسَى بْنُ أَنَسٍ: فَرَجَعَ الْمَرَّةَ الْآخِرَةَ بِبِشَارَةٍ عَظِيْمَةٍ، فَقَالَ: اذْهَبْ إِلَيْهِ، فَقُلْ لَهُ: إِنَّكَ لَسْتَ مِنْ أَهْلِ النَّارِ، وَلَكِنْ مِنْ أَهْلِ الْجَنَّةِ.

رَوَاهُ الْبُخَارِيُّ.

104/104. According to Anas b. Mālik ﷺ:

"Allah's Messenger ﷺ found Thābit b. Qays ﷺ absent. A man said: 'O Allah's Messenger! I will bring you his news.' So he went out and found him sitting home with his head bent down. He asked: 'What is the matter with you?' and he replied: 'I am miserable because I raised my voice louder than the Prophet's; all my pious deeds have gone void and I am one of the inmates of Hell.' The man came back and submitted his case before the Presence of Allah's Messenger. According to Mūsā b. Anas, the man once again went back to him with a glad tidings. The Messenger of Allah said: 'Go and tell him: "You are not the resident of Hell; you are of the people of Paradise."'"

Reported by al-Bukhārī.

١٠٥/١٠٥. عَنِ السَّائِبِ بْنِ يَزِيْدَ ﷺ قَالَ: كُنْتُ قَائِمًا فِي الْمَسْجِدِ فَحَصَبَنِي رَجُلٌ فَنَظَرْتُ فَإِذَا عُمَرُ بْنُ الْخَطَّابِ ﷺ فَقَالَ: اذْهَبْ فَأْتِنِي بِهَذَيْنِ. فَجِئْتُهُ بِهِمَا

[104] Set forth by •al-Bukhārī in *al-Ṣaḥīḥ*: Bk.: *al-Manāqib* [Virtues] Ch: *ʿAlāmāt al-Nubuwwa fī al-Islām* [Signs of Prophethood in Islam], 3/1322 §3417, Bk.: *Tafsīr al-Qurʾān*, Ch: *La tarfaʿū aṣwātakum fauqa ṣaut al-Nabiyyi* [Raise not your voice louder than the Messenger of Allah ﷺ, 4/1833 §4565.

قَالَ: مَنْ أَنْتُمَا أَوْ مِنْ أَيْنَ أَنْتُمَا؟ قَالَا: مِنْ أَهْلِ الطَّائِفِ. قَالَ: لَوْ كُنْتُمَا مِنْ أَهْلِ الْبَلَدِ لَأَوْجَعْتُكُمَا؛ تَرْفَعَانِ أَصْوَاتَكُمَا فِي مَسْجِدِ رَسُوْلِ اللهِ ﷺ.

رَوَاهُ الْبُخَارِيُّ.

105/105. According to Sāʾib b. Yazīd ﷺ:

"I was standing in the mosque when somebody threw a stone at me. I looked around and found ʿUmar b. al-Khaṭṭāb ﷺ there. He said: 'Go and fetch those two men to me.' I fetched both of them. He said: 'Who are you or which area do you come from?' Both of them said: 'We are from Ṭāʾif.' He said: 'Had you been of the residents of the city (Medina), I would have punished you for loudening your voices in Allah's Messenger's mosque.'"

Reported by al-Bukhārī.

١٠٦/١٠٦. عَنْ أَنَسِ بْنِ مَالِكٍ ﷺ قَالَ: لَقَدْ رَأَيْتُ رَسُوْلَ اللهِ ﷺ وَالْحَلَّاقُ يَحْلِقُهُ وَأَطَافَ بِهِ أَصْحَابُهُ. فَمَا يُرِيْدُوْنَ أَنْ تَقَعَ شَعْرَةٌ إِلَّا فِي يَدِ رَجُلٍ.

رَوَاهُ مُسْلِمٌ وَأَحْمَدُ.

106/106. According to Anas b. Mālik ﷺ:

"I saw Allah's Messenger ﷺ when the barber was cutting his hair and his Companions were moving around him. Every one of them was in an effort to ensure that not a single hair (of Allah's Messenger) drops on the ground and it goes into the hand of one of them."

---

105 Set forth by •al-Bukhārī in *al-Ṣaḥīḥ*: Bk.: *al-Ṣalāh* [Ritual Prayer] Ch: *Rafʿ al-Ṣawt fi al-Masājid* [Raising voice in the mosques], 1/179 §458. •al-Bayhaqī in *al-Sunan al-Kubrā*, 2/447 §4143•Ibn Kathīr in *Tafsīr al-Qurʾān al-ʿAẓīm*, 3/294.

106 Set forth by •Muslim in *al-Ṣaḥīḥ*: Bk.: *al-Faḍāʾil* [Excellent Merits], Ch.: The nearness of the Prophet ﷺ to the people, and their enjoyment of its blessing, 4/1812 §2325. •Aḥmad b. Ḥanbal in *al-Musnad*, 3/133, 137 §12423. •ʿAbd b. Ḥumayd in *al-Musnad*, 1/380 §1273.

Reported by Muslim and Aḥmad.

١٠٧/١٠٧. عَنِ ابْنِ شِمَاسَةَ الْـمَهْرِيِّ ﴿ قَالَ: حَضَرْنَا عَمْرَو بْنَ الْعَاصِ ﴿ ـ
وَهُوَ فِي سِيَاقَةِ الْـمَوْتِ ـ فَبَكَى طَوِيلاً، وَقَالَ: وَمَا كَانَ أَحَدٌ أَحَبَّ إِلَيَّ مِنْ رَسُولِ اللهِ
﴿، وَلاَ أَجَلَّ فِي عَيْنِي مِنْهُ. وَمَا كُنْتُ أُطِيقُ أَنْ أَمْلَأَ عَيْنَيَّ مِنْهُ إِجْلاَلاً لَهُ، وَلَوْ سُئِلْتُ
أَنْ أَصِفَهُ مَا أَطَقْتُ لِأَنِّي لَـمْ أَكُنْ أَمْلَأُ عَيْنَيَّ مِنْهُ.

رَوَاهُ مُسْلِمٌ.

107/107. According to Ibn Shimāsa al-Mahrī ﴿:

"We went to ʿAmr b. al-ʿĀṣ ﴿ to enquire about his well-being while he was in the death throes. So he kept weeping for quite some time, then said: 'There has been no one dearer to me than Allah's Messenger ﴿, and no one more exalted and venerated than he. I was unable to fill my eyes with him, in honour and majesty of him, and if asked to describe him, I could not do so, because I did not fill my eyes with him.'"

Reported by Muslim.

١٠٨/١٠٨. عَنْ عَبْدِ الرَّحْمَنِ ابْنِ أَبِي لَيْلَى ﴿ أَنَّ عَبْدَ اللهِ بْنَ عُمَرَ ﴿ حَدَّثَهُ
وَذَكَرَ قِصَّةً. قَالَ: فَدَنَوْنَا يَعْنِي مِنَ النَّبِيِّ ﴿، فَقَبَّلْنَا يَدَهُ.

رَوَاهُ أَبُوْ دَاوُدَ وَالْبَيْهَقِيُّ.

108/108. According to ʿAbd al-Raḥmān b. Abī Laylā ﴿, ʿAbd Allāh b. ʿUmar ﴿ spoke to him and told him a story. He said:

---

[107] Set forth by •Muslim in al-Ṣaḥīḥ: Bk.: al-Īmān [Faith], Ch.: The fact that Islam demolishes what preceded it, and likewise the Emigration [Hijra] and the Pilgrimage, 1/112 §121. •Ibn Manda in al-Īmān, 2/420 §270. •Abū ʿAwāna in al-Musnad, 1/70 §200. •Ibn Saʿd in al-Ṭabaqāt, 4/259. •al-Ḥusaynī in al-Bayān wa al-Taʿrīf, 1/157 §418. •al-Munāwī in Fayḍ al-Qadīr, /167.

[108] Set forth by •Abū Dāwūd in al-Sunan: Bk.: al-Adab [Proper Conduct], Ch.: Kissing the hand, 4/356 §5223. •al-Bayhaqī in al-Sunan al-Kubrā, 7/101

"We drew near," meaning to the Prophet ﷺ, "and we kissed his hand."

Reported by Abū Dāwūd and al-Bayhaqī.

١٠٩/١٠٩. عَنْ زَارِعٍ ﵁ (وَكَانَ فِي وَفْدِ عَبْدِ الْقَيْسِ) قَالَ: لَمَّا قَدِمْنَا الْمَدِيْنَةَ فَجَعَلْنَا نَتَبَادَرُ مِنْ رَوَاحِلِنَا، فَنُقَبِّلُ يَدَ رَسُوْلِ اللهِ ﷺ وَرِجْلَيْهِ.

رَوَاهُ أَبُوْ دَاوُدَ وَالْبُخَارِيُّ فِي الْأَدَبِ.

109/109. According to Zāriʿ ﵁ (while he was in the delegation of ʿAbd al-Qays):

"As soon as we reached Medina, we quickly dismounted our riding animals and, reaching him, we started kissing (the blessed) hands and feet of Allah's Messenger ﷺ."

Reported by Abū Dāwūd and al-Bukharī in *al-Adab.*

١١٠/١١٠. عَنْ عَبْدِ اللهِ بْنِ عُمَرَ ﵄ قَالَ: كُنَّا فِي غَزْوَةٍ، فَحَاصَ النَّاسُ حَيْصَةً. قُلْنَا: كَيْفَ نَلْقَى النَّبِيَّ ﷺ وَقَدْ فَرَرْنَا؟ فَنَزَلَتْ: ﴿إِلَّا مُتَحَرِّفًا لِّقِتَالٍ﴾ (الأنفال، ٨: ١٦). فَقُلْنَا: لَا نَقْدَمُ الْمَدِيْنَةَ فَلَا يَرَانَا أَحَدٌ. فَقُلْنَا: لَوْ قَدِمْنَا. فَخَرَجَ النَّبِيُّ ﷺ مِنْ صَلَاةِ الْفَجْرِ، قُلْنَا: نَحْنُ الْفَرَّارُوْنَ. قَالَ: أَنْتُمُ الْعَكَّارُوْنَ. قَالَ: فَدَنَوْنَا فَقَبَّلْنَا يَدَهُ، فَقَالَ: أَنَا فِئَةُ الْمُسْلِمِيْنَ.

رَوَاهُ أَبُوْ دَاوُدَ وَأَحْمَدُ وَالْبُخَارِيُّ فِي الْأَدَبِ وَاللَّفْظُ لَهُ.

---

§13362, & in *Shuʿab al-Īmān*, 6/476 §8965.

109 Set forth by •Abū Dāwūd in *al-Sunan*, Bk.: *al-Adab* [Proper Conduct], Ch.: Kissing the body, 4/357 §5225. •al-Bukhārī in *al-Adab al-Mufrad*, 1/339 §975. •al-Ṭabarānī in *al-Muʿjam al-Kabīr*, 5/275 §5313. •al-Bayhaqī in *Shuʿab al-Īmān*, 6/141 §7729. •al-Haythamī in *Majmaʿ al-Zawāʾid*, 9/2. •al-Ḥusaynī in *al-Bayān wa al-Taʿrīf*, 1/241. •al-Muqriʾ in *Taqbīl al-Yad*, 1/80 §20.

110/110. According to ʿAbd Allāh b. ʿUmar ﵄:

"We were engaged in a military expedition, when the people disintegrated and retreated from the front. We said: 'What face shall we show to Allah's Messenger ﷺ, for we have run away?' Then down came the revelation (Q.8:16): 'Except those who manoeuver for battle *[illā mutaḥarrifan li-qitālin]*,' so we said: 'We shall not approach Medina, so that no one may see us.' Then we had a second thought to go to Medina. The Prophet ﷺ came out for the morning ritual prayer, so we (approached and) said: 'We are the deserters!' He said: 'No, rather you are those who return to the fight after running away!' We drew near and kissed his hand, so he said: 'I am the refuge for all the Muslims!'"

Reported by Abū Dāwūd and Aḥmad and al-Bukhārī in *al-Adab* (the wording is his).

١١١/١١١. عَنْ مُوْسَى بْنِ عُقْبَةَ ﵁ في رواية طويلة أَرْسَلَ رَسُوْلُ اللهِ ﷺ عُثْمَانَ بْنَ عَفَّانَ ﵁ إِلَى قُرَيْشٍ ... فَدَعُوْا عُثْمَانَ بْنَ عَفَّانَ ﵁ لِيَطُوْفَ بِالْبَيْتِ فَأَبَى أَنْ يَطُوْفَ وَقَالَ: كُنْتُ لاَ أَطُوْفُ بِهِ حَتَّى يَطُوْفَ بِهِ رَسُوْلُ اللهِ ﷺ. فَرَجَعَ إِلَى رَسُوْلِ اللهِ ﷺ.

رَوَاهُ الْبَيْهَقِيُّ.

111/111. According to Mūsā b. ʿUqba ﵁, in the course of a detailed story:

"Allah's Messenger ﷺ sent ʿUthmān b. ʿAffān ﵁ as an ambassador to Quraysh (on the occasion of Ḥudaybiya agreement).... (After the negotiations) they offered ʿUthmān b. ʿAffān ﵁ to circumambulate the Sacred House [the Kaʿba], but he refused to circumambulate and said: 'I will not circumambulate it until Allah's Messenger

---

110 Set forth by •Abū Dāwūd in *al-Sunan*: Bk.: *al-Jihād* [The Sacred Struggle], Ch.: Turning one's back on the day of battle, 3/46 §2647. •Ibn Abī Shayba in *al-Muṣannaf*, 6/541 §33686. •Aḥmad b. Ḥanbal in *al-Musnad*, 2/70 §5384. •al-Bukhārī in *al-Adab al-Mufrad*, 1/338 §972. •al-Ḥusaynī in *al-Bayān wa al-Taʿrīf*, 1/295 §786.

111 Set forth by •al-Bayhaqī in *al-Sunan al-Kubrā*, 9/221. •Abū al-Maḥāsin in *Muʿtaṣar al-Mukhtaṣar*, 2/369.

ﷺ circumambulates it!' Then he returned to Allah's Messenger ﷺ (without circumambulating)."

Reported by al-Bayhaqī.

١١٢/١١٢. عَنْ أَسْمَاءَ بِنْتِ عُمَيْسٍ رضي الله عنها قَالَتْ: كَانَ رَسُوْلُ اللهِ ﷺ يُوْحَى إِلَيْهِ وَرَأْسُهُ فِي حِجْرِ عَلِيٍّ رضي الله عنه فَلَمْ يُصَلِّ الْعَصْرَ حَتَّى غَرَبَتِ الشَّمْسُ. فَقَالَ رَسُوْلُ اللهِ ﷺ: اَللَّهُمَّ، إِنَّ عَلِيًّا كَانَ فِي طَاعَتِكَ وَطَاعَةِ رَسُوْلِكَ فَارْدُدْ عَلَيْهِ الشَّمْسَ. قَالَتْ أَسْمَاءُ رضي الله عنها: فَرَأَيْتُهَا غَرَبَتْ وَرَأَيْتُهَا طَلَعَتْ بَعْدَ مَا غَرَبَتْ.

رَوَاهُ الطَّبَرَانِيُّ.

112/112. According to Asmā', the daughter of ʿUmays رضي الله عنها:

"Allah's Messenger ﷺ was receiving revelation and his head was

---

[112] Set forth by •al-Ṭabarānī in *al-Muʿjam al-Kabīr*, 24/147 §390. •al-Haythamī in *Majmaʿ al-Zawā'id*, 8/297. •Ibn Kathīr in *al-Bidāya wa al-Nihāya*, 6/83. •al-Qāḍī ʿIyāḍ in *al-Shifā*, 1/400. •al-Suyūṭī in *al-Khaṣā'iṣ al-Kubrā*, 2/137. •al-Ḥalabī in *al-Sīrat al-Ḥalabiyya*, 2/103. •al-Qurṭubī in *al-Jāmiʿ li-Aḥkām al-Qur'ān*, 15/197.

It has been reported by al-Ṭabarānī with chains of transmission, one of which has authentic sources, as well as Ibrāhīm b. Ḥasan, and he is a reliable source, confirmed by Ibn Ḥibbān. It has also been reported by al-Ṭahāwī in *Mushkil al-Āthār* (2/9; 4/388–389). The tradition also has other tracks, from Asmā', Abū Hurayra, ʿAlī b. Abī Ṭālib and Abū Saʿīd al-Khudrī رضي الله عنهم.

Its tracks had been collected by Abū al-Ḥasan al-Faḍlī, by ʿUbayd Allāh al-Ḥaskā, who died in the year A.H. 480, in *Mas'ala fī Taṣḥīḥ Ḥadīth Radd al-Shams*, and by al-Suyūṭī in *Kashf al-Labs ʿan Ḥadīth al-Shams*. According to al-Suyūṭī in *al-Khaṣā'iṣ al-Kubrā* (2/137): "It has been set forth by Ibn Manda, Ibn Shāhayn and al-Ṭabarānī, with chains of transmission, some of which are in compliance with the stipulation of authenticity." According to al-Shaybānī in *Ḥadā'iq al-Anwār* (1/193): "It has been set forth by al-Ṭahāwī in *Mushkil al-Ḥadīth / al-Āthār*, with two authentic chains of transmission."

According to al-Imam al-Nawawī in *Sharḥ Muslim* (12/52): "As stated by al-Qaḍī رحمه الله: 'The sun was arrested twice for our Prophet ﷺ....'" That was mentioned by al-Ṭahāwī, and he said: "Its reports are reliable."

It has also been declared fine by al-Ḥāfiẓ Abū Zurʿa in the supplement of his father's book entitled *Ṭarḥ al-Tathrīb* (7/274).

in the lap of ʿAlī ﷺ. So he could not perform the afternoon ritual prayer until the sun had set. Allah's Messenger supplicated ﷺ: 'O Allah! ʿAlī was in obedience to You and Your Messenger, so return the sun to him!'" Asmāʾ ﷺ said: "I saw it set, and I saw it rise after it had set!"

Reported by al-Ṭabarānī.

١١٣/١١٣. عَنْ قَيْسِ بْنِ مَخْرَمَةَ ﷺ قَالَ: وُلِدْتُ أَنَا وَرَسُوْلُ اللهِ ﷺ عَامَ الْفِيْلِ. قَالَ: وَسَأَلَ عُثْمَانُ بْنُ عَفَّانَ ﷺ قُبَاثَ بْنَ أَشْيَمَ أَخَا بَنِي يَعْمَرَ بْنِ لَيْثٍ: أَأَنْتَ أَكْبَرُ أَمْ رَسُوْلُ اللهِ؟ فَقَالَ: رَسُوْلُ اللهِ ﷺ أَكْبَرُ مِنِّي وَأَنَا أَقْدَمُ مِنْهُ فِي الْمِيْلَادِ.

رَوَاهُ التِّرْمِذِيُّ وَالْحَاكِمُ، وَقَالَ أَبُوْ عِيْسَى: هَذَا حَدِيْثٌ حَسَنٌ.

113/113. According to Qays b. Makhrama ﷺ:

"Both I and Allah's Messenger ﷺ were born in the Year of the Elephant. ʿUthmān b. ʿAffān ﷺ asked Qubāth b. Ashaym, the brother of the sons of Yaʿmar b. Layth: 'Are you older, or Allah's Messenger?' He said: 'Allah's Messenger ﷺ is older than I; I was only born before him!'"

Reported by al-Tirmidhī and al-Ḥākim. According to Abū ʿĪsā: "This is a fine tradition."

١١٤/١١٤. عَنْ مُغِيْرَةَ بْنِ أَبِي رَزِيْنٍ ﷺ قَالَ: قِيْلَ لِلْعَبَّاسِ بْنِ عَبْدِ الْمُطَّلِبِ ﷺ: أَيُّمَا أَكْبَرُ، أَنْتَ أَمِ النَّبِيُّ ﷺ؟ فَقَالَ: هُوَ أَكْبَرُ مِنِّي وَأَنَا وُلِدْتُ قَبْلَهُ.

رَوَاهُ الْحَاكِمُ وَابْنُ أَبِي شَيْبَةَ. وَرِجَالُهُ رِجَالُ الصَّحِيْحِ.

---

[113] Set forth by •al-Tirmidhī in *al-Sunan*: Bk.: *al-Faḍāʾil* [Excellent Merits] according to Allah's Messenger ﷺ, Ch.: What has come to us about the birthday of the Prophet ﷺ, 5/589 §3619. •al-Ḥākim in *al-Mustadrak*, 3/724 §6624. •al-Ṭabarānī in *al-Muʿjam al-Kabīr*, 19/37 §75. •al-Shaybānī in *al-Āḥād wa al-Mathānī*, 1/407 §566, 927.

114/114. According to Mughīra b. Abī Razīn 🙏:

"Someone asked al-ʿAbbās b. ʿAbd al-Muṭṭalib 🙏: 'Who is older, you or the Prophet 🙏?' He said: 'He is older than I; I was merely born before him!'"

> Reported by al-Ḥākim and Ibn Abī Shayba, and its sources are authentic.

---

[114] Set forth by •al-Ḥākim in *al-Mustadrak*, 3/362 §5398. •Ibn Abī Shayba in *al-Muṣannaf*, 5/296 §26256; 7/18 §33921. •al-Shaybānī in *al-Āḥād wa al-Mathānī*, 1/269 §350. •al-Haythamī in *Majmaʿ al-Zawāʾid*, 9/270. He said: "It has been reported by al-Ṭabarānī, whose sources are authentic."

الْبَابُ الثَّانِي

جَامِعُ الْمَنَاقِبِ

Chapter 2

Compendium of the Noble Virtues

اَلْفَصْلُ الْأَوَّلُ

فَصْلٌ فِي مَنَاقِبِ أَهْلِ الْبَيْتِ وَقَرَابَةِ الرَّسُوْلِ

Section 1

The Virtues of the Members of the Family and the Kindred of the Messenger

١/١١٥. عَنْ زَيْدِ بْنِ أَرْقَمَ ﵁ قَالَ: قَامَ رَسُوْلُ اللهِ ﷺ يَوْمًا فِيْنَا خَطِيْبًا، بِمَاءٍ يُدْعَى خُمًّا، بَيْنَ مَكَّةَ وَالْمَدِيْنَةِ. فَحَمِدَ اللهَ وَأَثْنَى عَلَيْهِ، وَوَعَظَ وَذَكَّرَ ثُمَّ قَالَ: أَمَّا بَعْدُ. أَلَا، أَيُّهَا النَّاسُ، فَإِنَّمَا أَنَا بَشَرٌ؛ يُوْشِكُ أَنْ يَأْتِيَ رَسُوْلُ رَبِّي فَأُجِيْبُ؛ وَأَنَا تَارِكٌ فِيْكُمْ ثَقَلَيْنِ: أَوَّلُهُمَا كِتَابُ اللهِ فِيْهِ الْهُدَى وَالنُّوْرُ فَخُذُوْا بِكِتَابِ اللهِ وَاسْتَمْسِكُوْا بِهِ. فَحَثَّ عَلَى كِتَابِ اللهِ وَرَغَّبَ فِيْهِ. ثُمَّ قَالَ: وَأَهْلُ بَيْتِي. أُذَكِّرُكُمُ اللهَ فِي أَهْلِ بَيْتِي. أُذَكِّرُكُمُ اللهَ فِي أَهْلِ بَيْتِي. أُذَكِّرُكُمُ اللهَ فِي أَهْلِ بَيْتِي.

رَوَاهُ مُسْلِمٌ.

115/1. According to Zayd b. Arqam ﵁:

"Allah's Messenger ﷺ stood up one day in our midst to deliver a sermon, beside a pond called 'Khum', between Mecca and Medina. He praised Allah and extolled Him, admonished, directed, guided

[115] Set forth by •Muslim in *al-Ṣaḥīḥ*: Bk.: *Faḍāʾil al-Ṣaḥāba* [The Excellent Merits of the Companions], Ch.: The excellent merits of ʿAlī b. Abī Ṭālib ﵁, 3/1873 §2408. •Aḥmad b. Ḥanbal in *al-Musnad*, 4/366 §19265. •al-Bayhaqī in *al-Sunan al-Kubrā*, 2/148 §2679. •Ibn Ḥibbān in *al-Ṣaḥīḥ*, 1/145 §123. •Ibn Khuzayma in *al-Ṣaḥīḥ* 4/62 §2357. •Abū al-Qāsim Hibat Allāh al-Lālakāʾī in *Iʿtiqād Ahl al-Sunna*, 1/79 §88. •Ibn Kathīr in *Tafsīr al-Qurʾān al-ʿAẓīm*, 3/487.

and then said: 'Furthermore, beware, O people, I am merely a human being! The messenger of my Lord (the angel of death) is about to come, so I shall respond. I am leaving you with two great things. The first of them is the Book of Allah, which contains guidance and light, so you must grasp the Book of Allah and adhere to it!' He ordained to follow the teachings contained in the Book of Allah and motivated (to put its teachings into practice). Then he said: '(Secondly) also the people of my household. I am reminding you of Allah for the sake of the people of my household! I am reminding you of Allah for the sake of the people of my household! I am reminding you of Allah for the sake of the people of my household!'"

Reported by Muslim.

١١٦/ ٢. عَنْ زَيْدِ بْنِ أَرْقَمَ ﷺ قَالَ: قَالَ رَسُوْلُ اللهِ ﷺ: إِنِّي تَارِكٌ فِيْكُم مَا إِنْ تَمَسَّكْتُمْ بِهِ لَنْ تَضِلُّوْا بَعْدِي. أَحَدُهُمَا أَعْظَمُ مِنَ الآخَرِ: كِتَابُ اللهِ حَبْلٌ مَمْدُوْدٌ مِنَ السَّمَاءِ إِلَى الْأَرْضِ وَعِتْرَتِي أَهْلُ بَيْتِي. وَلَنْ يَتَفَرَّقَا حَتَّى يَرِدَا عَلَيَّ الْحَوْضَ فَانْظُرُوْا كَيْفَ تَخْلُفُوْنِي فِيْهِمَا.

رَوَاهُ التِّرْمِذِيُّ وَحَسَّنَهُ وَالنَّسَائِيُّ.

116/2. According to Zayd b. Arqam ﷺ:

"Allah's Messenger ﷺ said: 'I am leaving you with two bequests, which are such that if you adhere to them, you will never go astray after me. The first of them is more important than the second: (1)

---

[116] Set forth by •al-Tirmidhī in *al-Sunan*: Bk.: *al-Manāqib* [Virtues] according to Allah's Messenger ﷺ, Ch.: The virtues of the family of the Prophet ﷺ, 5/663 §3786–3788. •al-Nasā'ī in *al-Sunan al-Kubrā*, 5/45 §8148, 8464. •al-Ḥākim in *al-Mustadrak*, 3/118 §4576. •al-Ṭabarānī, on the authority of Abū Saʿīd ﷺ, in *al-Muʿjam al-Awsaṭ*, 3/374 §3439, & in *al-Muʿjam al-Ṣaghīr*, 1/226 §323. •Aḥmad b. Ḥanbal in *al-Musnad*, 3/14 26, 59 §11119, 11227, 11578. •Abū Yaʿlā in *al-Musnad*, 2/303 §10267, 1140. •al-Ṭabarānī in *al-Muʿjam al-Kabīr*, 3/65 §2678. •Ibn Abī Shayba in *al-Muṣannaf*, 6/133 §30081. •Ibn Abī ʿĀṣim in *al-Sunna*, 2/644 §1553.

the Book of Allah, which is a rope extended from heaven to the earth, and (2) my relatives, the people of my household. The two will not separate until they reach me at the Basin [in Paradise], so be watchful how you follow me and act with regard to them both!'"

Reported and declared fine by al-Tirmidhī, and reported by al-Nasā'ī.

١١٧/ ٣. عَنْ جَابِرِ بْنِ عَبْدِ اللهِ ﷺ قَالَ: سَمِعْتُ رَسُوْلَ اللهِ ﷺ يَقُوْلُ: يَا أَيُّهَا النَّاسُ، إِنِّي قَدْ تَرَكْتُ فِيْكُمْ مَا إِنْ أَخَذْتُمْ بِهِ لَنْ تَضِلُّوْا: كِتَابَ اللهِ، وَعِتْرَتِي أَهْلَ بَيْتِي.

رَوَاهُ التِّرْمِذِيُّ وَحَسَّنَهُ.

117/3. According to Jābir b. ʿAbd Allāh ﷺ:

"I heard Allah's Messenger ﷺ say: 'O people, I am leaving among you things which if you adhere to, you will never go astray: the first one is the Book of Allah and the second one, my relatives, the people of my household!'"

Reported and declared fine by al-Tirmidhī.

١١٨/ ٤. عَنْ عَائِشَةَ ﷺ قَالَتْ: خَرَجَ النَّبِيُّ ﷺ غَدَاةً وَعَلَيْهِ مِرْطٌ مُرَحَّلٌ مِنْ شَعَرٍ أَسْوَدَ. فَجَاءَ الْحَسَنُ بْنُ عَلِيٍّ ﷺ فَأَدْخَلَهُ، ثُمَّ جَاءَ الْحُسَيْنُ ﷺ فَدَخَلَ مَعَهُ، ثُمَّ جَاءَتْ فَاطِمَةُ ﷺ فَأَدْخَلَهَا، ثُمَّ جَاءَ عَلِيٌّ ﷺ فَأَدْخَلَهُ، ثُمَّ قَالَ: ﴿إِنَّمَا يُرِيدُ ٱللَّهُ لِيُذْهِبَ عَنكُمُ ٱلرِّجْسَ أَهْلَ ٱلْبَيْتِ وَيُطَهِّرَكُمْ تَطْهِيرًا﴾. (الأحزاب، ٣٣: ٣٣).

رَوَاهُ مُسْلِمٌ.

117 Set forth by •al-Tirmidhī in *al-Sunan*: Bk.: *al-Manāqib* [Virtues] according to Allah's Messenger ﷺ, Ch.: The virtues of the family of the Prophet ﷺ, 5/662 §3786. •al-Ṭabarānī in *al-Muʿjam al-Awsaṭ*, 5/89 §4757, & in *al-Muʿjam al-Kabīr*, 3/66 §2680. •Ibn Kathīr in *Tafsīr al-Qurʾān al-ʿAẓīm*, 4/114.

118/4. According to ʿĀʾisha ؓ:

"The Prophet ﷺ went outside in the early morning, and he was wearing a black embroidered fur wrapper. Then along came Ḥasan b. ʿAlī ؓ: so he tucked him inside [the wrapper]. Then along came Ḥusayn ؓ: so he got inside with him. Then along came Fāṭima ؓ: so he tucked her inside. Then along came ʿAlī ؓ: so he tucked him inside. Then he said: 'Allah seeks only to remove uncleanliness from you, O Members of the Household, and to cleanse you with a thorough cleansing *[inna-mā yurīdu ʾllāhu li-yudhhiba ʿan-kumu al-rijsa Ahl al-Bayti wa yuṭahhira-kum taṭhīrā].*'" (Q.33:33).

Reporting by Muslim.

١١٩/ ٥. عَنْ عُمَرَ بْنِ أَبِي سَلَمَةَ ؓ رَبِيْبِ النَّبِيِّ ﷺ قَالَ: لَـمَّا نَزَلَتْ هَذِهِ الْآيَةُ عَلَى النَّبِيِّ ﷺ: ﴿إِنَّمَا يُرِيدُ ٱللَّهُ لِيُذْهِبَ عَنكُمُ ٱلرِّجْسَ أَهْلَ ٱلْبَيْتِ وَيُطَهِّرَكُمْ تَطْهِيرًا﴾ (الأحزاب، ٣٣: ٣٣)، فِي بَيْتِ أُمِّ سَلَمَةَ فَدَعَا فَاطِمَةَ، وَحَسَنًا، وَحُسَيْنًا، فَجَلَّلَهُمْ بِكِسَاءٍ، وَعَلِيٌّ خَلْفَ ظَهْرِهِ فَجَلَّلَهُ بِكِسَاءٍ، ثُمَّ قَالَ: اللَّهُمَّ، هَؤُلَاءِ أَهْلُ بَيْتِي، فَأَذْهِبْ عَنْهُمُ الرِّجْسَ وَطَهِّرْهُمْ تَطْهِيْرًا. قَالَتْ أُمُّ سَلَمَةَ: وَأَنَا مَعَهُمْ، يَا نَبِيَّ اللهِ. قَالَ: أَنْتِ عَلَى مَكَانِكِ وَأَنْتِ عَلَى خَيْرٍ.

رَوَاهُ التِّرْمِذِيُّ، وَقَالَ: هَذَا حَدِيْثٌ حَسَنٌ. وَفِي الْبَابِ عَنْ أُمِّ سَلَمَةَ وَأَنَسِ ابْنِ مَالِكٍ وَأَبِي الْحَمْرَاءِ وَمَعْقَلِ بْنِ يَسَارٍ وَعَائِشَةَ.

119/5. According to ʿUmar b. Abī Salama ؓ brought up by the

---

118 Set forth by •Muslim in *al-Ṣaḥīḥ*: Bk.: *Faḍāʾil al-Ṣaḥāba* [The Excellent Merits of the Companions], Ch.: The excellent merits of the family of the Prophet ﷺ, 4/1883, 2424. •al-Ḥākim in *al-Mustadrak*, 3/159 §4707–4709. He said: "This is an authentic tradition." •al-Bayhaqī in *al-Sunan al-Kubrā*, 2/149 §2680. •Ibn Abī Shayba in *al-Muṣannaf*, 6/370 §32102.

119 Set forth by •al-Tirmidhī in *al-Sunan*: Bk.: *Tafsīr al-Qurʾān* [Interpretation of the Qurʾān] according to Allah's Messenger ﷺ, Ch.: From *Sūrat al-Aḥzāb*, 5/351 §3205, & Bk.: *al-Manāqib* [Virtues] according to Allah's Messenger ﷺ, Ch.: The excellent merit of Fāṭima, the daughter of Muhammad ﷺ, 5/699

Prophet ﷺ:

"When this Qur'ānic Verse was revealed to the Prophet ﷺ in the home of the mother of the believers Umm Salama ﵂: 'Allah seeks only to remove uncleanliness from you, O Members of the Household, and to cleanse you with a thorough cleansing *[inna-mā yurīdu 'llāhu li-yudhhiba 'an-kumu al-rijsa Ahl al-Bayti wa yuṭahhira-kum taṭhīrā].'*" (Q.33:33)—he summoned Fāṭima, Ḥasan and Ḥusayn, then he enveloped them with a mantle. 'Alī was behind his back, so he enveloped him also with the same mantle. Then he said: 'O Allah, these are the Members of my Household, so remove uncleanliness from them and cleanse them with a thorough cleansing!' Umm Salama ﵂ said: 'I am (also) with them, O Prophet of Allah!' He said: 'You are worthy of your place, and you are at a better station!'"

> Reported by al-Tirmidhī, and he said: "This is a fine tradition," and there are traditions on this subject on the authority of Umm Salama, Anas b. Mālik, Abū al-Ḥamrā', Ma'qal b. Yasār and 'Ā'isha."

١٢٠/٦. عَنْ سَعْدِ بْنِ أَبِي وَقَّاصٍ ﵁ قَالَ: لَـمَّا نَزَلَتْ هَذِهِ الْآيَةُ: ﴿فَقُلْ تَعَالَوْا نَدْعُ أَبْنَآءَنَا وَأَبْنَآءَكُمْ﴾. (آل عمران، ٣:٦١)، دَعَا رَسُوْلُ اللهِ ﷺ عَلِيًّا وَفَاطِمَةَ وَحَسَنًا وَحُسَيْنًا فَقَالَ: اَللَّهُمَّ، هَؤُلَاءِ أَهْلِي.

رَوَاهُ مُسْلِمٌ وَالتِّرْمِذِيُّ، وَقَالَ أَبُوْ عِيْسَى: هَذَا حَدِيْثٌ حَسَنٌ.

120/6. According to Sa'd b. Abī Waqqāṣ ﵁:

---

§3871. •al-Ṭabarānī in *al-Mu'jam al-Awsaṭ*, 4/134 §3799.

[120] Set forth by •Muslim in *al-Ṣaḥīḥ*: Bk.: *Faḍā'il al-Ṣaḥāba* [The Excellent Merits of the Companions], Ch.: The excellent merits of 'Alī b. Abī Ṭālib ﵁, 4/1871 §2404. •al-Tirmidhī in *al-Sunan*: Bk.: *Tafsīr al-Qur'ān* [Interpretation of the Qur'ān] according to Allah's Messenger ﷺ, Ch.: From *Sūra Āl 'Imrān*, 5/225 §2999, & Bk.: *al-Manāqib* [Virtues] according to Allah's Messenger ﷺ, Ch.: (21), 5/638 §3724. •Aḥmad b. Ḥanbal in *al-Musnad*, 1/185 §1608. •al-Bayhaqī in *al-Sunan al-Kubrā*, 7/63 §13169–13170. •al-Nasā'ī in *al-Sunan al-Kubrā*, 5/107 §8399. •al-Ḥākim in *al-Mustadrak*, 3/163 §4719.

"When this Qur'ānic Verse (Q.3:61) was revealed: 'Say: "Come, we will summon our sons and your sons *[fa-qul taʿālaw nadʿu abnā'a-nā wa abnā'a-kum]*,'" Allah's Messenger ﷺ summoned ʿAlī, Fāṭima, Ḥasan and Ḥusayn, then he said: 'O Allah, these are my family!'"

Reported by Muslim and al-Tirmidhī. Abū ʿĪsā said: "This is a fine tradition."

١٢١/٧. عَنِ الْعَبَّاسِ بْنِ عَبْدِ الْـمُطَّلِبِ رضي الله عنهما قَالَ: قُلْتُ: يَا رَسُوْلَ اللهِ، إِنَّ قُرَيْشًا إِذَا لَقِيَ بَعْضُهُمْ بَعضًا لَقُوْهُمْ بِبِشْرٍ حَسَنٍ، وَإِذَا لَقُوْنَا لَقُوْنَا بِوُجُوْهٍ لاَ نَعْرِفُهَا. قَالَ: فَغَضِبَ النَّبِيُّ ﷺ غَضَبًا شَدِيْدًا، وَقَالَ: وَالَّذِي نَفْسِي بِيَدِهِ، لاَ يَدْخُلُ قَلْبَ رَجُلٍ الإِيْمَانُ حَتَّى يُحِبَّكُمْ لِلّٰهِ وَلِرَسُوْلِهِ وَلِقَرَابَتِي.

رَوَاهُ أَحْمَدُ وَالنَّسَائِيُّ وَالْحَاكِمُ وَالْبَزَّارُ.

وفي رواية: قَالَ: وَاللهِ، لاَ يَدْخُلُ قَلْبَ امْرِىءٍ إِيْمَانٌ حَتَّى يُحِبَّكُمْ لِلّٰهِ وَلِقَرَابَتِي.

121/7. According to al-ʿAbbās b. ʿAbd al-Muṭṭalib رضي الله عنهما:

"I said: 'O Messenger of Allah, when Quraysh meet one another, they meet them with good cheer, but when they meet us, they meet us with faces (void of feelings that) we do not recognize!' The Prophet ﷺ felt extremely annoyed, and said: 'By the One in whose Hand is my soul, faith will not enter a man's heart, until he loves you for the sake of Allah, for the sake of His Messenger, and for the sake of my kindred!'"

Reported by Aḥmad, al-Nasā'ī, al-Ḥākim and al-Bazzār.

According to one report: "He said: "By Allah, faith cannot enter anyone's heart until he loves you for the sake of Allah and

---

[121] Set forth by •Aḥmad b. Ḥanbal in *al-Musnad*, 1/207 §1772, 1777, 17656–17658. •al-Ḥākim in *al-Mustadrak*, 3/376 §5433, 2960. •al-Nasā'ī in *al-Sunan al-Kubrā*, 5/51 §8176. •al-Bazzār in *al-Musnad*, 6/131 §2175. •al-Bayhaqī in *Shuʿab al-Īmān*, 2/188 §1501. •al-Daylamī in *al-Firdaws bi-Ma'thūr al-Khiṭāb*, 4/361 §7037.

for the sake of my kindred.'"

١٢٢/ ٨. عَنِ الْعَبَّاسِ بْنِ عَبْدِ الْـمُطَّلِبِ ﵄ قَالَ: كُنَّا نَلْقَى النَّفَرَ مِنْ قُرَيْشٍ، وَهُمْ يَتَحَدَّثُوْنَ فَيَقْطَعُوْنَ حَدِيْثَهُمْ. فَذَكَرْنَا ذَلِكَ لِرَسُوْلِ اللهِ ﷺ، فَقَالَ: مَا بَالُ أَقْوَامٍ يَتَحَدَّثُوْنَ فَإِذَا رَأَوْا الرَّجُلَ مِنْ أَهْلِ بَيْتِي قَطَعُوْا حَدِيْثَهُمْ. وَاللهِ، لَا يَدْخُلُ قَلْبَ رَجُلٍ الإِيْمَانُ حَتَّى يُحِبَّهُمْ لِلّٰهِ وَلِقَرَابَتِهِمْ مِنِّي.

رَوَاهُ ابْنُ مَاجَه وَالْحَاكِمُ.

122/8. According to al-ʿAbbās b. ʿAbd al-Muṭṭalib ﵄:

"When we used to meet the people of Quraysh while they were conversing, they would stop their conversation. When we mentioned that to Allah's Messenger ﷺ, he said: 'What is the matter with the people? When they see the man from among the people of my household, they stop talking. By Allah, faith will not enter anyone's heart, until he loves my kindred for the sake of Allah and for the sake of their kinship with me!'"

Reported by Ibn Mājah and al-Ḥākim.

١٢٣/ ٩. عَنِ ابْنِ عَبَّاسٍ ﵄ قَالَ: قَالَ رَسُوْلُ اللهِ ﷺ: مَثَلُ أَهْلِ بَيْتِي مَثَلُ سَفِينَةِ نُوْحٍ. مَنْ رَكِبَ فِيْهَا نَجَا، وَمَنْ تَخَلَّفَ عَنْهَا غَرِقَ.

رَوَاهُ الطَّبَرَانِيُّ وَالْبَزَّارُ وَالْحَاكِمُ.

وفي رواية: عَنْ عَبْدِ اللهِ بْنِ الزُّبَيْرِ ﵄ قَالَ: مَنْ رَكِبَهَا سَلِمَ، وَمَنْ تَرَكَهَا غَرِقَ.

123/9. According to Ibn ʿAbbās ﵄:

---

[122] Set forth by •Ibn Mājah in *al-Sunan*, Introduction: Ch.: The excellent merit of al-ʿAbbās b. ʿAbd al-Muṭṭalib ﵁, 1/50 §140. •al-Ḥākim in *al-Mustadrak*, 4/85 §6960. •al-Maqdisī in *al-Aḥādīth al-Mukhtāra*, 8/382 §472. •al-Daylamī in *al-Firdaws bi-Maʾthūr al-Khiṭāb*, 4/113 §6350.

[123] Set forth by •al-Ṭabarānī in *al-Muʿjam al-Kabīr*, 12/34 §2388, 2638, 2636, & in *al-Muʿjam al-Awsaṭ*, 4/10 §3478; 5/355 §5536; 6/85 §5870, & in

"Allah's Messenger ﷺ said: 'The likeness of the people of my household is the likeness of Noah's ark. If someone sails upon it, he will be granted salvation, and if someone fails to board it, he will drown.'

Reported by al-Ṭabarānī, al-Bazzār and al-Ḥākim.

In one report: According to ʿAbd Allāh b. al-Zubayr ﷺ:

"If someone sails upon it, he will be safe and sound, and if someone abandons it, he will drown."

١٢٤/ ١٠. عَنْ عُمَرَ بْنِ الْخَطَّابِ ﷺ قَالَ: سَمِعْتُ رَسُوْلَ اللهِ ﷺ يَقُوْلُ: كُلُّ سَبَبٍ وَنَسَبٍ يَنْقَطِعُ يَوْمَ الْقِيَامَةِ إِلاَّ مَا كَانَ مِنْ سَبَبِي وَنَسَبِي.

رَوَاهُ الْحَاكِمُ وَالطَّبَرَانِيُّ. إِسْنَادُهُ حَسَنٌ.

124/10. According to ʿUmar b. al-Khaṭṭāb ﷺ:

"I heard Allah's Messenger ﷺ say: 'Every lineage and kinship will be discontinued on the Day of Resurrection except my lineage and my kinship.'"

Reported by al-Ḥākim and al-Ṭabarānī with an excellent chain of transmission.

١٢٥/ ١١. عَنْ جَابِرٍ ﷺ قَالَ: قَالَ رَسُوْلُ اللهِ ﷺ: لِكُلِّ بَنِي أُمٍّ عَصَبَةٌ يَنْتَمُوْنَ إِلَيْهِمْ إِلاَّ ابْنَي فَاطِمَةَ فَأَنَا وَلِيُّهُمَا وَعَصَبَتُهُمَا.

رَوَاهُ الْحَاكِمُ وَأَبُوْ يَعْلَى. وَقَالَ الْحَاكِمُ: هَذَا حَدِيْثٌ صَحِيْحُ الإِسْنَادِ.

---

al-Muʿjam al-Ṣaghīr, 1/240 §391; 2/84 §825. •al-Ḥākim in *al-Mustadrak*, 3/163 §4720. •al-Bazzār in *al-Musnad*, 9/343 §3900. •al-Daylamī in *al-Firdaws bi-Maʾthūr al-Khiṭāb*, 1/238 §916.

124 Set forth by •al-Ḥākim in *al-Mustadrak*, 3/153 §4684. •al-Ṭabarānī in *al-Muʿjam al-Kabīr*, 3/44 §2633–2635, & in *al-Muʿjam al-Awsaṭ*, 5/376 §5606. •ʿAbd al-Razzāq in *al-Muṣannaf*, 6/163 §10354. •al-Bayhaqī in *al-Sunan al-Kubrā*, 7/63 §13171. •al-Maqdisī in *al-Aḥādīth al-Mukhtāra*, 1/197 §101. He said: "Its chain of transmission is excellent." •al-Haythamī in *Majmaʿ al-Zawāʾid*, 9/173. He said: "Its chain of transmission is excellent."

125/11. According to Jābir ﵁:

"Allah's Messenger ﷺ said: 'All the sons of a mother have paternal kindred by whom they are recognized, except the two sons of Fāṭima, for I am their guardian and their paternal kindred!'"

Reported by al-Ḥākim and Abū Yaʿlā. Al-Ḥākim said: "This is a tradition with an authentic chain of transmission."

١٢٦/ ١٢. عَنْ عُمَرَ ﵁ قَالَ: سَمِعْتُ رَسُوْلَ اللهِ ﷺ يَقُوْلُ: كُلُّ بَنِي أُنْثَى فَإِنَّ عَصَبَتَهُمْ لِأَبِيْهِمْ مَا خَلاَ بَنِي فَاطِمَةَ، فَإِنِّي أَنَا عَصَبَتُهُمْ وَأَنَا أَبُوْهُمْ.

رَوَاهُ الدَّيْلَمِيُّ.

126/12. According to ʿUmar ﵁:

"I heard Allah's Messenger ﷺ say: 'All the sons of a female are attributed to their fathers, apart from the sons of Fāṭima, for I am their guardian and paternal kindred!'"

Reported by al-Daylamī.

١٢٧/ ١٣. عَنْ جَابِرٍ ﵁ قَالَ: قَالَ رَسُوْلُ اللهِ ﷺ: إِنَّ اللهَ ﷻ جَعَلَ ذُرِّيَّةَ كُلِّ نَبِيٍّ فِي صُلْبِهِ، وَإِنَّ اللهَ جَعَلَ ذُرِيَّتِي فِي صُلْبِ عَلِيِّ بْنِ أَبِي طَالِبٍ ﵁.

رَوَاهُ الطَّبَرَانِيُّ.

127/13. According to Jābir ﵁:

---

[125] Set forth by •al-Ḥākim in *al-Mustadrak*, 3/179 §4770. •Abū Yaʿlā in *al-Musnad*, 2/109 §6741. •al-Ṭabarānī in *al-Muʿjam al-Kabīr*, 3/44 §2631–2632.

[126] Set forth by •al-Daylamī in *al-Firdaws bi-Maʾthūr al-Khiṭāb*, 3/234 §4787. •al-Haythamī in *Majmaʿ al-Zawāʾid*, 4/224.

[127] Set forth by •al-Ṭabarānī in *al-Muʿjam al-Kabīr*, 3/43 §2630. •al-Daylamī in *al-Firdaws bi-Maʾthūr al-Khiṭāb*, 1/172 §643. •al-Haythamī in *Majmaʿ al-Zawāʾid*, 9/172. •al-Munāwī in *Fayḍ al-Qadīr*, 2/223.

"Allah's Messenger ﷺ said: 'Allah ﷻ has assigned the progeny of every Prophet to his own loins, but Allah has assigned my progeny to the loins of ʿAlī b. Abī Ṭālib ؓ!'"

Reported by al-Ṭabarānī.

١٢٨/ ١٤. عَنْ أَبِي مَسْعُوْدٍ الْأَنْصَارِيِّ ؓ قَالَ: قَالَ رَسُوْلُ اللهِ ﷺ: مَنْ صَلَّى صَلَاةً لَمْ يُصَلِّ فِيْهَا عَلَيَّ وَعَلَى أَهْلِ بَيْتِي، لَمْ تُقْبَلْ مِنْهُ.

وَقَالَ أَبُوْ مَسْعُوْدٍ ؓ: لَوْ صَلَّيْتُ صَلَاةً لَا أُصَلِّي فِيْهَا عَلَى مُحَمَّدٍ، مَا رَأَيْتُ أَنَّ صَلَاتِي تَتِمُّ.

رَوَاهُ الدَّارَقُطْنِيُّ وَالْبَيْهَقِيُّ.

128/14. According to Abū Masʿūd al-Anṣārī ؓ:

"Allah's Messenger ﷺ said: 'If someone performs a ritual prayer in which he does not invoke blessing upon me and upon the people of my household, it will not be accepted from him!'"

Abū Masʿūd ؓ also said: "If I performed a ritual prayer in which I failed to invoke blessing upon Muhammad, I would not consider my that ritual prayer to be complete!"

Reported by al-Dāraquṭnī and al-Bayhaqī.

١٢٩/ ١٥. عَنْ حُذَيْفَةَ ؓ قَالَ: قَالَ: رَسُوْلُ اللهِ ﷺ: إِنَّ هَذَا مَلَكٌ لَمْ يَنْزِلِ الْأَرْضَ قَطُّ قَبْلَ هَذِهِ اللَّيْلَةِ اسْتَأْذَنَ رَبَّهُ أَنْ يُسَلِّمَ عَلَيَّ وَيُبَشِّرَنِي بِأَنَّ فَاطِمَةَ سَيِّدَةُ نِسَاءِ أَهْلِ الْجَنَّةِ وَأَنَّ الْحَسَنَ وَالْحُسَيْنَ سَيِّدَا شَبَابِ أَهْلِ الْجَنَّةِ.

رَوَاهُ التِّرْمِذِيُّ وَالنَّسَائِيُّ وَأَحْمَدُ، وَقَالَ التِّرْمِذِيُّ: هَذَا حَدِيْثٌ حَسَنٌ.

---

128 Set forth by •al-Dāraquṭnī in *al-Sunan*, 1/355 §6–7. •al-Bayhaqī in *al-Sunan al-Kubrā*, 2/530 §3969. •Ibn al-Jawzī in *al-Taḥqīq fī Aḥādīth al-Khilāf*, 1/402 §544. •al-Shawkānī in *Nayl al-Awṭār*, 2/322.

129/15. According to Ḥudhayfa ﵁:

"Allah's Messenger ﷺ said: 'This angel never descended to the earth before tonight; he sought his Lord's permission to greet me with the salutation of peace, and to give me the glad tidings that Fāṭima is the mistress of the women of the people of the Garden of Paradise, and that Ḥasan and Ḥusayn are the chieftains of the youths of the people of the Garden of Paradise.'"

Reported by al-Tirmidhī, al-Nasāʾī and Aḥmad, and al-Tirmidhī said: "This is a fine tradition."

١٣٠/ ١٦. عَنْ عَلِيٍّ ﵁ أَنَّهُ دَخَلَ عَلَى النَّبِيِّ ﷺ، وَقَدْ بَسَطَ شَمْلَةً، فَجَلَسَ عَلَيْهَا هُوَ وَفَاطِمَةُ وَعَلِيٌّ وَالْحَسَنُ وَالْحُسَيْنُ، ثُمَّ أَخَذَ النَّبِيُّ ﷺ بِمَجَامِعِهِ فَعَقَدَ عَلَيْهِمْ ثُمَّ قَالَ: اَللّٰهُمَّ، ارْضَ عَنْهُمْ كَمَا أَنَا عَنْهُمْ رَاضٍ.

رَوَاهُ الطَّبَرَانِيُّ.

130/16. According to ʿAlī ﵁, he entered the presence of the Prophet ﷺ. He had spread a wrapper, so he (himself) and Fāṭima and ʿAlī and Ḥasan and Ḥusayn sat on it. Then the Prophet ﷺ grasped the corners of the wrapper (and pulled it over them) and tied the corners into a knot. Then he said: "O Allah, be well pleased with them, just as I am well pleased with them!"

Reported by al-Ṭabarānī.

---

[129] Set forth by •al-Tirmidhī in *al-Sunan*: Bk.: *al-Manāqib* [Virtues] according to Allah's Messenger ﷺ, Ch.: The virtues of al-Ḥasan and al-Ḥusayn ﵄, 5/660 §3781. •al-Nasāʾī in *al-Sunan al-Kubrā*, 80, 95 §8298, 8365 & in *Faḍāʾil al-Ṣaḥāba*, 1/58, 76 §193, 260. •Aḥmad b. Ḥanbal in *al-Musnad*,5/391 §23369 & in *Faḍāʾil al-Ṣaḥāba*, 2/788, §1406 •Ibn Abī Shayba in *al-Muṣannaf*, 6/388 §32271. •al-Ḥākim in *al-Mustadrak*, 3/164 §4721–4722. •al-Ṭabarānī in *al-Muʿjam al-Kabīr*, 22/402 §1005. •Abū Nuʿaym in *Ḥilya al-Awliyāʾ*, 4/190. •al-Bayhaqī in *al-Iʿtiqād*, 328.

[130] Set forth by •al-Ṭabarānī in *al-Muʿjam al-Awsaṭ*, 5/348 §5514. •al-Haythamī in *Majmaʿ al-Zawāʾid*, 9/169.

١٧/١٣١ . عَنْ عُمَرَ ﷺ أَنَّهُ دَخَلَ عَلَى فَاطِمَةَ بِنْتِ رَسُوْلِ اللهِ ﷺ فَقَالَ: يَا فَاطِمَةُ، وَاللهِ، مَا رَأَيْتُ أَحَدًا أَحَبَّ إِلَى رَسُوْلِ اللهِ ﷺ مِنْكِ. وَاللهِ، مَا كَانَ أَحَدٌ مِنَ النَّاسِ بَعْدَ أَبِيْكِ ﷺ أَحَبَّ إِلَيَّ مِنْكِ.

رَوَاهُ الْحَاكِمُ وَابْنُ أَبِي شَيْبَةَ.

131/17. According to ʿUmar ﷺ, he came to Fāṭima, the daughter of Allah's Messenger ﷺ, and said: "O Fāṭima! By Allah! I have not seen anyone dearer to Allah's Messenger ﷺ than you. By Allah! Not one of the people, after your father ﷺ, has been dearer to me than you!"

Reported by al-Ḥākim and Ibn Abī Shayba.

١٨/١٣٢ . عَنْ عَلِيٍّ ﷺ قَالَ: اَلْحَسَنُ أَشْبَهُ بِرَسُوْلِ اللهِ ﷺ مَا بَيْنَ الصَّدْرِ إِلَى الرَّأْسِ، وَالْحُسَيْنُ أَشْبَهُ بِالنَّبِيِّ ﷺ مَا كَانَ أَسْفَلَ مِنْ ذَلِكَ.

رَوَاهُ التِّرْمِذِيُّ وَأَحْمَدُ وَابْنُ حِبَّانَ، وَقَالَ أَبُوْ عِيْسَى: هَذَا حَدِيْثٌ حَسَنٌ صَحِيْحٌ.

132/18. According to ʿAlī ﷺ:

"Ḥasan bears a very close resemblance to Allah's Messenger ﷺ from the breast to the head, and Ḥusayn bears a very close resemblance to the Prophet ﷺ in the area below that."

Reported by al-Tirmidhī, Aḥmad and Ibn Ḥibbān. Abū ʿĪsā said: "This is a fine authentic tradition."

---

[131] Set forth by •al-Ḥākim in *al-Mustadrak*, 3/168 §4736. •Ibn Abī Shayba in *al-Muṣannaf*, 7/432 §37045. •Aḥmad b. Ḥanbal in *Faḍāʾil al-Ṣaḥāba*, 1/364. •al-Shaybānī in *al-Āḥād wa al-Mathānī*, 5/360 §2952. •al-Khaṭīb Baghdādī in *Tārīkh Baghdād*, 4/401.

[132] Set forth by •al-Tirmidhī in *al-Sunan*: Bk.: *al-Manāqib* [Virtues] according to Allah's Messenger ﷺ, Ch.: The virtues of al-Ḥasan and al-Ḥusayn, 5/660 §3779. •Aḥmad b. Ḥanbal in *al-Musnad*, 1/99 §774, 854. •Ibn Ḥibbān in *al-Ṣaḥīḥ*, 15/430 §6974. •al-Ṭayālisī in *al-Musnad*, 1/91 §130. •al-Maqdisī in *al-Aḥādīth al-Mukhtāra*, 2/394 §780.

١٣٣/ ١٩. عَنْ شُعْبَةَ عَنْ سَلَمَةَ بْنِ كُهَيْلٍ، قَالَ: سَمِعْتُ أَبَا الطُّفَيْلِ يُحَدِّثُ عَنْ أَبِي سَرِيْحَةَ ــ أَوْ زَيْدِ بْنِ أَرْقَمَ، (شَكَّ شُعْبَةُ) ــ عَنِ النَّبِيِّ ﷺ، قَالَ: مَنْ كُنْتُ مَوْلَاهُ فَعَلِيٌّ مَوْلَاهُ.

وَقَدْ رَوَى شُعْبَةُ هَذَا الْحَدِيْثَ عَنْ مَيْمُوْنٍ أَبِي عَبْدِ اللهِ عَنْ زَيْدِ بْنِ أَرْقَمَ عَنِ النَّبِيِّ ﷺ. رَوَاهُ التِّرْمِذِيُّ. وَقَالَ: هَذَا حَدِيْثٌ حَسَنٌ صَحِيْحٌ.

133/19. According to Shuʿba:

"Salama b. Kuhayl said: 'I heard Abū al-Ṭufayl saying on the authority of Abū Sarīḥa—or of Zayd b. Arqam (Shuʿba was

---

133 Set forth by •al-Tirmidhī in *al-Sunan*: Bk.: *al-Manāqib* [Virtues] according to Allah's Messenger ﷺ, Ch.: The virtues of ʿAlī b. Abī Ṭālib ؓ, 5/633 §3713. •al-Ṭabarānī in *al-Muʿjam al-Kabīr*, 5/195, 204 §5071, 5096.

This tradition has been reported on the authority of Ḥubshā b. Janāda in the following books: •al-Ḥākim in *al-Mustadrak*, 3/134 §4652. •al-Ṭabarānī in *al-Muʿjam al-Kabīr*, 12/78 §12593. •al-Khaṭīb al-Baghdādī in *Tārīkh Baghdād*, 12/343. •Ibn ʿAsākir in *Tārīkh Dimashq al-Kabīr*, 45/77, 144. •Ibn Kathīr in *al-Bidāya wa al-Nihāya*, 5/451. •al-Haythamī in *Majmaʿ al-Zawāʾid*, 9/108.

This tradition has been reported on the authority of Jābir b. ʿAbd Allāh ؓ in the following books: •Ibn Abī ʿĀṣim in *al-Sunna*, 602 §1355.

This tradition has also been reported on the authority of Ayyūb al-Anṣārī in the following books: •Ibn Abī Shayba in *al-Muṣannaf*, 6/366 §32072. •Ibn Abī ʿĀṣim in *al-Sunna*, 602 §1354. •al-Ṭabarānī in *al-Muʿjam al-Kabīr*, 4/173 §4052. •al-Ṭabarānī in *al-Muʿjam al-Awsaṭ*, 1/229 §348.

This tradition has also been reported on the authority of Burayda in the following books: •ʿAbd al-Razzāq in *al-Muṣannaf*, 11/225 §20388. •al-Ṭabarānī in *al-Muʿjam al-Ṣaghīr*, 1/71. •Ibn ʿAsākir in *Tārīkh Dimashq al-Kabīr*, 45/143.

This tradition has also been reported on the authority of Burayda in the following books: •Ibn Abī ʿĀṣim in *al-Sunna*, 601 §1353. •Ibn ʿAsākir in *Tārīkh Dimashq al-Kabīr*, 45/146. •Ibn Kathīr in *al-Bidāya wa al-Nihāya*, 5/457. •Ḥuṣām al-Dīn Hindī in *Kanz al-ʿUmmāl*, 11/602 §32904.

This tradition has also been reported on the authority of Mālik b. Ḥuwayrath in the following books: •al-Ṭabarānī in *al-Muʿjam al-Kabīr*, 19/252 §646. •Ibn ʿAsākir in *Tārīkh Dimashq al-Kabīr*, 45/177. •al-Haythamī in *Majmaʿ al-Zawāʾid*, 9/106.

doubtful)—that the Prophet ﷺ said: "If I am someone's Protector, ʿAlī is his Protector."'

Shuʿba has reported this hadith from Maymūn Abū ʿAbd Allāh who narrated it on the authority of Zayd b. Arqam who narrated it from Allah's Messenger ﷺ.

Reported by al-Tirmidhī who said: "This is a fine authentic tradition."

١٣٤/ ٢٠. عَنْ جُمَيْعِ بْنِ عُمَيْرٍ التَّمِيْمِيِّ ؓ قَالَ: دَخَلْتُ مَعَ عَمَّتِي عَلَى عَائِشَةَ ؓا فَسُئِلَتْ: أَيُّ النَّاسِ كَانَ أَحَبَّ إِلَى رَسُوْلِ اللهِ ﷺ؟ قَالَتْ: فَاطِمَةُ. فَقِيْلَ: مِنَ الرِّجَالِ؟ قَالَتْ: زَوْجُهَا. إِنْ كَانَ مَا عَلِمْتُ صَوَّامًا قَوَّامًا.

رَوَاهُ التِّرْمِذِيُّ وَقَالَ: هَذَا حَدِيْثٌ حَسَنٌ.

134/20. According to Jumayʿ b. ʿUmayr al-Tamīmī ؓ:

"Together with my paternal aunt, I came to ʿĀʾisha ؓ, and she was asked: 'Which of the people was dearest to Allah's Messenger ﷺ?' She said: 'Fāṭima!' Then she was asked: 'Which of the men?' She said: 'Her husband who was, as I knew him, a devout keeper of the fast and night vigil!'"

Reported by al-Tirmidhī and said: "This is a fine tradition."

١٣٥/ ٢١. عَنْ زَيْدِ بْنِ أَرْقَمَ ؓ أَنَّ رَسُوْلَ اللهِ ﷺ قَالَ لِعَلِيٍّ وَفَاطِمَةَ وَالْحَسَنِ وَالْحُسَيْنِ ؓ: أَنَا حَرْبٌ لِمَنْ حَارَبْتُمْ، وَسِلْمٌ لِمَنْ سَالَمْتُمْ.

رَوَاهُ التِّرْمِذِيُّ وَابْنُ مَاجَه.

---

[134] Set forth by •al-Tirmidhī in *al-Sunan*: Bk.: *al-Manāqib* [Virtues] according to Allah's Messenger ﷺ, Ch.: The excellent merit of Fāṭima, the daughter of Muhammad ﷺ, 5/701 §3874. •al-Ṭabarānī in *al-Muʿjam al-Kabīr*, 22/403–404 §1008–1009. •al-Ḥākim in *al-Mustadrak*, 3/171 §4744. •Abū Yaʿlā in *al-Muʿjam*, 1/128 §235.

135/21. According to Zayd b. Arqam ؓ:

"Allah's Messenger ﷺ said to ʿAlī, Fāṭima, Ḥasan and Ḥusayn ؑ: 'I am at war with those with whom you wage war, and at peace with those with whom you are at peace!'"

Reported by al-Tirmidhī and Ibn Mājah.

١٣٦/ ٢٢. عَنْ عَبْدِ الرَّحْمَنِ بْنِ أَبِـي لَيْلَى عَنْ أَبِيْهِ قَالَ: قَالَ رَسُوْلُ اللهِ ﷺ: لَا يُؤْمِنُ عَبْدٌ حَتَّى أَكُوْنَ أَحَبَّ إِلَيْهِ مِنْ نَفْسِهِ وَأَهْلِي أَحَبَّ إِلَيْهِ مِنْ أَهْلِهِ وَعِتْرَتِي أَحَبَّ إِلَيْهِ مِنْ عِتْرَتِهِ وَذَاتِي أَحَبَّ إِلَيْهِ مِنْ ذَاتِهِ.

رَوَاهُ الطَّبَرَانِيُّ وَالْبَيْهَقِيُّ.

136/22. According to ʿAbd al-Raḥmān b. Abī Laylā, his father said:

"Allah's Messenger ﷺ said: 'A servant does not truly believe until I am dearer to him than himself, and my family is dearer to him than his own family, and my relatives are dearer to him than his own relatives, and my person is dearer to him than his own person.'"

Reported by al-Ṭabarānī and al-Bayhaqī.

---

[135] Set forth by •al-Tirmidhī in *al-Sunan*: Bk.: *al-Manāqib* [Virtues] according to Allah's Messenger ﷺ, Ch.: The excellent merit of Fāṭima, the daughter of Muhammad ﷺ, 5/699 §3870. •Ibn Mājah in *al-Sunan*, Introduction: The excellent merit of al-Ḥasan and al-Ḥusayn, the sons of ʿAlī b. Abī Ṭālib ؓ, 1/52 §145. •al-Ḥākim in *al-Mustadrak*, 3/161 §4714. •al-Ṭabarānī in *al-Muʿjam al-Awsaṭ*, 5/182 §5015, & in *al-Muʿjam al-Kabīr*, 3/40 §2620. •al-Ṣaydāwī in *Muʿjam al-Shuyūkh*, 1/133 §85.

[136] Set forth by •al-Ṭabarānī in *al-Muʿjam al-Kabīr*, 7/75 §6416, & in *al-Muʿjam al-Awsaṭ*, 6/59 §5790. •al-Bayhaqī in *Shuʿab al-Īmān*, 2/189 §1505. •al-Daylamī in *al-Firdaws bi-Maʾthūr al-Khiṭāb*, 5/154 §7795. •al-Haythamī in *Majmaʿ al-Zawāʾid*, 1/88.

اَلْفَصْلُ الثَّانِي

فَصْلٌ فِي مَنَاقِبِ الْخُلَفَاءِ وَصَحَابَةِ الرَّسُوْلِ

Section 2

The Virtues of the Caliphs and the Companions of the Messenger

١٣٧/ ٢٣. عَنْ أَبِي سَعِيْدٍ الْخُدْرِيِّ ﷺ قَالَ: قَالَ النَّبِيُّ ﷺ: لاَ تَسُبُّوْا أَصْحَابِي، فَلَوْ أَنَّ أَحَدَكُمْ أَنْفَقَ مِثْلَ أُحُدٍ ذَهَبًا، مَا بَلَغَ مُدَّ أَحَدِهِمْ وَلاَ نَصِيْفَهُ.

رَوَاهُ الْبُخَارِيُّ.

ورواه مسلم عن أبي هريرة ﷺ: لاَ تَسُبُّوْا أَصْحَابِي! لاَ تَسُبُّوْا أَصْحَابِي، فَوَالَّذِي نَفْسِي بِيَدِهِ. ثُمَّ سَاقَ الْحَدِيْثَ بِنَحْوِهِ.

137/23. According to Abū Saʿīd al-Khudrī ﷺ:

---

[137] Set forth by •al-Bukhārī in *al-Ṣaḥīḥ*: Bk.: *Faḍā'il al-Ṣaḥāba* [The Excellent Merits of the Companions], Ch.: The saying of the Prophet ﷺ: "If you were chosen as a bosom friend," 3/1343 §3470. •Muslim in *al-Ṣaḥīḥ*: Bk.: *Faḍā'il al-Ṣaḥāba* [The Excellent Merits of the Companions], Ch.: Prohibition of maligning the Companions 4/1967 §2540. •al-Tirmidhī in *al-Sunan*: Bk.: *al-Manāqib* [Virtues] according to Allah's Messenger ﷺ, Ch.: (59), 5/695 §3861. He said: "This is a fine authentic tradition." •Ibn Mājah in *al-Sunan*: Ch.: The Excellent Merits of the Companions of Allah's Messenger ﷺ, Ch.: The excellent merit of the people of Badr, 1/57 §161. •al-Nasā'ī in *al-Sunan al-Kubrā*, 5/84 §8308. •Ibn Ḥibbān in *al-Ṣaḥīḥ*, 16/238 §7253. •Aḥmad b. Ḥanbal in *al-Musnad*, 3/11 §11094, 11534–11535, 11626. •Abū Yaʿlā in *al-Musnad*, 2/342 §1087. •Ibn Abī Shayba in *al-Muṣannaf*, 6/404 §32404. •al-Ṭabarānī in *al-Muʿjam al-Awsaṭ*, 1/212 §687.

"The Prophet ﷺ said: 'You must not revile my Companions, for even if one of you spent the equivalent of [Mount] Uḥud in gold, it would not reach the measure of one of them, nor half of it!'

Reported by al-Bukhārī.

Muslim also reported the above on the authority of Abū Hurayra ؓ, and he added to it:

"You must not revile my Companions! You must not revile my Companions, for by the One in whose Hand my soul is," then he cited the tradition in similar form.

١٣٨/ ٢٤. عَنْ عَبْدِ اللهِ بْنِ مُغَفَّلٍ ؓ، قَالَ: قَال رَسُوْلُ اللهِ ﷺ: اللهَ اللهَ فِي أَصْحَابِي. لاَ تَتَّخِذُوْهُمْ غَرَضًا بَعْدِي. فَمَنْ أَحَبَّهُمْ فَبِحُبِّي أَحَبَّهُمْ، وَمَنْ أَبْغَضَهُمْ فَبِبُغْضِي أَبْغَضَهُمْ، وَمَنْ آذَاهُمْ فَقَدْ آذَانِي، وَمَنْ آذَانِي فَقَدْ آذَى اللهَ، وَمَنْ آذَى اللهَ فَيُوْشِكُ أَنْ يَأْخُذَهُ.

رَوَاهُ التِّرْمِذِيُّ، وَقَالَ: هَذَا حَدِيْثٌ حَسَنٌ.

138/24. According to ʿAbd Allāh b. Mughaffal ؓ:

"Allah's Messenger ﷺ said: 'Fear Allah, fear Allah, with regard to my Companions and do not select them as a target of criticism after me! If someone loves them, he loves them because of loving me, and if someone hates them, he hates them because of hating me. If someone wrongs them, he has wronged me. If someone wrongs me, he has wronged Allah, and if someone wrongs Allah, He is about to seize him!'"

Reported by al-Tirmidhī, and said: "This is a fine tradition.

[138] Set forth by •al-Tirmidhī in *al-Sunan*: Bk.: *al-Manāqib* [Virtues] according to Allah's Messenger ﷺ, Ch.: Concerning someone who maligns the Companions of Allah's Messenger ﷺ, 5/696 §3862. •Aḥmad b. Ḥanbal in *al-Musnad*, 5/54, 57 §20549, 20578. •al-Bayhaqī in *Shuʿab al-Īmān*, 2/191 §1511. •Ibn Abī ʿĀṣim in *al-Sunna*, 2/479 §992. •al-Rūyānī in *al-Musnad*, 2/92 §882. •al-Daylamī in *al-Firdaws bi-Maʾthūr al-Khiṭāb*, 1/146 §525. •al-Haythamī in *Mawārid al-Ẓamʾān*, 1/568 §2284.

١٣٩/ ٢٥. عَنِ ابْنِ عُمَرَ ﵄ قَالَ: قَالَ رَسُوْلُ اللهِ ﷺ: إِذَا رَأَيْتُمُ الَّذِيْنَ يَسُبُّوْنَ أَصْحَابِي، فَقُوْلُوْا: لَعْنَةُ اللهِ عَلَى شَرِّكُمْ.

رَوَاهُ التِّرْمِذِيُّ.

139/25. According to Ibn ʿUmar ﵄:

"Allah's Messenger ﷺ said: 'If you see those who revile my Companions, say: "May Allah's curse be upon your evilness!"'"

Reported by al-Tirmidhī.

١٤٠/ ٢٦. عَنِ ابْنِ عَبَّاسٍ ﵄ قَالَ: قَالَ رَسُوْلُ اللهِ ﷺ: مَنْ سَبَّ أَصْحَابِي، فَعَلَيْهِ لَعْنَةُ اللهِ وَالْـمَلَائِكَةِ وَالنَّاسِ أَجْمَعِيْنَ.

رَوَاهُ الطَّبَرَانِيُّ.

140/26. According to Ibn ʿAbbās ﵄:

"Allah's Messenger ﷺ said: 'If someone reviles my Companions, upon him be the curse of Allah, the angels and all human beings!'"

Reported by al-Ṭabarānī.

---

139 Set forth by •al-Tirmidhī in *al-Sunan*: Bk.: *al-Manāqib* [Virtues] according to Allah's Messenger ﷺ, Ch.: What has come to us about the excellent merit of someone who sees the Prophet ﷺ and becomes his Companion, 5/697 §3866. •al-Ṭabarānī in *al-Muʿjam al-Awsaṭ*, 8/191 §8366. •al-Daylamī in *al-Firdaws bi-Maʾthūr al-Khiṭāb*, 1/263 §1022.

140 Set forth by •al-Ṭabarānī in *al-Muʿjam al-Kabīr*, 12/142 §12709, & on the authority of Abū Saʿīd ﵁ in *al-Muʿjam al-Awsaṭ*, 5/94 §4771. •al-Haythamī in *Majma al-Zawaʾid*, 10/21. •Ibn Abī Shayba, on the authority of ʿAṭāʾ b. Abī Rabāḥ, in *al-Muṣannaf*, 6/405 §32419. •al-Khilāl in *al-Sunna*, 3/515 §833. •Ibn Abī ʿĀṣim in *al-Sunna*, 2/483 §1001. •Ibn al-Jaʿd in *al-Musnad*, 1/296 §2010. •al-Daylamī in *al-Firdaws bi-Maʾthūr al-Khiṭāb*, 5/14 §7302. •al-Munāwī in *Fayḍ al-Qadīr*, 5/274.

١٤١ / ٢٧. عَنْ عِمْرَانَ بْنِ حُصَيْنٍ ﵄ يَقُوْلُ: قَالَ رَسُوْلُ اللهِ ﷺ: خَيْرُ أُمَّتِي قَرْنِي، ثُمَّ الَّذِيْنَ يَلُوْنَهُمْ، ثُمَّ الَّذِيْنَ يَلُوْنَهُمْ. قَالَ عِمْرَانُ: فَلاَ أَدْرِي أَذَكَرَ بَعْدَ قَرْنِهِ قَرْنَيْنِ أَوْ ثَلاَثاً. ثُمَّ إِنَّ بَعْدَكُمْ قَوْمًا يَشْهَدُوْنَ وَلاَ يُسْتَشْهَدُوْنَ، وَيَخُوْنُوْنَ وَلاَ يُؤْتَمَنُوْنَ، وَيَنْذُرُوْنَ وَلاَ يَفُوْنَ، وَيَظْهَرُ فِيْهِمُ السِّمَنُ.

مُتَّفَقٌ عَلَيْهِ.

141/27. According to ʿImrān b. Ḥuṣayn ﵄:

"Allah's Messenger ﷺ said: 'The best of my Community are my generation, then those who will follow them, then those who will follow them!' (ʿImrān said: I do not remember whether he mentioned two generations or three after his generation.) 'Then, after you, there will be a group of people who will bear witness whereas they will not be asked to do. They will be dishonest and

[141] Set forth by •al-Bukhārī in *al-Ṣaḥīḥ*: Bk.: *Faḍā'il al-Ṣaḥāba* [The Excellent Merits of the Companions], Ch.: The excellent merits of the Companions of the Prophet ﷺ, 3/1335 §3450, & Bk.: *al-Riqāq* [The Softening of Hearts], Ch.: Wariness of the splendour of this world and competition for it, 5/2362 §6064, & Bk.: *al-Aymān wa al-Nudhūr* [Oaths and Vows], Ch.: The sin of someone who does not fulfil the vow, 6/2463 §6317. •Muslim in *al-Ṣaḥīḥ*: Bk.: *Faḍā'il al-Ṣaḥāba* [The Excellent Merits of the Companions], Ch.: The excellent merit of the Companions, then those who follow them, then those who follow them, 4/1964 §5235. •al-Tirmidhī in *al-Sunan*: Bk.: *al-Fitan* [Troubles] according to Allah's Messenger ﷺ, Ch.: What has come to us about the 3rd Century, 4/500 §2302–2303, & Bk.: *al-Munāqib* [Virtues] according to Allah's Messenger, Ch.: What has come to us about the excellent merit of someone who saw the Messenger of Allah ﷺ and the excellent merit of the Companiopns, 5/695, §3859. •al-Nasā'ī in *al-Sunan*: Bk.: *al-Aymān wa al-Nudhūr* [Oaths and Vows], Ch.: Fulfilment of the vow, 7/17 §3809. •Ibn Mājah in *al-Sunan*: Bk.: *al-Aḥkām* [The Rules of Law], Ch.: Abhorrence of testimony by someone who is not called as a witness, 2/791 §2362. •al-Bayhaqī in *al-Sunan al-Kubrā*: Bk.: *al-Nudhūr* [Vows], Ch.: Fulfilment of the vow, 10/74. •al-Bazzār in *al-Musnad*, 9/18 §3521. •Aḥmad b. Ḥanbal in *al-Musnad*, 4/427 §19835. •al-Ṭabarānī in *al-Muʿjam al-Kabīr*, 18/233 §581. •al-Ṭayālisī in *al-Musnad*, 1/113 §841. •al-Ṭaḥāwī in *Sharḥ Maʿāni al-Āthār*, 4/151. •al-Mundhirī in *al-Targhīb wa al-Tarhīb*, 4/5 §4546.

will not be relied on. They will vow but will not fulfil, and obesity will become manifest in them.'"

Agreed upon by al-Bukhārī and Muslim.

١٤٢/ ٢٨. عَنْ عَبْدِ اللهِ ﷺ قَالَ: قَالَ رَسُوْلُ اللهِ ﷺ: خَيْرُ أُمَّتِي الْقَرْنُ الَّذِيْنَ يَلُوْنِي ثُمَّ الَّذِيْنَ يَلُوْنَهُمْ ثُمَّ الَّذِيْنَ يَلُوْنَهُمْ.

مُتَّفَقٌ عَلَيْهِ.

142/28. According to ʿAbd Allāh ﷺ:

"Allah's Messenger ﷺ said: 'The best of my *Umma* (Community) are the people who are closer to me, then those who are closer to them, then those who are closer to them.'"

Agreed upon by al-Bukhārī and Muslim.

١٤٣/ ٢٩. عَنْ عَائِشَةَ ﷺ قَالَتْ: سَأَلَ رَجُلٌ النَّبِيَّ ﷺ: أَيُّ النَّاسِ خَيْرٌ؟ قَالَ الْقَرْنُ الَّذِي أَنَا فِيْهِ ثُمَّ الثَّانِي ثُمَّ الثَّالِثُ.

رَوَاهُ مُسْلِمٌ.

143/29. According to ʿĀʾisha ﷺ:

---

[142] Set forth by •al-Bukhārī in *al-Ṣaḥīḥ*: & Bk.: *al-Shahādāt* [Testimonies], Ch.: One must not testify unjustly when one testifies, 2/938 §2509, & Bk.: *Faḍāʾil al-Ṣaḥāba* [The Excellent Merits of the Companions], Ch.: [The excellent merits of the Companions of the Prophet ﷺ, 3/1335 §3451, & Bk.: *al-Riqāq* [The Softening of Hearts], Ch.: Wariness of the splendour of this world and competition for it, 5/2362 §6065, & Bk.: *al-Aymān wa al-Nudhūr* [Oaths and Vows], Ch.: If someone says: "I testify by Allah [*Ashhadu bi Allāh*]," or "I have testified by Allah [*Ashhadtu bi Allāh*]," 6/2452 §2682. •Muslim in *al-Ṣaḥīḥ*: Bk.: *Faḍāʾil al-Ṣaḥāba* [The Excellent Merits of the Companions], Ch.: The excellent merit of the Companions, then those who follow them, then those who follow them, 4/1962 §2533. •Ibn Abī Shayba in *al-Muṣannaf*, 6/404 §3240. •Abū Yaʿlā in *al-Musnad*, 9/40 §5103.

[143] Set forth by •Muslim in *al-Ṣaḥīḥ*: Bk.: *Faḍāʾil al-Ṣaḥāba* [The Excellent Merits of the Companions], Ch.: The excellent merit of the Companions, then

"A man asked the Prophet ﷺ: 'Which of the people are best?'
He said: 'The generation in which I am included, then the second,
then the third.'"

Reported by Muslim.

٣٠ / ١٤٤. عَنْ جَابِرِ بْنِ عَبْدِ اللهِ ﵁ قَالَ: قَالَ لَنَا رَسُولُ اللهِ ﷺ يَوْمَ الْحُدَيْبِيَةِ:
أَنْتُمْ خَيْرُ أَهْلِ الْأَرْضِ، وَكُنَّا أَلْفاً وَأَرْبَعَ مِائَةٍ، وَلَوْ كُنْتُ أُبْصِرُ الْيَوْمَ لَأَرَيْتُكُمْ مَكَانَ
الشَّجَرَةِ.

مُتَّفَقٌ عَلَيْهِ.

144/30. According to Jābir b. ʿAbd Allāh ﵁:

"Allāh's Messenger ﷺ said to us on the Day of al-Ḥudaybiya:
'You are the best of the people of the earth.' We were then a
thousand and four hundred. And if I could see today, I would
surely show you the place of that tree!" (By that time Jābir had lost
his vision.)

Agreed upon by al-Bukhārī and Muslim.

---

those who follow them, then those who follow them, 4/1965 §2536. •Aḥmad
b. Ḥanbal in al-Musnad, 6/156 §25272. •Ibn Abī Shayba in al-Muṣannaf,
6/404 §32409. •Ibn Abī ʿĀṣim in al-Sunna, 2/629 §1475.

144 Set forth by •al-Bukhārī in al-Ṣaḥīḥ: Bk.: al-Maghāzī [Military
Expeditions], Ch.: The Campaign of al-Ḥudaybiya, 4/1526 §3923. •Muslim
in al-Ṣaḥīḥ: Bk.: al-Imāra [The Emirate; Imperial Authority], Ch.:
Commendation of the pledge of allegiance to the commander of the army,
when fighting is intended, and explanation of paying homage beneath the tree,
3/1484 §1856. •Aḥmad b. Ḥanbal in al-Musnad, 3/308 §14352. •al-Shāfiʿī in
al-Musnad, 1/217. •Abū ʿAwāna in al-Musnad, 4/301 §6818. •al-Bayhaqī in
al-Sunan al-Kubrā, 5/235 §9981. •al-Khurāsānī in Kitāb al-Sunan, 2/367
§2885. •Ibn Abī Shayba in al-Muṣannaf, 7/385 §36849. §

١٤٥/ ٣١. عَنْ عَلِيٍّ ﵁ قَالَ: قَالَ النَّبِيُّ ﷺ لِأَهْلِ بَدْرٍ: فَلَعَلَّ اللهَ اطَّلَعَ إِلَى أَهْلِ بَدْرٍ فَقَالَ: اعْمَلُوْا مَا شِئْتُمْ فَقَدْ وَجَبَتْ لَكُمُ الْجَنَّةُ، أَوْ فَقَدْ غَفَرْتُ لَكُمْ.

مُتَّفَقٌ عَلَيْهِ.

145/31. According to ʿAlī ﵁:

"The Prophet ﷺ said pertaining to the people of Badr: 'Allah looked with pity on the people of Badr and said: 'Do whatever you wish, for the Garden of Paradise is necessarily yours,' or: 'for I have already forgiven you!'"

Agreed upon by al-Bukhārī and Muslim.

١٤٦/ ٣٢. عَنْ جَابِرِ بْنِ سَمُرَةَ ﵁ قَالَ: خَطَبَنَا عُمَرُ بْنُ الْخَطَّابِ بِالْجَابِيَةِ فَقَالَ: إِنَّ رَسُوْلَ اللهِ ﷺ قَامَ فِيْنَا مِثْلَ مُقَامِي فِيْكُمْ فَقَالَ: احْفَظُوْنِي فِي أَصْحَابِي، ثُمَّ الَّذِيْنَ يَلُوْنَهُمْ، ثُمَّ الَّذِيْنَ يَلُوْنَهُمْ.

رَوَاهُ ابْنُ مَاجَه وَالْحَاكِمُ.

وفي رواية: عَنِ ابْنِ عُمَرَ ﵄: فَقَالَ: اسْتَوْصُوْا بِأَصْحَابِي خَيْرًا.

146/32. According to Jābir b. Samura ﵁:

---

145 Set forth by •al-Bukhārī in *al-Ṣaḥīḥ*: Bk.: *al-Maghāzī* [Military Expeditions], Ch.: The excellent merit of someone present at Badr, 4/1463 §3762, & Bk.: *al-Jihād* [The Sacred Struggle], Ch.: The spy, 3/1095 §2845, & Bk.: *al-Maghāzī* [Military Expeditions], Ch.: What Ḥāṭib b. Abī Baltaʿa was sent with to the people of Mecca, to inform them of the expedition of the Prophet ﷺ, 4/1557 §4025. •Muslim in *al-Ṣaḥīḥ*: Bk.: *Faḍāʾil al-Ṣaḥāba* [The Excellent Merits of the Companions], Ch.: The excellent merits of the people of Badr ﵃, and the story of Ḥāṭib b. Abī Baltaʿa ﵁, 4/1941 §2494. •al-Tirmidhī in *al-Sunan*: Bk.: *Tafsīr al-Qurʾan* [Interpretation of the Qurʾān] according to Allah's Messenger ﷺ, Ch.: From *Sūrat al-Mumtaḥana*, 5/409 §3305. •al-Dārimī in *al-Sunan*, 2/404 §2761.

146 Set forth by •Ibn Mājah in *al-Sunan*: Bk.: *al-Aḥkām* [The Rules of Law], Ch.: Abhorrence of testimony by someone who is not called as a witness, 2/791

"ʿUmar b. al-Khaṭṭāb addressed us at al-Jābiya; he said: 'Allah's Messenger ﷺ stayed among us as I am standing among you, for he ﷺ said: "Take care of me with regard to my Companions (i.e., venerate them), then those who follow them, then those who follow them!'"

Reported by Ibn Mājah and al-Ḥākim.

In one report: According to Ibn ʿUmar ﷺ: "He said: 'Treat my Companions with good intent!'"

١٤٧/ ٣٣. عَنْ جَابِرٍ ﷺ عَنِ النَّبِيِّ ﷺ قَالَ: لَا تَمَسُّ النَّارُ مُسْلِمًا رَآنِي أَوْ رَآى مَنْ رَآنِي.

رَوَاهُ التِّرْمِذِيُّ وَالطَّبَرَانِيُّ، وَقَالَ التِّرْمِذِيُّ: هَذَا حَدِيْثٌ حَسَنٌ.

147/33. According to Jābir ﷺ:

"The Prophet ﷺ said: 'The Fire of Hell will not touch a Muslim who has seen me, or has seen someone who has seen me (i.e., my Companion)!'"

Reported by al-Tirmidhī and al-Ṭabarānī, and al-Tirmidhī said: "This is a fine tradition."

١٤٨/ ٣٤. عَنْ أَبِي سَعِيْدٍ الْخُدْرِيِّ ﷺ قَالَ: قَالَ رَسُوْلُ اللهِ ﷺ: مَا مِنْ نَبِيٍّ إِلَّا لَهُ وَزِيْرَانِ مِنْ أَهْلِ السَّمَاءِ وَوَزِيْرَانِ مِنْ أَهْلِ الْأَرْضِ. فَأَمَّا وَزِيْرَايَ مِنْ أَهْلِ السَّمَاءِ

---

§2363. •al-Ḥākim in *al-Mustadrak*, 1/198–199 §388, 390. •al-Ṭabarānī in *al-Muʿjam al-Awsaṭ*, 6/306 §6483. •Aḥmad b. Ḥanbal in *al-Musnad*, 1/18 §114. •al-Bayhaqī in *al-Sunan al-Kubrā*, 7/91 §13299. •Abū al-Qāsim Hibat Allāh in *Iʿtiqād Ahl al-Sunna*, 1/106 §155. •al-Ḥusaynī in *al-Bayān wa al-Taʿrīf*, 2/219 §1546.

[147] Set forth by •al-Tirmidhī in *al-Sunan*: Bk.: *al-Manāqib* [Virtues] according to Allah's Messenger ﷺ, Ch.: What has come to us about the excellent merit of someone who sees the Prophet ﷺ and becomes his Companion, 5/694 §3858. •al-Ṭabarānī in *al-Muʿjam al-Kabīr*, 17/357 §983, & in *al-Muʿjam al-Awsaṭ*, 1/308 §1036. •al-Haythamī in *Majmaʿ al-Zawāʾid*, 10/21. •al-Daylamī in *al-Firdaws bi-Maʾthūr al-Khiṭāb*, 5/116 §7659. •Ibn Abī ʿĀṣim in *al-Sunna*, 2/630 §1484.

فَجِبْرِيلُ وَمِيكَائِيلُ، وَأَمَّا وَزِيرَايَ مِنْ أَهْلِ الْأَرْضِ فَأَبُوبَكْرٍ وَعُمَرُ.

رَوَاهُ التِّرْمِذِيُّ، وَقَالَ: هَذَا حَدِيثٌ حَسَنٌ. وَقَالَ الْحَاكِمُ: هَذَا حَدِيثٌ صَحِيحُ الْإِسْنَادِ.

148/34. According to Abū Saʿīd al-Khudrī ☺:

"Allah's Messenger ☺ said: 'No Prophet is without two viziers among the people of heaven and two viziers among the people of the earth. As for my two viziers among the people of heaven, they are Gabriel and Michael, and as for my two viziers among the people of the earth, they are Abū Bakr and ʿUmar!'"

Reported by al-Tirmidhī, and according to him, this is a fine tradition, and, according to al-Ḥākim, this is a tradition with an authentic chain of transmission.

١٤٩ / ٣٥. عَنْ عَبْدِ اللهِ بْنِ حَنْطَبٍ ☺ أَنَّ رَسُولَ اللهِ ☺ رَأَى أَبَا بَكْرٍ وَعُمَرَ فَقَالَ: هَذَانِ السَّمْعُ وَالْبَصَرُ.

رَوَاهُ التِّرْمِذِيُّ.

149/35. According to ʿAbd Allāh b. Ḥanṭab ☺:

"Allah's Messenger ☺ saw Abū Bakr and ʿUmar, so he said: 'These two are (for me) the hearing and the eyesight!'"

Reported by al-Tirmidhī.

---

[148] Set forth by •al-Tirmidhī in *al-Sunan*: Bk.: *al-Manāqib* [Virtues] according to Allah's Messenger ☺, Ch.: The virtues of Abū Bakr and ʿUmar ☺, 5/616 §3680. •al-Ḥākim in *al-Mustadrak*, 2/290 §3047. •Ibn al-Jaʿd in *al-Musnad*, 1/298 §2026. •al-Daylamī in *al-Firdaws bi-Maʾthūr al-Khiṭāb*, 4/382 §7111. •al-Mubārakfūrī in *Tuḥfat al-Aḥwadhī*, 10/114.

[149] Set forth by •al-Tirmidhī in *al-Sunan*: Bk.: *al-Manāqib* [Virtues] according to Allah's Messenger ☺, Ch.: Concerning the virtues of Abū Bakr and ʿUmar ☺, 5/613 §3671.

١٥٠ / ٣٦. عَنْ أَنَسِ بْنِ مَالِكٍ ﷺ قَالَ: إِنَّ النَّبِيَّ ﷺ صَعِدَ أُحُدًا، وَأَبُوْ بَكْرٍ وَعُمَرُ وَعُثْمَانُ. فَرَجَفَ بِهِمْ، فَقَالَ: اثْبُتْ، أُحُدُ، فَإِنَّمَا عَلَيْكَ نَبِيٌّ وَصِدِّيْقٌ وَشَهِيْدَانِ.

رَوَاهُ الْبُخَارِيُّ وَالتِّرْمِذِيُّ.

150/36. According to Anas b. Mālik ﷺ:

"The Prophet ﷺ ascended Uḥud, and so did Abū Bakr, ʿUmar and ʿUthmān. (Overjoyed) it started swinging (on their arrival), so he said: 'Stay firm, Uḥud, for you have on you a Prophet, a champion of the truth and two martyrs!'"

Reported by al-Bukhārī and al-Tirmidhī.

١٥١ / ٣٧. عَنْ أَنَسٍ ﷺ قَالَ: قَالَ رَسُوْلُ اللهِ ﷺ لِأَبِي بَكْرٍ وَعُمَرَ ﷺ: هَذَانِ سَيِّدَا كُهُوْلِ أَهْلِ الْجَنَّةِ مِنَ الْأَوَّلِيْنَ وَالْآخِرِيْنَ إِلاَّ النَّبِيِّيْنَ وَالْمُرْسَلِيْنَ.

رَوَاهُ التِّرْمِذِيُّ وَحَسَّنَهُ.

151/37. According to Anas ﷺ:

---

[150] Set forth by •al-Bukhārī in *al-Ṣaḥīḥ*: Bk.: *Faḍāʾil al-Ṣaḥāba* [The Excellent Merits of the Companions], Ch.: The saying of the Prophet ﷺ: "If you were chosen as a bosom friend," 3/1344 §3472, & Ch.: The virtues of ʿUthmān b. ʿAffān Abū ʿAmr al-Qurashī ﷺ, 3/1344 §3496, & Ch.: Concerning the virtues of ʿUmar b. Abī Ḥafṣ al-Qurashī al-ʿAdawī ﷺ, 3/1346 §3483. •al-Tirmidhī in *al-Sunan*: *al-Manāqib* [Virtues] according to Allah's Messenger ﷺ, Ch.: The virtues of ʿUthmān b. ʿAffān ﷺ, 5/624 §3697. •Abū Dāwūd in *al-Sunan*: Bk.: The Sunna, Ch.: Concerning the Caliphs. 4/212 §4651. •al-Nasāʾī in *al-Sunan al-Kubrā*, 5/43 §8135. •Aḥmad b. Ḥanbal in *al-Musnad*, 3/112 §12127, 22862. •al-Ṭabarānī in *al-Muʿjam al-Awsaṭ*, 6/338 §6566. •Ibn Ḥibbān in *al-Ṣaḥīḥ*, 14/415 §6492. •Abū Yaʿlā in *al-Musnad*, 5/289 §2910.

[151] Set forth by •al-Tirmidhī in *al-Sunan*: Bk.: *al-Manāqib* [Virtues] according to Allah's Messenger ﷺ, Ch.: Concerning the virtues of Abū Bakr and ʿUmar ﷺ, 5/610 §3664–3665. •Ibn Mājah in *al-Sunan*, Introduction: Ch.: The excellent merits of the Companions of Allah's Messenger ﷺ, 1/36 §95–100. •Ibn Ḥibbān in *al-Ṣaḥīḥ*, 15/330 §6904. •al-Bazzār in *al-Musnad*, 2/132 §490. •Aḥmad b. Ḥanbal in *al-Musnad*, 1/80 §602. •Abū Yaʿlā in *al-*

"Allah's Messenger ﷺ said in favour of Abū Bakr and ʿUmar ﷺ: 'These two are the chieftains of the elderly people of the Garden of Paradise, among the first and the last, apart from the Prophets and the Messengers!'"

Reported by al-Tirmidhī and he declared it fine.

١٥٢ / ٣٨. عَنْ أَبِي هُرَيْرَةَ ﷺ أَنَّ رَسُوْلَ اللهِ ﷺ كَانَ عَلَى حِرَاءٍ هُوَ وَأَبُوْ بَكْرٍ وَعُمَرُ وَعُثْمَانُ وَعَلِيٌّ وَطَلْحَةُ وَالزُّبَيْرُ. فَتَحَرَّكَتِ الصَّخْرَةُ. فَقَالَ النَّبِيُّ ﷺ: اهْدَأْ، فَمَا عَلَيْكَ إِلاَّ نَبِيٌّ أَوْ صِدِّيْقٌ أَوْ شَهِيْدٌ.

رَوَاهُ مُسْلِمٌ وَالتِّرْمِذِيُّ، وَقَالَ التِّرْمِذِيُّ: هَذَا حَدِيْثٌ صَحِيْحٌ.

152/38. According to Abū Hurayra ﷺ:

"Allah's Messenger ﷺ was on [Mount] Ḥirāʾ. With him were Abū Bakr, ʿUmar, ʿUthmān, ʿAlī, Ṭalḥa and al-Zubayr. So the mountain moved. The Prophet ﷺ said: 'Be still, for there is none on you except a Prophet, a champion of the truth and a martyr!'"

Reported by Muslim and al-Tirmidhī. According to al-Tirmidhī: "This is an authentic tradition."

١٥٣ / ٣٩. عَنْ عَبْدِ اللهِ بْنِ مَسْعُوْدٍ ﷺ قَالَ: إِنَّ اللهَ نَظَرَ فِي قُلُوْبِ الْعِبَادِ، فَوَجَدَ قَلْبَ مُحَمَّدٍ ﷺ خَيْرَ قُلُوْبِ الْعِبَادِ، فَاصْطَفَاهُ لِنَفْسِهِ، فَابْتَعَثَهُ اللهُ بِرِسَالَتِهِ، ثُمَّ نَظَرَ فِي قُلُوْبِ الْعِبَادِ بَعْدَ قَلْبِ مُحَمَّدٍ، فَوَجَدَ قُلُوْبَ أَصْحَابِهِ خَيْرَ قُلُوْبِ الْعِبَادِ، فَجَعَلَهُمْ

Musnad, 1/405 §533. •Ibn Abī ʿĀṣim in *al-Sunna*, 2/617 §1419. •al-Ṭabarānī in *al-Muʿjam al-Awsaṭ*, 2/91 §1348; 7/68 §6873, & in *al-Muʿjam al-Ṣaghīr*, 2/173 §976.

[152] Set forth by •Muslim in *al-Ṣaḥīḥ*: Bk.: *Faḍāʾil al-Ṣaḥāba* [The Excellent Merits of the Companions], Ch.: The excellent merits of Ṭalḥa and al-Zubayr ﷺ, 4/1880 §2417. •al-Tirmidhī in *al-Sunan*: Bk.: *al-Manāqib* [Virtues] according to Allah's Messenger ﷺ, Ch.: Concerning the virtues of ʿUthmān b. ʿAffān ﷺ, 5/624 §3696. •Ibn Ḥibbān in *al-Ṣaḥīḥ*, 15/441 §6983. •al-Nasāʾī in *al-Sunan al-Kubrā*, 5/59 §8207. •Aḥmad b. Ḥanbal in *al-Musnad*, 2/419 §9420. •Ibn Abī ʿĀṣim in *al-Sunna*, 2/621 §1441.

وُزَرَاءَ نَبِيِّهِ، يُقَاتِلُوْنَ عَلَى دِيْنِهِ (وَفِي رِوَايَةٍ: فَجَعَلَهُمْ أَنْصَارَ دِيْنِهِ) فَمَا رَأَى الْمُسْلِمُوْنَ
حَسَنًا، فَهُوَ عِنْدَ اللهِ حَسَنٌ، وَمَا رَأَوْا سَيِّئًا، فَهُوَ عِنْدَ اللهِ سَيِّئٌ.

رَوَاهُ أَحْمَدُ وَالْبَزَّارُ. وَقَالَ الْهَيْثَمِيُّ: رِجَالُهُ مُوَثَّقُوْنَ.

153/39. According to ʿAbd Allāh b. Masʿūd :

"Allah examined the hearts of the servants, so He found the heart of Muhammad ﷺ to be the best of the hearts of the servants, so He chose him for Himself. Allah therefore raised him as His Messenger. Then He examined the hearts of the servants after Muhammad, so He found the hearts of his Companions to be the best of the hearts of the servants. He therefore made them the viziers of His Prophet, who fight in defence of His Religion (in one report: 'He therefore made them the helpers of His Religion'). So whatever Muslims regard as good, it is good in the sight of Allah, and whatever they regard as bad is bad in the sight of Allah.'"

Reported by Aḥmad and al-Bazzār. According to al-Haythamī: "Its sources are reliable."

١٥٤ / ٤٠. عَنِ ابْنِ عَبَّاسٍ قَالَ: قَالَ رَسُوْلُ اللهِ ﷺ: مَهْمَا أُوْتِيْتُمْ مِنْ كِتَابِ اللهِ
فَالْعَمَلُ بِهِ لَا عُذْرَ لِأَحَدٍ فِي تَرْكِهِ. فَإِنْ لَمْ يَكُنْ فِي كِتَابِ اللهِ فَسُنَّةٌ مِنِّي مَاضِيَةٌ. فَإِنْ
لَمْ يَكُنْ سُنَّتِي فَمَا قَالَ أَصْحَابِي. إِنَّ أَصْحَابِي بِمَنْزِلَةِ النُّجُوْمِ فِي السَّمَاءِ. فَأَيَّمَا أَخَذْتُمْ
بِهِ اهْتَدَيْتُمْ وَاخْتِلَافُ أَصْحَابِي لَكُمْ رَحْمَةٌ.

رَوَاهُ الْبَيْهَقِيُّ.

154/40. According to Ibn ʿAbbās :

153 Set forth by •Aḥmad b. Ḥanbal in *al-Musnad*, 1/379 §3600. •al-Bazzār in *al-Musnad*, 5/212 §1816, 1702. •al-Ṭabarānī in *al-Muʿjam al-Awsaṭ*, 4/58 §3602, & in *al-Muʿjam al-Kabīr*, 9/112, 115 §8582, 8593. •al-Bayhaqī in *al-Iʿtiqād*, 1/322. •al-Haythamī in *Majmaʿ al-Zawāʾid*, 1/177; 8/212.

154 Set forth by •al-Bayhaqī in *al-Madkhal ilā al-Sunan al-Kubrā*, 1/162 §152. •ʿAbd b. Ḥumayd likewise in *al-Musnad*, 1/250 §783. •al-Qaḍāʿī in

"Allah's Messenger ﷺ said: 'Whenever a command is given to you from the Book of Allah, no excuse will be accepted from anyone for refraining from acting upon it. If a command is not found in the Book of Allah (pertaining to an issue), it should be searched in my custom (Sunna); and if it is not found even in my custom [Sunna], then look for (the solution to the problem) according to what my Companions have said. My Companions are like stars in the sky; (they provide the same light) so whoever of them you follow, you will be rightly guided, and the diversity (i.e., disagreement) of my Companions is also a mercy for you.'"

Reported by al-Bayhaqī.

١٥٥ / ٤١. عَنْ نُسَيْرِ بْنِ ذُعْلُوقٍ ﷺ قَالَ: كَانَ ابْنُ عُمَرَ ﷺ يَقُوْلُ: لَا تَسُبُّوا أَصْحَابَ مُحَمَّدٍ ﷺ، فَلَمُقَامُ أَحَدِهِمْ سَاعَةً خَيْرٌ مِنْ عَمَلِ أَحَدِكُمْ عُمْرَهُ.

رَوَاهُ ابْنُ مَاجَه وَابْنُ أَبِي شَيْبَةَ.

155/41. According to Nusayr b. Dhuʿlūq ﷺ:

"Ibn ʿUmar ﷺ used to say: 'You must not revile the Companions of Muhammad ﷺ, for a moment they spent in the companionship of Allah's Messenger ﷺ is far greater in value than the work of one of you throughout his lifetime.'"

Reported by Ibn Mājah and Ibn Abī Shayba.

Musnad al-Shihāb: Ch.: The likeness of my Companions is the likeness of the stars, 2/275 §1346. •al-Daylamī in *al-Firdaws bi-Maʾthūr al-Khiṭāb*, 4/160 §6497. •al-Dhahabī in *Mīzān al-Iʿtidāl*, 2/142; 8/73, & in *Lisān al-Mīzān*, 2/118, 137 §594. •al-Khaṭīb Baghdādī in *al-Kifāya fī ʿIlm al-Riwāya*, 1/48. •al-Suyūṭī in *Miftāḥ al-Janna*, 1/45. •Ibn al-Mulaqqin in *Khalāṣat al-Badr al-Munīr*, 2/431 §2868. •Ibn ʿAbd al-Barr in *al-Tamhīd*, 4/263. •al-ʿAsqalānī in *Fatḥ al-Bārī*, 4/57. •Ibn Qudāma in *al-Mughnī*, 3/2109. •Āmadī in *al-Iḥkām*, 1/290. •Ibn Ḥazm in *al-Iḥkām*, 5/61.

[155] Set forth by •Ibn Mājah in *al-Sunan*, Introduction: Ch.: The excellent merit of the people of Badr, 1/57 §162. •Ibn Abī Shayba in *al-Muṣannaf*, 6/405 §32415. •Ibn Abī ʿĀṣim in *Kitāb al-Sunna*, 2/484 §1006.

١٥٦/ ٤٢. عَنِ الْعِرْبَاضِ بْنِ سَارِيَةَ ﵁ قَالَ: وَعَظَنَا رَسُوْلُ اللهِ ﷺ يَوْمًا بَعْدَ صَلَاةِ الْغَدَاةِ مَوْعِظَةً بَلِيْغَةً ذَرَفَتْ مِنْهَا الْعُيُوْنُ وَوَجِلَتْ مِنْهَا الْقُلُوْبُ، فَقَالَ رَجُلٌ: إِنَّ هَذِهِ مَوْعِظَةُ مُوَدِّعٍ فَمَاذَا تَعْهَدُ إِلَيْنَا، يَا رَسُوْلَ اللهِ؟ قَالَ: أُوْصِيكُمْ بِتَقْوَى اللهِ وَالسَّمْعِ وَالطَّاعَةِ وَإِنْ عَبْدٌ حَبَشِيٌّ، فَإِنَّهُ مَنْ يَعِشْ مِنْكُمْ يَرَى اخْتِلَافًا كَثِيْرًا. وَإِيَّاكُمْ وَمُحْدَثَاتِ الْأُمُوْرِ، فَإِنَّهَا ضَلَالَةٌ. فَمَنْ أَدْرَكَ ذَلِكَ مِنْكُمْ، فَعَلَيْهِ بِسُنَّتِي وَسُنَّةِ الْخُلَفَاءِ الرَّاشِدِيْنَ الْمَهْدِيِّيْنَ. عَضُّوْا عَلَيْهَا بِالنَّوَاجِذِ.

رَوَاهُ التِّرْمِذِيُّ وَابْنُ مَاجَه، وَقَالَ التِّرْمِذِيُّ: هَذَا حَدِيْثٌ حَسَنٌ صَحِيْحٌ.

156/42. According to al-ʿIrbāḍ b. Sāriya ﵁:

"Allah's Messenger ﷺ addressed us one day, after the early morning ritual prayer, with an eloquent sermon, due to which the eyes welled with tears and the hearts tremoured (with the fear of Allah), so a man said: 'This is the sermon of someone bidding farewell, so what are you entrusting to us, O Messenger of Allah?' He said: 'I am charging you with pious devotion to Allah and with hearing and obedience, even if [your leader is] an Abyssinian slave, for if one of you lives long, he will observe great dissension. You must beware of the innovated matters (contradicting Shariah), for they lead to error. If someone among you comes upon that time, he must adhere to my exemplary custom (Sunna) and the exemplary custom of the rightly guided Caliphs. So clench the Sunna firmly with your teeth (i.e., hold fast to it tenaciously)!'"

Reported by al-Tirmidhī and Ibn Mājah. According to al-Tirmidhī: "This is a fine authentic tradition."

---

[156] Set forth by •al-Tirmidhī in *al-Sunan*: Bk.: *al-ʿIlm* [Knowledge] according to Allah's Messenger ﷺ, Ch.: What has come to us about adherence to the Sunna and avoidance of innovations, 5/44 §2676. •Abū Dāwūd in *al-Sunan*: Bk.: The Sunna, Ch.: The necessity of the Sunna, 4/200 §4607. •Ibn Mājah in *al-Sunan*: Introduction: Following the Sunna of the rightly guided Caliphs, 1/15 §42. •Aḥmad b. Ḥanbal in *al-Musnad*, 4/126. •Ibn Ḥibbān in *al-Ṣaḥīḥ*, 1/178 §5. •al-Ḥākim in *al-Mustadrak*, 1/174 §329. This is a faultless authentic tradition." •al-Ṭabarānī in *al-Muʿjam al-Kabīr*, 18/246 §618.

١٥٧/ ٤٣. عَنِ ابْنِ عُمَرَ رضي الله عنهما أَنَّ رَسُوْلَ اللهِ ﷺ قَالَ: إِنَّ اللهَ جَعَلَ الْحَقَّ (وفي رواية: وَضَعَ الْحَقَّ) عَلَى لِسَانِ عُمَرَ وَقَلْبِهِ.

وَقَالَ ابْنُ عُمَرَ رضي الله عنهما: مَا نَزَلَ بِالنَّاسِ أَمْرٌ قَطُّ فَقَالُوْا فِيْهِ وَقَالَ فِيْهِ عُمَرُ أَوْ قَالَ ابْنُ الْخَطَّابِ فِيْهِ، (شَكَّ خَارِجَةُ) إِلاَّ نَزَلَ فِيْهِ الْقُرْآنُ عَلَى نَحْوِ مَا قَالَ عُمَرُ.

رَوَاهُ التِّرْمِذِيُّ وَأَبُوْ دَاوُدَ. وَقَالَ أَبُوْ عِيْسَى: هَذَا حَدِيْثٌ حَسَنٌ. وَقَالَ الْحَاكِمُ: هَذَا حَدِيْثٌ صَحِيْحٌ.

157/43. According to Ibn ʿUmar ﷺ:

"Allah's Messenger ﷺ said: 'Allah has placed the truth on the tongue of ʿUmar and in his heart!'"

Ibn ʿUmar ﷺ also said: "Whenever some problem raised its head and the people gave their opinion about that and ʿUmar or Ibn al-Khaṭṭāb also spoke about it (Khārija was doubtful), the Qurʾān (in that matter) was revealed congruous to what ʿUmar opined."

> Reported by al-Tirmidhī and Abū Dāwūd. Abū ʿĪsā said: "This is a fine tradition," and al-Ḥākim said: "This is an authentic tradition."

---

157 Set forth by •al-Tirmidhī in *al-Sunan*: Bk.: *al-Manāqib* [Virtues] according to Allah's Messenger ﷺ, Ch.: Concerning the virtues of ʿUmar b. al-Khaṭṭāb ﷺ, 5/617 §3682. •Abū Dāwūd in *al-Sunan*: Bk.: *al-Kharāj wa al-Imāra wa al-Fay'* [The Land Tax, Imperial Authority and the Bestowal of Booty], Ch. The registration of the grant, 3/138 §2961–2962. •Ibn Mājah in *al-Sunan*: Introduction: Ch.: The Excellent Merits of the Companions of Allah's Messenger ﷺ, 1/40 §108. •Aḥmad b. Ḥanbal in *al-Musnad*, 2/53 §5145. •Ibn Ḥibbān in *al-Ṣaḥīḥ*, 15/312 §6889. •al-Ḥākim in *al-Mustadrak*, 3/93 §4501. •al-Bayhaqī in *al-Sunan al-Kubrā*, 6/295 §12503.

اَلْفَصْلُ الثَّالِثُ

فَصْلٌ فِي مَنَاقِبِ الإِمَامِ الْمَهْدِيِّ الْمُنْتَظَرِ عليه السلام

Section 3

The Virtues of the Awaited Imām, the Mahdī عليه السلام

١٥٨/ ٤٤. عَنْ أَبِي هُرَيْرَةَ رضي الله عنه قَالَ: قَالَ رَسُوْلُ اللهِ صلى الله عليه وآله وسلم: كَيْفَ أَنْتُمْ إِذَا نَزَلَ ابْنُ مَرْيَمَ فِيْكُمْ وَإِمَامُكُمْ مِنْكُمْ!

مُتَّفَقٌ عَلَيْهِ.

158/44. According to Abū Hurayra رضي الله عنه:

"Allah's Messenger صلى الله عليه وآله وسلم said: 'What will be your state (of joy and pleasure) when the son of Mary comes down among you (from the sky), and your Imam will be from among you!'"

Agreed upon by al-Bukhārī and Muslim.

١٥٩/ ٤٥. عَنْ جَابِرِ بْنِ عَبْدِ اللهِ الأَنْصَارِيِّ رضي الله عنهما قَالَ: سَمِعْتُ رَسُوْلَ اللهِ صلى الله عليه وآله وسلم يَقُوْلُ: لاَ تَزَالُ طَائِفَةٌ مِنْ أُمَّتِي يُقَاتِلُوْنَ عَلَى الْحَقِّ ظَاهِرِيْنَ إِلَى يَوْمِ الْقِيَامَةِ. قَالَ:

---

158 Set forth by •al-Bukhārī in *al-Ṣaḥīḥ*: Bk.: *al-Anbiyā'* [The Prophets], Ch.: The descent of Jesus the son of Mary عليه السلام, 3/1272 §3265. •Muslim in *al-Ṣaḥīḥ*: Bk.: *al-Īmān* [Faith], Ch.: The descent of Jesus the son of Mary as an administrator of the Sacred Law of our Prophet Muhammad صلى الله عليه وآله وسلم, 1/136 §155. •Ibn Ḥibbān in *al-Ṣaḥīḥ*, 15/213 §6802. •al-ʿAsqalānī in *Fatḥ al-Bārī*, 6/493.

فَيَنْزِلُ عِيْسَى ابْنُ مَرْيَمَ ﷺ فَيَقُوْلُ أَمِيْرُهُمْ: تَعَالَ صَلِّ لَنَا. فَيَقُوْلُ: لاَ، إِنَّ بَعْضَكُمْ عَلَى بَعْضٍ أُمَرَاءُ تَكْرِمَةَ اللهِ هَذِهِ الْأُمَّةَ.

رَوَاهُ مُسْلِمٌ وَأَحْمَدُ وَابْنُ حِبَّانَ.

159/45. According to Jābir b. ʿAbd Allāh al-Anṣārī ﷺ:

"I heard Allah's Messenger ﷺ say: 'A party among my *Umma* (Community) will not cease fighting to establish and enforce the truth triumphantly, until the Day of Resurrection.' (According to Jābir, subsequent to these blessed words) he said: 'Mary's son Jesus ﷺ will descend, and the Commander of the Muslims will say: "Come and lead our ritual prayer!" He will say, replying: 'No! I will not lead your ritual prayer for the fact that you are commanders in charge of one another and due to the superiority and grandeur which Allah has bestowed upon this *Umma* (so ʿĪsā will not accept to lead the ritual prayer)!'

Reported by Muslim, Aḥmad and Ibn Ḥibbān.

١٦٠/ ٤٦. عَنْ عَبْدِ اللهِ ﷺ عَنِ النَّبِيِّ ﷺ قَالَ: يَلِي رَجُلٌ مِنْ أَهْلِ بَيْتِي يُوَاطِئُ اسْمُهُ اسْمِي. قَالَ عَاصِمٌ: وَحَدَّثَنَا أَبُوْ صَالِحٍ عَنْ أَبِي هُرَيْرَةَ ﷺ قَالَ: لَوْ لَمْ يَبْقَ مِنَ الدُّنْيَا إِلاَّ يَوْمٌ لَطَوَّلَ اللهُ ذَلِكَ الْيَوْمَ حَتَّى يَلِيَ.

رَوَاهُ التِّرْمِذِيُّ وَأَبُوْ دَاوُدَ وَأَحْمَدُ. وَقَالَ أَبُوْ عِيْسَى: هَذَا حَدِيْثٌ حَسَنٌ صَحِيْحٌ.

160/46. According to ʿAbd Allāh ﷺ:

---

[159] Set forth by •Muslim in *al-Ṣaḥīḥ*: Bk.: *al-Īmān* [Faith], Ch.: The descent of Jesus the son of Mary as an administrator of the Sacred Law of our Prophet Muhammad ﷺ, 1/137 §156. •Ibn Ḥibbān in *al-Ṣaḥīḥ*, 15/231 §6819. •Aḥmad b. Ḥanbal in *al-Musnad*, 3/345. •Ibn al-Jārūd in *Kitāb al-Muntaqā*, 1/257 §1031. •al-Bayhaqī in *al-Sunan al-Kubrā*, 9/180. •Abū ʿAwāna in *al-Musnad*, 1/99 §317. •Ibn Manda in *al-Īmān*, 1/517 §518.

[160] Set forth by •al-Tirmidhī in *al-Sunan*: Bk.: *al-Fitan* [Troubles] according to Allah's Messenger ﷺ, Ch.: What has come to us about the Mahdī, 4/505 §2231. •Abū Dāwūd in *al-Sunan*: Bk.: The Mahdī, 4/236 §4282. •Aḥmad

"The Prophet ﷺ said: 'From among the people of my household, there will be eventually raised a man whose name coincides with my name (and he will become the Caliph).'"

ʿĀṣim said: "Abū Ṣāliḥ told us, on the authority of Abū Hurayra ؓ: 'If nothing but a day remains of this world, Allah will prolong that day till he (the Mahdī) eventually arrives and takes over as Caliph!'"

Reported by al-Tirmidhī, Abū Dāwūd and Aḥmad. Abū ʿĪsā said: "This is a fine authentic tradition."

١٦١/٤٧. عَنْ عَبْدِ اللهِ ؓ قَالَ: قَالَ رَسُوْلُ اللهِ ﷺ: لَا تَذْهَبُ الدُّنْيَا حَتَّى يَمْلِكَ الْعَرَبَ رَجُلٌ مِنْ أَهْلِ بَيْتِي؛ يُوَاطِئُ اسْمُهُ اسْمِي.

رَوَاهُ التِّرْمِذِيُّ وَأَبُوْ دَاوُدَ وَأَحْمَدُ. وَقَالَ أَبُوْ عِيْسَى: هَذَا حَدِيْثٌ حَسَنٌ صَحِيْحٌ.

161/47. According to ʿAbd Allāh ؓ:

"Allah's Messenger ﷺ said: 'This world will not cease to exist until a man from among the people of my household, whose name (Muhammad) will coincide with my name, becomes the ruler of Arabs!'"

Reported by al-Tirmidhī, Abū Dāwūd and Aḥmad. Abū ʿĪsā said: "This is a fine authentic tradition."

---

b. Ḥanbal in *al-Musnad*, 1/376 §3571. •al-Ṭabarānī in *al-Muʿjam al-Kabīr*, 10/133 §10215. •al-Haythamī in *Mawārid al-Ẓamʾān*, 1/464 §1877. •al-Muqriʿ in *al-Sunan al-Wārida fī al-Fitan*, 5/104, §562.

[161] Set forth by •al-Tirmidhī in *al-Sunan*: Bk.: *al-Fitan* [Troubles] according to Allah's Messenger, Ch.: What has come to us about the Mahdī, 4/505 §2230. •al-Ḥākim in *al-Mustadrak*, 4/488 §8364. •Abū Dāwūd in *al-Sunan*: Bk.: The Mahdī, 4/106 §4282. •al-Bazzār in *al-Musnad*, 5/204 §1804. •Aḥmad b. Ḥanbal in *al-Musnad*, 1/448 §4279. •al-Ṭabarānī in *al-Muʿjam al-Kabīr*, 10/435 §10223. •al-Shāshī in *al-Musnad*, 2/110 §235.

٤٨/١٦٢. عَنْ أَبِي سَعِيدٍ الْخُدْرِيِّ ۞ قَالَ: قَالَ رَسُولُ اللهِ ۞: اَلْمَهْدِيُّ مِنِّي:
أَجْلَى الْجَبْهَةِ، أَقْنَى الْأَنْفِ. يَمْلَأُ الْأَرْضَ قِسْطًا وَعَدْلاً كَمَا مُلِئَتْ ظُلْمًا وَجَوْرًا،
وَيَمْلِكُ سَبْعَ سِنِينَ.

رَوَاهُ أَبُوْ دَاوُدَ.

162/48. According to Abū Saʿīd al-Khudrī ۞:

"Allah's Messenger ۞ said: 'The (Imam) Mahdī will be descended from me (i.e., from my lineage), endowed with (an illumined complexion,) bright face and a fine and sublime nose. He will fill the earth with equity and justice, as it was filled with tyranny and injustice (before), and he will rule for seven years (as Caliph).'"

Reported by Abū Dāwūd.

٤٩/١٦٣. عَنْ عَلِيٍّ ۞ قَالَ: قَالَ رَسُولُ اللهِ ۞: اَلْمَهْدِيُّ مِنَّا أَهْلَ الْبَيْتِ.
يُصْلِحُهُ اللهُ تَعَالَى فِي لَيْلَةٍ.

رَوَاهُ ابْنُ مَاجَه وَأَحْمَدُ.

163/49. According to ʿAlī ۞:

"Allah's Messenger ۞ said: 'The (Imam) Mahdī will descend from the people of my household. Allah Most High will raise him to the station of piety overnight (i.e., Allah will elevate him to the lofty station of His divine friendship [wilāya], which he will be in need of, in a night's time).'"

---

[162] Set forth by •Abū Dāwūd in al-Sunan: Bk.: The Mahdī, 4/107 §428. •al-Ḥākim in al-Mustadrak, 4/512 §8438. •al-Ṭabarānī in al-Muʿjam al-Awsaṭ, 9/176 §9460.

[163] Set forth by •Ibn Mājah in al-Sunan: Bk.: al-Fitan [Troubles], Ch.: The emergence of the Mahdī, 2/1367 §4085. •Aḥmad b. Ḥanbal in al-Musnad, 1/84 §645. •Abū Yaʿlā in al-Musnad, 1/359 §465. •Ibn Abī Shayba in al-Muṣannaf, 7/513 §37644.

Reported by Ibn Mājah and Aḥmad.

١٦٤/ ٥٠. عَنْ أُمِّ سَلَمَةَ ﵂ قَالَتْ: سَمِعْتُ رَسُوْلَ اللهِ ﷺ يَقُوْلُ: اَلْـمَهْدِيُّ مِنْ عِتْرَتِي مِنْ وَلَدِ فَاطِمَةَ.

رَوَاهُ أَبُوْ دَاوُدَ.

164/50. According to Umm Salama ﵂:

"I heard Allah's Messenger ﷺ say: 'The (Imam) Mahdī is one of my descendants from the offspring of Fāṭima.'"

Reported by Abū Dāwūd.

١٦٥/ ٥١. عَنْ أَبِي إِسْحَاقَ ﵀ قَالَ: قَالَ عَلِيٌّ ﵁، وَنَظَرَ إِلَى ابْنِهِ الْحَسَنِ، فَقَالَ: إِنَّ ابْنِي هَذَا سَيِّدٌ كَمَا سَمَّاهُ النَّبِيُّ ﷺ، وَسَيَخْرُجُ مِنْ صُلْبِهِ رَجُلٌ يُسَمَّى بِاسْمِ نَبِيِّكُمْ ﷺ يُشْبِهُهُ فِي الْخُلْقِ وَلَا يُشْبِهُهُ فِي الْخَلْقِ. ثُمَّ ذَكَرَ قِصَّةَ يَمْلَأُ الْأَرْضَ عَدْلًا.

رَوَاهُ أَبُوْ دَاوُدَ.

165/51. According to Abū Isḥāq ﵀:

"Alī ﵁ looked at his son Ḥasan and said: 'This son of mine is a chieftain, as the Prophet ﷺ has called him, and from his loins there will soon emerge a man called by the name of your Prophet ﷺ, whom he will resemble in moral character, but whom he will not resemble in physical constitution.' Then he related the account that he will fill the earth with justice."

Reported by Abū Dāwūd.

---

164 Set forth by •Abū Dāwūd in *al-Sunan*: Bk.: The Mahdī, 4/107 §4284. •al-Muqri' in *al-Sunan al-Wārida fī al-Fitan*, 5/1057 §575. •al-ʿAẓīm Ābādī in *ʿAwn al-Maʿbūd*, 11/251. •al-Munāwī in *Fayḍ al-Qadīr*, 6/277.

165 Set forth by •Abū Dāwūd in *al-Sunan*: Bk.: The Mahdī, 4/108 §4290. •al-ʿAẓīm Ābādī in *ʿAwn al-Maʿbūd*, 11/257. •al-Mubārakfūrī in *Tuḥfat al-Aḥwadhī*, 6/403. •al-Suyūṭī in *Sharḥ Sunan Ibn Mājah*, 1/300 §4085.

١٦٦/ ٥٢. عَنْ جَابِرِ بْنِ سَمُرَةَ ﷺ قَالَ: سَمِعْتُ رَسُوْلَ اللهِ ﷺ يَقُوْلُ: لَا يَزَالُ الإِسْلَامُ عَزِيْزًا إِلَى اثْنَي عَشَرَ خَلِيْفَةً ثُمَّ قَالَ كَلِمَةً لَمْ أَفْهَمْهَا. فَقُلْتُ لِأَبِي: مَا قَالَ؟ فَقَالَ: كُلُّهُمْ مِنْ قُرَيْشٍ.

رَوَاهُ مُسْلِمٌ وَأَحْمَدُ.

166/52. According to Jābir b. Samura ﷺ:

"I heard Allah's Messenger ﷺ say: 'Islam will not cease to dominate (and prevail) till there have been twelve Caliphs.' Then he uttered something that I could not understand, so I asked my father: 'What did he say?' He told me: 'All of them (the Caliphs) will be from Quraysh.'"

Reported by Muslim and Aḥmad.

١٦٧/ ٥٣. عَنْ أَبِي سَعِيْدٍ الْخُدْرِيِّ ﷺ قَالَ: قَالَ رَسُوْلُ اللهِ ﷺ: لَا تَقُوْمُ السَّاعَةُ حَتَّى تُمْلَأَ الْأَرْضُ ظُلْمًا وَجَوْرًا وَعُدْوَانًا ثُمَّ يَخْرُجُ مِنْ أَهْلِ بَيْتِي مَنْ يَمْلَأُهَا قِسْطًا وَعَدْلًا.

رَوَاهُ الْحَاكِمُ، وَقَالَ: صَحِيْحٌ عَلَى شَرْطِهِمَا وَوَافَقَهُ الذَّهَبِيُّ.

167/53. According to Abū Saʿīd al-Khudrī ﷺ:

"Allah's Messenger ﷺ said: 'The Final Hour will not occur until the earth is filled with tyranny, injustice and enmity. Then, from the people of my household, there will emerge a man (Mahdī) who

---

166 Set forth by •Muslim in *al-Ṣaḥīḥ*: Bk.: *al-Imāra* [The Emirate; Imperial Authority], Ch.: The people are subservient to Quraysh and the Caliphate of Quraysh, 3/1453 §1821. •Ibn Ḥibbān in *al-Ṣaḥīḥ*, 15/44 §6662. •Abū ʿAwāna in *al-Musnad*, 4/370 §6982. •Aḥmad b. Ḥanbal in *al-Musnad*, 5/106 §21058. •al-Ṭabarānī in *al-Muʿjam al-Kabīr*, 2/195 §1792. •al-Shaybānī in *al-Āḥād wa al-Mathānī*, 3/126 §1448. •al-ʿAsqalānī in *Fatḥ al-Bārī*, 13/211.

167 Set forth by •al-Ḥākim in *al-Mustadrak*, 4/600 §8669. •al-Haythamī in *Mawārid al-Ẓamʾān*, 1/464 §1880.

will fill it with equity and justice (i.e., the Final Hour will not occur until the Mahdī does not become a Caliph).'"

Reported by al-Ḥākim, who said: "It is authentic in conformity with the stipulation of al-Bukhārī and Muslim, and confirmed by al-Dhahabī."

١٦٨/ ٥٤. عَنْ أَنَسِ بْنِ مَالِكٍ ﵁ قَالَ: سَمِعْتُ رَسُوْلَ اللهِ ﷺ يَقُولُ: نَحْنُ وَلَدَ عَبْدِ الْـمُطَّلِبِ سَادَةُ أَهْلِ الْجَنَّةِ: أَنَا وَحَمْزَةُ وَعَلِيٌّ وَجَعْفَرٌ وَالْحَسَنُ وَالْحُسَيْنُ وَالْـمَهْدِيُّ.

رَوَاهُ ابْنُ مَاجَه.

168/54. According to Anas b. Mālik ﵁:

"I heard Allah's Messenger ﷺ say: 'We the offspring of ʿAbd al-Muṭallib are the chieftains of the Garden of Paradise: I and Ḥamza and ʿAlī and Jaʿfar and Ḥasan and Ḥusayn and the Mahdī.'"

Reported by Ibn Mājah.

١٦٩/ ٥٥. عَنْ أُمِّ سَلَمَةَ ﵂ قَالَتْ: قَالَ رَسُوْلُ اللهِ ﷺ: يُبَايَعُ رَجُلٌ مِنْ أُمَّتِي بَيْنَ الرُّكْنِ وَالْـمَقَامِ كَعِدَّةِ أَهْلِ بَدْرٍ، فَيَأْتِيْهِ عَصَبُ الْعِرَاقِ وَأَبْدَالُ الشَّامِ.

رَوَاهُ الْحَاكِمُ وَابْنُ أَبِـي شَيْبَةَ.

169/55. According to Umm Salama ﵂:

"Allah's Messenger ﷺ said: 'Allegiance will be pledged with a man (Mahdī) from among my *Umma* between the Corner-stone [of the Kaʿba] and the Station [of Abraham], exactly equal in number to the number of the people of Badr (313). Later, the divine friends of Allah (*awliyāʾ*) from Iraq and the substitute-saints (*abdāl*) from Syria will come to him (for the oath of allegiance).'"

Reported by al-Ḥākim and Ibn Abī Shayba.

168 Set forth by •Ibn Mājah in *al-Sunan*: Bk.: *al-Fitan* [Troubles], Ch.: The emergence of the Mahdi, 2/1368 §4087.

169 Set forth by •al-Ḥākim in *al-Mustadrak*, 4/478 §8328. •Ibn Abī Shayba in *al-Muṣannaf*, 7/460 §37223.

الْفَصْلُ الرَّابِعُ

فَصْلٌ فِي مَنَاقِبِ الْأَئِمَّةِ الْفُقَهَاءِ الْمُجْتَهِدِيْنَ رضي الله عنهم

Section 4

The Virtues of the Imams and Painstaking Jurists ﵃

١٧٠/ ٥٦. عَنْ أَبِي هُرَيْرَةَ رضي الله عنه قَالَ: كُنَّا جُلُوْسًا عِنْدَ النَّبِيِّ ﷺ فَأُنْزِلَتْ عَلَيْهِ سُوْرَةُ الْجُمُعَةِ: ﴿وَءَاخَرِينَ مِنْهُمْ لَمَّا يَلْحَقُواْ بِهِمْ﴾. (الجمعة، ٦٢: ٣). قَالَ: قُلْتُ: مَنْ هُمْ، يَا رَسُوْلَ اللهِ؟ فَلَمْ يُرَاجِعْهُ حَتَّى سَأَلَ ثَلَاثًا، وَفِيْنَا سَلْمَانُ الْفَارِسِيُّ. وَضَعَ رَسُوْلُ اللهِ ﷺ يَدَهُ عَلَى سَلْمَانَ، ثُمَّ قَالَ: لَوْ كَانَ الإِيْمَانُ عِنْدَ الثُّرَيَّا، لَنَالَهُ رِجَالٌ، أَوْ رَجُلٌ، مِنْ هَؤُلَاءِ.

مُتَّفَقٌ عَلَيْهِ وَهَذَا لَفْظُ الْبُخَارِيِّ.

170/56. According to Abū Hurayra ﵁:

---

[170] Set forth by •al-Bukhārī in *al-Ṣaḥīḥ*, 16/298, Bk.: *Tafsīr al-Jumuʿa* [Interpretation/*Sūrat al-Jumuʿa*], Ch.: Allah's saying: "As well as others of them who have not yet joined them [*wa ākharīna min-hum lammā yalḥaqū bi-him*]." (Q.62:3), 3, 4/1858 §4615. •Muslim in *al-Ṣaḥīḥ*: Bk.: *Faḍāʾil al-Ṣaḥāba* [The Excellent Merits of the Companions], Ch.: The excellence of Persia, 4/1972 §2546. •al-Tirmidhī in *al-Sunan*: Bk.: *al-Manāqib* [Virtues] according to Allah's Messenger ﷺ, Ch.: The excellent merit of the Persians, 5/725 §3942, & Bk.: Interpretation of the Qurʾān according to Allah's Messenger ﷺ, Ch.: From *Sūra Muhammad* ﷺ, 5/384 §3260–3261, & Ch.: From *Sūrat al-Jumuʿa*, 5/413 §3310. •Ibn Ḥibbān in *al-Ṣaḥīḥ*, 16/298 §7308. •al-Daylamī in *al-Firdaws bi-Maʾthūr al-Khiṭāb*, 4/367 §7060. •Abū Nuʿaym in *Ḥilya al-Awliyāʾ*, 6/64. •al-ʿAsqalānī in *Fatḥ al-Bārī*, 8/642 §4615. •al-Ḥusaynī in *al-Bayān wa al-Taʿrīf*, 2/170 §1399. •Ibn Kathīr in *Tafsīr al-Qurʾān al-ʿAẓīm*, 4/364 §4797. •al-Ṭabarānī in *Jāmiʿ al-Bayān*, 28/96. •al-

"We were sitting in the presence of the Prophet ﷺ, when (this Verse of) the *Sūra al-Jumuʿa* (Friday) was revealed to him: '(And He has sent this Messenger for purification and education among) others of them also who have not yet joined these people (that are present now i.e., they will come after them in the time to come). *[wa ākharīna min-hum lammā yalḥaqū bi-him]*' (Q.62:3). I said: 'Who are they, O Messenger of Allah?' He did not respond until he was asked three times, and Salmān al-Fārisī was among us. Allah's Messenger ﷺ placed his hand on (the shoulders of) Salmān, then said: 'If faith were beside the Pleiades (the highest station in the heaven), some among these (Persian) men, or a man (the reporter is in doubt), would attain to it!'"

Agreed upon by al-Bukhārī and Muslim (this is the wording of al-Bukhārī).

١٧١ / ٥٧. عَنْ أَبِي هُرَيْرَةَ رضي الله عنه قَالَ: قَالَ رَسُوْلُ اللهِ ﷺ: لَوْ كَانَ الدِّيْنُ عِنْدَ الثُّرَيَّا لَذَهَبَ بِهِ رَجُلٌ مِنْ فَارِسَ، أَوْ قَالَ، مِنْ أَبْنَاءِ فَارِسَ حَتَّى يَتَنَاوَلَهُ.

رَوَاهُ مُسْلِمٌ.

171/57. According to Abū Hurayra رضي الله عنه:

"Allah's Messenger ﷺ said: 'If the Religion were beside the Pleiades, a man from Persia,' or he said, 'from among the sons of (the people of) Persia would surely have attained to it!'"

Reported by Muslim.

Qurṭubī in *al-Jāmiʿ li-Aḥkām al-Qurʾān*, 18/93.

171 Set forth by •Muslim in *al-Ṣaḥīḥ*: Bk.: *Faḍāʾil al-Ṣaḥāba* [The Excellent Merits of the Companions], Ch.: The excellence of Persia, 4/1972 §2546. •al-Haythamī in *Majmaʿ al-Zawāʾid*, Ch.: What has come to us about some people among the Persians, 10/64. •al-Muqriʾ in *al-Sunan al-Wārida fī al-Fitan*, 3/744 §366. •Ibn ʿAsākir in *Tārīkh Dimashq al-Kabīr*, 23/218. •al-Ḥusaynī in *al-Bayān wa al-Taʿrīf*, 2/170 §1399. •al-Munāwī in *Fayḍ al-Qadīr*, 5/322. •al-Qurṭubī in *al-Jāmiʿ li-Aḥkām al-Qurʾān*, 18/93.

١٧٢/ ٥٨. عَنْ أَبِي هُرَيْرَةَ ﷺ قَالَ: قَالَ رَسُوْلُ اللهِ ﷺ: لَوْ كَانَ الدِّيْنُ عِنْدَ الثُّرَيَّا، لَذَهَبَ رَجُلٌ مِنْ فَارِسَ أَوْ أَبْنَاءِ فَارِسَ حَتَّى يَتَنَاوَلَهُ.

رَوَاهُ أَحْمَدُ.

172/58. According to Abū Hurayra ﷺ:

"Allah's Messenger ﷺ said: 'If the Religion were beside the Pleiades, a man from Persia, or the sons of (the people of) Persia, would surely have attained to it!'"

Reported by Aḥmad.

١٧٣/ ٥٩. عَنْ عَبْدِ اللهِ ﷺ قَالَ: قَالَ رَسُوْلُ اللهِ ﷺ: لَوْكَانَ الدِّيْنُ مُعَلَّقاً بِالثُّرَيَّا، لَتَنَاوَلَهُ نَاسٌ مِنْ أَبْنَاءِ فَارِسَ.

رَوَاهُ الطَّبَرَانِيُّ وَابْنُ أَبِي شَيْبَةَ.

173/59. According to ʿAbd Allāh ﷺ:

"Allah's Messenger ﷺ said: 'If the Religion were attached to the Pleiades, some people from among the people of Persia would surely have acquired it even from there!'"

Reported by al-Ṭabarānī and Ibn Abī Shayba.

١٧٤/ ٦٠. عَنْ أَبِي هُرَيْرَةَ ﷺ قَالَ: قَالَ رَسُوْلُ اللهِ ﷺ: لَوْ كَانَ الْعِلْمُ بِالثُّرَيَّا، لَتَنَاوَلَهُ نَاسٌ مِنْ أَهْلِ (أَبْنَاءِ) فَارِسَ.

---

172 Set forth by •Aḥmad b. Ḥanbal in *al-Musnad*, 2/308 §8067.

173 Set forth by •al-Ṭabarānī in *al-Muʿjam al-Kabīr*, 10/204 §10470. •Ibn Abī Shayba in *al-Muṣannaf*: Ch.: What has come to us about the Persians, 6/415 §32515–32516. •al-Daylamī in *al-Firdaws bi-Maʾthūr al-Khiṭāb*, 3/360 §5084. •Ibn ʿAsākir in *Tārīkh Dimashq al-Kabīr*, 23/218. •al-Wāsiṭī in *Tārīkh Wāsiṭ*, 1/220. •al-Khaṭīb al-Baghdādī in *Tārīkh Baghdād*, 10/312 §5460. •Ibn Qāniʿ in *Muʿjam al-Ṣaḥāba*, 3/129 §1102. •al-ʿAsqalānī in *al-Iṣāba*, 6/213 §8217. •al-Haythamī in *Majmaʿ al-Zawāʾid*: Ch.: What has come to us about some people among the Persians, 10/65.

رَوَاهُ أَحْمَدُ وَابْنُ حِبَّانَ، وَقَالَ الْهَيْثَمِيُّ: رَوَاهُ أَبُوْ يَعْلَى وَالْبَزَّارُ وَالطَّبَرَانِيُّ وَرِجَالُهُمْ

رِجَالُ الصَّحِيْحِ.

174/60. According to Abū Hurayra ﷺ:

"Allah's Messenger ﷺ said: 'If knowledge were suspended with the Pleiades, some people among the inhabitants of Persia would surely have acquired it!'"

Reported by Aḥmad and Ibn Ḥibbān. According to al-Haythamī: "It has been reported by Abū Yaʿlā, al-Bazzār and al-Ṭabarānī, and their narrators are authentic."

١٧٥ / ٦١. عَنْ أَبِي هُرَيْرَةَ ﵁ عَنِ النَّبِيِّ ﷺ قَالَ: وَيْلٌ لِلْعَرَبِ مِنْ شَرٍّ قَدِ اقْتَرَبَ!

أَفْلَحَ مَنْ كَفَّ يَدَهُ! تَقَرَّبُوا، يَا بَنِي فَرُّوْخَ، إِلَى اللهِ، فَإِنَّ الْعَرَبَ قَدْ أَعْرَضَتْ. وَوَاللهِ،

إِنَّ مِنْكُمْ لَرِجَالاً لَوْكَانَ الْعِلْمُ بِالثُّرَيَّا لَنَالُوْهُ.

رَوَاهُ الطَّحَاوِيُّ.

175/61. According to Abū Hurayra ﷺ:

"The Prophet ﷺ said: 'Woe to the Arabs, because of an evil that is imminent! Successful is he who withholds his hand from it! O Banū Farrūkh, acquire nearness to Allah, for the Arabs have turned away (from Him). By Allah! If knowledge were in the Pleiades, some men among you would surely have attained to it!'"

Reported by al-Ṭaḥāwī.

---

174 Set forth by •Aḥmad b. Ḥanbal in *al-Musnad*, 2/420 §9430, 7937, 9454, 10059. •al-Bazzār in *al-Musnad*, 9/195 §3741. •Ibn Ḥibbān in *al-Ṣaḥīḥ*: Ch.: His reference ﷺ to the Persians when speaking of faith and the truth, 16/299 §7309. •al-Haythamī in *Mawārid al-Ẓamʾān*: Ch.: Concerning some people among the natives of Persia, 1/574 §2309, & in *Majmaʿ al-Zawāʾid*: Ch.: What has come to us about some people among the natives of Persia, 10/64. •al-Ḥārith in *Musnad Zawāʾid al-Haythamī*, 2/943. •al-Qaysarānī in *Tadhkirat al-Ḥuffāẓ*, 3/972 §912. •al-Dhahabī in *Siyar Aʿlām al-Nubalāʾ*, 10/210. •Ibn ʿAsākir in *Tārīkh Dimashq al-Kabīr*, 51/140.

175 Set forth by •al-Ṭaḥāwī in *Mushkil al-Āthār*, 3/94.

١٧٦/ ٦٢. عَنْ أَبِي هُرَيْرَةَ ﵁ عَنِ النَّبِيِّ ﷺ قَالَ: اقْتَرِبُوْا، يَا بَنِي فَرُّوخَ، إِلَى الذِّكْرِ. وَاللهِ، إِنَّ مِنْكُمْ لَرِجَالاً لَوْ أَنَّ الْعِلْمَ كَانَ مُعَلَّقًا بِالثُّرَيَّا لَتَنَاوَلُوْهُ.

رَوَاهُ الْبَيْهَقِيُّ.

176/62. According to Abū Hurayra ﵁:

"The Prophet ﷺ said: 'Draw near, O Banū Farrūkh, to the remembrance of Allah! By Allah! If knowledge were attached to the Pleiades, some men among you would surely have attained to it!'"

Reported by al-Bayhaqī.

١٧٧/ ٦٣. عَنْ أَبِي هُرَيْرَةَ ﵁ قَالَ: قَالَ رَسُوْلُ اللهِ ﷺ: ادْنُوْا، يَا مَعْشَرَ الْمَوَالِيِّ، إِلَى الذِّكْرِ، فَإِنَّ الْعَرَبَ قَدْ أَعْرَضَتْ، وَإِنَّ الإِيْمَانَ لَوْ كَانَ مُعَلَّقًا بِالْعَرْشِ كَانَ مِنْكُمْ مَنْ يَطْلُبُهُ.

رَوَاهُ أَبُوْ نُعَيْمٍ فِي تَارِيْخِهِ.

177/63. According to Abū Hurayra ﵁:

"Allah's Messenger ﷺ said: 'Draw near, O company of the *mawalī* (non-Arabs), to the remembrance, for the Arabs have surely turned their faces away. If faith were attached to the Heavenly Throne, some of you would surely struggle for it!'"

Reported by Abū Nuʿaym in his *Tārīkh* [History].

١٧٨/ ٦٤. عَنْ أَبِي هُرَيْرَةَ ﵁ فِي رِوَايَةٍ: يُوْشِكُ أَنْ يَضْرِبَ النَّاسُ (الرَّجُلُ) أَكْبَادَ الإِبِلِ يَطْلُبُوْنَ الْعِلْمَ. وفي رواية: يَخْرُجُ النَّاسُ مِنَ الْمَشْرِقِ وَالْمَغْرِبِ، فَلاَ يَجِدُوْنَ أَحَدًا أَعْلَمَ مِنْ عَالِمِ الْمَدِيْنَةِ.

[176] Set forth by •al-Bayhaqī in *Shuʿab al-Īmān*, 4/342 §5330.

[177] Set forth by •Abū Nuʿaym in *Tārīkh Iṣbahān*, 1/6.

رَوَاهُ التِّرْمِذِيُّ وَالنَّسَائِيُّ وَالْحَاكِمُ. وَقَالَ أَبُوْ عِيْسَى: هَذَا حَدِيْثٌ حَسَنٌ. وَقَالَ الْحَاكِمُ: هَذَا حَدِيْثٌ صَحِيْحٌ.

178/64. According to Abū Hurayra ﵁, in one report:

"The people are (the man is) on the verge of striking the livers of the camels in search of knowledge (i.e., will travel very fast)," and in another report: "The people go forth from the east and the west, but they will not find anyone more knowledgeable than the scholar of Medina."

Reported by al-Tirmidhī, al-Nasāʾī and al-Ḥākim. Abū ʿĪsā said: "This is a fine tradition." And al-Ḥākim said: "This is an authentic tradition."

١٧٩/ ٦٥. عَنْ عَبْدِ اللهِ ﵁ قَالَ: قَالَ رَسُوْلُ اللهِ ﷺ: لَا تَسُبُّوْا قُرَيْشًا، فَإِنَّ عَالِمَهَا يَمْلَأُ طِبَاقَ الْأَرْضِ عِلْمًا.

رَوَاهُ الطَّيَالِسِيُّ وَابْنُ أَبِي عَاصِمٍ وَالْخَطِيْبُ.

179/65. According to ʿAbd Allāh ﵁:

---

178 Set forth by •al-Tirmidhī in *al-Sunan*: Bk.: *al-ʿIlm* [Knowledge] according to Allah's Messenger ﷺ, Ch.: What has come to us about the scholar of Medina, 5/57 §2680. •al-Nasāʾī in *al-Sunan al-Kubrā*: Ch.: The scholar of Medina, 2/489 §4291. •al-Ḥākim in *al-Mustadrak*, 1/168 §2308. •al-Bayhaqī in *al-Sunan al-Kubrā*, 1/385 §1681. •Abū al-Maḥāsin in *Muʿtaṣar al-Mukhtaṣar*, 2/339. •al-Khaṭīb in *Tārīkh Baghdād*, 5/306, 1/195 §90. •al-Haythamī in *Majmaʿ al-Zawāʾid*, 1/134. •Ibn ʿAbd al-Barr in *al-Tamhīd*, 1/84. •al-Dhahabī in *Siyar Aʿlām al-Nubalāʾ*, 8/55. •al-ʿAsqalānī in *Tahdhīb al-Tahdhīb*, 10/7. •al-Mizzī in *Tahdhīb al-Kamāl*, 27/117.

179 Set forth by •al-Ṭayālisī in *al-Musnad*, 1/39 §309. •Ibn Abī ʿĀṣim in *al-Sunna*, 2/637 §1523. •al-Khaṭīb in *Tārīkh Baghdād*, 2/61. •Abū Nuʿaym in *Ḥilya al-Awliyāʾ*, 6/295, 9/65. •al-Daylamī in *al-Firdaws bi-Maʾthūr al-Khiṭāb*, 5/12 §7295. •al-Bayhaqī in *Bayān man akhṭaʾ ʿalā al-Shāfiʿī*, 1/94. •al-ʿAsqalānī in *Tahdhīb al-Tahdhīb*, 9/24 & in *Lisān al-Mīzān*, 6/159 §566. •al-Mizzī in *Tahdhīb al-Kamāl*, 24/364. •al-Munāwī in *Fayḍ al-Qadīr*, 2/105. •al-Shāshī in *al-Musnad*, 2/169 §728. •al-Dhahabī in *Mīzān al-Iʿtidal*, 7/27.

"Allah's Messenger ﷺ said: 'You must not revile Quraysh, for their scholar will fill the strata of the earth with (the light of) knowledge.'"

Reported by al-Ṭayālisī, Ibn Abī ʿĀṣim and al-Khaṭīb.

اَلْفَصْلُ الْخَامِسُ

فَصْلٌ فِي مَنَاقِبِ الْأَوْلِيَاءِ وَالصَّالِحِيْنَ رضي الله عنهم

Section 5

The Virtues of the Saints and the Righteous رضي الله عنهم

١٨٠/٦٦. عَنْ أَبِي هُرَيْرَةَ رضي الله عنه عَنِ النَّبِيِّ ﷺ قَالَ: إِذَا أَحَبَّ اللهُ الْعَبْدَ، نَادَى جِبْرِيْلَ: إِنَّ اللهَ يُحِبُّ فُلَانًا، فَأَحْبِبْهُ. فَيُحِبُّهُ جِبْرِيْلُ، فَيُنَادِي جِبْرِيْلُ فِي أَهْلِ السَّمَاءِ: إِنَّ اللهَ يُحِبُّ فُلَانًا، فَأَحِبُّوْهُ. فَيُحِبُّهُ أَهْلُ السَّمَاءِ، ثُمَّ يُوْضَعُ لَهُ الْقَبُوْلُ فِي الْأَرْضِ.

مُتَّفَقٌ عَلَيْهِ.

180/66. According to Abū Hurayra رضي الله عنه:

"The Prophet ﷺ said: 'When Allah loves the servant, He calls on Gabriel: "Allah loves So-and-so! You must therefore love him (the servant)!" So Gabriel loves him! Then Gabriel announces to the people of heaven: "Allah loves So-and-so! You must therefore love him!" So the people of heaven, too, love him! Acceptance (and popularity) is then established for him (in the hearts of the people) on the earth.'"

Agreed upon by al-Bukhārī and Muslim.

---

[180] Set forth by •al-Bukhārī in *al-Ṣaḥīḥ*: Bk.: *Bad' al-Khalq* [The Beginning of Creation], Ch.: Concerning the angels, 3/1175 §3037, & Bk.: *al-Adab* [Proper Conduct], Ch.: Hatred of Allah تعالى, 5/2246 §5293, & Bk.: *al-Tawḥīd* [The Affirmation of Oneness], Ch.: The Lord's conversation with Gabriel and Allah's summoning the angels, 6/2721 §7047. •Muslim in *al-Ṣaḥīḥ*: Bk.: *al-Birr wa al-Ṣila wa al-Ādāb* [Piety, Affinity and Good Manners], Ch.: If Allah loves a servant, He endears him to His servants, 4/2030 §2637. •Mālik in *al-Muwaṭṭa'*, 2/953 §1710.

١٨١/ ٦٧. عَنْ أَبِي هُرَيْرَةَ ﵁ قَالَ: قَالَ رَسُوْلُ اللهِ ﷺ: إِنَّ اللهَ قَالَ: مَنْ عَادَى لِي وَلِيًّا، فَقَدْ آذَنْتُهُ بِالْحَرْبِ. وَمَا تَقَرَّبَ إِلَيَّ عَبْدِي بِشَيْءٍ أَحَبَّ إِلَيَّ مِمَّا افْتَرَضْتُ عَلَيْهِ. وَمَا يَزَالُ عَبْدِي يَتَقَرَّبُ إِلَيَّ بِالنَّوَافِلِ حَتَّى أُحِبَّهُ، فَإِذَا أَحْبَبْتُهُ كُنْتُ سَمْعَهُ الَّذِي يَسْمَعُ بِهِ، وَبَصَرَهُ الَّذِي يُبْصِرُ بِهِ، وَيَدَهُ الَّتِي يَبْطِشُ بِهَا، وَرِجْلَهُ الَّتِي يَمْشِي بِهَا. وإِنْ سَأَلَنِي، لَأُعْطِيَنَّهُ، وَلَئِنِ اسْتَعَاذَنِي، لَأُعِيذَنَّهُ. وَمَا تَرَدَّدْتُ عَنْ شَيْءٍ أَنَا فَاعِلُهُ تَرَدُّدِي عَنْ نَفْسِ الْمُؤْمِنِ. يَكْرَهُ الْمَوْتَ وَأَنَا أَكْرَهُ مَسَاءَتَهُ.

رَوَاهُ الْبُخَارِيُّ.

181/67. According to Abū Hurayra ﵁:

"Allah's Messenger ﷺ said: 'Allah has said: "If someone treats a friend of Mine as an enemy, I have declared war on him. My servant does not draw near to Me by means of anything dearer to Me than that which I have made incumbent upon him. My servant does not cease to attain to My nearness by means of supererogatory devotions, until I love him, and when I love him, I become his hearing with which he hears, his sight with which he sees, his hand with which he holds, and his foot with which he walks. If he asks of Me, I surely grant him, and if he appeals to Me for refuge, I surely grant him refuge. I do not vacillate about anything of which I am the Doer. My vacillation is about taking the soul of the believer. He dislikes death and I dislike his pain.'""

Reported by al-Bukhārī.

١٨٢/ ٦٨. عَنْ عُمَرَ بْنِ الْخَطَّابِ ﵁ قَالَ: قَالَ النَّبِيُّ ﷺ: إِنَّ مِنْ عِبَادِ اللهِ لَأُنَاسًا مَا هُمْ بِأَنْبِيَاءَ وَلَا شُهَدَاءَ. يَغْبِطُهُمُ الْأَنْبِيَاءُ وَالشُّهَدَاءُ يَوْمَ الْقِيَامَةِ بِمَكَانِهِمْ مِنَ اللهِ. قَالُوْا: يَا رَسُوْلَ اللهِ، تُخْبِرُنَا مَنْ هُمْ؟ قَالَ: هُمْ قَوْمٌ تَحَابُّوْا بِرُوْحِ اللهِ عَلَى غَيْرِ أَرْحَامٍ

[181] Set forth by •al-Bukhārī in *al-Ṣaḥīḥ*: Bk.: *al-Riqāq* [The Softening of Hearts], Ch.: Humility, 5/2384 §6137. •Ibn Ḥibbān in *al-Ṣaḥīḥ*, 2/58 §347. •al-Bayhaqī in *al-Sunan al-Kubrā*, 10/219, Ch.: (60), & in *Kitāb al-Zuhd al-Kabīr*, 2/269 §696.

بَيْنَهُمْ، وَلاَ أَمْوَالٍ يَتَعَاطُوْنَهَا. فَوَاللهِ، إِنَّ وُجُوْهَهُمْ لَنُوْرٌ وَإِنَّهُمْ لَعَلَى نُوْرٍ. لاَ يَخَافُوْنَ إِذَا خَافَ النَّاسُ، وَلاَ يَحْزَنُوْنَ إِذَا حَزِنَ النَّاسُ، وَقَرَأَ هَذِهِ الْآيَةَ: ﴿أَلَآ إِنَّ أَوْلِيَآءَ ٱللَّهِ لَا خَوْفٌ عَلَيْهِمْ وَلَا هُمْ يَحْزَنُونَ﴾. (يونس، ١٠: ٦٢).

رَوَاهُ أَبُوْ دَاوُدَ وَالنَّسَائِيُّ.

182/68. According to ʿUmar b. al-Khaṭṭāb ﵁:

"The Prophet ﷺ said: 'Among Allah's exalted servants there are some people who are neither Prophets not martyrs. The Prophets and the martyrs will envy them on the Day of Resurrection for the dignity they receive from Allah.' The Companions said: 'O Messenger of Allah, will you tell us who they are?' He said: 'They are people who love one another for the sake of Allah, not because of close family ties, and not because of money transactions (or properties they share). By Allah, their faces will be (full of) light, and they are in a state of light (over the pulpits of light)! They will not fear when other people fear, and they will not grieve when other people grieve.' Then he recited this Qurʾānic Verse: 'Beware! Surely there shall be no fear upon the friends of Allah (*awliyāʾ*), nor shall they grieve *[a-lā inna awliyāʾa ʾllāhi lā khawfun ʿalayhim wa lā hum yaḥzanūn]*.'" (Q.10:62).

Reported by Abū Dāwūd and al-Nasāʾī.

١٨٣ / ٦٩. عَنْ أَبِي هُرَيْرَةَ ﵁ قَالَ: قَالَ رَسُوْلُ اللهِ ﷺ: إِنَّ مِنْ عِبَادِ اللهِ عِبَادًا لَيْسُوْا بِأَنْبِيَاءَ. يَغْبِطُهُمُ الْأَنْبِيَاءُ وَالشُّهَدَاءُ. قِيْلَ: مَنْ هُمْ لَعَلَّنَا نُحِبُّهُمْ؟ قَالَ: هُمْ قَوْمٌ تَحَابُّوْا بِرُوْحِ اللهِ مِنْ غَيْرِ أَرْحَامٍ وَلاَ انْتِسَابٍ. وُجُوْهُهُمْ نُوْرٌ عَلَى مَنَابِرَ مِنْ نُوْرٍ. لاَ يَخَافُوْنَ إِذَا خَافَ النَّاسُ، وَلاَ يَحْزَنُوْنَ إِذَا حَزِنَ النَّاسُ، ثُمَّ قَرَأَ: ﴿أَلَآ إِنَّ أَوْلِيَآءَ ٱللَّهِ لَا خَوْفٌ عَلَيْهِمْ وَلَا هُمْ يَحْزَنُونَ﴾. (يونس، ١٠: ٦٢).

---

182 Set forth by •Abū Dāwūd in *al-Sunan*: Bk.: *al-Buyūʿ* [Sales], Ch.: Pawning [*al-rahn*], 3/288 §3527. •al-Nasāʾī in *al-Sunan al-Kubrā*, *Sūra Yūnus*, 6/362 §11236. •al-Bayhaqī in *Shuʿab al-Īmān*, 6/486 §8998.

رَوَاهُ ابْنُ حِبَّانَ وَأَبُوْ يَعْلَى وَالْبَيْهَقِيُّ.

183/69. According to Abū Hurayra ﷺ:

"Allah's Messenger ﷺ said: 'Among Allah's servants there are some who are not Prophets and whom the Prophets and the martyrs envy.' He was asked: '(O Messenger of Allah,) who are they (enlighten us on their attributes), so that we may love them?' He said: 'They are people who love one another for the sake of Allah, without having family ties and without common ancestry. Their faces will be full of light and they will be sitting (making disclosures of radiant light) on the pulpits of light. They will not fear when other people fear, and they will not grieve when other people grieve.' Then he recited: 'Beware! Surely there shall be no fear upon the friends of Allah (*awliyā*ʾ), nor shall they grieve *[a-lā inna awliyāʾa ʾllāhi lā khawfun ʿalay-him wa lā hum yaḥzanūn].*'" (Q.10:62).

Reported by Ibn Ḥibbān, Abū Yaʿlā and al-Bayhaqī.

١٨٤/ ٧٠. عَنْ أَسْمَاءَ بِنْتِ يَزِيْدَ ﷺ قَالَتْ: سَمِعْتُ رَسُولَ اللهِ ﷺ يَقُوْلُ: أَلاَ أُنَبِّئُكُمْ بِخِيَارِكُمْ؟ قَالُوْا: بَلَى، يَا رَسُوْلَ اللهِ. قَالَ: خِيَارُكُمُ الَّذِيْنَ إِذَا رُؤُوْا ذُكِرَ اللهُ.

رَوَاهُ ابْنُ مَاجَه وَأَحْمَدُ وَالْبُخَارِيُّ فِي الأَدَبِ.

184/70. According to Asmāʾ, the daughter of Yazīd ﷺ:

"I heard Allah's Messenger ﷺ say: 'Shall I not inform you of the best of you?' They said: 'Of course, O Messenger of Allah!' He said: 'The best of you are those that, when they are seen, Allah is remembered!'"

---

[183] Set forth by •Ibn Ḥibbān in *al-Ṣaḥīḥ*, 2/332 §573. •Abū Yaʿlā in *al-Musnad*, 10/495 §6110. •al-Bayhaqī in *Shuʿab al-Īmān*, 6/485 §8997–8999. •al-Mundhirī in *al-Targhīb wa al-Tarhīb*, 4/12 §4580.

[184] Set forth by •Ibn Mājah in *al-Sunan*: Bk.: *al-Zuhd* [Abstinence], Ch.: Someone to whom no attention is paid, 2/1379 §4119. •Aḥmad b. Ḥanbal in *al-Musnad*, 6/459 §27640. •al-Bukhārī in *al-Adab al-Mufrad*, 1/119 §323. •al-Ṭabarānī in *al-Muʿjam al-Kabīr*, 24/167 §423.

Reported by Ibn Mājah, Aḥmad and al-Bukhārī in *al-Adab*.

١٨٥ / ٧١. عَنِ ابْنِ عَبَّاسٍ ﷺ، قَالَ: سُئِلَ رَسُوْلُ اللهِ ﷺ عَنْ أَوْلِيَاءِ اللهِ. فَقَالَ: الَّذِيْنَ إِذَا رُؤُوْا، ذُكِرَ اللهُ تعالى.

رَوَاهُ النَّسَائِيُّ. وَقَالَ الْهَيْثَمِيُّ: رَوَاهُ الْبَزَّارُ وَوَثَّقَهُ.

185/71. According to Ibn ʿAbbās ﷺ:

"Allah's Messenger ﷺ was asked about the friends of Allah, so he said: 'They are those that, when they are seen, Allah ﷻ is remembered!'"

Reported by an Nasāʾī. Al-Haythamī said: "Reported and confirmed by al-Bazzar."

١٨٦ / ٧٢. عَنْ عَبْدِ اللهِ بْنِ مَسْعُوْدٍ ﷺ قَالَ: قَالَ رَسُوْلُ اللهِ ﷺ: إِنَّ مِنَ النَّاسِ مَفَاتِيْحَ لِذِكْرِ اللهِ. إِذَا رُؤُوْا، ذُكِرَ اللهُ.

رَوَاهُ الطَّبَرَانِيُّ وَالْبَيْهَقِيُّ وَابْنُ أَبِي الدُّنْيَا.

186/72. According to ʿAbd Allāh b. Masʿūd ﷺ:

"Allah's Messenger ﷺ said: 'Some of the people are keys of the remembrance of Allah, for when they are seen, Allah is remembered.'"

Reported by al-Ṭabarānī, al-Bayhaqī and Ibn Abī al-Dunyā.

١٨٧ / ٧٣. عَنْ عَمْرِو بْنِ الْحَمِقِ ﷺ قَالَ: قَالَ رَسُوْلُ اللهِ ﷺ: لَا يُحِقُّ الْعَبْدُ حَقِيقَةَ

[185] Set forth by •al-Nasāʾī in *al-Sunan al-Kubrā*: *Sūra Yūnus*, 6/362 §11235. •Ibn al-Mubārak in *Kitāb al-Zuhd*, 1/72 §217. •al-Maqdisī in *al-Aḥādīth al-Mukhtāra*, 10/108 §105. •al-Ḥakīm al-Tirmidhī in *Nawādir al-Uṣūl*, 2/39. •al-Haythamī in *Majmaʿ al-Zawāʾid*, 10/78.

[186] Set forth by •al-Ṭabarānī in *al-Muʿjam al-Kabīr*, 10/205 §10476. •al-Bayhaqī in *Shuʿab al-Īmān*, 1/455 §499. •Ibn Abī al-Dunyā in *Kitāb al-Awliyāʾ*, 1/17 §26. •al-Haythamī in *Majmaʿ al-Zawāʾid*, 10/78. He confirmed its authenticity.

الإِيْمَانِ حَتَّى يَغْضَبَ لِلّٰهِ وَيَرْضَى لِلّٰهِ. فَإِذَا فَعَلَ ذَلِكَ، اسْتَحَقَّ حَقِيْقَةَ الإِيْمَانِ. وَإِنَّ أَحِبَّائِي وَأَوْلِيَائِي الَّذِيْنَ يُذْكَرُوْنَ بِذِكْرِي وَأُذْكَرُ بِذِكْرِهِمْ.

رَوَاهُ الطَّبَرَانِيُّ وَأَحْمَدُ.

187/73. According to ʿAmr b. al-Ḥamiq ﷺ:

"Allah's Messenger ﷺ said: 'The servant does not truly find the reality of faith, until he is angry for the sake of Allah and pleased for the sake of Allah (i.e., his pleasure is tightly fastened to Allah's pleasure). And when he does that, he finds the reality of faith. (Allah proclaimed:) My loved ones and My friends are those who are remembered when I am remembered, and I am remembered when they are remembered (My remembrance is theirs and their remembrance is Mine)!'"

Reported by al-Ṭabarānī and Aḥmad.

١٨٨/ ٧٤. عَنْ عُمَرَ بْنِ الْخَطَّابِ ﷺ عَنْ مُعَاذِ بْنِ جَبَلٍ ﷺ قَالَ: سَمِعْتُ رَسُوْلَ اللهِ ﷺ يَقُولُ: إِنَّ يَسِيْرَ الرِّيَاءِ شِرْكٌ، وَإِنَّ مَنْ عَادَى لِلّٰهِ وَلِيًّا، فَقَدْ بَارَزَ اللهَ بِالْمُحَارَبَةِ. إِنَّ اللهَ يُحِبُّ الْأَبْرَارَ الْأَتْقِيَاءَ الْأَخْفِيَاءَ، الَّذِيْنَ إِذَا غَابُوْا لَمْ يُفْتَقَدُوْا، وَإِنْ حَضَرُوْا لَمْ يُدْعَوْا وَلَمْ يُعْرَفُوْا. قُلُوْبُهُمْ مَصَابِيْحُ الْهُدَى؛ يَخْرُجُوْنَ مِنْ كُلِّ غَبْرَاءَ مُظْلِمَةٍ.

رَوَاهُ ابْنُ مَاجَه وَالْحَاكِمُ. وَقَالَ الْحَاكِمُ: هَذَا حَدِيْثٌ صَحِيْحٌ.

188/74. According to ʿUmar b. al-Khaṭṭāb ﷺ, Muʿādh b. Jabal ﷺ said:

---

[187] Set forth by •al-Ṭabarānī in *al-Muʿjam al-Awsaṭ*, 1/203 §651. •al-Haythamī in *Majmaʿ al-Zawāʾid*, 1/58. •Aḥmad b. Ḥanbal in *al-Musnad*, 3/430 §15634. •Ibn Rajab in *Jāmiʿ al-ʿUlūm wa al-Ḥikam*, 1/365. •Ibn Abī al-Dunyā in *Kitāb al-Awliyāʾ*, 1/15 §19. •al-Daylamī in *al-Firdaws bi-Maʾthūr al-Khiṭāb*, 5/152 §7789. •al-Mundhirī in *al-Targhīb wa al-Tarhīb*, 4/14 §4589.

[188] Set forth by •Ibn Mājah in *al-Sunan*: Bk.: *al-Fitan* [Troubles], Ch.: Someone for whom safety from troubles is hoped, 2/1320 §3989. •al-Ḥākim in *al-Mustadrak*, 1/44 §4; 4/364 §7933. •al-Ṭabarānī in *al-Muʿjam al-Ṣaghīr*,

"I heard Allah's Messenger ﷺ say: 'The slightest pretence (and showiness) is also a form of polytheism. If someone treats a friend of Allah as an enemy, he has waged war on Allah. Surely, Allah loves those pious devotees who remain hidden. When they are absent they are not looked for, and when they are present, they are not invited and are not recognized (in any meeting or gathering or for some assignment). Their hearts are the lamps of right guidance, and they get rid of every trial or saddening disruption (and stay safe and sound).'"

Reported by Ibn Mājah and al-Ḥākim, who said: "This is an authentic tradition."

١٨٩/ ٧٥. عَنِ ابْنِ عَبَّاسٍ رضي الله عنهما قَالَ: قِيْلَ: يَا رَسُوْلَ اللهِ، أَيُّ جُلَسَائِنَا خَيْرٌ؟ قَالَ: مَنْ ذَكَّرَكُمُ اللهَ رُؤْيَتُهُ وَزَادَ فِي عِلْمِكُمْ مَنْطِقُهُ وَذَكَرَكُمْ بِالْآخِرَةِ عَمَلُهُ.

رَوَاهُ أَبُوْ يَعْلَى وَعَبْدُ بْنُ حُمَيْدٍ وَنَحْوَهُ أَبُوْ نُعَيْمٍ.

189/75. According to Ibn ʿAbbās رضي الله عنهما:

"Someone said: 'O Messenger of Allah, which of our social companions are best?' He said: 'The one whose sight reminds you of Allah, whose speech increases your knowledge, and whose conduct reminds you of the Hereafter!'"

Reported by Abū Yaʿlā and ʿAbd b. Ḥumayd, and in similar form by Abū Nuʿaym.

2/122 §892. •al-Daylamī in *al-Firdaws bi-Maʾthūr al-Khiṭāb*, 5/548 §9049. •al-Mundhirī in *al-Targhīb wa al-Tarhīb*, 1/34 §49.

[189] Set forth by •Abū Yaʿlā in *al-Musnad*, 4/326 §2437. •ʿAbd b. Ḥumayd in *al-Musnad*, 1/213 §631. •Abū Nuʿaym in *Ḥilya al-Awliyāʾ*, 7/46. •Ibn al-Mubārak in *al-Zuhd*, 1/121 §355. •Ibn Abī al-Dunyā in *al-Awliyāʾ*, 1/17 §25. •al-Mundhirī in *al-Targhīb wa al-Tarhīb*, 1/63 §163. •al-Hindī in *Kanz al-ʿUmmāl*, 9/28, 37 §24764, 24820. •al-Ḥusaynī in *al-Bayān wa al-Taʿrīf*, 2/39 §994. •al-Zurqānī in *Sharḥ ʿalā al- Muwaṭṭaʾ*, 4/553. •al-Munāwī in *Fayḍ al-Qadīr*, 3/467.

اَلْفَصْلُ السَّادِسُ

فَصْلٌ فِي مَا أَعَدَّهُ اللهُ مِنْ قُرَّةِ أَعْيُنٍ لِعِبَادِهِ الصَّالِحِيْنَ

Section 6

What Allāh has Prepared as Comfort for the Righteous Servants

١٩٠/٧٦. عَنْ أَبِي هُرَيْرَةَ ﷺ قَالَ: قَالَ رَسُوْلُ اللهِ ﷺ: قَالَ اللهُ ﷻ: أَعْدَدْتُ لِعِبَادِيَ الصَّالِحِيْنَ مَا لَا عَيْنٌ رَأَتْ، وَلَا أُذُنٌ سَمِعَتْ، وَلَا خَطَرَ عَلَى قَلْبِ بَشَرٍ. فَاقْرَؤُوْا إِنْ شِئْتُمْ: ﴿فَلَا تَعْلَمُ نَفْسٌ مَّآ أُخْفِىَ لَهُم مِّن قُرَّةِ أَعْيُنٍ جَزَآءًۢ بِمَا كَانُوا۟ يَعْمَلُونَ﴾. (السجدة، ٣٢: ١٧).

مُتَّفَقٌ عَلَيْهِ.

190/76. According to Abū Hurayra ﷺ:

---

[190] Set forth by •al-Bukhārī in *al-Ṣaḥīḥ*: Bk.: *Bad᾿ al-Khalq* [The Beginning of Creation], Ch.: What has come to us about the quality of the Garden of Paradise, and the fact that it was created, 3/1185 §3072, & Bk.: *Tafsīr al-Sajda* [Interpretation/*Sūrat al-Sajda*], Ch.: Allah's saying: "So no soul knows what comfort is kept secretly in store for them [*fa-lā taʿlamu nafsun mā ukhfiya lahum min qurrati aʿyun*]." (Q.32:17), 4/1794 §4501–4502, & Bk.: *al-Tawḥīd* [The Affirmation of Oneness], Ch.: His saying: "They wish to change the verdict of Allah [*yurīdūna an yubaddilū Kalāma Allāh*]." (Q.48:15), 6/2723 §7059. •Muslim in *al-Ṣaḥīḥ*: Bk.: The Quality of the Garden of Paradise and its Felicity, Ch.: (51), 4/2174–2175 §2824. •al-Tirmidhī in *al-Sunan*: Bk.: *Tafsīr al-Qur᾿an* [Interpretation of the Qur᾿ān] according to Allah's Messenger ﷺ, Ch.: From *Sūrat al-Sajda*, 5/346 §3197, & Ch.: From *Sūrat al-Wāqiʿa*, 5/400 §3292. Abū ʿĪsā said: "This is a fine authentic tradition." •Ibn Mājah in *al-Sunan*: Bk.: *al-Zuhd* [Abstinence], Ch.: The quality of the Garden of Paradise, 2/1447 §4328. •al-Nasā᾿ī in *al-Sunan al-Kubrā*, 6/317 §11085. •Aḥmad b. Ḥanbal in *al-Musnad*, 2/438 §10428, 9647, 22877. •Ibn

"Allah's Messenger ﷺ said: 'Allah ﷻ has said: "I have prepared for My righteous servants favours that no eye has seen, and no ear has heard, and which have never occurred to the heart of a human being. So recite if you will: 'So no soul knows what eye-cooling bliss is kept in store for them, as a reward for what they used to do *[fa-lā taʿlamu nafsun mā ukhfiya la-hum min qurrati aʿyun: jazāʾan bi-mā kānū yaʿmalūn].*' (Q.32:17).""'

Agreed upon by al-Bukhārī and Muslim.

١٩١ / ٧٧. عَنْ أَبِي سَعِيْدِ الْخُدْرِيِّ رضي الله عنه قَالَ: قَالَ رَسُوْلُ اللهِ ﷺ: إِنَّ اللهَ تعالى يَقُوْلُ لِأَهْلِ الْجَنَّةِ: يَا أَهْلَ الْجَنَّةِ، فَيَقُوْلُوْنَ: لَبَّيْكَ، رَبَّنَا، وَسَعْدَيْكَ، وَالْخَيْرُ فِي يَدَيْكَ. فَيَقُوْلُ: هَلْ رَضِيْتُمْ؟ فَيَقُوْلُوْنَ: وَمَا لَنَا لَا نَرْضَى، يَا رَبِّ، وَقَدْ أَعْطَيْتَنَا مَا لَمْ تُعْطِ أَحَدًا مِنْ خَلْقِكَ؟ فَيَقُوْلُ: أَلَا أُعْطِيْكُمْ أَفْضَلَ مِنْ ذَلِكَ؟ فَيَقُوْلُوْنَ: يَا رَبِّ، وَأَيُّ شَيْءٍ أَفْضَلُ مِنْ ذَلِكَ؟ فَيَقُوْلُ: أُحِلُّ عَلَيْكُمْ رِضْوَانِي، فَلَا أَسْخَطُ عَلَيْكُمْ بَعْدَهُ أَبَدًا.

مُتَّفَقٌ عَلَيْهِ.

191/77. According to Abū Saʿīd al-Khudrī رضي الله عنه:

"Allah's Messenger ﷺ said: 'Allah ﷻ will say to the people of the Garden of Paradise: "O people of the Garden of Paradise!"

Ḥibbān in *al-Ṣaḥīḥ*, 2/91 §369. •al-Ḥākim in *al-Mustadrak*, 2/448 §3549–3550. He said: "This is a tradition with an authentic chain of transmission."

[191] Set forth by •al-Bukhārī in *al-Ṣaḥīḥ*: Bk.: *al-Riqāq* [The Softening of Hearts], Ch.: The quality of the Garden of Paradise and the Fire of Hell, 5/2398 §6183, & Bk.: *al-Tawḥīd* [The Affirmation of Oneness], Ch.: The Lord's conversation with the inhabitants of the Garden of Paradise, 6/2732 §7080. •Muslim in *al-Ṣaḥīḥ*: Bk.: The Garden of Paradise and the Quality of its Felicity, Ch.: The bestowal of good pleasure upon the inhabitants of the Garden of Paradise, 4/2176 §2829. •al-Tirmidhī in *al-Sunan*: Bk.: *Ṣifat al-Janna* [The Quality of the Garden of Paradise] according to Allah's Messenger ﷺ, Ch.: (18). •al-Nasāʾī in *al-Sunan al-Kubrā*, 4/416 §7749. •Aḥmad b. Ḥanbal in *al-Musnad*, 3/88 §11853. •Ibn Ḥibbān in *al-Ṣaḥīḥ*, 16/470 §7440. •Ibn al-Mubārak in *al-Zuhd*, 1/129 §430. •al-Mundhirī in *al-Targhīb wa al-Tarhīb*, 4/313 §5750.

They will say: "At Your service, our Lord, we totally submit to You in obedience over and over again and seek twofold pleasure! And every kind of goodness is in Your Hands!" He will say: "Are you well pleased?" They will say: "How could we not be well pleased, O our Lord, when You have given us that which You have given to none of Your creatures?" He will say: "Should I not give you something superior to that?" They will say: "O my Lord, what thing is superior to that?" He will then say: "I bestow My good pleasure upon you, so I shall never inflict My displeasure upon you again!"'"

Agreed upon by al-Bukhārī and Muslim.

١٩٢ / ٧٨. عَنْ أَنَسِ بْنِ مَالِكٍ ﵁ أَنَّ رَسُوْلَ اللهِ ﷺ قَالَ: إِنَّ فِي الْجَنَّةِ لَسُوْقًا يَأْتُوْنَهَا كُلَّ جُمُعَةٍ فَتَهُبُّ رِيْحُ الشِّمَالِ فَتَحْثُوْ فِي وُجُوْهِهِمْ وَثِيَابِهِمْ، فَيَزْدَادُوْنَ حُسْنًا وَجَمَالاً. فَيَرْجِعُوْنَ إِلَى أَهْلِيْهِمْ وَقَدِ ازْدَادُوْا حُسْنًا وَجَمَالا. فَيَقُوْلُ لَهُمْ أَهْلُوْهُمْ: وَاللهِ، لَقَدِ ازْدَدْتُمْ بَعْدَنَا حُسْنًا وَجَمَالاً. فَيَقُوْلُوْنَ: وَأَنْتُمْ، وَاللهِ، لَقَدْ ازْدَدْتُمْ بَعْدَنَا حُسْنًا وَجَمَالاً.

رَوَاهُ مُسْلِمٌ وَالدَّارِمِيُّ.

192/78. According to Anas b. Mālik ﵁:

"Allah's Messenger ﷺ said: 'There is a market in the Garden of Paradise, where they will come every Friday (the Day of Congregation). So the north wind will blow and throw its effect on their clothes and faces increasing their handsomeness and beauty. When they return to their families, their families will say to them seeing their increased handsomeness and beauty: "By Allah, you have increased in handsomeness and beauty after going away from us," and they will say: "You too! By Allah, you have increased after us in handsomeness and beauty!"'"

[192] Set forth by •Muslim in *al-Ṣaḥīḥ*: Bk.: The Quality of the Garden of Paradise and its Felicity, Ch.: The market of the Garden of Paradise, and the bliss and beauty they obtain therein, 4/2178 §2833. •al-Dārimī in *al-Sunan*, 2/436 §2841. •Ibn al-Mubārak in *al-Zuhd*, 1/524 §1491. •al-Mundhirī in *al-Targhīb wa al-Tarhīb*, 4/301 §5727.

Reported by Muslim and al-Dārimī.

١٩٣/ ٧٩. عَنْ صُهَيْب ﷺ عَنِ النَّبِيِّ ﷺ قَالَ: إِذَا دَخَلَ أَهْلُ الْجَنَّةِ الْجَنَّةَ، قَالَ: يَقُوْلُ اللهُ ﷻ: تُرِيْدُوْنَ شَيْئًا أَزِيْدُكُمْ؟ فَيَقُوْلُوْنَ: أَلَمْ تُبَيِّضْ وُجُوْهَنَا؟ أَلَمْ تُدْخِلْنَا الْجَنَّةَ وَتُنَجِّنَا مِنَ النَّارِ؟ قَالَ: فَيَكْشِفُ الْحِجَابَ فَمَا أُعْطُوْا شَيْئًا أَحَبَّ إِلَيْهِمْ مِنَ النَّظَرِ إِلَى رَبِّهِمْ ﷻ ثُمَّ تَلاَ هَذِهِ الآيَةَ: ﴿لِّلَّذِينَ أَحْسَنُواْ ٱلْحُسْنَىٰ وَزِيَادَةٌ﴾. (يونس، ١٠:٢٦).

رَوَاهُ مُسْلِمٌ وَالتِّرْمِذِيُّ.

193/79. According to Ṣuhayb ﷺ:

"The Prophet ﷺ said: 'When the people of the Garden of Paradise enter the Garden of Paradise, Allah ﷻ will say: "Do you wish for something extra that I shall give you?" They will say: "(O our Lord,) have You not brightened our faces? Have You not caused us to enter the Garden of Paradise, and saved us from the Fire of Hell?" He will therefore remove the veil; they will not have been given anything dearer to them than the sight of their Lord ﷻ.' Then he recited this Qurʾānic Verse: 'For those who do good is the reward most fair and even more besides *[liʾlladhīna aḥsanu al-ḥusnā wa ziyāda]*.'" (Q.10:26).

Reported by Muslim and al-Tirmidhī.

١٩٤/ ٨٠. عَنْ سَعِيْدِ بْنِ الْمُسَيِّبِ أَنَّهُ لَقِيَ أَبَا هُرَيْرَةَ ﷺ فَقَالَ أَبُوْ هُرَيْرَةَ ﷺ: أَسْأَلُ اللهَ أَنْ يَجْمَعَ بَيْنِي وَبَيْنَكَ فِي سُوْقِ الْجَنَّةِ. فَقَالَ سَعِيْدٌ: أَوَ فِيْهَا سُوْقٌ؟ قَالَ: نَعَمْ، أَخْبَرَنِي رَسُوْلُ اللهِ ﷺ أَنَّ أَهْلَ الْجَنَّةِ إِذَا دَخَلُوْهَا نَزَلُوْا فِيْهَا بِفَضْلِ أَعْمَالِهِمْ. فَيُؤْذَنُ لَهُمْ فِي مِقْدَارِ يَوْمِ الْجُمُعَةِ مِنْ أَيَّامِ الدُّنْيَا فَيَزُوْرُوْنَ رَبَّهُمْ، وَيُبْرِزُ لَهُمْ عَرْشَهُ.

193 Set forth by •Muslim in *al-Ṣaḥīḥ*: Bk.: *al-Īmān* [Faith], Ch.: Proof of the believers' seeing their Lord in the Hereafter, 1/163 §181. •al-Tirmidhī in *al-Sunan*: Bk.: *Tafsīr al-Qurʾān* [Interpretation of the Qurʾān] according to Allah's Messenger ﷺ, Ch.: From *Sūra Yūnus*, 5/286 §3105. •Aḥmad b. Ḥanbal in *al-Musnad*, 4/332. •ʿAbd Allāh b. Aḥmad in *al-Sunan*, 1/245 §449. •al-Mundhirī in *al-Targhīb wa al-Tarhīb*, 4/309 §5744.

قَالَ أَبُو هُرَيْرَةَ: قُلْتُ: يَا رَسُوْلَ اللهِ، وَهَلْ نَرَى رَبَّنَا؟ قَالَ: نَعَمْ، هَلْ تَتَمَارَوْنَ فِي رُؤْيَةِ الشَّمْسِ وَالْقَمَرِ لَيْلَةَ الْبَدْرِ؟ قُلْنَا: لَا. قَالَ: كَذٰلِكَ لَا تَتَمَارَوْنَ فِي رُؤْيَةِ رَبِّكُمْ ﷻ وَلَا يَبْقَى فِي ذٰلِكَ الْمَجْلِسِ رَجُلٌ إِلَّا حَاضَرَهُ اللهُ مُحَاضَرَةً...

ثُمَّ نَنْصَرِفُ إِلَى مَنَازِلِنَا، فَيَتَلَقَّانَا أَزْوَاجُنَا فَيَقُلْنَ: مَرْحَبًا وَأَهْلًا! لَقَدْ جِئْتَ وَإِنَّ بِكَ مِنَ الْجَمَالِ وَالطِّيْبِ أَفْضَلَ مِمَّا فَارَقْتَنَا عَلَيْهِ. فَيَقُوْلُ: إِنَّا جَالَسْنَا الْيَوْمَ رَبَّنَا الْجَبَّارَ ﷻ، وَيَحِقُّ لَنَا أَنْ نَنْقَلِبَ بِمِثْلِ مَا انْقَلَبْنَا.

رَوَاهُ التِّرْمِذِيُّ وَابْنُ مَاجَه.

194/80. According to Saʿīd b. al-Musayyib, he encountered Abū Hurayra ؓ, so Abū Hurayra ؓ said:

"I supplicate Allah to bring me and you together in the market of the Garden of Paradise!" Saʿīd said: "Is there a market in it?" He said: "Yes, Allah's Messenger ﷺ informed me that when the people of the Garden of Paradise will enter it, they will be given ranks according to the most superior and the best of their deeds. So, it will be permitted to them to the extent of the Day of Congregation (Friday) among the days of this world to behold the countenance of their Lord. And He will make His Throne appear to them."

Abū Hurayra said: "I said: 'O Messenger of Allah, shall we see our Lord?' He said: 'Yes, would you doubt about the sighting of the sun and the full moon?' We said: 'No!' He said: 'You will likewise not argue about the sighting of your Lord ﷻ, and no man will remain in that meeting place without Allah conversing with him directly....'"

---

194 Set forth by •al-Tirmidhī in *al-Sunan*: Bk.: The Quality of the Garden of Paradise according to Allah's Messenger ﷺ, Ch.: What has come to us about the market of the Garden of Paradise, 4/685 §2549. •Ibn Mājah in *al-Sunan*: Bk.: *al-Zuhd* [Abstinence], Ch.: The quality of the Garden of Paradise, 2/1450 §4336. •Ibn Ḥibbān in *al-Ṣaḥīḥ*, 16/464–467 §7437. •Ibn Abī ʿĀṣim in *al-Sunna*, 1/258 §585–586. •al-Mundhirī in *al-Targhīb wa al-Tarhīb*, 4/301 §5728.

"We shall then go away to our dwellings, so our wives will receive us, saying: 'Welcome! You have come home with beauty and goodness finer than the state in which you parted from us!' He will say: 'We sat today in the company of our Lord, the All-Compelling ﷻ, and we deserved to be transformed into this (beautiful) form and figure.'"

Reported by al-Tirmidhī and Ibn Mājah.

١٩٥/ ٨١. عَنْ أَبِي سَعِيْدٍ الْخُدْرِيِّ رضي الله عنه قَالَ: قَالَ رَسُوْلُ اللهِ ﷺ: إِنَّ اللهَ تعالى أَحَاطَ حَائِطَ الْجَنَّةِ لَبِنَةً مِنْ ذَهَبٍ وَلَبِنَةً مِنْ فِضَّةٍ ثُمَّ شَقَّقَ فِيْهَا الأَنْهَارَ وَغَرَسَ الأَشْجَارَ. فَلَمَّا نَظَرَتِ الْمَلاَئِكَةُ إِلَى حُسْنِهَا قَالَتْ: طُوْبَى لَكِ مَنَازِلَ الْمُلُوْكِ.

رَوَاهُ الطَّبَرَانِيُّ وَالْبَزَّارُ وَأَحْمَدُ مُخْتَصَرًا.

195/81. According to Abū Saʿīd al-Khudrī رضي الله عنه:

"Allah's Messenger ﷺ said: 'Allah ﷻ made the wall of the Garden of Paradise with some adobe of gold and some adobe of silver, then He made the streams flow in it and planted the trees. So when the angels looked at its loveliness, they said: "Blessing for you!" O dwelling of the kings (of the realms of spiritualism and divine friendship of Allah)!'"

Reported by al-Ṭabarānī, al-Bazzār and Aḥmad in brief.

١٩٦/ ٨٢. عَنْ حُذَيْفَةَ رضي الله عنه في رواية طويلة قَالَ: قَالَ رَسُوْلُ اللهِ ﷺ: فَيَكُوْنُ أَوَّلُ مَا يَسْمَعُوْنَ مِنْهُ أَنْ يَقُوْلَ: أَيْنَ عِبَادِيَ الَّذِيْنَ أَطَاعُوْنِي بِالْغَيْبِ وَلَمْ يَرَوْنِي وَصَدَّقُوْا

---

195 Set forth by •al-Bazzār in *al-Musnad* (*Kashf al-Astār*), 4/189. •al-Haythamī in *Majmaʿ al-Zawāʾid*, 1/397. He said: "It has been reported by al-Bazzār with both full and limited transmission, and by al-Ṭabarānī in *al-Muʿjam al-Awsaṭ*, with limited sources and authentic sources." •Aḥmad b. Ḥanbal in *al-Musnad*, 2/362. •al-Ṭabarānī in *al-Muʿjam al-Awsaṭ*, 3/74 §2532. •al-Ḥumaydī summarily in *al-Musnad*, 2/486 §1150. •al-Daylamī in *al-Firdaws bi-Maʾthūr al-Khiṭāb*, 1/178 §664; 2/115 §2605. •Ibn al-Mubārak in *al-Zuhd*, 1/512 §1457. •al-Mundhirī in *al-Targhīb wa al-Tarhīb*, 4/282 §5650. He said: "It has been set forth by al-Bayhaqī."

رُسُلِي وَاتَّبَعُوْا امْرِي؟ فَسَلُوْنِي فَهٰذَا يَوْمُ الْـمَزِيْدِ. قَالَ: فَيَجْتَمِعُوْنَ عَلَى كَلِمَةٍ وَاحِدَةٍ: رَبِّ، رَضِيْنَا عَنْكَ فَارْضَ عَنَّا. قَالَ: فَيَرْجِعُ اللهُ تَعَالَى فِي قَوْلِهِمْ أَنْ يَا أَهْلَ الْجَنَّةِ، إِنِّي لَوْ لَـمْ أَرْضَ عَنْكُمْ لَـمَّا أَسْكَنْتُكُمْ جَنَّتِي. فَسَلُوْنِي فَهٰذَا يَوْمُ الْـمَزِيْدِ. قَالَ: فَيَجْتَمِعُوْنَ عَلَى كَلِمَةٍ وَاحِدَةٍ: رَبِّ، وَجْهَكَ أَرِنَا نَنْظُرْ إِلَيْهِ. قَالَ: فَكَشَفَ اللهُ تُبَارَكَ وَتَعَالَى تِلْكَ الْحُجُبَ وَيَتَجَلَّى لَهُمْ شَيْءٌ. لَوْلَا أَنَّهُ قَضَى عَلَيْهِمْ أَنْ لَا يَحْتَرِقُوْا، لَاحْتَرَقُوْا مِمَّا غَشِيَهُمْ مِنْ نُوْرِهِ فَيَغْشَاهُمْ مِنْ نُوْرِهِ.

قَالَ: فَيَرْجِعُونَ إِلَى مَنَازِلِهِمْ وَقَدْ خَفُوْا عَلَى أَزْوَاجِهِمْ وَخَفِيْنَ عَلَيْهِمْ مِمَّا غَشِيَهُمْ مِنْ نُوْرِهِ. فَإِذَا صَارُوْا إِلَى مَنَازِلِهِمْ تَرَادَّ النُّوْرُ وَأَمْكَنَ وَتَرَادَّ وَأَمْكَنَ حَتَّى يَرْجِعُوْا إِلَى صُوَرِهِمُ الَّتِي كَانُوْا عَلَيْهَا. قَالَ: فَيَقُوْلُ لَهُمْ أَزْوَاجُهُمْ: لَقَدْ خَرَجْتُمْ مِنْ عِنْدِنَا عَلَى صُوْرَةٍ وَرَجَعْتُمْ عَلَى غَيْرِهَا. قَالَ: فَيَقُوْلُوْنَ: ذٰلِكَ بِأَنَّ اللهَ تَجَلَّى لَنَا فَنَظَرْنَا مِنْهُ إِلَى مَا خَفِيْنَا بِهِ عَلَيْكُمْ. قَالَ: فَلَهُمْ فِي كُلِّ سَبْعَةٍ أَيَّامٍ الضِّعْفُ عَلَى مَا كَانُوْا. قَالَ: وَذٰلِكَ قَوْلُهُ: ﴿فَلَا تَعْلَمُ نَفْسٌ مَّآ أُخْفِىَ لَهُم مِّن قُرَّةِ أَعْيُنٍ جَزَآءًۢ بِمَا كَانُوا۟ يَعْمَلُونَ﴾. (السجدة، ٣٢: ١٧).

رَوَاهُ الْبَزَّارُ.

196/82. According to Ḥudhayfa ﷺ, in the course of a detailed report:

"Allah's Messenger ﷺ said: 'As for what they will hear from Him first of all, it is that He will say: "Where are My servants who have obeyed Me without having seen Me, and who have believed My Messengers and complied with My commandments? Entreat Me, for this is the day of the surplus (the day of showering My

---

[196] Set forth by •al-Bazzār in *al-Musnad*, 7/288 §2881. •al-Mundhirī in *al-Targhīb wa al-Tarhīb*, 4/311 §5748. •al-Haythamī in *Majmaʿ al-Zawāʾid*, 10/422.

blessings on you)!" They will therefore join together in uttering a single entreaty: "O Lord! We have been well pleased with You, so be well pleased with us!" Allah Most High will reiterate: "O people of the Garden of Paradise, if I had not been well pleased with you, I would not have lodged you in the Garden of My Paradise! Entreat Me, for this is the day of the surplus!" They will, then, join together in uttering a single entreaty: "O Lord! Show us Your Countenance, so that we may behold You!" Allah Most High will then remove those veils and something will be manifested to them. If He had not decreed for them that they would not be burned, they would surely be burned by what they were enveloped from. Then Allah's Light will stretch over them its shade.

"'They will then return to their dwellings. Their wives will be unaware of the Light they have acquired from Allah. And they will also be unaware about their wives. When they reach their dwellings, the Light will gradually increase and grow firm until they return to their previous forms. Their wives will say to them: "You went away from our presence in a particular form, and you have come back in another!" They will say: "That is because Allah has unveiled Himself to us, so we have seen from Him what remained concealed from you."

"'In every seven days, they will have twice as much as they used to have (of beholding Him), and that is in accordance with His saying: "So no soul knows what eye-cooling bliss is kept secretly in store for them, as a reward for what they used to do *[fa-lā taʿlamu nafsun mā ukhfiya la-hum min qurrati aʿyun: jazāʾan bi-mā kānū yaʿmalūn]*."'" (Q.32:17).

Reported by al-Bazzār.

اَلْبَابُ الثَّالِثُ

اَلْمُعْجِزَاتُ وَالْكَرَامَاتُ

CHAPTER 3

MIRACLES AND MIRACULOUS VIRTUES

الْفَصْلُ الأَوَّلُ

فَصْلٌ فِي مُعْجِزَاتِ النَّبِيِّ ﷺ

Section 1

The Miracles of the Prophet ﷺ

١٩٧/١. عَنْ عَبْدِ اللهِ بْنِ مَسْعُودٍ رضي الله عنه قَالَ: انْشَقَّ الْقَمَرُ عَلَى عَهْدِ رَسُوْلِ اللهِ ﷺ فِلْقَتَيْنِ. فَسَتَرَ الْجَبَلُ فِلْقَةً وَكَانَتْ فِلْقَةٌ فَوْقَ الْجَبَلِ. فَقَالَ رَسُوْلُ اللهِ ﷺ: اَللَّهُمَّ، اشْهَدْ.

مُتَّفَقٌ عَلَيْهِ وَهَذَا لَفْظُ مُسْلِمٍ.

وفي رواية: عَنْ أَنَسِ بْنِ مَالِكٍ رضي الله عنه أَنَّ أَهْلَ مَكَّةَ سَأَلُوْا رَسُوْلَ اللهِ ﷺ أَنْ يُرِيَهُمْ آيَةً، فَأَرَاهُمُ انْشِقَاقَ الْقَمَرِ مَرَّتَيْنِ.

مُتَّفَقٌ عَلَيْهِ وَهَذَا لَفْظُ مُسْلِمٍ.

197/1. According to ʿAbd Allāh b. Masʿūd رضي الله عنه:

---

[197] Set forth by •al-Bukhārī in *al-Ṣaḥīḥ*: Bk.: *al-Manāqib* [Virtues], Ch.: The polytheists' asking the Prophet ﷺ to show them a miraculous sign, so he showed them the splitting of the moon, 3/1330 §3437–3439, & Bk.: *al-Tafsīr al-Qamar* [Interpretation/Sūra of the Moon], Ch.: "The moon has been split in two, yet if they see a miraculous sign, they turn away [*wa ʾnshaqqa al-qamar. wa in yaraw āyatan yuʿriḍū*]." (Q.54:1–2), 4/1843 §4583–4587. •Muslim in *al-Ṣaḥīḥ*: Bk.: The Characteristics of the Hypocrites and their Rules, Ch.: The splitting of the moon, 4/2158–2159 §2800–2801. •al-Tirmidhī in *al-Sunan*: Bk.: The Interpretation of the Qurʾān according to Allah's Messenger ﷺ, Ch.: From the Sūra of the Moon, 5/398 §3285–3289. •al-Nasāʾī in *al-Sunan al-Kubrā*, 6/476 §1552–1553. •Ibn Ḥibbān in *al-Ṣaḥīḥ*, 4/420 §6495. •al-Ḥākim in *al-Mustadrak*, 2/513 §3758–3761. He said: "This is an authentic tradition." •al-Bazzār in *al-Musnad*, 5/202 §1801–1802. •Aḥmad b. Ḥanbal

"The moon split into two halves during the days of Allah's Messenger ﷺ, so the mountain covered one half and one half was above the mountain. Allah's Messenger ﷺ said: 'O Allah, bear witness!'"

Agreed upon by al-Bukhārī and Muslim, and this is the wording of Muslim.

In one report: According to Anas b. Mālik ﵁:

"The people of Mecca asked Allah's Messenger ﷺ to show them a sign, so he showed them the splitting of the moon into two halves two times."

Agreed upon by al-Bukhārī and Muslim, and this is the wording of Muslim.

١٩٨/ ٢. عَنْ أَنَسٍ ﵁ أَنَّ رَجُلاً جَاءَ إِلَى النَّبِيِّ ﷺ يَوْمَ الْجُمُعَةِ وَهُوَ يَخْطُبُ بِالْمَدِيْنَةِ، فَقَالَ: قَحَطَ الْمَطَرُ، فَاسْتَسْقِ رَبَّكَ. فَنَظَرَ إِلَى السَّمَاءِ وَمَا نَرَى مِنْ سَحَابٍ، فَاسْتَسْقَى. فَنَشَأَ السَّحَابُ بَعْضُهُ إِلَى بَعْضٍ، ثُمَّ مُطِرُوْا حَتَّى سَالَتْ مَثَاعِبُ الْمَدِيْنَةِ. فَمَا زَالَتْ إِلَى الْجُمُعَةِ الْمُقْبِلَةِ مَا تُقْلِعُ، ثُمَّ قَامَ ذَلِكَ الرَّجُلُ أَوْ غَيْرُهُ وَالنَّبِيُّ ﷺ يَخْطُبُ، فَقَالَ: غَرِقْنَا، فَادْعُ رَبَّكَ يَحْبِسْهَا عَنَّا. فَضَحِكَ ثُمَّ قَالَ: اَللَّهُمَّ، حَوَالَيْنَا وَلاَ عَلَيْنَا. مَرَّتَيْنِ أَوْ ثَلاَثًا. فَجَعَلَ السَّحَابُ يَتَصَدَّعُ عَنِ الْمَدِيْنَةِ يَمِيْنًا وَشِمَالاً، يُمْطَرُ مَا حَوَالَيْنَا وَلاَ يُمْطَرُ مِنْهَا شَيْءٌ، يُرِيْهِمُ اللهُ كَرَامَةَ نَبِيِّهِ ﷺ وَإِجَابَةَ دَعْوَتِهِ.

مُتَّفَقٌ عَلَيْهِ.

198/2. According to Anas ﵁:

---

in *al-Musnad*, 1/377 §3583, 3924, 4360. •Abū Yaʿlā in *al-Musnad*, 5/306 §2929. •al-Ṭabarānī in *al-Muʿjam al-Kabīr*, 2/132 §1559–1561. •al-Ṭayālisī in *al-Musnad*, 1/37 §280. •al-Shāshī in *al-Musnad*, 1/402 §404.

198 Set forth by •al-Bukhārī in *al-Ṣaḥīḥ*: Bk.: *al-Adab* [Proper Conduct], Ch.: Smiling and laughing, 5/2261 §5742, & Bk.: *al-Daʿawāt* [Supplications], Ch.: The supplication made while not facing the Qibla [direction of ritual prayer], 5/2335 §5982, & Bk.: *al-Jumuʿa* [Friday Congregational Prayer], Ch.: The prayer for rain [*al-istisqāʾ*] in the sermon on the day of the congregational

"A man came to the Prophet ﷺ on Friday, the Day of Congregation, while he was delivering the Friday sermon in Medina. He said: '(O Messenger of Allah,) the absence of rain has caused drought and famine; so, pray to your Lord for rain!' Then he looked towards the sky, and we saw no trace of clouds, so he prayed for rain. The clouds arose, bit by bit, then the rain poured down until the drains of Medina overflowed. The rain continued incessantly until the following Friday, then that man or another stood up and sought to submit while the Prophet ﷺ was delivering a sermon. The man said: '(O Messenger of Allah,) we are nearly drowned, so beseech your Lord to check the rainfall from us!' He smiled then said: 'O Allah, [let it rain] around us, not on us!' He said that twice or thrice. So the clouds started splitting away from Medina to right and left. The rain was falling on our surroundings but not on us (on the city of Medina). So Allah shows His Prophet's ﷺ blessing and miracle and the response to his supplication."

Agreed upon by al-Bukhārī and Muslim.

---

prayer, 1/315 §891, & Bk.: The Prayer for Rain, Ch.: The prayer for rain in the congregational mosque, 1/343 §967, & Ch.: The prayer for rain in the sermon, while facing the Qibla, 1/344 §968, & Ch.: If the polytheists seek the intercession of the Muslims during the drought, 1/346 §974, & Ch.: Someone who is showered with rain until it wets his beard, 1/349 §986, & Bk.: *al-Manāqib* [Virtues], Ch.: The signs of Prophethood in Islam, 3/1313 §3389. •Muslim in *al-Ṣaḥīḥ*: Bk.: *al-Istisqāʾ* [The Prayer for Rain], Ch.: Supplication [*al-Duʿāʾ*] in the prayer for rain, 2/612–614 §897. •Abū Dāwūd in *al-Sunan*: Bk.: The Prayer for Rain, Ch.: Raising the hands in the prayer for rain, 1/304 §1174. •al-Nasāʾī in *al-Sunan*: Bk.: The Prayer for Rain, Ch.: How to perform it, 3/159–166 §1515, 1517, 1527, 1528. •Ibn Mājah in *al-Sunan*: Bk.: Performance of the Ritual Prayer and the Sunna therein, Ch.: What has come to us about supplication in the prayer for rain, 1/404 §1269. •al-Nasāʾī in *al-Sunan al-Kubrā*, 1/558 §1818. •Ibn al-Jārūd in *al-Muntaqā*, 1/75 §256. •Ibn Khuzayma in *al-Ṣaḥīḥ*, 2/338 §1423. •Ibn Ḥibbān in *al-Ṣaḥīḥ*, 3/272 §992. •ʿAbd al-Razzāq in *al-Muṣannaf*, 3/92 §4911. •Aḥmad b. Ḥanbal in *al-Musnad*, 3/104 §12038. •al-Bayhaqī in *al-Sunan al-Kubrā*, 3/221 §5630. •Ibn Abī Shayba in *al-Muṣannaf*, 6/28 §29225. •al-Ṭaḥāwī in *Sharḥ Maʿānī al-Āthār*, 1/321. •al-Ṭabarānī in *al-Muʿjam al-Awsaṭ*, 1/187 §592, & in *al-Muʿjam al-Kabīr*, 10/285 §10673. •Abū Yaʿlā in *al-Musnad*, 6/82 §3334.

١٩٩/ ٣. عَنْ عَبْدِ اللهِ ابْنِ عَبَّاسٍ رضي الله عنهما قَالَ: خَسَفَتِ الشَّمْسُ عَلَى عَهْدِ رَسُوْلِ اللهِ ﷺ فَصَلَّى. قَالُوْا: يَا رَسُوْلَ اللهِ، رَأَيْنَاكَ تَنَاوَلُ شَيْئًا فِي مَقَامِكَ ثُمَّ رَأَيْنَاكَ تَكَعْكَعْتَ. فَقَالَ: إِنِّي أُرِيْتُ الْجَنَّةَ، فَتَنَاوَلْتُ مِنْهَا عُنْقُوْدًا. وَلَوْ أَخَذْتُهُ لَأَكَلْتُمْ مِنْهُ، مَا بَقِيَتِ الدُّنْيَا.

مُتَّفَقٌ عَلَيْهِ.

199/3. According to ʿAbd Allāh b. ʿAbbās ﷺ:

"Once the sun was eclipsed during the days of Allah's Messenger ﷺ, and he offered the ritual prayer (for eclipse). The Companions said: 'O Messenger of Allah, we saw you taking hold of something while standing, then we saw you slightly withdrawing!' He said: 'I was shown the Garden of Paradise, so I caught a bunch of grapes. Had I plucked it, you would surely have eaten from it as long as this world survives!'"

Agreed upon by al-Bukhārī and Muslim.

٢٠٠/ ٤. عَنْ جَابِرِ بْنِ عَبْدِ اللهِ رضي الله عنهما قَالَ: عَطِشَ النَّاسُ يَوْمَ الْحُدَيْبِيَةِ، وَالنَّبِيُّ ﷺ بَيْنَ يَدَيْهِ رِكْوَةٌ فَتَوَضَّأَ. فَجَهِشَ النَّاسُ نَحْوَهُ، فَقَالَ: مَا لَكُمْ؟ قَالُوْا: لَيْسَ عِنْدَنَا مَاءٌ نَتَوَضَّأُ وَلَا نَشْرَبُ إِلَّا مَا بَيْنَ يَدَيْكَ. فَوَضَعَ يَدَهُ فِي الرِّكْوَةِ، فَجَعَلَ الْمَاءُ يَثُوْرُ بَيْنَ

[199] Set forth by •al-Bukhārī in *al-Ṣaḥīḥ*: Bk.: The Quality of the Ritual Prayer, Ch.: Looking up towards the Imam in the ritual prayer, 1/261 §715, & Bk.: *al-Kusūf* [The Solar Eclipse], Ch.: The prayer of the solar eclipse performed in congregation, 1/357 §1004, & Bk.: *al-Nikāḥ* [Marriage], Ch.: The unbelief of the companion, 5/1994 §4901. •Muslim in *al-Ṣaḥīḥ*: Bk.: *al-Kusūf* [The Solar Eclipse], Ch.: What was shown to the Prophet ﷺ in the prayer of the solar eclipse, with regard to the Garden of Paradise and the Fire of Hell, 2/627 §904. •al-Nasāʾī in *al-Sunan*: Bk.: *al-Kusūf* [The Solar Eclipse], Ch.: The value of recitation in the prayer of the solar eclipse, 3/147 §1493, & in *al-Sunan al-Kubrā*, 1/578 §1878. •Mālik in *al-Muwaṭṭā*ʾ, 1/186 §445. •Ibn Ḥibbān in *al-Ṣaḥīḥ*, 7/73 §2832, 2853. •Aḥmad b. Ḥanbal in *al-Musnad*, 1/298 §2711, 3374. •ʿAbd al-Razzāq in *al-Muṣannaf*, 3/98 §4925. •al-Bayhaqī in *al-Sunan al-Kubrā*, 3/321 §6096. •al-Shāfiʿī in *al-Sunan al-Maʾthūra*, 1/140 §47.

أَصَابِعِهِ كَأَمْثَالِ الْعُيُوْنِ، فَشَرِبْنَا وَتَوَضَّأْنَا. قُلْتُ: كَمْ كُنْتُمْ؟ قَالَ: لَوْ كُنَّا مِائَةَ أَلْفٍ

لَكَفَانَا. كُنَّا خَمْسَ عَشْرَةَ مِائَةً.

رَوَاهُ الْبُخَارِيُّ وَأَحْمَدُ.

200/4. According to Jābir b. ʿAbd Allāh 🕮:

"The people felt thirsty on the Day of al-Ḥudaybiya, and there was a small flask of water lying in front of Allah's Messenger 🕮 and he performed the minor ritual ablution. The people rushed towards him so he asked: 'What is the matter with you?' The Companions submitted: 'O Messenger of Allah, we have no water with which to perform the minor ritual ablution, nor any to drink, except what is lying with you!' (Hearing this) he put his hand into the flask. The water began to gush forth between his fingers like fountainheads, so we drank (to our fill) and performed the minor ritual ablution as well. I said: 'How many were you?' He said: 'If we had been a hundred thousand, it would have sufficed us, whereas we were only fifteen hundred.'"

Reported by al-Bukhārī and Aḥmad.

٢٠١ / ٥. عَنْ جَابِرِ بْنِ عَبْدِ الله 🕮 أَنَّ امْرَأَةً مِنَ الْأَنْصَارِ قَالَتْ لِرَسُولِ الله 🕮: يَا

رَسُولَ الله، أَلَا أَجْعَلُ لَكَ شَيْئًا تَقْعُدُ عَلَيْهِ، فَإِنَّ لِي غُلَامًا نَجَّارًا؟ قَالَ: إِنْ شِئْتِ. قَالَ:

فَعَمِلَتْ لَهُ الْمِنْبَرَ. فَلَمَّا كَانَ يَوْمُ الْجُمُعَةِ، قَعَدَ النَّبِيُّ 🕮 عَلَى الْمِنْبَرِ الَّذِي صُنِعَ.

---

²⁰⁰ Set forth by •al-Bukhārī in al-Ṣaḥīḥ: Bk.: al-Manāqib [Virtues], Ch.: The signs of Prophethood in Islam, 3/1310 §3383, & Bk.: al-Maghāzī [Military Expeditions], Ch.: The Campaign of al-Ḥudaybiya, 4/1526 §3921–3923, & Bk.: al-Ashriba [Beverages], Ch.: The drink of blessing and the water of the blessed, 5/2135, §5316 & Bk.: al-Tafsīr al-Fatḥ [Interpretation/The Sūra of Victory], Ch.: "When they swore allegiance to you beneath the tree [idh yubāyiʿūna-ka taḥta al-shajarati]." (Q.48:18), 4/1831 §4560. •Aḥmad b. Ḥanbal in al-Musnad, 3/329 §14562. •Ibn Khuzayma in al-Ṣaḥīḥ, 1/65 §125. •Ibn Ḥibbān in al-Ṣaḥīḥ, 14/480 §6542. •al-Dārimī in al-Sunan, 1/21 §27. •Abū Yaʿlā in al-Musnad, 4/82 §2107. •al-Bayhaqī in al-Iʿtiqād, 1/272. •Ibn al-Jaʿd in al-Musnad 1/29 §82.

فَصَاحَتِ النَّخْلَةُ الَّتِي كَانَ يَخْطُبُ عِنْدَهَا، حَتَّى كَادَتْ أَنْ تَنْشَقَّ، فَنَزَلَ النَّبِيُّ ﷺ حَتَّى أَخَذَهَا فَضَمَّهَا إِلَيْهِ، فَجَعَلَتْ تَئِنُّ أَنِينَ الصَّبِيِّ الَّذِي يُسَكَّتُ، حَتَّى اسْتَقَرَّتْ.

رَوَاهُ الْبُخَارِيُّ وَالتِّرْمِذِيُّ وَالنَّسَائِيُّ وَابْنُ مَاجَه. وَقَالَ التِّرْمِذِيُّ: هَذَا حَدِيْثٌ حَسَنٌ صَحِيْحٌ.

201/5. According to Jābir b. ʿAbd Allāh ﷺ:

"A woman from among the Anṣār said to Allah's Messenger ﷺ: 'O Messenger of Allah, should I not provide you with something for you to sit upon, for I have a servant who is a carpenter?' He said: 'If you wish (do it),' so she had a pulpit made for him. Then, when the Day of Congregation arrived, the Prophet ﷺ sat on the pulpit that had been constructed. (But due to this seat taken by the Holy Prophet ﷺ) the date palm he used to lean on while preaching screamed and wept (with pangs of love), until it almost split. On this the Prophet ﷺ descended from the pulpit and embraced the date palm. Then it started moaning like the child who is patted with love and caressed to become quiet, until it finally felt soothed."

Reported by al-Bukhārī, al-Tirmidhī, al-Nasāʾī and Ibn Majah. According to al-Tirmidhī: "This is a fine authentic tradition."

---

[201] Set forth by •al-Bukhārī in *al-Ṣaḥīḥ*: Bk.: *al-Buyūʿ* [Sales], Ch.: The carpenter [*al-Najjār*], 2/378 §1989, & Bk.: *al-Manāqib* [Virtues], Ch.: The signs of Prophethood in Islam, 3/1314 §3391–3392, & Bk.: *al-Masājid* [Mosques], Ch.: Seeking assistance of the carpenter and the craftsman in the structures of the pulpit and the mosque, 1/172 §438. •al-Tirmidhī in *al-Sunan*: Bk.: Virtues according to Allah's Messenger ﷺ, Ch.: (6), 5/594 §3627. •al-Nasāʾī in *al-Sunan*: Bk.: *al-Jumuʿa* [Friday Congregational Prayer], Ch.: The place of the Imam during the sermon, 3/102 §1396. •Ibn Mājah in *al-Sunan*: Bk.: Performance of the Ritual Prayer and the Sunna therein, Ch.: What has come to us about the origin of the importance of the pulpit, 1/454 §1414–1417. •Aḥmad b. Ḥanbal in *al-Musnad*, 3/226. •al-Dārimī likewise in *al-Sunan*, 1/23 §42. •Ibn Khuzayma in *al-Ṣaḥīḥ*, 3/139 §1776–1777. •ʿAbd al-Razzāq in *al-Muṣannaf*, 3/186 §5253. •Ibn Ḥibbān in *al-Ṣaḥīḥ*, 14/43, 48. §6506. •Abū Yaʿlā in *al-Musnad*, 6/114 §3384.

٦/٢٠٢. عَنْ أَبِي هُرَيْرَةَ ﷺ قَالَ: أَتَيْتُ النَّبِيَّ ﷺ، بِتَمَرَاتٍ، فَقُلْتُ: يَا رَسُوْلَ اللهِ، ادْعُ اللهَ فِيْهِنَّ بِالْبَرَكَةِ. فَضَمَّهُنَّ ثُمَّ دَعَا لِي فِيْهِنَّ بِالْبَرَكَةِ، فَقَالَ: خُذْهُنَّ وَاجْعَلْهُنَّ فِي مِزْوَدِكَ هَذَا أَوْ فِي هَذَا الْمِزْوَدِ. كُلَّمَا أَرَدْتَ أَنْ تَأْخُذَ مِنْهُ شَيْئًا، فَأَدْخِلْ فِيْهِ يَدَكَ فَخُذْهُ وَلاَ تَنْثُرْهُ نَثْرًا. فَقَدْ حَمَلْتُ مِنْ ذَلِكَ التَّمْرِ كَذَا وَكَذَا مِنْ وَسْقٍ فِي سَبِيْلِ اللهِ، فَكُنَّا نَأْكُلُ مِنْهُ وَنُطْعِمُ. وَكَانَ لاَ يُفَارِقُ حِقْوِي حَتَّى كَانَ يَوْمُ قَتْلِ عُثْمَانَ ﷺ فَإِنَّهُ انْقَطَعَ.

رَوَاهُ التِّرْمِذِيُّ وَأَحْمَدُ وَابْنُ حِبَّانَ. وَقَالَ أَبُوْعِيْسَى: هَذَا حَدِيْثٌ حَسَنٌ.

202/6. According to Abū Hurayra ﷺ:

"I came to the Prophet ﷺ with some dates and submitted: 'Supplicate Allah for blessing upon them!' The Messenger of Allah collected them and supplicated on my behalf for blessing upon them, then said to me: 'Take them and put them in this haversack of yours. Whenever you wish to eat something from it, insert your hand into it, then take it and do not unfold it.' Then I spent from these dates so-and-so many camel-loads (*wasqs*—one *wasq* measures 240 kg.) in the cause of Allah. We used to eat from it and served others as well to eat. That haversack (full of dates) would always be tied to my waist, never detached until the day when ʿUthmān ﷺ was martyred; it, then, got detached from me."

Reported by al-Tirmidhī, Aḥmad and Ibn Ḥibbān. Abū ʿĪsā said: "This is a fine tradition."

٧/٢٠٣. عَنْ عَبْدِ اللهِ ﷺ قَالَ: كُنَّا نَعُدُّ الآيَاتِ بَرَكَةً، وَأَنْتُمْ تَعُدُّوْنَهَا تَخْوِيْفًا. كُنَّا مَعَ رَسُوْلِ اللهِ ﷺ فِي سَفَرٍ، فَقَلَّ الْمَاءُ، فَقَالَ: اطْلُبُوا فَضْلَةً مِنْ مَاءٍ. فَجَاؤُوْا بِإِنَاءٍ فِيْهِ

[202] Set forth by •al-Tirmidhī in *al-Sunan*: Bk.: Virtues according to Allah's Messenger ﷺ, Ch.: The virtues of Abū Hurayra, 5/685 §3839. •Aḥmad b. Ḥanbal in *al-Musnad*, 2/352 §8613. •Ibn Ḥibbān in *al-Ṣaḥīḥ*, 14/467 §6532. •al-Haythamī in *Mawārid al-Ẓamʾān*, 1/527 §2150. •Ibn Rāhawayh in *al-Musnad*, 1/75 §3. •Ibn Kathīr in *al-Bidāya wa al-Nihāya*, 6/117. •al-Dhahabī in *Siyar Aʿlām al-Nubalāʾ*, 2/231. •al-Suyūṭī in *al-Khaṣāʾiṣ al-Kubrā*, 2/85.

مَاءٌ قَلِيْلٌ، فَأَدْخَلَ يَدَهُ فِي الْإِنَاءِ ثُمَّ قَالَ: حَيَّ عَلَى الطَّهُوْرِ الْـمُبَارَكِ، وَالْبَرَكَةُ مِنَ اللهِ. فَلَقَدْ رَأَيْتُ الْـمَاءَ يَنْبُعُ مِنْ بَيْنِ أَصَابِعِ رَسُوْلِ اللهِ ﷺ، وَلَقَدْ كُنَّا نَسْمَعُ تَسْبِيْحَ الطَّعَامِ وَهُوَ يُؤْكَلُ.

رَوَاهُ الْبُخَارِيُّ وَالتِّرْمِذِيُّ. وَقَالَ أَبُوْ عِيْسَى: هَذَا حَدِيْثٌ حَسَنٌ صَحِيْحٌ.

203/7. According to ʿAbd Allāh ﷺ:

"We used to count the miraculous signs as a blessing, and you count them as stimulants of fear. We were with Allah's Messenger ﷺ on a journey, and water was in short supply, so he said: 'Fetch some remaining water!' Some Companions brought a vessel containing a small amount of water, so he inserted his hand into the vessel, and said: 'Come quickly to the blessed water and the blessing is from Allah!' I saw the water gushing forth like a fountain between the fingers of Allah's Messenger ﷺ. Moreover, we used to hear glorification of Allah sounded from the food while it was being eaten."

Reported by al-Bukhārī and al-Tirmidhī. Abū ʿĪsā said: "This is a fine authentic tradition."

٢٠٤/ ٨. عَنْ أَنَسٍ ﷺ قَالَ: أُتِيَ النَّبِيُّ ﷺ بِإِنَاءٍ، وَهُوَ بِالزَّوْرَاءِ. فَوَضَعَ يَدَهُ فِي الْإِنَاءِ، فَجَعَلَ الْـمَاءُ يَنْبُعُ مِنْ بَيْنِ أَصَابِعِهِ، فَتَوَضَّأَ الْقَوْمُ.

---

[203] Set forth by •al-Bukhārī in *al-Ṣaḥīḥ*: Bk.: *al-Manāqib* [Virtues], Ch.: The signs of Prophethood in Islam, 3/1312 §3386. •al-Tirmidhī in *al-Sunan*: Bk.: Virtues according to Allah's Messenger ﷺ, Ch.: (6) 5/597 §3633. •Aḥmad b. Ḥanbal in *al-Musnad*, 1/460 §4393. •Ibn Khuzayma in *al-Ṣaḥīḥ*, 1/102 §204. •al-Dārimī in *al-Sunan*, 1/28 §29. •Ibn Abī Shayba in *al-Muṣannaf*, 6/316 §31722. •al-Bazzār in *al-Musnad*, 4/301 §1978. •al-Ṭabarānī in *al-Muʿjam al-Awsaṭ*, 4/384 §4501. •Abū Yaʿlā in *al-Musnad*, 9/253 §5372. •al-Shāshī in *al-Musnad*, 1/358 §346. •Abū al-Qāsim Hibat Allāh in *Iʿtiqād Ahl al-Sunna*, 4/803 §1479. •Abū al-Maḥāsin in *Muʿtaṣar al-Mukhtaṣar*, 1/8. •al-Bayhaqī in *al-Iʿtiqād*, 1/272.

قَالَ قَتَادَةُ: قُلْتُ لِأَنَسٍ: كَمْ كُنْتُمْ؟ قَالَ: ثَلَاثَ مِائَةٍ، أَوْ زُهَاءَ ثَلَاثِ مِائَةٍ.

مُتَّفَقٌ عَلَيْهِ.

204/8. According to Anas ﷺ:

"A water vessel was presented before the Prophet ﷺ while he was in al-Zawrā' [a place with a deep well]. He put his hand into the vessel and water started gushing forth between his fingers. So the people performed the minor ritual ablution."

Qatāda said: "I asked Anas: 'How many were you?' He said: 'Three hundred, or about three hundred.'"

Agreed upon by al-Bukhārī and Muslim.

٢٠٥/٩. عَنِ الْبَرَاءِ ﷺ قَالَ: كُنَّا يَوْمَ الْحُدَيْبِيَةِ أَرْبَعَ عَشْرَةَ مِائَةً وَالْحُدَيْبِيَةُ بِئْرٌ. فَنَزَحْنَاهَا حَتَّى لَمْ نَتْرُكْ فِيهَا قَطْرَةً. فَجَلَسَ النَّبِيُّ ﷺ عَلَى شَفِيرِ الْبِئْرِ فَدَعَا بِمَاءٍ، فَمَضْمَضَ وَمَجَّ فِي الْبِئْرِ. فَمَكَثْنَا غَيْرَ بَعِيدٍ، ثُمَّ اسْتَقَيْنَا حَتَّى رَوِينَا، وَرَوَتْ أَوْ صَدَرَتْ رَكَائِبُنَا.

رَوَاهُ الْبُخَارِيُّ.

205/9. According to al-Barā' ﷺ:

"We numbered fourteen hundred on the Day of al-Ḥudaybiya, and al-Ḥudaybiyya has a water well. So we drew water out of it leaving not even a drop of water in it. (The Companions, worried

---

[204] Set forth by •al-Bukhārī in *al-Ṣaḥīḥ*: Bk.: *al-Manāqib* [Virtues], Ch.: The signs of Prophethood in Islam, 3/1309–1310 §3379, 3380, 5316. •Muslim in *al-Ṣaḥīḥ*: Bk.: *al-Faḍā'il* [Excellent Merits], Ch.: The miracles of the Prophet ﷺ, 4/1783 §2279. •al-Tirmidhī in *al-Sunan*: Bk.: Virtues according to Allah's Messenger ﷺ, Ch.: (6), 5/596 §3631. •Mālik in *al-Muwaṭṭā'*, 1/32 §62. •al-Shāfi'ī in *al-Musnad*, 1/15. •Aḥmad b. Ḥanbal in *al-Musnad*, 3/132 §12370. •al-Bayhaqī in *al-Sunan al-Kubrā*, 1/193 §878. •Ibn Abī Shayba in *al-Muṣannaf*, 6/316 §31724.

[205] Set forth bya •al-Bukhārī in *al-Ṣaḥīḥ*: Bk.: *al-Manāqib* [Virtues], Ch.: The signs of Prophethood in Islam, 3/1311 §3384.

about finishing of water, submitted their concern before the presence of the Messenger of Allah ﷺ). Then the Prophet ﷺ sat on the edge of the well and asked for water. He rinsed his holy mouth and spat it (the water) into the well and we stayed not far away. Then we drew water until we quenched our thirst, and our riding animals too quenched their thirst."

Reported by al-Bukhārī.

٢٠٦/ ١٠. عَنْ جَابِرٍ ﵄ أَنَّ أَبَاهُ تُوُفِّيَ وَعَلَيْهِ دَيْنٌ، فَأَتَيْتُ النَّبِيَّ ﷺ فَقُلْتُ: إِنَّ أَبِي تَرَكَ عَلَيْهِ دَيْنًا، وَلَيْسَ عِنْدِي إِلاَّ مَا يُخْرِجُ نَخْلُهُ، وَلاَ يَبْلُغُ مَا يُخْرِجُ سِنِيْنَ مَا عَلَيْهِ. فَانْطَلِقْ مَعِي لِكَيْ لاَ يُفْحِشَ عَلَيَّ الْغُرَمَاءُ. فَمَشَى حَوْلَ بَيْدَرٍ مِنْ بَيَادِرِ التَّمْرِ فَدَعَا، ثُمَّ آخَرَ، ثُمَّ جَلَسَ عَلَيْهِ، فَقَالَ: انْزِعُوْهُ. فَأَوْفَاهُمُ الَّذِي لَهُمْ، وَبَقِيَ مِثْلُ مَا أَعْطَاهُمْ.

رَوَاهُ الْبُخَارِيُّ وَأَحْمَدُ.

206/10. According to Jābir (b. ʿAbd Allāh) ﵄, whose father died owing a debt:

"I came to the Prophet ﷺ and said: 'My father has left a debt unpaid, and I have nothing except what his date palm yields, and his date palm will not yield in many years the equivalent of what he owes. Accompany me so that the creditors do not treat me harshly.' (He, therefore, moved away with him, so that the creditors would not treat him roughly.) He walked around one heap of the dates and made a supplication and then another heap (and supplicated). Then he sat on it and said: 'Measure and give away to the creditors what is their due.' So, he settled what was due to them, and the equivalent of what he gave them remained intact."

Reported by al-Bukhārī and Aḥmād.

---

[206] Set forth by •al-Bukhārī in *al-Ṣaḥīḥ*: Bk.: *al-Manāqib* [Virtues], Ch.: The signs of Prophethood in Islam, 3/1312 §3387, & Bk.: *al-Buyūʿ* [Sales], Ch.: The measure incumbent on the seller and the giver, 2/748 §2020. al-Nasāʾī in *al-Sunan*: Bk.: *Wasaya* Ch.: Paying back the debt before distribution of inheritance, 6/245 §3637 •Aḥmad b. Ḥanbal in *al-Musnad*, 3/365 §14977.

٢٠٧/١١. عَنْ أَسْمَاءَ بِنْتِ عُمَيْسٍ ﵂ قَالَتْ: كَانَ رَسُوْلُ اللهِ ﷺ يُوْحَى إِلَيْهِ وَرَأْسُهُ فِي حِجْرِ عَلِيٍّ ﵁. فَلَمْ يُصَلِّ الْعَصْرَ حَتَّى غَرَبَتِ الشَّمْسُ. فَقَالَ رَسُوْلُ اللهِ ﷺ: اَللَّهُمَّ، إِنَّ عَلِيًّا فِي طَاعَتِكَ وَطَاعَةِ رَسُوْلِكَ فَارْدُدْ عَلَيْهِ الشَّمْسَ. قَالَتْ أَسْمَاءُ ﵂: فَرَأَيْتُهَا غَرَبَتْ وَرَأَيْتُهَا طَلَعَتْ بَعْدَ مَا غَرَبَتْ.

رَوَاهُ الطَّحَاوِيُّ وَالطَّبَرَانِيُّ وَاللَّفْظُ لَهُ وَرِجَالُهُ رِجَالُ الصَّحِيْحِ.

207/11. According to Asmā᾿, the daughter of ʿUmays ﵂:

"Allah's Messenger ﷺ was receiving revelation while his holy head was in the lap of ʿAlī ﵁. So he could not perform the afternoon ritual prayer until the sun had set. Allah's Messenger ﷺ therefore prayed: 'O Allah, ʿAlī is obedient to You and obedient to Your Messenger, so bring the sun back to him!'" Asmā᾿ ﵂ said: "So I saw it set and I saw it rise after it had set!"

---

[207] Set forth by •al-Ṭabarānī in *al-Muʿjam al-Kabīr*, 24/147 §390. •al-Haythamī in *Majmaʿ al-Zawā᾿id*, 8/297. •al-Dhahabī in *Mīzān al-Iʿtidal*, 5/205. •Ibn Kathīr in *al-Bidāya wa al-Nihāya*, 6/83. •al-Qāḍī ʿIyāḍ in *al-Shifā*, 1/400. •al-Suyūṭī in *al-Khaṣā᾿iṣ al-Kubrā*, 2/137. •al-Ḥalabī in *al-Sīrat al-Ḥalabiyya*, 2/103. •al-Qurṭubī in *al-Jāmiʿ li-Aḥkām al-Qur᾿ān*, 10/197.

It has been reported by al-Tabarānī with several chains of transmission, and the sources of one of them are the sources of the *Ṣaḥīḥ*, apart from Ibrāhīm b. Ḥasan, whose reliability has been confirmed by Ibn Ḥibbān. It has also been reported by al-Ṭaḥāwī in *Mushkil al-Āthār* (2/9, 4/388–9), and the tradition has other paths of transmission, from Asmā᾿, Abū Hurayra, ʿAlī b. Abī Ṭālib and Abū Saʿīd al-Khudrī ﵃.

Its paths of transmission have been collected by Abū al-Ḥasan al-Faḍlī, by ʿAbd Allāh al-Ḥasakā, who died in A.H. 470, in *Mas᾿ala fī Taṣḥīḥ Ḥadīth Radd al-Shams*, and by al-Suyūṭī in *Kashf al-Libs ʿan Ḥadīth al-Shams*. According to al-Suyūṭī, in *al-Khaṣā᾿iṣ al-Kubrā* (2/137): "It has been set forth by Ibn Manda, Ibn Shāhīn and al-Tabarānī with chains of transmission, some of which meet the precondition of the Ṣaḥīḥ." According to al-Shaybānī in *Ḥadā᾿iq al-Anwār* (1/193): "It has been set forth by al-Ṭaḥāwī in *Mushkil al-Āthār*, with two authentic chains of transmission."

Imam al-Nawawī has said in Sharḥ Muslim (12/52): "According to al-Qāḍī ﵀, the sun was arrested twice for our Prophet ﷺ. " That was mentioned by al-Ṭaḥāwī, and he said: "Its narrators are reliable."

Reported by at-Ṭaḥāwī and al-Ṭabarānī (the wording is his) and the chains of transmission are authentic.

٢٠٨/ ١٢. عَنْ أَنَسٍ ﷺ قَالَ: كَانَ أَهْلُ بَيْتٍ مِنَ الْأَنْصَارِ لَهُمْ جَمَلٌ يَسْنُوْنَ عَلَيْهِ، وَإِنَّ الْجَمَلَ اسْتُصْعِبَ عَلَيْهِمْ فَمَنَعَهُمْ ظَهْرَهُ. وَإِنَّ الْأَنْصَارَ جَاؤُوْا إِلَى رَسُوْلِ اللهِ ﷺ فَقَالُوْا: إِنَّهُ كَانَ لَنَا جَمَلٌ نُسْنِي عَلَيْهِ وَإِنَّهُ اسْتُصْعِبَ عَلَيْنَا وَمَنَعَنَا ظَهْرَهُ، وَقَدْ عَطَشَ الزَّرْعُ وَالنَّخْلُ. فَقَالَ رَسُوْلُ اللهِ ﷺ لِأَصْحَابِهِ: قُوْمُوْا. فَقَامُوْا فَدَخَلَ الْحَائِطَ وَالْجَمَلُ فِي نَاحِيَةٍ، فَمَشَى النَّبِيُّ ﷺ نَحْوَهُ. فَقَالَتِ الْأَنْصَارُ: يَا نَبِيَّ اللهِ، إِنَّهُ قَدْ صَارَ مِثْلَ الْكَلْبِ، وَإِنَّا نَخَافُ عَلَيْكَ صَوْلَتَهُ. فَقَالَ: لَيْسَ عَلَيَّ مِنْهُ بَأْسٌ. فَلَمَّا نَظَرَ الْجَمَلُ إِلَى رَسُوْلِ اللهِ ﷺ أَقْبَلَ نَحْوَهُ حَتَّى خَرَّ سَاجِدًا بَيْنَ يَدَيْهِ، فَأَخَذَ رَسُوْلُ اللهِ ﷺ بِنَاصِيَتِهِ أَذَلَّ مَا كَانَتْ قَطُّ حَتَّى أَدْخَلَهُ فِي الْعَمَلِ. فَقَالَ لَهُ أَصْحَابُهُ: يَا رَسُوْلَ اللهِ، هَذِهِ بَهِيْمَةٌ؛ لَا تَعْقِلُ؛ تَسْجُدُ لَكَ وَنَحْنُ نَعْقِلُ فَنَحْنُ أَحَقُّ أَنْ نَسْجُدَ لَكَ. وَفِي رِوَايَةٍ: قَالُوْا: يَا رَسُوْلَ اللهِ، نَحْنُ أَحَقُّ بِالسُّجُوْدِ لَكَ مِنَ الْبَهَائِمِ. فَقَالَ: لَا يَصْلُحُ لِبَشَرٍ أَنْ يَسْجُدَ لِبَشَرٍ. وَلَوْ صَلَحَ لِبَشَرٍ أَنْ يَسْجُدَ لِبَشَرٍ، لَأَمَرْتُ الْمَرْأَةَ أَنْ تَسْجُدَ لِزَوْجِهَا مِنْ عِظَمِ حَقِّهِ عَلَيْهَا.

رَوَاهُ أَحْمَدُ وَنَحْوَهُ الدَّارِمِيُّ وَالطَّبَرَانِيُّ وَإِسْنَادُهُ حَسَنٌ.

208/12. According to Anas ﷺ:

"The members of a household among the Anṣār had a camel on which they used to carry water for the purpose of irrigation, but the camel became rebellious and refused to yield its back to carry

[208] Set forth by •Aḥmad b. Ḥanbal in *al-Musnad*, 3/158 §12635. •al-Dārimī in *al-Sunan*: Ch.: (4), What Allah conferred upon His Prophet, including the belief in him of the trees, the beasts and the jinn, 1/22 §17. •al-Ṭabarānī in *al-Muʿjam al-Awsaṭ*, 9/81 §9189. •ʿAbd b. Ḥumayd in *al-Musnad*, 1/320 §1053. •al-Mundhirī in *al-Targhīb wa al-Tarhīb*, 3/35 §2977. •al-Haythamī in *Majmaʿ al-Zawāʾid*, 9/4, 9. •al-Ḥusaynī in *al-Bayān wa al-Taʿrīf*, 2/171. •al-Munāwī in *Fayḍ al-Qadīr*, 5/329.

water. The Anṣār Companions came to Allah's Messenger ﷺ and said: 'We have a camel on which we draw water for the purpose of irrigation, but it has rebelled and does not let us engage him in any labour and the crops and the date palm orchard have become dry (due to shortage of water)!' Allah's Messenger ﷺ asked the Companions: 'Rise.' So they got up (and went to that Anṣārī's home). So he entered the garden and the camel was in a corner. The Prophet ﷺ walked towards it, so the Anṣār said: 'O Prophet of Allah, it has become mad like the dog, and we are afraid of its attacking you!' He said: 'No harm will come to me from it!' Then, when the camel caught sight of Allah's Messenger ﷺ, it moved towards him until it sank to the ground, prostrating itself in front of him. Allah's Messenger ﷺ then held it by its forelock, as gently as ever, and put it back to work. (Seeing this) his Companions said to him: 'O Messenger of Allah, it prostrates itself before you even though it is an unintelligent animal! We are intelligent, so we are more entitled to prostrate ourselves before you!'"

In one report: "They said: 'O Messenger of Allah, we are more entitled to prostration before you than are the animals (and the beasts).' So he said: 'It is not lawful for a human being to prostrate himself before a human being. If it were lawful for a human being to prostrate himself before a human being, I would have commanded the wife to prostrate herself before her husband, because of his higher degree and rank over her!'"

Reported by Aḥmad and in similar form by al-Dārimī and al-Ṭabarānī with a fine chain of transmission.

٢٠٩/ ١٣. عَنْ جَابِرٍ رضي الله عنه أَنَّ أُمَّ مَالِك كَانَتْ تُهْدِي لِلنَّبِيِّ ﷺ فِي عُكَّةٍ لَهَا سَمْنًا. فَيَأْتِيهَا بَنُوهَا فَيَسْأَلُونَ الْأُدْمَ. وَلَيْسَ عِنْدَهُمْ شَيْءٌ، فَتَعْمِدُ إِلَى الَّذِي كَانَتْ تُهْدِي فِيهِ لِلنَّبِيِّ ﷺ، فَتَجِدُ فِيهِ سَمْنًا. فَمَا زَالَ يُقِيمُ لَهَا أُدْمَ بَيْتِهَا حَتَّى عَصَرَتْهُ، فَأَتَتِ النَّبِيَّ ﷺ فَقَالَ: عَصَرْتِيهَا؟ قَالَتْ: نَعَمْ. قَالَ: لَوْ تَرَكْتِيهَا مَا زَالَ قَائِمًا.

رَوَاهُ مُسْلِمٌ وَأَحْمَدُ.

209/13. According to Jābir ﵁:

"Umm Mālik used to present the Prophet ﷺ with clarified butter in a butter-skin of hers. Her sons would come to her and ask for curry when they had nothing. She would pick up the skin in which she used to send her gift for the Prophet ﷺ. And she would find clarified butter in it. The problem of curry in their home was always solved in like manner until (one day when) she squeezed it. Then she came to the Prophet ﷺ, and he said: 'Did you squeeze it?' When she said: 'Yes,' he said: 'If you had left it as it was, it would not have ceased providing you (butter)!'"

Reported by Muslim and Aḥmad.

٢١٠/ ١٤. عَنْ جَابِرٍ ﵁ أَنَّ رَجُلاً أَتَى النَّبِيَّ ﷺ يَسْتَطْعِمُهُ، فَأَطْعَمَهُ شَطْرَ وَسْقِ شَعِيرٍ. فَمَا زَالَ الرَّجُلُ يَأْكُلُ مِنْهُ وَامْرَأَتُهُ وَضَيْفُهُمَا حَتَّى كَالَهُ. فَأَتَى النَّبِيَّ ﷺ فَقَالَ: لَوْ لَمْ تَكِلْهُ، لَأَكَلْتُمْ مِنْهُ وَلَقَامَ لَكُمْ.

رَوَاهُ مُسْلِمٌ وَأَحْمَدُ.

210/14. According to Jābir ﵁:

"A man came to the Prophet ﷺ, asking him for food, so he provided him with half a camel-load of barley corn. The man kept eating from it, as well as his wife and their guest until he measured it one day. Then he came to the Prophet ﷺ, who said: 'If you had not measured it, you would have always eaten from it and it would have been replenished for you (forever)!'"

Reported by Muslim and Aḥmad.

٢١١/ ١٥. عَنْ سَعْدِ بْنِ أَبِي وَقَّاصٍ ﵁ قَالَ: رَأَيْتُ رَسُوْلَ اللهِ ﷺ يَوْمَ أُحُدٍ،

[209] Set forth by •Muslim in *al-Ṣaḥīḥ*: Bk.: *al-Faḍā'il* [Excellent Merits], Ch.: The miracles of the Prophet ﷺ, 4/1784 §2280. •Aḥmad b. Ḥanbal in *al-Musnad*, 3/340, 347 §14705, 14782. •al-ʿAsqalānī in *Tahdhīb al-Tahdhīb*, 12/505 §2984, & in *Fatḥ al-Bārī*, 11/281, & in *al-Iṣāba*, 8/298 §12239.

[210] Set forth by •Muslim in *al-Ṣaḥīḥ*: Bk.: *al-Faḍā'il* [Excellent Merits], Ch.: The miracles of the Prophet ﷺ, 4/1784 §2281. •Aḥmad b. Ḥanbal in *al-Musnad*, 3/337, 347 §14661, 14783.

وَمَعَهُ رَجُلاَنِ يُقَاتِلاَنِ عَنْهُ. عَلَيْهِمَا ثِيَابُ بِيْضٌ، كَأَشَدِّ الْقِتَالِ. مَا رَأَيْتُهُمَا قَبْلُ وَلاَ بَعْدُ يَعْنِي جِبْرِيْلَ وَمِيْكَائِيْلَ عليهما السلام.

مُتَّفَقٌ عَلَيْهِ.

211/15. According to Saʿd b. Abī Waqqāṣ ﷺ:

"I saw Allah's Messenger ﷺ on the Day of Uḥud, and he was accompanied by two men fighting from his side (in his defence). They were dressed in white clothes and fighting valiantly. I have not seen them before or after, meaning Gabriel and Michael."

Agreed upon by al-Bukhārī and Muslim.

٢١٢/١٦. عَنْ أَنَسٍ رضي الله عنه في رواية طويلة أَنَّ رَسُوْلَ اللهِ ﷺ شَاوَرَ، حِيْنَ بَلَغَنَا إِقْبَالُ أَبِـي سُفْيَانَ. وَقَامَ سَعْدُ بْنُ عُبَادَةَ رضي الله عنه فَقَالَ: وَالَّذِي نَفْسِي بِيَدِهِ، لَوْ أَمَرْتَنَا أَنْ نُخِيْضَهَا الْبَحْرَ لَأَخَضْنَاهَا. وَلَوْ أَمَرْتَنَا أَنْ نَضْرِبَ أَكْبَادَهَا إِلَى بَرْكِ الْغِمَادِ لَفَعَلْنَا. قَالَ: فَنَدَبَ رَسُوْلُ اللهِ ﷺ النَّاسَ، فَانْطَلَقُوْا حَتَّى نَزَلُوْا بَدْرًا. فَقَالَ رَسُوْلُ اللهِ ﷺ: هَذَا مَصْرَعُ فُلاَنٍ. قَالَ: وَيَضَعُ يَدَهُ عَلَى الْأَرْضِ، هَاهُنَا وَهَاهُنَا. قَالَ: فَمَا مَاتَ أَحَدُهُمْ عَنْ مَوضِعِ يَدِ رَسُوْلِ اللهِ ﷺ.

رَوَاهُ مُسْلِمٌ وَأَبُوْ دَاوُدَ.

---

[211] Set forth by •al-Bukhārī in *al-Ṣaḥīḥ*: Bk.: *al-Maghāzī* [Military Expeditions], Ch.: "When the two parties of you almost lost courage, and Allah was their Protecting Friend [*idh hammat ṭāʾifatāni min-kum an tafshalā wa ʾllāhu Waliyyu-humā*]." (Q.3:122), 4/1489 §3828, & Bk.: *al-Libās* [Clothing], Ch.: White garments, 5/2192 §5488. •Muslim in *al-Ṣaḥīḥ*: Bk.: *al-Faḍāʾil* [Excellent Merits], Ch.: The battle of Gabriel and Michael in defence of the Prophet ﷺ on the Day of Uḥud, 4/1802 §2306. •Aḥmad b. Ḥanbal in *al-Musnad*, 1/171 §1468. •al-Shāshī in *al-Musnad*, 1/185 §133. •al-Dhahabī in *Siyar Aʿlām al-Nubalāʾ*, 1/107. •al-Iṣbahānī in *Dalāʾil al-Nubuwwa*, 1/51 §34. •al-Khaṭīb al-Tabrīzī in *Mishkāt al-Maṣābīḥ*, 2/382 §7575.

212/16. According to Anas ﵁, in the course of a detailed report:

"Allah's Messenger ﷺ sought counsel, when we received news of the approach of Abū Sufyān (and his party from Syria). Saʿd b. ʿUbāda ﵁ stood up and said: 'By the One in whose Hand my soul is, if you had commanded us to plunge our horses into the sea, we would have plunged them, and if you had commanded us to thump their livers against the rocks of Bark al-Ghimād, we would have done so!' Allah's Messenger ﷺ then summoned the people, and they (came and) set off until they reached Badr. Allah's Messenger ﷺ said: 'This is the place of So-and-so's slaughter,' and he placed his hand on the ground, here and there. (The next day during the battle) not one of the unbelievers died away from the spot where Allah's Messenger ﷺ had laid his hand!"

Reported by Muslim and Abū Dāwūd.

٢١٣/ ١٧. عَنْ جَابِرٍ ﵁ فِي رواية طويلة قَالَ: سِرْنَا مَعَ رَسُوْلِ اللهِ ﷺ حَتَّى نَزَلَ وَادِيًا أَفْيَحَ. فَذَهَبَ رَسُوْلُ اللهِ ﷺ يَقْضِي حَاجَتَهُ. فَاتَّبَعْتُهُ بِإِدَاوَةٍ مِنْ مَاءٍ. فَنَظَرَ رَسُوْلُ اللهِ ﷺ فَلَمْ يَرَ شَيْئًا يَسْتَتِرُ بِهِ. فَإِذَا شَجَرَتَانِ بِشَاطِئِ الْوَادِي. فَانْطَلَقَ رَسُوْلُ اللهِ ﷺ إِلَى إِحْدَاهُمَا فَأَخَذَ بِغُصْنٍ مِنْ أَغْصَانِهَا. فَقَالَ: انْقَادِي عَلَيَّ بِإِذْنِ اللهِ – فَانْقَادَتْ مَعَهُ كَالْبَعِيْرِ الْمَخْشُوْشِ الَّذِي يُصَانِعُ قَائِدَهُ – حَتَّى أَتَى الشَّجَرَةَ الْأُخْرَى. فَأَخَذَ

[212] Set forth by •Muslim in *al-Ṣaḥīḥ*: Bk.: *al-Jihād wa al-Siyar* [The Sacred Struggle and the Campaigns], Ch.: The Campaign of Badr, 3/1403 §1779, & similarly in Bk.: The Garden of Paradise and the Qualities of its Felicity and its Inhabitants, Ch.: Demonstration of the seat of the deceased in the Garden of Paradise or the Fire of Hell, and confirmation of the torment of the grave and taking refuge therefrom, 4/2202 §2873. •Abū Dāwūd in *al-Sunan*: Bk.: *al-Jihād* [The Sacred Struggle], Ch.: The prisoner of war is disarmed, beaten and bound, 3/58 §2071. •al-Nasāʾī in *al-Sunan*: Bk.: *al-Janāʾiz* [Funeral Ceremonies], Ch.: The spirits of the believers, 4/108 §2074, & in *al-Sunan al-Kubrā*, 1/665 §2201. •Ibn Ḥibbān in *al-Ṣaḥīḥ*, 11/24 §4722. •Aḥmad b. Ḥanbal in *al-Musnad*, 3/219 §13320. •al-Bazzār in *al-Musnad*, 1/340 §222. •Ibn Abī Shayba in *al-Muṣannaf*, 7/362 §36708. •al-Ṭabarānī in *al-Muʿjam al-Awsaṭ*, 8/219 §8453, & in *al-Muʿjam al-Ṣaghīr*, 2/233 §1085. •Abū Yaʿlā in *al-Musnad*, 6/69 §3322. •Ibn al-Jawzī in *Ṣafwat al-Ṣafwa*, 1/102. •al-Khaṭīb al-Tabrīzī in *Mishkāt al-Maṣābīḥ*, 2/381 §5871.

بِغُصْنٍ مِنْ أَغْصَانِهَا. فَقَالَ: انْقَادِي عَلَيَّ بِإِذْنِ اللهِ. فَانْقَادَتْ مَعَهُ كَذَلِكَ، حَتَّى إِذَا كَانَ بِالْـمُنْصَفِ مِمَّا بَيْنَهُمَا، قَالَ: الْتَئِمَا عَلَيَّ بِإِذْنِ اللهِ، فَالْتَأَمَتَا. فَجَلَسْتُ أُحَدِّثُ نَفْسِي. فَحَانَتْ مِنِّي لَفْتَةٌ، فَإِذَا أَنَا بِرَسُوْلِ اللهِ ﷺ مُقْبِلاً. وَإِذَا الشَّجَرَتَانِ قَدِ افْتَرَقَتَا. فَقَامَتْ كُلُّ وَاحِدَةٍ مِنْهُمَا عَلَى سَاقٍ. فَقَالَ رَسُوْلُ اللهِ ﷺ: يَا جَابِرُ، هَلْ رَأَيْتَ مَقَامِي؟ قُلْتُ: نَعَمْ، يَا رَسُوْلَ اللهِ، قَالَ: فَانْطَلِقْ إِلَى الشَّجَرَتَيْنِ فَاقْطَعْ مِنْ كُلِّ وَاحِدَةٍ مِنْهُمَا غُصْنًا فَأَقْبِلْ بِهِمَا. حَتَّى إِذَا قُمْتَ مَقَامِي فَأَرْسِلْ غُصْنًا عَنْ يَمِيْنِكَ وَعَنْ يَسَارِكَ.

قَالَ جَابِرٌ: فَقُمْتُ فَأَخَذْتُ حَجَرًا فَكَسَرْتُهُ وَحَسَرْتُهُ، فَانْذَلَقَ لِي. فَأَتَيْتُ الشَّجَرَتَيْنِ فَقَطَعْتُ مِنْ كُلِّ وَاحِدَةٍ مِنْهُمَا غُصْنًا. ثُمَّ أَقْبَلْتُ أَجُرُّهُمَا حَتَّى قُمْتُ مَقَامَ رَسُوْلِ اللهِ ﷺ؛ أَرْسَلْتُ غُصْنًا عَنْ يَمِيْنِي وَغُصْنًا عَنْ يَسَارِي، ثُمَّ لَحِقْتُهُ فَقُلْتُ: قَدْ فَعَلْتُ، يَا رَسُوْلَ اللهِ، فَعَمَّ ذَاكَ؟ قَالَ: إِنِّي مَرَرْتُ بِقَبْرَيْنِ يُعَذَّبَانِ، فَأَحْبَبْتُ بِشَفَاعَتِي أَنْ يُرَفَّهَ عَنْهُمَا مَا دَامَ الْغُصْنَانِ رَطْبَيْنِ.

رَوَاهُ مُسْلِمٌ وَابْنُ حِبَّانَ.

213/17. According to Jābir ؓ, in the course of a detailed report:

"We set off with Allah's Messenger ﷺ (for a battle) until we alighted in a wide valley. Allah's Messenger ﷺ then went to relieve himself, and I followed him with a water bag. Allah's Messenger ﷺ looked around, but he did not see anything with which to screen himself. There were two trees on the rim of the valley, so Allah's Messenger ﷺ went over to one of them and grasped one of its branches. He said: 'Be compliant with me, by Allah's leave,' so

---

[213] Set forth by •Muslim in *al-Ṣaḥīḥ*: Bk.: *al-Zuhd wa al-Raqāʾiq* [Abstinence and the Softening of Hearts], Ch.: The long tradition of Jābir and the story of Abū al-Yasar, 4/2306 §3012. •Ibn Ḥibbān in *al-Ṣaḥīḥ*, 14/455–456 §6524. •al-Bayhaqī in *al-Sunan al-Kubrā*, 1/94 §452. •al-Iṣbahānī in *Dalāʾil al-Nubuwwa*, 1/53–55 §37. •Ibn ʿAbd al-Barr in *al-Tamhīd*, 1/222. •al-Khaṭīb al-Tabrīzī in *Mishkāt al-Maṣābīḥ*, 2/283 §5885.

the tree was duly compliant with him, like the camel with a stick inserted in the bone of its nose, which obeys its rider. Then, when he came to the other tree, he grasped one of its branches and said: 'Be compliant with me, by Allah's leave,' so it was duly compliant with him like the first tree. Then, when he reached the middle of the space between them, he said: 'Come close together over me, by Allah's leave,' so they duly came close together. Sitting there, I was talking to myself. I happened to glance around, and there was I with Allah's Messenger approaching ﷺ! The two trees had also separated, so each one of them stood in its previous position! Allah's Messenger ﷺ said: 'O Jābir, have you noticed the place where I was standing?' I said: 'Yes, O Messenger of Allah!' He said: 'Go over to the two trees, lop a branch off each one of them, and fetch them both. Then, when you reach my place, cast one branch to your right and one to your left.'"

Jābir said: "I therefore stood up, grabbed a stone, broke it and tugged it out, so it became sharp for me. Then I came to the two trees and lopped a branch off each one of them. Then I dragged the pair of them until I reached the place of Allah's Messenger ﷺ, where I cast a branch to my right and a branch to my left. Then I joined him and said: 'I have done [what you told me], O Messenger of Allah, but what is the point in doing that?' He said: 'I passed by two graves inflicting torment, so I wished through my intercession that their torment might be mitigated as long as the two branches are fresh and green!'"

Reported by Muslim and Ibn Ḥibbān.

٢١٤/١٨. عَنْ أَنَسٍ رضي الله عنه أَنَّ النَّبِيَّ ﷺ نَعَى زَيْدًا وَجَعْفَرًا وَابْنَ رَوَاحَةَ لِلنَّاسِ قَبْلَ أَنْ يَأْتِيَهُمْ خَبَرُهُمْ. فَقَالَ: أَخَذَ الرَّايَةَ زَيْدٌ فَأُصِيبَ، ثُمَّ أَخَذَ جَعْفَرٌ فَأُصِيبَ، ثُمَّ أَخَذَ ابْنُ رَوَاحَةَ فَأُصِيبَ - وَعَيْنَاهُ تَذْرِفَانِ - حَتَّى أَخَذَ الرَّايَةَ سَيْفٌ مِنْ سُيُوْفِ اللهِ حَتَّى فَتَحَ اللهُ عَلَيْهِمْ.

رَوَاهُ الْبُخَارِيُّ وَالنَّسَائِيُّ وَأَحْمَدُ.

214/18. According to Anas ﵁:

"The Prophet ﷺ announced the death of Zayd, Jaʿfar and Ibn Rawāḥa to the people, before the news of their martyrdom reached them. So he said: 'Zayd held the standard, so he was slain. Then Jaʿfar held it, so he was slain. Then Ibn Rawāḥa held it, so he was slain.' With his eyes shedding tears, he went on to say: 'Until one of Allah's swords (Khālid b. al-Walīd) held the standard, and Allah granted victory over them!'"

Reported by al-Bukhārī, al-Nasāʾī and Aḥmad.

١٩/٢١٥. عَنْ أَنَسِ بْنِ مَالِكٍ ﵁ في رواية طويلة قَالَ: إِنَّ رَجُلاً كَانَ يَكْتُبُ لِرَسُوْلِ اللهِ ﷺ فَارْتَدَّ عَنِ الإِسْلَامِ، وَلَحِقَ بِالْـمُشْرِكِيْنَ، وَقَالَ: أَنَا أَعْلَمُكُمْ بِمُحَمَّدٍ. إِنْ كُنْتُ لَأَكْتُبُ مَا شِئْتُ. فَمَاتَ ذَلِكَ الرَّجُلُ فَقَالَ النَّبِيُّ ﷺ: إِنَّ الْأَرْضَ لَـمْ تَقْبَلْهُ.

وَقَالَ أَنَسٌ: فَأَخْبَرَنِي أَبُوْطَلْحَةَ أَنَّهُ أَتَى الْأَرْضَ الَّتِي مَاتَ فِيْهَا فَوَجَدَهُ مَنْبُوْذًا، فَقَالَ: مَا شَأْنُ هَذَا؟ فَقَالُوْا: دَفَنَّاهُ مِرَارًا فَلَمْ تَقْبَلْهُ الْأَرْضُ.

رَوَاهُ مُسْلِمٌ وَأَحْمَدُ وَاللَّفْظُ لَهُ وَالْبَيْهَقِيُّ.

---

[214] Set forth by •al-Bukhārī in *al-Ṣaḥīḥ*: Bk.: *al-Maghāzī* [Military Expeditions], Ch.: The Battle of Muʾta from the land of Syria, 4/1554 §4014, & Bk.: *al-Janāʾiz* [Funeral Ceremonies], Ch.: The man should announce the death to the family of the deceased in person, 1/420 §1189, & Bk.: *al-Jihād* [The Sacred Struggle], Ch.: The desire for martyrdom, 3/1030 §2645, & Ch.: Someone who behaves imperiously in war without official authority, if he is afraid of the enemy, 3/1115 §2898, & Bk.: *al-Manāqib* [Virtues], Ch.: The signs of Prophethood in Islam, 3/1328 §3431, & Bk.: *Faḍāʾil al-Ṣaḥāba* [The Excellent Merits of the Companions], Ch.: The virtues of Khālid b. al-Walīd ﵁, 3/1372 §3547. •al-Nasāʾī likewise in *al-Sunan al-Kubrā*, 5/180 §8604. •Aḥmad b. Ḥanbal in *al-Musnad*, 1/204 §1750. •al-Ḥākim in *al-Mustadrak*, 3/337 §5295. He said: "This is a tradition with an authentic chain of transmission." •al-Ṭabarānī in *al-Muʿjam al-Kabīr,* 2/105, §1459–1461 •al-Khaṭīb al-Tabrīzī in *Mishkāt al-Maṣābīḥ*, 2/384 §5887.

215/19. According to Anas b. Mālik ﷺ, in the course of a detailed report:

"A man used to work as a scribe for Allah's Messenger ﷺ, but he apostatized from Islam and joined the polytheists, and he said: 'I am the one of you most knowledgeable of Muhammad. So I would write what I wanted to.' That man then died, so the Prophet ﷺ said: 'The earth has not accepted him!'"

Anas also said: "Abū Ṭalḥa informed me that he came to the land where he died, and he found his corpse lying outside the grave, so he said: 'What is the matter with (the dead body of) this person?' They said: 'We buried him several times, but the earth did not accept him!'"

Reported by Muslim, Aḥmad (the wording is his) and al-Bayhaqī.

٢١٦/ ٢٠. عَنِ ابْنِ عَبَّاس رضي الله عنهما قَالَ: جَاءَ أَعْرَابِيٌّ إِلَى رَسُوْلِ اللهِ ﷺ فَقَالَ: بِمَ أَعْرِفُ أَنَّكَ نَبِيٌّ؟ قَالَ: إِنْ دَعَوْتُ هَذَا الْعِذْقَ مِنْ هَذِهِ النَّخْلَةِ، أَتَشْهَدُ أَنِّي رَسُوْلُ اللهِ؟ فَدَعَاهُ رَسُوْلُ اللهِ ﷺ فَجَعَلَ يَنْزِلُ مِنَ النَّخْلَةِ حَتَّى سَقَطَ إِلَى النَّبِيِّ ﷺ ثُمَّ قَالَ: ارْجِعْ. فَعَادَ، فَأَسْلَمَ الْأَعْرَابِيُّ.

رَوَاهُ التِّرْمِذِيُّ وَالْحَاكِمُ وَالطَّبَرَانِيُّ. وَقَالَ أَبُوْعِيْسَى: هَذَا حَدِيْثٌ حَسَنٌ صَحِيْحٌ.

216/20. According to Ibn ʿAbbās رضي الله عنهما:

"A Bedouin came to Allah's Messenger ﷺ and said: 'How can I

---

[215] Set forth by •Muslim in *al-Ṣaḥīḥ*: Bk.: The Characteristics of the Hypocrites and their Rules, 4/2145 §2781. •Aḥmad b. Ḥanbal in *al-Musnad*, 3/120 §12236, 13348. •al-Bayhaqī in al-Sunan al-Ṣughrā, 1/568 §1054. •ʿAbd b. Ḥumayd in *al-Musnad*, 1/381 §1278. •Abū al-Maḥāsin in *Muʿtaṣar al-Mukhtaṣar*, 2/188. •al-Khaṭīb al-Tabrīzī in *Mishkāt al-Maṣābīḥ*, 2/387 §5798.

[216] Set forth by •al-Tirmidhī in *al-Sunan*: Bk.: *al-Manāqib* [Virtues] according to Allah's Messenger ﷺ, Ch.: 5/594 §3628. •al-Ḥākim in *al-Mustadrak*, 2/676 §4237. •al-Ṭabarānī in *al-Muʿjam al-Kabīr*, 12/110 §12622. •al-Maqdisī in *al-Aḥādīth al-Mukhtāra*, 9/538–539 §527. •al-Bayhaqī in *al-Iʿtiqād*, 1/48. •al-Khaṭīb al-Tabrīzī in *Mishkāt al-Maṣābīḥ*, 2/394 §5924.

know that you are a Prophet?' He replied: 'If I summon this bunch of dates from this date palm, will you bear witness that I am the Messenger of Allah?' Then Allah's Messenger ﷺ summoned it, so it set about descending from the date palm, until it dropped down to (the holy feet of) the Prophet ﷺ. Then he told it to go back and it returned, so the Bedouin embraced Islam (beholding the love and obedience of the vegetable world for Allah's Messenger)!"

Reported by al-Tirmidhī, al-Ḥākim and al-Ṭabarānī. Abū ʿĪsā said: "This is a fine authentic tradition."

٢١٧/ ٢١. عَنْ أَبِي زَيْدِ بْنِ أَخْطَبَ ﵁ قَالَ: مَسَحَ رَسُوْلُ اللهِ ﷺ يَدَهُ عَلَى وَجْهِي وَدَعَا لِي.

قَالَ عَزْرَةُ: إِنَّهُ عَاشَ مِائَةً وَعِشْرِيْنَ سَنَةً وَلَيْسَ فِي رَأْسِهِ إِلاَّ شَعَرَاتٌ بِيْضٌ.

رَوَاهُ التِّرْمِذِيُّ وَالطَّبَرَانِيُّ. وَقَالَ أَبُوْ عِيْسَى: هَذَا حَدِيْثٌ حَسَنٌ.

217/21. According to Abū Zayd b. Akhṭab ﵁:

"Allah's Messenger ﷺ wiped his hand over my face and supplicated on my behalf."

ʿAzra said: "He lived for a hundred and twenty years, and there were only a few white hairs in his head!"

Reported by al-Tirmidhī and al-Ṭabarānī. Abū ʿĪsā said: "This is a fine tradition."

٢١٨/ ٢٢. عَنْ قَتَادَةَ بْنِ النُّعْمَانِ ﵁ أَنَّهُ أُصِيْبَتْ عَيْنُهُ يَوْمَ بَدْرٍ، فَسَالَتْ حَدَقَتُهُ عَلَى وَجْنَتِهِ. فَأَرَادُوْا أَنْ يَقْطَعُوْهَا، فَسَأَلُوْا رَسُوْلَ اللهِ ﷺ فَقَالَ: لاَ. فَدَعَا بِهِ، فَغَمَزَ حَدَقَتَهُ

---

[217] Set forth by •al-Tirmidhī in *al-Sunan*: Bk.: *al-Manāqib* [Virtues] according to Allah's Messenger ﷺ, Ch.: (6), 5/594 §3629. •al-Ṭabarānī in *al-Muʿjam al-Kabīr*, 17/27 §45, & likewise in *al-Muʿjam al-Kabīr*, 18/21 §35. •al-Shaybānī in *al-Āḥād wa al-Mathānī*, 4/199 §2182. •al-Haythamī in *Majmaʿ al-Zawāʾid*, 9/412.

بِرَاحَتِهِ، فَكَانَ لَا يُدْرَى أَيُّ عَيْنَيْهِ أُصِيبَتْ.

رَوَاهُ أَبُو يَعْلَى.

218/22. According to Qatāda b. al-Nuʿmān ☙, his eye was wounded on the Day of Badr (by an arrow), so its pupil dangled over his face. The Companions wanted to cut it off, so they asked Allah's Messenger ☙, but he said: "No!" Then he supplicated for him and placed the pupil into its socket with the palm of his hand. Qatāda's eye convalesced to its normal position so naturally that there was no way of knowing which of his eyes had been wounded!

Reported by Abū Yaʿlā.

٢٣/٢١٩. عَنِ الْبَرَاءِ بْنِ عَازِبٍ ﵄ قَالَ: بَعَثَ رَسُولُ اللهِ ﷺ إِلَى أَبِي رَافِعٍ الْيَهُودِيِّ رِجَالاً مِنَ الْأَنْصَارِ، فَأَمَّرَ عَلَيْهِمْ عَبْدَ اللهِ بْنَ عَتِيكٍ ﵄، وَكَانَ أَبُو رَافِعٍ يُؤْذِي رَسُولَ اللهِ ﷺ وَيُعِينُ عَلَيْهِ، وَكَانَ فِي حِصْنٍ لَهُ بِأَرْضِ الْحِجَازِ... (قَالَ عَبْدُ اللهِ بْنُ عَتِيكٍ ﵄ فِي قِصَّةِ قَتْلِ أَبِي رَافِعٍ:) فَعَرَفْتُ أَنِّي قَتَلْتُهُ: فَجَعَلْتُ أَفْتَحُ الْأَبْوَابَ بَابًا بَابًا، حَتَّى انْتَهَيْتُ إِلَى دَرَجَةٍ لَهُ فَوَضَعْتُ رِجْلِي وَأَنَا أَرَى قَدِ انْتَهَيْتُ إِلَى الْأَرْضِ، فَوَقَعْتُ فِي لَيْلَةٍ مُقْمِرَةٍ فَانْكَسَرَتْ سَاقِي فَعَصَبْتُهَا بِعِمَامَةٍ... فَانْتَهَيْتُ إِلَى النَّبِيِّ ﷺ فَحَدَّثْتُهُ، فَقَالَ: ابْسُطْ رِجْلَكَ. فَبَسَطْتُ رِجْلِي فَمَسَحَهَا، فَكَأَنَّمَا لَمْ أَشْتَكِهَا قَطُّ.

رَوَاهُ الْبُخَارِيُّ.

219/23. According to al-Barā' b. ʿĀzib ☙:

---

218 Set forth by •Abū Yaʿlā in al-Musnad, 3/120 §1549. •Abū ʿAwāna in al-Musnad, 4/348 §6929. •al-Haythamī in Majmaʿ al-Zawāʾid, 8/297. •Ibn Saʿd in al-Ṭabaqāt al-Kubrā, 1/187. •al-Dhahabī in Siyar Aʿlām al-Nubalāʾ, 2/333. •al-ʿAsqalānī in Tahdhīb al-Tahdhīb, 7/430 §814, & in al-Iṣāba, 4/208 §4888. •Ibn Qāniʿ in Muʿjam al-Ṣaḥāba, 2/361. •Ibn Kathīr in al-Bidāya wa al-Nihāya, 3/291.

219 Set forth by •al-Bukhārī in al-Ṣaḥīḥ: Bk.: al-Maghāzī [Military Expeditions], Ch.: The killing of Abū Rāfiʿ ʿAbd Allāh b. Abī al-Ḥuqayq,

"Allah's Messenger ﷺ sent some men from among the Anṣār to Abū Rāfiʿ, the Jew (to take him to task). He appointed ʿAbd Allāh b. ʿAtīk as their commander, for Abū Rāfiʿ used to molest Allah's Messenger ﷺ and provide assistance (to the unbelievers) against him (and the Muslim Community). He was in his fortress in the land of Ḥijāz.... (Relating the killing of Abū Rāfiʿ the Jew, ʿAbd Allāh b. ʿAtīk said): 'I felt sure that I had killed him, so I set about opening the gates, gate after gate, until I finally reached a staircase, so I stamped my foot and I had obviously reached the ground. It was a moonlit night. I fell down and broke my lower leg, so I bandaged it with a turban.... I came to the Prophet ﷺ and narrated the whole incident. He said: "Stretch out your leg!" I stretched out my leg, and he wiped it with his compassionate hand. (The fractured shin bone united there and then.) I have never complained about it since then.'"

Reported by al-Bukhārī.

٢٢٠/ ٢٤. عَنْ عَائِشَةَ قَالَتْ: كَانَ لِآلِ رَسُوْلِ اللهِ ﷺ وَحْشٌ. فَإِذَا خَرَجَ رَسُوْلُ اللهِ ﷺ، لَعِبَ وَاشْتَدَّ وَأَقْبَلَ وَأَدْبَرَ. فَإِذَا أَحَسَّ بِرَسُوْلِ اللهِ ﷺ قَدْ دَخَلَ، رَبَضَ فَلَمْ يَتَرَمْرَمْ، مَا دَامَ رَسُوْلُ اللهِ ﷺ فِي الْبَيْتِ، كَرَاهِيَةَ أَنْ يُؤْذِيَهُ.

رَوَاهُ أَحْمَدُ وَأَبُوْ يَعْلَى.

220/24. According to ʿĀʾisha:

"An ox was kept for the family of Allah's Messenger ﷺ. When the Messenger of Allah ﷺ would come out, it used to jump, dance

---

4/1482 §3813. •al-Bayhaqī in *al-Sunan al-Kubrā*, 9/80. •al-Iṣbahānī in *Dalāʾil al-Nubuwwa*, 1/125. •Ibn ʿAbd al-Barr in *al-Istīʿāb*, 3/946. •al-Ṭabarī in *Tārīkh al-Umam wa al-Mulūk*, 2/56. •Ibn Kathīr in *al-Bidāya wa al-Nihāya*, 4/139. •Ibn Taymiyya in *al-Ṣārim al-Maslūl*, 2/294.

[220] Set forth by •Aḥmad b. Ḥanbal, in *al-Musnad*, 6/112, 150 §24862, 25210. •Abū Yaʿlā in *al-Musnad*, 8/121 §4660. •Ibn Rāhuwiyā in *al-Musnad*, 3/617 §1192. •al-Ṭaḥāwī in *Sharḥ Maʿānī al-āthār*, 4/195 •al-Bayhaqī in *Dalāʾil al-Nubuwwa*, 6/31. •Ibn ʿAbd al-Barr in *al-Tamhīd*, 6/314 •al-Haythamī in *Majmaʿ al-Zawāid*, 9/3.

and rejoice, and would swing to and fro (in ecstasy). When it would feel that Allah's Messenger ﷺ had gone inside, it would stand still and make no movement at all. Then so long as the Prophet would stay home, it would remain calm, fearing it might cause him discomfort."

Reported by Aḥmad and Abū Yaʿlā.

٢٢١/ ٢٥. عَنْ أَبِي هُرَيْرَةَ ؓ قَالَ: قُلْتُ: يَا رَسُوْلَ اللهِ، إِنِّي أَسْمَعُ مِنْكَ حَدِيْثًا كَثِيْرًا أَنْسَاهُ. قَالَ: ابْسُطْ رِدَاءَكَ. فَبَسَطْتُهُ. قَالَ: فَغَرَفَ بِيَدَيْهِ، ثُمَّ قَالَ: ضُمَّهُ. فَضَمَمْتُهُ، فَمَا نَسِيْتُ شَيْئًا بَعْدَهُ.

مُتَّفَقٌ عَلَيْهِ وَهَذَا لَفْظُ الْبُخَارِيِّ.

221/25. According to Abū Hurayra ؓ:

"I said: 'O Messenger of Allah, I hear many a saying from you, but forget it!' He said: 'Spread out your sheet of wrapper,' so I spread it out and he measured full cups of his hands (from the air and cast into my sheet). Then he said: 'Fold it to your breast,' so I obeyed, and I have never forgotten anything since then!'"

Agreed upon by al-Bukhārī and Muslim, and this is the wording of al-Bukhārī.

٢٢٢/ ٢٦. عَنْ جَابِرِ بْنِ عَبْدِ اللهِ ؓ أَنَّ يَهُوْدِيَّةً مِنْ أَهْلِ خَيْبَرَ سَمَّتْ شَاةً مَصْلِيَةً ثُمَّ أَهْدَتْهَا لِرَسُوْلِ اللهِ ﷺ فَأَخَذَ رَسُوْلُ اللهِ ﷺ الذِّرَاعَ فَأَكَلَ مِنْهَا وَأَكَلَ رَهْطٌ مِنْ أَصْحَابِهِ مَعَهُ، ثُمَّ قَالَ لَهُمْ رَسُوْلُ اللهِ ﷺ: ارْفَعُوْا أَيْدِيَكُمْ. وَأَرْسَلَ رَسُوْلُ اللهِ ﷺ إِلَى الْيَهُوْدِيَّةِ فَدَعَاهَا فَقَالَ لَهَا: أَسَمَمْتِ هَذِهِ الشَّاةَ؟ قَالَتِ الْيَهُوْدِيَّةُ: مَنْ أَخْبَرَكَ؟ قَالَ:

221 Set forth by •al-Bukhārī in *al-Ṣaḥīḥ*: Bk.: *al-ʿIlm* [Knowledge], Ch.: The preservation of knowledge, 1/56 §119. •Muslim in *al-Ṣaḥīḥ*: Bk.: *Faḍāʾil al-Ṣaḥāba* [The Excellent Merits of the Companions], Ch.: The excellent merits of Abū Hurayra al-Dawsī ؓ, 4/1939 §2491. •al-Tirmidhī in *al-Sunan*: Bk.: *al-Manāqib* [Virtues] according to Allah's Messenger ﷺ, Ch.: The virtues of Abū Hurayra ؓ, 5/684 §3834–3835. •al-Ṭabarānī in *al-Muʿjam al-Awsaṭ*, 1/247 §881. •Abū Yaʿlā in *al-Musnad*, 11/121 §6248.

أَخبرَتْني هَذِهِ فِي يَدِي لِلذِّرَاعِ. قَالَتْ: نَعَمْ. قَالَ: فَمَا أَرَدْتِ إِلَى ذَلِكَ؟ قَالَتْ: إِنْ كَانَ نَبِيًّا فَلَنْ يَضُرَّهُ وَإِنْ لَمْ يَكُنْ نَبِيًّا اسْتَرَحْنَا مِنْهُ. فَعَفَا عَنْهَا رَسُوْلُ اللهِ ﷺ وَلَمْ يُعَاقِبْهَا.

رَوَاهُ أَبُوْ دَاوُدَ وَالدَّارِمِيُّ.

222/26. According to Jābir b. ʿAbd Allāh ﷺ:

"A Jewess from among the people of Khaybar poisoned a roast sheep and presented it to Allah's Messenger ﷺ, so Allah's Messenger ﷺ took the foreleg and ate from it, and a group of his Companions also ate with him. Then Allah's Messenger ﷺ said to them: 'Hold back your hands!' Allah's Messenger ﷺ sent for the Jewess and asked her: 'Did you poison this sheep?' The Jewess said: 'Who informed you?' He said: 'This foreleg in my hand informed me!' She said: 'Yes, [I did poison it]!' He said: 'What did you intend by that?' She said: 'If he is a Prophet, it will not harm him, and if he is not a Prophet, we shall be rid of him!' Allah's Messenger ﷺ therefore pardoned her and did not punish her."

Reported by Abū Dāwūd and al-Dārimī.

٢٢٣/٢٧. عَنْ أَبِي زَيْدٍ الْأَنْصَارِيِّ ﷺ قَالَ: قَالَ لِي رَسُوْلُ اللهِ ﷺ: ادْنُ مِنِّي. قَالَ: فَمَسَحَ بِيَدِهِ عَلَى رَأْسِهِ وَلِحْيَتِهِ. قَالَ: ثُمَّ قَالَ: اَللَّهُمَّ، جَمِّلْهُ وَأَدِمْ جَمَالَهُ. قَالَ: فَلَقَدْ بَلَغَ بِضْعًا وَمِئَةَ سَنَةٍ، وَمَا فِي رَأْسِهِ وَلِحْيَتِهِ بَيَاضٌ إِلاَّ نَبْذٌ يَسِيْرٌ وَلَقَدْ كَانَ مُنْبَسِطَ الْوَجْهِ وَلَمْ يَنْقَبِضْ وَجْهُهُ حَتَّى مَاتَ.

رَوَاهُ أَحْمَدُ.

223/27. According to Abū Zayd al-Anṣārī ﷺ:

---

[222] Set forth by •Abū Dāwūd in *al-Sunan*: Bk.: *al-Diyyāt* [Blood Money], Ch.: A warning to beware of someone who gives a man poison to drink or eat, so he dies, 4/18 §4510. •al-Dārimī in *al-Sunan*, 1/46 §68. •al-Bayhaqī in *al-Sunan al-Kubrā*, 8/46.

[223] Set forth by •Aḥmad b. Ḥanbal in *al-Musnad*, 5/77 §21013. •al-ʿAsqalānī in *al-Iṣāba*, 4/599 §5763. •al-Mizzī in *Tahdhīb al-Kamāl*, 21/542 §4326.

"Allah's Messenger ﷺ said to me: 'Come close to me!'" (The reporter said:) "He wiped his hand over his head and his beard, then said: 'O Allah, beautify him and perpetuate his beauty!' He reached the age of slightly more than a hundred years, with no whiteness in the hair of his head and his beard, apart from a tiny amount. His face remained clear and bright and did not shrivel at all until he died."

Reported by Aḥmad.

الْفَصْلُ الثَّانِي

فَصْلٌ فِي كَرَامَاتِ الْأَوْلِيَاءِ وَالصَّالِحِيْنَ رضي الله عنهم

SECTION 2

THE MIRACULOUS VIRTUES OF THE FRIENDS OF ALLAH AND SAINTS رضي الله عنهم

٢٢٤/ ٢٨. عَنْ عَائِشَةَ رضي الله عنها زَوْجِ النَّبِيِّ ﷺ أَنَّهَا قَالَتْ: إِنَّ أَبَا بَكْرٍ الصِّدِّيْقَ رضي الله عنه كَانَ نَحَلَهَا جَادَّ عِشْرِيْنَ وَسْقًا مِنْ مَالِهِ بِالْغَابَةِ.

فَلَمَّا حَضَرَتْهُ الْوَفَاةُ قَالَ: وَاللهِ، يَا بُنَيَّةُ، مَا مِنَ النَّاسِ أَحَدٌ أَحَبُّ إِلَيَّ غِنًى بَعْدِي مِنْكِ وَلَا أَعَزُّ عَلَيَّ فَقْرًا بَعْدِي مِنْكِ. وَإِنِّي كُنْتُ نَحَلْتُكِ جَادَّ عِشْرِيْنَ وَسْقًا. فَلَوْ كُنْتِ جَدَدْتِيْهِ وَاحْتَزْتِيْهِ كَانَ لَكِ وَإِنَّمَا هُوَ الْيَوْمَ مَالُ وَارِثٍ. وَإِنَّمَا هُوَ أَخَوَاكِ وَأُخْتَاكِ، فَاقْتَسِمُوْهُ عَلَى كِتَابِ اللهِ.

قَالَتْ عَائِشَةُ رضي الله عنها: فَقُلْتُ: يَا أَبَتِ، وَاللهِ، لَوْ كَانَ كَذَا وَكَذَا لَتَرَكْتُهُ؛ إِنَّمَا هِيَ أَسْمَاءُ، فَمَنِ الْأُخْرَى؟ فَقَالَ أَبُوْ بَكْرٍ رضي الله عنه: ذُوْبَطْنِ بِنْتِ خَارِجَةَ أُرَاهَا جَارِيَةً فَوَلَدَتْ أُمَّ كُلْثُوْمٍ.

رَوَاهُ مَالِكٌ وَالطَّحَاوِيُّ وَالْبَيْهَقِيُّ.

224/28. According to ʿĀʾisha رضي الله عنها, the wife of the Prophet ﷺ:

---

224 Set forth by •Mālik in *al-Muwaṭṭāʾ*: Bk.: *al-Aqḍiya* [Judgements], Ch.: Gifts that are not permissible, 2/752 §1438. •al-Bayhaqī in *al-Sunan al-Kubrā*, 6/169 §11728, 12267. •al-Ṭaḥāwī in *Sharḥ Maʿāni al-Āthār*, 4/88. •Abū al-Qāsim Hibat Allāh in *Karāmāt al-Awliyāʾ*, 1/177 §62. •al-ʿAsqalānī in *al-Iṣāba*, 7/575 §11023. •al-Nawawī in *Tahdhīb al-Asmāʾ*, 2/574 §1030,

"Abū Bakr al-Ṣiddīq ﵁ had presented her with a gift of some date palm trees from his property in al-Ghāba (valley). They would yield dates equal to twenty camel-loads (*wasqs*—one *wasq* measures 240 kg.).

"So when death drew near, he said: 'By Allah, O my little daughter, there is no one among humankind dearer to me than you to become affluent after me, and there is no one more distressing to me to become poor after me than you! I presented you with date palms yielding twenty camel-loads of dates. If you had taken over the trees, they would have been yours. But today they are simply the property of an heir. Your two brothers and your two sisters are also the inheritors, so you must share and distribute them in accordance with the Book of Allah.'"

ʿĀʾisha ﵂ said: "O my father, by Allah, if it were such and such, I would relinquish it but I have only one sister; she is Asmāʾ; who is the other one?" Abū Bakr ﵁ said: "The occupant of the daughter of Khārija's womb. I see her as a girl." Then she gave birth to Umm Kulthūm.

Reported by Mālik, al-Ṭaḥāwī and al-Bayhaqī.

٢٢٥/ ٢٩. عَنْ عَبْدِ الرَّحْـمَنِ بنْ أَبِـي بَكْرٍ ﵄ فِي رواية طويلة: فَدَعَا (أَيِ أَبُوْ بَكْرٍ ﵁) بِالطَّعَامِ فَأَكَلَ وَأَكَلُوْا. فَجَعَلُوْا لاَ يَرْفَعُوْنَ لُقْمَةً إِلاَّ رَبَا مِنْ أَسْفَلِهَا أَكْثَرُ مِنْهَا، فَقَالَ: يَا أُخْتَ بَنِي فِرَاسٍ، مَا هَذَا؟ قَالَتْ: لاَ وَقُرَّةِ عَيْنِي، لَهِيَ الآنَ أَكْثَرُ مِنْهَا قَبْلَ ذَلِكَ بِثَلاَثِ مَرَّاتٍ. فَأَكَلُوْا وَبَعَثَ بِهَا إِلَى النَّبِيِّ ﷺ فَذَكَرَ أَنَّهُ أَكَلَ مِنْهَا.

مُتَّفَقٌ عَلَيْهِ.

225/29. According to ʿAbd al-Raḥmān b. Abī Bakr ﵄, in the course of a detailed report:

1239. •al-Zaylaʿī in *Naṣb al-Rāya*, 4/122. •Abū Jaʿfar al-Ṭabarī in *al-Riyāḍ al-Naḍra*, 2/123, 257. •Ibn Saʿd in *al-Ṭabaqāt al-Kubrā*, 3/194.

[225] Set forth by •al-Bukhārī in *al-Ṣaḥīḥ*: Bk.: *Mawāqīt al-Ṣalāt* [Set Times of the Ritual Prayer], Ch.: Evening conversations with the guest and the family, 1/216 §577, & Bk.: *al-Manāqib* [Virtues], Ch.: The signs of Prophethood in

"He (Abū Bakr ﵁) invited the Companions (of Suffa) to food and he himself also joined them. Every time they picked up a morsel, more food would sprout from beneath it, so Abū Bakr ﵁ said: 'O sister of the Banū Firās, what is this?' She said: 'O the coolness of my eyes, there is now three times more of food than there was before!' So the Companions ate to their fill. He also sent it to the Prophet ﷺ, and he also ate of it."

Agreed upon by al-Bukhārī and Muslim.

٢٢٦/ ٣٠. عَنِ ابْنِ عُمَرَ ﵄ قَالَ: مَا سَمِعْتُ عُمَرَ لِشَيْءٍ قَطُّ يَقُوْلُ: إِنِّي لَأَظُنُّهُ كَذَا إِلاَّ كَانَ كَمَا يَظُنُّ.

رَوَاهُ الْبُخَارِيُّ.

226/30. According to Ibn ʿUmar ﵄:

"I never heard ʿUmar say about something: 'I really do think it is such-and-such,' without its being exactly compatible with what he thought!"

Reported by al-Bukhārī.

٢٢٧/ ٣١. عَنْ أَبِي هُرَيْرَةَ ﵁ قَالَ: قَالَ رَسُوْلُ اللهِ ﷺ: لَقَدْ كَانَ فِيْمَا قَبْلَكُمْ مِنَ الْأُمَمِ نَاسٌ مُحَدَّثُوْنَ، فَإِنْ يَكُ فِي أُمَّتِي أَحَدٌ فَإِنَّهُ عُمَرُ أَي مُلْهَمُوْنَ.

Islam, 3/1312 §3388, & Bk.: *al-Adab* [Proper Conduct], Ch.: The repugnance of anger and worry in the presence of the guest, 5/2274 §5789, & Bk.: *al-Adab* [Proper Conduct], Ch.: The guest's saying to his companion: "I shall not eat until you eat!" 5/2274 §5790. •Muslim in *al-Ṣaḥīḥ*: Bk.: *al-Ashriba* [Beverages], Ch.: Honouring the guest, and the excellent merit of treating him preferentially, 3/1627 §2057. •al-Bazzār in *al-Musnad*, 6/228 §2263. •Aḥmad b. Ḥanbal in *al-Musnad*, 1/197 §1702, 1712.

226 Set forth by •al-Bukhārī in *al-Ṣaḥīḥ*: Bk.: *Faḍā'il al-Ṣaḥāba* [The Excellent Merits of the Companions], Ch.: The embracing of Islam by ʿUmar b. al-Khaṭṭāb ﵁, 3/1403 §3653. •al-Ḥākim in *al-Mustadrak*, 3/94 §4503. •Abū al-Qāsim Hibat Allāh in *Karāmāt al-Awliyā'*, 1/119 §65. •al-Nawawī in *Riyāḍ al-Ṣāliḥīn*, 1/568 §1510.

رَوَاهُ الْبُخَارِيُّ وَرَوَاهُ مُسْلِمٌ مِنْ رِوَايَةِ عَائِشَةَ ﵂. وقَالَ أَبُوْ عِيْسَى: هَذَا حَدِيْثٌ صَحِيْحٌ.

وفي رواية: عَنْ أَبِي سَعِيْدٍ الْخُدْرِيِّ ﵁ قَالُوْا: يَا رَسُوْلَ اللهِ، كَيْفَ مُحَدَّثٌ؟ قَالَ: تَتَكَلَّمُ الْمَلَائِكَةُ عَلَى لِسَانِهِ.

رَوَاهُ الطَّبَرَانِيُّ وَإِسْنَادُهُ حَسَنٌ.

227/31. According to Abū Hurayra ﵁:

"Allah's Messenger ﷺ said: 'In the communities that preceded you there were people Allah would pour things into their hearts (i.e., they would become conscious of things spiritually). And if there is one in my Community, it is ʿUmar!'"

Reported by al-Bukhārī, and by Muslim from the report of ʿĀʾisha ﵂. Abū ʿĪsā said: "This is an authentic tradition."

In one report: According to Abū Saʿīd al-Khudrī ﵁:

"They said: 'O Messenger of Allah, what state it is when

---

227 Set forth by •al-Bukhārī in *al-Ṣaḥīḥ*: Bk.: *Faḍāʾil al-Ṣaḥāba* [The Excellent Merits of the Companions], Ch.: The virtues of ʿUmar b. al-Khaṭṭāb ﵁, 3/1349 §3486, & Bk.: *al-Anbiyāʾ* [The Prophets], Ch.: "Or do you think that the Companions of the Cave and the Inscription are a wonder among Our signs? [*am ḥasibta anna aṣḥāba al-kahfi wa al-raqīmi kānū min āyāti-nā ʿajabā*]." (Q.18:9), 3/1279 §3282. •Muslim in *al-Ṣaḥīḥ*: Bk.: *Faḍāʾil al-Ṣaḥāba* [The Excellent Merits of the Companions], Ch.: The excellent merits of ʿUmar ﵁, 4/1864 §2398. •al-Tirmidhī in *al-Sunan*: Bk.:. *al-Manāqib* [Virtues] according to Allah's Messenger ﷺ, Ch.: The virtues of ʿUmar b. al-Khaṭṭāb ﵁, 5/622 §3693. •Ibn Ḥibbān in *al-Ṣaḥīḥ*, 15/317 §6894. •al-Ḥākim in *al-Mustadrak*, 3/92 §4499. He said: "This is a tradition with an authentic chain of transmission." •Aḥmad b. Ḥanbal in *al-Musnad*, 6/55 §24330. •al-Bayhaqī in *Shuʿab al-Īmān*, 5/48 §5734. •al-Ṭabarānī in *al-Muʿjam al-Awsaṭ*, 7/18 §6726. •al-Daylamī in *al-Firdaws bi-Maʾthūr al-Khiṭāb*, 3/278 §4839. •Isḥāq b. Rāhawayh in *al-Musnad*, 2/479 §1058. •al-Ḥakīm al-Tirmidhī in *Nawādir al-Uṣūl*, 3/138. •al-Nawawī in *Riyāḍ al-Ṣāliḥīn*, 1/564 §1504. •al-Haythamī in *Majmaʿ al-Zawāʾid*, 9/69. •al-Bayhaqī in *al-Iʿtiqād*, 1/315. •al-ʿAsqalānī in *Fatḥ al-Bārī*, 7/50. •al-Mubārakfūrī in *Tuḥfat al-Aḥwadhī*, 10/125.

someone receives spiritual consciousness?' He said: 'The angels speak on his tongue!'"

Reported by al-Ṭabarānī and its chain of transmission is excellent.

٢٢٨/ ٣٢. عَنْ عَائِشَةَ ﵂ قَالَتْ: قَالَ رَسُوْلُ اللهِ ﷺ: إِنِّي لَأَنْظُرُ إِلَى شَيَاطِيْنِ الإِنْسِ وَالْجِنِّ قَدْ فَرُّوْا مِنْ عُمَرَ.

وفي رواية: قَالَ: إِنَّ الشَّيْطَانَ لَيَخَافُ (أَوْ لَيَفْرَقُ) مِنْكَ، يَا عُمَرُ.

رَوَاهُ التِّرْمِذِيُّ وَالنَّسَائِيُّ وَأَحْمَدُ، وَقَالَ أَبُوْ عِيْسَى: هَذَا حَدِيْثٌ صَحِيْحٌ.

228/32. According to ʿĀʾisha ﵂:

"Allah's Messenger ﷺ said: 'I see that the satans of humankind and the jinn have fled from ʿUmar (in fear)!'"

In one report: "He said: 'Satan is surely afraid (or terrified) of you, O ʿUmar!'"

Reported by al-Tirmidhī, al-Nasāʾī and Aḥmad. Abū ʿĪsā said: "This is an authentic tradition."

٢٢٩/ ٣٣. عَنِ ابْنِ عُمَرَ ﵄ أَنَّ عُمَرَ بَعَثَ جَيْشًا وَأَمَّرَ عَلَيْهِمْ رَجُلاً يُدْعَى سَارِيَةَ، فَبَيْنَمَا عُمَرُ يَخْطُبُ فَجَعَلَ يَصِيْحُ: يَا سَارِيُّ، الْجَبَلَ. فَقَدِمَ رَسُوْلٌ مِنَ الْجَيْشِ فَقَالَ: يَا أَمِيْرَ الْمُؤْمِنِيْنَ، لَقِيْنَا عَدُوَّنَا فَهَزَمُوْنَا فَإِذَا بِصَائِحٍ يَصِيْحُ: يَا سَارِيُّ، الْجَبَلَ. فَأَسْنَدْنَا ظُهُوْرَنَا إِلَى الْجَبَلِ فَهَزَمَهُمُ اللهُ تَعَالَى.

رَوَاهُ أَحْمَدُ فِي الْفَضَائِلِ وَالْبَيْهَقِيُّ وَأَبُوْ نُعَيْمٍ.

---

228 Set forth by •al-Tirmidhī in *al-Sunan*: Bk.: *al-Manāqib* [Virtues] according to Allah's Messenger ﷺ, Ch.: The virtues of ʿUmar b. al-Khaṭṭāb ﵁, 5/621 §3690–3691. •al-Nasāʾī in *al-Sunan al-Kubrā*, 5/309 §5957. •Aḥmad b. Ḥanbal in *al-Musnad*, 5/353 §23039, & in *Faḍāʾil al-Ṣaḥāba*, 1/333 §480. •al-Bayhaqī in *al-Sunan al-Kubrā*, 10/77. •Ibn Ḥibbān in *al-Ṣaḥīḥ*, 10/231 §4386.

229/33. According to Ibn ʿUmar ﷺ:

"ʿUmar dispatched an army, and he appointed as their commander a man called Sāriya. Then, one day while delivering his sermon, ʿUmar called out: 'O Sāriya! Take cover of the mountain!' A messenger from that army came (after the war) and said: 'O Commander of the Believers! We were engaged in fighting the enemy who had nearly put us to flight, when suddenly a caller called: 'O Sāriya! Take cover of the mountain!' So we turned our backs towards the mountain. Then Allah Most High put our enemy to flight (and bestowed victory upon us)!'"

Reported by Aḥmad in *al-Faḍāʾil*, al-Bayhaqī and Abū Nuʿaym.

٢٣٠/ ٣٤. عَنْ قَيْسِ بْنِ الْحَجَّاجِ عَمَّنْ حَدَّثَهُ قَالَ: لَـمَّا فُتِحَتْ مِصْرُ أَتَى أَهْلُهَا إِلَى عَمْرِو بْنِ الْعَاصِ رضي الله عنه حِيْنَ دَخَلَ بُوْنَةَ مِنْ أَشْهُرِ الْعَجَمِ. فَقَالُوْا: أَيُّهَا الْأَمِيْرُ، إِنَّ لِنِيْلِنَا هَذَا سُنَّةً لَا يَجْرِي إِلَّا بِهَا. فَقَالَ: وَمَا ذَاكَ؟ قَالُوْا: إِذَا كَانَ ثَنْتَا عَشْرَةَ لَيْلَةً خَلَوْنَ مِنْ هَذَا الشَّهْرِ عَمَدْنَا إِلَى جَارِيَةٍ بِكْرٍ مِنْ أَبَوَيْهَا فَأَرْضَيْنَا أَبَوَيْهَا وَجَعَلْنَا عَلَيْهَا مِنَ الْحُلِيِّ وَالثِّيَابِ أَفْضَلُ مَا يَكُوْنُ ثُمَّ أَلْقَيْنَاهَا فِي هَذَا النِّيْلِ. فَقَالَ لَهُمْ عَمْرٌو رضي الله عنه: إِنَّ هَذَا مِمَّا لَا يَكُوْنُ فِي الْإِسْلَامِ. إِنَّ الْإِسْلَامَ يَهْدِمُ مَا كَانَ قَبْلَهُ.

قَالَ: فَأَقَامُوْا بُوْنَةَ وَأَبِيْبَ وَمَسْرَى وَالنِّيْلُ لَا يَجْرِي قَلِيْلاً وَلَا كَثِيْرًا حَتَّى هَمُّوْا بِالْجَلَاءِ. فَلَـمَّا رَأَى ذَلِكَ عَمْرٌو رضي الله عنه كَتَبَ بِذَلِكَ إِلَى عُمَرَ بْنِ الْخَطَّابِ رضي الله عنه، فَكَتَبَ: إِنَّكَ قَدْ أَصَبْتَ بِالَّذِي فَعَلْتَ وَإِنَّ الْإِسْلَامَ يَعْتَدِمُ مَا قَبْلَهُ وَإِنِّي قَدْ بَعَثْتُ إِلَيْكَ بِبِطَاقَةٍ دَاخِلَ كِتَابِي هَذَا فَأَلْقِهَا فِي النِّيْلِ. فَلَـمَّا قَدِمَ كِتَابُ عُمَرَ رضي الله عنه إِلَى عَمْرِو بْنِ الْعَاصِ رضي الله عنه، وَأَخَذَ الْبِطَاقَةَ فَفَتَحَهَا فَإِذَا فِيْهَا:

---

[229] Set forth by •Aḥmad b. Ḥanbal in *Faḍāʾil al-Ṣaḥāba*, 1/219 §355. •al-Bayhaqī in *Dalāʾil al-Nubuwwa*, 6/370, & in *al-Iʿtiqād*, 1/314. •Abū Nuʿaym in *Dalāʾil al-Nubuwwa*, 3/210–211. •al-Khaṭīb al-Tabrīzī in *Mishkāt al-Maṣābīḥ*, 2/410 §5954. •al-Rāzī in *al-Tafsīr al-Kabīr*, 21/87.

مِنْ عَبْدِ الله عُمَرَ أَمِيرِ الْمُؤْمِنِينَ إِلَى نِيلِ مِصْرَ. أَمَّا بَعْدُ! فَإِنْ كُنْتَ إِنَّمَا تَجْرِي مِنْ
قِبَلِكَ فَلَا تَجْرِ. وَإِنْ كَانَ اللهُ الْوَاحِدُ الْقَهَّارُ هُوَ الَّذِي يُجْرِيكَ فَنَسْأَلُ اللهَ الْوَاحِدَ الْقَهَّارَ
أَنْ يُجْرِيَكَ.

قَالَ: فَأَلْقَى الْبِطَاقَةَ فِي النِّيلِ فَلَمَّا أَلْقَى الْبِطَاقَةَ أَصْبَحُوا يَوْمَ السَّبْتِ وَقَدْ أَجْرَاهُ
اللهُ تَعَالَى سِتَّةَ عَشَرَ ذِرَاعًا فِي لَيْلَةٍ وَاحِدَةٍ وَقَطَعَ اللهُ تَعَالَى تِلْكَ السُّنَّةَ عَنْ أَهْلِ مِصْرَ
إِلَى الْيَوْمِ.

رَوَاهُ اللَّالَكَائِيُّ وَالْقُرْطَبِيُّ وَابْنُ كَثِيرٍ وَأَبُو الشَّيْخِ فِي كِتَابِ الْعَظَمَةِ.

230/34. According to Qays b. al-Ḥajjāj ⬦, someone told him:

"When Egypt was conquered, its inhabitants came to (the Governor of Egypt) ʿAmr b. al-ʿĀṣ ⬦ at the beginning of Būna, one of the months of the Copts. They said: 'O Commander, this river Nile of ours has a custom without which it does not flow.' He asked them: 'What is that custom?' They said: 'When twelve nights of this month have elapsed, we take a virgin girl from her parents with their consent. Then we adorn her with the finest ornaments and clothing and throw her into the Nile.' ʿAmr ⬦ told them: 'This custom will never be accepted (and practised) in Islam, for Islam abolishes what (absurd customs) existed before it (in the days of ignorance)!'

"The inhabitants of Egypt abided by this command for three months, Būna, Abīb and Masrā. The Nile flowed neither little nor much, so the local inhabitants prepared for evacuation. ʿAmr b. al-ʿĀṣ ⬦ observed that state of affairs, and described it in a letter to ʿUmar b. al-Khaṭṭāb ⬦, who wrote back to him: 'You have acted correctly in what you have done, for Islam has rooted out the (absurd) customs that preceded it. I have enclosed a written note

---

230 Set forth by •Abū al-Qāsim Hibat Allāh in *Karāmāt al-Awliyāʾ*, 1/119 §66. •al-Qurṭubī in *al-Jāmiʿ li-Aḥkām al-Qurʾān*, 13/103. •Ibn Kathīr in *Tafsīr al-Qurʾān al-ʿAẓīm*, 3/465. •al-Rāzī in *al-Tafsīr al-Kabīr*, 21/88. •al-Ḥamawī in *Muʿjam al-Buldān*, 5/335.

inside this letter of mine, so throw it into the Nile!' When ʿUmar's letter reached ʿAmr b. ʿĀṣ, he took out that note and spread it open. He found these words inscribed upon it:

"'From Allah's servant ʿUmar, the Commander of the Believers, to the Nile of Egypt. Now, if you used to flow of your own accord, you must not flow! If it was Allah, the One, the All-Compelling, who used to make you flow, we beseech Allah, the One, the All-Compelling, to make you flow!'

"He promptly threw the slip of paper into the Nile, and when Saturday morning dawned, Allah Most High had caused it to flow sixteen cubits (higher than before) in a single night! Allah Most High has abolished that custom from the people of Egypt ever since."

Reported by al-Lālakāʾī, al-Qurṭabī, Ibn Kathīr, and Abū al-Shaykh in *Kitāb al-ʿAẓama*.

٢٣١/ ٣٥. عَنْ مَالِكٍ ﷺ قَالَ فِي رِوَايَةٍ طَوِيلَةٍ: قُتِلَ عُثْمَانُ ﷺ وَإِنَّ رَأْسَهُ عَلَى الْبَابِ لَيَقُوْلُ: طُقْ طُقْ حَتَّى صَارُوْا بِهِ إِلَى حَشِّ كَوْكَبٍ فَاحْتَفَرُوا لَهُ.

رَوَاهُ الطَّبَرَانِيُّ وَابْنُ عَسَاكِرَ.

231/35. According to Mālik ﷺ, in the course of a detailed report:

"ʿUthmān ﷺ was martyred, and his head was on the gate, calling out: 'Bury me, bury me,' until his companions brought him to Kaukab-garden where they dug a grave for him (and buried him)."

Reported by al-Ṭabarānī and Ibn ʿAsākir.

٢٣٢/ ٣٦. عَنْ مَالِكٍ ﷺ قَالَ: كَانَ عُثْمَانُ ﷺ يَمُرُّ بِحَشِّ كَوْكَبٍ فَيَقُوْلُ: لَيُدْفَنَنَّ رَجُلٌ صَالِحٌ.

---

[231] Set forth by •al-Ṭabarānī in *al-Muʿjam al-Kabīr*, 1/78 §109. •Ibn ʿAsākir in *Tārīkh Dimashq al-Kabīr*, 39/532. •al-Haythamī in *Majmaʿ al-Zawāʾid*, 9/95. •Ibn ʿAbd al-Barr in *al-Istīʿāb*, 3/1047. •Ibn Saʿd in *al-Ṭabaqāt al-Kubrā*, 3/77. •al-Mizzī in *Tahdhīb al-Kamāl*, 19/457. •al-ʿAsqalānī in *Talkhīṣ al-Ḥabīr*, 2/145.

رَوَاهُ الطَّبَرَانِيُّ وَابْنُ عَسَاكِرَ.

232/36. According to Mālik 🙽:

"When ʿUthmān 🙽 used to pass by Kawkab-garden, he would say: 'A righteous man will surely be buried (here and he was himself buried there)!'"

Reported by al-Ṭabarānī and Ibn ʿAsākir.

٢٣٣/ ٣٧. عَنِ ابْنِ عُمَرَ 🙽 قَالَ: إِنَّ عُثْمَانَ 🙽 أَصْبَحَ فَحَدَّثَ فَقَالَ: إِنِّي رَأَيْتُ النَّبِيَّ 🙽 فِي الْمَنَامِ اللَّيْلَةَ فَقَالَ: يَا عُثْمَانُ، أَفْطِرْ عِنْدَنَا. فَأَصْبَحَ عُثْمَانُ 🙽 صَائِمًا فَقُتِلَ مِنْ يَوْمِهِ.

رَوَاهُ الْحَاكِمُ وَابْنُ أَبِي شَيْبَةَ. وَقَالَ الْحَاكِمُ: هَذَا حَدِيثٌ صَحِيحُ الْإِسْنَادِ.

233/37. According to Ibn ʿUmar 🙽:

"ʿUthmān 🙽 entered the morning (of the day he was martyred) and related an experience. He said: 'I saw the Prophet 🙽 in a dream tonight, so he said: 'O ʿUthmān, break fast with us today!' ʿUthmān therefore entered the morning fasting; he was martyred the same day!"

Reported by al-Ḥakim and Ibn Abī Shayba. According to al-Ḥakim: "This is a tradition with an authentic chain of transmission."

---

232 Set forth by •al-Ṭabarānī in *al-Muʿjam al-Kabīr*, 1/78 §109. •Ibn ʿAsākir in *Tārīkh Dimashq al-Kabīr*, 39/532. •al-Haythamī in *Majmaʿ al-Zawāʾid*, 9/95. •Ibn ʿAbd al-Barr in *al-Istīʿāb*, 3/1047. •Ibn Saʿd in *al-Ṭabaqāt*, 3/77. •al-Mizzī in *Tahdhīb al-Kamāl*, 19/457.

233 Set forth by •al-Ḥakim in *al-Mustadrak*, 3/110 §4554. •Ibn Abī Shayba in *al-Muṣannaf*, 6/181 §30510–30511; 7/442 §37085. •al-Haythamī in *Majmaʿ al-Zawāʾid*, 7/232. •Ibn Saʿd in *al-Ṭabaqāt al-Kubrā*, 3/74. •Ibn Ḥayyān in *Ṭabaqāt al-Muḥaddithīn bi-Aṣbahān*, 2/298 §182. •Ibn ʿAsākir in *Tārīkh Dimashq al-Kabīr*, 39, 384.

٢٣٤/ ٣٨. وفي رواية: عَنِ امْرَأَةِ عُثْمَانَ قَالَتْ: قَالَ: رَأَيْتُ رَسُوْلَ اللهِ ﷺ وَأَبَا بَكْرٍ وَعُمَرَ ﵄ قَالُوْا: إِنَّكَ تُفْطِرُ عِنْدَنَا اللَّيْلَةَ.

رَوَاهُ ابْنُ أَبِـي شَيْبَةَ وَابْنُ سَعْدٍ.

234/38. In one report: ʿUthmān's wife said:

"He (ʿUthmān) said: 'I saw Allah's Messenger ﷺ and Abū Bakr and ʿUmar ﵄. They said: "You are going to break fast with us tonight!"'"

Reported by Ibn Abī Shayba and Ibn Saʿd.

٢٣٥/ ٣٩. عَنْ سُلَيْمَانَ ابْنِ يَسَارٍ ﵁ أَنَّ جَهْجَاهَ الْغِفَارِيَّ أَخَذَ عَصَا عُثْمَانَ الَّتِي يَتَخَصَّرُ بِهَا فَكَسَرَهَا عَلَى رَكْبَتِهِ فَوَقَعَتْ فِي رَكْبَتِهِ الآكِلَةُ.

رَوَاهُ ابْنُ عَسَاكِرَ وَاللاَّلَكَائِيُّ.

235/39. According to Sulaymān b. Yasār ﵁:

"Jahjāh al-Ghafārī took ʿUthmān's staff on which he was leaning, and broke it on his knee (arrogantly), so gangrene infected his knee."

Reported by Ibn ʿAsākir and al-Lālakāʾī.

٢٣٦/ ٤٠. عَنْ أَبِـي رَافِعٍ ﵁ مَوْلَى رَسُوْلِ اللهِ ﷺ، قَالَ: خَرَجْنَا مَعَ عَلِيٍّ ﵁ حِيْنَ بَعَثَهُ رَسُوْلُ اللهِ ﷺ بِرَأْيَتِهِ، فَلَـمَّا دَنَا مِنَ الْحِصْنِ، خَرَجَ إِلَيْهِ أَهْلُهُ فَقَاتَلَهُمْ. فَضَرَبَهُ

---

[234] Set forth by •al-Ḥākim in *al-Mustadrak*, 3/110 §4554. •Ibn Abī Shayba in *al-Muṣannaf*, 6/181 §30510–30511; 7/442 §37085. •al-Haythamī in *Majmaʿ al-Zawāʾid*, 7/232. •Ibn Saʿd in *al-Ṭabaqāt al-Kubrā*, 3/74. •Ibn Ḥayyān in *Ṭabaqāt al-Muḥaddithīn bi-Aṣbahān*, 2/298 §182. •Ibn ʿAsākir in *Tārīkh Dimashq al-Kabīr*, 39, 384.

[235] Set forth by •Ibn ʿAsākir in *Tārīkh Dimashq al-Kabīr*, 39/329. •Abū al-Qāsim Hibat Allāh in *Karāmāt al-Awliyāʾ*, 1/124 §70. •Ibn ʿAbd al-Barr in *al-Istīʿāb*, 1/269. •al-Rāzī in *al-Tafsīr al-Kabīr*, 21/88.

رَجُلٌ مِنْ يَهُوْدٍ فَطَرَحَ تُرْسَهُ مِنْ يَدِهِ، فَتَنَاوَلَ عَلِيٌّ ﷺ بَابًا كَانَ عِنْدَ الْحِصْنِ، فَتَرَّسَ بِهِ نَفْسَهُ. فَلَمْ يَزَلْ فِي يَدِهِ وَهُوَ يُقَاتِلُ حَتَّى فَتَحَ اللهُ عَلَيْهِ. ثُمَّ أَلْقَاهُ مِنْ يَدَيْهِ حِيْنَ فَرَغَ. فَلَقَدْ رَأَيْتُنِي فِي نَفَرٍ مَعِي سَبْعَةٌ أَنَا ثَامِنُهُمْ، نَجْهَدُ عَلَى أَنْ نَقْلِبَ ذَلِكَ الْبَابَ فَمَا نَقْلِبُهُ.

رَوَاهُ أَحْمَدُ.

236/40. According to Abū Rāfiʿ ﷺ, the freedman of Allah's Messenger ﷺ:

"We set out with ʿAlī ﷺ, when Allah's Messenger ﷺ dispatched him with his standard (to Khaybar). Then, when he drew near to Khaybar fortress (not distant from Medina), its occupants came out and attacked him suddenly. (He was fighting valiantly when) a man from among the Jews struck him, and threw his shield from his hand. ʿAlī ﷺ then reached a gate that was next to the fortress, so he (pulled it and) armed himself with it as his shield, and it remained in his hand while he fought, until Allah granted him victory. Then he threw that gate from his hand when war finished. I had a troop of seven men and I was the eighth. We eight strived to topple that gate but could not topple it (which ʿAlī pulled alone and used as his shield)."

Reported by Aḥmad.

٢٣٧/ ٤١. عَنْ جَابِرٍ ﷺ أَنَّ عَلِيًّا ﷺ حَمَلَ الْبَابَ يَوْمَ خَيْبَرَ حَتَّى صَعِدَ الْمُسْلِمُوْنَ فَفَتَحُوْهَا وَأَنَّهُ جُرِّبَ فَلَمْ يَحْمِلْهُ إِلاَّ أَرْبَعُوْنَ رَجُلاً.

رَوَاهُ ابْنُ أَبِي شَيْبَةَ. وَقَالَ الْعَسْقَلَانِيُّ: رَوَاهُ الْحَاكِمُ.

237/41. According to Jābir ﷺ:

---

236 Set forth by •Aḥmad b. Ḥanbal in *al-Musnad*, 6/8 §23909. •al-Haythamī in *Majmaʿ al-Zawāʾid*, 6/152. •al-Ṭabarī in *Tārīkh al-Umam wa al-Mulūk*, 2/137. •Ibn Hishām in *al-Sīrat al-Nabawiyya*, 4/306.

237 Set forth by •Ibn Abī Shayba in *al-Muṣannaf*, 6/374 §32139. •al-ʿAsqalānī in *Fatḥ al-Bārī*, 7/478. •al-Ṭabarī in *Tārīkh al-Umam wa al-Mulūk*, 2/137.

"ʿAlī ﷺ carried the gate on the Day of Khaybar, until the Muslims climbed up and conquered the fort. It was then tested that as many as forty men struggled jointly to lift that gate!"

Reported by Ibn Abī Shayba, and according to al-ʿAsqalānī, it was reported by al-Ḥākim.

٤٢/٢٣٨. عَنْ زَاذَانَ ﵁ أَنَّ عَلِيًّا ﵁ حَدَّثَ حَدِيثًا فَكَذَّبَهُ رَجُلٌ. فَقَالَ لَهُ عَلِيٌّ ﵁: أَدْعُوْ عَلَيْكَ إِنْ قُلْتَ كَاذِبًا. قَالَ: أُدْعُ فَدَعَا عَلَيْهِ فَلَمْ يَبْرَحْ حَتَّى ذَهَبَ بَصَرُهُ.

رَوَاهُ الطَّبَرَانِيُّ.

238/42. According to Zādān ﵁:

"ʿAlī ﷺ made a discourse and a man accused him of lying. So ʿAlī ﷺ said to him: 'I shall curse you if you are a liar!' The man said: 'Curse!' so he cursed him, and he did not even leave that assembly until he became blind."

Reported by al-Ṭabarānī.

٤٣/٢٣٩. عَنْ عَاصِمِ بْنِ ضَمْرَةَ ﵁ قَالَ: خَطَبَ الْحَسَنُ بْنُ عَلِيٍّ ﵄ حِيْنَ قُتِلَ عَلِيٌّ ﵁ فَقَالَ: يَا أَهْلَ الْكُوْفَةِ ـ أَوْ ـ يَا أَهْلَ الْعِرَاقِ، لَقَدْ كَانَ بَيْنَ أَظْهُرِكُمْ رَجُلٌ قُتِلَ اللَّيْلَةَ أَوْ أُصِيْبَ الْيَوْمَ؛ لَـمْ يَسْبِقْهُ الْأَوَّلُوْنَ بِعِلْمٍ وَلَا يُدْرِكُهُ الْآخَرُوْنَ؛ كَانَ النَّبِيُّ ﷺ إِذَا بَعَثَهُ فِي سَرِيَّةٍ كَانَ جِبْرِيْلُ ﵇ عَنْ يَمِيْنِهِ وَمِيْكَايِلُ ﵇ عَنْ يَسَارِهِ فَلَا يَرْجِعُ حَتَّى يَفْتَحَ اللهُ عَلَيْهِ.

رَوَاهُ ابْنُ أَبِي شَيْبَةَ.

239/43. According to ʿĀṣim b. Ḍamra ﵁:

•Ibn Hishām in al-Sīrat al-Nabawiyya, 4/306.

238 Set forth by •al-Ṭabarānī in al-Muʿjam al-Awsaṭ, 2/219 §1791. •al-Haythamī in Majmaʿ al-Zawāʾid, 9/116. •al-Lālakāʾī in Karāmāt al-Awliyāʾ, 1/126 §73.

239 Set forth by •Ibn Abī Shayba in al-Muṣannaf, 6/369 §32094. •al-Hindī

"ʿAlī's son Ḥasan ﵁ delivered a sermon when ʿAlī ﵁ was martyred. He said: 'O people of Kūfa! (or) O people of Iraq! A man amongst you has been martyred tonight or killed today whom the forerunners (of *Umma*) did not surpass in knowledge, and whom the latecomers will not be able to overtake. Whenever the Messenger of Allah ﷺ sent him to a war front, Gabriel ﵇ was on his right and Michael ﵇ was on his left, so he would never return until Allah granted him victory!'"

Reported by Ibn Abī Shayba.

٢٤٠/ ٤٤. عَنْ أُمِّ سَلْمَى ﵂ قَالَتْ: اشْتَكَتْ فَاطِمَةُ سلام الله عليها شَكْوَاهَا الَّتِي قُبِضَتْ فِيْهِ، فَكُنْتُ أُمَرِّضُهَا. فَأَصْبَحَتْ يَوْمًا كَأَمْثَلِ مَا رَأَيْتُهَا فِي شَكْوَاهَا تِلْكَ. قَالَتْ: وَخَرَجَ عَلِيٌّ ﵁ لِبَعْضِ حَاجَتِهِ، فَقَالَتْ: يَا أُمَّهْ، اسْكُبِي لِي غُسْلاً. فَسَكَبْتُ لَهَا غُسْلاً فَاغْتَسَلَتْ كَأَحْسَنِ مَا رَأَيْتُهَا تَغْتَسِلُ. ثُمَّ قَالَتْ: يَا أُمَّهْ، أَعْطِيْنِي ثِيَابِي الْجُدُدَ. فَأَعْطَيْتُهَا، فَلَبِسَتْهَا، ثُمَّ قَالَتْ: يَا أُمَّهْ، قَدِّمِي لِي فِرَاشِي وَسَطَ الْبَيْتِ. فَفَعَلْتُ وَاضْطَجَعَتْ وَاسْتَقْبَلَتِ الْقِبْلَةَ، وَجَعَلَتْ يَدَهَا تَحْتَ خَدِّهَا. ثُمَّ قَالَتْ: يَا أُمَّهْ، إِنِّي مَقْبُوْضَةٌ الآنَ، وَقَدْ تَطَهَّرْتُ فَلاَ يَكْشِفْنِي أَحَدٌ. فَقُبِضَتْ مَكَانَهَا. قَالَتْ: فَجَاءَ عَلِيٌّ ﵁ فَأَخْبَرْتُهُ.

رَوَاهُ أَحْمَدُ.

240/44. According to Umm Salmā ﵂:

"When Sayyida Fāṭima ﵂ had illness in which she departed this life, I used to nurse her. I think one morning she was as near to perfection as I ever saw her during the period of her ailment.

---

in *Kanz al-ʿUmmāl*, 6/412.

240 Set forth by •Aḥmad b. Ḥanbal in *al-Musnad*, 6/461 §27656–27657. •al-Dūlābī in *al-Dhurriyat al-Ṭāhira*, 1/113. •al-Zaylaʿī in *Naṣb al-Rāya*, 2/250. •*Muḥḥīb al-Dīn* in *Dhakhāʾir al-ʿUqbā*, 1/103. •al-Haythamī in *Majmaʿ al-Zawāʾid*, 9/210. •Ibn al-Athīr in *Usud al-Ghāba fī Maʿrifat al-Ṣaḥāba*, 7/221.

ʿAlī ﵁ went out to attend to some need of his, so she said: 'O Umm [Salmā], bring some bathwater for me!' I brought her some bathwater, and she performed the major ablution as well as I ever saw her perform it. Then she said: 'O Umm, bring me the new dress.' I obeyed. She put it on and then she said: 'O Umm, spread my mattress for me in the middle of the house!' I acted accordingly, and she lay down and turned towards the *Qibla* [the direction of prayer], placing her hand beneath her cheek. Then she said: 'O Umm, I will now pass away. I have purified myself (taking a bath), so no one should examine me,' and she died on the spot. Then ʿAlī ﵁ arrived, and I told him the whole thing."

Reported by Aḥmad.

٢٤١/ ٤٥. عَنْ عُمَارَةَ بْنِ عُمَيْرٍ ﵁ قَالَ: لَـمَّا جِيءَ بِرَأْسِ عُبَيْدِ اللهِ بْنِ زِيَادٍ وَأَصْحَابِهِ، نُضِّدَتْ فِي الْـمَسْجِدِ فِي الرَّحَبَةِ. فَانْتَهَيْتُ إِلَيْهِمْ وَهُمْ يَقُوْلُوْنَ: قَدْ جَاءَتْ قَدْ! جَاءَتْ! فَإِذَا حَيَّةٌ قَدْ جَاءَتْ تَخَلَّلُ الرُّؤُوْسَ حَتَّى دَخَلَتْ فِي مِنْخَرَي عُبَيْدِ اللهِ بْنِ زِيَادٍ فَمَكَثَتْ هُنَيْهَةً ثُمَّ خَرَجَتْ فَذَهَبَتْ حَتَّى تَغَيَّبَتْ. ثُمَّ قَالُوْا: قَدْ جَاءَتْ! قَدْ جَاءَتْ! فَفَعَلَتْ ذَلِكَ مَرَّتَيْنِ أَوْ ثَلَاثًا.

رَوَاهُ التِّرْمِذِيُّ وَالطَّبَرَانِيُّ، وَقَالَ أَبُوْ عِيْسَى: هَذَا حَدِيْثٌ حَسَنٌ صَحِيْحٌ.

241/45. According to ʿUmāra b. ʿUmayr ﵁:

"When the head of ʿUbayd Allāh b. Ziyād (the assassin of Imam Ḥusayn) and the heads of his companions were brought, they were arrayed in the mosque, in the veranda. I eventually reached them when they were saying: 'It has come! It has come!' Lo and behold, a snake had come and penetrated the heads, until it entered the nostrils of ʿUbayd Allāh b. Ziyād and stayed there. Then it came

---

241 Set forth by •al-Tirmidhī in *al-Sunan*: Bk.: *al-Manāqib* [Virtues], Ch.: The virtues of al-Ḥasan and al-Ḥusayn ﵄, 5/660 §3780. •al-Ṭabarānī in *al-Muʿjam al-Kabīr*, 3/112 §2832. •al-Mubārakfūrī in *Tuḥfat al-Aḥwadhī*, 10/193.

out and went away until it disappeared. Then they said: ‘It has come! It has come!’ It did that twice or thrice.”

Reported by al-Tirmidhī and al-Ṭabarānī. Abū ʿĪsā said: “This is a fine authentic tradition.”

٢٤٢/ ٤٦. عَنْ قُرَّةَ بْنِ خَالِدٍ قَالَ: سَمِعْتُ أَبَا رَجَاءٍ الْعَطَارِدِيَّ ﵀ يَقُوْلُ: لاَ تَسُبُّوْا عَلِيًّا ﵇ وَلاَ أَهْلَ هَذَا الْبَيْتِ فَإِنَّ جَارًا لَنَا مِنْ بِلْهَجِيْمِ قَالَ: أَلَمْ تَرَوْا إِلَى هَذَا الْفَاسِقِ الْحُسَيْنِ بْنِ عَلِيٍّ قَتَلَهُ اللهُ. فَرَمَاهُ اللهُ بِكَوْكَبَيْنِ فِي عَيْنَيْهِ فَطَمَسَ اللهُ بَصَرَهُ.

رَوَاهُ الطَّبَرَانِيُّ؛ إِسْنَادُهُ حَسَنٌ وَرِجَالُهُ رِجَالُ الصَّحِيْحِ.

242/46. According to Qurra b. Khālid:

“I heard Abū Rajāʾ al-ʿAṭāridī ﵀ say: ‘You must not vilify ʿAlī ﵇, nor the people of the household (of Allah’s Messenger ﷺ), for a neighbour of ours from Bilhajīm said: “Have you not considered this (God forbid!) profligate, Ḥusayn b. ʿAlī ﵇? Allah has killed him!” Allah then hit him [that vilifier] with two stars (from the sky) in his eyes, and obliterated his sight!’”

Reported by al-Ṭabarānī, with a fine chain of transmission. And its narrators are authentic.

٢٤٣/ ٤٧. عَنْ خَيْثَمَةَ ﵀ قَالَ: أُتِيَ خَالِدُ بْنُ الْوَلِيْدِ ﵁ بِرَجُلٍ وَمَعَهُ زِقُّ خَمْرٍ. فَقَالَ: اَللَّهُمَّ، اجْعَلْهُ عَسَلاً، فَصَارَ عَسَلاً.

وَفِي رِوَايَةٍ: لَـمَّا قَدِمَ خَالِدُ بْنُ الْوَلِيْدِ الْحِرَّةَ، أُتِيَ بِسُمٍّ فَوَضَعَهُ فِي رَاحَتِهِ ثُمَّ سَمَّى وَشَرِبَهُ.

رَوَاهُ اللاَّلَكَائِيُّ وَالذَّهَبِيُّ وَالْعَسْقَلاَنِيُّ. وَقَالَ: رَوَاهُ أَبُوْ يَعْلَى وَابْنُ سَعْدٍ وَابْنُ أَبِي الدُّنْيَا بِإِسْنَادٍ صَحِيْحٍ.

---

242 Set forth by •al-Ṭabarānī in *al-Muʿjam al-Kabīr*, 3/112 §2830. •al-Haythamī in *Majmaʿ al-Zawāʾid*, 9/196. He said: “Its sources are authentic.”

243/47. According to Ḥaythama ﵁:

"Khālid b. al-Walīd ﵁ was brought a man who had a jar of wine with him. He said: 'O Allah, turn it into honey!' It thereupon became honey."

In one report: "When Khālid b. al-Walīd reached Ḥarrā, he was brought some poison, so he put it in the palm of his hand, then invoked the Name of Allah and drank it. (The poison proved absolutely ineffective.)"

> Reported by al-Lālakā'ī, al-Dhahabī and al-ʿAsqalānī. He also said: "It has been reported by Abū Yaʿlā, Ibn Saʿd and Ibn Abī al-Dunyā, with an authentic chain of transmission."

٢٤٤/٤٨. عَنْ أَبِي خَلْدَةَ قَالَ: قُلْتُ لِأَبِي الْعَالِيَةِ: سَمِعَ أَنَسٌ ﵁ مِنَ النَّبِيِّ ﷺ؟ قَالَ: خَدَمَهُ عَشْرَ سِنِينَ وَدَعَا لَهُ النَّبِيُّ ﷺ وَكَانَ لَهُ بُسْتَانٌ يَحْمِلُ فِي السَّنَةِ الْفَاكِهَةَ مَرَّتَيْنِ، وَكَانَ فِيهَا رَيْحَانٌ؛ كَانَ يَجِيءُ مِنْهُ رِيحُ الْمِسْكِ.

رَوَاهُ التِّرْمِذِيُّ وَقَالَ: هَذَا حَدِيثٌ حَسَنٌ.

244/48. According to Abū Khalda ﵁:

"I said to Abū al-ʿĀliya: 'Has Anas ﵁ heard traditions from the Prophet ﷺ?' He said: 'He served him for ten years, and the Prophet ﷺ supplicated on his behalf so the orchard he had used to bear fruit twice a year. And it contained sweet basil which used to smell the scent of musk.'"

> Reported by al-Tirmidhī and he said: "This is a fine tradition."

---

243 Set forth by •Abū al-Qāsim Hibat Allāh in *Karāmāt al-Awliyā'*, 2/254 §94–97. •al-Dhahabī in *Siyar Aʿlām al-Nubalā'*, 1/375–376. •al-ʿAsqalānī in *al-Iṣāba*, 2/254. •al-Rāzī in *al-Tafsīr al-Kabīr*, 21/89.

244 Set forth by •al-Tirmidhī in *al-Sunan*: Bk.: *al-Manāqib* [Virtues] according to Allah's Messenger ﷺ, Ch.: The virtues of Anas b. Mālik ﵁, 5/683 §3833. •al-Dhahabī in *Siyar Aʿlām al-Nubalā'*, 3/400. •al-ʿAsqalānī in *al-Iṣāba*, 1/127. •al-Khaṭīb al-Tabrīzī in *Mishkāt al-Maṣābīḥ*, 2/401 §5952.

٢٤٥/ ٤٩. عَنْ أَبِي هُرَيْرَةَ ﵁ في رواية طويلة وَكَانَ خُبَيْبٌ هُوَ قَتَلَ الْحَارِثَ يَوْمَ بَدْرٍ، فَمَكَثَ عِنْدَهُمْ أَسِيْرًا... وَكَانَتْ تَقُوْلُ مِنْ بَعْضِ بَنَاتِ الْحَارِثِ: مَا رَأَيْتُ أَسِيْرًا قَطُّ خَيْرًا مِنْ خُبَيْبٍ. لَقَدْ رَأَيْتُهُ يَأْكُلُ مِنْ قِطْفِ عِنَبٍ وَمَا بِمَكَّةَ يَوْمَئِذٍ ثَمَرَةٌ، وَإِنَّهُ لَمُوْثَقٌ فِي الْحَدِيْدِ، وَمَا كَانَ رِزْقٌ إِلاَّ رَزَقَهُ اللهُ.

رَوَاهُ الْبُخَارِيُّ وَأَحْمَدُ.

245/49. According to Abū Hurayra ﵁, in the course of a detailed report:

"Khubayb was the one who killed al-Ḥārith (a chieftain of Quraysh) on the Day of Badr. (Later) he (was caught in an episode and) remained in their custody as a prisoner of war.... One of al-Ḥārith's daughters used to say: 'I have never seen a prisoner better than Khubayb. I once saw him eating bunches of grapes, when there was no fruit in Mecca at the time (it was not the season of fruits) and he was fettered in iron too. So this was the sustenance Allah used to provide (from the unseen).'"

Reported by al-Bukhārī and Aḥmad.

٢٤٦/ ٥٠. عَنْ أَبِي هُرَيْرَةَ ﵁ في رواية طويلة وَبَعَثَ قُرَيْشٌ إِلَى عَاصِمٍ لِيُؤْتُوْا بِشَيْءٍ مِنْ جَسَدِهِ يَعْرِفُوْنَهُ وَكَانَ عَاصِمٌ قَتَلَ عَظِيْمًا مِنْ عُظَمَائِهِمْ يَوْمَ بَدْرٍ. فَبَعَثَ اللهُ عَلَيْهِ مِثْلَ الظُّلَّةِ مِنَ الدَّبْرِ، فَحَمَتْهُ مِنْ رُسُلِهِمْ فَلَمْ يَقْدِرُوْا مِنْهُ عَلَى شَيْءٍ.

---

245 Set forth by •al-Bukhārī in *al-Ṣaḥīḥ*: Bk.: *al-Maghāzī* [Military Expeditions], Ch.: The campaigns of al-Rajīʿ, Riʿl, Dhakawān and Biʾr Maʿūna, 4/1499 §3858, & Bk.: *al-Jihād* [The Sacred Struggle], Ch.: Whether the man should give himself up as a prisoner, someone who does not give himself up as a prisoner, and someone who performs two cycles of ritual prayer at the time of killing, 3/1108 §2880. •Aḥmad b. Ḥanbal in *al-Musnad*, 2/310 §8082. •ʿAbd al-Razzāq in *al-Muṣannaf*, 5/353 §9730. •al-Ṭabarānī in *al-Muʿjam al-Kabīr*, 4/221 §4191. •Abū al-Qāsim Hibat Allāh in *Karāmāt al-Awliyāʾ*, 1/101 §53. •al-ʿAsqalānī in *Fatḥ al-Bārī*, 7/384. •Ibn ʿAbd al-Barr in *al-Istīʿāb*, 2/779 §1305. •al-Ṭabarī in *Tārīkh al-Umam wa al-Mulūk*, 2/78.

رَوَاهُ الْبُخَارِيُّ وَأَحْمَدُ.

246/50. According to Abū Hurayra ﷺ, in the course of a detailed report:

"(After slaying him by deceit,) the Quraysh sent a few militants to ʿĀṣim's dead body in order to bring some portion of his corpse for recognition. The venerable ʿĀṣim ﷺ had killed one of their noblemen on the Day of Badr. Allah therefore bestowed upon him shelter from the rear in the form of a swarm of bees. It protected him from their agents (and allowed none even to get closer to him). They could not do anything to his body."

Reported by al-Bukhārī and Aḥmad.

٢٤٧/ ٥١. عَنْ جَابِرٍ ﷺ قَالَ: لَمَّا حَضَرَ أُحُدٌ، دَعَانِي أَبِي مِنَ اللَّيْلِ، فَقَالَ: مَا أُرَانِي إِلَّا مَقْتُوْلاً فِي أَوَّلِ مَنْ يُقْتَلُ مِنْ أَصْحَابِ النَّبِيِّ ﷺ، وَإِنِّي لَا أَتْرُكُ بَعْدِي أَعَزَّ عَلَيَّ مِنْكَ غَيْرَ نَفْسِ رَسُوْلِ اللهِ ﷺ. فَإِنَّ عَلَيَّ دَيْنًا، فَاقْضِ، وَاسْتَوْصِ بِأَخَوَاتِكَ خَيْرًا. فَأَصْبَحْنَا، فَكَانَ أَوَّلَ قَتِيْلٍ، وَدُفِنَ مَعَهُ آخَرُ فِي قَبْرٍ، ثُمَّ لَمْ تَطِبْ نَفْسِي أَنْ أَتْرُكَهُ مَعَ الْآخَرِ، فَاسْتَخْرَجْتُهُ بَعْدَ سِتَّةِ أَشْهُرٍ، فَإِذَا هُوَ كَيَوْمِ وَضَعْتُهُ هُنَيَّةً، غَيْرَ أُذُنِهِ.

رَوَاهُ الْبُخَارِيُّ، وَقَالَ الْحَاكِمُ: هَذَا حَدِيْثٌ صَحِيْحٌ عَلَى شَرْطِ مُسْلِمٍ.

247/51. According to Jābir ﷺ:

---

246 Set forth by •al-Bukhārī in *al-Ṣaḥīḥ*: Bk.: *al-Maghāzī* [Military Expeditions], Ch.: The campaigns of al-Rajīʿ, Riʿl, Dhakawān and Biʾr Maʿūna, 4/1499 §3858, & Bk.: *al-Jihād* [The Sacred Struggle], Ch.: Whether the man should give himself up as a prisoner, someone who does not give himself up as a prisoner, and someone who performs two cycles of ritual prayer at the time of killing, 3/1108 §2880. •Aḥmad b. Ḥanbal in *al-Musnad*, 2/310 §8082. •ʿAbd al-Razzāq in *al-Muṣannaf*, 5/353 §9730. •al-Ṭabarānī in *al-Muʿjam al-Kabīr*, 4/221 §4191. •Abū al-Qāsim Hibat Allāh in *Karāmāt al-Awliyāʾ*, 1/101 §53.

247 Set forth by •al-Bukhārī in *al-Ṣaḥīḥ*: *al-Janāʾiz* [Funeral Ceremonies], Ch.: Whether the corpse should be removed from the grave and the tomb because of a reason, 1/453 §1286. •al-Ḥākim in *al-Mustadrak*, 3/224

"When time for the battle of Uḥud came, my father called me at night, and said: 'I do not see myself except as someone killed as the first of the Companions of the Prophet ﷺ to be killed. I am leaving no one after me who is dearer to me than you, apart from Allah's Messenger ﷺ. I owe a debt, so you must settle it, and you must behave nicely with your sisters.' Then we entered the morning, and he was the first one to be martyred and was buried with another (martyr), but I did not feel happy about leaving him with the other, so I excavated him after six months, and lo and behold, he was almost as he was on the day when I laid him to rest, apart from his ear (that was wounded while fighting)!'"

Reported by al-Bukhārī. According to al-Ḥākim: "This is an authentic tradition in conformity with the stipulation of Muslim."

٢٤٨/ ٥٢. عَنْ أَنَسٍ رضي الله عنه أَنَّ رَجُلَيْنِ خَرَجَا مِنْ عِنْدِ النَّبِيِّ ﷺ فِي لَيْلَةٍ مُظْلِمَةٍ، وَإِذَا نُوْرٌ بَيْنَ أَيْدِيْهِمَا حَتَّى تَفَرَّقَا فَتَفَرَّقَ النُّوْرُ مَعَهُمَا.

عَنْ أَنَسٍ رضي الله عنه كَانَ أُسَيْدُ بْنُ حُضَيْرٍ وَعَبَّادُ بْنُ بِشْرٍ عِنْدَ النَّبِيِّ ﷺ.

رَوَاهُ الْبُخَارِيُّ وَأَبُوْ يَعْلَى.

248/52. According to Anas رضي الله عنه:

§4913. •al-Bayhaqī in *al-Sunan al-Kubrā*, 6/285 §12459, •al-ʿAsqalānī in *Muqaddima Fatḥ al-Bārī*, 1/270. •al-Khaṭīb al-Tabrīzī in *Mishkāt al-Maṣābīḥ*, 2/399 §5945.

[248] Set forth by •al-Bukhārī in *al-Ṣaḥīḥ*: Chs.: *al- Masājid* [The Mosques], Ch.: Installing the camel in the mosque because of a reason, 1/177 §453, & Bk.: *al-Manāqib* [Virtues], Ch.: The polytheists' asking the Prophet ﷺ to show them a miraculous sign, so he showed them the splitting of the moon, 3/1331 §3440, & Bk.: *Faḍā'il al-Ṣaḥāba* [The Excellent Merits of the Companions], Ch.: The virtue of Asyad b. Ḥuḍayr and ʿAbbād b. Bishr رضي الله عنهما, 3/1384 §3594. •Abū Yaʿlā in *al-Musnad*, 5/361 §3007. •al-Bayhaqī in *al-Iʿtiqād*, 1/310. •al-Nawawī in *Riyāḍ al-Ṣāliḥīn*, 1/566 §1506. •al-Khaṭīb al-Tabrīzī in *Mishkāt al-Maṣābīḥ*, 2/399 §5944.

"Two men from among the Companions of the Prophet ﷺ went out from the presence of the Prophet ﷺ (to go home after the session was over). It was a murky night. (On the way back home) a light appeared in front of them suddenly (illumining their path). When they both got apart (in different directions towards their respective homes), the light also split into two accompanying both of them."

According to Anas ﷺ: "These two companions were Usayd b. Ḥuḍayr and ʿAbbād b. Bishr."

Reported by al-Bukhārī and Abū Yaʿlā.

٢٤٩/ ٥٣. عَنْ عَائِشَةَ رضي الله عنها قَالَتْ: لَـمَّا مَاتَ النَّجَاشِيُّ، كُنَّا نَتَحَدَّثُ أَنَّهُ لاَ يَزَالُ يُرَى عَلَى قَبْرِهِ نُورٌ.

رَوَاهُ أَبُو دَاوُدَ.

249/53. According to ʿĀʾisha ﷺ:

"When al-Najāshī (the King of Abyssinia) died, we were saying that a light would not cease to be seen on his tomb."

Reported by Abū Dāwūd.

٢٥٠/ ٥٤. عَنْ سَفِينَةَ رضي الله عنه قَالَ: رَكِبْتُ الْبَحْرَ فِي سَفِيْنَةٍ فَانْكَسَرَتْ فَرَكِبْتُ لَوْحًا مِنْهَا فَطَرَحَنِي فِي أَجَمَةٍ فِيْهَا أَسَدٌ فَلَمْ يَرُعْنِي إِلاَّ بِهِ فَقُلْتُ: يَا أَبَا الْحَارِثِ، أَنَا مَوْلَى رَسُوْلِ اللهِ ﷺ. فَطَأْطَأَ رَأْسَهُ وَغَمَزَ بِمَنْكَبِهِ شِقِّي. فَمَا زَالَ يَغْمِزُنِي وَيَهْدِيْنِي إِلَى الطَّرِيْقِ حَتَّى وَضَعَنِي عَلَى الطَّرِيْقِ. فَلَـمَّا وَضَعَنِي هَمْهَمَ فَظَنَنْتُ أَنَّهُ يُوَدِّعُنِي.

رَوَاهُ الْحَاكِمُ وَالْبُخَارِيُّ فِي الْكَبِيْرِ وَالطَّبَرَانِيُّ وَالْبَغَوِيُّ فِي شَرْحِ السُّنَّةِ. وَقَالَ الْحَاكِمُ: هَذَا حَدِيْثٌ صَحِيْحُ الإِسْنَادِ.

---

249 Set forth by •Abū Dāwūd in *al-Sunan*: Bk.: *al-Jihād* [The Sacred Struggle], Ch.: Light is seen beside the grave of the martyr, 3/16 §2523. •al-Dhahabī in *Siyar Aʿlām al-Nubalāʾ*, 1/430. •al-ʿAsqalānī in *al-Iṣāba*, 1/206. •al-Khaṭīb al-Tabrīzī in *Mishkāt al-Maṣābīḥ*, 2/400 §5949.

250/54. According to Safīna ﷺ:

"I boarded a ship in the sea but it broke up, so I floated on a plank detached from it. It landed me at a place which was a den of a lion. Then the same happened as I feared: the lion was right in front of me. (I had no means of self-protection) so I said: 'O Abū al-Ḥārith,* I am the slave of Allah's Messenger ﷺ!' The lion lowered his head and pressed my side with his shoulder, then he kept pressing me and guiding me towards the road, until he set me down on the road. Then, when he set me down, he growled, so I assumed that he was bidding me farewell!'"

Reported by al-Ḥākim, al-Bukhārī in *al-Kabīr*, al-Ṭabarānī, and al-Baghwī in *Sharḥ al-Sunna*. According to al-Ḥākim: "This is a tradition with an authentic chain of transmission."

٢٥١/ ٥٥. عَنِ ابْنِ عُمَرَ رضي الله عنهما عَنْ رَسُوْلِ اللهِ ﷺ قَالَ: هٰذَا الَّذِي تَحَرَّكَ لَهُ الْعَرْشُ، وَفُتِحَتْ لَهُ أَبْوَابُ السَّمَاءِ، وَشَهِدَهُ سَبْعُوْنَ أَلْفًا مِنَ الْمَلَائِكَةِ. لَقَدْ ضُمَّ ضَمَّةً ثُمَّ فُرِّجَ عَنْهُ.

وفي رواية: قَالَ: اَلْحَمْدُ لِلّٰهِ، لَوْ نَجَا أَحَدٌ مِنْ ضُمَّةِ الْقَبْرِ، لَنَجَا مِنْهَا سَعْدُ بْنُ مُعَاذٍ رضي الله عنه.

رَوَاهُ النَّسَائِيُّ وَالطَّبَرَانِيُّ. وَقَالَ الْعَسْقَلَانِيُّ: وَرِجَالُهُ ثِقَاتٌ مُحْتَجٌّ بِهِمْ فِي الصَّحِيْحِ.

251/55. According to Ibn ʿUmar ﷺ:

---

250 Set forth by •al-Ḥākim in *al-Mustadrak*, 2/675 §4235; 3/702 §6550. •al-Bukhārī in *al-Tārīkh al-Kabīr*, 3/195 §663. •al-Ṭabarānī in *al-Muʿjam al-Kabīr*, 7/80 §6432. •Ibn Rāshid in *al-Jāmiʿ*, 11/281. •Abū al-Qāsim Hibat Allāh in *Karāmāt al-Awliyā'*, 1/158 §114. •al-Baghawī in *Sharḥ al-Sunna*, 13/313 §3732. •al-Khaṭīb al-Tabrīzī in *Mishkāt al-Maṣābīḥ*, 2/400 §5949.

* The lion is called Abū al-Ḥārith by the Arabs, because he is the prince of the beasts of prey.

251 Set forth by •al-Nasā'ī in *al-Sunan*: Bk.: *al-Janā'iz* [Funeral Ceremonies],

"Allah's Messenger ﷺ said: 'This (Saʿd b. Muʿādh al-Anṣārī) is the one whose death moved the Throne, for whom the gates of heaven were opened, and for whom seventy thousand angels performed the funeral ritual prayer. The grave subjected him to severe constraint but only once and then it was widened.'"

In one report: "He said: 'Praise be to Allah! If anyone were to be delivered from the pressing of the grave, Saʿd b. Muʿādh would be delivered from it (pressing by the grave is soothing for the believers and the pious; it is a motherly embrace)!'"

> Reported by al-Nasāʾī and al-Ṭabarānī. According to al-ʿAsqalānī: "Its sources are reliable as evidence of its authenticity."

٢٥٢/ ٥٦. عَنِ ابْنِ عَبَّاسٍ ﵄ قَالَ: ضَرَبَ بَعْضُ أَصْحَابِ النَّبِيِّ ﷺ خِبَاءَهُ عَلَى قَبْرٍ وَهُوَ لَا يَحْسِبُ أَنَّهُ قَبْرٌ، فَإِذَا فِيهِ إِنْسَانٌ يَقْرَأُ سُورَةَ تَبَارَكَ الَّذِي بِيَدِهِ الْمُلْكُ حَتَّى خَتَمَهَا، فَأَتَى النَّبِيَّ ﷺ فَقَالَ: يَا رَسُوْلَ اللهِ، إِنِّي ضَرَبْتُ خِبَائِي عَلَى قَبْرٍ وَأَنَا لَا أَحْسِبُ أَنَّهُ قَبْرٌ، فَإِذَا فِيهِ إِنْسَانٌ يَقْرَأُ سُوْرَةَ الْمُلْكِ حَتَّى خَتَمَهَا. فَقَالَ رَسُوْلُ اللهِ ﷺ: هِيَ الْمَانِعَةُ، هِيَ الْمُنْجِيَةُ، تُنْجِيهِ مِنْ عَذَابِ الْقَبْرِ.

رَوَاهُ التِّرْمِذِيُّ وَالْبَيْهَقِيُّ. وَقَالَ أَبُوْ عِيْسَى: هَذَا حَدِيْثٌ حَسَنٌ.

252/56. According to Ibn ʿAbbās ﵄:

Ch.: The pressing of the grave, 4/100 §2055, & in *al-Sunan al-Kubrā*, 1/660 §8182. •al-Ṭabarānī in *al-Muʿjam al-Awsaṭ*, 2/199 §1707, & in *al-Muʿjam al-Kabīr*, 6/10 §5333. •Ibn Rāhawayh likewise in *al-Musnad*, 2/552 §1127. •al-Zaylaʿī in *Naṣb al-Rāya*, 2/286. •al-Suyūṭī in *Sharḥ ʿalā Sunan al-Nasāʾī*, 4/101 §2055. •al-ʿAsqalānī in *al-Qawl al-Musaddad*, 1/81.

[252] Set forth by •al-Tirmidhī in *al-Sunan*: Bk.: *Faḍāʾil al-Qurʾān* [The Excellent Merits of the Qurʾān] according to Allah's Messenger ﷺ, Ch.: What has come to us about the excellence of *Sūrat al-Mulk*, 5/164 §2890. •al-Bayhaqī in *Shuʿab al-Īmān*, 2/495 §2510. •al-Mundhirī in *al-Targhīb wa al-Tarhīb*, 2/247 §2266. •al-Qurṭubī in *al-Jāmiʿ li-Aḥkām al-Qurʾān*, 18/205. •Ibn Kathīr in *Tafsīr al-Qurʾān al-ʿAẓīm*, 4/396. •al-Khaṭīb al-Tabrīzī in *Mishkāt al-Maṣābīḥ*: Bk.: *Faḍāʾil al-Qurʾān* [The Excellent Merits of the

"One of the Companions of the Prophet ﷺ pitched his tent on a grave, though he had no idea that it was a grave. Then he suddenly heard a person inside it, reciting *Sūra al-Mulk* (Q.61): 'Blessed is He in whose Hand is the Sovereignty *[tabāraka ʾlladhī bi-yadi-hī al-mulk]...*' through to the end, so he went to the Prophet ﷺ and said: 'O Messenger of Allah, I pitched my tent on a grave (unintentionally), and I had no idea that it was a grave. Then suddenly I heard a person inside it, reciting the *Sūra of Sovereignty [Sūrat al-Mulk]* from beginning to end!' Allah's Messenger ﷺ said: 'It is the preventive; it is the saviour that saves him from the torment of the grave!'"

Reported by al-Tirmidhī and al-Bayhaqī. Abū ʿĪsā said: "This is a fine tradition."

Qurʾān], second section, 1/405 §2153.

اَلْبَابُ الرَّابِعُ

شَرَفُ هَذِهِ الْأُمَّةِ

Chapter 4

The Nobility of this *Umma*

اَلْفَصْلُ الْأَوَّلُ

فَصْلٌ فِي شَرَفِ الْأُمَّةِ الْمُحَمَّدِيَّةِ

SECTION 1
THE NOBILITY OF MUHAMMAD'S *UMMA*

١/٢٥٣. عَنِ ابْنِ عَبَّاسٍ رضي الله عنهما قَالَ: قَالَ النَّبِيُّ ﷺ: عُرِضَتْ عَلَيَّ الْأُمَمُ، فَأَجِدُ النَّبِيَّ يَمُرُّ مَعَهُ الْأُمَّةُ، وَالنَّبِيُّ يَمُرُّ مَعَهُ النَّفَرُ، وَالنَّبِيُّ يَمُرُّ مَعَهُ الْعَشَرَةُ، وَالنَّبِيُّ يَمُرُّ مَعَهُ الْخَمْسَةُ، وَالنَّبِيُّ يَمُرُّ وَحْدَهُ. فَنَظَرْتُ فَإِذَا سَوَادٌ كَثِيْرٌ، قُلْتُ: يَا جِبْرِيْلُ، هَؤُلَاءِ أُمَّتِي؟ قَالَ: لَا، وَلَكِنِ انْظُرْ إِلَى الْأُفُقِ. فَنَظَرْتُ فَإِذَا سَوَادٌ كَثِيْرٌ. قَالَ: هَؤُلَاءِ أُمَّتُكَ، وَهَؤُلَاءِ سَبْعُوْنَ أَلْفًا قُدَّامَهُمْ لَا حِسَابَ عَلَيْهِمْ وَلَا عَذَابَ. قُلْتُ: وَلِمَ؟ قَالَ: كَانُوْا لَا يَكْتَوُوْنَ وَلَا يَسْتَرْقُوْنَ. وَلَا يَتَطَيَّرُوْنَ وَعَلَى رَبِّهِمْ يَتَوَكَّلُوْنَ.

فَقَامَ إِلَيْهِ عُكَّاشَةُ بْنُ مِحْصَنٍ فَقَالَ: ادْعُ اللهَ أَنْ يَجْعَلَنِي مِنْهُمْ. قَالَ: اَللَّهُمَّ، اجْعَلْهُ مِنْهُمْ. ثُمَّ قَامَ إِلَيْهِ رَجُلٌ آخَرُ قَالَ: ادْعُ اللهَ أَنْ يَجْعَلَنِي مِنْهُمْ. قَالَ: سَبَقَكَ بِهَا عُكَّاشَةُ.

مُتَّفَقٌ عَلَيْهِ.

253/1. According to Ibn ʿAbbās رضي الله عنهما:

---

253 Set forth by •al-Bukhārī in *al-Ṣaḥīḥ*: Bk.: The Softening of Hearts [*al-Riqāq*], Ch: Seventy thousand will enter the Garden of Paradise without reckoning, 5/2396 §6175, & in *al-Ṣaḥīḥ*: Bk.: Medicine [*al-Ṭibb*], Ch.: Someone who is cauterized or cauterizes another person, 5/2157 §5378, & in *al-Ṣaḥīḥ*: Bk.: Medicine [*al-Ṭibb*], Ch.: Someone who does not use magic, 5/2170 §5420, & in Bk.: The Prophets [*al-Anbiyāʾ*], Ch.: The death of Moses, and his subsequent remembrance, 3/1251 §3229. •Muslim in *al-Ṣaḥīḥ*: Bk.: Faith [*al-Īmān*], Ch.: Evidence of the entry of groups of the Muslims into the Garden of Paradise, without reckoning and without punishment, 1/179–

"The Prophet said: '(All) the religious communities were shown to me. So I would find a Prophet passing by along with his *Umma* (Community). Then anoher Prophet passed with only a few people with him. Then there were still others passing by, one had ten people with him and another five and yet another was all by himself. I looked, therefore, and lo and behold, there was a great multitude! I said: "O Gabriel, are these my people?" He said: "No, but look towards the horizon!" I looked, therefore, and lo and behold, there was a great multitude! He said: "These are your *Umma* (Community), and these seventy thousand ahead of them will face neither reckoning nor torment." I said: "Why?" He said: "They were not given to branding themselves, nor seeking unlawful magical (and superstitious) cures, nor taking evil omen, and they placed (perfect) trust in their Lord."'

"ʿUkkāsha b. Miḥṣan then stood up and said: '(O Messenger of Allah,) beseech Allah to include me among them!' He said: 'O Allah, include him among them!' Then another man stood up and submitted: 'Beseech Allah to include me too among them!' He said: ʿUkkāsha has surpassed you!'"

Agreed upon by al-Bukhārī and Muslim.

٢٥٤/ ٢. عَنْ عَبْدِ اللهِ رضي الله عنه قَالَ: كُنَّا مَعَ النَّبِيِّ ﷺ فِي قُبَّةٍ، فَقَالَ: أَتَرْضَوْنَ أَنْ تَكُوْنُوْا ثُلُثَ أَهْلِ الْجَنَّةِ؟ قُلْنَا: نَعَمْ. قَالَ: وَالَّذِي نَفْسُ مُحَمَّدٍ بِيَدِهِ، إِنِّي لَأَرْجُوْ أَنْ تَكُوْنُوْا نِصْفَ أَهْلِ الْجَنَّةِ، وَذَلِكَ أَنَّ الْجَنَّةَ لَا يَدْخُلُهَا إِلَّا نَفْسٌ مُسْلِمَةٌ، وَمَا أَنْتُمْ فِي أَهْلِ الشِّرْكِ إِلَّا كَالشَّعْرَةِ الْبَيْضَاءِ فِي جِلْدِ الثَّوْرِ الْأَسْوَدِ، أَوْ كَالشَّعْرَةِ السَّوْدَاءِ فِي جِلْدِ الثَّوْرِ الْأَحْمَرِ.

---

199 §216–220. •al-Tirmidhī in *al-Sunan*: Bk.: The attributes of the Day of Resurrection, the softening of hearts and Godwariness, according to Allah's Messenger, Ch.: (16) 4/631 §2446. •al-Nasāʾī in *al-Sunan al-Kubrā*, 4/378 §7604. •Ibn Ḥibbān in *al-Ṣaḥīḥ*, 13/447–448 §6084, 6430. •al-Dārimī in *al-Sunan*, 2/422 §2807. •Aḥmad b. Ḥanbal in *al-Musnad*, 1/271 §2448. •Abū Yaʿlā in *al-Musnad*, 9/233 §5340. •al-Ṭabarānī in *al-Muʿjam al-Kabīr*, 18/241 §605.

مُتَّفَقٌ عَلَيْهِ.

254/2. According to ʿAbd Allāh ﵁:

"We were together with the Prophet ﷺ in a pavilion, so he said: 'Would you be content with being one-third of the people of the Garden of Paradise?' When we said: 'Yes,' he said: 'By the One in whose Hand the soul of Muhammad is, I do hope that you will be half of the people of the Garden of Paradise! That is to say, no one will enter the Garden of Paradise except a Muslim, and in the midst of the people of polytheism you are just like the white hair in the hide of the black bull, or like the black hair in the hide of the red bull!'"

Agreed upon by al-Bukhārī and Muslim.

٣/٢٥٥. عَنْ سُلَيْمَانَ بْنِ بُرَيْدَةَ ﵄ عَنْ أَبِيْهِ، قَالَ: قَالَ رَسُوْلُ اللهِ ﷺ: أَهْلُ الْجَنَّةِ عِشْرُوْنَ وَمِائَةُ صَفٍّ. ثَمَانُوْنَ مِنْهَا مِنْ هَذِهِ الْأُمَّةِ، وَأَرْبَعُوْنَ مِنْ سَائِرِ الْأُمَمِ.

رَوَاهُ التِّرْمِذِيُّ وَابْنُ مَاجَه. وَقَالَ أَبُوْ عِيْسَى: هَذَا حَدِيْثٌ حَسَنٌ. وَقَالَ الْحَاكِمُ: هَذَا حَدِيْثٌ صَحِيْحٌ.

255/3. According to Sulaymān b. Burayda ﵄, his father said:

---

[254] Set forth by •al-Bukhārī in *al-Ṣaḥīḥ*, Bk.: *al-Riqāq* [The Softening of Hearts], Ch.: The manner of the gathering [at the Resurrection], 5/2392 §6163, & Bk.: *al-Aymān wa al-Nudhūr* [Oaths and Vows], Ch.: The manner of the oath of the Prophet ﷺ, 6/2448 §6266. •Muslim in *al-Ṣaḥīḥ*: Bk.: *al-Īmān* [Faith], Ch.: The fact that this *Umma* (Community) constitutes half of the inhabitants of the Garden of Paradise, 1/200 §221. •al-Tirmidhī in *al-Sunan*: Bk.: The quality of the Garden of Paradise, according to Allah's Messenger ﷺ, Ch.: What has come to us concerning the rank of the inhabitants of the Garden of Paradise, 4/684 §2547. He said: "This is a fine authentic tradition." •Ibn Mājah in *al-Sunan*: Bk.: *al-Zuhd* [Abstinence], Ch.: The quality of the *Umma* (Community) of Muhammad ﷺ, 2/1432 §4283. •al-Nasāʾī in *al-Sunan al-Kubrā*, 6/409 §11339. •Aḥmad b. Ḥanbal in *al-Musnad*, 1/386 §3661. •al-Bazzār in *al-Musnad*, 5/237 §1850.

[255] Set forth by •al-Tirmidhī in *al-Sunan*: Bk.: The Quality of the Garden of Paradise, according to Allah's Messenger ﷺ, Ch.: What has come to us

"Allah's Messenger ﷺ said: 'The people of the Garden of Paradise are a hundred and twenty rows, eighty of them from my *Umma* (Community) and forty from the other communities.'"

Reported by al-Tirmidhī and Ibn Mājah. Abū ʿĪsā said: "This is a fine tradition," and al-Ḥākim said: "This is an authentic tradition."

٢٥٦/ ٤. عَنْ عُمَرَ بْنِ الْخَطَّابِ ﷺ عَنْ رَسُوْلِ اللهِ ﷺ قَالَ: اَلْجَنَّةُ حُرِّمَتْ عَلَى الْأَنْبِيَاءِ حَتَّى أَدْخُلَهَا، وَحُرِّمَتْ عَلَى الْأُمَمِ حَتَّى تَدْخُلَهَا أُمَّتِي.

رَوَاهُ الطَّبَرَانِيُّ.

256/4. According to ʿUmar b. al-Khaṭṭāb ﷺ:

"Allah's Messenger ﷺ said: 'The Garden of Paradise is forbidden to all the Prophets until I enter it, and it is forbidden to the communities until my *Umma* (Community) enters it.'"

Reported by al-Ṭabarānī.

٢٥٧/ ٥. عَنْ أَبِي ذَرٍّ الْغِفَارِيِّ ﷺ قَالَ: قَالَ رَسُوْلُ اللهِ ﷺ: إِنَّ اللهَ تَجَاوَزَ عَنْ أُمَّتِي الْخَطَأَ وَالنِّسْيَانَ، وَمَا اسْتُكْرِهُوْا عَلَيْهِ.

---

about the number of the ranks of the people of the Garden of Paradise, 4/683 §2546. He said: "This is a fine authentic tradition." •Ibn Mājah in *al-Sunan*: Bk.: *al-Zuhd* [Abstinence], Ch.: The quality of the *Umma* (Community) of Muhammad ﷺ, 2/1434 §4289. •al-Ḥākim in *al-Mustadrak*, 1/155 §273. •al-Dārimī in *al-Sunan*, 2/434 §2835. •Ibn Ḥibbān in *al-Ṣaḥīḥ*, 16/498 §7459. •Aḥmad b. Ḥanbal in *al-Musnad*, 5/347 §22990, 23052, 23111. •al-Bazzār in *al-Musnad*, 5/368 §1999. •Ibn Abī Shayba in *al-Muṣannaf*, 6/315 §31713. •al-Ṭabarānī in *al-Muʿjam al-Ṣaghīr*, 1/67 §82, *al-Muʿjam al-Awsaṭ*, 2/77 §1310, & in *al-Muʿjam al-Kabīr*, 10/184 §10398. •Abū Yaʿlā in *al-Musnad*, 1/183 §211.

[256] Set forth by •al-Ṭabarānī in *al-Muʿjam al-Awsaṭ*, 1/289 §942. •al-Haythamī in *Majmaʿ al-Zawāʾid*, 10/69. •al-Hindī in *Kanz al-ʿUmmāl*, 11/416 §31953.

رَوَاهُ ابْنُ مَاجه وَابْنُ حِبَّانَ وَالْبَيْهَقِيُّ وَالطَّبَرَانِيُّ فِي الثَّلَاثَةِ. وَقَالَ الْحَاكِمُ: هَذَا حَدِيْثٌ صَحِيْحٌ.

257/5. According to Abū Dharr al-Ghifārī ﵁:

"Allah's Messenger ﷺ said: 'Allah has overlooked the error and forgetfulness of my *Umma* (Community), and what they have done under oppression and coercion.'"

Reported by Ibn Mājah, Ibn Ḥibbān, al-Bayhaqī, and al-Ṭabarānī in his three collections. According to al-Ḥākim: "This is an authentic tradition."

٢٥٨/٦. عَنْ أَبِي هُرَيْرَةَ ﵁ قَالَ: قَالَ رَسُوْلُ اللهِ ﷺ: إِنَّ اللهَ ﷻ تَجَاوَزَ لِأُمَّتِي عَمَّا حَدَّثَتْ بِهِ أَنْفُسُهَا مَا لَمْ تَعْمَلْ أَوْ تَكَلَّمْ بِهِ.

رَوَاهُ مُسْلِمٌ وَالنَّسَائِيُّ وَابْنُ مَاجه.

258/6. According to Abū Hurayra ﵁:

"Allah's Messenger ﷺ said: 'Allah ﷻ has overlooked what the

---

[257] Set forth by •Ibn Mājah in *al-Sunan*: Bk.: *al-Ṭalāq* [Divorce], Ch.: The divorce of the coerced and the procrastinator, 1/659 §2043. •Ibn Ḥibbān, on the authority of Ibn ʿAbbās ﵄, in *al-Ṣaḥīḥ*, 16/202 §7219. •al-Ḥākim in *al-Mustadrak*, 2/216 §2801. •al-Bayhaqī in *al-Sunan al-Kubrā*, 7/356 §14871. •al-Dāraquṭnī in *al-Sunan*, 4/170 §33. •Ibn Abī Shayba in *al-Muṣannaf*, 4/172 §204. •ʿAbd al-Razzāq likewise in *al-Muṣannaf*, 6/410 §11417. •al-Ṭaḥāwī in *Sharḥ Maʿānī al-Āthār*, 3/95. •al-Ṭabarānī in *al-Muʿjam al-Ṣaghīr*, 2/52 §766, & in *al-Muʿjam al-Awsaṭ*, 8/161 §8273, & in *al-Muʿjam al-Kabīr*, 2/97 §1430, & in *Musnad al-Shāmiyyīn*, 2/152 §1090.

[258] Set forth by •Muslim in *al-Ṣaḥīḥ*: Bk.: *al-Īmān* [Faith], Ch.: Allah disregards the speech of the soul and the notions of the heart, if they are not firmly established, 1/116 §127. •Ibn Mājah in *al-Sunan*: Bk.: *al-Ṭalāq* [Divorce], Ch.: Someone who divorces within himself, but does not speak of it, 1/658 §2040. •al-Nasāʾī in *al-Sunan al-Kubrā*, 3/360 §5628. •Ibn Khuzayma in *al-Ṣaḥīḥ*, 2/52 §898. •Ibn Ḥibbān, in *al-Ṣaḥīḥ*, 10/179 §4335. •Aḥmad b. Ḥanbal in *al-Musnad*, 2/255 §7464. •Ibn Abī Shayba in *al-Muṣannaf*, 4/85. •Abū Yaʿlā in *al-Musnad*, 11/276 §6389. •al-Bayhaqī in *Shuʿab al-Īmān*, 1/299 §332.

members of my *Umma* (Community) talked about within their inner beings (i.e., mistrusts and misgivings in hearts), so long as they do not act upon it or utter with tongue.'"

Reported by Muslim, al-Nasāʾī and Ibn Mājah.

٢٥٩/ ٧. عَنْ مِحْجَنِ بْنِ الْأَدْرَعِ السُّلَمِيِّ ﷺ قَالَ: قَالَ رَسُوْلُ اللهِ ﷺ: إِنَّ اللهَ رَضِيَ لِهَذِهِ الأُمَّةِ الْيُسْرَ وَكَرِهَ لَهَا الْعُسْرَ — قَالَهَا ثَلَاثًا.

رَوَاهُ الطَّبَرَانِيُّ بِرِجَالِ الصَّحِيْحِ.

259/7. According to Miḥjan b. al-Adraʿ al-Sulamī ﷺ:

"Allah's Messenger ﷺ said: 'Allah has liked (and approved of) ease for this *Umma* (Community) and has disliked (and disapproved of) hardship for it.' He said this three times."

Reported by al-Ṭabarānī with authentic narrators.

٢٦٠/ ٨. عَنْ حُذَيْفَةَ ﷺ قَالَ: غَابَ عَنَّا رَسُوْلُ اللهِ ﷺ يَوْمًا فَلَمْ يَخْرُجْ حَتَّى ظَنَنَّا أَنَّهُ لَنْ يَخْرُجَ. فَلَمَّا خَرَجَ، سَجَدَ سَجْدَةً فَظَنَنَّا أَنَّ نَفْسَهُ قُبِضَتْ فِيهَا. فَلَمَّا رَفَعَ رَأْسَهُ، قَالَ: إِنَّ رَبِّي تَبَارَكَ وَتَعَالَى اسْتَشَارَنِي فِي أُمَّتِي وَفِيْهِ: وَأَحَلَّ لَنَا كَثِيْرًا مِمَّا شَدَّدَ عَلَى مَنْ قَبْلَنَا وَلَمْ يَجْعَلْ عَلَيْنَا مِنْ حَرَجٍ.

رَوَاهُ أَحْمَدُ.

260/8. According to Ḥudhayfa ﷺ:

"One day Allah's Messenger ﷺ did not come out until we thought probably he would never come out. Then when he came out, he prostrated himself continually until we thought probably

---

259 Set forth by •al-Ṭabarānī in *al-Muʿjam al-Kabīr*, 20/298 §707. •al-Haythamī in *Majmaʿ al-Zawāʾid*, 4/15. •al-Ḥārith in *al-Musnad* (*Zawāʾid al-Haythamī*), 1/343 §237.

260 Set forth by •Aḥmad b. Ḥanbal in *al-Musnad*, 5/393 §23384. •al-Haythamī in *Majmaʿ al-Zawāʾid*, 10/68.

his soul had been taken away. Then, when he raised his holy head from prostration, he said: 'My Lord has consulted me about my *Umma* (Community),' and stated: 'He has made lawful for us much of what He strictly prohibited to those before us, and He has not placed any difficulty upon us in this world.'"

Reported by Aḥmad.

٢٦١/ ٩. عَنْ أَبِي الدَّرْدَاءِ (رضي الله عنه) قَالَ: قَالَ رَسُوْلُ اللهِ ﷺ: أَنَا أَوَّلُ مَنْ يُؤْذَنُ لَهُ بِالسُّجُوْدِ يَوْمَ الْقِيَامَةِ، وَأَنَا أَوَّلُ مَنْ يُؤْذَنُ لَهُ أَنْ يَرْفَعَ رَأْسَهُ، فَأَنْظُرَ إِلَى بَيْنَ يَدَيَّ، فَأَعْرِفَ أُمَّتِي مِنْ بَيْنِ الْأُمَمِ، وَمِنْ خَلْفِي مِثْلُ ذَلِكَ، وَعَنْ يَمِيْنِي مِثْلُ ذَلِكَ. فَقَالَ لَهُ رَجُلٌ: يَا رَسُوْلَ اللهِ، كَيْفَ تَعْرِفُ أُمَّتَكَ مِنْ بَيْنِ الْأُمَمِ فِيْمَا بَيْنَ نُوْحٍ إِلَى أُمَّتِكَ؟ قَالَ: هُمْ غُرٌّ مُحَجَّلُوْنَ مِنْ أَثَرِ الْوُضُوْءِ. لَيْسَ أَحَدٌ كَذَلِكَ غَيْرُهُمْ، وَأَعْرِفُهُمْ أَنَّهُمْ يُؤْتَوْنَ كُتُبَهُمْ بِأَيْمَانِهِمْ، وَأَعْرِفُهُمْ يَسْعَى بَيْنَ أَيْدِيْهِمْ ذُرِّيَّتُهُمْ.

رَوَاهُ أَحْمَدُ وَالْحَاكِمُ وَالْبَيْهَقِيُّ. وَقَالَ الْحَاكِمُ: هَذَا حَدِيْثٌ صَحِيْحُ الإِسْنَادِ.

261/9. According to Abū al-Dardāʾ (رضي الله عنه):

"Allah's Messenger ﷺ said: 'I shall be the first who is permitted to prostrate himself on the Day of Resurrection, and I shall be the first who is allowed to raise his head. So I shall therefore look in front of me, and I shall distinguish my *Umma* (Community) from among the communities, and likewise behind me, and likewise to my right.' A man said to him: 'O Messenger of Allah! How will you distinguish your *Umma* (Community) from among the communities, while there will be people of the communities from Noah to your *Umma* (Community)?' He said: '(They will be unique:) their limbs will be shining due to the effect of the

---

261 Set forth by •Aḥmad b. Ḥanbal in *al-Musnad*, 5/199 §21785. •al-Ḥākim in *al-Mustadrak*, 2/520 §3784. •al-Bayhaqī in *Shuʿab al-Īmān*, 3/17 §2745. •al-Ṭayālisī in *al-Musnad*, 1/48 §361. •Ibn Ḥibbān likewise in *al-Ṣaḥīḥ*, 3/324 §1049. •al-Mundhirī in *al-Targhīb wa al-Tarhīb*, 1/91 §286. •al-Haythamī in *Majmaʿ al-Zawāʾid*, 1/225; 2/250; 10/344. He said: "It was reported by al-Ṭabarānī."

minor ritual ablution *[wuḍū']*. None (of the other communities) will be like that except them. I shall also distinguish them because they will carry their records (of deeds) in their right hands, and I shall distinguish them because their offspring will run in front of them!'"

Reported by Aḥmad, al-Ḥākim and al-Bayhaqī. According to al-Ḥākim: "This is a tradition with an authentic chain of transmission."

٢٦٢/ ١٠. عَنْ أَبِي ذَرٍّ وَأَبِي الدَّرْدَاءِ ﷺ أَنَّ رَسُوْلَ اللهِ ﷺ قَالَ: إِنِّي لَأَعْرِفُ أُمَّتِي يَوْمَ الْقِيَامَةِ مِنْ بَيْنِ الْأُمَمِ. قَالُوْا: يَا رَسُوْلَ اللهِ، وَكَيْفَ تَعْرِفُ أُمَّتَكَ؟ قَالَ: أَعْرِفُهُمْ يُؤْتَوْنَ كُتُبَهُمْ بِأَيْمَانِهِمْ، وَأَعْرِفُهُمْ بِسِيْمَاهُمْ فِي وُجُوْهِهِمْ مِنْ أَثَرِ السُّجُوْدِ، وَأَعْرِفُهُمْ بِنُوْرِهِمْ يَسْعَى بَيْنَ أَيْدِيْهِمْ.

رَوَاهُ أَحْمَدُ بِإِسْنَادٍ جَيِّدٍ.

262/10. According to Abū Dharr and Abū al-Dardā' ﷺ:

"Allah's Messenger ﷺ said: 'I shall surely distinguish my *Umma* (Community) on the Day of Resurrection from among the communities.' They said: 'O Messenger of Allah, and how will you distinguish your *Umma* (Community)?' He said: 'I shall recognize them because they will be given their records in their right hands, and there will be marks on their foreheads from the effect of the prostration, and I shall distinguish them by their light running in front of them.'"

Reported by Aḥmad with a perfect chain of transmission.

٢٦٣/ ١١. عَنْ أَبِي أُمَامَةَ الْبَاهِلِيِّ ﷺ يَقُوْلُ: تَخْرُجُ يَوْمَ الْقِيَامَةِ ثُلَّةٌ غُرٌّ مُحَجَّلُوْنَ. يَسُدُّ الْأُفُقَ نُوْرُهُمْ مِثْلُ الشَّمْسِ. فَيُنَادِيْ مُنَادٍ: اَلنَّبِيُّ الْأُمِّيُّ فَيَتَحَسَّسُ لَهَا كُلُّ نَبِيٍّ أُمِّيٍّ، فَيُقَالُ: مُحَمَّدٌ وَأُمَّتُهُ. فَيَدْخُلُوْنَ الْجَنَّةَ لَيْسَ عَلَيْهِمْ حِسَابٌ وَلَا عَذَابٌ. ثُمَّ تَخْرُجُ

[262] Set forth by •Aḥmad b. Ḥanbal in *al-Musnad*, 5/199 §21788.

ثُلَّةٌ أُخْرَى غُرٌّ مُحَجَّلُوْنَ نُوْرُهُم مِثْلُ الْقَمَرِ لَيْلَةَ الْبَدْرِ يَسُدُّ الأُفُقَ نُوْرُهُمْ. فَيُنَادِي مُنَادٍ: اَلنَّبِيُّ الأُمِّيُّ. فَيَتَحَسَّسُ لَهَا كُلُّ نَبِيٍّ أُمِّيٍّ، فَيُقَالُ: مُحَمَّدٌ وَأُمَّتُهُ. فَيَدْخُلُوْنَ الْجَنَّةَ بِغَيْرِ حِسَابٍ وَلاَ عَذَابٍ. ثُمَّ تَخْرُجُ ثُلَّةٌ أُخْرَى غُرٌّ مُحَجَّلُوْنَ نُوْرُهُمْ مِثْلُ أَعْظَمِ كَوْكَبٍ فِي السَّمَاءِ. يَسُدُّ الأُفُقَ نُوْرُهُمْ. فَيُنَادِي مُنَادٍ: اَلنَّبِيُّ الأُمِّيُّ. فَيَتَحَسَّسُ لَهَا كُلُّ نَبِيٍّ أُمِّيٍّ فَيُقَالُ: مُحَمَّدٌ وَأُمَّتُهُ. فَيَدْخُلُوْنَ الْجَنَّةَ بِغَيْرِ حِسَابٍ وَلاَ عَذَابٍ، ثُمَّ يَجِيءُ رَبُّكَ ثُمَّ يُوْضَعُ الْمِيْزَانُ وَالْحِسَابُ.

رَوَاهُ الطَّبَرَانِيُّ.

263/11. According to Abū Umāma al-Bāhilī رضي الله عنه:

"A unique people will emerge on the Day of Resurrection, with illumined foreheads and shining extremeties. Their light will fill the horizon like the light of the sun. Then a herald will cry: 'The untaught Prophet!' Every untaught Prophet will give heed to it, but it will be said: 'Muhammad and his *Umma* (Community).' So they will enter the Garden of Paradise without being subjected to any reckoning, nor to any torment! Then another unique people will emerge, with illumined foreheads and shining extremeties and with their light filling the horizon like the light of the moon on the full moon night. Then a herald will cry: 'The untaught Prophet!' Every untaught Prophet will give heed to it, but it will be said: 'Muhammad and his *Umma* (Community).' So they will enter the Garden of Paradise without being subjected to any reckoning, nor to any torment! In like manner there will emerge another unique people, with illumined foreheads and shining extremeties and with their light filling the horizon like the light of the greatest star. Then a herald will cry: 'The untaught Prophet!' Every untaught Prophet will give heed to it, so it will be said: 'Muhammad and his *Umma* (Community).' So they will enter the Garden of Paradise

[263] Set forth by •al-Ṭabarānī in *al-Muʿjam al-Kabīr*, 8/173 §7723, & in *Musnad al-Shāmiyyīn*, 2/201 §1185. •al-Haythamī in *Majmaʿ al-Zawāʾid*, 10/409.

without being subjected to any reckoning, nor to any torment! Then your Lord will come (matching His Glory). The balance and the reckoning will then be established."

Reported by al-Ṭabarānī.

٢٦٤/ ١٢. عَنْ بَهْزِ بْنِ حَكِيْمٍ، عَنْ أَبِيْهِ عَنْ جَدِّهِ، أَنَّهُ سَمِعَ النَّبِيَّ ﷺ يَقُوْلُ فِي قَوْلِهِ تَعَالَى: ﴿كُنتُمْ خَيْرَ أُمَّةٍ أُخْرِجَتْ لِلنَّاسِ﴾. (آل عمران، ٣:١١٠). قَالَ: إِنَّكُمْ تُتِمُّوْنَ سَبْعِيْنَ أُمَّةً. أَنْتُمْ خَيْرُهَا وَأَكْرَمُهَا عَلَى اللهِ.

رَوَاهُ التِّرْمِذِيُّ وَابْنُ مَاجَه وَأَحْمَدُ. وَقَالَ التِّرْمِذِيُّ: هَذَا حَدِيْثٌ حَسَنٌ. وَقَالَ الْحَاكِمُ: هَذَا حَدِيْثٌ صَحِيْحُ الإِسْنَادِ.

264/12. According to Bahz b. Ḥakīm, on the authority of his father, his grandfather said that he heard the Prophet ﷺ saying about Allah's decree: "You are the best *Umma* (Community) that has been brought forth for (the guidance of) humankind *[kuntum khayra ummatin ukhrijat li-ʾn-nāsi]*." (Q.3:110). He, then, said: "You are complementing seventy communities. You are the best of them and the noblest of them in the sight of Allah!"

Reported by al-Tirmidhī, Ibn Mājah and Aḥmad. According to al-Tirmidhī: "This is a fine tradition," and al-Ḥākim said: "This is a tradition with an authentic chain of transmission."

٢٦٥/ ١٣. عَنْ بَهْزِ بْنِ حَكِيْمٍ، عَنْ أَبِيْهِ عَنْ جَدِّهِ قَالَ: قَالَ رَسُوْلُ اللهِ ﷺ: نُكَمِّلُ، يَوْمَ الْقِيَامَةِ، سَبْعِيْنَ أُمَّةً. نَحْنُ آخِرُهَا وَخَيْرُهَا.

---

[264] Set forth by •al-Tirmidhī in *al-Sunan*: Bk.: Interpretation of the Qurʾān according to Allah's Messenger ﷺ, Ch.: From the Sūra of Āl ʿImrān, (Q.3), 5/226 §3001. •Ibn Mājah in *al-Sunan*: Bk.: *al-Zuhd* [Abstinence], Ch.: The quality of the *Umma* (Community) of Muhammad ﷺ, 2/1433 §4287, 4288. •al-Ḥākim in *al-Mustadrak*, 4/94 §6987. •Aḥmad b. Ḥanbal in *al-Musnad*, 3/61 §4/11604; 4/447; 5/3. •al-Bayhaqī in *al-Sunan al-Kubrā*, 9/5. •al-Ṭabarānī in *al-Muʿjam al-Kabīr*, 19/419 §1012, 1023. •ʿAbd b. Ḥumayd in *al-Musnad*, 1/156 §411. •al-Rūyānī in *al-Musnad*, 2/115 §924. •Ibn al-Mubārak in *al-Zuhd*, 1/114 §382.

رَوَاهُ ابْنُ مَاجَه.

265/13. According to Bahz b. Ḥakīm, on the authority of his father, his grandfather said:

"Allah's Messenger ﷺ said: 'We shall accomplish, on the Day of Resurrection, seventy communities. We are the last of them, and the best of them!'"

Reported by Ibn Mājah.

٢٦٦/ ١٤. عَنْ عَلِيِّ بْنِ أَبِي طَالِبٍ رضي الله عنه يَقُوْلُ: قَالَ رَسُوْلُ اللهِ ﷺ: أُعْطِيْتُ مَا لَمْ يُعْطَ أَحَدٌ مِنَ الْأَنْبِيَاءِ. فَقُلْنَا: يَا رَسُوْلَ اللهِ، مَا هُوَ؟ قَالَ: نُصِرْتُ بِالرُّعْبِ وَأُعْطِيْتُ مَفَاتِيْحَ الْأَرْضِ وَسُمِّيْتُ أَحْمَدَ وَجُعِلَ التُّرَابُ لِي طَهُوْرًا وَجُعِلَتْ أُمَّتِي خَيْرَ الْأُمَمِ.

رَوَاهُ ابْنُ أَبِي شَيْبَةَ وَأَحْمَدُ بِإِسْنَادٍ جَيِّدٍ.

266/14. According to ʿAlī b. Abī Ṭālib رضي الله عنه:

"Allah's Messenger ﷺ said: 'I have been given what none of the Prophets was given.' We said: 'O Messenger of Allah! What is it?' He said: 'I have been assisted with awesomeness (i.e., over-dominant, ever-prevailing and impressive posture). I have been given the keys of (all the treasures of) the earth. I have been named as Aḥmad [Most Praiseworthy]. The soil has been rendered pure for me, and my *Umma* (Community) has been made the best of the communities!'"

Reported by Ibn Abī Shayba and Aḥmad, with a perfect chain of transmission.

---

265 Set forth by •Ibn Mājah in *al-Sunan*: Bk.: *al-Zuhd* [Abstinence], Ch.: The quality of the *Umma* (Community) of Muhammad ﷺ, 2/1433 §4287.

266 Set forth by •Ibn Abī Shayba in *al-Muṣannaf*, 6/304 §31647. •Aḥmad b. Ḥanbal in *al-Musnad*, 1/98 §763, 1361. •al-Bayhaqī in *al-Sunan al-Kubrā*, 1/213 §965. •Abū al-Qāsim Hibat Allāh in *Iʿtiqād Ahl al-Sunna*, 4/783 §1443, 1447. •al-Maqdisī in *al-Aḥādīth al-Mukhtāra*, 2/348 §728–729. •al-Haythamī in *Majmaʿ al-Zawāʾid*, 1/260, 8/269.

٢٦٧/ ١٥. عَنْ ثَوْبَانَ ﵁ قَالَ: قَالَ رَسُوْلُ اللهِ ﷺ: إِنَّ اللهَ زَوَى لِيَ الْأَرْضَ. فَرَأَيْتُ مَشَارِقَهَا وَمَغَارِبَهَا. وَإِنَّ أُمَّتِي سَيَبْلُغُ مُلْكُهَا مَا زُوِيَ لِي مِنْهَا وَأُعْطِيْتُ الْكَنْزَيْنِ الْأَحْمَرَ وَالْأَبْيَضَ. وَإِنِّي سَأَلْتُ رَبِّي لِأُمَّتِي أَنْ لَا يُهْلِكَهَا بِسَنَةٍ عَامَّةٍ، وَأَنْ لَا يُسَلِّطَ عَلَيْهِمْ عَدُوًّا مِنْ سِوَى أَنْفُسِهِمْ، فَيَسْتَبِيْحَ بَيْضَتَهُمْ وَإِنَّ رَبِّي قَالَ: يَا مُحَمَّدُ، إِنِّي إِذَا قَضَيْتُ فَإِنَّهُ لَا يُرَدُّ. وَإِنِّي أَعْطَيْتُكَ لِأُمَّتِكَ أَنْ لَا أُهْلِكَهُمْ بِسَنَةٍ عَامَّةٍ وَأَنْ لَا أُسَلِّطَ عَلَيْهِمْ عَدُوًّا مِنْ سِوَى أَنْفُسِهِمْ يَسْتَبِيْحُ بَيْضَتَهُمْ وَلَو اجْتَمَعَ عَلَيْهِمْ مَنْ بِأَقْطَارِهَا أَوْ قَالَ: مَنْ بَيْنَ أَقْطَارِهَا حَتَّى يَكُوْنَ بَعْضُهُمْ يُهْلِكُ بَعْضًا وَيَسْبِي بَعْضُهُمْ بَعْضًا.

رَوَاهُ مُسْلِمٌ وَالتِّرْمِذِيُّ وَأَبُوْ دَاوُدَ. وَقَالَ التِّرْمِذِيُّ: هَذَا حَدِيْثٌ حَسَنٌ صَحِيْحٌ. وَقَالَ الْحَاكِمُ: هَذَا حَدِيْثٌ صَحِيْحٌ.

267/15. According to Thawbān ﵁:

"Allah's Messenger ﷺ said: 'Allah collected the earth together for me, so I beheld both its eastern regions and its western regions. Soon the domain of my *Umma* (Community) will surely reach that extent to which the earth has been collected together for me. I was granted both the red and the white treasures. I begged my Lord not to destroy my *Umma* (Community) with a drought (and famine), and not to allow an enemy from other than themselves to seize power over them by invading their territory and annihilate

267 Set forth by •Muslim in *al-Ṣaḥīḥ*: Bk.: *al-Fitan wa Ashrāṭ al-Sāʿa* [Troubles and the Portents of the Final Hour], Ch.: The mutual destruction of the members of this *Umma* (Community), 4/2215 §2889. •al-Tirmidhī in *al-Sunan*: Bk.: *al-Fitan* [Troubles] according to Allah's Messenger ﷺ, Ch.: What has come to us concerning the Prophet's questioning three times about his *Umma* (Community) ﷺ, 4/472 §2176. •Abū Dāwūd in *al-Sunan*: Bk.: *al-Fitan wa al-Malāḥim* [Troubles and Massacres], Ch.: Discussion of troubles and their signs, 4/97 §4252. •Aḥmad b. Ḥanbal in *al-Musnad*, 5/278 §22448, 22505. •al-Bazzār in *al-Musnad*, 8/413 §3487. •al-Ḥākim in *al-Mustadrak*, 4/496 §8390. •Ibn Abī Shayba in *al-Muṣannaf*, 6/311 §31694. •Ibn Ḥibbān in *al-Ṣaḥīḥ*, 15/109 §6714. •al-Bayhaqī in *al-Sunan al-Kubrā*, 9/181. •al-Daylamī in *al-Firdaws bi-Maʾthūr al-Khiṭāb*, 2/296 §3347.

them. My Lord said: 'O Muhammad, once I have issued a decree, it will not be reversed! For the sake of your *Umma* (Community), I have granted you the assurance that I will not destroy it with a universal drought, and that I will not allow an enemy from other than themselves to seize power over them by invading their territory and annihilate them, even if they (enemies) unite against them (from all directions), so much so that one of them will not kill another and one of them will not imprison another.'"

Reported by Muslim, al-Tirmidhī and Abū Dāwūd. According to al-Tirmidhī: "This is a fine authentic tradition," and al-Ḥākim said: "This is an authentic tradition."

٢٦٨/١٦. عَنْ عَمْرِو بْنِ قَيْسٍ ﷺ أَنَّ رَسُوْلَ اللهِ ﷺ قَالَ: إِنَّ اللهَ أَدْرَكَ بِيَ الْأَجَلَ الْـمَرْحُومَ وَاخْتَصَرَ لِي اخْتِصَارًا. فَنَحْنُ الْآخِرُوْنَ وَنَحْنُ السَّابِقُوْنَ يَوْمَ الْقِيَامَةِ. وَإِنِّي قَائِلٌ قَوْلاً غَيْرَ فَخْرٍ. إِبْرَاهِيْمُ خَلِيْلُ اللهِ، وَمُوْسَى صَفِيُّ اللهِ، وَأَنَا حَبِيْبُ اللهِ. وَمَعِي لِوَاءُ الْحَمْدِ يَوْمَ الْقِيَامَةِ. وَإِنَّ اللهَ وَعَدَنِي فِي أُمَّتِي وَأَجَارَهُمْ مِنْ ثَلَاثٍ: لَا يَعُمُّهُمْ بِسَنَةٍ وَلَا يَسْتَأْصِلُهُمْ عَدُوٌّ، وَلَا يَجْمَعُهُمْ عَلَى ضَلَالَةٍ.

رَوَاهُ الدَّارِمِيُّ.

268/16. According to ʿAmr b. Qays ﷺ:

"Allah's Messenger ﷺ said: 'Allah has granted my *Umma* (Community) His Mercy and has made its life span brief. So, we are the last [people of this world,] and we are the pioneers on the Day of Resurrection. I am uttering a statement that is no boast! Abraham is the Bosom Friend of Allah *[Khalīl Allāh]*, Moses is the True Friend of Allah *[Ṣafiyy Allāh]*, and I am the Beloved Friend of Allah *[Ḥabīb Allāh]*. With me is the banner of praise on the Day of Resurrection. Allah has promised me benefit for my *Umma* (Community), and He has protected them from three things, so that (1) He will not make

---

[268] Set forth by •al-Dārimī in *al-Sunan*: Ch.: (8), The excellent merit that was given to the Prophet ﷺ, 1/42 §54. •al-Mubārakfūrī in *Tuḥfat al-Aḥwadhī*, 6/323.

them suffer a universal drought, (2) an enemy will not exterminate them, and (3) He will not unify them to go astray.'"

Reported by al-Dārimī.

١٧/٢٦٩. عَنْ أَبِي مَالِكٍ الْأَشْعَرِيِّ ﷺ قَالَ: قَالَ رَسُوْلُ اللهِ ﷺ: إِنَّ اللهَ أَجَارَكُمْ مِنْ ثَلَاثِ خِلَالٍ: أَنْ لَا يَدْعُوَ عَلَيْكُمْ نَبِيُّكُمْ فَتَهْلِكُوْا جَمِيْعًا، وَأَنْ لَا يَظْهَرَ أَهْلُ الْبَاطِلِ عَلَى أَهْلِ الْحَقِّ، وَأَنْ لَا تَجْتَمِعُوْا عَلَى ضَلَالَةٍ.

رَوَاهُ أَبُوْ دَاوُدَ وَالطَّبَرَانِيُّ.

269/17. According to Abū Mālik al-Ashʿarī ﷺ:

"Allah's Messenger ﷺ said: 'Allah has protected you from three afflictions, so that (1) your Prophet will not curse you, causing all of you to perish collectively, (2) the people of falsehood will not triumph over the people of the truth, and (3) collectively you will never unite over an error.'"

Reported by Abū Dāwūd and al-Ṭabarānī.

١٨/٢٧٠. عَنْ أَنَسِ بْنِ مَالِكٍ ﷺ قَالَ: قَالَ رَسُوْلُ اللهِ ﷺ: إِنَّ هَذِهِ الْأُمَّةَ مَرْحُوْمَةٌ. عَذَابُهَا بِأَيْدِيْهَا. فَإِذَا كَانَ يَوْمُ الْقِيَامَةِ، دُفِعَ إِلَى كُلِّ رَجُلٍ مِنَ الْمُسْلِمِيْنَ رَجُلٌ مِنَ الْمُشْرِكِيْنَ، فَيُقَالُ: هَذَا فِدَاؤُكَ مِنَ النَّارِ.

رَوَاهُ أَبُوْ حَنِيْفَةَ وَابْنُ مَاجَه وَاللَّفْظُ لَهُ.

270/18. According to Anas b. Mālik ﷺ:

---

269 Set forth by •Abū Dāwūd in *al-Sunan*: Bk.: *al-Fitan* [Troubles] Ch.: Discussion of troubles and their signs, 4/98 §4253. •al-Ṭabarānī in *al-Muʿjam al-Kabīr*, 3/292 §3440, & in *Musnad al-Shāmiyyīn*, 2/442 §1663.

270 Set forth by •Ibn Mājah in *al-Sunan*: Bk.: *al-Zuhd* [Abstinence], Ch.: The quality of the *Umma* (Community) of Muhammad ﷺ, 2/1434 §4292. •Abū Ḥanīfa, on the authority of Abū Mūsā, in *al-Musnad*, 1/155. •ʿAbd b. Ḥumayd in *al-Musnad*, 1/190 §537. •al-Marwazī in *al-Fitan*, 2/618 §1722.

"Allah's Messenger ﷺ said: 'This *Umma* (Muslim Community) is the (fortunate) one Allah has blessed with (special) mercy. Its torment is at its disposal. When the Day of Resurrection arrives, a man among the polytheists will be pushed towards each man among the Muslims, and it will be said: 'This is your ransom from the Fire of Hell!'"

Reported by Abū Ḥanīfa and Ibn Mājah (the wording is his).

اَلْفَصْلُ الثَّانِي

فَصْلٌ فِي فَضْلِ آخِرِ الْأُمَّةِ الْمُحَمَّدِيَّةِ

Section 2
The Excellence of Muhammad's *Umma* in Final Days

١٩/٢٧١. عَنْ مُعَاوِيَةَ ﵁، قَالَ: سَمِعْتُ النَّبِيَّ ﷺ يَقُوْلُ: لَا يَزَالُ مِنْ أُمَّتِي أُمَّةٌ قَائِمَةٌ بِأَمْرِ اللهِ. لَا يَضُرُّهُمْ مَنْ خَذَلَهُمْ وَلَا مَنْ خَالَفَهُمْ حَتَّى يَأْتِيَهُمْ أَمْرُ اللهِ وَهُمْ عَلَى ذَلِكَ.

مُتَّفَقٌ عَلَيْهِ وَهَذَا لَفْظُ الْبُخَارِيِّ.

271/19. According to Muʿāwiya ﵁:

"I heard the Prophet ﷺ say: 'Among my *Umma* (people), there will not cease to be a group of people obedient to Allah's commandment. Those who abandon them will not harm them, nor will those who oppose them, until Allah's commandment (the

[271] Set forth by •al-Bukhārī in *al-Ṣaḥīḥ*: Bk.: *al-Manāqib* [Virtues], Ch.: The polytheists asked the Prophet ﷺ to show them a sign, so he showed them the splitting of the moon, 3/1331 §3442, & Bk.: *al-Tawḥīd* [The Affirmation of Oneness], Ch.: Allah's saying: "And Our word to a thing, when We intend it, is only that We say to it: 'Be!' and it is. [*inna-mā qawlu-nā li-shayʾin idhā aradnā-hu an naqūla la-hu kun fa-yakūn*]." (Q.16:40), 6/2714 §7022. •Muslim in *al-Ṣaḥīḥ*: Bk.: *al-Imāra* [The Emirate; Imperial Authority], Ch.: He [the Prophet ﷺ] said: "A group from my *Umma* (Community) will not cease to recognize the truth, unharmed by those who oppose them." 3/1524 §1037. •Aḥmad b. Ḥanbal in *al-Musnad*, 4/101. •Abū Yaʿlā in *al-Musnad*, 13/375 §7383. •al-Ṭabarānī in *al-Muʿjam al-Kabīr*, 19/380 §893. •al-Lālakāʾī in *Iʿtiqād Ahl al-Sunna*, 1/110 §144.

Day of Resurrection) comes to them and they will be in the same state.'"

Agreed upon by al-Bukhārī and Muslim, and this is the wording of al-Bukhārī.

٢٧٢/ ٢٠. عَنْ أَبِي هُرَيْرَةَ ﷺ قَالَ: قَالَ رَسُوْلُ اللهِ ﷺ: وَالَّذِي نَفْسُ مُحَمَّدٍ بِيَدِهِ، لَيَأْتِيَنَّ عَلَى أَحَدِكُمْ يَوْمٌ وَلَا يَرَانِي، ثُمَّ لَأَنْ يَرَانِي أَحَبُّ إِلَيْهِ مِنْ أَهْلِهِ وَمَالِهِ مَعَهُمْ.

مُتَّفَقٌ عَلَيْهِ وَهَذَا لَفْظُ مُسْلِمٍ.

272/20. According to Abū Hurayra ﷺ:

"Allah's Messenger ﷺ said: 'By the One in whose Hand the soul of Muhammad is, a day will come when you will not be able to see me, but seeing me will then be dearer to him than his family and his property.'"

Agreed upon by al-Bukhārī and Muslim, and this is the wording of Muslim.

٢٧٣/ ٢١. عَنْ بَهْزِ بْنِ حَكِيْمٍ، عَنْ أَبِيْهِ، عَنْ جَدِّهِ، أَنَّهُ سَمِعَ النَّبِيَّ ﷺ يَقُوْلُ فِي قَوْلِهِ تَعَالَى: ﴿كُنتُمْ خَيْرَ أُمَّةٍ أُخْرِجَتْ لِلنَّاسِ﴾. (آل عمران، ٣: ١١٠)، قَالَ: إِنَّكُمْ تُتِمُّوْنَ سَبْعِيْنَ أُمَّةً. أَنْتُمْ خَيْرُهَا وَأَكْرَمُهَا عَلَى اللهِ.

رَوَاهُ التِّرْمِذِيُّ وَابْنُ مَاجَه وَأَحْمَدُ وَالْحَاكِمُ. وَقَالَ الْحَاكِمُ: هَذَا حَدِيْثٌ صَحِيْحُ الْإِسْنَادِ.

---

272 Set forth by •al-Bukhārī in *al-Ṣaḥīḥ*: Bk.: *al-Manāqib* [Virtues], Ch.: The signs of Prophethood in Islam, 3/315 §3394. •Muslim in *al-Ṣaḥīḥ*: Bk.: *al-Faḍā'il* [Excellent Merits], Ch.: The merit of beholding him ﷺ and longing for him, 4/1836 §2364. •Ibn Ḥibbān in *al-Ṣaḥīḥ*, 15/167 §6765. •Aḥmad b. Ḥanbal in *al-Musnad*, 2/313 §8126. •al-ʿAsqalānī in *Fatḥ al-Bārī*, 6/607. •al-Nawawī in *Sharḥ ʿalā Ṣaḥīḥ Muslim*, 15/118. •al-Suyūṭī in *al-Dībāj*, 6/348 §2364.

273/21. According to Bahz b. Ḥakīm, on the authority of his father, his grandfather said that he heard the Prophet ﷺ saying about Allah's decree:

"You are the best *Umma* (Community) that has been brought forth for (the guidance of) humankind *[kuntum khayra ummatin ukhrijat li 'n-nāsi]*." (Q.3:110). He, then, said: "You are complementing seventy communities. You are the best of them and the noblest of them in the estimation of Allah!"

Reported by al-Tirmidhī, Ibn Mājah, Aḥmad and al-Ḥākim, who said: "This is a tradition with an authentic chain of transmission."

٢٧٤/ ٢٢. عَنْ أَبِي هُرَيْرَةَ ﷺ أَنَّ رَسُوْلَ اللهِ ﷺ قَالَ: مِنْ أَشَدِّ أُمَّتِي لِي حُبًّا نَاسٌ يَكُوْنُوْنَ بَعْدِي. يَوَدُّ أَحَدُهُمْ لَوْ رَآنِي بِأَهْلِهِ وَمَالِهِ.

رَوَاهُ مُسْلِمٌ وَأَحْمَدُ.

274/22. According to Abū Hurayra ﷺ:

"Allah's Messenger ﷺ said: 'Among my *Umma* (Community) the most intensely in love with me there are some people who will come after me. Every one of them would dearly wish that he could purchase the sight of me with his family and his wealth!'"

Reported by Muslim and Aḥmad.

---

[273] Set forth by •al-Tirmidhī in *al-Sunan*: Bk.: *al-Tafsīr* [Interpretation] according to Allah's Messenger ﷺ, Ch.: From the Sūra of Āl ʿImrān, (Q.3), 5/226 §3001. •Ibn Mājah in *al-Sunan*, Bk.: *al-Zuhd* [Abstinence], Ch.: The quality of the *Umma* (Community) of Muhammad ﷺ, 2/1433 §4288. •al-Ḥākim in *al-Mustadrak*, 4/94 §6987. •Aḥmad b. Ḥanbal in *al-Musnad*, 5/3. •al-Ṭabarānī in *al-Muʿjam al-Kabīr*, 19/422 §1023. •al-Bayhaqī in *al-Sunan al-Kubrā*, 9/5. •al-Rūyānī in *al-Musnad*, 2/115 §924. •ʿAbd b. Ḥumayd in *al-Musnad*, 1/156 §411. •Ibn al-Mubārak in *al-Zuhd*, 1/114 §382. •al-Ḥakīm al-Tirmidhī in *Nawādir al-Uṣūl*, 1/153.

[274] Set forth by •Muslim in *al-Ṣaḥīḥ*: Bk.: The Garden of Paradise and the Quality of its Felicity and its Inhabitants, Ch.: Concerning someone who wishes for the vision of the Prophet ﷺ with his family and his wealth, 4/2178 §2832. •Aḥmad b. Ḥanbal in *al-Musnad*, 2/417 §9388. •Ibn Ḥibbān in *al-Ṣaḥīḥ*, 16/214 §7231.

٢٧٥/ ٢٣. عَنْ أَنَسٍ ﷺ قَالَ: قَالَ رَسُوْلُ اللهِ ﷺ: مَثَلُ أُمَّتِي مَثَلُ الْمَطَرِ. لَا يُدْرَى أَوَّلُهُ خَيْرٌ أَمْ آخِرُهُ.

رَوَاهُ التِّرْمِذِيُّ وَحَسَّنَهُ وَأَحْمَدُ وَالْبَزَّارُ.

275/23. According to Anas ﷺ:

"Allah's Messenger ﷺ said: 'The likeness of my *Umma* (Community) is the likeness of the rain. There is no knowing whether the first of it is a blessing, or the last of it!'"

Reported by al-Tirmidhī, Aḥmad and al-Bazzār and al-Tirmidhī declared it fine.

٢٧٦/ ٢٤. عَنْ أَبِي هُرَيْرَةَ ﷺ قَالَ: قَالَ رَسُوْلُ اللهِ ﷺ: إِنَّ أُنَاسًا مِنْ أُمَّتِي يَأْتُوْنَ بَعْدِي. يَوَدُّ أَحَدُهُمْ لَوِ اشْتَرَى رُؤْيَتِي بِأَهْلِهِ وَمَالِهِ.

رَوَاهُ الْحَاكِمُ، وَقَالَ: هَذَا حَدِيْثٌ صَحِيْحُ الإِسْنَادِ.

276/24. According to Abū Hurayra ﷺ:

"Allah's Messenger ﷺ said: 'There will be people of my *Umma* (Community) who will come after me, every one of them charged with the only longing that he could purchase the sight of me with his family and his wealth (i.e., see me once by even sacrificing his family and assets)!'"

Reported by al-Ḥākim, who said: "This is a tradition with an authentic chain of transmission."

٢٧٧/ ٢٥. عَنْ عَمْرِو بْنِ شُعَيْبٍ، عَنْ أَبِيْهِ، عَنْ جَدِّهِ ﷺ قَالَ: قَالَ رَسُوْلُ اللهِ ﷺ:

---

[275] Set forth by •al-Tirmidhī in *al-Sunan*: Bk.: *al-Amthāl* [Parables] according to Allah's Messenger ﷺ, Ch.: The parable of the five ritual prayers, 5/152 §2869. •al-Bazzār in *al-Musnad*, 9/23 §3527. •Aḥmad b. Ḥanbal in *al-Musnad*, 3/130, 143 §12349, 12483. •al-Ṭayālisī in *al-Musnad*, 1/90 §647. •al-Quḍāʿī in *Musnad al-Shihāb*, 2/277 §1352. •Abū Yaʿlā in *al-Musnad*, 6/380 §3717.

[276] Set forth by •al-Ḥākim in *al-Mustadrak*, 4/95 §6991.

أَيُّ الْخَلْقِ أَعْجَبُ إِلَيْكُمْ إِيْمَانًا؟ قَالُوْا: اَلْـمَلاَئِكَةُ. قَالَ: وَمَا لَهُمْ لاَ يُؤْمِنُوْنَ وَهُمْ عِنْدَ رَبِّهِمْ؟ قَالُوْا: فَالنَّبِيُّوْنَ. قَالَ: وَمَا لَهُمْ لاَ يُؤْمِنُوْنَ وَالْوَحْيُ يَنْزِلُ عَلَيْهِمْ؟ قَالُوْا: فَنَحْنُ. قَالَ: وَمَا لَكُمْ لاَ تُؤْمِنُوْنَ وَأَنَا بَيْنَ أَظْهُرِكُمْ؟ فَقَالَ رَسُوْلُ اللهِ ﷺ: إِنَّ أَعْجَبَ الْخَلْقِ إِلَيَّ إِيْمَانًا لَقَوْمٌ يَكُوْنُوْنَ مِنْ بَعْدِي. يَجِدُوْنَ صُحُفًا فِيْهَا كِتَابٌ يُؤْمِنُوْنَ بِمَا فِيْهَا.

رَوَاهُ الطَّبَرَانِيُّ وَأَبُوْ يَعْلَى وَالْحَاكِمُ، وَقَالَ الْحَاكِمُ: هَذَا حَدِيْثٌ صَحِيحُ الْإِسْنَادِ.

277/25. According to ʿAmr b. Shuʿāyb, on the authority of his father, his grandfather ﷺ said:

"Allah's Messenger ﷺ said: 'As for faith, which of all creatures are the most remarkable to you?' They said: 'The angels!' He said: 'How could they not believe, for they are in the presence of their Lord (every moment)?' They said: 'Then what about the Prophets?' He said: 'How could they not believe, for the revelation descends upon them?' They said: 'Then what about us?' He said: 'How could you not believe, for I am in your midst?' Allah's Messenger ﷺ then said: 'The most remarkable of all creatures to me, where faith is concerned, are the people who will come after me, for they will find many books but will put (unseen) faith only in the contents of (my) Book.'"

Reported by al-Ṭabarānī, Abū Yaʿlā and al-Ḥākim, who said: "This is a tradition with an authentic chain of transmission."

٢٧٨/٢٦. عَنْ أَنَسِ بْنِ مَالِكٍ ﷺ قَالَ: قَالَ رَسُوْلُ اللهِ ﷺ: وَدِدْتُ أَنِّي لَقِيْتُ إِخْوَانِي. قَالَ: فَقَالَ أَصْحَابُ النَّبِيِّ ﷺ: أَوَ لَيْسَ نَحْنُ إِخْوَانَكَ؟ قَالَ: أَنْتُمْ أَصْحَابِي، وَلَكِنْ إِخْوَانِي الَّذِيْنَ آمَنُوْا بِـي وَلَـمْ يَرَوْنِي.

[277] Set forth by •al-Ṭabarānī in *al-Muʿjam al-Kabīr*, 12/87 §12560. •Abū Yaʿlā, on the authority of ʿUmar b. al-Khaṭṭāb ﷺ, in *al-Musnad*, 1/147 §160. •al-Ḥākim in *al-Mustadrak*, 4/96 §6993. •al-Khaṭīb in *Mishkāt al-Maṣābīḥ*, 3/403 §6288. •al-Haythamī, on the authority of ʿUmar b. al-Khaṭṭāb ﷺ, in *Majmaʿ al-Zawāʾid*, 8/330; 6/65. He said: "It has been reported by al-Bazzār and Aḥmad." •al-Ḥusaynī in *al-Bayān wa al-Taʿrīf*, 1/130 §346.

رَوَاهُ أَحْمَدُ وَالطَّبَرَانِيُّ.

278/26. According to Anas b. Mālik ﷺ:

"Allah's Messenger ﷺ said: 'I would have loved to meet my brethren,' so the Companions of the Prophet ﷺ said: 'Are we not your brethren?' He said: 'You are my Companions, but my brethren are those who have believed in me although they have not seen me.'"

Reported by Aḥmad and al-Ṭabarānī.

٢٧٩/ ٢٧. عَنْ عَبْدِ الرَّحْمَنِ بْنِ أَبِي عُمْرَةَ الْأَنْصَارِيِّ ﷺ عَنْ أَبِيْهِ أَنَّهُ قَالَ لِرَسُوْلِ اللهِ ﷺ: (يَا رَسُوْلَ اللهِ،) أَرَأَيْتَ مَنْ آمَنَ بِكَ وَلَمْ يَرَكَ وَصَدَّقَكَ وَلَمْ يَرَكَ؟ قَالَ: طُوْبَى لَهُمْ! طُوْبَى لَهُمْ! أُوْلَئِكَ مِنَّا.

رَوَاهُ الطَّبَرَانِيُّ.

279/27. According to ʿAbd al-Rahman b. Abī ʿUmra al-Anṣārī on the authority of his father ﷺ:

"He submitted to Allah's Messenger ﷺ asking: '(O Messenger of Allah,) what do you say about those who believe in you although they have not seen you, and they have confirmed faith in you although they have not seen you?' He said: 'Blessed are they, blessed are they! They belong to us!'"

Reported by al-Ṭabarānī.

٢٨٠/ ٢٨. عَنْ أَبِي أُمَامَةَ ﷺ أَنَّ رَسُوْلَ اللهِ ﷺ قَالَ: طُوْبَى لِمَنْ رَآنِي وَآمَنَ بِي وَطُوْبَى سَبْعَ مَرَّاتٍ لِمَنْ لَمْ يَرَنِي وَآمَنَ بِي.

---

278 Set forth by •Aḥmad b. Ḥanbal in *al-Musnad*, 3/155 §12601. •al-Ṭabarānī in *al-Muʿjam al-Kabīr*, 1/212 §576. •al-Haythamī in *Majmaʿ al-Zawāʾid*, 10/67. •al-Ḥusaynī in *al-Bayān wa al-Taʿrīf*, 1/32 §60; 2/94 §1161.

279 Set forth by •al-Ṭabarānī in *al-Muʿjam al-Awsaṭ*, 8/276 §8624.

رَوَاهُ أَحْمَدُ وَابْنُ حِبَّانَ.

280/28. According to Abū Umāma ؓ:

"Allah's Messenger ﷺ said: 'Blessed is the one who has seen me and believed in me, and seven times blessed is the one who has not seen me, yet he has believed in me!'"

Reported by Aḥmad and Ibn Ḥibbān.

٢٨١/ ٢٩. عَنْ أَبِي جُمُعَةَ ؓ قَالَ: تَغَدَّيْنَا مَعَ رَسُوْلِ اللهِ ﷺ وَمَعَنَا أَبُوْ عُبَيْدَةَ بْنُ الْجَرَّاحِ. قَالَ: قَالَ: يَا رَسُوْلَ اللهِ، هَلْ أَحَدٌ خَيْرٌ مِنَّا؟ أَسْلَمْنَا مَعَكَ، وَجَاهَدْنَا مَعَكَ. قَالَ: نَعَمْ، قَوْمٌ يَكُوْنُوْنَ مِنْ بَعْدِكُمْ يُؤْمِنُوْنَ بِي وَلَمْ يَرَوْنِي.

رَوَاهُ أَحْمَدُ وَالدَّارِمِيُّ وَالطَّبَرَانِيُّ، وَقَالَ الْهَيْثَمِيُّ: رِجَالُهُ ثِقَاتٌ.

281/29. According to Abū Jumuʿa ؓ:

"We had dinner with Allah's Messenger ﷺ, and with us was Abū ʿUbayda b. al-Jarrāḥ, who said: 'O Messenger of Allah, is anyone better than us? We have embraced Islam with you, and we have waged the sacred struggle together with you!' He said: 'Yes, the people who will come after you, for they will believe in me although they have not seen me (from this standpoint they will be better than you)!'"

Reported by Aḥmad, al-Dārimī and al-Ṭabarānī, and according to al-Haythamī its narrators are reliable.

---

[280] Set forth by •Aḥmad b. Ḥanbal in *al-Musnad*, 5/257 §22268, 22192, 22331. •Ibn Ḥibbān in *al-Ṣaḥīḥ*, 16/216 §7233. •al-Ḥākim, on the authority of ʿAbd Allāh b. Busr, in *al-Mustadrak*, 4/96 §6994. •al-Ṭabarānī in *al-Muʿjam al-Kabīr*, 8/259 §8009 & in *al-Muʿjam al-Ṣaghīr*, 2/104 §858. •Abū Yaʿlā, on the authority of Anas b. Mālik ؓ, in *al-Musnad*, 6/119 §3391. •al-Maqdisī in *al-Aḥādīth al-Mukhtāra*, 9/99 §87. •al-Rūyānī in *al-Musnad*, 2/311 §1266.

[281] Set forth by •al-Dārimī in *al-Sunan*, 2/398 §2844. •Aḥmad b. Ḥanbal in *al-Musnad*, 4/106 §17017. •al-Ṭabarānī in *al-Muʿjam al-Kabīr*, 4/22 §3537. •Abū Yaʿlā in *al-Musnad*, 3/128 §1559. •Ibn Manda in *Kitāb al-Īmān*, 1/372 §210. •al-Haythamī in *Majmaʿ al-Zawāʾid*, 10/66.

٢٨٢/ ٣٠. عَنْ عَبْدِ الرَّحْمَنِ بْنِ الْعَلَاءِ الْحَضْرَمِيِّ ﷺ قَالَ: حَدَّثَنِي مَنْ سَمِعَ النَّبِيَّ ﷺ يَقُوْلُ: إِنَّهُ سَيَكُوْنُ فِي آخِرِ هَذِهِ الْأُمَّةِ قَوْمٌ لَهُمْ مِثْلُ أَجْرِ أَوَّلِهِمْ. يَأْمُرُوْنَ بِالْمَعْرُوْفِ وَيَنْهَوْنَ عَنِ الْمُنْكَرِ وَيُقَاتِلُوْنَ أَهْلَ الْفِتَنِ.

رَوَاهُ الْبَيْهَقِيُّ.

282/30. According to ʿAbd al-Raḥmān b. al-ʿAlāʾ al-Ḥaḍaramī ﷺ:

"Someone told me that he heard the Prophet ﷺ say: 'In the final era of this *Umma* (Community), surely there will be people who are entitled to the same reward as (that of the people of the) first (era). They will enjoin what is right and forbid what is wrong, and they will fight the troublemakers (and mischief-mongers).'"

Reported by al-Bayhaqī.

[282] Set forth by •al-Bayhaqī in *Dalāʾil al-Nubuwwa*, 6/513. •al-Suyūṭī in *Miftāḥ al-Janna*, 1/68.

اَلْفَصْلُ الثَّالِثُ

فَصْلٌ فِي أَنَّ هَذِهِ الأُمَّةَ لَا تَجْتَمِعُ عَلَى الضَّلَالَةِ

SECTION 3

THIS *UMMA* (COMMUNITY) WILL NOT AGREE UPON AN ERROR

٢٨٣/ ٣١. عَنِ ابْنِ عُمَرَ ﵄ قَالَ: قَالَ رَسُوْلُ اللهِ ﷺ: إِنَّ اللهَ لَا يَجْمَعُ أُمَّتِي (أَوْ قَالَ أُمَّةَ مُحَمَّدٍ) عَلَى ضَلَالَةٍ، وَيَدُ اللهِ مَعَ الْجَمَاعَةِ، وَمَنْ شَذَّ شَذَّ إِلَى النَّارِ.

رَوَاهُ التِّرْمِذِيُّ وَالْحَاكِمُ.

283/31. According to Ibn ʿUmar ﵄:

"Allah's Messenger ﷺ said: 'Allah will not unite my *Umma* (Community)—or he may have said: the *Umma* (Community) of Muhammad ﷺ—in agreement upon an error. The Hand of (the protection of) Allah is with the collective body, and the one who leaves the party deviates towards the Fire of Hell.'"

Reported by al-Tirmidhī and al-Ḥākim.

٢٨٤/ ٣٢. عَنِ الْحَارِثِ الْأَشْعَرِيِّ ﵁ قَالَ: قَالَ رَسُوْلُ اللهِ ﷺ: بِخَمْسِ كَلِمَاتٍ أَمَرَنِي اللهُ بِهِنَّ: الْجَمَاعَةِ وَالسَّمْعِ وَالطَّاعَةِ وَالْهِجْرَةِ وَالْجِهَادِ فِي سَبِيْلِ اللهِ. فَمَنْ خَرَجَ مِنَ الْجَمَاعَةِ قِيْدَ شِبْرٍ فَقَدْ خَلَعَ رِبْقَةَ الْإِسْلَامِ مِنْ رَأْسِهِ إِلَّا أَنْ يَرْجِعَ.

---

[283] Set forth by •al-Tirmidhī in *al-Sunan*: Bk.: *al-Fitan* [Troubles] according to Allah's Messenger ﷺ, Ch.: What has come to us about the necessity of sticking to the congregation, 4/466 §2167. •al-Ḥākim in *al-Mustadrak*, 1/201 §397. •al-Munāwī in *Fayḍ al-Qadīr*, 2/271.

رَوَاهُ الْحَاكِمُ وَابْنُ خُزَيْمَةَ، وَقَالَ الْحَاكِمُ: هَذَا حَدِيْثٌ صَحِيْحٌ.

284/32. According to al-Ḥārith al-Ashʿarī ﵁:

"Allah's Messenger ﷺ said: 'There are five things Allah has commanded me: (1) Collective body, (2) Hearing the advice, (3) Obedience, (4) Emigration, and (5) Struggle in the cause of Allah. If someone departs from collective body as far as the distance between the tip of the thumb and the tip of the little finger (the span of the stretched hand), he has removed the noose of Islam from his head (or removed the strap of obedience and slavery to Islam from his neck) unless he returns (back to community organization to ever remain a part of it).'"

Reported by al-Ḥākim and Ibn Khuzayma. According to al-Ḥākim: "This is an authentic tradition."

٢٨٥/ ٣٣. عَنِ ابْنِ عُمَرَ ﵄ في رواية طويلة قَالَ: خَطَبَنَا عُمَرُ بِالْجَابِيَةِ فَقَالَ: يَأَيُّهَا النَّاسُ، إِنِّي قُمْتُ فِيْكُمْ كَمَقَامِ رَسُوْلِ اللهِ ﷺ فِيْنَا فَقَالَ: عَلَيْكُمْ بِالْجَمَاعَةِ، وَإِيَّاكُمْ وَالْفُرْقَةَ، فَإِنَّ الشَّيْطَانَ مَعَ الْوَاحِدِ، وَهُوَ مِنَ الاثْنَيْنِ أَبْعَدُ. مَنْ أَرَادَ بُحْبُوحَةَ الْجَنَّةِ فَلْيَلْزَمِ الْجَمَاعَةَ. مَنْ سَرَّتْهُ حَسَنَتُهُ وَسَاءَتْهُ سَيِّئَتُهُ فَذَلِكُمُ الْمُؤْمِنُ.

رَوَاهُ التِّرْمِذِيُّ وَالنَّسَائِيُّ وَأَحْمَدُ. وَقَالَ التِّرْمِذِيُّ: هَذَا حَدِيْثٌ حَسَنٌ صَحِيْحٌ.

285/33. According to Ibn ʿUmar ﵄, in the course of a detailed report:

---

[284] Set forth by •al-Ḥākim in *al-Mustadrak*, 1/204, 582 §404, 1534. •Ibn Khuzayma in *al-Ṣaḥīḥ*, 3/195 §1895. •al-Bayhaqī in *al-Sunan al-Kubrā*, 8/157. •al-Ṭabarānī in *al-Muʿjam al-Kabīr*, 3/286, 287, 289 §3427, 3430, 3431. •Abū Yaʿlā in *al-Musnad*, 3/140 §1571.

[285] Set forth by •al-Tirmidhī in *al-Sunan*: Bk.: *al-Fitan* [Troubles] according to Allah's Messenger ﷺ, Ch.: What has come to us about the necessity of sticking to the congregation, 4/465 §2165. •al-Nasāʾī in *al-Sunan al-Kubrā*, 5/388 §9225. •Ibn Abī ʿĀṣim in *al-Sunna*, 1/42 §88. •Aḥmad b. Ḥanbal in *al-Musnad*, 5/370 §23194. •al-ʿAsqalānī in *Fatḥ al-Bārī*, 13/316. •al-Mubārakfūrī in *Tuḥfat al-Aḥwadhī*, 6/320.

"ʿUmar addressed us at Jābiya, and said: 'O people, I am standing at a place among you where Allah's Messenger ﷺ used to stand among us (or I have assumed a stance towards you that Allah's Messenger ﷺ assumed towards us), for he said: "Collective body (party or community organization) is incumbent upon you, and you must be on guard against separatism, for Satan is with the solitary or lone, but remains far from two (or more). If someone seeks the hub (i.e., affluence) of the Garden of Paradise, clinging to the party is inevitable for him. The one who feels pleased on his good deed and displeased on his bad act is the (true) believer."'"

Reported by al-Tirmidhī, al-Nasāʾī and Aḥmad. According to al-Tirmidhī: "This is a fine authentic tradition."

٢٨٦/ ٣٤. عَنِ ابْنِ عُمَرَ رضي الله عنهما قَالَ: قَالَ رَسُوْلُ اللهِ ﷺ: لَا يَجْمَعُ اللهُ هَذِهِ الْأُمَّةَ عَلَى الضَّلَالَةِ أَبَدًا وَقَالَ: يَدُ اللهِ عَلَى الْجَمَاعَةِ فَاتَّبِعُوْا السَّوَادَ الْأَعْظَمَ فَإِنَّهُ مَنْ شَذَّ شَذَّ فِي النَّارِ.

رَوَاهُ الْحَاكِمُ وَابْنُ أَبِي عَاصِمٍ.

286/34. According to Ibn ʿUmar رضي الله عنهما:

"Allah's Messenger ﷺ said: 'Allah will not unite this *Umma* (Community) in agreement upon an error.' He also said: 'Allah's Hand (of Power and Protection) is upon the collective body, so follow the great majority, for the one who breaks away (from the collective body) is cast into the Fire of Hell.'"

Reported by al-Ḥākim and Ibn Abī ʿĀṣim.

---

[286] Set forth by •al-Ḥākim in *al-Mustadrak*, 1/119–201 §391–397. •Ibn Abī ʿĀṣim in *al-Sunna*, 1/39 §80. •al-Lālakāʾī in *Iʿtiqād Ahl al-Sunna*, 1/106 §154. •al-Daylamī in *al-Firdaws bi-Maʾthūr al-Khiṭāb*, 5/258 §8116. •al-Ḥakīm al-Tirmidhī in *Nawādir al-Uṣūl*, 1/4222. •Abū Nuʿaym in *Ḥilya al-Awliyāʾ*, 3/37 •al-Munāwī in *Fayḍ al-Qadīr*, 2/271.

٢٨٧/ ٣٥. عَنْ أَنَسِ بْنِ مَالِكٍ ﷺ قَالَ: قَالَ رَسُوْلُ اللهِ ﷺ: إِنَّ أُمَّتِي لاَ تَجْتَمِعُ عَلَى ضَلاَلَةٍ فَإِذَا رَأَيْتُمُ اخْتِلاَفًا فَعَلَيْكُمْ بِالسَّوَادِ الْأَعْظَمِ.

رَوَاهُ ابْنُ مَاجَه وَالطَّبَرَانِيُّ.

287/35. According to Anas b. Mālik ﷺ:

"Allah's Messenger ﷺ said: 'My *Umma* (Community) will not agree (collectively) upon an error, so if you notice a disagreement, then it is inevitable for you to adhere to the great majority (i.e., collective body).'"

Reported by Ibn Mājah and al-Ṭabarānī.

٢٨٨/ ٣٦. عَنْ أَنَسِ بْنِ مَالِكٍ ﷺ قَالَ: قَالَ رَسُوْلُ اللهِ ﷺ: إِنَّ بَنِي إِسْرَائِيْلَ افْتَرَقَتْ عَلَى إِحْدَى وَسَبْعِيْنَ فِرْقَةً. وَإِنَّ أُمَّتِي سَتَفْتَرِقُ عَلَى ثِنْتَيْنِ وَسَبْعِيْنَ فِرْقَةً. كُلُّهَا فِي النَّارِ إِلاَّ وَاحِدَةً وَهِيَ الْجَمَاعَةُ.

رَوَاهُ ابْنُ مَاجَه وَأَحْمَدُ وَأَبُوْ يَعْلَى.

288/36. According to Anas b. Mālik ﷺ:

"Allah's Messenger ﷺ said: 'The Children of Israel split into seventy-one groups, and my *Umma* (Community) will split into seventy-two groups, all of them in the Fire of Hell, except one, that being the great majority group.'"

Reported by Ibn Mājah and Aḥmad and Abū Yaʿlā.

---

287 Set forth by •Ibn Mājah in *al-Sunan*: Bk.: *al-Fitan* [Troubles] according to Allah's Messenger ﷺ, Ch.: *al-Sawād al-Aʿẓam* [The great majority], 4/367 §3950. •al-Ṭabarānī in *al-Muʿjam al-Kabīr*, 12/447 §13623. •al-Kinānī in *Miṣbāḥ al-Zujāja*, 4/169 §1395.

288 Set forth by •Ibn Mājah in *al-Sunan*: Bk.: *al-Fitan* [Troubles], Ch.: Separation of the Communities, 2/1322 §3991–3993. •Aḥmad b. Ḥanbal in *al-Musnad*, 3/145 §12501. •Abū Yaʿlā in *al-Musnad*, 7/36 §3944. •al-Maqdisī in *al-Aḥādīth al-Mukhtāra*, 7/90 §2499. •Ibn Abī ʿĀṣim in *al-Sunna*, 1/32 §64. •al-Marwazī in *al-Sunna*, 1/21 §53.

٢٨٩/٣٧. عَنْ أَبِي ذَرٍّ ﷺ عَنِ النَّبِيِّ ﷺ أَنَّهُ قَالَ: اثْنَانِ خَيْرٌ مِنْ وَاحِدٍ، وَثَلَاثَةٌ خَيْرٌ مِنِ اثْنَيْنِ، وَأَرْبَعَةٌ خَيْرٌ مِنْ ثَلَاثَةٍ. فَعَلَيْكُمْ بِالْجَمَاعَةِ، فَإِنَّ اللهَ ﷻ لَنْ يَجْمَعَ أُمَّتِي إِلَّا عَلَى هُدًى.

رَوَاهُ أَحْمَدُ.

289/37. According to Abū Dharr ﷺ:

"The Prophet ﷺ said: 'Two are better than one, three are better than two, and four are better than three. You must therefore adhere to the collective body, for Allah ﷻ will never unite my *Umma* (Community) except in agreement upon right guidance.'"

Reported by Aḥmad.

---

[289] Set forth by •Aḥmad b. Ḥanbal in *al-Musnad*, 5/145 §21331. •al-Haythamī in *Majma' al-Zawā'id*, 1/177; 5/218. •al-Mubārakfūrī in *Tuḥfat al-Aḥwadhī*, 6/323.

اَلْفَصْلُ الرَّابِعُ

فَصْلٌ فِي أَنَّ النَّبِيَّ ﷺ كَانَ لَا يَخْشَى عَلَى أُمَّتِهِ أَنْ تُشْرِكَ بَعْدَهُ

SECTION 4

THE PROPHET ﷺ NEVER FEARED THAT HIS UMMA (COMMUNITY) MIGHT BECOME POLYTHEISTIC AFTER HIM

٢٩٠/٣٨. عَنْ عُقْبَةَ بْنِ عَامِرٍ ﵁، قَالَ: صَلَّى رَسُولُ اللهِ ﷺ عَلَى قَتْلَى أُحُدٍ، بَعْدَ ثَمَانِي سِنِينَ كَالْمُوَدِّعِ لِلْأَحْيَاءِ وَالْأَمْوَاتِ، ثُمَّ طَلَعَ الْـمِنْبَرَ، فَقَالَ: إِنِّي بَيْنَ أَيْدِيكُمْ فَرَطٌ وَأَنَا عَلَيْكُمْ شَهِيدٌ، وَإِنَّ مَوْعِدَكُمُ الْحَوْضُ، وَإِنِّي لَأَنْظُرُ إِلَيْهِ مِنْ مَقَامِي هَذَا. وَإِنِّي لَسْتُ أَخْشَى عَلَيْكُمْ أَنْ تُشْرِكُوا، وَلَكِنِّي أَخْشَى عَلَيْكُمُ الدُّنْيَا أَنْ تَنَافَسُوهَا. قَالَ: فَكَانَتْ آخِرَ نَظْرَةٍ نَظَرْتُهَا إِلَى رَسُولِ اللهِ ﷺ.

مُتَّفَقٌ عَلَيْهِ وَاللَّفْظُ لِلْبُخَارِيِّ.

290/38. According to ʿUqba b. ʿĀmir ﵁:

---

290 Set forth by •al-Bukhārī in al-Ṣaḥīḥ: Bk.: al-Maghāzī [Military Expeditions], Ch.: The Campaign of Uḥud, 4/1486 §3816. •Muslim in al-Ṣaḥīḥ: Bk.: al-Faḍāʾil [Excellent Merits], Ch.: Establishment of the Basin [Ḥawḍ] of our Prophet ﷺ and its qualities, 4/1796 §2296. •Abū Dāwūd in al-Sunan: Bk.: al-Janāʾiz [Funeral Ceremonies], Ch.: The ritual prayer is performed on the grave of the deceased after a time, 3/216 §3224. •al-Ṭabarānī in al-Muʿjam al-Kabīr, 17/279 §768. •al-Bayhaqī in al-Sunan al-Kubrā, 4/14 §6601. •al-Shaybānī in al-Āḥād wa al-Mathānī, 5/45 §2583. •Aḥmad b. Ḥanbal in al-Musnad, 4/154.

"Allah's Messenger ﷺ prayed over the martyres of Uḥud, after eight years, like the bidder of farewell to the living and the dead. Then he mounted the pulpit and said: 'I am your forerunner in front of you, and I am a witness over you. Your rendezvous is the Basin [*al-Ḥawḍ*], and I am looking towards it from this station of mine. I have not been afraid that you might become polytheists, but I am afraid that you might get in love with the worldly possessions and pursuits.' That was the last time I had the (eye-cooling and heart-soothing) sight of Allah's Messenger ﷺ."

Agreed upon by al-Bukhārī and Muslim, and this is the wording of al-Bukhārī.

٢٩١/ ٣٩. عَنْ عُقْبَةَ بْنِ عَامِرٍ رضي الله عنه قَالَ: قَالَ رَسُوْلُ اللهِ ﷺ: إِنِّي فَرَطٌ لَكُمْ وَأَنَا شَهِيدٌ عَلَيْكُمْ وَإِنِّي وَاللهِ، لَأَنْظُرُ إِلَى حَوْضِي الآنَ. وَإِنِّي أُعْطِيْتُ مَفَاتِيحَ خَزَائِنِ الْأَرْضِ، أَوْ مَفَاتِيحَ الْأَرْضِ. وَإِنِّي وَاللهِ، مَا أَخَافُ عَلَيْكُمْ أَنْ تُشْرِكُوْا بَعْدِي وَلَكِنْ أَخَافُ عَلَيْكُمْ أَنْ تَتَنَافَسُوْا فِيهَا.

مُتَّفَقٌ عَلَيْهِ.

291/39. According to ʿUqba b. ʿĀmir رضي الله عنه:

"Allah's Messenger ﷺ said: 'I am your forerunner, and I am a witness over you. By Allah, I am looking towards the Basin [*al-Ḥawḍ*] even now, and I have been given the keys of the treasures of the earth (or: 'the keys of the earth'). By Allah, I am not afraid that you might become polytheists after me, but I am afraid that you might get in love with the world (and its pleasures and pursuits).'"

Agreed upon by al-Bukhārī and Muslim.

---

[291] Set forth by •al-Bukhārī in *al-Ṣaḥīḥ*: Bk.: *al-Manāqib* [Virtues], Ch.: The signs of Prophethood in Islam, 3/1317 §3401, & Bk.: *al-Riqāq* [The Softening of Hearts], Ch.: Warning against the charm of this world and competition for it, 5/2361 §6061. •Muslim in *al-Ṣaḥīḥ*: Bk.: *al-Faḍāʾil* [Excellent Merits], Ch.: Establishment of the Basin [*Ḥawḍ*] of our Prophet ﷺ and its qualities, 4/1795 §2296. •Aḥmad b. Ḥanbal in *al-Musnad*, 4/153.

٢٩٢/ ٤٠. عَنْ عُقْبَةَ بْنِ عَامِرٍ ﷺ قَالَ: قَالَ رَسُوْلُ اللهِ ﷺ: إِنِّي لَسْتُ أَخْشَى عَلَيْكُمْ أَنْ تُشْرِكُوْا بَعْدِي، وَلَكِنِّي أَخْشَى عَلَيْكُمُ الدُّنْيَا أَنْ تَنَافَسُوْا فِيْهَا، وَتَقْتَتِلُوْا فَتَهْلِكُوْا كَمَا هَلَكَ مَنْ كَانَ قَبْلَكُمْ. قَالَ عُقْبَةُ: فَكَانَ آخِرَ مَا رَأَيْتُ رَسُوْلَ اللهِ ﷺ عَلَى الْمِنْبَرِ.

رَوَاهُ مُسْلِمٌ.

292/40. According to ʿUqba b. ʿĀmir ﷺ:

"Allah's Messenger ﷺ said: 'I have not been afraid that you might become polytheists after me, but I am afraid that you might be captivated by love of the world and that you might combat one another and perish, as perished those who were before you.'"

ʿUqba said: "That was the last time I saw the effulgent appearance of Allah's Messenger ﷺ upon the pulpit." (He departed life soon after that).

Reported by Muslim.

[292] Set forth by •Muslim in *al-Ṣaḥīḥ*: Bk.: *al-Faḍā'il* [Excellent Merits], Ch.: Establishment of the Basin [*Ḥawḍ*] of our Prophet ﷺ and its qualities, 4/1796 §2296. •al-Ṭabarānī in *al-Muʿjam al-Kabīr*, 17/279 §769. •al-Shaybānī in *al-Āḥād wa al-Mathānī*, 5/45 §2583.

اَلْفَصْلُ الْخَامِسُ

فَصْلٌ فِي بَعْثِ الْأَئِمَّةِ الْمُجَدِّدِيْنَ لِهَذِهِ الْأُمَّةِ

Section 5

The Sending of the Reviving Imams to this *Umma* (Community)

٢٩٣/ ٤١. عَنْ أَبِي هُرَيْرَةَ رضي الله عنه فِيمَا أَعْلَمُ عَنْ رَسُوْلِ اللهِ صلى الله عليه وآله وسلم قَالَ: إِنَّ اللهَ تعالى يَبْعَثُ لِهَذِهِ الْأُمَّةِ عَلَى رَأْسِ كُلِّ مِائَةِ سَنَةٍ مَنْ يُجَدِّدُ لَهَا دِيْنَهَا.

رَوَاهُ أَبُوْ دَاوُدَ وَالْحَاكِمُ وَالطَّبَرَانِيُّ.

293/41. According to Abū Hurayra ﷺ:

"Among what (knowledge) I learnt from Allah's Messenger ﷺ is that he said: 'Indeed, Allah ﷻ will send to this *Umma* (Community), at the beginning of every hundred years, someone who will renew its *Dīn* (Religion) for it.'"

Reported by Abū Dāwūd, al-Ḥākim and al-Ṭabarānī.

٢٩٤/ ٤٢. عَنْ مُعَاذِ بْنِ جَبَلٍ رضي الله عنه قَالَ: قَالَ رَسُوْلُ اللهِ صلى الله عليه وآله وسلم: إِنَّ أَدْنَى الرِّيَاءِ شِرْكٌ وَأَحَبَّ الْعَبِيْدِ إِلَى اللهِ تَبَارَكَ وَتَعَالَى الْأَتْقِيَاءُ الْأَخْفِيَاءُ الَّذِيْنَ إِذَا غَابُوْا لَمْ يُفْتَقَدُوْا وَإِذَا شَهِدُوْا لَمْ يُعْرَفُوْا. أُوْلَئِكَ أَئِمَّةُ الْهُدَى وَمَصَابِيْحُ الْعِلْمِ.

---

293 Set forth by •Abū Dāwūd in *al-Sunan*: Bk.: *al-Malāḥim*, Ch.: Discussion about the century, 4/109 §4291. •al-Ḥākim in *al-Mustadrak*, 4/567–568 §8592–8593. •al-Ṭabarānī in *al-Muʿjam al-Awsaṭ*, 6/223 §6527. •al-Daylamī in *al-Firdaws bi-Maʾthūr al-Khiṭāb*, 1/148 §532. •al-Muqriʾ in *al-Sunan al-Wārida fī al-Fitan*, 3/742 §364. •Ibn ʿAsākir in *Tārīkh Dimashq al-Kabīr*, 51/341, 388. •al-Khaṭīb al-Baghdādī in *Tārīkh Baghdād*, 2/61.

رَوَاهُ الْحَاكِمُ وَالطَّبَرَانِيُّ. وَقَالَ الْحَاكِمُ: هَذَاحَدِيْثٌ صَحِيْحٌ.

294/42. According to Muʿādh b. Jabal ﷺ:

"Allah's Messenger ﷺ said: 'Even an ordinary pretence (and showiness) is a form of polytheism, and the dearest of the servants to Allah Most High are the most self-protecting and retiring devotees, who are not searched for when they are absent, and are not recognized when they are present. It is they who are the imams of right guidance and the lanterns of knowledge.'"

Reported by al-Ḥākim and al-Ṭabarānī. According to al-Ḥākim: "This is an authentic tradition."

٢٩٥/ ٤٣. عَنِ ابْنِ عَبَّاسٍ ﷺ قَالَ: قَالَ رَسُوْلُ اللهِ ﷺ: مَنْ تَمَسَّكَ بِسُنَّتِي عِنْدَ فَسَادِ أُمَّتِي، فَلَهُ أَجْرُ مِائَةِ شَهِيْدٍ.

رَوَاهُ أَبُوْ نُعَيْمٍ وَالْبَيْهَقِيُّ وَالدَّيْلَمِيُّ.

295/43. According to Ibn ʿAbbās ﷺ:

"Allah's Messenger ﷺ said: 'If someone adheres to my Sunna and holds it firmly when my *Umma* (Community) falls prey to mischief and disruption, he is entitled to the reward of a hundred martyrs.'"

Reported by Abū Nuʿaym, al-Bayhaqī and al-Daylamī.

٢٩٦/ ٤٤. عَنِ الْحَسَنِ بْنِ عَلِيٍّ ﷺ قَالَ: قَالَ رَسُوْلُ اللهِ ﷺ: مَنْ جَاءَهُ الْمَوْتُ

---

294 Set forth by •al-Ḥākim in *al-Mustadrak*, 3/303 §5182. •al-Ṭabarānī in *al-Muʿjam al-Awsaṭ*, 5/163 §4950, & in *al-Muʿjam al-Kabīr*, 20/36 §53. •al-Quḍāʿī in *Musnad al-Shihāb*, 2/252 §1298. •al-Bayhaqī in *Kitāb al-Zuhd*, 2/112.

295 Set forth by •Abū Nuʿaym in *Ḥilya al-Awliyāʾ*, 8/200. •al-Bayhaqī in *Kitāb al-Zuhd al-Kabīr*, 2/118 §207. •al-Daylamī in *al-Firdaws bi-Maʾthūr al-Khiṭāb*, 4/198 §6608. •al-Mundhirī in *al-Targhīb wa al-Tarhīb*, 1/41 §65. •al-Mizzī in *Tahdhīb al-Kamāl*, 24/364. •al-Dhahabī in *Mīzān al-Iʿtidāl*, 2/270.

وَهُوَ يَطْلُبُ الْعِلْمَ لِيُحْيِيَ بِهِ الإِسْلَامَ فَبَيْنَهُ وَبَيْنَ النَّبِيِّيْنَ دَرَجَةٌ وَاحِدَةٌ فِي الْجَنَّةِ.

رَوَاهُ الدَّارِمِيُّ وَالطَّبَرَانِيُّ.

296/44. According to al-Ḥasan b. ʿAlī ﵄:

"Allah's Messenger ﷺ said: 'If death comes to someone who is striving to acquire knowledge with the intention that he will revive Islam by means of that knowledge, the difference between him and the Prophets in the Garden of Paradise will only be of a single degree!'"

Reported by al-Dārimī and al-Ṭabarānī.

٢٩٧/ ٤٥. عَنْ أَبِي هُرَيْرَةَ ﵁، عَنْ رَسُوْلِ اللهِ ﷺ أَنَّهُ قَالَ: لَا نَبِيَّ بَعْدِي. قَالُوْا: فَمَا يَكُوْنُ، يَا رَسُوْلَ اللهِ؟ قَالَ: يَكُوْنُ خُلَفَاءُ بَعْضُهُمْ عَلَى أَثَرِ بَعْضٍ فَمَنِ اسْتَقَامَ مِنْهُمْ فَفُوْا لَهُمْ بَيْعَتَهُمْ، وَمَنْ لَمْ يَسْتَقِمْ فَأَدُّوْا إِلَيْهِمْ حَقَّهُمْ وَسَلُوا اللهَ الَّذِي لَكُمْ.

رَوَاهُ ابْنُ رَاهَوَيْهِ.

297/45. According to Abū Hurayra ﵁:

"Allah's Messenger ﷺ said: '(Know that) there is no Prophet after me.' The Companions submitted: 'So what will there be, O Messenger of Allah?' He said: 'There will be (my) Caliphs and (subsequently) their Caliphs. For those of them you find on the straight path, you must fulfil their pledge of allegiance (the covenant of faithfulness), and for those who do not follow the straight path, you must discharge their rightful due, and ask Allah for what is your rightful due.'"

---

296 Set forth by •al-Dārimī in *al-Sunan*, Ch.: The excellence of knowledge and the scholar, 1/112 §354. •Ibn ʿAsākir in *Tārīkh Dimashq al-Kabīr*, 51/61. •al-Ṭabarānī in *al-Muʿjam al-Awsaṭ*, 9/174 §9454. •al-Haythamī in *Majmaʿ al-Zawāʾid*, 1/123. •Ibn ʿAbd al-Barr in *Jāmiʿ Bayān al-ʿIlm wa Faḍ li-h*, 1/46. •al-Zubaydī in *Ittiḥāf Sādat al-Muttaqīn*, 1/100. •al-Mundhirī in *al-Targhīb wa al-Tarhīb*, 1/53 §110.

297 Set forth by •Ibn Rāhawayh in *al-Musnad*, 1/257 §223.

Reported by Ibn Rāhawayh.

٢٩٨/ ٤٦. عَنْ كَثِيْرِ بْنِ عَبْدِ اللهِ الْـمُزَنِيِّ عَنْ أَبِيْهِ عَنْ جَدِّهِ ﷺ قَالَ: قَالَ رَسُوْلُ اللهِ ﷺ: إِنَّ الدِّيْنَ (أَوْ قَالَ: إِنَّ الإِسْلَامَ) بَدَأَ غَرِيْبًا وَسَيَعُوْدُ غَرِيْبًا كَمَا بَدَأَ؛ فَطُوْبَى لِلْغُرَبَاءِ؛ قِيْلَ: يَا رَسُوْلَ اللهِ، مَنِ الْغُرَبَاءُ؟ قَالَ: الَّذِيْنَ يُحْيُوْنَ سُنَّتِي وَيُعَلِّمُوْنَهَا عِبَادَ اللهِ.

رَوَاهُ التِّرْمِذِيُّ وَالْقُضَاعِيُّ وَاللَّفْظُ لَهُ وَالْبَيْهَقِيُّ فِي الزُّهْدِ.

298/46. According to Kathīr b. ʿAbd Allāh al-Muzanī, on the authority of his father, his grandfather ﷺ said:

"Allah's Messenger ﷺ said: 'Certainly, the *Dīn* (Religion) (or he may have said: Islam) began as a stranger (i.e., the followers of *Dīn* seemed strangers, or it also means that the spread of Islam started from wayfaring and emigration). And (a time will also come when) this Religion will once again appear alien (to society) as it used to look like in the beginning. And there is good news for those who get isolated (to work for the promotion of *Dīn* with concentration). He was asked: 'O Messenger of Allah, who are the strangers?' He said: 'Those who revive my Sunna and teach it to the servants of Allah!'"

Reported by al-Tirmidhī, al-Quḍāʿī (the wording is his) and al-Bayhaqī in *al-Zuhd*.

٢٩٩/ ٤٧. عَنْ سَعِيْدِ بْنِ الْـمُسَيَّبِ ﷺ أَنَّ رَسُوْلَ اللهِ ﷺ قَالَ: مَنْ تَعَلَّمَ الْعِلْمَ يُحْيِي بِهِ الإِسْلَامَ لَـمْ يَكُنْ بَيْنَهُ وَبَيْنَ الْأَنْبِيَاءِ إِلاَّ دَرَجَةٌ.

---

[298] Set forth by •al-Tirmidhī in *al-Sunan*: Bk.: *al-Imān* [Faith], Ch.: What has come to us that Islam began with the poor, and it will return to the poor just as it began, 5/18 §2840. •al-Quḍāʿī in *Musnad al-Shihāb*, 2/138 §1052–1053. •Ibn Abī Shayba in *al-Muṣannaf*, 7/83 §34367. •al-Ṭabarānī in *al-Muʿjam al-Kabīr*, 17/16 §11. •Abū Nuʿaym in *Ḥilya al-Awliyāʾ*, 2/10. •al-Bayhaqī in *Kitāb al-Zuhd al-Kabīr*, 2/117 §205. •al-Haythamī in *Majmaʿ al-Zawāʾid*, 7/318. •al-Suyūṭī in *Miftāḥ al-Janna*, 1/67.

رَوَاهُ ابْنُ عَبْدِ الْبَرِّ.

299/47. According to Saʿīd b. al-Musayyib ﷺ:

"Allah's Messenger ﷺ said: 'If someone acquires knowledge with which to revive Islam, there will not be any difference between him and the Prophets except by only one degree.'"

Reported by Ibn ʿAbd al-Barr.

٣٠٠/٤٨. عَنِ الْحَسَنِ ابْنِ عَلِيٍّ عليهما السلام قَالَ: قَالَ رَسُوْلُ اللهِ ﷺ: رَحْمَةُ اللهِ عَلَى خُلَفَائِي، ثَلَاثَ مَرَّاتٍ. قَالُوْا: وَمَنْ خُلَفَاؤُكَ، يَا رَسُوْلَ اللهِ؟ قَالَ: الَّذِيْنَ يُحْيُوْنَ سُنَّتِي وَيُعَلِّمُوْنَهَا النَّاسَ.

رَوَاهُ ابْنُ عَسَاكِرَ وَابْنُ عَبْدِ الْبَرِّ وَالْهِنْدِيُّ.

300/48. According to al-Ḥasan b. ʿAlī ﷺ:

"Allah's Messenger ﷺ said three times: 'May Allah's mercy be upon my Caliphs.' The Companions said: 'And who are your Caliphs, O Messenger of Allah?' He said: 'Those who revive my Sunna and teach it to the people!'"

Reported by Ibn ʿAsākir, Ibn ʿAbd al-Barr and al-Hindī.

٣٠١/ ٤٩. عَنْ أَبِي سَعِيْدٍ الْفَرْيَابِيِّ رحمه الله قَالَ: قَالَ أَحْمَدُ بْنُ حَنْبَلٍ رحمه الله: إِنَّ اللهَ يُقَيِّضُ لِلنَّاسِ فِي كُلِّ رَأْسِ مِائَةِ سَنَةٍ مَنْ يُعَلِّمُهُمُ السُّنَنَ وَيَنْفِي عَنْ رَسُوْلِ اللهِ ﷺ الْكِذْبَ.

رَوَاهُ الْمِزِّيُّ وَالْخَطِيْبُ وَالْعَسْقَلَانِيُّ.

301/49. According to Ibn Saʿīd al-Faryābī ﷺ:

---

299 Set forth by •Ibn ʿAbd al-Barr in *Jāmiʿ Bayān al-ʿIlm wa Faḍli-h*, 46/1.

300 Set forth by •Ibn ʿAsākir in *Tārīkh Dimashq al-Kabīr*, 51/61. •Ibn ʿAbd al-Barr in *Jāmiʿ Bayān al-ʿIlm wa Faḍli-h*, 1/46. •al-Hindī in *Kanz al-ʿUmmāl*, 10/229 §29209.

301 Set forth by •al-Mizzī in *Tahdhīb al-Kamāl*, 24/365. •al-ʿAsqalānī in *Tahdhīb al-Tahdhīb*, 9/25. •al-Khaṭīb in *Tārīkh Baghdād*, 2/62. •al-ʿAẓīm

"Aḥmad b. Ḥanbal ﵀ said: 'Allah sends to the people, at the beginning of every hundred years, someone who teaches them the practices of Sunna, and refutes the lies ascribed to Allah's Messenger ﷺ.'"

Reported by al-Mizzī, al-Khaṭīb and al-ʿAsqalānī.

Ābādī in *ʿAwn al-Maʿbūd*, 11/261.

الْبَابُ الْخَامِسُ

حُكْمُ الْخَوَارِجِ وَالْمُرْتَدِّيْنَ وَالْمُتَنَقِّصِيْنَ النَّبِيَّ ﷺ

CHAPTER 5

THE KHAWĀRIJ, THE APOSTATES AND THE DENIGRATORS OF THE PROPHET ﷺ

١/٣٠٢. عَنْ أَبِي سَعِيْدٍ الْخُدْرِيِّ رضي الله عنه يَقُوْلُ: بَعَثَ عَلِيُّ بْنُ أَبِي طَالِبٍ رضي الله عنهما إِلَى رَسُوْلِ اللهِ ﷺ مِنَ الْيَمَنِ بِذُهَيْبَةٍ فِي أَدِيْمٍ مَقْرُوْظٍ لَمْ تُحَصَّلْ مِنْ تُرَابِهَا. قَالَ: فَقَسَمَهَا بَيْنَ أَرْبَعَةِ نَفَرٍ بَيْنَ عُيَيْنَةَ ابْنِ بَدْرٍ وَأَقْرَعَ بْنِ حَابِسٍ وَزَيْدِ الْخَيْلِ وَالرَّابِعُ إِمَّا عَلْقَمَةُ وَإِمَّا عَامِرُ بْنُ الطُّفَيْلِ. فَقَالَ رَجُلٌ مِنْ أَصْحَابِهِ: كُنَّا نَحْنُ أَحَقَّ بِهَذَا مِنْ هَؤُلَاءِ. قَالَ: فَبَلَغَ ذَلِكَ النَّبِيَّ ﷺ، فَقَالَ: أَلَا تَأْمَنُوْنِي وَأَنَا أَمِيْنُ مَنْ فِي السَّمَاءِ؟ يَأْتِيْنِي خَبَرُ السَّمَاءِ صَبَاحًا وَمَسَاءً.

قَالَ: فَقَامَ رَجُلٌ غَائِرُ الْعَيْنَيْنِ، مُشْرِفُ الْوَجْنَتَيْنِ، نَاشِزُ الْجَبْهَةِ، كَثُّ اللِّحْيَةِ، مَحْلُوْقُ الرَّأْسِ، مُشَمَّرُ الْإِزَارِ. فَقَالَ: يَا رَسُوْلَ اللهِ، اتَّقِ اللهَ. قَالَ: وَيْلَكَ أَوَلَسْتُ أَحَقَّ أَهْلِ الْأَرْضِ أَنْ يَتَّقِيَ اللهَ؟

قَالَ: ثُمَّ وَلَّى الرَّجُلُ. قَالَ خَالِدُ بْنُ الْوَلِيْدِ: يَا رَسُوْلَ اللهِ، أَلَا أَضْرِبُ عُنُقَهُ؟ قَالَ: لَا، لَعَلَّهُ أَنْ يَكُوْنَ يُصَلِّي. فَقَالَ خَالِدٌ: وَكَمْ مِنْ مُصَلٍّ يَقُوْلُ بِلِسَانِهِ مَا لَيْسَ فِي قَلْبِهِ.

قَالَ رَسُوْلُ اللهِ ﷺ: إِنِّي لَـمْ أُوْمَرْ أَنْ أَنْقُبَ عَنْ قُلُوْبِ النَّاسِ، وَلاَ أَشُقَّ بُطُوْنَهُمْ.

قَالَ: ثُمَّ نَظَرَ إِلَيْهِ وَهُوَ مُقَفٍّ، فَقَالَ: إِنَّهُ يَخْرُجُ مِنْ ضِئْضِيءِ هَذَا قَوْمٌ يَتْلُوْنَ كِتَابَ اللهِ رَطْبًا لاَ يُجَاوِزُ حَنَاجِرَهُمْ. يَمْرُقُوْنَ مِنَ الدِّيْنِ كَما يَمْرُقُ السَّهْمُ مِنَ الرَّمِيَّةِ. وَأَظُنُّهُ قَالَ: لَئِنْ أَدْرَكْتُهُمْ، لَأَقْتُلَنَّهُمْ قَتْلَ ثَمُوْدَ.

مُتَّفَقٌ عَلَيْهِ.

302/1. According to Abū Saʿīd al-Khudrī ﷺ:

"ʿAlī b. Abī Ṭālib ﷺ sent to Allah's Messenger ﷺ from Yemen, in a tanned leather skin, a small piece of gold from which even the soil had not yet been removed. He distributed it among these four individuals: (1) ʿUyayna b. Badr, (2) Aqraʿ b. Ḥābis, (3) Zayd al-Khayl, and (4) either ʿAlqama or ʿĀmir b. al-Ṭufayl. A man from among his Companions said: 'We were more deserving of this than these!' When that reached the Prophet ﷺ, he said: 'Do you not trust me while I am the trustee of those in heaven? The news of heaven comes to me in the morning and in the evening!'

"Then stood up a man with deep sunken eyes, raised cheek bones, a bulging forehead, a thick and bulky beard, a shaven head and a waist sheet that was lifted above his knees. He said: 'O Messenger of Allah, fear Allah!' He said: 'Woe to you! Am I not the worthiest of the people of the earth, with regard to wariness of Allah?'

"So when the man turned to go away, Khālid b. al-Walīd said:

---

[302] Set forth by •al-Bukhārī in *al-Ṣaḥīḥ*, Bk.: *al-Maghāzī* [Military Expeditions], Ch.: The sending of ʿAlī b. Abī Ṭālib and Khālid b. al-Walīd ﷺ to Yemen before the Farewell Pilgimage, 4/1581 §4094. •Muslim in *al-Ṣaḥīḥ*, Bk.: *al-Zakāt* [The Alms-due], Ch.: Discussion of the Khawārij and their qualities, 2/742 §1064. •Aḥmad b. Ḥanbal in *al-Musnad*, 3/4 §11021. •Ibn Khuzayma in *al-Ṣaḥīḥ*, 4/71 §2373. •Ibn Ḥibbān in *al-Ṣaḥīḥ*, 1/205 §25. •Abū Yaʿlā in *al-Musnad*, 2/390. •Abū Nuʿaym in *al-Musnad al-Mustakhraj* 3/128 §2375, & in *Ḥilya al-Awliyā*ʾ, 5/71. •al-ʿAsqalānī in *Fatḥ al-Bārī*, 8/68 §4094. •*Ḥāshiya Ibn al-Qayyim*, 13/16. •al-Suyūṭī in *al-Dībāj*, 3/160 §1064. •Ibn Taymiyya in *al-Ṣārim al-Maslūl*, 1/188, 192.

'O Messenger of Allah, shall I not strike his neck?' He said: 'No, perhaps he is a performer of the ritual prayer!' Khālid submitted: 'Many a performer of the ritual prayer says with his tongue what is not in his heart!' Allah's Messenger ﷺ said: 'I have not been commanded to break into people's hearts, nor to cut open their bellies!'

"Then the Prophet ﷺ looked towards him and he (the man) had turned his back towards him, so he said: 'From the offspring of this man, there will emerge a set of people who will recite the Book of Allah as a tune, but the Qurʾān will not pass beyond their throats. They will dart through the Religion as the arrow darts through the game animal.' I also think that he said: 'If I was present in their time, I would surely kill them like the slaughter of Thamūd!'"

Agreed upon by al-Bukhārī and Muslim.

٣٠٣/ ٢. وفي رواية مسلم زاد: فَقَامَ إِلَيْهِ عُمَرُ بْنُ الْخَطَّابِ ﵁، فَقَالَ: يَا رَسُوْلَ اللهِ، أَلَا أَضْرِبُ عُنُقَهُ؟ قَالَ: لَا. قَالَ: ثُمَّ أَدْبَرَ فَقَامَ إِلَيْهِ خَالِدٌ سَيْفُ اللهِ. فَقَالَ: يَا رَسُوْلَ اللهِ، أَلَا أَضْرِبُ عُنُقَهُ؟ قَالَ: لَا. فَقَالَ: إِنَّهُ سَيَخْرُجُ مِنْ ضِئْضِئِ هٰذَا قَوْمٌ يَتْلُوْنَ كِتَابَ اللهِ لَيِّنًا رَطْبًا، (وَقَالَ: قَالَ عُمَارَةُ: حَسِبْتُهُ) قَالَ: لَئِنْ أَدْرَكْتُهُمْ، لَأَقْتُلَنَّهُمْ قَتْلَ ثَمُوْدَ.

303/2. In the report of Muslim, he added: "ʿUmar b. al-Khaṭṭāb ﵁ stood up and submitted: 'O Messenger of Allah, shall I not strike off his (the hypocrite's) neck?' He said: 'No!' Then the man turned away, so Khālid Sayf Allah stood up and submitted: 'O Messenger of Allah, shall I not strike off his (the hypocrite's) neck?' He said: 'No!' Then he said: 'From the offspring of this man, there will emerge a set of people who will recite the Book of Allah as a gentle and pleasing tune.' (According to ʿUmāra, he supposed that) he said: 'If I was present in their time, I would certainly kill them like the slaughter of Thamūd!'"

---

[303] Set forth by •Muslim in *al-Ṣaḥīḥ*, Bk.: *al-Zakāt* [The Alms-due], Ch.: Discussion of the Khawārij and their qualities, 2/743 §1064.

٣/٣٠٤. عَنْ أَبِي سَعِيْدٍ الْخُدْرِيِّ ﷺ قَالَ: بَيْنَا النَّبِيُّ ﷺ يَقْسِمُ ذَاتَ يَوْمٍ قِسْمًا فَقَالَ ذُوالْخُوَيْصَرَةِ رَجُلٌ مِنْ بَنِي تَمِيْمٍ: يَا رَسُوْلَ اللهِ، اعْدِلْ. قَالَ: وَيْلَكَ مَنْ يَعْدِلُ إِذَا لَمْ أَعْدِلْ! فَقَالَ عُمَرُ: ائْذَنْ لِي فَلأَضْرِبْ عُنُقَهُ. قَالَ: لاَ، إِنَّ لَهُ أَصْحَابًا يَحْقِرُ أَحَدُكُمْ صَلاَتَهُ مَعَ صَلاَتِهِمْ، وَصِيَامَهُ مَعَ صِيَامِهِمْ. يَمْرُقُوْنَ مِنَ الدِّيْنِ كَمُرُوْقِ السَّهْمِ مِنَ الرَّمِيَّةِ. يَنْظُرُ إِلَى نَصْلِهِ فَلاَ يُوْجَدُ فِيْهِ شَيْءٌ ثُمَّ يَنْظُرُ إِلَى رِصَافِهِ فَلاَ يُوْجَدُ فِيْهِ شَيْءٌ ثُمَّ يَنْظُرُ إِلَى نَضِيِّهِ فَلاَ يُوْجَدُ فِيْهِ شَيْءٌ ثُمَّ يَنْظُرُ إِلَى قُذَذِهِ فَلاَ يُوْجَدُ فِيْهِ شَيْءٌ. قَدْ سَبَقَ الْفَرْثَ وَالدَّمَ. يَخْرُجُوْنَ عَلَى حِيْنِ فُرْقَةٍ مِنَ النَّاسِ. آيَتُهُمْ رَجُلٌ إِحْدَى يَدَيْهِ مِثْلُ ثَدْيِ الْمَرْأَةِ أَوْ مِثْلُ الْبَضْعَةِ تَدَرْدَرُ.

قَالَ أَبُوْ سَعِيْدٍ: أَشْهَدُ لَسَمِعْتُهُ مِنَ النَّبِيِّ ﷺ، وَأَشْهَدُ أَنِّي كُنْتُ مَعَ عَلِيٍّ حِيْنَ قَاتَلَهُمْ. فَالْتُمِسَ فِي الْقَتْلَى فَأُتِيَ بِهِ عَلَى النَّعْتِ الَّذِي نَعَتَ النَّبِيُّ ﷺ.

مُتَّفَقٌ عَلَيْهِ.

304/3. According to Abū Saʿīd al-Khudrī ﷺ:

"While the Prophet ﷺ was distributing the war gains among us one day, Dhū al-Khuwayṣira, a man from the Banū Tamīm tribe, said: 'O Messenger of Allah, act fairly!' He replied: 'Woe to you! Who acts fairly, if I do not act fairly?' ʿUmar then said: '(O Messenger of Allah!) Give me permission to strike his neck off!' He said: 'No! He has companions as well who would perform the

304 Set forth by •al-Bukhārī in *al-Ṣaḥīḥ*, Bk.: *al-Adab* [Proper Conduct], Ch.: What has come to us about the man's saying: "Woe to you!" 5/2281 §5811, & in Bk.: Calling on the apostates and the intransigents to repent, and fighting them, Ch.: & Someone who refrains from fighting the Khawārij because of sympathy, and so that the people will not shun him, 6/2540 §6534. •Muslim in *al-Ṣaḥīḥ*, Bk.: *al-Zakāt* [The Alms-due], Ch.: Discussion of the Khawārij and their qualities, 2/744 §1064. •al-Nasāʾī in *al-Sunan al-Kubrā*, 5/159 §8560–8561; 6/355 §11220. •Aḥmad b. Ḥanbal in *al-Musnad*, 3/65 §11639. •Ibn Ḥibbān in *al-Ṣaḥīḥ*, 15/140 §6741. •al-Bayhaqī in *al-Sunan al-Kubrā*, 8/171. •ʿAbd al-Razzāq in *al-Muṣannaf*, 10/146.

ritual prayers which if any one of you would compare with his own he would consider it inferior to theirs and his fasting inferior to theirs. But they would stray from the Religion like darting of the arrow through the game animal—the hunter examines the head of the arrow, but finds nothing on it. Then he examines its cord, but there is nothing on it. Then he examines its shaft, but there is nothing on it. Then he examines its feather, but there is nothing on it. It flies past missing the faeces and the blood (of the game animal too fast to take any smear). They will emerge at the time of a disintegration of people into sects (to fuel this dissension). Their signs include a man who has one hand like the breast of a woman, or like a quivering lump of flesh.'"

Abū Saʿīd said: "I bear witness that I heard it from the Prophet ﷺ, and I bear witness that I was together with ʿAlī when he fought them (the Khawārij). The man described by the Prophet ﷺ was searched among the killed and was found; he was exactly the same as the Prophet ﷺ had described him."

Agreed upon by al-Bukhārī and Muslim.

٣٠٥/ ٤. عَنْ أَبِي سَعِيْدٍ الْخُدْرِيِّ رضي الله عنه قَالَ: بَعَثَ عَلِيٌّ رضي الله عنه وَهُوَ بِالْيَمَنِ إِلَى النَّبِيِّ ﷺ بِذُهَيْبَةٍ فِي تُرْبَتِهَا فَقَسَمَهَا بَيْنَ الْأَقْرَعِ بْنِ حَابِسٍ الْحَنْظَلِيِّ ثُمَّ أَحَدِ بَنِي مُجَاشِعٍ وَبَيْنَ عُيَيْنَةَ بْنِ بَدْرٍ الْفَزَارِيِّ وَبَيْنَ عَلْقَمَةَ بْنِ عُلَاثَةَ الْعَامِرِيِّ ثُمَّ أَحَدِ بَنِي كِلَابٍ وَبَيْنَ زَيْدِ الْخَيْلِ الطَّائِيِّ ثُمَّ أَحَدِ بَنِي نَبْهَانَ فَتَغَيَّظَتْ قُرَيْشٌ وَالْأَنْصَارُ فَقَالُوْا: يُعْطِيْهِ صَنَادِيْدَ أَهْلِ نَجْدٍ وَيَدَعُنَا. قَالَ: إِنَّمَا أَتَأَلَّفُهُمْ. فَأَقْبَلَ رَجُلٌ غَائِرُ الْعَيْنَيْنِ، نَاتِئُ الْجَبِيْنِ، كَثُّ اللِّحْيَةِ، مُشْرِفُ الْوَجْنَتَيْنِ، مَحْلُوْقُ الرَّأْسِ، فَقَالَ: يَا مُحَمَّدُ، اتَّقِ اللهَ. فَقَالَ النَّبِيُّ ﷺ: فَمَنْ يُطِيْعُ اللهَ إِذَا عَصَيْتُهُ فَيَأْمَنُنِي عَلَى أَهْلِ الْأَرْضِ وَلَا تَأْمَنُوْنِي؟ فَسَأَلَ رَجُلٌ مِنَ الْقَوْمِ قَتْلَهُ - أُرَاهُ خَالِدَ بْنَ الْوَلِيْدِ - فَمَنَعَهُ النَّبِيُّ ﷺ (وفي روية أبي نعيم: فَقَالَ: يَا مُحَمَّدُ، اتَّقِ اللهَ وَاعْدِلْ. فَقَالَ رَسُوْلُ اللهِ ﷺ: يَأْمَنُنِي أَهْلُ السَّمَاءِ وَلَا تَأْمَنُوْنِي؟ فَقَالَ أَبُوْ بَكْرٍ: أَضْرِبُ رَقَبَتَهُ، يَا رَسُوْلَ اللهِ؟ قَالَ: نَعَمْ، فَذَهَبَ فَوَجَدَهُ يُصَلِّي، فَجَاءَ النَّبِيَّ

ﷺ فَقَالَ: وَجَدْتُهُ يُصَلِّي. فَقَالَ آخَرُ: أَنَا أَضْرِبُ رَقَبَتَهُ؟) فَلَـمَّا وَلَّى قَالَ النَّبِيُّ ﷺ: إِنَّ مِنْ ضِئْضِيءِ هَذَا قَوْمًا يَقْرَءُوْنَ الْقُرْآنَ؛ لاَ يُجَاوِزُ حَنَاجِرَهُمْ. يَمْرُقُوْنَ مِنَ الإِسْلاَمِ مُرُوْقَ السَّهْمِ مِنَ الرَّمِيَّةِ. يَقْتُلُوْنَ أَهْلَ الإِسْلاَمِ وَيَدَعُوْنَ أَهْلَ الْأَوْثَانِ. لَئِنْ أَدْرَكْتُهُمْ، لأَقْتُلَنَّهُمْ قَتْلَ عَادٍ.

مُتَّفَقٌ عَلَيْهِ وَهَذَا لَفْظُ الْبُخَارِيِّ.

305/4. According to Abū Saʿīd al-Khudrī ؓ:

"While ʿAlī ؑ was in Yemen, he sent to the Prophet ﷺ a small piece of unclean gold, so he distributed it among the following: al-Aqraʿ b. Ḥābis al-Ḥanẓalī, then a member of the Banū Mujāshiʿ tribe and ʿUyayna b. Badr al-Fazārī and ʿAlqama b. ʿUlātha al-ʿĀmirī, then a member of the Banū Kilāb and Zayd al-Khayl al-Ṭāʾī, then a member of the Banū Nabhān. Quraysh and the Anṣār felt annoyed on this, so they said: 'He is giving it to the chieftains of the people of Najd and leaving us out!' He said: 'I am simply bringing their hearts together!' Then along came a man with sunken eyes, a bulging forehead, a thick and bulky beard,

---

[305] Set forth by •al-Bukhārī in *al-Ṣaḥīḥ*, Bk.: *al-Tawḥīd* [The Affirmation of Oneness], Ch.: Allah's saying: "The angels and the Spirit ascend to Him [*taʿruju al-malāʾikatu wa al-rūḥu ilay-hi*]." (Q.70:4), 6/2702 §6995, & Bk.: *al-Anbiyāʾ* [The Prophets], Ch.: Allah's saying: "And as for ʿĀd, they were destroyed by a fierce roaring wind [*wa ammā ʿĀdun fa-uhlikū bi-rīḥin ṣarṣarun ʿātiya*]." (Q.69:6), 3/1219 §3166. •Muslim in *al-Ṣaḥīḥ*, Bk.: *al-Zakāt* [The Alms-due], Ch.: Discussion of the Khawārij and their qualities, 2/741 §1064. •Abū Dāwūd in *al-Sunan*, Bk.: The Sunna, Ch.: Fighting the Khawārij, 4/243 §4764. •al-Nasāʾī in *al-Sunan*, Bk.: The Prohibition of Bloodshed, Ch.: Someone who unsheathes his sword, then thrusts it into the people, 7/118 §4101, & Bk.: The Alms-due, Ch.: That which appeases their hearts, 5/87 §2578, & in *al-Sunan al-Kubrā*, 6/356 §11221. •Abū Nuʿaym in *al-Musnad al-Mustakhraj*, 3/127 §2373. •Aḥmad b. Ḥanbal in *al-Musnad*, 3/68, 73 §11666, 11713. •ʿAbd al-Razzāq in *al-Muṣannaf*, 10/156. •al-Bayhaqī in *al-Sunan al-Kubrā*, 6/339 §12724; 7/18 §12926. •Ibn Manṣūr in *Kitāb a-Sunan*, 2/373 §2903. •Abū Nuʿaym in *Ḥilya al-Awliyāʾ*, 5/72. •al-Shawkānī in *Nayl al-Awṭār*, 7/345. •Ibn Taymiyya in *al-Ṣārim al-Maslūl*, 1/196.

raised cheek bones and a shaven head. He said: 'O Muhammad, fear Allah!' The Prophet ﷺ said: 'Who obeys Allah if I disobey Him? He entrusts me with the people of the earth, but do you not trust me?' One of the Companions asked permission to kill him—I think he was Khālid b. al-Walīd—but the Prophet ﷺ prevented him." (In the report of Abū Nuʿāym): "He said: 'O Muhammad, beware of Allah and act fairly,' so Allah's Messenger ﷺ said: 'I am the trustee of those in heaven, but do you not trust me?' Abū Bakr then submitted: 'Shall I strike his neck, O Messenger of Allah?' He said yes, so he went and found him performing the ritual prayer. Then he came to the Prophet ﷺ and submitted: 'I found him performing the ritual prayer (so I did not kill him)!' Then some other Companion submitted: 'Shall I strike his neck off?' When he went away, the Prophet ﷺ said: 'Among the offspring of this man, there will emerge a set of people who will recite the Qurʾān but it will not pass beyond their throats. They will get away from Islam as the arrow darts through the game animal. They will kill the Muslims and leave the idolators. If I was in their time, I would surely kill them like the slaughter of ʿĀd!'"

Agreed upon by al-Bukhārī and Muslim, and this is the wording of al-Bukhārī.

٣٠٦/ ٥. عَنْ عَلِيٍّ رضي الله عنه قَالَ: إِنِّي سَمِعْتُ رَسُوْلَ اللهِ ﷺ يَقُوْلُ: سَيَخْرُجُ قَوْمٌ فِي آخِرِ الزَّمَانِ أَحْدَاثُ الْأَسْنَانِ، سُفَهَاءُ الْأَحْلَامِ. يَقُوْلُوْنَ مِنْ خَيْرِ قَوْلِ الْبَرِيَّةِ؛ لَا يُجَاوِزُ إِيْمَانُهُمْ حَنَاجِرَهُمْ؛ يَمْرُقُوْنَ مِنَ الدِّيْنِ كَمَا يَمْرُقُ السَّهْمُ مِنَ الرَّمِيَّةِ؛ فَأَيْنَمَا لَقِيْتُمُوْهُمْ فَاقْتُلُوْهُمْ، فَإِنَّ فِي قَتْلِهِمْ أَجْرًا لِمَنْ قَتَلَهُمْ يَوْمَ الْقِيَامَةِ. مُتَّفَقٌ عَلَيْهِ.

وَأَخْرَجَهُ أَبُو عِيْسَى التِّرْمِذِيُّ عَنْ عَبْدِ اللهِ بْنِ مَسْعُوْدٍ رضي الله عنهما فِي سُنَنِهِ، وَقَالَ: وَفِي الْبَابِ عَنْ عَلِيٍّ وَأَبِي سَعِيْدٍ وَأَبِي ذَرٍّ رضي الله عنهم، وَهَذَا حَدِيْثٌ حَسَنٌ صَحِيْحٌ. وَقَدْ رُوِيَ فِي غَيْرِ هَذَا الْحَدِيْثِ: عَنِ النَّبِيِّ ﷺ حَيْثُ وَصَفَ هَؤُلَاءِ الْقَوْمَ الَّذِيْنَ يَقْرَءُونَ الْقُرْآنَ

لَا يُجَاوِزُ تَرَاقِيَهُمْ. يَمْرُقُونَ مِنَ الدِّينِ كَمَا يَمْرُقُ السَّهْمُ مِنَ الرَّمِيَّةِ. إِنَّمَا هُمُ الْـخَوَارِجُ الْـحَرُورِيَّةُ وَغَيْرُهُمْ مِنَ الْـخَوَارِجِ.

306/5. According to ʿAlī:

"I heard Allah's Messenger say: 'Soon at the end of time, there will appear or emerge some people who will be young in age and empty of reason. They will utter some of the best words of all humankind (the traditions of the Holy Prophet), but their faith will not pass beyond their throats. They will go out of *Dīn* [Religion] as the arrow darts through the game animal. So wherever you encounter them, kill them, for if someone kills them, he is entitled to a reward on the Day of Resurrection for having killed them.'"

Agreed upon by al-Bukhārī and Muslim.

This has also been set forth by Abū ʿĪsā al-Tirmidhī, on the authority of ʿAbd Allāh b. Masʿūd, in his *al-Sunan*. He has also said that there are traditions on this subject on the authority of ʿAlī, Abū Saʿīd and Abū Dharr: "This is a fine authentic tradition." It has also been reported in another tradition that the Prophet said, whenever he described this set of people: 'They are those who will recite the Qur'ān, but it will not pass beyond

---

[306] Set forth by •al-Bukhārī in *al-Ṣaḥīḥ*: Bk.: Calling on the apostates and the intransigents to repent, and fighting them, Ch.: Killing the Khawārij and the heretics after establishing the evidence against them, 6/2539 §6531. •Muslim in *al-Ṣaḥīḥ*: Bk.: *al-Zakāt* [The Alms-due], Ch.: Urging the killing of the Khawārij, 2/746 §1066. •al-Tirmidhī in *al-Sunan*: Bk.: *al-Fitan* [Troubles] according to Allah's Messenger, Ch.: The quality of the renegades [*al-māriqa*] 4/481 §2188. •al-Nasā'ī in *al-Sunan*, Bk.: The Prohibition of Bloodshed, Ch.: Someone who unsheathes his sword, then thrusts it into the people, 7/119 §4102. •Ibn Mājah in *al-Sunan*: Introduction, Ch.: Discussion of the Khawārij, 1/59 §168. •Aḥmad b. Ḥanbal in *al-Musnad*, 1/81, 113, 131 §616, 912, 1086. •Ibn Abī Shayba in *al-Muṣannaf*, 7/553 §37883. •ʿAbd al-Razzāq in *al-Muṣannaf*, 10/157. •al-Bazzār in *al-Musnad*, 2/188 §568. •Abū Yaʿlā in *al-Musnad*, 1/273 §324. •al-Bayhaqī in *al-Sunan al-Kubrā*, 8/170. •al-Ṭabarānī in *al-Muʿjam aṣ-Ṣaghīr*, 2/213 §1049. •ʿAbd Allāh b. Aḥmad in *al-Sunna*, 2/443 §914. •al-Ṭayālisī in *al-Musnad*, 1/24 §168.

their throats. They will stray from the Religion as the arrow darts through the game animal.' They are al-Ḥarūriyya and others (comprising different sects) among the Khawārij."

٦/٣٠٧. عَنْ أَبِي سَعِيْدٍ رضي الله عنه قَالَ: بَيْنَا النَّبِيُّ ﷺ يَقْسِمُ، جَاءَ عَبْدُ اللهِ بْنُ ذِي الْخُوَيْصِرَةِ التَّمِيْمِيُّ فَقَالَ: اعْدِلْ، يَا رَسُوْلَ اللهِ! قَالَ: وَيْحَكَ، وَمَنْ يَعْدِلُ إِذَا لَمْ أَعْدِلْ؟ قَالَ عُمَرُ بْنُ الْخَطَّابِ: ائْذَنْ لِي فَأَضْرِبَ عُنُقَهُ. قَالَ: دَعْهُ، فَإِنَّ لَهُ أَصْحَابًا. يَحْقِرُ أَحَدُكُمْ صَلَاتَهُ مَعَ صَلَاتِهِ وَصِيَامَهُ مَعَ صِيَامِهِ. يَمْرُقُوْنَ مِنَ الدِّيْنِ كَمَا يَمْرُقُ السَّهْمُ مِنَ الرَّمِيَّةِ. يُنْظَرُ فِي قُذَذِهِ فَلَا يُوْجَدُ فِيْهِ شَيْءٌ، ثُمَّ يُنْظَرُ فِي نَصْلِهِ فَلَا يُوْجَدُ فِيْهِ شَيْءٌ ثُمَّ يُنْظَرُ فِي رِصَافِهِ فَلَا يُوْجَدُ فِيْهِ شَيْءٌ، ثُمَّ يُنْظَرُ فِي نَضِيِّهِ فَلَا يُوْجَدُ فِيْهِ شَيْءٌ. قَدْ سَبَقَ الْفَرْثَ وَالدَّمَ.

مُتَّفَقٌ عَلَيْهِ.

307/6. According to Abū Saʿīd رضي الله عنه:

[307] Set forth by •al-Bukhārī in *al-Ṣaḥīḥ*, Bk.: Calling on the apostates and the intransigents to repent, and fighting them, Ch.: Someone who refrains from fighting the Khawārij because of sympathy, and so that the people will not shun him, 6/2540 §6532, 6534, & Bk.: *al-Manāqib* [Virtues], Ch.: The signs of Prophethood in Islam, 3/1321 §3414, & Bk.: *Faḍāʾil al-Qurʾān* [The Excellent Merits of the Qurʾān], Ch.: Weeping during the recitation of the Qurʾān, 4/1928 §4771, & Bk.: *al-Adab* [Proper Conduct], Ch.: What has come to us about the man's saying: "Woe to you!" 5/2281 §5811. •Muslim in *al-Ṣaḥīḥ*, Bk.: *al-Zakāt* [The Alms-due], Ch.: Discussion of the Khawārij and their qualities, 2/744 §1064. •al-Nasāʾī likewise, on the authority of Abū Barza رضي الله عنه, in *al-Sunan*, Bk.: The Prohibition of Bloodshed, Ch.: Someone who unsheathes his sword, then thrusts it into the people, 7/119 §4103, & in *al-Sunan al-Kubrā*, 6/355 §11220. •Ibn Mājah in *al-Sunan*: Introduction, Ch.: Discussion of the Khawārij, 1/61 §172. •Ibn al-Jārūd in *al-Muntaqā*, 1/272 §1083. •Ibn Ḥibbān in *al-Ṣaḥīḥ*, 15/140 §6741. •al-Ḥākim, on the authority of Abū Barza رضي الله عنه, in *al-Mustadrak*, 2/160 §2647. He said: "This is an authentic tradition." •Aḥmad b. Ḥanbal in *al-Musnad*, 3/56 §11554, 14861. •al-Bayhaqī in *al-Sunan al-Kubrā*, 8/171. •Ibn Abī Shayba in *al-Muṣannaf*: 7/562 §37932. •ʿAbd al-Razzāq in *al-Muṣannaf*, 10/146. •al-Bazzār likewise, on the authority of Abū Barza رضي الله عنه, in *al-Musnad*, 9//305 §3846. •al-Ṭabarānī

"While the Prophet ﷺ was distributing shares (of the battle gains), ʿAbd Allāh b. Dhū al-Khuwayṣira al-Tamīmī came and said: 'Act fairly, O Messenger of Allah!' (On this scorn) he said: 'Woe to you! You damned! Who acts fairly, if I do not act fairly?' ʿUmar b. al-Khaṭṭāb submitted: 'Give me permission to strike off his neck (the evil hypocrite)!' He said: 'Leave him, for he has (or will have) companions that if you compare your *ṣalāh* (ritual prayer) and your *ṣiyām* (fasting) with theirs, you will look down upon your prayer and fasting in comparison to theirs. Yet they will go out of the Religion as the arrow darts through the game animal. (If after slinging the arrow) its feather is examined, no mark of blood is found on it. Then its head is examined, but there is nothing on it. Then its cord is examined, but there is nothing on it. Then its shaft is examined, but there is nothing on it. The arrow has been too fast to be smeared by dung and blood.'" [That is the true example of these evil hypocrites—they will have no association with the *Dīn* (Religion) of Islam].

Agreed upon by al-Bukhārī and Muslim.

٣٠٨/ ٧. عَنْ جَابِرٍ رضي الله عنه يَقُوْلُ: بَصَرَ عَيْنِي وَسَمِعَ أُذُنِي رَسُوْلَ اللهِ ﷺ بِالْجِعْرَانَةِ وَفِي ثَوْبِ بِلَالٍ فِضَّةٌ وَرَسُوْلُ اللهِ ﷺ يَقْبِضُهَا لِلنَّاسِ يُعْطِيْهِمْ، فَقَالَ رَجُلٌ: اعْدِلْ. قَالَ: وَيْلَكَ، وَمَنْ يَعْدِلُ إِذَا لَمْ أَكُنْ أَعْدِلُ؟ قَالَ عُمَرُ بْنُ الْخَطَّابِ: يَارَسُوْلَ اللهِ، دَعْنِي أَقْتُلْ هَذَا الْمُنَافِقَ الْخَبِيْثَ. فَقَالَ رَسُوْلُ اللهِ ﷺ: مَعَاذَ اللهِ أَنْ يَتَحَدَّثَ النَّاسُ أَنِّي أَقْتُلُ أَصْحَابِي. إِنَّ هَذَا وَأَصْحَابَهُ يَقْرَءُوْنَ الْقُرْآنَ لَا يُجَاوِزُ تَرَاقِيَهُمْ. يَمْرُقُوْنَ مِنَ الدِّيْنِ كَمَا يَمْرُقُ السَّهْمُ مِنَ الرَّمِيَّةِ.

رَوَاهُ أَحْمَدُ وَأَبُوْ نُعَيْمٍ.

308/7. According to Jābir رضي الله عنه:

in *al-Muʿjam al-Awsaṭ*, 9/35 §9060. •Abū Yaʿlā in *al-Musnad*, 2/298 §1022. •al-Bukhārī, on the authority of Jābir رضي الله عنه, in *al-Adab al-Mufrad*, 1/270 §774.

[308] Set forth by •Aḥmad b. Ḥanbal in *al-Musnad*, 3/354 §1461. •Abū

"My eye beheld and my ear heard Allah's Messenger ﷺ in al-Jiʿrāna. There was some silver in Bilāl's apparel (lap), and Allah's Messenger ﷺ was taking handfuls of it to give to the people. A man said: 'Act fairly!' He said: 'Woe to you! Who acts fairly, if I do not act fairly?' ʿUmar b. al-Khaṭṭāb submitted: 'O Messenger of Allah, allow me to kill this wicked hypocrite!' Allah's Messenger ﷺ said: 'I take refuge with Allah from having people say that I kill my Companions! This man and his companions will recite the Qurʾān, but it will not pass beyond their throats. They will deviate from *Dīn* [Religion] as the arrow shoots through the game animal.'"

Reported by Aḥmad and Abū Nuʿaym.

٨/٣٠٩. عَنْ أَبِي سَعِيْدٍ الْخُدْرِيِّ ؓ عَنِ النَّبِيِّ ﷺ قَالَ: يَخْرُجُ نَاسٌ مِنْ قِبَلِ الْمَشْرِقِ وَيَقْرَءُوْنَ الْقُرْآنَ؛ لَا يُجَاوِزُ تَرَاقِيَهُمْ. يَمْرُقُوْنَ مِنَ الدِّيْنِ كَمَا يَمْرُقُ السَّهْمُ مِنَ الرَّمِيَّةِ، ثُمَّ لَا يَعُوْدُوْنَ فِيْهِ حَتَّى يَعُوْدَ السَّهْمُ إِلَى فُوْقِهِ. قِيْلَ: مَا سِيْمَاهُمْ؟ قَالَ: سِيْمَاهُمُ التَّحْلِيْقُ أَوْ قَالَ: التَّسْبِيْدُ.

رَوَاهُ الْبُخَارِيُّ.

وفي رواية: عَنْ يُسَيْرِ بْنِ عَمْرٍو، قَالَ: سَأَلْتُ سَهْلَ بْنَ حُنَيْفٍ ؓ: هَلْ سَمِعْتَ النَّبِيَّ ﷺ يَذْكُرُ الْخَوَارِجَ؟ فَقَالَ: سَمِعْتُهُ وَأَشَارَ بِيَدِهِ نَحْوَ الْمَشْرِقِ: قَوْمٌ يَقْرَءُوْنَ الْقُرْآنَ بِأَلْسِنَتِهِمْ لَا يَعْدُوْ تَرَاقِيَهُمْ. يَمْرُقُوْنَ مِنَ الدِّيْنِ كَمَا يَمْرُقُ السَّهْمُ مِنَ الرَّمِيَّةِ.

رَوَاهُ مُسْلِمٌ.

309/8. According to Abū Saʿīd al-Khudrī ؓ:

Nuʿaym in *al-Musnad al-Mustakhraj*, 3/127 §2372.

309 Set forth by •al-Bukhārī in *al-Ṣaḥīḥ*, Bk.: *al-Tawḥīd* [The Affirmation of Oneness], Ch.: The Qurʾānic recitation of the profligate and the hypocrite, their voices and their reading do not pass beyond their larynxes, 6/2748 §7123. •Muslim in *al-Ṣaḥīḥ*: Bk.: *al-Zakāt* [The Alms-due], Ch.: The Khawārij are the worst of the people, 2/750 §1068. •Aḥmad b. Ḥanbal in *al-Musnad*, 3/64

"The Prophet ﷺ said: 'Some people will emerge from the direction of the east, and they will recite the Qur'ān, but it will not pass beyond their throats. They will go out of the Religion as the arrow zooms through the game animal. Then they will not return to it until the arrow returns to its notch (i.e., they will never come back to the fold of Islam).' He was asked: 'What is their distinctive feature?' He said: 'Their distinctive feature will be shaving the head,' or he may have said: 'Their distinctive feature will be the habit of shaving the hair close to the skin.'"

Reported by al-Bukhārī.

In one report, Yusayr b. ʿAmr said:

"I asked Sahl b. Ḥunayf ؓ: 'Did you hear the Prophet ﷺ mention the Khawārij?' He said: 'I heard him say (they will emerge from this direction), while pointing his hand towards the east: "A set of people will recite the Qur'ān with their tongues, but it will not get beyond their throats. They will go out of the Religion as the arrow passes through the game animal."'"

Reported by Muslim.

٩/٣١٠. عَنْ زَيْدِ بْنِ وَهْبٍ الْجُهَنِيِّ أَنَّهُ كَانَ فِي الْجَيْشِ الَّذِيْنَ كَانُوْا مَعَ عَلِيٍّ ؓ الَّذِيْنَ سَارُوْا إِلَى الْخَوَارِجِ، فَقَالَ عَلِيٌّ ؓ: أَيُّهَا النَّاسُ، إِنِّي سَمِعْتُ رَسُوْلَ اللهِ ﷺ يَقُوْلُ: يَخْرُجُ قَوْمٌ مِنْ أُمَّتِي. يَقْرَءُوْنَ الْقُرْآنَ لَيْسَ قِرَاءَتُكُمْ إِلَى قِرَاءَتِهِمْ بِشَيءٍ وَلَا صَلَاتُكُمْ إِلَى صَلَاتِهِمْ بِشَيءٍ وَلَا صِيَامُكُمْ إِلَى صِيَامِهِمْ بِشَيءٍ. يَقْرَءُوْنَ الْقُرْآنَ يَحْسِبُوْنَ أَنَّهُ لَهُمْ، وَهُوَ عَلَيْهِمْ. لَا تُجَاوِزُ صَلَاتُهُمْ تَرَاقِيَهُمْ. يَمْرُقُوْنَ مِنَ الإِسْلَامِ كَمَا يَمْرُقُ السَّهْمُ مِنَ الرَّمِيَّةِ.

رَوَاهُ مُسْلِمٌ وَأَبُوْ دَاوُدَ.

---

§11632; 3/486. •Ibn Abī Shayba in *al-Muṣannaf*, 7/563 §37397. •Abū Yaʿlā in *al-Musnad*, 2/408 §1193. •al-Ṭabarānī in *al-Muʿjam al-Kabīr*, 6/91 §5609. •Ibn Abī ʿĀṣim in *al-Sunna*, 2/490 §909. He said: "Its chain of transmission is authentic." •Abū Nuʿaym in *al-Musnad al-Mustakhraj*, 3/135 §2390.

310/9. According to Zayd b. Wahb al-Juhanī:

"He was among those in the army who were allied with ʿAlī ؓ, and they went to fight against the Khawārij, so ʿAlī ؓ said: 'O people, I once heard Allah's Messenger ﷺ say: "A set of people will come out from my Community. They will recite the Qurʾān, but your recitation is nothing like their recitation, your ritual prayer is nothing like their ritual prayer, and your fasting is nothing like their fasting. They will recite the Qurʾān, supposing that it is to their credit, when actually that is to their debit. Their ritual prayer will not pass beyond their throats. They will flee from the ambit of Islam as the arrow rips through the game animal."'"

Reported by Muslim and Abū Dawud.

١٠/٣١١. عَنْ أَبِي سَعِيْدٍ ؓ أَنَّ النَّبِيَّ ﷺ ذَكَرَ قَوماً يَكُوْنُوْنَ فِي أُمَّتِهِ؛ يَخْرُجُوْنَ فِي فُرْقَةٍ مِنَ النَّاسِ. سِيْمَاهُمُ التَّحَالُقُ. قَالَ: هُمْ شَرُّ الْخَلْقِ (أَوْ مِنْ أَشَرِّ الْخَلْقِ). يَقْتُلُهُمْ أَدْنَى الطَّائِفَتَيْنِ إِلَى الْحَقِّ. قَالَ: فَضَرَبَ النَّبِيُّ ﷺ لَهُمْ مَثَلاً أَوْ قَالَ قَوْلاً: الرَّجُلُ يَرْمِي الرَّمِيَّةَ (أَوْ قَالَ: الْغَرَضَ) فَيَنْظُرُ فِي النَّصْلِ فَلاَ يَرَى بَصِيْرَةً وَيَنْظُرُ فِي النَّضِيِّ فَلاَ يَرَى بَصِيْرَةً وَيَنْظُرُ فِي الْفُوْقِ فَلاَ يَرَى بَصِيْرَةً.

رَوَاهُ مُسْلِمٌ وَأَحْمَدُ.

311/10. According to Abū Saʿīd ؓ:

---

310 Set forth by •Muslim in *al-Ṣaḥīḥ*, Bk.: *al-Zakāt* [The Alms-due], Ch.: Urging the killing of the Khawārij, 2/748 §1066. •Abū Dāwūd in *al-Sunan*, Bk.: The Sunna, Ch.: Fighting the Khawārij, 4/244 §4768. •al-Nasāʾī in *al-Sunan al-Kubrā*, 5/163 §8571. •Aḥmad b. Ḥanbal in *al-Musnad*, 1/91 §706. •ʿAbd al-Razzāq in *al-Muṣannaf*, 10/147. •al-Bazzār in *al-Musnad*, 2/197 §581. •Ibn Abī ʿĀṣim in *al-Sunna*, 2/445–446. •al-Bayhaqī in *al-Sunan al-Kubrā*, 8/170.

311 Set forth by •Muslim in *al-Ṣaḥīḥ*, Bk.: *al-Zakāt* [The Alms-due], Ch.: Discussion of the Khawārij and their qualities, 2/745 §1065. •Aḥmad b. Ḥanbal in *al-Musnad*, 3/5 §11031. •ʿAbd Allāh b. Aḥmad in *al-Sunan*, 2/622 §1482. He said: "Its chain of transmission is authentic."

"The Prophet ﷺ mentioned that a group in his Community will emerge when people will disintegrate into sects; their distinctive feature would be the shaven heads. He (Abū Saʿīd) said: 'They are the worse (or among the worst) of creatures. The group out of the two, closest to the truth, will kill them.' The Prophet ﷺ then gave an example for them: 'The man shoots an arrow at the game animal (or he may have said 'the target'), then he examines the head of the arrow, but he does not see any blood. He likewise examines the shaft, but he does not see any blood. He also examines the notch, but he does not see any blood. (This is how they will go out of the ambit of Islam).'"

Reported by Muslim and Ahmad.

٣١٢/ ١١. عَنْ أَبِـي سَلَمَةَ وَعَطَاء بْنِ يَسَار أَنَّـهُمَا أَتَيَا أَبَا سَعِيْدٍ الْخُدْرِيَّ رضي الله عنه فَسَأَلاَهُ عَنِ الْحَرُوْرِيَّةِ: أَسَمِعْتَ النَّبِيَّ ﷺ؟ قَالَ: لاَ أَدْرِي مَا الْحَرُوْرِيَّةُ. سَمِعْتُ النَّبِيَّ ﷺ يَقُوْلُ: يَخْرُجُ فِي هَذِهِ الْأُمَّةِ، وَلَـمْ يَقُلْ مِنْهَا، قَوْمٌ تَحْقِرُوْنَ صَلاَتَكُمْ مَعَ صَلاَتِهِمْ؛ يَقْرَءُوْنَ الْقُرْآنَ لاَ يُجَاوِزُ حُلُوْقَهُمْ أَوْ حَنَاجِرَهُمْ؛ يَمْرُقُوْنَ مِنَ الدِّيْنِ مُرُوْقَ السَّهْمِ مِنَ الرَّمِيَّةِ.

مُتَّفَقٌ عَلَيْهِ.

312/11. According to Abū Salama and ʿAṭāʾ b. Yasār, they came

---

[312] Set forth by •al-Bukhārī in *al-Ṣaḥīḥ*, Bk.: Calling on the apostates and the intransigents to repent, and fighting them, Ch.: Killing the Khawārij and the heretics after establishing the evidence against them, 6/2540 §6532, & Bk.: *Faḍāʾil al-Qurʾān* [The Excellent Merits of the Qurʾān], Ch.: The sin committed by someone who makes a show of reciting the Qurʾān, or gains by it some worldly benefit, or boasts of it, 4/1928 §4771. •Muslim in *al-Ṣaḥīḥ*, Bk.: *al-Zakāt* [The Alms-due], Ch.: Discussion of the Khawārij and their qualities, 2/743 §1064. •Mālik in *al-Muwaṭṭāʾ*: Bk.: The Qurʾān, Ch.: What has come to us about the Qurʾān, 1/204 §478. •al-Nasāʾī in *al-Sunan al-Kubrā*, 3/31 §8089. •Aḥmad b. Ḥanbal in *al-Musnad*, 3/60 §11596. •Ibn Ḥibbān in *al-Ṣaḥīḥ*, 15/132 §6737. •al-Bukhārī in *Khalq Afʿāl al-ʿIbād*, 1/53. •Ibn Abī Shayba in *al-Muṣannaf*, 7/560 §37920. •Abū Yaʿlā in *al-Musnad*,

to Abū Saʿīd al-Khudrī ؓ and asked him about the al-Ḥarūriyya. They said: "Did you hear the Prophet ﷺ say (anything about them)?" He replied, "I do not know what the al-Ḥarūriyya are! But I heard the Prophet say ﷺ: 'There will emerge in this Community (he did not say from it) a set of people in contrast with whose ritual prayer you will consider your own ritual prayer inferior. They will recite the Qurʾān, but it will not pass beyond their throats (or their larynxes). They will flee from the Religion as the arrow rips through the game animal.'"

Agreed upon by al-Bukhārī and Muslim.

٣١٣/ ١٢. عَنْ أَبِـي سَعِيْدٍ الْخُدْرِيِّ وَأَنَس بْن مَالك ؆ عَنْ رَسُوْل الله ﷺ قَالَ: سَيَكُوْنُ فِي أُمَّتِي اخْتِلَافٌ وَفُرْقَةٌ. قَوْمٌ يُحْسِنُوْنَ الْقِيْلَ وَيُسِيْئُوْنَ الْفِعْلَ. يَقْرَءُوْنَ الْقُرْآنَ لاَ يُجَاوِزُ تَرَاقِيَهُمْ (وفي رواية: يَحْقِرُ أَحَدُكُمْ صَلَاتَهُ مَعَ صَلَاتِهِمْ وَصِيَامَهُ مَعَ صِيَامِهِمْ). يَمْرُقُوْنَ مِنَ الدِّيْنِ مُرُوْقَ السَّهْمِ مِنَ الرَّمِيَّةِ. لاَ يَرْجِعُوْنَ حَتَّى يَرْتَدَّ عَلَى فُوْقِهِ. هُمْ شَرُّ الْخَلْقِ وَالْخَلِيْقَةِ. طُوْبَى لِمَنْ قَتَلَهُمْ وَقَتَلُوْهُ. يَدْعُوْنَ إِلَى كِتَابِ اللهِ وَلَيْسُوْا مِنْهُ فِي شَيْءٍ. مَنْ قَاتَلَهُمْ كَانَ أَوْلَى بِاللهِ مِنْهُمْ. قَالُوْا: يَارَسُوْلَ اللهِ، مَا سِيْمَاهُمْ؟ قَالَ: اَلتَّحْلِيْقُ.

وفي رواية: عَنْ أَنَسٍ ؓ أَنَّ رَسُوْلَ اللهِ ﷺ قَالَ نَحْوَهُ: سِيْمَاهُمْ التَّحْلِيْقُ وَالتَّسْبِيْدُ.

رَوَاهُ أَبُوْ دَاوُدَ وَابْنُ مَاجه مُخْتَصَرًا وَأَحْمَدُ وَالْحَاكِمُ.

313/12. According to Abū Saʿīd al-Khudrī and Anas b. Mālik ؆:

2/430 §1233.

313 Set forth by •Abū Dāwūd in *al-Sunan*, Bk.: The Sunna, Ch.: Fighting the Khawārij, 4/243 §4765. •Ibn Mājah in *al-Sunan*: Introduction, Ch.: Discussion of the Khawārij, 1/60 §169. •Aḥmad b. Ḥanbal in *al-Musnad*, 3/224 §13362. •al-Ḥākim in *al-Mustadrak*, 2/161 §2649. •al-Bayhaqī in *al-Sunan al-Kubrā*, 8/171. •al-Maqdisī in *al-Aḥādīth al-Mukhtāra*, 7/15 §2391–2392. He said: "Its chain of transmission is authentic." •Abū Yaʿlā in *al-Musnad*, 5/426,§3117 •al-Ṭabarānī likewise in *al-Muʿjam al-Kabīr*, 8/121

"Allah's Messenger ﷺ said: 'Soon my Community will fall prey to dissension and sectarianism. There will be a group of people who will speak well and act badly. They will recite the Qur'ān, but it will not pass beyond their throats.' (And in one report: 'You will consider your own ritual prayer inferior to their ritual prayer, and your own fast inferior to their fast.') They will go out of the Religion as the arrow shoots through the game animal, and they will not return (to Islam) until the arrow returns to its notch. They are the worst of creatures and the creation. Glad tidings to the one who kills them and whom they kill! They will call to the Book of Allah, but they will have nothing to do with it. If someone fights them, he will be nearer to Allah than they are.' They said: 'O Messenger of Allah, what is their distinctive feature?' He said: 'Shaving the head!'"

In one report: According to Anas ؓ: "Allah's Messenger ﷺ said in the same way: 'Their distinctive feature is shaving the head and shaving the hair close to the skin (and keeping it frequently shaved).'"

Reported by Abū Dāwūd, Ibn Mājah in brief, Aḥmad and al-Ḥākim.

١٣/٣١٤. عَنْ شَرِيْك بْنِ شِهَاب قَالَ: كُنْتُ أَتَمَنَّى أَنْ أَلْقَى رَجُلاً مِنْ أَصْحَابِ النَّبِيِّ ﷺ أَسْأَلُهُ عَنِ الْخَوَارِجِ، فَلَقِيْتُ أَبَا بَرْزَةَ فِي يَوم عِيْدٍ فِي نَفَرٍ مِنْ أَصْحَابِهِ فَقُلْتُ لَهُ: هَلْ سَمِعْتَ رَسُوْلَ اللهِ ﷺ يَذْكُرُ الْخَوَارِجَ؟ فَقَالَ: نَعَمْ، سَمِعْتُ رَسُوْلَ اللهِ ﷺ بِأُذُنِي وَرَأَيْتُهُ بِعَيْنِي. أُتِيَ رَسُوْلُ اللهِ ﷺ بِمَالٍ فَقَسَمَهُ. فَأَعْطَى مَنْ عَنْ يَمِيْنِهِ وَمَنْ عَنْ شِمَالِهِ، وَلَمْ يُعْطِ مَنْ وَرَاءَهُ شَيْئًا، فَقَامَ رَجُلٌ مِنْ وَرَائِهِ. فَقَالَ: يَا مُحَمَّدُ، مَا عَدَلْتَ فِي الْقِسْمَةِ. رَجُلٌ أَسْوَدُ مَطْمُوْمُ الشَّعْرِ، عَلَيْهِ ثَوْبَانِ أَبْيَضَانِ (وزاد أحمد: بَيْنَ عَيْنَيْهِ أَثَرُ السُّجُوْدِ)، فَغَضِبَ رَسُوْلُ اللهِ ﷺ غَضَبًا شَدِيْدًا، وَقَالَ: وَاللهِ، لاَ تَجِدُوْنَ بَعْدِي رَجُلاً هُوَ أَعْدَلُ مِنِّي. ثُمَّ قَالَ: يَخْرُجُ فِي آخِرِ الزَّمَانِ قَوْمٌ كَأَنَّ هَذَا مِنْهُمْ (وفي رواية:

§7553. •al-Marwazī in *al-Sunna*, 1/20 §52.

قَالَ: يَخْرُجُ مِنْ قِبَلِ الْـمَشْرِقِ رِجَالٌ كَانَ هَذَا مِنْهُمْ هَدْيُهُمْ هَكَذَا). يَقْرَءُوْنَ الْقُرْآنَ لَا يُجَاوِزُ تَرَاقِيَهُمْ. يَمْرُقُوْنَ مِنَ الإِسْلَامِ كَمَا يَمْرُقُ السَّهْمُ مِنَ الرَّمِيَّةِ. سِيْمَاهُمُ التَّحْلِيْقُ. لَا يَزَالُوْنَ يَخْرُجُوْنَ حَتَّى يَخْرُجَ آخِرُهُمْ مَعَ الْـمَسِيْحِ الدَّجَّالِ. فَإِذَا لَقِيْتُمُوْهُمْ فَاقْتُلُوْهُمْ. هُمْ شَرُّ الْخَلْقِ وَالْخَلِيْقَةِ.

رَوَاهُ النَّسَائِيُّ وَأَحْمَدُ وَالْبَزَّارُ وَالْحَاكِمُ، وَقَالَ الْحَاكِمُ: هَذَا حَدِيْثٌ صَحِيْحٌ. وَرِجَالُهُ رِجَالُ الصَّحِيْحِ كَمَا قَالَ الْهَيْثَمِيُّ.

314/13. According to Sharīk b. Shihāb:

"I was eager to meet with a man from among the Companions of the Prophet ﷺ, in order to ask him about the Khawārij, so I met with Abū Barza on ʿĪd Day (Festival), in a group of his Companions, and I asked him: 'Have you heard Allah's Messenger ﷺ mentioning the Khawārij?' He said: 'Yes, I have heard Allah's Messenger ﷺ with my ear and seen him with my eye. Allah's Messenger ﷺ was brought some property, so he shared it out. He gave to those on his right and those on his left, but did not give anything to those behind him, so a man approached from behind him and said: "O Muhammad, you have not been fair in the distribution!" He was a closely shaven Negro, wearing two white garments (and Imam Aḥmad b. Ḥunbal added: 'Between his eyes [on the forehead] was the mark of prostration.') Allah's Messenger ﷺ was intensely angry, and he said: "By Allah! You will not find after me any man who is fairer than I am!" Then he said: "There will emerge a set of people, at the end of time, and this is also one of them. (And according to one report, he said: 'From the directions of the east, there will

---

314 Set forth by •al-Nasāʾī in *al-Sunan*: Bk.: The Prohibition of Bloodshed, Ch.: Someone who unsheathes his sword, then thrusts it into the people, 7/119 §4103, & in *al-Sunan al-Kubrā*, 2/312 §3566. •Aḥmad b. Ḥanbal in *al-Musnad*, 4/421. •al-Bazzār in *al-Musnad*, 9/294, 305 §3846. •al-Ḥākim in *al-Mustadrak*, 2/160 §2647. •Ibn Abī Shayba in *al-Muṣannaf*, 7/559 §37917. •Ibn Abī ʿĀṣim in *al-Sunna*, 2/452 §927. •al-Ṭayālisī in *al-Musnad*, 1/124 §923. •al-ʿAsqalānī in *Fatḥ al-Bārī*, 12/292. •al-Qaysarānī in *Tadhkirat al-Ḥuffāẓ*, 3/1101. •Ibn Taymiyya in *al-Ṣārim al-Maslūl*, 1/188.

emerge men of whom this was one, such being their style.') They will recite the Qur'ān, but it will not pass beyond their throats. They will flee from Islam as the arrow darts through the game animal. Their distinctive feature is shaving the head. They will not cease to emerge, until the last group of them emerges with the False Messiah, so if you encounter them, you must kill them. They are the worst of creatures and the creation!"'"

> Reported by al-Nasā'ī, Aḥmad, al-Bazzār and al-Ḥākim. According to al-Ḥākim, this is an authentic tradition, and its narrators are reliable, as al-Haythamī said.

١٤/٣١٥. عَنْ أَبِي سَلَمَةَ قَالَ: قُلْتُ لِأَبِي سَعِيْدٍ الْخُدْرِيِّ رضي الله عنه: هَلْ سَمِعْتَ رَسُوْلَ اللهِ ﷺ يَذْكُرُ فِي الْحَرُورِيَّةِ شَيْئًا؟ فَقَالَ: سَمِعْتُهُ يَذْكُرُ قَوْمًا يَتَعَبَّدُونَ (وفي رواية أحمد: يَتَعَمَّقُوْنَ فِي الدِّيْنِ). يَحْقِرُ أَحَدُكُمْ صَلَاتَهُ مَعَ صَلَاتِهِمْ وَصَومَهُ مَعَ صَومِهِمْ. يَمْرُقُونَ مِنَ الدِّيْنِ كَمَا يَمْرُقُ السَّهْمُ مِنَ الرَّمِيَّةِ. أَخَذَ سَهْمَهُ فَنَظَرَ فِي نَصْلِهِ فَلَمْ يَرَ شَيْئًا، فَنَظَرَ فِي رِصَافِهِ فَلَمْ يَرَ شَيْئًا فَنَظَرَ فِي قِدْحِهِ فَلَمْ يَرَ شَيْئًا، فَنَظَرَ فِي الْقُذَذِ فَتَمَارَى هَلْ يَرَى شَيْئًا أَمْ لَا.

رَوَاهُ ابْنُ مَاجَه وَأَحْمَدُ.

315/14. According to Abū Salama:

"I said to Abū Sa'īd al-Khudrī رضي الله عنه: 'Have you heard Allah's Messenger ﷺ mentioning anything about al-Ḥarūriyya (Khawārij)?' He said: 'I heard him mention a group of people who will devote themselves to acts of worship (in Aḥmad's report: who will immerse themselves in the Religion). One of you will disdain his own ritual prayer in contrast with their ritual prayer, and his own fasting in contrast with their fasting. They will go out of the Religion as the arrow darts through the game animal. The hunter

---

[315] Set forth by •Ibn Mājah in *al-Sunan*: Introduction Ch.: Discussion of the Khawārij, 1/60 §169. •Aḥmad b. Ḥanbal in *al-Musnad*, 3/33 §11309. •Ibn Abī Shayba in *al-Muṣannaf*, 7/557 §37909.

took his arrow and examined its head, but he did not see anything. Then he examined its cord, but he did not see anything. Then he examined its shaft, but he did not see anything. Then he examined its feather, wondering whether or not he would see something.'"

Reported by Ibn Mājah and Aḥmad.

١٥/٣١٦. عَنْ عَبْدِ اللهِ بْنِ عُمَرَ ﵂ قَالَ: سَمِعْتُ رَسُولَ اللهِ ﷺ يَقُولُ وَهُوَ عَلَى الْمِنْبَرِ: أَلاَ إِنَّ الْفِتْنَةَ هَاهُنَا ـ يُشِيرُ إِلَى الْـمَشْرِقِ ـ مِنْ حَيْثُ يَطْلُعُ قَرْنُ الشَّيْطَانِ.

مُتَّفَقٌ عَلَيْهِ وَهَذَا لَفْظُ الْبُخَارِيِّ.

316/15. According to ʿAbd Allāh b. ʿUmar ﵂:

"I heard Allah's Messenger ﷺ say, while he was on the pulpit: 'Beware! The trouble is here'—pointing towards the east—'from whence will arise the horn (i.e., the generation) of Satan!'"

Agreed upon by al-Bukhārī and Muslim, and this is the wording of al-Bukhārī.

١٦/٣١٧. عَنِ ابْنِ عُمَرَ ﵂ أَنَّهُ سَمِعَ رَسُولَ اللهِ ﷺ وَهُوَ مُسْتَقْبِلُ الْـمَشْرِقِ يَقُولُ: أَلاَ إِنَّ الْفِتْنَةَ هَاهُنَا مِنْ حَيْثُ يَطْلُعُ قَرْنُ الشَّيْطَانِ.

مُتَّفَقٌ عَلَيْهِ.

317/16. According to Ibn ʿUmar ﵂, he heard Allah's Messenger ﷺ

---

316 Set forth by •al-Bukhārī in al-Ṣaḥīḥ: Bk.: al-Manāqib [Virtues], Ch.: Yemen's relationship to Ishmael, 3/1293 §3320, & Bk.: Bad' al-Khalq [The Beginning of Creation], Ch.: The character of Iblīs and his armies, 3/1195 §3105. •Muslim in al-Ṣaḥīḥ, Bk.: al-Fitan wa Ashrāṭ al-Sāʿa [Troubles and the Portents of the Final Hour], Ch.: Trouble is from the east, from whence the horns of Satan emerge, 4/2229 §2905. •Mālik in al-Muwaṭṭā': Bk.: al-Isti'dhān [Taking Leave], Ch.: What has come to us about the east, 2/975 §1757. •Aḥmad b. Ḥanbal in al-Musnad, 2/73 §5428. •Ibn Ḥibbān in al-Ṣaḥīḥ, 15/25 §6649.

317 Set forth by •al-Bukhārī in al-Ṣaḥīḥ: Bk.: al-Fitan [Troubles], Ch.: The saying of the Prophet ﷺ: "Trouble is from the direction of the east," 6/2598

say, while he was facing the east:

"Beware! The trouble is here, from whence will arise the horn (i.e., the generation) of Satan!"

Agreed upon by al-Bukhārī and Muslim.

٣١٨/ ١٧. عَنِ ابْنِ عُمَرَ رضي الله عنهما قَالَ ذَكَرَ النَّبِيُّ ﷺ: اَللّٰهُمَّ، بَارِكْ لَنَا فِي شَامِنَا! اَللّٰهُمَّ، بَارِكْ لَنَا فِي يَمَنِنَا! قَالُوْا: يَارَسُوْلَ اللهِ، وَفِي نَجْدِنَا؟ قَالَ: اَللّٰهُمَّ، بَارِكْ لَنَا فِي شَامِنَا! اَللّٰهُمَّ، بَارِكْ لَنَا فِي يَمَنِنَا! قَالُوْا: يَارَسُوْلَ اللهِ، وَفِي نَجْدِنَا؟ فَأَظُنُّهُ قَالَ فِي الثَّالِثَةِ: هُنَاكَ الزَّلَازِلُ وَالْفِتَنُ، وَبِهَا يَطْلُعُ قَرْنُ الشَّيْطَانِ.

رَوَاهُ الْبُخَارِيُّ وَالتِّرْمِذِيُّ وَأَحْمَدُ، وَقَالَ التِّرْمِذِيُّ: هَذَا حَدِيْثٌ حَسَنٌ صَحِيْحٌ.

318/17. According to Ibn ʿUmar رضي الله عنهما:

"The Prophet exclaimed ﷺ: 'O Allah, bless us in our Syria! O Allah, bless us in our Yemen!' They said: 'O Messenger of Allah, and in our Najd?' He said: 'O Allah, bless us in our Syria! O Allah, bless us in our Yemen!' They said: 'O Messenger of Allah, and in our Najd?' Then I think he said in the third repetition: 'Over there are the earthquakes and the troubles, and in it will arise the horn of Satan (i.e., the disruption of the Khawārij)!'"

Reported by al-Bukhārī, al-Tirmidhī and Aḥmad. Al-

---

§6680. •Muslim in *al-Ṣaḥīḥ*: Bk.: *al-Fitan wa Ashrāṭ al-Sāʿa* [Troubles and the Portents of the Final Hour], Ch.: Trouble is from the east, from whence the horns of Satan emerge, 4/2228 §2905. •Aḥmad b. Ḥanbal in *al-Musnad*, 2/91 §5659. •al-Ṭabarānī in *al-Muʿjam al-Awsaṭ*, 1/122 §387. •al-Muqriʾ in *al-Sunan al-Wārida*, 1/246 §43.

[318] Set forth by •al-Bukhārī in *al-Ṣaḥīḥ*: Bk.: *al-Fitan* [Troubles]; Ch.:The saying of the Prophet ﷺ: "Trouble is from the direction of the east," 6/2598 §6681, & Bk.: *al-Istisqāʾ* [The Prayer for Rain], Ch.: What has been said about the earthquakes and the signs, 1/351 §990. •al-Tirmidhī in *al-Sunan*: Bk.: *al-Manāqib* [Virtues] according to Allah's Messenger ﷺ, Ch.: The Excellence of Syria and Yemen, 5/733 §3953. •Aḥmad b. Ḥanbal in *al-Musnad*, 2/118 §5987. •Ibn Ḥibbān in *al-Ṣaḥīḥ*, 16/290 §7301 •al-Ṭabarānī in *al-Muʿjam al-Kabīr*, 12/384 §13422. •al-Muqriʾ in *al-Sunan al-Wārida fī al-Fitan*, 1/251 §46. •al-Mundhirī in *al-Targhīb wa al-Tarhīb*, 4/29 §4666.

Tirmidhī said: "This is a fine authentic tradition."

٣١٩/ ١٨. أخرج البخاري في صحيحه في ترجمة الباب: قَوْلُ اللهِ تَعَالَى: ﴿وَمَا كَانَ ٱللَّهُ لِيُضِلَّ قَوْمًۢا بَعْدَ إِذْ هَدَىٰهُمْ حَتَّىٰ يُبَيِّنَ لَهُم مَّا يَتَّقُونَ﴾. (التوبة، ٩/ ١١٥). وَكَانَ ابْنُ عُمَرَ رضي الله عنهما يَرَاهُمْ شِرَارَ خَلْقِ اللهِ، وَقَالَ: إِنَّهُمُ انْطَلَقُوْا إِلَى آيَاتٍ نَزَلَتْ فِي الْكُفَّارِ فَجَعَلُوْهَا عَلَى الْـمُؤْمِنِيْنَ.

وَقَالَ الْعَسْقَلَانِيُّ فِي الْفَتْحِ: وَصَلَهُ الطَّبَرِيُّ فِي مُسْنَدِ عَلِيٍّ مِنْ تَهْذِيْبِ الْآثَارِ مِنْ طَرِيْقِ بُكَيْرِ بْنِ عَبْدِ اللهِ بْنِ الْأَشَجِّ: أَنَّهُ سَأَلَ نَافِعًا: كَيْفَ كَانَ رَأَى ابْنُ عُمَرَ فِي الْحَرُوْرِيَّةِ؟ قَالَ: كَانَ يَرَاهُمْ شِرَارَ خَلْقِ اللهِ. انْطَلَقُوْا إِلَى آيَاتِ الْكُفَّارِ فَجَعَلُوْهَا فِي الْـمُؤْمِنِيْنَ.

قُلْتُ: وَسَنَدُهُ صَحِيْحٌ، وَقَدْ ثَبَتَ فِي الْـحَدِيْثِ الصَّحِيْحِ الْـمَرْفُوْعِ عِنْدَ مُسْلِمٍ مِنْ حَدِيْثِ أَبِـي ذَرٍّ رضي الله عنه فِي وَصْفِ الْـخَوَارِجِ: هُمْ شِرَارُ الْخَلْقِ وَالْخَلِيْقَةِ. وَعِنْدَ أَحْمَدَ بِسَنَدٍ جَيِّدٍ عَنْ أَنَسٍ مَرْفُوْعًا مِثْلَهُ.

وَعِنْدَ الْبَزَّارِ مِنْ طَرِيْقِ الشَّعْبِيِّ عَنْ عَائِشَةَ رضي الله عنها قَالَتْ: ذَكَرَ رَسُوْلُ اللهِ ﷺ الْخَوَارِجَ فَقَالَ: هُمْ شِرَارُ أُمَّتِي. يَقْتُلُهُمْ خِيَارُ أُمَّتِي. وَسَنَدُهُ حَسَنٌ.

وَعِنْدَ الطَّبَرَانِيِّ مِنْ هَذَا الْوَجْهِ مَرْفُوْعًا: هُمْ شِرَارُ الْخَلْقِ وَالْخَلِيْقَةِ يَقْتُلُهُمْ خَيْرُ الْخَلْقِ وَالْخَلِيْقَةِ. وَفِي حَدِيْثِ أَبِـي سَعِيْدٍ رضي الله عنه عِنْدَ أَحْمَدَ: هُمْ شَرُّ الْبَرِيَّةِ.

وَفِي رِوَايَةِ عُبَيْدِ اللهِ بْنِ أَبِـي رَافِعٍ عَنْ عَلِيٍّ رضي الله عنه عِنْدَ مُسْلِمٍ: مِنْ أَبْغَضِ خَلْقِ اللهِ إِلَيْهِ.

وَفِي حَدِيْثِ عَبْدِ اللهِ بْنِ خَبَّابٍ رضي الله عنهما يَعْنِي عَنْ أَبِيْهِ عِنْدَ الطَّبَرَانِيِّ: شَرُّ قَتْلَى أَظَلَّتْهُمْ

السَّماءُ وَأَقَلَّتْهُمُ الْأَرْضُ. وَفِي حَدِيْثِ أَبِـي أُمَامَةَ ﷺ نَحْوَهُ.

وَعِنْدَ أَحْمَدَ وَابْنِ أَبِـي شَيْبَةَ مِنْ حَدِيْثِ أَبِـي بَرْزَةَ مَرْفُوْعًا فِي ذِكْرِ الْـخَوَارِجِ: شَرُّ الْخَلْقِ وَالْخَلِيْقَةِ يَقُولُهَا ثَلاَثًا.

وَعِنْدَ ابْنِ أَبِـي شَيْبَةَ مِنْ طَرِيْقِ عُمَيْرِ بْنِ إِسْحَاقَ عَنْ أَبِـي هُرَيْرَةَ ﷺ: هُمْ شَرُّ الْخَلْقِ. وَهَذَا مِمَّا يُؤَيِّدُ قَوْلَ مَنْ قَالَ بِكُفْرِهِمْ.

319/18. According to al-Bukhārī in his *Ṣaḥīḥ*, in the interpretation of the Chapter: Allah's saying: "Allah would never send a people astray after He had guided them, until He had made clear to them what they should avoid *[wa mā kāna ʾllāhu li-yuḍilla qawman baʿda idh hadā-hum ḥattā yubayyina la-hum mā yattaqūn]*." (Q.9:115): "Ibn ʿUmar ﷺ used to regard them (the Khawārij) as the worst of Allah's creatures, and he said: 'They have seized upon the Qurʾānic Verses revealed concerning the unbelievers, and applied them to the believers.'"

---

319 Set forth by •al-Bukhārī in *al-Ṣaḥīḥ*, Bk.: Calling on the apostates and the intransigents to repent, and fighting them, Ch.: (5) Killing the Khawārij and the heretics after establishing the evidence against them, 6/2539. •Muslim in *al-Ṣaḥīḥ*, Bk.: *al-Zakāt* [The Alms-due], Ch.: The Khawārij are the worst of the people, 2/750 §1067, & Bk.: *al-Zakāt* [The Alms-due], Ch.: Urging the killing of the Khawārij, 2/749 §1066. •Abū Dāwūd in *al-Sunan*, Bk.: The Sunna, Ch.: Fighting the Khawārij, 4/243 §4765. •al-Nasāʾī in *al-Sunan*, Bk.: The Prohibition of Bloodshed, Ch.: Someone who unsheathes his sword, then thrusts it into the people, 7/119–120 §4103. •Ibn Mājah in al-Sunan: Introduction, Ch.: Discussion of the Khawārij, 1/60 §170. •Aḥmad b. Ḥanbal in *al-Musnad*, 3/15, 224 §11133, 13362; 4/421, 423; 5/31, 176 §21571. •Ibn Ḥibbān in *al-Ṣaḥīḥ*, 15/387 §6939. •Ibn Abī Shayba in *al-Muṣannaf*, 7/557, 559 §37905, 37917. •al-Bazzār in *al-Musnad*, 9/294, 305 §3846. •al-Ḥākim in *al-Mustadrak*, 2/167 §2659. •al-Ṭabarānī in *al-Muʿjam al-Awsaṭ*, 6/186 §6142; 7/335 §7660, & in *al-Muʿjam a√-Ṣaghīr*, 1/42 §33, & in *al-Muʿjam al-Kabīr*, 5/19 §4461; 8/266 §8033. •al-Bayhaqī in *al-Sunan al-Kubrā*, 8/188. •Abū Yaʿlā in *al-Musnad*, 5/337 §2963. •al-Haythamī in *Majmaʿ al-Zawāʾid*, 6/230, 239. •al-ʿAsqalānī in *Fatḥ al-Bārī*, 12/286 §6532, & in *Taghlīq al-Taʿlīq*, 5/259. •Ibn ʿAbd al-Barr in *al-Tamhīd*, 23/335.

According to al-ʿAsqalānī in *al-Fatḥ*: "Al-Ṭabarānī has traced it by way of Bakīr b. ʿAbd Allāh b. al-Ashajj from *Tahdhīb al-Āthār* and included in *Musnad ʿAlī* that he asked Nāfiʿ: 'How did Ibn ʿUmar regard the al-Ḥarūriyya (Khawārij)?' He said: 'He used to regard them as the worst of Allah's creatures. They have seized upon the Qurʾānic Verses concerning the unbelievers and applied them to the believers.'"

I (ʿAsqalānī) have remarked: "Its chain of transmission is authentic, for it has been established in the authentic tradition traced to its ultimate source, according to Muslim, from the tradition of Abū Dharr ﷺ concerning the description of the Khawārij: 'They are the worst of creatures and the creation.' According to Aḥmad, it is similarly traced to its ultimate source with a perfect chain of transmission, on the authority of Anas."

According to al-Bazzār, by way of al-Shaʿbī on the authority of ʿĀʾisha ﷺ, she said: "Allah's Messenger ﷺ mentioned the Khawārij, and he said: 'They are the worst of my Community. The best of my Community will slay them.'" Its chain of transmission is excellent.

According to al-Ṭabārānī, tracing in this manner to the ultimate source [the wording is]: "They (Khawārij) are the worst of creatures and the creation. The best of creatures and the creation will slay them."

In the report of ʿUbayd Allāh b. Abī Rāfiʿ, on the authority of ʿAlī ﷺ, according to Muslim [the wording is]: "They (Khawārij) are among the most hateful of Allah's creatures towards Him."

In the tradition of ʿAbd Allāh b. Khabbāb ﷺ, i.e., on the authority of his father, according to al-Ṭabārānī [the wording is]: "They (Khawārij) are the worst of the slain whom the sky has shaded and the earth has carried." Likewise in the tradition of Abū Umāma ﷺ.

According to Aḥmad and Ibn Abī Shayba, from the tradition of Abū Barza traced to its ultimate source, on the subject of the Khawārij [the wording is]: "The worst of creatures and the creation," said three times.

According to Ibn Abī Shayba, by way of ʿUmayr b. Isḥāq on the authority of Abū Hurayra ﷺ [the wording is]: "They are the worst of creatures." This contributes support to the allegation of those who allege their unbelief.

٣٢٠/ ١٩. عَنْ أَبِي غَالِبٍ قَالَ: رَأَى أَبُوْ أُمَامَةَ ﷺ رُءُوْسًا مَنْصُوْبَةً عَلَى دَرَجِ مَسْجِدِ دِمَشْقَ، فَقَالَ أَبُوْ أُمَامَةَ ﷺ: كِلَابُ النَّارِ شَرُّ قَتْلَى تَحْتَ أَدِيْمِ السَّمَاءِ؛ خَيْرُ قَتْلَى مَنْ قَتَلُوْهُ ثُمَّ قَرَأَ: ﴿يَوْمَ تَبْيَضُّ وُجُوهٌ وَتَسْوَدُّ وُجُوهٌ﴾ إِلَى آخِرِ الآيَةِ (آل عمران، ٣/ ١٠٦). قُلْتُ لِأَبِي أُمَامَةَ: أَنْتَ سَمِعْتَهُ مِنْ رَسُوْلِ اللهِ ﷺ؟ قَالَ: لَوْ لَمْ أَسْمَعْهُ إِلاَّ مَرَّةً أَوْ مَرَّتَيْنِ أَوْ ثَلَاثًا أَوْ أَرْبَعًا حَتَّى عَدَّ سَبْعًا مَا حَدَّثْتُكُمُوْهُ.

رَوَاهُ التِّرْمِذِيُّ وَأَحْمَدُ وَالْحَاكِمُ. وَقَالَ أَبُوْ عِيْسَى: هَذَا حَدِيْثٌ حَسَنٌ، وَقَالَ الْحَاكِمُ: هَذَا حَدِيْثٌ صَحِيْحٌ.

320/19. According to Abū Ghālib: "Abū Umāma ﷺ saw the heads (of Khawārij) displayed on the stairs of the mosque of Damascus, so Abū Umāma ﷺ said: '(These) dogs of the Fire of Hell are the worst of the slain beneath the surface of the sky. The best of the slain is the one whom they slay, then he recited this Verse: "On the day when many faces will be whitened and many faces will be blackened *[yawma tabyaḍḍu wujūhun wa taswaddu wujūh]*."'" (Q.3:106). I said to Abū Umāma: "Did you hear it from Allah's Messenger ﷺ?" He said: "If I had heard it only once or twice, or three or four times..."—he counted up to seven—"I would not have related it to you (i.e., not twice or thrice, I heard it frequently)!"

Reported by al-Tirmidhī, Aḥmad and al-Ḥākim. Abū ʿĪsā said: "This is an excellent tradition," and al-Ḥākim said:

---

320 Set forth by •al-Tirmidhī in *al-Sunan*, Bk.: Interpretation of the Qurʾān according to Allah's Messenger ﷺ, Ch.: From the Sūra of Āl ʿImrān, (Q.3), 5/226 §3000. •Aḥmad b. Ḥanbal in *al-Musnad*, 5/256 §22262. •al-Ḥākim in *al-Mustadrak*, 2/163 §2655. •al-Bayhaqī in *al-Sunan al-Kubrā*, 8/188. •al-Ṭabarānī in *Musnad al-Shāmiyyīn*, 2/248 §1279, & in *al-Muʿjam al-Kabīr*, 8/271 §8044. •al-Maḥāmilī in *al-Amālī*, 1/408 §478–479. •ʿAbd Allāh b. Aḥmad in *al-Sunna*, 2/643 §1542–1546. He said: "Its chain of transmission is authentic." •Ibn Taymiyya in *al-Ṣārim al-Maslūl*, 1/189.

"This is an authentic tradition."

٣٢١/ ٢٠. عَنِ ابْنِ عُمَرَ رضي الله عنهما عَنِ النَّبِيِّ ﷺ أَنَّهُ كَانَ قَائِمًا عِنْدَ بَابِ عَائِشَةَ رضي الله عنها فَأَشَارَ بِيَدِهِ نَحْوَ الْـمَشْرِقِ فَقَالَ: اَلْفِتْنَةُ هَاهُنَا حَيْثُ يَطْلُعُ قَرْنُ الشَّيْطَانِ.

رَوَاهُ الْبُخَارِيُّ وَأَحْمَدُ وَاللَّفْظُ لَهُ.

321/20. According to Ibn ʿUmar رضي الله عنهما:

"The Prophet ﷺ was standing beside the door of ʿĀʾisha رضي الله عنها, when he pointed his hand towards the east and said: 'The trouble is here, from whence will arise the horn (i.e., the generation) of Satan!'"

Reported by al-Bukhārī and Aḥmad (the wording is his).

٣٢٢/ ٢١. عَنِ ابْنِ عُمَرَ رضي الله عنهما أَنَّ رَسُوْلَ اللهِ ﷺ قَامَ عِنْدَ بَابِ حَفْصَةَ فَقَالَ بِيَدِهِ نَحْوَ الْـمَشْرِقِ: اَلْفِتْنَةُ هَاهُنَا مِنْ حَيْثُ يَطْلُعُ قَرْنُ الشَّيْطَانِ. قَالَهَا مَرَّتَيْنِ أَوْ ثَلَاثًا.

رَوَاهُ مُسْلِمٌ.

322/21. According to Ibn ʿUmar رضي الله عنهما:

"Allah's Messenger ﷺ stood beside the door of Ḥafṣa, and he said, with his hand pointing towards the east: 'The trouble is here, from whence will arise the horn (i.e., the generation) of Satan!' He said it two or three times."

Reported by Muslim.

٣٢٣/ ٢٢. عَنِ ابْنِ عُمَرَ رضي الله عنهما أَنَّ رَسُوْلَ اللهِ ﷺ قَالَ: اَللَّهُمَّ، بَارِكْ لَنَا فِي شَامِنَا

---

321 Set forth by •al-Bukhārī in *al-Ṣaḥīḥ*, Bk.: *al-Khumus* [One-fifth spoils of war], Ch.: What has come to us about the houses of the wives of the Prophet ﷺ, and what part of the houses was assigned to them, 3/1130 §2937. •Aḥmad b. Ḥanbal in *al-Musnad*, 2/18 §4679. •al-Muqriʾ in *al-Sunan al-Wārida fī al-Fitan*, 1/245 §42.

322 Set forth by •Muslim in *al-Ṣaḥīḥ*, Bk.: *al-Fitan wa Ashrāṭ al-Sāʿa* [Troubles and the Portents of the Final Hour], Ch.: The trouble from whence the horns of Satan emerge, 4/2229 §2905.

وَيَمَنِنَا، مَرَّتَيْنِ. فَقَالَ رَجُلٌ: وَفِي مَشْرِقِنَا، يَا رَسُوْلَ اللهِ؟ فَقَالَ رَسُوْلُ اللهِ ﷺ: مِنْ
هُنَالِكَ يَطْلُعُ قَرْنُ الشَّيْطَانِ وَلَهَا تِسْعَةُ أَعْشَارِ الشَّرِّ.

رَوَاهُ أَحْمَدُ وَالطَّبَرَانِيُّ.

323/22. According to Ibn ʿUmar :

"Allah's Messenger said twice: 'O Allah, bless our Syria and
our Yemen!' A man then said: 'And in our east, O Messenger of
Allah?' Allah's Messenger said: 'Over there will arise the horn
(i.e., the generation) of Satan, and it will possess nine tenths of
evil!'"

Reported by Aḥmad and al-Ṭabarānī.

٣٢٤ / ٢٣. عَنْ أَنَسٍ ﷺ قَالَ: ذُكِرَ لِي أَنَّ رَسُوْلَ اللهِ ﷺ قَالَ: وَلَـمْ أَسْمَعْهُ مِنْهُ: إِنَّ
فِيْكُمْ قَوْمًا يَعْبُدُوْنَ وَيَدْأَبُوْنَ حَتَّى يُعْجَبَ بِهِمُ النَّاسُ وَتُعْجِبَهُمْ نُفُوْسُهُمْ. يَمْرُقُوْنَ
مِنَ الدِّيْنِ مُرُوْقَ السَّهْمِ مِنَ الرَّمِيَّةِ.

رَوَاهُ أَحْمَدُ وَرِجَالُهُ رِجَالُ الصَّحِيْحِ.

324/23. According to Anas :

"I was told that Allah's Messenger said, though I did not
hear it from him: 'Surely, among you there is a group of people
who worship and practise devotion so much that the people admire
them and their own selves admire them (and their ritual prayer).
But they will go out of the Religion as the arrow darts through the
game animal.'"

---

323 Set forth by •Aḥmad b. Ḥanbal in *al-Musnad*, 2/90 §5642. •al-Ṭabarānī
in *al-Muʿjam al-Awsaṭ*, 2/249 §1889. •al-Rūyānī in *al-Musnad*, 2/421 §1433.
•al-Haythamī in *Majmaʿ al-Zawāʾid*, 10/57. He said: "Aḥmad's narrators are
the narrators of ʿAbd al-Raḥmān b. ʿAṭāʾ, and he is reliable."

324 Set forth by •Aḥmad b. Ḥanbal in *al-Musnad*, 3/183 §12909. •al-
Haythamī in *Majmaʿ al-Zawāʾid*, 6/229. He said: "It has been reported by
Aḥmad, and his narrators are authentic."

Reported by Aḥmad and his narrators are authentic.

٣٢٥/ ٢٤. عَنْ عَبْدِ اللهِ بْنِ رَبَاحِ الْأَنْصَارِيِّ رضي الله عنه قَالَ: سَمِعْتُ كَعْبًا رضي الله عنه يَقُوْلُ: لِلشَّهِيْدِ نُوْرٌ وَلِمَنْ قَاتَلَ الْحَرُوْرِيَّةَ عَشْرَةُ أَنْوَارٍ (وفي رواية ابن أبي شيبة: فَضْلُ ثَمَانِيَةِ أَنْوَارٍ عَلَى نُوْرِ الشُّهَدَاءِ) وَكَانَ يَقُوْلُ: لِجَهَنَّمَ سَبْعَةُ أَبْوَابٍ ثَلَاثَةٌ مِنْهَا لِلْحَرُوْرِيَّةِ.

رَوَاهُ عَبْدُ الرَّزَّاقِ وَابْنُ أَبِي شَيْبَةَ.

325/24. According to ʿAbd Allāh b. Rabāḥ al-Anṣārī ﷺ:

"I heard Kaʿb say ﷺ: 'The martyr has a light, and someone who kills the al-Ḥarūriyya [Khawārij] has ten lights (in the report of Ibn Abī Shayba: eight lights in addition to the light of the martyr),' and he used to say: 'Hell has seven gates, three of them (prefixed) for the al-Ḥarūriyya [Khawārij].'"

Reported by ʿAbd al-Razzāq and Ibn Abī Shayba.

٣٢٦/ ٢٥. عَنْ حُذَيْفَةَ رضي الله عنه قَالَ: قَالَ رَسُوْلُ اللهِ ﷺ: إِنَّ مَا أَتَخَوَّفُ عَلَيْكُمْ رَجُلٌ قَرَأَ الْقُرْآنَ حَتَّى إِذَا رُئِيَتْ بَهْجَتُهُ عَلَيْهِ وَكَانَ رِدْئًا لِلْإِسْلَامِ غَيْرَهُ إِلَى مَاشَاءَ اللهُ فَانْسَلَخَ مِنْهُ وَنَبَذَهُ وَرَاءَ ظَهْرِهِ وَسَعَى عَلَى جَارِهِ بِالسَّيْفِ وَرَمَاهُ بِالشِّرْكِ. قَالَ: قُلْتُ: يَا نَبِيَّ اللهِ، أَيُّهُمَا أَوْلَى بِالشِّرْكِ الْمَرْمِيُّ أَمِ الرَّامِي؟ قَالَ: بَلِ الرَّامِي.

رَوَاهُ ابْنُ حِبَّانَ وَالْبَزَّارُ وَالْبُخَارِيُّ فِي الْكَبِيْرِ؛ إِسْنَادُهُ حَسَنٌ.

326/25. According to Ḥudhayfa ﷺ:

---

325 Set forth by •ʿAbd al-Razzāq in *al-Muṣannaf*, 10/155. •Ibn Abī Shayba in *al-Muṣannaf*, 7/557 §37911.

326 Set forth by •Ibn Ḥibbān in *al-Ṣaḥīḥ*, 1/282 §81. •al-Bazzār in *al-Musnad*, 7/220 §2793. •al-Bukhārī in *Tarīkh al-Kabīr*, 4/301 §2907. •al-Ṭabarānī, on the authority of Muʿādh b. Jabal ﷺ, in *al-Muʿjam al-Kabīr*, 20/88 §169, & in *Musnad al-Shāmiyyīn*, 2/254 §1291. •Ibn Abī ʿĀṣim in *al-Sunna*, 1/24 §43. •al-Haythamī in *Majmaʿ al-Zawāʾid*, 1/188. He said: "Its chain of transmission is excellent." •Ibn Kathīr in *Tafsīr al-Qurʾān al-ʿAẓīm*, 2/266.

"Allah's Messenger ﷺ said: 'What I fear for you is a man who reads the Qurʾān until its splendour is visible upon him, and who is a support for others for the cause of Islam, as long as Allah wills, then he abandons it (the Qurʾān) and throws it behind his back, attacks his neighbour with the sword and accuses him of polytheism.' I said: 'O Prophet of Allah, which of the two is more guilty of polytheism, the accused or the accuser?' He said: 'The accuser, of course!'"

Reported by Ibn Ḥibbān, al-Bazzār and al-Bukhārī in *al-Tārīkh*; its chain of transmission is excellent.

٣٢٧/ ٢٦. عَنِ ابْنِ عُمَرَ رضي الله عنهما قَالَ: سَمِعْتُ رَسُوْلَ اللهِ ﷺ عِنْدَ حُجْرَةِ عَائِشَةَ رضي الله عنها يَدْعُوْ: اَللّٰهُمَّ، بَارِكْ لَنَا فِي مُدِّنَا وَبَارِكْ لَنَا فِي صَاعِنَا وَبَارِكْ لَنَا فِي شَامِنَا وَيَمَنِنَا. ثُمَّ اسْتَقْبَلَ الْمَشْرِقَ فَقَالَ: مِنْ هَاهُنَا يَخْرُجُ قَرْنُ الشَّيْطَانِ وَالزَّلَازِلُ وَالْفِتَنُ وَمِنْ هَاهُنَا الْفَدَّادُوْنَ.

رَوَاهُ الطَّبَرَانِيُّ.

327/26. According to Ibn ʿUmar ﷺ:

"I heard Allah's Messenger ﷺ beside the room of ʿĀʾisha ﷺ, offering the supplication: 'O Allah, bless us in our *mudd* (handful) and bless us in our *ṣāʿ* (cubic) measure! Bless us in our Syria and our Yemen!' Then he turned to face the east and said: 'From here will emerge the horn (i.e., the generation) of Satan, the earthquakes and the troubles, and from here [will emerge] the stern-spoken and arrogant boasters with conceited gait.'"

Reported by al-Ṭabarānī.

٣٢٨/ ٢٧. عَنْ عَبْدِ اللهِ بْنِ عَمْرِو بْنِ الْعَاصِ رضي الله عنهما قَالَ: سَمِعْتُ رَسُوْلَ اللهِ ﷺ يَقُوْلُ: سَيَخْرُجُ أُنَاسٌ مِنْ أُمَّتِي مِنْ قِبَلِ الْمَشْرِقِ، يَقْرَءُوْنَ الْقُرْآنَ، لَا يُجَاوِزُ تَرَاقِيَهُمْ.

---

327 Set forth by •al-Ṭabarānī in *al-Muʿjam al-Awsaṭ*, 7/252 §7421. •Abū Nuʿaym in *al-Musnad al-Mustakhraj*, 4/44 §3183.

كُلَّمَا خَرَجَ مِنْهُمْ قَرْنٌ قُطِعَ، كُلَّمَا خَرَجَ مِنْهُمْ قَرْنٌ قُطِعَ، حَتَّى عَدَّهَا زِيَادَةً عَلَى عَشْرَةِ مَرَّاتٍ كُلَّمَا خَرَجَ مِنْهُمْ قَرْنٌ قُطِعَ، حَتَّى يَخْرُجُ الدَّجَّالُ فِي بَقِيَّتِهِمْ.

رَوَاهُ أَحْمَدُ وَالْحَاكِمُ.

328/27. According to ʿAbd Allāh b. ʿAmr b. al-ʿĀṣ ﷺ:

"I heard Allah's Messenger ﷺ saying: 'Some people from my Community will emerge from the direction of the east, reciting the Qurʾān, which will not pass beyond their throats. Whenever a horn (i.e., a generation) emerges from them, it will be cut short. Whenever a horn (i.e., a generation) emerges from them, it will be cut short; the Prophet ﷺ repeated it over ten times and said: Whenever a generation emerges from them, it will be cut short, until the Antichrist emerges in their last remnant.'"

Reported by Aḥmad and al-Ḥākim.

٣٢٩/ ٢٨. عَنْ عَبْدِ اللهِ بْنِ عَمْرٍو ﷺ قَالَ: يَأْتِي عَلَى النَّاسِ زَمَانٌ يَجْتَمِعُوْنَ وَيُصَلُّوْنَ فِي الْمَسَاجِدِ وَلَيْسَ فِيْهِمْ مُؤْمِنٌ.

رَوَاهُ ابْنُ أَبِي شَيْبَةَ وَالْحَاكِمُ، وَقَالَ الْحَاكِمُ: هَذَا حَدِيْثٌ صَحِيْحُ الإِسْنَادِ عَلَى شَرْطِ الشَّيْخَيْنِ.

329/28. According to ʿAbd Allāh b. ʿAmr ﷺ:

"There will come upon the people a time when they congregate and perform the ritual prayer in the mosques, and there will not be a believer among them!'"

328 Set forth by •Aḥmad b. Ḥanbal in *al-Musnad*, 2/198 §6871. •al-Ḥākim in *al-Mustadrak*, 4/553 §8497. •Ibn Ḥammād in *al-Fitan*, 2/532. •Ibn Rāshid in *al-Jāmiʿ*, 11/377. •al-Ajrī in *al-Sharīʿa*, 1/113 §260. •al-Haythamī in *Majmaʿ al-Zawāʾid*, 6/228.

329 Set forth by •Ibn Abī Shayba in *al-Muṣannaf*, 6/163 §30355; 7/505 §37586. •al-Ḥākim in *al-Mustadrak*, 4/489 §8365. •al-Daylamī in *al-Firdaws bi-Maʾthūr al-Khiṭāb*, 5/441 §8086. •Abū al-Maḥāsin in *Muʿtaṣar al-Mukhtaṣar*, 2/266. •al-Faryābī in *Ṣifat al-Munafiq*, 1/80 §108–110.

Reported by Ibn Abī Shayba and al-Ḥākim, who said: "This is a tradition with an authentic chain of transmission, in conformity with the stipulation of al-Bukhārī and Muslim."

٣٣٠/ ٢٩. عَنْ أَبِي هُرَيْرَةَ رضي الله عنه يَقُوْلُ: قَالَ رَسُوْلُ اللهِ ﷺ: يَخْرُجُ فِي آخِرِ الزَّمَانِ رِجَالٌ يَخْتِلُوْنَ الدُّنْيَا بِالدِّيْنِ. يَلْبَسُوْنَ لِلنَّاسِ جُلُوْدَ الضَّأْنِ مِنَ اللِّيْنِ. أَلْسِنَتُهُمْ أَحْلَى مِنَ السُّكَّرِ (وفي رواية: أَلْسِنَتُهُمْ أَحْلَى مِنَ الْعَسَلِ) وَقُلُوْبُهُمْ قُلُوْبُ الذِّئَابِ. يَقُوْلُ اللهُ ﷻ: أَبِي يَغْتَرُّوْنَ أَمْ عَلَيَّ يَجْتَرِءُوْنَ؟ فَبِي حَلَفْتُ لَأَبْعَثَنَّ عَلَى أُوْلَئِكَ مِنْهُمْ فِتْنَةً تَدَعُ الْحَلِيْمَ مِنْهُمْ حَيْرَانًا.

رَوَاهُ التِّرْمِذِيُّ، وَقَالَ أَبُوْ عِيْسَى: هَذَا حَدِيْثٌ حَسَنٌ.

330/29. According to Abū Hurayra (may Allah be pleased with him):

"Allah's Messenger ﷺ said: 'At the end of time, there will emerge some men who will acquire this world by means of the Religion. They will clothe themselves for the people with the sheepskins of gentility. Their tongues will be sweeter than sugar (in one version: Their tongues will be sweeter than honey), but their hearts will be (blood-seekers like) the hearts of wolves. Allah ﷻ will say: "Are they deceiving Me, or are they treating Me audaciously? I have sworn by Me that I will surely inflict upon these among them calamities that will leave even the forbearing among them bewildered!"'"

Reported by al-Tirmidhī. Abū ʿĪsā said: "This is an excellent tradition."

---

330 Set forth by •al-Tirmidhī in *al-Sunan*, Bk.: *al-Zuhd* [Abstinence] according to Allah's Messenger ﷺ, Ch.: (59), 4/604 §2404–2405. •Ibn Abī Shayba in *al-Muṣannaf*, 7/235 §35624. •al-Bayhaqī in *Shuʿab al-Īmān*, 5/362 §6956. •al-Ṭabarānī in *al-Muʿjam al-Awsaṭ*, 8/379. •Ibn al-Mubārak in *al-Zuhd*, 1/17 §50. •al-Daylamī in *al-Firdaws bi-Maʾthūr al-Khiṭāb*, 5/510 §8919. •al-Mundhirī in *al-Targhīb wa al-Tarhīb*, 1/32 §41. •Ibn Hanād in *al-Zuhd*, 2/437 §860.

٣٣١/ ٣٠. عَنْ أَبِي بَكْرَةَ رضي الله عنه قَالَ: قَالَ رَسُوْلُ اللهِ ﷺ: سَيَخْرُجُ قَوْمٌ أَحْدَاثٌ أَحِدَّاءُ أَشِدَّاءُ ذَلِقَةٌ أَلْسِنَتُهُمْ بِالْقُرْآنِ يَقْرَءُوْنَهُ لَا يُجَاوِزُ تَرَاقِيَهُمْ. فَإِذَا لَقِيْتُمُوْهُمْ فَأَنِيمُوْهُمْ ثُمَّ إِذَا لَقِيْتُمُوْهُمْ فَاقْتُلُوْهُمْ فَإِنَّهُ يُؤْجَرُ قَاتِلُهُمْ.

رَوَاهُ أَحْمَدُ وَالْحَاكِمُ وَابْنُ أَبِي عَاصِمٍ. رِجَالُ أَحْمَدَ رِجَالُ الصَّحِيْحِ، وَقَالَ ابْنُ أَبِي عَاصِمٍ: إِسْنَادُهُ صَحِيْحٌ، وَقَالَ الْحَاكِمُ: هَذَا حَدِيْثٌ صَحِيْحٌ.

331/30. According to Abū Bakra رضي الله عنه:

"Allah's Messenger ﷺ said: 'There will emerge a group of people who are youthful, sharp-witted and vehement. They will recite the Qurʾān distinctly and expressly, but it will not pass beyond their throats. If you encounter them, you must put them to sleep. Then, if you encounter (another group of) them again, you must kill them, for their killer will be rewarded!'

Reported by Aḥmad, al-Ḥākim and Ibn Abī ʿĀṣim. Aḥmad's narrators are authentic. Ibn Abī ʿĀṣim said: "Its chain of transmission is authentic," and al-Ḥākim said: "This is an authentic tradition."

٣٣٢/ ٣١. عَنْ أَبِي سَعِيدٍ الْخُدْرِيِّ رضي الله عنه أَنَّ أَبَا بَكْرٍ رضي الله عنه جَاءَ إِلَى رَسُوْلِ اللهِ ﷺ، فَقَالَ: يَا رَسُوْلَ اللهِ، إِنِّي مَرَرْتُ بِوَادِ كَذَا وَكَذَا فَإِذَا رَجُلٌ مُتَخَشِّعٌ، حَسَنُ الْهَيْئَةِ، يُصَلِّي. فَقَالَ لَهُ النَّبِيُّ ﷺ: اذْهَبْ إِلَيْهِ، فَاقْتُلْهُ. قَالَ: فَذَهَبَ إِلَيْهِ أَبُو بَكْرٍ، فَلَمَّا رَآهُ عَلَى تِلْكَ الْحَالِ كَرِهَ أَنْ يَقْتُلَهُ، فَرَجَعَ إِلَى رَسُوْلِ اللهِ ﷺ، قَالَ: فَقَالَ النَّبِيُّ ﷺ لِعُمَرَ: اذْهَبْ فَاقْتُلْهُ. فَذَهَبَ عُمَرُ فَرَآهُ عَلَى تِلْكَ الْحَالِ الَّتِي رَآهُ أَبُوْ بَكْرٍ. قَالَ: فَكَرِهَ أَنْ يَقْتُلَهُ.

[331] Set forth by •Aḥmad b. Ḥanbal in *al-Musnad*, 5/36, 44. •al-Ḥākim in *al-Mustadrak*, 2/159 §2645. •Ibn Abī ʿĀṣim in *al-Sunna*, 2/456 §937. •ʿAbd Allāh b. Aḥmad in *al-Sunan*, 2/637 §1519. He said: "Its chain of transmission is excellent." •al-Bayhaqī in *al-Sunan al-Kubrā*, 8/187. •al-Daylamī in *al-Firdaws bi-Maʾthūr al-Khiṭāb*, 2/322 §3460. •al-Haythamī in *Majmaʿ al-Zawāʾid*, 6/230. •al-Ḥārith in *al-Musnad*, (*Zawāʾid al-Haythamī*), 2/714 §704.

قَالَ: فَرَجَعَ فَقَالَ: يَا رَسُوْلَ اللهِ، إِنِّي رَأَيْتُهُ يُصَلِّي مُتَخَشِّعًا فَكَرِهْتُ أَنْ أَقْتُلَهُ. قَالَ: يَا عَلِيُّ، اِذْهَبْ فَاقْتُلْهُ. قَالَ: فَذَهَبَ عَلِيٌّ، فَلَمْ يَرَهُ فَرَجَعَ عَلِيٌّ، فَقَالَ: يَا رَسُوْلَ اللهِ، إِنَّهُ لَـمْ يَرَهْ. قَالَ: فَقَالَ النَّبِيُّ ﷺ: إِنَّ هَذَا وَأَصْحَابَهُ يَقْرَءُوْنَ الْقُرْآنَ لَا يُجَاوِزُ تَرَاقِيَهُمْ. يَمْرُقُوْنَ مِنَ الدِّيْنِ كَمَا يَمْرُقُ السَّهْمُ مِنَ الرَّمِيَّةِ ثُمَّ لَا يَعُوْدُوْنَ فِيْهِ حَتَّى يَعُوْدَ السَّهْمُ فِي فُوْقِهِ. فَاقْتُلُوْهُمْ هُمْ شَرُّ الْبَرِيَّةِ.

رَوَاهُ أَحْمَدُ، وَرِجَالُهُ ثِقَاتٌ.

332/31. According to Abū Saʿīd al-Khudrī ﵁:

"Abū Bakr ﵁ came to Allah's Messenger ﷺ and said: 'O Messenger of Allah, I passed by the valley of Such-and-such, and lo and behold, there was a humble, good-looking man, performing the ritual prayer!' The Prophet ﷺ told him: 'Go to him, for you must kill him!' Abū Bakr therefore went to him, but when he saw him in that state (of submissiveness and devotion while praying), he found it heavy to kill him, so he returned to Allah's Messenger ﷺ. The Prophet ﷺ then said to ʿUmar: 'Go and kill him!' ʿUmar went, but he saw him in that state in which Abū Bakr had seen him, and he too found it burdensome to kill him, so he came back and said: 'O Messenger of Allah, I saw him humbly performing the ritual prayer, so I was averse to killing him.' He then said: 'O ʿAlī, go and kill him!' ʿAlī went, but he did not see him, so he came back and said: 'O Messenger of Allah, he is not seen around!' The Prophet ﷺ then said: 'This man and his companions recite the Qurʾān, but it does not pass beyond their throats. They flee from the Religion as the arrow zooms through the game animal. Then they will not return to it until the arrow returns to its notch (i.e., their come-back to the Religion is not likely), so you must kill them (whenever you find them during war), for they are the worst of creatures!'

---

[332] Set forth by •Aḥmad b. Ḥanbal in *al-Musnad*, 3/15 §11133. •al-Haythamī in *Majmaʿ al-Zawāʾid*, 6/225. He said: "Its narrators are reliable." •al-ʿAsqalānī in *Fatḥ al-Bārī*, 12/229. •Ibn Ḥazm in *al-Muḥlī*, 11/104. •al-Shawkānī in *Nayl al-Awṭār*, 7/351.

Reported by Aḥmad and his narrators are reliable.

٣٣٣/ ٣٢. عَنْ أَبِي بَكْرَةَ رضي الله عنه أَنَّ نَبِيَّ اللهِ ﷺ مَرَّ بِرَجُلٍ سَاجِدٍ وَهُوَ يَنْطَلِقُ إِلَى الصَّلَاةِ فَقَضَى الصَّلَاةَ وَرَجَعَ عَلَيْهِ وَهُوَ سَاجِدٌ. فَقَامَ النَّبِيُّ ﷺ، فَقَالَ: مَنْ يَقْتُلُ هَذَا؟ فَقَامَ رَجُلٌ فَحَسَرَ عَنْ يَدَيْهِ فَاخْتَرَطَ سَيْفَهُ وَهَزَّهُ ثُمَّ قَالَ: يَا نَبِيَّ اللهِ، بِأَبِي أَنْتَ وَأُمِّي، كَيْفَ أَقْتُلُ رَجُلاً سَاجِدًا يَشْهَدُ أَنْ لَا إِلَهَ إِلاَّ اللهُ وَأَنَّ مُحَمَّدًا عَبْدُهُ وَرَسُوْلُهُ؟ ثُمَّ قَالَ: مَنْ يَقْتُلُ هَذَا؟ فَقَامَ رَجُلٌ، فَقَالَ: أَنَا فَحَسَرَ عَنْ ذِرَاعَيْهِ وَاخْتَرَطَ سَيْفَهُ وَهَزَّهُ حَتَّى أَرْعَدَتْ يَدُهُ. فَقَالَ: يَا نَبِيَّ اللهِ، كَيْفَ أَقْتُلُ رَجُلاً سَاجِدًا يَشْهَدُ أَنْ لَا إِلَهَ إِلاَّ اللهُ وَأَنَّ مُحَمَّدًا عَبْدُهُ وَرَسُوْلُهُ؟ فَقَالَ النَّبِيُّ ﷺ: وَالَّذِي نَفْسُ مُحَمَّدٍ بِيَدِهِ، لَوْ قَتَلْتُمُوْهُ لَكَانَ أَوَّلَ فِتْنَةٍ وَآخِرَهَا.

رَوَاهُ أَحْمَدُ وَابْنُ أَبِي عَاصِمٍ. إِسْنَادُهُ صَحِيْحٌ وَرِجَالُهُ كُلُّهُمْ ثِقَاتٌ كَمَا قَالَ ابْنُ أَبِي عَاصِمٍ وَالْهَيْثَمِيُّ.

333/32. According to Abū Bakra رضي الله عنه:

"The Prophet ﷺ passed by a man who was prostrating himself. And he was on his way to the ritual prayer, so he performed his ritual prayer and came back to that man, who was still in (the state of) prostration. The Prophet ﷺ stopped there and said: 'Who will kill this man?' A man volunteered, so he pulled up his sleeves and bared his hands, unsheathed his sword and brandished it, but then (looked at him and affected by his appearance) said: 'O Prophet of Allah, I appeal to you by my father and my mother! How can I kill a man who is prostrating himself, bearing witness that there is no God but Allah, and that Muhammad is His servant and His Messenger?' Then he said again: 'Who will kill this man?'

333 Set forth by •Aḥmad b. Ḥanbal in *al-Musnad*, 5/42 §19536. •Ibn Abī ʿĀṣim in *al-Sunna*, 2/457 §938. •al-Haythamī in *Majmaʿ al-Zawāʾid*, 6/225. He said: "It has been reported by Aḥmad and al-Ṭabarānī, and Aḥmad's narrators are authentic." •al-Ḥārith in *al-Musnad* (*Zawāʾid al-Haythamī*), 2/713 §703. •Ibn Rajab in *Jāmiʿ al-ʿUlūm wa al-Ḥikam*, 1/131.

Another man volunteered and said: 'I will.' So he laid his hands bare, unsheathed his sword and brandished it (and was about to kill him when) his hand trembled, and then he said: 'How can I kill a man who is prostrating himself, bearing witness that there is no God but Allah, and that Muhammad is His servant and His Messenger?' The Prophet ﷺ then said: 'By the One in whose Hand the soul of Muhammad is, if you had killed him, it would have been the beginning and the end of a trouble (the disruption of Khawārij would have ended)!'"

> Reported by Aḥmad and Ibn Abī ʿĀṣim. Its chain of transmission is authentic, and all its sources are reliable, as stated by Ibn Abī ʿĀṣim and al-Haythamī.

٣٣٤/ ٣٣. عَنْ أَنَسِ بْنِ مَالِكٍ ﵁ قَالَ: كَانَ فِي عَهْدِ رَسُوْلِ اللهِ ﷺ رَجُلٌ يُعْجِبُنَا تَعَبُّدُهُ وَاجْتِهَادُهُ (وَفِي رِوَايَةٍ: حَتَّى جَعَلَ بَعْضُ أَصْحَابِ النَّبِيِّ ﷺ أَنَّ لَهُ فَضْلاً عَلَيْهِمْ). قَدْ عَرَّفْنَاهُ لِرَسُوْلِ اللهِ ﷺ بِاسْمِهِ وَوَصَفْنَاهُ بِصِفَتِهِ. فَبَيْنَمَا نَحْنُ نَذْكُرُهُ إِذْ طَلَعَ الرَّجُلُ. قُلْنَا: هُوَ، هَذَا. قَالَ: إِنَّكُمْ لَتُخْبِرُوْنَ عَنْ رَجُلٍ إِنَّ عَلَى وَجْهِهِ سُفْعَةً مِنَ الشَّيْطَانِ. فَأَقْبَلَ حَتَّى وَقَفَ عَلَيْهِمْ وَلَمْ يُسَلِّمْ. فَقَالَ لَهُ رَسُوْلُ اللهِ ﷺ: أَنْشُدُكَ بِاللهِ، هَلْ قُلْتَ فِي نَفْسِكَ حِيْنَ وَقَفْتَ عَلَى الْمَجْلِسِ: مَا فِي الْقَوْمِ أَحَدٌ أَفْضَلُ أَوْ أَخْيَرُ مِنِّي؟ قَالَ: اَللَّهُمَّ، نَعَمْ. ثُمَّ دَخَلَ يُصَلِّي (وَفِي رِوَايَةٍ: ثُمَّ انْصَرَفَ فَأَتَى نَاحِيَةً مِنَ الْمَسْجِدِ فَخَطَّ خَطًّا بِرِجْلِهِ ثُمَّ صَفَّ كَعْبَيْهِ فَقَامَ يُصَلِّي) فَقَالَ رَسُوْلُ اللهِ ﷺ: مَنْ يَقْتُلُ الرَّجُلَ؟ فَقَالَ أَبُوْ بَكْرٍ: أَنَا. فَدَخَلَ عَلَيْهِ فَوَجَدَهُ يُصَلِّي فَقَالَ: سُبْحَانَ اللهِ أَقْتُلُ رَجُلاً يُصَلِّي! وَقَدْ نَهَى رَسُوْلُ اللهِ ﷺ عَنْ ضَرْبِ الْمُصَلِّيْنَ. فَخَرَجَ، فَقَالَ رَسُوْلُ اللهِ ﷺ: مَا فَعَلْتَ؟ قَالَ: كَرِهْتُ أَنْ أَقْتُلَهُ وَهُوَ يُصَلِّي، وَقَدْ نَهَيْتَ عَنْ ضَرْبِ الْمُصَلِّيْنَ. قَالَ: مَنْ يَقْتُلُ الرَّجُلَ؟ قَالَ عُمَرُ: أَنَا. فَدَخَلَ فَوَجَدَهُ وَاضِعًا وَجْهَهُ. قَالَ عُمَرُ: أَبُوْ بَكْرٍ أَفْضَلُ مِنِّي. فَخَرَجَ، فَقَالَ رَسُوْلُ اللهِ ﷺ: مَا فَعَلْتَ؟ قَالَ: وَجَدْتُهُ وَاضِعًا وَجْهَهُ للهِ فَكَرِهْتُ أَنْ أَقْتُلَهُ. قَالَ: مَنْ يَقْتُلُ الرَّجُلَ؟ فَقَالَ عَلِيٌّ: أَنَا. قَالَ: أَنْتَ

لَهُ إِنْ أَدْرَكْتَهُ. قَالَ: فَدَخَلَ عَلَيْهِ فَوَجَدَهُ قَدْ خَرَجَ فَرَجَعَ إِلَى رَسُوْلِ اللهِ ﷺ فَقَالَ: مَا فَعَلْتَ؟ قَالَ: وَجَدْتُهُ وَقَدْ خَرَجَ. قَالَ: لَوْ قُتِلَ مَا اخْتَلَفَ فِي أُمَّتِي رَجُلَانِ كَانَ أَوَّلُهُمْ وَآخِرُهُمْ. قَالَ مُوْسَى: سَمِعْتُ مُحَمَّدَ بْنَ كَعْبٍ يَقُوْلُ: هُوَ الَّذِي قَتَلَهُ عَلِيٌّ رضي الله عنه ذَا الثَّدْيَةِ.

وفي رواية: فَقَالَ النَّبِيُّ ﷺ: هَذَا أَوَّلُ قَرْنٍ مِنَ الشَّيْطَانِ طَلَعَ فِي أُمَّتِي (أَوْ أَوَّلُ قَرْنٍ طَلَعَ مِنْ أُمَّتِي). أَمَّا إِنَّكُمْ لَوْ قَتَلْتُمُوهُ، مَا اخْتَلَفَ مِنْكُمْ رَجُلَانِ. إِنَّ بَنِي إِسْرَائِيْلَ اخْتَلَفُوْا عَلَى إِحْدَى أَوِ اثْنَتَيْنِ وَسَبْعِيْنَ فِرْقَةً، وَإِنَّكُمْ سَتَخْتَلِفُوْنَ مِثْلَهُمْ أَوْ أَكْثَرَ. لَيْسَ مِنْهَا صَوَابٌ إِلاَّ وَاحِدَةٌ. قِيْلَ: يَا رَسُوْلَ اللهِ، وَمَا هَذِهِ الْوَاحِدَةُ؟ قَالَ: الْجَمَاعَةُ، وَآخِرُهَا فِي النَّارِ.

رَوَاهُ أَبُوْ يَعْلَى وَعَبْدُ الرَّزَّاقِ وَأَبُوْ نُعَيْمٍ، وَرِجَالُهُ رِجَالُ الصَّحِيْحِ كَمَا قَالَ الْهَيْثَمِيُّ. وَإِسْنَادُهُ صَحِيْحٌ.

334/33. According to Anas b. Mālik رضي الله عنه:

"In the time of Allah's Messenger ﷺ, there was a man whose worship and hard labour (in seeking Allah's pleasure) amazed us, (in one report: to the point where some of the Companions of the Prophet ﷺ credited him with a superiority over them). We made him known to Allah's Messenger ﷺ by his name and described him by his characteristic. Then, while we were mentioning him, the man suddenly appeared. We said: (O Messenger of Allah,) 'this is he!' He said: 'You are telling about a man whose face bears a tint of Satan!' Then he approached until he stood over them, and he did not give the salutation of peace, so Allah's Messenger ﷺ said to him: 'I adjure you by Allah! (Speak the truth.) Did you

---

334 Set forth by •Abū Yaʿlā in *al-Musnad*, 1/90 §90; 7/155, 168 §4127, 4143. •ʿAbd al-Razzāq in *al-Muṣannaf*, 1/155 §18674. •Abū Nuʿaym in *Ḥilya al-Awliyāʾ*, 3/52. •al-Marwazī in *al-Sunna*, 1/21 §53. •al-Maqdisī in *al-Aḥādīth al-Mukhtāra*, 17/69 §2499. •al-Haythamī in *Majmaʿ al-Zawāʾid*, 6/226.

say in your heart, when you attended the meeting: "There is no one here among the people superior to or better than I am!"?' He said: 'By Allah, yes (I said it with myself)!' Then he entered (the mosque and) set about performing the ritual prayer. (In one report: Then he turned, came to the compound of the mosque, aligned his heels and set about performing the ritual prayer.) Allah's Messenger ﷺ said: 'Who will kill the man?' Abū Bakr said: 'I will!' Then he entered his presence and found him performing the ritual prayer, so he said: 'Glory be to Allah! Am I going to kill a man who is performing the ritual prayer?' Allah's Messenger ﷺ had forbidden striking those performing the ritual prayer, so he withdrew (without killing him). Allah's Messenger ﷺ said: 'What have you done?' He said: 'I was averse to killing him while he was performing the ritual prayer, for you had forbidden striking those performing the ritual prayer.' He said again: 'Who will kill the man?' ʿUmar said: 'I will!' Then he entered and found him humbling his face before Allah. ʿUmar said: 'Abū Bakr is more meritorious than I am,' so he too withdrew (without killing him). Allah's Messenger ﷺ said: 'What have you done?' He said: 'I found him humbling his face to Allah, so I was averse to killing him (in this state).' He said yet again: 'Who will kill the man?' ʿAlī said: 'I will!' He said: 'You are entitled to (killing) him, if you catch up with him!' Then he entered his place and found that he had left, so he returned to Allah's Messenger ﷺ, who said: 'What have you done?' He said: 'I discovered that he had left.' Allah's Messenger ﷺ said: 'If he were killed, no two men in my Community would have disagreement, for he would be the first and the last of them (to cause disruption).' Mūsā said: 'I heard Muhammad b. Kaʿb say: "He was the man with one hand like a woman's breast (*dhū al-thadya*), whom ʿAlī ؓ killed.'"

In one report: "The Prophet ﷺ said: 'This first generation of Satan has arisen in my Community (or: A first generation has arisen in my Community). If only you killed him, no two men among you would differ! The Children of Israel split up into seventy-one or seventy-two sects, and you will surely split up like them, or into even more divisions, none of them correct except one.' He was asked: 'What is this one?' He said: 'The united congregation (the largest party), and the rest will end up in the Fire of Hell!'"

Reported by Abū Yaʿlā, ʿAbd al-Razzāq and Abū Nuʿaym. Its narrators are reliable, as al-Haythamī said, and its chain of transmission is authentic.

٣٣٥/ ٣٤. عَنْ طَارِقِ بْنِ زِيَادٍ قَالَ: خَرَجْنَا مَعَ عَلِيٍّ ﷺ إِلَى الْخَوَارِجِ فَقَتَلَهُمْ، ثُمَّ قَالَ: انْظُرُوْا فَإِنَّ نَبِيَّ اللهِ ﷺ قَالَ: إِنَّهُ سَيَخْرُجُ قَوْمٌ يَتَكَلَّمُوْنَ بِالْحَقِّ لَا يُجَاوِزُ حَلْقَهُمْ. يَخْرُجُوْنَ مِنَ الْحَقِّ كَمَا يَخْرُجُ السَّهْمُ مِنَ الرَّمِيَّةِ.

رَوَاهُ النَّسَائِيُّ وَأَحْمَدُ.

335/34. According to Ṭāriq b. Ziyād:

"We went out with ʿAlī ﷺ towards the Khawārij (to fight them), so he slew them. Then he said: 'Observe, for the Prophet ﷺ said: "Soon there will emerge a group of people who will talk about the truth, but it will not pass beyond their throats. They will exit from the truth as the arrow exits from the game animal."'"

Reported by al-Nasāʾī and Aḥmad.

٣٣٦/ ٣٥. عَنْ مِقْسَمٍ أَبِي الْقَاسِمِ مَوْلَى عَبْدِ اللهِ بْنِ الْحَارِثِ بْنِ نَوْفَلٍ عَنْ عَبْدِ اللهِ بْنِ عَمْرِو بْنِ الْعَاصِ ﷺ... فَذَكَرَ الْحَدِيْثَ وَفِيْهِ: قَالَ: قَالَ رَسُوْلُ اللهِ ﷺ: فَإِنَّهُ سَيَكُوْنُ لَهُ شِيعَةٌ يَتَعَمَّقُوْنَ فِي الدِّيْنِ حَتَّى يَخْرُجُوْا مِنْهُ كَمَا يَخْرُجُ السَّهْمُ مِنَ الرَّمِيَّةِ... وَذَكَرَ تَمَامَ الْحَدِيْثِ.

رَوَاهُ أَحْمَدُ وَابْنُ أَبِي عَاصِمٍ، وَقَالَ ابْنُ أَبِي عَاصِمٍ: إِسْنَادُهُ جَيِّدٌ وَرِجَالُهُ كُلُّهُمْ

---

335 Set forth by •al-Nasāʾī in *al-Suna al-Kubrā*, 5/161 §8566. •Aḥmad b. Ḥanbal in *al-Musnad*, 1/107 §848, & in *Faḍāʾil al-Ṣaḥāba*, 2/714 §1224. •al-Khaṭīb al-Baghdādī in *Tārīkh Baghdād*, 14/362 §7689. •al-Marwazī in *Taʿẓīm Qadr al-Ṣalāt*, 1/256 §247. •al-Mizzī in *Tahdhīb al-Kamāl*, 13/338 §2948.

ثِقَاتٌ.

336/35. According to Miqsam Abū al-Qāsim, the freedman of ʿAbd Allāh b. al-Ḥārith b. Nawfil, on the authority of ʿAbd Allāh b. ʿAmr b. al-ʿĀṣ ﷺ:

"Allah's Messenger ﷺ said: '... Soon it will have a sect whose members (apparently) immerse themselves in the Religion, but they will exit from it as the arrow exits from the game animal....'" (He cited the whole tradition.)

> Reported by Aḥmad and Ibn Abī ʿĀṣim. Ibn Abī ʿĀṣim said: "Its chain of transmission is perfect, and all of its narrators are reliable."

٣٣٧/ ٣٦. عَنْ عُقْبَةَ بْنِ عَامِرٍ ﷺ قَالَ: قَالَ رَسُوْلُ اللهِ ﷺ: سَيَخْرُجُ أَقْوَامٌ مِنْ أُمَّتِي يَشْرَبُوْنَ الْقُرْآنَ كَشُرْبِهِمُ اللَّبَنَ.

رَوَاهُ الطَّبَرَانِيُّ وَرِجَالُهُ ثِقَاتٌ كَمَا قَالَ الْهَيْثَمِيُّ وَالْمُنَاوِيُّ.

337/36. According to ʿUqba b. ʿĀmir ﷺ:

"Allah's Messenger ﷺ said: 'Soon there will emerge from my Community some groups of people who will recite the Qurʾān as if they were gulping down their drink of milk!'"

> Reported by al-Ṭabarānī, whose narrators are reliable, according to al-Haythamī and al-Munāwī.

٣٣٨/ ٣٧. عَنْ أَنَسِ بْنِ مَالِكٍ ﷺ أَنَّ رَسُوْلَ اللهِ ﷺ دَخَلَ عَامَ الْفَتْحِ وَعَلَى رَأْسِهِ

---

336 Set forth by •Aḥmad b. Ḥanbal in *al-Musnad*, 2/219 §7038. •Ibn Abī ʿĀṣim in *al-Sunna*, 2/453–454 §929–930. •ʿAbd Allāh b. Aḥmad in *al-Sunna*, 2/631 §1504. •Ibn Taymiyya in *al-Ṣārim al-Maslūl*, 1/237. •al-ʿAsqalānī in *Fatḥ al-Bārī*, 12/292. •al-Ṭabarī in *Tārīkh al-Umam wa al-Mulūk*, 2/176.

337 Set forth by •al-Ṭabarānī in *al-Muʿjam al-Kabīr*, 17/297 §821. •al-Haythamī in *Majmaʿ al-Zawāʾid*, 6/229. •al-Munāwī in *Fayḍ al-Qadīr*, 4/118.

الْـمِغْفَرُ. فَلَمَّا نَزَعَهُ جَاءَ رَجُلٌ فَقَالَ: إِنَّ ابْنَ خَطَلٍ مُتَعَلِّقٌ بِأَسْتَارِ الْكَعْبَةِ فَقَالَ: اقْتُلُوْهُ.

مُتَّفَقٌ عَلَيْهِ.

338/37. According to Anas b. Mālik ﷺ:

"Allah's Messenger ﷺ entered (the Ennobled Mecca) the Year of Victory with the helmet on his head. Then, when he took it off, a man came and said: '(Your denigrator) Ibn Khaṭl is hanging attached to the curtains of the Kaᶜba (to save his life),' so he said: 'Kill him!'"

Agreed upon by al-Bukhārī and Muslim.

٣٣٩/ ٣٨. عَنْ عُرْوَةَ بْنِ مُحَمَّدٍ عَنْ رَجُلٍ مِنْ بِلْقِيْنَ: أَنَّ امْرَأَةً كَانَتْ تَسُبُّ النَّبِيَّ ﷺ. فَقَالَ النَّبِيُّ ﷺ: مَنْ يَكْفِيْنِي عَدُوِّي؟ فَخَرَجَ إِلَيْهَا خَالِدُ بْنُ الْوَلِيْدِ ﷺ فَقَتَلَهَا.

رَوَاهُ عَبْدُ الرَّزَّاقِ وَالْبَيْهَقِيُّ.

339/38. According to ᶜUrwa b. Muhammad, a man from Bilqīn

338 Set forth by •al-Bukhārī in *al-Ṣaḥīḥ*: Bk.: *al-Ḥajj* [The Pilgrimage], Ch.: Entering the Sanctuary [*al-Ḥaram*] and Mecca without ritual consecration [*iḥrām*], 2/655 §1749, & Bk.: *al-Jihād wa al-Siyar* [The Sacred Struggle and the Campaigns], 3/1107 §2879, & Bk.: *al-Maghāzī* [The Military Expeditions], Ch.: Where the Prophet ﷺ planted the banner on the Day of Victory, 4/1561 §4035. •Muslim in *al-Ṣaḥīḥ*: Bk.: *al-Ḥajj* [The Pilgrimage], Ch.: The permissibility of entering Mecca without ritual consecration, 2/989 §1357. •al-Tirmidhī in *al-Sunan*: Bk.: The Sacred Struggle according to Allah's Messenger ﷺ, Ch.: What has come to us about the helmet [*mighfar*]. He said: "This is a fine authentic tradition." 4/202 §1693. •Abū Dāwūd in *al-Sunan*: Bk.: *al-Jihād*, Ch.: Killing the prisoner of war, 3/60 §2685. •al-Nasāʾī in *al-Sunan*: Bk.: *Manāsik al-Ḥajj* [The Rites of the Pilgrimage], Ch.: Entering Mecca without ritual consecration [*iḥrām*], 5/200 §2867, & in *al-Sunan al-Kubrā*, 2/382 §3850. •Aḥmad b. Ḥanbal in *al-Musnad*, 3/185, 231–232 §12955, 13437, 13461, 13542. •Ibn Ḥibbān in *al-Ṣaḥīḥ*, 9/37 §3721. •al-Ṭaḥāwī in *Sharḥ Maᶜānī al-Āthār*, 2/259. •al-Ṭabarānī in *al-Muᶜjam al-Awsaṭ*, 9/29 §9034.

339 Set forth by •ᶜAbd al-Razzāq in *al-Muṣannaf*, 5/307 §9705. •al-Bayhaqī in *al-Sunan al-Kubrā*, 8/202. •Ibn Taymiyya in *al-Ṣārim al-Maslūl*, 1/140.

said:

"A woman used to malign the Prophet ﷺ, so the Prophet ﷺ said: 'Who will take revenge on my enemy?' Khālid b. al-Walīd ؓ went out to her and killed her."

Reported by ʿAbd al-Razzāq and al-Bayhaqī.

٣٤٠ / ٣٩. عَنِ ابْنِ عَبَّاسٍ ؓ أَنَّ رَجُلاً مِنَ الْـمُشْرِكِيْنَ شَتَمَ النَّبِيَّ ﷺ فَقَالَ النَّبِيُّ ﷺ: مَنْ يَكْفِيْنِي عَدُوِّي؟ فَقَالَ الزُّبَيْرُ: أَنَا. فَبَارَزَهُ، فَقَتَلَهُ. فَأَعْطَاهُ رَسُوْلُ اللهِ ﷺ سَلَبَهُ.

رَوَاهُ عَبْدُ الرَّزَّاقِ وَأَبُوْ نُعَيْمٍ.

340/39. According to Ibn ʿAbbās ؓ:

"A man from among the polytheists vilified the Prophet ﷺ, so the Prophet ﷺ said: 'Who will take revenge on my enemy?' 'I will,' said al-Zubayr, so he fought a duel with him and killed him. Allah's Messenger ﷺ then gave al-Zubayr the war gains acquired from his dead body."

Reported by ʿAbd al-Razzāq and Abū Nuʿaym.

٣٤١ / ٤٠. عَنِ ابْنِ عَبَّاسٍ ؓ قَالَ: قَالَ رَسُوْلُ اللهِ ﷺ: مَنْ بَدَّلَ دِيْنَهُ فَاقْتُلُوْهُ.

رَوَاهُ الْبُخَارِيُّ وَالتِّرْمِذِيُّ وَأَبُوْ دَاوُدَ وَالنَّسَائِيُّ وَابْنُ مَاجَه وَاللَّفْظُ لَـهُمَا.

341/40. According to Ibn ʿAbbās ؓ:

---

340 Set forth by •ʿAbd al-Razzāq in *al-Muṣannaf*, 5/237, 307 §9477, 9704. •Abū Nuʿaym in *Ḥilya al-Awliyā'*, 8/45. •Ibn Taymiyya in *al-Ṣārim al-Maslūl*, 1/154.

341 Set forth by •al-Bukhārī in *al-Ṣaḥīḥ*: Bk.: *al-Jihād wa al-Siyar* [The Sacred Struggle and the Campaigns], Ch.: May he not suffer the chastisement of Allah, 3/1098 §2854. •al-Tirmidhī in *al-Sunan*: Bk.: The Penalties according to Allah's Messenger ﷺ, Ch.: What has come to us about the apostate, 4/59 §1458. •Abū Dāwūd in *al-Sunan*: Bk.: *al-Ḥudūd* [The Penalties], Ch.: The verdict on someone who apostatizes. 4/126 §4351. •al-Nasā'ī in *al-Sunan*: Bk.: *Taḥrīm al-Dam* [The Prohibition of Bloodshed], Ch.: The verdict on

"Allah's Messenger ﷺ said: 'If someone alters his Religion, you must kill him.'"

Reported by al-Bukhārī, al-Tirmidhī, Abū Dāwūd, al-Nasāʾī and Ibn Mājah (this is the wording of al-Nasāʾī and Ibn Mājah).

٣٤٢/ ٤١. عَنْ عَبْدِ الْمَلِكِ عَنْ أَبِي حُرَّةَ أَنَّ عَلِيًّا رضي الله عنه لَمَّا بَعَثَ أَبَا مُوْسَى لِإِنْفَاذِ الْحُكُوْمَةِ، اجْتَمَعَ الْخَوَارِجُ فِي مَنْزِلِ عَبْدِ اللهِ بْنِ وَهْبِ الرَّاسِبِيِّ مِنْ رُؤُوْسِ الْخَوَارِجِ. فَخَطَبَهُمْ خُطْبَةً بَلِيْغَةً؛ زَهَّدَهُمْ فِي هَذِهِ الدُّنْيَا وَرَغَّبَهُمْ فِي الْآخِرَةِ وَالْجَنَّةِ وَحَثَّهُمْ عَلَى الْأَمْرِ بِالْمَعْرُوْفِ وَالنَّهْيِ عَنِ الْمُنْكَرِ. ثُمَّ قَالَ: فَاخْرُجُوْا بِنَا إِخْوَانَنَا مِنْ هَذِهِ الْقَرْيَةِ الظَّالِمِ أَهْلُهَا إِلَى جَانِبِ هَذَا السَّوَادِ إِلَى بَعْضِ كُوَرِ الْجِبَالِ أَوْ بَعْضِ هَذِهِ الْمَدَائِنِ مُنْكِرِيْنَ لِهَذِهِ الْبِدَعِ الْمُضِلَّةِ.... ثُمَّ اجْتَمَعُوْا فِي مَنْزِلِ شُرَيْحِ بْنِ أَوْفَى الْعَبَسِيِّ. فَقَالَ ابْنُ وَهْبٍ: اشْخَصُوْا بِنَا إِلَى بَلْدَةٍ نَجْتَمِعُ فِيْهَا لِإِنْفَاذِ حُكْمِ اللهِ فَإِنَّكُمْ أَهْلُ الْحَقِّ.

رَوَاهُ ابْنُ جَرِيْرٍ وَابْنُ الْأَثِيْرِ وَابْنُ كَثِيْرٍ.

342/41. According to ʿAbd al-Mālik, Abū Ḥurra said:

"When ʿAlī رضي الله عنه sent Abū Mūsā (al-Ashʿarī) رضي الله عنه to take charge of the government (as Governer), the Khawārij assembled in the residence of ʿAbd Allāh b. Wahab al-Rāsibī, one of the chieftains of the Khawārij. He addressed them with an eloquent sermon, instructing them to abstain from this world, urging them to prefer the Hereafter and the Garden of Paradise, and inciting them to enjoin what is right and forbid what is wrong. Then he said: 'The people of this iniquitous town must go out from it, with us as

---

the apostate, 7/103 §4059. •Ibn Mājah in *al-Sunan*, Bk.: *al-Ḥudūd* [The Penalties], Ch.: The Apostate from his Religion, 2/848 §2535. •Aḥmad b. Ḥanbal in *al-Musnad*, 1/322 §2968. •Ibn Ḥibbān in *al-Ṣaḥīḥ*, 10/327 §4475.

[342] Set forth by •Ibn Jarīr al-Ṭabarī in *Tarīkh al-Umam wa al-Mulūk*, 3/115. •Ibn al-Athīr in *al-Kāmil*, 3/213–214. •Ibn Kathīr in *al-Bidāya wa al-Nihāya*, 7/285–286. •Ibn al-Jawzī in *al-Muntaẓim fī Tārīkh al-Umam wa al-Mulūk* [History of the Communities and the Kings], 5/130–131.

brethren, in the direction of some of the mountain villages, or some other cities so that our disapproval of the misleading innovations is proved....' Then they assembled in the residence of Shurayḥ b. Awfā al-ʿAbasī, and Ibn Wahab said: 'We should now look for a town in which (setting up our centre) we shall all forgather to enforce the rule of Allah, for now it is you who are the people of the truth!'"

Reported by Ibn Jarīr, Ibn al-Athīr and Ibn Kathīr.

٣٤٣/ ٤٢. ذكر ابن الأثير في الكامل: خَرَجَ الْأَشْعَثُ بِالْكِتَابِ يَقْرَؤُهُ عَلَى النَّاسِ حَتَّى مَرَّ عَلَى طَائِفَةٍ مِنْ بَنِي تَمِيْمٍ فِيْهِمْ عُرْوَةُ بْنُ أُدَيَّةَ أَخُوْ أَبِـي بِلاَلٍ فَقَرَأَ عَلَيْهِمْ، فَقَالَ عُرْوَةُ: تُحَكِّمُوْنَ فِي أَمْرِ اللهِ الرِّجَالَ؟ لاَ حُكْمَ إِلاَّ لِلهِ.

343/42. According to Ibn al-Athīr in *al-Kāmil*:

"Al-Ashʿath went out with the written agreement (signed between ʿAlī and Muʿāwiya ﵄), reciting it to the people of all the tribes until he came upon a group of the Banū Tamīm, among whom was ʿUrwa b. Udayya/Udhayna (al-Khārijī), the brother of Abū Bilāl. When he recited to them the agreement, ʿUrwa said: 'Do you make men pass arbitrary judgement on the business of Allah? There is no one to decree apart from Allah!'"

٣٤٤/ ٤٣. عَنْ عَلِيٍّ ﷺ أَنَّهُ كَتَبَ إِلَى الْخَوَارِجِ بِالنَّهْرِ: بِسْمِ اللهِ الرَّحْمَنِ الرَّحِيْمِ. مِنْ عَبْدِ اللهِ عَلِيٍّ أَمِيْرِ الْـمُؤْمِنِيْنَ إِلَى زَيْدِ بْنِ حُصَيْنٍ وَعَبْدِ اللهِ بْنِ وَهْبٍ وَمَنْ مَعَهُمَا مِنَ النَّاسِ. أَمَّا بَعْدُ فَإِنَّ هَذَيْنِ الرَّجُلَيْنِ اللَّذَيْنِ ارْتَضَيْنَا حَكَمَيْنِ. قَدْ خَالَفَا كِتَابَ اللهِ وَاتَّبَعَا هَوَاهُمَا بِغَيْرِ هُدًى مِنَ اللهِ فَلَمْ يَعْمَلاَ بِالسُّنَّةِ وَلَـمْ يُنْفِذَا الْقُرْآنَ حُكْمًا. فَبَرِىءَ اللهُ مِنْهُمَا وَرَسُوْلُهُ وَالْـمُؤْمِنُوْنَ، فَإِذَا بَلَغَكُمْ كِتَابِـي هَذَا فَأَقْبِلُوْا إِلَيْنَا فَإِنَّا سَائِرُوْنَ إِلَى عَدُوِّنَا وَعَدُوِّكُمْ وَنَحْنُ عَلَى الْأَمْرِ الْأَوَّلِ الَّذِي كُنَّا عَلَيْهِ.

---

343 Set forth by •Ibn al-Athīr in *al-Kāmil*, 3/196. •Ibn al-Jawzī in *al-Muntaẓim fī Tārīkh al-Umam wa al-Mulūk*, [History of the Communities and the Kings], 5/123.

فَكَتَبُوْا (الخوارج) إِلَيْهِ: أَمَّا بَعْدُ، فَإِنَّكَ لَمْ تَغْضَبْ لِرَبِّكَ وَإِنَّمَا غَضِبْتَ لِنَفْسِكَ، فَإِنْ شَهِدْتَ عَلَى نَفْسِكَ بِالْكُفْرِ، وَاسْتَقْبَلْتَ التَّوْبَةَ، نَظَرْنَا فِيْمَا بَيْنَنَا وَبَيْنَكَ، وَإِلاَّ فَقَدْ نَبَذْنَاكَ عَلَى سَوَاءٍ؛ إِنَّ اللهَ لاَ يُحِبُّ الْخَائِنِيْنَ.

فَلَمَّا قَرَأَ كِتَابَهُمْ أَيِسَ مِنْهُمْ وَرَأَى أَنْ يَدَعَهُمْ وَيَمْضِيَ بِالنَّاسِ حَتَّى يَلْقَى أَهْلَ الشَّامِ حَتَّى يَلْقَاهُمْ.

رَوَاهُ ابْنُ جَرِيْرٍ وَابْنُ الأَثِيْرِ وَابْنُ كَثِيْرٍ.

344/43. As reported on the authority of ʿAlī ﷺ, he wrote to the Khawārij at Nahrawan:

"In the Name of Allah, the All-Compassionate, the Ever-Merciful! From the servant of Allah ʿAlī ﷺ, the Commander of the Believers, to Zayd b. Ḥuṣayn, ʿAbd Allāh b. Wahab, and their followers.

"These are the two men whom we have preferred as mediators. They have contradicted the Book of Allah, and followed their passionate desire without guidance from Allah, for they have not acted in accordance with the Sunna and they have not complied with the Qurʾān as a rule of law. Allah has therefore washed His hands of them, and His Messenger and the true believers have done likewise.

"If this letter reaches you all, you must draw near to us, for we are travelling towards our enemy and your enemy, and we are engaged in the most important business in which we have been engaged.'"

They (the Kharijites) wrote to ʿAlī ﷺ in reply: "Now your wrath is not for Allah, for there is personal desire in it. If you bear testimony to your diselief and repent afresh we can see to it, otherwise we reject you because Allah does not keep betrayers His

---

344 Set forth by •Ibn Jarīr al-Ṭabarī in *Tārīkh al-Umam wa al-Mulūk*, 3/117. •Ibn al-Athīr in *al-Kāmil*, 3/216. •Ibn Kathīr in *al-Bidāya wa al-Nihāya*, 7/287. •Ibn al-Jawzī in *al-Muntaẓim*, 5/132.

friends."

When ʿAlī read their reply, he lost hope (of their coming back to guidance), so he decided to leave them in that state and joined the people of Syria along with the troops.

Reported by Ibn Jarīr, Ibn al-Athīr and Ibn Kathīr.

٣٤٥/ ٤٤. عَنْ زِيَادِ بْنِ أَبِيْهِ أَنَّ عُرْوَةَ بْنَ حُدَيْرٍ (الخارجي) نَجَا بَعْدَ ذَلِكَ مِنْ حَرْبِ النَّهْرَوَانِ وَبَقِيَ إِلَى أَيَّامِ مُعَاوِيَةَ ﷺ. ثُمَّ أَتَى إِلَى زِيَادِ بْنِ أَبِيْهِ وَمَعَهُ مَولًى لَهُ، فَسَأَلَهُ زِيَادٌ عَنْ عُثْمَانَ ﷺ، فَقَالَ: كُنْتُ أَوَالِي عُثْمَانَ عَلَى أَحْوَالِهِ فِي خِلَافَتِهِ سِتَّ سِنِيْنَ. ثُمَّ تَبَرَّأْتُ مِنْهُ بَعْدَ ذَلِكَ لِلْأَحْدَاثِ الَّتِي أَحْدَثَهَا، وَشَهِدَ عَلَيْهِ بِالْكُفْرِ. وَسَأَلَهُ عَنْ أَمِيْرِ الْمُؤْمِنِيْنَ عَلِيٍّ ﷺ فَقَالَ: كُنْتُ أَتَوَلَّاهُ إِلَى أَنْ حَكَمَ الْحَكَمَيْنِ، ثُمَّ تَبَرَّأْتُ مِنْهُ بَعْدَ ذَلِكَ، وَشَهِدَ عَلَيْهِ بِالْكُفْرِ وَسَأَلَهُ عَنْ مُعَاوِيَةَ ﷺ فَسَبَّهُ سَبًّا قَبِيْحًا... فَأَمَرَ زِيَادُ بِضَرْبِ عُنُقِهِ.

رَوَاهُ الشَّهْرَسْتَانِيُّ.

345/44. As reported on the authority of Ziyād b. Abīh:

"Urwa b. Ḥudayr (al-Khārijī) escaped from the battle of Nahrawan and survived until the days of Muʿāwiya ﷺ. Then he came to Ziyād b. Abīh, accompanied by a freedman of his, so Ziyād asked him about ʿUthmān ﷺ. He said: 'I used to be a close supporter of ʿUthmān in his states of being, for six years during his Caliphate. Then I washed my hands of him after that, because of the innovations that he invented.' He testified against him on the charge of unbelief. When Ziyād asked him about ʿAlī, the Commander of the Believers ﷺ, he said: 'I used to be his close supporter, until he appointed the arbitrators, then I washed my hands of him after that.' He testified against him on the charge of unbelief. Then he asked him about Muʿāwiya ﷺ, and he reviled

345 Set forth by •ʿAbd al-Karīm al-Shahrastānī in *al-Milal wa al-Niḥal*, 1/137.

him ignominiously, so Ziyād commanded that his neck be struck off."

Reported by al-Shahrastānī.

٣٤٦/ ٤٥. عَنْ أَبِي الطُّفَيْلِ أَنَّ رَجُلاً وُلِدَ لَهُ غُلَامٌ عَلَى عَهْدِ رَسُوْلِ اللهِ ﷺ فَأَتَى النَّبِيَّ ﷺ فَأَخَذَ بِبَشَرَةِ وَجْهِهِ وَدَعَا لَهُ بِالْبَرَكَةِ. قَالَ: فَنَبَتَتْ شَعَرَةٌ فِي جَبْهَتِهِ كَهَيْئَةِ الْقَوْسِ وَشَبَّ الْغُلَامُ. فَلَمَّا كَانَ زَمَنُ الْخَوَارِجِ، أَحَبَّهُمْ فَسَقَطَتِ الشَّعَرَةُ عَنْ جَبْهَتِهِ. فَأَخَذَهُ أَبُوْهُ فَقَيَّدَهُ وَحَبَسَهُ مَخَافَةَ أَنْ يَلْحَقَ بِهِمْ. قَالَ: فَدَخَلْنَا عَلَيْهِ فَوَعَظْنَاهُ وَقُلْنَا لَهُ فِيمَا نَقُولُ: أَلَمْ تَرَ أَنَّ بَرَكَةَ دَعْوَةِ رَسُوْلِ اللهِ ﷺ قَدْ وَقَعَتْ عَنْ جَبْهَتِكَ؟ فَمَا زِلْنَا بِهِ حَتَّى رَجَعَ عَنْ رَأْيِهِمْ. فَرَدَّ اللهُ عَلَيْهِ الشَّعَرَةَ بَعْدُ فِي جَبْهَتِهِ وَتَابَ.

رَوَاهُ أَحْمَدُ وَابْنُ أَبِي شَيْبَةَ.

346/45. According to Abū al-Ṭufayl:

"A son was born to a man in the time of Allah's Messenger ﷺ, so he brought him to the Prophet ﷺ, who took hold of the skin of his face and invoked blessing for him. Some hair then sprouted on his forehead distinct from all his hair. The boy grew up, and when came the time of the Khawārij, he fell in love with them, so the hair dropped off his forehead. His father grabbed him, tied him up and imprisoned him, for fear that he might become attached to them (and join them)."

Abū al-Ṭufayl says: "We therefore went to him and admonished him. We said to him, for instance: 'Have you not noticed that since your inclining to these people, the blessing invoked by Allah's Messenger ﷺ has dropped off your forehead?' We persisted and

346 Set forth by •Aḥmad b. Ḥanbal in *al-Musnad*, 5/456 §23856. •Ibn Abī Shayba in *al-Muṣannaf*, 7/556 §37904. •al-Iṣbahānī in *Dalāʾil al-Nubuwwa*, Bk.: 1/174 §220. •al-Haythamī in *Majmaʿ al-Zawāʾid*, 6/243; 10/270. He said: "It has been reported by Aḥmad and al-Ṭabarānī, whose narrators are the sources ʿAlī b. Zayd, and it has been authenticated." •al-ʿAsqalānī in *al-Iṣāba*, 95/359 §6972.

did not leave him until he renounced their opinion. The liking for the Khawārij then vacated his heart, so Allah restored to him the blessed hair on his forehead and he repented the true repentance."

Reported by Aḥmad and Ibn Abī Shayba.

٣٤٧/ ٤٦. عَنْ سَعِيْدِ بْنِ جُهْمَانَ قَالَ: كَانَتِ الْخَوَارِجُ قَدْ تَدْعُوْنِي حَتَّى كِدْتُ أَنْ أَدْخُلَ فِيْهِمْ. فَرَأَتْ أُخْتُ أَبِي بِلَالٍ فِي النَّوْمِ أَنَّ أَبَا بِلَالٍ كَلْبٌ أَهْلَبُ أَسْوَدُ عَيْنَاهُ تَذْرِفَانِ. فَقَالَتْ: بِأَبِي أَنْتَ، يَا أَبَا بِلَالٍ، مَا شَأْنُكَ أَرَاكَ هَكَذَا؟ قَالَ: جُعِلْنَا بَعْدَكُمْ كِلَابَ النَّارِ. وَكَانَ أَبُوْ بِلَالٍ مِنْ رُؤُوْسِ الْخَوَارِجِ.

رَوَاهُ ابْنُ أَبِي شَيْبَةَ وَابْنُ أَبِي عَاصِمٍ وَاللَّفْظُ لَهُ؛ إِسْنَادُهُ صَحِيْحٌ.

347/46. According to Saʿīd b. Juhmān:

"The Khawārij kept inviting me until I (feeling influenced) nearly entered their company. Then the sister of Abū Bilāl saw in her sleep that Abū Bilāl was a shaggy black dog, whose eyes were tearful, so she said: 'I appeal to you by my father, O Abū Bilāl! What is the matter with you, that I should see you like this?' He replied: 'We have been made the dogs of Hell Fire after you.' Abū Bilāl was one of the chieftains of the Khawārij."

Reported by Ibn Abī Shayba and Ibn Abī ʿĀṣim (the wording is his and his chain of transmission is authentic).

٣٤٨/ ٤٧. عَنْ أَبِي عُثْمَانَ النَّهْدِيِّ: سَأَلَ رَجُلٌ مِنْ بَنِي يَرْبُوعٍ، أَوْ مِنْ بَنِي تَمِيْمٍ. عُمَرَ بْنَ الْخَطَّابِ ﷺ عَنِ ﴿الذَّارِيَاتِ﴾ وَ ﴿الْمُرْسَلَاتِ﴾ وَ ﴿النَّازِعَاتِ﴾. أَوْ عَنْ بَعْضِهِنَّ. فَقَالَ عُمَرُ: ضَعْ عَنْ رَأْسِكَ. فَإِذَا لَهُ وَفْرَةٌ، فَقَالَ عُمَرُ ﷺ: أَمَا وَاللهِ، لَوْ رَأَيْتُكَ مَحْلُوقًا، لَضَرَبْتُ الَّذِي فِيْهِ عَيْنَاكَ. ثُمَّ قَالَ: ثُمَّ كَتَبَ إِلَى أَهْلِ الْبَصْرَةِ أَوْ قَالَ

---

[347] Set forth by •Ibn Abī Shayba in *al-Muṣannaf*, 7/555 §37895. •Ibn Abī ʿĀṣim in *al-Sunna*, 2/634 §1509.

إِلَيْنَا. أَنْ لاَ تُجَالِسُوْهُ. قَالَ: فَلَوْ جَاءَ وَنَحْنُ مِائَةٌ، تَفَرَّقْنَا.

رَوَاهُ سَعِيْدُ بْنُ يَحْيَى الأُمْوِيُّ وَغَيْرُهُ بِإِسْنَادٍ صَحِيْحٍ كَمَا قَالَ ابْنُ تَيْمِيَّةَ.

348/47. According to Abū ʿUthmān al-Nahdī:

"A man from the Banū Yarbūʿ, or from the Banū Tamīm, asked ʿUmar b. al-Khaṭṭāb ﷺ about the Qurʾānic terms *al-dhāriyyāt* [those that scatter (Sūra 51)], *al-mursalāt* [those sent forth (Sūra 77], and *al-nāziʿāt* [those that tear out (Sūra 79]—or about some of them. ʿUmar said: 'Remove the cover from your head.' (When he removed the head cover) he saw his hair drooping over the ears. He said: 'By Allah! If I had seen you shaven, I would have smitten this skull which contains your sunken eyes!' Then he wrote to the people of Baṣra, or said to us: 'You must not keep him company, so when he come we split up even while we were a hundred strong!'"

Reported by Saʿīd b. Yaḥyā al-Umwī and others, with an authentic chain of transmission, according to Ibn Taymiyya.

٣٤٩/ ٤٨. عَنِ السَّائِبِ بْنِ يَزِيْدَ: قَالَ: فَبَيْنَمَا عُمَرُ ﷺ ذَاتَ يَوْمٍ جَالِسًا يُغَدِّي النَّاسَ إِذَا جَاءَ رَجُلٌ عَلَيْهِ ثِيَابٌ وَعِمَامَةٌ. فَتَغَدَّى حَتَّى إِذَا فَرَغَ قَالَ: يَا أَمِيرَ الْمُؤْمِنِيْنَ، ﴿وَالذَّارِيَاتِ ذَرْوًا فَالْحَامِلاتِ وِقْرًا﴾ فَقَالَ عُمَرُ ﷺ: أَنْتَ هُوَ. فَقَامَ إِلَيْهِ وَحَسَرَ عَنْ ذِرَاعَيْهِ فَلَمْ يَزَلْ يَجْلِدُهُ حَتَّى سَقَطَتْ عِمَامَتُهُ. فَقَالَ: وَالَّذِي نَفْسُ عُمَرَ بِيَدِهِ، لَوْ وَجَدْتُكَ مَحْلُوْقًا، لَضَرَبْتُ رَأْسَكَ.

رَوَاهُ اللاَّلَكَائِيُّ.

349/48. According to al-Sāʾib b. Yazīd:

---

348 Set forth by •Ibn Taymiyya in *al-Ṣārim al-Maslūl*, 1/195.

349 Set forth by •al-Lālakāʾī in *Iʿtiqād Ahl al-Sunna*, 4/634 §1136. •al-Shawkānī in *Nayl al-Awṭār*, 1/155. •al-ʿAẓīm Ābādī in *ʿAwn al-Maʿbūd*, 11/166. •Ibn Qudāma in *al-Mughnī*, 1/65; 9/8.

"While ʿUmar ☥ was sitting one day, taking lunch with the people, along came a man wearing (fine) clothes and a turban. He also took lunch, then said after he had finished eating: 'O Commander of the Believers (what is the meaning of): "By those that scatter, and those that bear heavy loads [wa al-dhāriyāti dharwan fa al-ḥāmilāti wiqran]!" (Q.51:1–2). ʿUmar ☥ said: 'You are the same (denigrator)!' Then he approached him, laid his arms bare, and did not stop flogging him until his turban fell off. Then he said: 'By the One in whose Hand is ʿUmar's soul, if I had found you shaven, I would have smitten your head!'"

Reported by al-Lālakāʾī.

٣٥٠ / ٤٩. عَنْ أَبِي يَحْيَى قَالَ: سَمِعَ رَجُلًا مِنَ الْخَوَارِجِ وَهُوَ يُصَلِّي صَلَاةَ الْفَجْرِ يَقُولُ: ﴿وَلَقَدْ أُوحِيَ إِلَيْكَ وَإِلَى الَّذِينَ مِن قَبْلِكَ لَئِنْ أَشْرَكْتَ لَيَحْبَطَنَّ عَمَلُكَ وَلَتَكُونَنَّ مِنَ الْخَاسِرِينَ﴾. (الزمر، ٣٩: ٦٥)، قَالَ: فَتَرَكَ سُورَتَهُ الَّتِي كَانَتْ فِيهَا قَالَ: وَقَرَأَ ﴿فَاصْبِرْ إِنَّ وَعْدَ اللهِ حَقٌّ وَلَا يَسْتَخِفَّنَّكَ الَّذِينَ لَا يُوقِنُونَ﴾. (الروم، ٣٠: ٦٠).

رَوَاهُ ابْنُ أَبِي شَيْبَةَ.

350/49. According to Abū Yaḥyā, he heard a man from among the Khawārij saying, while he was performing the dawn ritual prayer: "And in truth (this) revelation has been sent to you and to those (Messengers as well) who were (raised) before you: '(O man,) if you associate partners with Allah, then all your works will go to waste and you will certainly be among the losers.'" [wa la-qad ūḥiya ilay-ka wa ila 'lladhīna min qabli-k: la-in ashrakta la-yaḥbaṭanna ʿamalu-ka wa la-takūnanna min al-khāsirīn]." (Q.39:65). He said: "So he omitted that Sūrā and recited this Verse of another Sūrā: 'So be steadfast. Verily, the Promise of Allah is true. Let not those who lack certitude of faith enfeeble you (on account of the grief over their straying and discomfort for their guidance.)' [fa-'ṣbir inna waʿda 'llāhi ḥaqqun wa lā yastakhiffanna-ka 'lladhīna lā

---

350 Set forth by •Ibn Abī Shayba in al-Muṣannaf, 7/554 §37891.

yūqinūn]." (Q.30:60). (The hypocrites singled out Qur'ānic Verses which they believed, might allude to the Prophet's imperfection. This tells us how polluted their minds were!)

Reported by Ibn Abī Shayba.

٣٥١/ ٥٠. عَنْ أَبِي غَالِبٍ قَالَ: كُنْتُ فِي مَسْجِدِ دِمَشْقَ فَجَاءُوا بِسَبْعِيْنَ رَأْسًا مِنْ رُؤُوْسِ الْحُرُوْرِيَّةِ فَنُصِبَتْ عَلَى دُرَجِ الْمَسْجِدِ. فَجَاءَ أَبُوْأُمَامَةَ ﵁ فَنَظَرَ إِلَيْهِمْ فَقَالَ: كِلَابُ جَهَنَّمَ، شَرُّ قَتْلَى قُتِلُوْا تَحْتَ ظِلِّ السَّمَاءِ، وَمَنْ قُتِلُوْا خَيْرُ قَتْلَى تَحْتَ السَّمَاءِ. وَبَكَى فَنَظَرَ إِلَيَّ وَقَالَ: يَا أَبَا غَالِبٍ، إِنَّكَ مِنْ بَلَدِ هَؤُلَاءِ؟ قُلْتُ: نَعَمْ. قَالَ: أَعَاذَكَ اللهُ مِنْهُمْ. قَالَ: تَقْرَأُ آلَ عِمْرَانَ؟ قُلْتُ: نَعَمْ. قَالَ: ﴿مِنْهُ ءَايَٰتٌ مُّحْكَمَٰتٌ هُنَّ أُمُّ ٱلْكِتَٰبِ وَأُخَرُ مُتَشَٰبِهَٰتٌ فَأَمَّا ٱلَّذِينَ فِى قُلُوبِهِمْ زَيْغٌ فَيَتَّبِعُونَ مَا تَشَٰبَهَ مِنْهُ ٱبْتِغَآءَ ٱلْفِتْنَةِ وَٱبْتِغَآءَ تَأْوِيلِهِۦ وَمَا يَعْلَمُ تَأْوِيلَهُۥٓ إِلَّا ٱللَّهُ وَٱلرَّٰسِخُونَ فِى ٱلْعِلْمِ﴾ (آل عمران، ٣:٧)، قَالَ: ﴿يَوْمَ تَبْيَضُّ وُجُوهٌ وَتَسْوَدُّ وُجُوهٌ فَأَمَّا ٱلَّذِينَ ٱسْوَدَّتْ وُجُوهُهُمْ أَكَفَرْتُم بَعْدَ إِيمَٰنِكُمْ فَذُوقُوا۟ ٱلْعَذَابَ بِمَا كُنتُمْ تَكْفُرُونَ﴾ (آل عمران، ٣:١٠٦)، قُلْتُ: يَا أَبَا أُمَامَةَ، إِنِّي رَأَيْتُكَ تُهَرِيْقُ عِبْرَتَكَ. قَالَ: نَعَمْ، رَحْمَةً لَهُمْ. إِنَّهُمْ كَانُوْا مِنْ أَهْلِ الإِسْلَامِ. قَالَ: افْتَرَقَتْ بَنُو إِسْرَائِيْلَ عَلَى وَاحِدَةٍ وَسَبْعِيْنَ فِرْقَةً، وَتَزِيْدُ هَذِهِ الأُمَّةُ فِرْقَةً وَاحِدَةً، كُلُّهَا فِي النَّارِ إِلاَّ السَّوَادَ الأَعْظَمَ. عَلَيْهِمْ مَا حُمِّلُوا وَعَلَيْكُمْ مَا حُمِّلْتُمْ، وَإِنْ تُطِيْعُوهُ تَهْتَدُوْا، وَمَا عَلَى الرَّسُوْلِ إِلاَّ الْبَلَاغُ. اَلسَّمْعُ وَالطَّاعَةُ خَيْرٌ مِنَ الْفِرْقَةِ وَالْمَعْصِيَةِ. فَقَالَ لَهُ رَجُلٌ: يَا أَبَا أُمَامَةَ، أَمِنْ رَأْيِكَ تَقُوْلُ أَمْ شَيْءٌ سَمِعْتَهُ مِنْ رَسُوْلِ اللهِ ﷺ؟ قَالَ: إِنِّي إِذًا لَجَرِيْءٌ. قَالَ: بَلْ سَمِعْتُهُ مِنْ رَسُوْلِ اللهِ ﷺ مَرَّةً وَلَا مَرَّتَيْنِ حَتَّى ذَكَرَ سَبْعًا.

رَوَاهُ ابْنُ أَبِي شَيْبَةَ وَالْبَيْهَقِيُّ وَالطَّبَرَانِيُّ.

351/50. According to Abū Ghālib: "I was in the mosque of

351 Set forth by •Ibn Abī Shayba in *al-Muṣannaf*, 7/554 §37892. •al-Bayhaqī in *al-Sunan al-Kubrā*, 8/188. •al-Ṭabarānī in *al-Muʿjam al-Kabīr*, 8/267–268

Damascus, when they brought seventy heads from the heads of al-Ḥarūriyya [Kharijites] and displayed them on the stairs of the mosque. Abū Umāma ﷺ came and looked at them, then said: 'The dogs of Hell, the worst of the slain, have been slain beneath the shade of the sky, and some of those who have been slain by them are the best of the slain beneath heaven.' He wept, then looked at me and said: 'O Abū Ghālib! Are you from the same country as these?' When I said yes, he said: 'May Allah protect you from them!'

"He said: 'Do you recite *Sūra Āl ʿImrān*?' When I said yes, he said: 'It contains clear and definite Verses—these Commands are the bases of the Book—and others that are allegorical (containing elusive and subtle connotations and implications). As for those in whose hearts is doubt, they pursue that which is allegorical, seeking dissension by seeking to explain it with the intention to derive the desired meaning instead of the real and original meaning, and no one knows its explanation except Allah and those who are firmly rooted in knowledge *[min-hu āyātun muḥkamātun hunna Ummu al-Kitābi wa ukharu mutashābihāt: fa-amma ʾlladhīna fī qulūbi-him zayghun fa-yattabiʿūna mā tashābaha min-huʾbtighāʾa al-fitnati wa ʾbtighāʾa taʾwīli-h: wa mā yaʿlamu taʾwīla-hu illa ʾllāh: wa al-rāsikhūna fī al-ʿilmi].*' (Q.3:7).

"He also said: 'On the day when faces will be whitened and faces will be blackened; and as for those whose faces have been blackened (they will be asked): "Did you disbelieve after your belief? Then taste the torment because you disbelieved *[yawma tabyaḍḍu wujūhun wa taswaddu wujūh: fa-amma ʾlladhīna ʾswaddat wujūhu-hum: a-kafartum baʿda īmāni-kum fa-dhūqu al-ʿadhāba bi-mā kuntum takfurūn].*"' (Q.3:106).

"I said: 'O Abū Umāma! I have seen you shedding your tears!' He said: 'Yes, a compassion for them! (Before fleeing from the *Dīn* they were among the people of Islam. The Children of Israel split into seventy-one sects, and this Community will add one sect (will divide into 72 sects), all of it in the Fire of Hell except the thronging majority (the largest party). They are responsible for

§8034–8035. •al-Ḥārith in *al-Musnad*, (*Zawāʾid al-Haythamī*), 2/716 §706.

that with which they have been charged, and you are responsible for that with which you have been charged, and if you obey him (the Messenger), you will be guided aright, but the Messenger has no other charge than to convey the message. To hear and obey is better than dissension and sinful disobedience.'

"Hearing this a man said to him: 'O Abū Umāma! Are you expressing your own opinion, or something you have heard from Allah's Messenger ﷺ?' He said: 'In the former case, I would be foolhardy. As a matter of fact, I have heard it from Allah's Messenger ﷺ.' He said that he had heard this not just once or twice but seven times."

Reported by Ibn Abī Shayba, al-Bayhaqī and al-Ṭabarānī.

Bibliography

The Holy Qur'ān.

Aḥmad b. Ḥanbal, Abū ʿAbd Allāh b. Muhammad (164–241/780–855), *al-Musnad,* Beirut, Lebanon: al-Maktab al-Islāmī, 1398/1978.

al-ʿAjlūnī, Abū al-Fidā' Ismāʿīl b. Muhammad b. ʿAbd al-Hādī b. ʿAbd al-Ghanī al-Jarrāḥī (1087–1162/1676–1749), *Kashf al-Khifā' wa Muzīl al-Ilbās,* Beirut, Lebanon: Mu'assisa al-Risāla, 1405/1985.

al-Albānī, Muhammad Nāṣir al-Dīn (1333–1420/1914–1999), *Silsilat al-Aḥādīth al-Ṣaḥīḥa,* Beirut, Lebanon: al-Maktab al-Islāmī, 1405/1985.

ʿAbd Allāh, Ibn Aḥmad b. Ḥanbal (213–290 AH), *al-Sunna,* Dammām: Dār Ibn Qayyim, 1406 AH.

al-Āmadī, Sayf al-Dīn Abū al-Ḥasan ʿAlī b. ʿAlī b. Muhammad (551–631/1156–1233), *al-Iḥkām fī Uṣūl al-Aḥkhām,* Beirut, Lebanon: Dār al-Kutub al-ʿIlmiyya, 1400/1980.

Ibn ʿAsākir, Abū al-Qāsim ʿAlī b. al-Ḥasan b. Hibat Allāh b. ʿAbd Allāh b. al-Ḥusayn al-Dimashqī (499–571/1105–1176), *Tārīkh Dimashq al-Kabīr,* generally known as *Tārīkh Ibn ʿAsākīr,* Beirut, Lebanon: Dār al-Iḥyā' al-Turāth al-ʿArabī, 1421/2001.

Ibn Abī ʿĀṣim, Abū Bakr b. ʿAmr al-Ḍaḥḥāk b. Makhlad al-Shaybānī (206–287/822–900), *al-Sunna,* Beirut, Lebanon: al-Maktab al-Islāmī 1400 AH.

——. *al-Zuhd,* Egypt, Cairo: Dār al-Riyān li al-Turāth, 1408 AH.

Ibn al-Athīr, Abū al-Ḥasan ʿAlī b. Muhammad b. ʿAbd al-Karīm b. ʿAbd al-Wāḥid al-Shaybānī al-Jazarī (555–630/1160–1233), *al-Kāmil fī al-Tārīkh,* Beirut, Lebanon: Dār al-Ṣādir, 1979.

——. *Usad al-Ghāba fī Maʿrifa al-Ṣaḥāba,* Beirut, Lebanon: Dār al-Kutub al-ʿIlmiyya.

Abū ʿAwāna, Yaʿqūb b. Isḥāq b. Ibrāhīm b. Zayd al-Naysabūrī (230–316/845–928), *al-Musnad,* Beirut, Lebanon: Dār al-Maʿrifa, 1998.

al-Azdī, Rabīʿ b. Ḥabīb b. ʿAmr al-Baṣrī (95–153/713–770), *al-Jāmiʿ al-Ṣaḥīḥ—Musnad al-Imām al-Rabīʿ b. al-Ḥabīb*, Beirut, Lebanon: Dār al-Ḥikma, 1415 AH.

al-ʿAẓīm Ābādī, Abū al-Ṭayyab Muhammad Shams al-Ḥaqq, *ʿAwn al-Maʿbūd Sharḥ Sunan Abī Dāwūd*, Beirut, Lebanon: Dār al-Kutub al-ʿIlmiyya, 1415 AH.

al-Baghawī, Abū Muhammad al-Ḥusayn b. Masʿūd b. Muhammad (436–516/1044–1122), *Sharḥ al-Sunna*, Beirut, Lebanon: al-Maktab al-Islāmī, 1403/1983.

Ibn ʿAbd al-Barr, Abū ʿUmar Yūsuf b. ʿAbd Allāh b. Muhammad (368–463/979–1071), *Jāmiʿ Bayān al-ʿIlm wa Faḍlih*, Beirut, Lebanon: Dār al-Kutub al-ʿIlmiyya, 1398/1978 AH.

——. *al-Istīʿāb fī Maʿrifa al-Aṣḥāb*, Beirut, Lebanon: Dār al-Jīl, 1412 AH.

——. *al-Tamhīd*, Maghrib, Marakish: Ministry for Religious Affairs, 1387 AH.

al-Bayhaqī, Abū Bakr Aḥmad b. al-Ḥusayn b. ʿAlī b. ʿAbd Allāh b. Mūsā (384–458/994–1066), *al-Iʿtiqād*, Beirut, Lebanon: Dār al-Āfāq al-Jadīd, 1401 AH.

——. *Bayān Khaṭāʾ man Akhṭaʾ ʿalā al-Shāfiʿī*, Beirut, Lebanon: Muʾassisa al-Risāla, 1402.

——. *Dalāʾil al-Nubuwwa*, Beirut, Lebanon: Dār al-Kutub al-ʿIlmiyya, 1405/1985.

——. *Shuʿab al-Īmān*, Beirut, Lebanon: Dār al-Kutub al-ʿIlmiyya, 1410/1990.

——. *al-Sunan al-Ṣughrā*, Medina, Saudi Arabia: Maktaba al-Dār, 1410/1989.

——. *al-Sunan al-Kubrā*, Mecca, Saudi Arabia: Maktaba Dār al-Bāz, 1414/1994.

——. *al-Zuhd al-Kabīr*, Beirut, Lebanon: Muʾassisa al-Kutub al-Thaqāfiyya, 1996.

al-Bazzār, Abū Bakr Aḥmad b. ʿAmr b. ʿAbd al-Khāliq al-Baṣrī (210–292/825–905), *al-Musnad*, Beirut, Lebanon: 1409 AH.

al-Bukhārī, Abū ʿAbd Allāh Muhammad b. Ismāʿīl b. Ibrahīm b. Mughīra (194–256/810–870), *al-Adab al-Mufrad*, Beirut, Lebanon: Dār al-Bashāʾir al-Islāmiyya, 1409/1989.

——. *al-Ṣaḥīḥ*, Beirut, Lebanon, Damascus, Syria: Dār al-Qalam, 1401/1981.

——. *al-Tārīkh al-Kabīr*, Beirut, Lebanon: Dār al-Kutub al-ᶜIlmiyya.

al-Dāraquṭnī, Abū al-Ḥasan ᶜAlī b. ᶜUmar b. Aḥmad b. al-Mahdī b. Masᶜūd b. al-Nuᶜmān (306–385/918–995), *al-Sunan*, Beirut, Lebanon: Dār al-Maᶜrifa, 1386/1966.

al-Dārimī, Abū Muhammad ᶜAbd Allāh b. ᶜAbd al-Raḥmān (181–255/797–869), *al-Sunan*, Beirut, Lebanon: Dār al-Kitāb al-ᶜArabī, 1407 AH.

Abū Dāwūd, Sulaymān b. Ashᶜath b. Isḥāq b. Bashīr al-Sijistānī (202–275/817–889), *al-Sunan*, Beirut, Lebanon: Dār al-Fikr, 1414/1994.

al-Daylamī, Abū Shujāᶜ Shīrawayh b. Shardār b. Shīrawayh al-Daylamī al-Hamdānī (445–509/1053–1115), *Musnad al-Firdaws*, Beirut, Lebanon: Dār al-Kutub al-ᶜIlmiyya, 1986.

al-Dhahabī, Shams al-Dīn Muhammad b. Aḥmad al-Dhahabī (673–748/1274–1348), *Mīzān al-Iᶜtidāl fī Naqd al-Rijāl*, Beirut, Lebanon: Dār al-Kutub al-ᶜIlmiyya, 1995.

——. *Siyar Aᶜlām al-Nubalā'*, Beirut, Lebanon: Mu'assisa al-Risāla, 1413 AH.

al-Dūlābī, Abū Bishr Muhammad b. Aḥmad b. Muhammad b. Ḥammād (224–310 AH), *al-Dhurriya al-Ṭāhira al-Nabawiyya*, Kuwait: Dār al-Salafiyya, 1407 AH.

Ibn Abī al-Dunyā, Abū Bakr ᶜAbd Allāh b. Muhammad b. al-Qurashī (208–281 AH), *al-Awliyā'*, Beirut, Lebanon: Mu'assisa al-Kutub al-Thaqāfiyya, 1413 AH.

al-Faryābī, Abū Bakr Jaᶜfar b. Muhammad b. al-Ḥasan (207–301 AH), *Ṣifat al-Munāfiq*, Mecca, Kuwait: Dār al-Khulafā' li al-Kitāb al-Islāmī, 1405 AH.

Ibn Ḥajar al-ᶜAsqalānī, Aḥmad b. ᶜAlī b. Muhammad b. Muhammad b. ᶜAlī b. Aḥmad al-Kinānī (773–852/1372–1449), *Fatḥ al-Bārī Sharḥ Ṣaḥīḥ al-Bukarī*, Lahore, Pakistan: Dār Nashr al-Kutub al-Islāmiyya, 1401/1981.

——. *Lisān al-Mīzān*, Beirut, Lebanon: Mu'assisa al-Aᶜlamī li al-Maṭbūᶜāt, 1406/1986.

——. *al-Qawl al-Musaddad fī al-Dhabb ʿan al-Musnad li al-Imām Aḥmad,* Cairo, Egypt: Maktaba Ibn Taymiyya, 1401/1981.

——. *Tahdhīb al-Tahdhīb,* Beirut, Lebanon: Dār al-Fikr, 1404/1984.

——. *Talkhīṣ al-Ḥabīr fī Aḥādīth al-Rāfiʿī al-Kabīr,* Medina, Saudi Arabia: 1384/1964.

al-Ḥākim, Abū ʿAbd Allāh Muhammad b. ʿAbd Allāh b. Muhammad (321–405/933–1014), *al-Mustadrak ʿalā al-Ṣaḥīḥayn,* Beirut, Lebanon: Dār al-Kutub al-ʿIlmiyya, 1411/1990.

al-Ḥakīm al-Tirmidhī, Abū ʿAbd Allāh Muhammad b. ʿAlī bin al-Ḥasan b. Bashir, *Nawādir al-Uṣūl fī Aḥadīth al-Rasūl,* Beirut, Lebanon: Dār al-Jīl, 1992.

al-Ḥalabī, ʿAlī ḅ. Burhān al-Dīn (d. 1404 AH), *al-Sīra al-Ḥalabiyya,* Beirut, Lebanon: Dār al-Maʿrifa, 1400 AH.

al-Ḥamawī, Yāqūt b. ʿAbd Allāh al-Ḥamawī Abū ʿAbd Allāh (d. 626 AH), *Muʿjam al-Buldān,* Beirut, Lebanon: Dār Iḥyāʾ al-Turāth, 1399/1979.

al-Hanād, Hanād b. al-Sarrī al-Kūfī (152–243 AH), *al-Zuhd,* Kuwait: Dār al-Khulafāʾ li al-Kitāb al-Islamī, 1406 AH.

al-Haythamī, Nūr al-Dīn Abū al-Ḥasan ʿAlī b. Abī Bakr b. Sulaymān (735–807/1335–1405), *Majmaʿ al-Zawāʾid,* Cairo, Egypt: Dār al-Riyān li al-Turāth & Beirut Lebanon: Dār al-Kitab al-ʿArabī, 1407/1987.

——. *Mawārid al-Zamʾān ilā Zawāʾid Ibn Ḥibbān,* Beirut, Lebanon: Dār al-Kutub al-ʿIlmiyya.

Ibn Ḥayyān, ʿAbd Allāh b. Muhammad b. Jaʿfar b. Ḥayyan al-Aṣbahānī Abū Muhammad (274–369 AH), *Ṭabaqāt al-Muḥaddithīn bi-Aṣbahān,* Beirut, Lebanon: Muʾassisa al-Risāla, 1408 AH.

Ibn Ḥazm, ʿAlī b. Aḥmad b. Saʿīd b. Ḥazm al-Andalusī (384–456/994–1064), *al-Iḥkām fī Uṣūl al-Aḥkām,* Faislabad, Pakistan: Ḍhiyāʾ al-Sunna Idāra al-Tarjama wa al-Taʿrīf, 1404 AH.

Ibn Ḥibbān, Abū Ḥātim Muhammad b. Ḥibbān b. Aḥmad b. Ḥibbān (270–354/884–965), *al-Ṣaḥīḥ,* Beirut, Lebanon: Muʾassisa al-Risāla, 1414/1993.

Ibn Hishām, Abū Muhammad ʿAbd al-Malik (d. 213/828), *al-Sīra al-Nabawiyya,* Beirut, Lebanon: Dār al-Jīl, 1411 AH.

ʿAbd b. Ḥumayd, Abū Muhammad b. Naṣr al-Kasī (d. 249/863), *al-Musnad,* Cairo, Egypt: Maktaba al-Sunna, 1408/1988.

al-Ḥusaynī, Ibrahīm b. Muhammad (1054–1120 AH), *al-Bayān wa al-Taʿrīf,* Beirut, Lebanon: Dār al-Kitāb al-ʿArabī 1401 AH.

Ḥussam al-Dīn al-Hindī, ʿAlāʾ al-Dīn ʿAlī al-Muttaqī (d. 975 AH), *Kanz al-ʿUmmāl fī Sunan al-Afāl wa al-Aqwāl,* Beirut, Lebanon: Muʾassisa al-Risāla, 1399/1979.

Ibn al-Jaʿd, Abū al-Ḥasan ʿAlī b. Jaʿd b. ʿUbayd Hāshimī (133–230/750–845), *al-Musnad,* Beirut, Lebanon: Muʾassisa Nādir, 1410/1990.

Ibn al-Jārūd, Abū Muhammad ʿAbd Allāh b. ʿAlī (d. 307/919), *al-Muntaqā min al-Sunan al-Musnadā,* Beirut, Lebanon: Muʾassisa al-Kitāb al-Thaqāfiyya, 1418/1988.

Ibn al-Jawzī, Abū al-Faraj ʿAbd al-Raḥmān b. ʿAlī b. Muhammad b. ʿAlī b. ʿUbayd Allāh (510–579/1116–1201), *al-Muntaẓim fī Tārīkh al-Mumlūk wa al-Umam,* Beirut, Lebanon: Dār al-Kutub al-ʿIlmiyya, 1409/1989.

——. *Ṣifa al-Ṣafwa,* Beirut, Lebanon: Dār al-Kutub al-ʿIlmiyya, 1409/1989.

——. *al-Wafā bi-Aḥwāl al-Muṣṭafā* ﷺ, Beirut, Lebanon: Dār al-Kutub al-ʿIlmiyya, 1408/1988.

al-Jurjānī, Abū al-Qāsim Ḥamza b. Yūsuf (345/428 AH), *Tārīkh Jurjān*, Beirut, Lebanon: ʿĀlim al-Kutub, 1401/1981.

Ibn Kathīr, Abū al-Fidāʾ Ismāʿīl b. ʿUmar (701–774/1301–1373), *al-Bidāya wa al-Nihāya,* Beirut, Lebanon: Dār al-Fikr, 1419/1998.

——. *Tafsīr al-Qurʾān al-ʿAẓīm,* Beirut, Lebanon: Dār al-Maʿrifa, 1400/1980.

Ibn Khallād, Abū al-Ḥasan b. ʿAbd al-Raḥmān b. Khallād al-Rāmahurmazī (202–275/817–889), *Amthāl al-Ḥadīth al-Marwiyya ʿan al-Nabī* ﷺ, Beirut, Lebanon: Muʾassisa al-Kitāb al-Thaqāfiyya, 1409 AH.

al-Khaṭīb al-Baghdādī, Abū Bakr Aḥmad b. ʿAlī b. Thābit b. Aḥmad b. al-Mahdī b. Thābit (392–463/1002–1071), *al-Kifāyat fī ʿIlm al-Riwāya,* Medina, Saudi Arabia: al-Maktaba al-ʿIlmiyya.

——. *Tārīkh Baghdād*, Beirut, Lebanon: Dār al Kutāb al-ʿIlmiyya.

al-Khaṭīb al-Tabrīzī (d. 741 AH), Walī al-Dīn Abū ʿAbd Allāh Muhammad b. ʿAbd Allāh, *Mishkāt al-Maṣābīḥ,* Beirut, Lebanon: Dār al-Kutub al-ʿIlmiyya, 1424/2003.

Ibn Khuzayma, Abū Bakr Muhammad b. Isḥāq (223–311/838–924), *al-Ṣaḥīḥ,* Beirut, Lebanon: al-Maktab al-Islāmī, 1390/1970.

al-Kinānī, Aḥmad b. Abī Bakr b. Ismāʿīl (762–840 AH), *Miṣbāḥ al-Zujāja fī Zawaʾid b. Māja,* Beirut, Lebanon: Dār al-ʿArabiyya, 1403 AH.

al-Lālakāʾī, Abū al-Qāsim Hibat Allāh b. al-Ḥasan b. al-Manṣūr (d. 418 AH), *Karāmāt al-Awliyāʾ,* Riyadh, Saudi Arabia, Dār al-Ṭayba, 1412 AH.

——. *Sharḥ Uṣūl Iʿtiqād Ahl al-Sunna wa al-Jamaʿa min al-Kitāb wa al-Sunna aw Ijmāʿ al-Ṣaḥāba,* Riyadh, Saudi Arabia, Dār al-Ṭayba, 1402 AH.

al-Maḥāmilī, Ḥusayn b. Ismāʿīl al-Ḍabbī Abū ʿAbd Allāh (235–330/849–941), *al-Amālī,* Damam & Jordan: Dār Ibn al-Qayyim, 1412 AH.

Abū al-Mahāsin, Yūsuf b. Mūsā al-Ḥanafī, *al-Muʿtaṣar min al-Mukhtasar min Mashkal al-Āthār,* Beirut, Lebanon: ʿĀlim al-Kutub.

Ibn Mājah, Abū ʿAbd Allāh Muhammad b. Yazīd al-Qazwīnī (209–273/824–887), *al-Sunan,* Beirut, Lebanon: Dār al-Kutub al-ʿIlmiyya, 1419/1998.

Mālik, Ibn Anas b. Mālik b. Abī ʿĀmir b. ʿAmr b. Ḥārith al-Aṣbaḥī (93–179/712–795), *al-Muwaṭṭāʾ,* Beirut, Lebanon: Dār Iḥyāʾ al-Turāth al-ʿArabī.

Ibn Manda, Abū ʿAbd Allāh Muhammad b. Isḥāq b. Yaḥyā (310–395/922–1005), *al-Īmān,* Beirut, Lebanon: Muʾassisa al-Risāla, 1406 AH.

al-Maqdisī, Muhammad b. ʿAbd al-Wāḥid al-Ḥanbalī, (567–643 AH), *al-Aḥādīth al-Mukhtāra,* Mecca, Saudi Arabia: Maktaba al-Nahda al-Ḥadīthiyya, 1410/1990.

al-Marwazī, Muhammad b. Naṣr b. al-Ḥajjāj Abū ʿAbd Allāh (d. 202–294 AH), *al-Sunna,* Beirut, Lebanon: Muʾassisa al-Kutub al-Thaqāfiyya, 1408 AH.

——. *Taʿẓīm Qadr al-Ṣalāt,* Medina, Saudi Arabia, Maktaba al-Dār, 1406 AH.

al-Mizzī, Abū al-Ḥajjāj Yūsuf b. Zakī ʿAbd al-Raḥmān b. Yūsuf b. ʿAbd al-Malik b. Yūsuf b. ʿAlī (654–742/1256–1341), *Tahdhīb al-Kamāl,* Beirut, Lebanon: Muʾassisa al-Risāla, 1400/1980.

——. *Tuḥfat al-Ashrāf bi-Maʿrifat al-Aṭrāf,* Mumbai, India: al-Dār al-Qayyyima & Beirut, Lebanon: Maktab al-Islāmī, 1403/1983.

Ibn al-Mubārak, Abū ʿAbd al-Raḥmān ʿAbd Allāh b. Wāḍiḥ al-Marwazī (118–181/736–798), *Kitāb al-Zuhd,* Beirut, Lebanon: Dār al-Kutub al-ʿIlmiyya.

al-Mubārakfūrī, Muhammad ʿAbd al-Raḥmān b. ʿAbd al-Raḥīm (1283–1353 AH), *Tuḥfa al-Aḥwadhī fī Sharḥ Jāmiʿ al-Tirmidhī,* Beirut, Lebanon: Dār al-Kutub al-ʿIlmiyya.

Ibn al-Mulaqqin, ʿUmar b. ʿAlī b. al-Mulaqqin al-Anṣārī (723–804 AH), *Khulāṣat al-Badr al-Munīr fī Takhrīj Kitāb al-Sharḥ al-Kabīr li al-Rāfiʿī,* Riyadh, Saudi Arabia: Maktaba al-Rushd, 1410 AH.

al-Munāwī, ʿAbd al-Rawf b. Tāj al-Ārifīn b. ʿAlī b. Zayn al-ʿAbidīn (952–1031/1545–1621), *Fayḍ al-Qadīr Sharḥ al-Jāmiʿ al-Ṣaghīr,* Egypt: Maktaba al-Tujjāriyya al-Kubrā, 1356 AH.

al-Mundhirī, Abū Muhammad ʿAbd al-Aẓīm b. ʿAbd al-Qawī b. ʿAbd Allāh b. Salama b. Saʿd (581–656/1185–1258), *al-Targhīb wa al-Tarhīb,* Beirut, Lebanon: Dār al-Kutub al-ʿIlmiyya, 1417 AH.

al-Muqriʾ, Abū ʿAmr ʿUthmān b. Saʿīd Dānī (371–444/981–1052), *al-Sunan al-Wārida fī al-Fitan,* Riyaḍ, Saudi Arabia: Dār al-ʿĀṣima, 1416 AH.

Muslim, Ibn al-Ḥajjāj Abū al-Ḥasan al-Qushayrī al-Naysābūrī (206–261/821–875), *al-Ṣaḥīḥ,* Beirut, Lebanon: Dār al-Iḥyāʾ al-Turāth al-ʿArabī.

al-Nasāʾī, Aḥmad b. Shuʿayb Abū ʿAbd al-Raḥmān (215–303/830–915), *al-Sunan,* Beirut, Lebanon: Dār al-Kutub al-ʿIlmiyya, 1416/1995.

——. *al-Sunan al-Kubrā,* Beirut, Lebanon: Dār al-Kutub al-ʿIlmiyya, 1411/1991.

al-Nawawī, Abū Zakariyyā Yaḥyā b. Sharaf b. Murrī b. al-Ḥasan b. al-Ḥusayn b. Muhammad b. Jumuʿa b. Ḥizām (631–677/1233–1278), *Riyāḍ al-Ṣāliḥīn min Kalām Sayyid al-Mursalīn* ﷺ, Beirut, Labanon: Dār al-Khayr, 1412/1991.

Abū Nuʿaym, Aḥmad b. ʿAbd Allāh b. Aḥmad b. Isḥāq b. Mūsā b. Mihrān al-Aṣbahānī (336–430/948–1038), *Ḥilya al-Awliyāʾ wa Ṭabaqāt al-Aṣfiyāʾ*, Beirut, Lebanon: Dār al-Kitāb al-ʿArabī, 1400/1980.

——. *Dalāʾil al-Nubuwwa,* Hyderabad, India: Majlis Dāʾira Maʿārif ʿUthmāniyya.

——. *al-Musnad al-Mustakhraj ʿalā Ṣaḥīḥ al-Imām Muslim,* Beirut, Lebanon: Dār al-Kutub al-ʿIlmiyya, 1996.

al-Qāḍī ʿIyāḍ, Abū al-Faḍl ʿIyāḍ b. Mūsā b. ʿIyāḍ b. ʿAmr b. Mūsā b. ʿIyāḍ b. Muhammad b. Mūsā b. ʿIyāḍ al-Yaḥṣubī (476–544/1083–1149), *al-Shifāʾ bi-Taʿrīf Ḥuqūq al-Muṣṭafā* ﷺ, Beirut, Lebanon: Dār al-Kitab al-ʿArabī.

Ibn Qāniʿ, Abū al-Ḥusayn ʿAbd al-Bāqī b. Qāniʿ (265/351 AH), *Muʿjam al-Ṣaḥāba,* Medina, Saudi Arabia: Maktaba al-Ghurabāʾ al-Athariyya, 1418 AH.

al-Qasṭallānī, Abū al-ʿAbbās Aḥmad b. Muhammad b. Abī Bakr b. ʿAbd al-Malik b. Aḥmad b. Muhammad b. Muhammad b. Ḥusayn b. ʿAlī (851–923/1448–1517), *al-Mawāhib al-Laduniyya bi al-Minḥ al-Muḥammadiyya,* Beirut, Lebanon: al-Maktab al-Islamī, 1412/1991.

Ibn al-Qaysarānī, Abū al-Faḍl Muhammad b. Ṭāhir b. ʿAlī b. Aḥmad al-Maqdasī (448–507/1056–1113), *Tadhkira al-Ḥuffāẓ,* Riyadh, Saudi Arabia: Dār al-Samiʿī, 1415 AH.

al-Qazwīnī, ʿAbd al-Karīm b. Muhammad Rāfiʿī, *al-Tadwīn fī Akhbār Qazwīn,* Beirut, Lebanon: Dār al-Kutub al-ʿIlmiyya, 1987.

Ibn Qudāma, Abū Muhammad ʿAbd Allāh b. Aḥmad al-Maqdasī (d. 620 AH), *al-Mughnī fī Fiqh al-Imām Aḥmad b. Ḥanbal al-Shaybānī,* Beirut, Lebanon: Dār al-Fikr, 1405 AH.

al-Qurṭubī, Abū ʿAbd Allāh Muhammad b. Aḥmad b. Muhammad b. Yaḥyā b. Mufarraj al-Umawī (d. 671 AH), *al-Jāmiʿ li-Ahkām al-Qurʾān,* Beirut, Lebanon: Dār al-Iḥyāʾ al-Turāth al-ʿArabī.

Ibn Rāhawayh, Abū Ya'qūb Isḥāq b. Ibrahīm b. Makhlad b. Ibrahīm b. 'Abd Allāh (161–237/778–851), *al-Musnad*, Medina, Saudi Arabia: Maktaba al-Īmān, 1412/1991.

Ibn Rajab al-Ḥanbalī, Abū al-Faraj 'Abd al-Raḥmān b. Aḥmad (736–795 AH), *Jāmi' al-'Ulūm wa al-Ḥikam fī Sharḥ Khamsīn Ḥadīth min Jawāmi' al-Kalim*, Beirut, Lebanon: Dār al-Ma'rifa, 1408 AH.

Ibn Rāshid, Ma'mar b. Rāshid al-Azdī (d. 151 AH), *al-Jāmi'*, Beirut, Lebanon: al-Maktab al-Islāmī, 1403 AH.

al-Rāzī, Muhammad b. 'Umar b. al-Ḥasan b. al-Ḥusayn b. 'Alī al-Tamīmī (543–606/1149–1210), *al-Tafsīr al-Kabīr*, Tehran, Iran: Dār al-Kutub al-'Ilmiyya.

'Abd al-Razzāq, Abū Bakr b. Hammām b. Nāfi' al-Ṣan'ānī (126–211/744–826), *al-Muṣannaf*, Beirut, Lebanon: al-Maktab al-Islāmī, 1403 AH.

al-Ruyānī, Abū Bakr Muhammad b. Hārūn (d. 307 AH), *al-Musnad*, Cairo, Egypt: Mu'assisa Cordoba, 1416 AH.

Sa'īd b. Manṣūr, Abū 'Uthmān al-Khurāsānī (d. 227 AH), *al-Sunan*, Riyadh, Saudi Arabia: Dār al-Aṣma'ī, 1414 AH.

al-Shāfi'ī, Abū 'Abd Allāh Muhammad b. Idrīs b. 'Abbās b. 'Uthmān b. al-Shāfi' al-Qurashī (150–204/767–819), *al-Musnad*, Beirut, Lebanon: Dār al-Kutub al-'Ilmiyya.

——. *al-Sunan al-Ma'thūra*, Beirut, Lebanon: Dār al-Ma'rifa, 1406 AH.

al-Shahrastānī, Abū al-Fatḥ Muhammad b. 'Abd al-Karīm b. Abī Bakr Aḥmad (479–548 AH), *al-Milal wa al-Niḥal*, Beirut, Lebanon: Dār al-Ma'rifa, 2001 AH.

al-Shāshī, Abū Sa'īd Haytham (d. 335/946 AH), *al-Musnad*, Medina, Saudi Arabia: Maktaba al-'Ulūm wa al-Ḥikam, 1410 AH.

al-Shawkānī, Muhammad b. 'Alī b. Muhammad (1173–1250/1760–1834), *Fatḥ al-Qadīr*, Beirut, Lebanon, Dār al-Fikr, 1402/1982.

——. *Nayl al-Awtār Sharḥ Muntaqā al-Akhbār*, Beirut, Lebanon: Dār al-Fikr, 1402/1982.

Ibn Abī Shayba, Abū Bakr 'Abd Allāh b. Muhammad b. Ibrahīm b. 'Uthmān al-Kūfī (159–235/776–850), *al-Muṣannaf*, Riyadh, Saudi Arabia: Maktaba al-Rushd, 1409 AH.

al-Shaybānī, Abū Bakr Aḥmad b. ʿAmr b. al-Ḍaḥḥāk b. Makhlad (206–287/822–900), *al-Āḥād wa al-Mathānī*, Riyadh, Saudi Arabia: Dār al-Rāya, 1411/1991.

al-Subkī, Taqī al-Dīn Abū al-Ḥasan ʿAlī b. ʿAbd al-Kāfī b. ʿAlī b. Tammām b. Yūsuf b. Mūsā b. Tammām al-Anṣārī (683–756/1284–1355), *Shifāʾ al-Saqām fī Ziyāra Khayr al-Anām*, Hyderabad, India: Dāʾira Maʿārif Niẓāmmiyya, 1315 AH.

——. *Shifāʾ al-Saqām fī Ziyārat Khayr al-Anām*, Hyderabad, India: Dāʾira Maʿārif Nizāmmiyya, 1315 AH.

Ibn al-Sunnī, Aḥmad b. Muhammad al-Daynūrī (284–364 AH), *ʿAmal al-Yawm wa al-Layla*, Beirut, Lebanon: Dār Ibn Ḥazm, 1425/2004.

al-Suyūṭī, Jalāl al-Dīn Abū al-Faḍl ʿAbd al-Raḥmān b. Abī Bakr b. Muhammad b. Abī Bakr b. ʿUthmān (849–911/1445–1505), *al-Dībāj ʿalā Ṣaḥīḥ Muslim*, al-Khūbar, Saudi Arabia: Dār Ibn ʿAffān, 1416/1996.

——. *al-Durr al-Manthūr fi al-Tafsīr bi al-Maʾthūr*, Beirut, Lebanon: Dār al-Maʿrifa.

——. *al-Jāmiʿ al-Ṣaghīr fī Aḥadīth al-Bashīr al-Nadhīr*, Beirut, Lebanon: Dār al-Kutub al-ʿIlmiyya.

——. *al-Khaṣāʾiṣ al-Kubrā*, Faisalabad, Pakistan: Maktaba al-Nūriyya al-Riḍwiyya.

——. *Miftāḥ al-Janna*, Medina, Saudi Arabia, al-Jāmiʿa al-Islāmiyya, 1399 AH.

——. *Sharḥ ʿalā Sunan al-Nasāʾī*, Ḥalb, Syria: Maktab al-Maṭbūʿāt al-Islamiyya, 1406/1986.

——. *Sharḥ Sunan Ibn Mājah*, Karachi, Pakistan: Qadīmī Kutub Khānā.

al-Ṭabarānī, Abū al-Qāsim Sulaymān b. Aḥmad b. Ayyūb b. Maṭīr al-Lakhmī (260–360/873–971), *al-Muʿjam al-Awsaṭ*, Riyadh, Saudi Arabia: Maktaba al-Maʿārif, 1405/1985.

——. *al-Muʿjam al-Kabīr*, Mosul, Iraq: Matbaʿa al-Zahrāʾ al-Ḥadītha.

——. *al-Muʿjam al-Kabīr*, Cairo, Egypt: Maktaba Ibn Taymiyya.

——. *al-Muʿjam al-Ṣaghīr*, Beirut, Lebanon: Dār al-Kutub al-ʿIlmiyya, 1403/1983.

——. *Musnad al-Shāmiyyīn,* Beirut, Lebanon: Muʾassisa al-Risāla, 1405/1985.

al-Ṭabarī, Abū ʿAbbās Aḥmad b. ʿAbd Allāh b. Muhammad b. Abī Bakr b. Muhammad b. Ibrahīm (615–694/1218–1295), *al-Riyāḍ al-Naḍra fī Manāqib al-ʿAshra,* Beirut, Lebanon, Dār al-Gharb al-Islāmī, 1996.

al-Ṭabarī, Abū Jaʿfar Aḥmad Muhammad b. Jarīr b. Yazīd (224–310/839–923), *Tārīkh al-Umam wa al-Mulūk,* Beirut, Lebanon: Dār al-Kutub al-ʿIlmiyya, 1407 AH.

al-Ṭaḥāwī, Abū Jaʿfar Aḥmad b. Muhammad b. Salama b. Salma b. ʿAbd al-Malik b. Salma (229–321/853–933), *Sharḥ Maʿānī al-Āthār,* Beirut, Lebanon: Dār al-Kutub al-ʿIlmiyya, 1399 AH.

al-Ṭayālisī, Abū Dāwūd Sulaymān b. Dāwūd al-Jārūd (133–204/751–819), *al-Musnad,* Beirut, Lebanon: Dār al-Maʿrifa.

Ibn Taymiyya, Aḥmad b. ʿAbd al-Ḥalīm b. ʿAbd al-Salām al-Ḥarānī (661–728/1263–1328), *Iqtiḍāʾ al-Ṣirāṭ al-Mustaqīm,* Lahore, Pakistan: al-Maktaba al-Salafiyya, 1398/1978.

——. *al-Ṣārim al-Maslūl,* Beirut, Lebanon, Dār Ibn Ḥazm, 1417 AH.

al-Wāsiṭī, Aslam b. Sahl Razār (d. 296 AH), *Tārīkh Wāsiṭ,* Beirut Lebanon, ʿAlām al-Kitab, 1406 AH.

Abū Yaʿlā, Aḥmad b. ʿAlī b. Mathnā b. Yaḥyā b. ʿĪsā b. al-Hilāl al-Mūṣilī al-Tamīmī (210–307/825–919), *al-Musnad,* Damascus, Syria: Dār al-Maʾmūn li al-Turāth, 1404/1984.

Yaḥyā b. Muʿīn, Abū Zakariyyā (158–233 AH), *al-Tārīkh,* Mecca, Saudi Arabia: Markaz al-Baḥth al-ʿIlmī wa Iḥyāʾ al-Turāth al-Islāmī, 1399/1979 AH.

al-Zaylaʿī, Abū Muhammad ʿAbd Allāh b. Yūsuf al-Ḥanafī (d. 762/1360), *Naṣb al-Rāya li-Aḥadīth al-Hidāya,* Egypt: Dār al-Ḥadīth, 1357/1938.

al-Zurqānī, Abū ʿAbd Allāh Muhammad b. ʿAbd al-Bāqī b. Yūsuf b. Aḥmad b. ʿAlwān Egyptian al-Azharī al-Mālikī (1055–1122/1645–1710), *Sharḥ al-Muwaṭṭāʿ,* Beirut, Lebanon: Dār al-Kutub al-ʿIlmiyya, 1411 AH.

Index

Yarbūʿ, Banū 325
Yazīd 45, 85, 174, 325
Yusayr b. ʿAmr 290
Yemen 280, 284, 297–298, 304, 306

Zādān 226
Zāriʿ 120
Zawrāʾ, al- 197
Zayd 55, 207
Zayd b. Arqam 127–128, 139–141
Zayd b. Ḥuṣayn 321
Zayd al-Khayl 280, 284
Zaylaʿī 216, 227, 236, 343
Ziyād b. Abīh 322
Zubayr, al- 134, 152, 318
Zurqānī, al- 24, 46, 97, 177